THUCYDIDES AND ATHENIAN IMPERIALISM

By JACQUELINE DE ROMILLY

Professor of Greek at the Sorbonne

Translated by
PHILIP THODY

OXFORD
BASIL BLACKWELL
MCMLXIII

© *in this translation*
J. de Romilly, 1963

First printed August 1963

PRINTED IN GREAT BRITAIN IN THE CITY OF OXFORD
AT THE ALDEN PRESS
BOUND AT THE KEMP HALL BINDERY OXFORD

ANALYTICAL TABLE OF CONTENTS

I. *The causes of the war*, pp. 17-36. — The incidents and the 'real cause' (17-18); possibility of seeing the 'real cause' from the very beginning of the war (18-20); its presence throughout Book I (20-24). — Necessary links between all the different elements and the early parts of the work: the first incidents (25), the final negotiations and Pericles' speech (26-27), the last speech of the Corinthians (27-29), the speech by Archidamus (29-32), the debate at Sparta as a whole (32-35). — The only passages which stand out are the speech by the Athenians and the Pentecontaëtia, which both insist more fully on the role of Athenian imperialism (35-36).

II. *The history of the war*, pp. 36-54. — The importance of Athenian imperialism as explaining all events and showing their connexion, in Books II (36-37), III (37-40), IV (40-44); where there are signs of passages having been rewritten, the role of Athenian imperialism seems to have been emphasized, as in the parts dealing with Brasidas (45-47). — Similarly in Books V (47-50), VI and VII (50-53), VIII (53-54).

Parallelism, throughout the work, between the arguments for and against Athenian imperialism (54-57).

I. *Athenian ambition*, pp. 58-86. — Justifiable simplification as regards its relationship with internal political disputes (59-65), its normal field of expansion (65-71), and its general aim, this being less to obtain supplies of corn (71-74), or to acquire wealth (74-77), than to secure the satisfaction of ruling over others (77-82). — Thucydides dismisses explanations based upon a policy of Ionian (83) or democratic (84) alliance, and by the use which he makes of parallel expressions underlines the general and universal nature of Athenian imperialism (85-86).

II. *The nature of Athenian rule*, pp. 86-97. — Evidence from the vocabulary (86-88). — Brevity of the indications given about the allies' military (88-89) and financial (89-92) obligations, as about the other grievances of Thucydides' contemporaries (92-96); explanation of this brevity (96-97).

CONCLUSION—THE POINT OF VIEW ADOPTED BY THUCYDIDES IN
HIS JUDGMENT ON ATHENIAN IMPERIALISM 98-104

The simplifications and omissions noted show that his judgment contains no moral considerations (98-100), no concern for Greek fraternity (100-101), and no bias related to internal Athenian politics (102-103).

PART TWO
THE SUCCESSIVE FORMS ASSUMED
BY ATHENIAN IMPERIALISM

Pericles before the war, pp. 110-111.
His speeches, as expressing both his ideas (comparison with contemporary works) and ideas approved of by Thucydides, pp. 111-141: — speech in Book I: first part (112-113), second part (113-119); last speech: Athenian rule over the whole of the sea (123-124), Athenian rule as tyrannical (124-128), the beauty of Athenian rule (126-130); the Funeral Oration (130-140). — Pericles' general position (140-141).
Date to be assigned to the different passages, pp. 142-153. — Speech in Book I (142-146); Funeral Oration (146-147); last speech (147-153).
General conclusions about the writing of the work (153-154) and results concerning Thucydides' views on Athenian imperialism (154-155).

I. *The defection of Mytilene*, pp. 156-171. — Composition of the two speeches and Thucydides' judgment (156-160); the view on Athenian empire in both speeches (160-163); parallel expressions used by Cleon and Pericles, difference of intention on Thucydides' part (163-167). — Date of composition (167-171).
II. *The affair of Pylos*, pp. 172-192. — Composition of the speech made by the Spartan ambassadors and Thucydides' judgment (172-179); difference between the ideas expressed in this passage and those put forward in the sections on Pericles (179-182); comparison with the views expressed by contemporary writers: Eupolis (183), Euripides (183-186), Aristophanes (186-187). — Date of composition (187-192).

GENERAL CONCLUSION

PREFACE

This book was first published in French, in 1947, under the title *Thucydides et l'imperialisme athénien — La Pensée de l'historien et la genèse de l'œuvre* (the sub-title indicating the character and scope of the work).

The text printed here is a translation. This means that, although I revised it myself and made here and there some slight alterations in detail, I did not attempt to change the original text, or to incorporate all the recent and most important research published on Thucydides: the reader will find at the end of the book a short survey and discussion of the studies which are particularly connected with the subject matter treated here, with references to the pages of the book (a sign alongside the page number will call his attention to this survey in appropriate cases).

The translation was not an easy undertaking, and I am all the more grateful to Mr Thody for all the trouble he has generously taken. I also want to thank the staff at Blackwell's for their precious help.

These acknowledgments must be joined to those in the French edition; for the book, which is dedicated to the memory of my father, Maxime David, owes a great deal to several scholars — the late Louis Bodin deserving among them a place of honour. To their names should now be added that of Sir Ronald Syme, who, in various ways, made the enterprise easier.

In Memoriam Patris

MAXIME DAVID

GENERAL INTRODUCTION

PERHAPS more than any other historical work, Thucydides' description of the Peloponnesian War differs from a simple collection of raw facts: every single word in it seems to imply choice and arrangement; and this gives the reader the impression that, from beginning to end, a sure and certain hand is guiding him towards definite conclusions. And yet, it seems unlikely that his work should have been written as a whole from the start; and many points suggest a composition by several stages, with possible false starts and revisions. For he was writing about a war which lasted twenty-seven years, and which was not ended when he set to work.[1] Furthermore, it was a war fought in two sections, a war which he might have thought definitely finished after the first ten years: in fact, when peace had been finally re-established, he still thought it original to have treated it as a single unit, and not as two separate wars with an interval of peace between them.[2] Also, his work was never completed, and this fact alone should lead us to look at it not as something final, freed from the circumstances of his life, but as something that was still alive, linked to the author's life and ideas, and dependent upon changes in his attitude.[3]

There are, indeed, some signs in the *History of the Peloponnesian War* which suggest that it is not quite homogeneous. Besides passages referring to the whole sequence of events up to 404 (e.g. the judgment on Pericles, in II. 65), we find other passages, such as the description of natural phenomena in I. 23, in which certain omissions as well as the general tone seem to imply that not all the events were yet fully known.[4] And in some passages, which in themselves do not

[1] He himself indicates at the very beginning of his work (I. 1. 1) that he set to work at the beginning of the war (ἀρξάμενος εὐθὺς καθισταμένου). Even if what he means there is only a preparatory sketch (cf. p. 347), it is likely that he should have at least started to organize his material — that is to say, to write his History — before the twenty-seven-year war came to a close.

[2] cf. V. 25. The case of the Peloponnesian War is not very different from the wars of 1914-1918 and 1939-1945, looked upon by some people as a new 'Thirty Years War'.

[3] In particular, if a work of more than a certain length contains during the period in which it is actually being written a number of disconnected elements which are intended to disappear later, those would obviously be more likely to subsist in a work that was left uncompleted.

[4] If it is taken by itself, this clue is not sufficient to support a whole theory. Nevertheless we can note that the dramatic eclipse (of the moon, it is true) which prevented Nicias from setting out in VII. 50. 4 is not even included in the list of these 'natural phenomena'

give any internal clues about the date when they were written, scholars have noticed contradictions, inconsistencies, or repetitions, which at least suggest that they were written at different times.[1] Consequently, whether we adopt a simple interpretation — like that put forward by Ullrich in 1846 — or whether we look for more complex interpretations — such as those proposed later — it is obvious that the composition of Thucydides' work poses a problem whose solution could clarify the meaning of the text, and which, therefore, is worth examining. I would even go so far as to say it is a problem that we cannot avoid examining. But once this has been assumed, the existence of such a problem must paralyse any study of Thucydides. It becomes impossible to study any question fully without having first of all settled the problem of the composition of the work; yet this cannot be settled without having already considered the other questions.

It is true that scholars have worked on particular questions of method or opinion, and have analysed particular speeches. On the whole some very interesting conclusions have been reached. But as soon as methods, opinions and intentions may be thought of as changing from one passage to another, we have first to decide whether that kind of explanation is to be accepted or not; and if it is, to what extent. Lange's interesting and penetrating study of Thucydides' political ideas is called into question by the work of Schwartz, for whereas Lange weighed certain judgments one against another, Schwartz established a chronological distinction. Similarly, a study such as Abbott's might appear superficial to a reader of Schadewaldt, for where Abbott describes a method as settled once for all, Schadewaldt shows how it was progressively expanded. Finally, detailed studies, such as that of Rose Zahn on the first speech of Pericles, or that of Landmann on the first speech of Hermocrates, cannot avoid the question of what was written before or after; and such an attempt always more or less presupposes that a general solution to the prob-

---

[1] Steup's edition notes a vast number of these contradictions, on which Schwartz bases his system. In the general opinion, the most surprising repetition (together with the 'doublets' of Book VIII) is that of the murder of the tyrants in Books I and VI.

In fact, when Thucydides does mention it in the narrative, he does so because of the influence which it had over the events and he does not now seem to consider such a phenomenon as a 'sign' deserving interest on its own account. On the other hand, in 404, after the general collapse, the role of the plague in Athens could well have passed into the background, whereas Thucydides says in I. 23. 3: ἡ οὐχ ἥκιστα βλάψασα καὶ μέρος τι φθείρασα ἡ λοιμώδης νόσος.

lem of the composition of Thucydides' work has been found. One can thus explain the attitude of Patzer, who, setting out to study the importance of certain ideas in Thucydides, was in fact obliged to dispose of the problem of composition in a preliminary work. And this also explains why almost everything written on Thucydides in the first half of the twentieth century should have been directed towards this problem.[1]

Nevertheless, although this discussion has been going on for a century and although an immense amount of work has been done in many places, and especially in Germany, no progress has been made; far from it. It seems as though the question has simply become more and more complicated, to such an extent that even after so many efforts have been made no firm basis has been acquired for future research, and no one point has been definitely established.[2] Ullrich, in 1846, would acknowledge only two stages in the writing of the work, separated by purely material factors: for him, Thucydides began to write the history of the war about 421 B.C., at the time when it was still only a ten-year war. When hostilities broke out again, and Thucydides thought they were likely to continue, he waited till 404 B.C., when they were over, before making a few corrections in the first part of his work and writing the second part. But after Ullrich, scholars began to discover more numerous and more subtle revisions in Thucydides' text. Ćwikliński, in 1877, maintained that the Sicilian episode had been written and published separately. In 1886 Schwartz admitted that Book I was made up of bits and pieces. Then Prenzel and Wilamowitz showed that Book VIII revealed the same disorder. In 1919, Schwartz published his long study of the whole work, in which he showed that the same disorder could be found everywhere. For him, Thucydides' work is often simply a series of notes and essays, inspired by different aims and ideas, and put together by a rather clumsy editor. But this view in turn provoked intense controversy. Schwartz, declared Pohlenz, had shown insufficient caution and been far too brutal in separating one part

---

[1] See later: *Bibliography*. The possibility naturally remains, on the one hand to bring new and valuable remarks to bear on the kind of problems just mentioned, or, on the other, to study some very general features of Thucydides' language and composition. I do not maintain that the problem of how the work was written has *entirely* paralysed work on Thucydides, but simply that its general effect has been to discourage and make it more difficult.

[2] Cf. J. David, *État présent des études relatives à Thucydide*, *Actes du Congrès de Strasbourg de l'Association Guillaume Budé*.

B

from another: for him, the work should be divided up quite differently, and he argued that it was neither the facts themselves nor Thucydides' opinion on them which had changed, but simply his way of looking at them and presenting their importance to his reader. Most scholars expressed similar criticism: Kolbe and Wilamowitz shared Pohlenz's opposition to this splitting up of the work into small pieces, while Aly and Momigliano explained the evolution of Thucydides' thought in a different way. Like that of Ullrich before him, Schwartz's system was gradually whittled away. Among the new suggestions put forward in the course of this reaction, Schadewaldt's seems the most interesting. He takes as his starting-point the Sicilian episode, distinguished from the others by its unity and finish: for him, these two qualities are explained by the evolution in Thucydides' mind of the idea of historical truth. This is yet another principle which enables one to discover different levels in the work. But his suggestion immediately raised as many difficulties as those of his predecessors. Rehm and Pohlenz did not agree with him, and soon Grosskinsky began to undermine the whole of his system by the interpretation of Chapter I. 22, in which Thucydides explains his method and the type of truth which he intended to discover. All that then remained of so many efforts was a confused tangle of all kinds of hypotheses, contested opinions and arguments twisted in every conceivable sense. The thesis of the work's essential unity, brilliantly defended by Meyer in 1899, still had supporters such as Patzer in 1937 and was soon to get more; whereas, in the same year, the example of Laqueur's work showed that scholars who maintained that the work had been written in different sections could still analyse the text away to nothing. Exhausting by the immense bibliography which it offers, completely negative in its results, the question of the composition of the work can at present be considered as the perfect example of a vain and insoluble problem.

This fact can be explained, for the poverty of the results stems from the uselessness of the methods employed. For on what can we base our arguments? On internal evidence? Everything shows how extremely difficult this is, for such evidence will always be very vague. Suppose, for example, that we want to prove that such and such a passage was written before a certain date. We generally have to base our reasoning on omissions and use the argument *ex silentio*. But, while many passages may have been written before a certain date, only a few will noticeably fail to mention a future event, and in practically no passage will such an omission be absolute proof of a mistake or lack of knowledge about the event. Suppose we try to prove that such and such a passage was written after a certain date: our task will be certainly much easier, but if the passage in question is included in a speech, Thucydides will have been careful to disguise the allusion in order to fit the idea to the circumstances in which it was expressed. Thus we can only be absolutely sure in those cases where Thucydides makes remarks in his own name, and we know that, acting as an authoritative but inconspicuous guide, he did his best to reduce both the number and the importance of such remarks. If, finally, we can fix a *terminus ante quem* or a *terminus post quem* for any particular passage, we shall not be very far advanced, for we shall still have to decide how long this particular passage is: the reference could be valid for a group of words, for a sentence, for a paragraph, or for a whole book. For example, in the Sicilian books, the mention of Aeginetans 'then installed in Aegina' indicates a date after 405. But while for Schadewaldt this reference is valid for the whole of books VI and VII, Schwartz thinks it valid only for the list of allies (VII. 57-58), and Rehm thinks it refers only to the part of the sentence which actually mentions Aeginetans. Thus one becomes involved in endless discussions about the composition of the work; and before we are able to discover a clue within the text itself and decide on its area of application, we ought to know first of all the ideas which could or could not have been expressed at such a moment, then Thucydides' own habits in composing his work and arranging ideas, and finally the arrangement prevailing in each particular case. Even then, it would be difficult to be certain: otherwise, it is impossible.

But, it may be said, one can at least base oneself on the contradictions, since these, although not establishing directly any dates, do nevertheless indicate fairly rigorous distinctions, and differences in the time of composition. In fact, they are no better, for, whatever Schwartz may say, they are just as vague and uncertain.

A moment's thought will make this clear. If it is an editor[1] who

---

[1] Thucydides' work certainly did have an editor. The final sentence is sufficient proof of this. But this sentence seems to indicate that the editor did not intend altering Thucydides' text. The chronological indication which he gives does not claim to be assimilated into the text, and some manuscripts even present it as being completely foreign to it. This is a reason for thinking that the editor did not play the important role attributed to him by some scholars in putting the work together. Other reasons can be found in the very characteristics of the work, and in the careful way in which it was constructed.

has brought together a number of different and unfinished essays written by Thucydides, his main aim must have been to fit them together in as convincing a manner as possible. If we suppose that he was prevented from doing so successfully by his own stupidity, he must at least have tried to smooth over the transitions and make the contradictions less glaring; thus we are unlikely to find abrupt transitions and flagrant omissions. And we shall certainly find nothing as clear cut as the divisions suggested by Schwartz. Let us suppose, on the other hand, that it was Thucydides himself who fitted the different parts together: if this is the case, then he must have done so correctly, and cannot have allowed a particular passage to exist side by side with the one intended to replace it. It is even probable that, if Thucydides carried out certain changes after the work was written, he bore the particular context in mind in each case, and established stylistic and factual relationships which now lead us astray. It may be added that even in those sections where there is a definite difficulty, we need to be sure that it is one which can be explained by considerations of chronology. Eduard Meyer has made a list of a whole series of contradictions in Thucydides' work which cannot conceivably be attributed to the circumstances under which it was written.[1] It is clear that here is yet another wide field for possible disagreement. And, once again, we can only approach the question if we already have clear and well-defined ideas about Thucydides' general habits and the way he deals with historical facts in the narration, or conducts an argument in the speeches. Finally, these are the questions to which any discussion inevitably returns, and which must first of all be clarified.

This seemed to me to be the situation facing any scholar who undertakes research on Thucydides. It is obviously a very difficult one, since each of these two lines of approach implies the other and is, taken by itself, both useless and doomed to failure. Such a view of it explains the problem I have undertaken to treat.

Since each line of approach necessarily implies the other, I felt it necessary to bring them together, and begin by presupposing the existence of two unknowns. Thus, by simultaneously pursuing two lines of approach, each would illuminate the other, so that

---

[1] *Forsch.*, II, pp. 286-7. In particular, he mentions certain difficulties connected with the text of treaties, the relations between Athens and other countries, the number of ships involved. Clearly, many works originally written 'at one sitting' contain imperfections of this type.

facts discovered about Thucydides' intellectual attitude might contribute to a more exact knowledge of how the work was written, while this knowledge, in turn, might be used to fit the ideas into the living reality in which they came to birth. In other words, it seemed to me that the best plan of approach was to study the way the work was written from the point of view of a particular idea, habit or principle peculiar to Thucydides; or, if one prefers, to study this idea, habit or principle by reference to the problem of the composition of the work.

The theme chosen still had to be suitable for a study of this nature. That is to say, traces of it had to be detectable in different parts of Thucydides' work. Such considerations eliminated all possible analyses concerned only with isolated sections of the work. It has been said already that such studies may well be of great interest but that their result is never complete. How is one to know whether the conclusions reached are applicable to the whole work? And yet they have to be: even at the risk of appearing highly imprudent, we cannot do without a synthesis, taking into consideration the composition of the whole History. By keeping in mind only one single problem, but one which affected a number of different passages, one might reduce to a minimum the criticism that one was being over-presumptuous.

One last condition still had to be fulfilled: the theme chosen had to be one where changes would be likely to show. It stands out clearly, from all the studies made of the style and language of Thucydides, that these remain basically the same throughout all his work.[1] Similarly, his general method does not change, in so far as it corresponds to his own basic intellectual disposition.[2] The realm of political judgment, on the contrary, would afford many opportunities for changes and evolution.

Here, one central fact stood out, a fact which more than any other was continuously present throughout the work and gave occasions for changes of opinion, since its own reality changed with time and demanded at each moment a new interpretation as well as a new judgment: this fact was Athenian imperialism.

It had the additional advantage of raising a question as obscure as it was important. Because it took various forms one after the other

---

[1] Cf. Jan Ros, S.J. *Die* Μεταβολή . . . , p. 457.

[2] That is why only studies of this type have been able to yield results without being hindered by the problem of how the work was written.

and because it brought into play a multiplicity of different circumstances, Athenian imperialism invited varied opinions; and
Thucydides' general attitude has been interpreted in a number of ways.
Some have made him an apostle of imperialism and others its
opponent. And those who have tried to find the key to these apparent
contradictions by studying the time of composition of the different
sections have presented very different views about the evolution of
Thucydides' thought on this particular subject. For Schwartz, the
unfinished work had, after 404, the tendency to become an apologia
for the imperialism which it had begun by criticizing. For Momigliano, the work begun as a defence of Athenian imperialism, later
tried to explain how it came to grief — a surprise for Thucydides
while he was actually writing the work. This study sets out to find
an answer to the different problems raised by these hypotheses.

Now if it is true that the historical, political and philosophical
thought of Thucydides centres on this one theme, then these questions
are of the utmost importance.

Needless to say, it is an extremely heavy task to treat such a
problem in its relationship with the way the work was written, but I
have already explained why, in my view, the two questions cannot
be treated separately. It is at least obvious that this task is sufficient
in itself, and that I cannot claim to exhaust all the problems raised by
the question of how and when the work was written. Many points
will not even be mentioned,[1] and many problems will be left without
a solution. I shall try to deal only with those that are directly related
to Thucydides' attitude towards Athenian imperialism. I hope that
my attempt to solve this particular problem will make a useful
contribution towards any new study of the composition of his work.
Nevertheless, this aspect will remain secondary in importance to the
precise question of the relationship between Thucydides and
Athenian imperialism, which will be treated in its entirety.

This order of importance is, after all, natural. The problem of the
way in which Thucydides wrote is of interest only in so far as it helps
us to understand his work. The point is to recapture the living nature
of the thought which we are studying. And such a subordination
fits in with the true function of philology which — it will be
remembered — should always remain a part of humanism.

---

[1] Thus the question of the text of the treaties, the chronology, the 'doublets'. These
different questions offer no means of arriving at valid conclusions; but there is no need to
prove it in this book.

Part One

The Data —
Athenian Imperialism in Thucydides' Work

INTRODUCTION

THERE is no word in Greek to express the idea of imperialism. There is simply one to indicate the fact of ruling over people, or to indicate the people ruled over taken as a group: that is the word ἀρχή. Nevertheless, imperialism, and especially Athenian imperialism, is a very precise idea for a Greek.[1]

Athenian imperialism began to show itself immediately after the Persian wars. It is legitimate to ask when it came to an end, and in particular whether we can still talk of Athenian imperialism at the beginning of the Peloponnesian War. Athens was then in possession of her whole empire,[2] and we can find little more than one or two annexations such as that of Melos while the war was actually going on. With the defeat of 404, this empire completely disintegrates. We might therefore think that Thucydides deals with Athenian imperialism only in the chapters of Book I which describe the fifty years leading up to the war, during the course of which this empire was acquired.[3] However, this is not at all the case, for although the empire had been acquired before 433, the policy of imperialism still continued to exist. Indeed, even omitting certain unsuccessful but clearly motivated attempts at new conquests – in Sicily, for example – it inspired all the political undertakings of that time. When the men who governed the city went to war against Sparta, when they put down a revolt, tried to annex new territories, or refused to negotiate under certain conditions, they were carrying on the tradition of those who had originally acquired the empire. Though faced with a more difficult situation, and although less successful in their enterprises, they were still obeying the same feelings and discussing the same problems. They were still inspired by the idea of Athens' ἀρχή, whether they were defending it by war, maintaining it by strict rule, or extending it by conquest. Thus, there is still an Athenian imperialism during the

---

[1] The idea is mainly expressed by paraphrases. The imperialists are called, for instance: οἱ ἄρχειν βουλόμενοι (IV. 61. 5) or: ὅσοι ἕτεροι ἑτέρων ἠξίωσαν ἄρχειν (II. 64. 5). Their attitude is also described with expressions of very general meaning, such as πλεονεξία or words of the same family.

[2] 446 marks the end of the actual period of conquest. But the authority of Athens continues to grow until 433.

[3] I. 97-118. This account is normally called the Fifty Years or the Pentecontaëtia.

Peloponnesian War, and an attitude which Thucydides adopts towards this imperialism; both of these will show in his work.

Before studying the changes in Thucydides' opinion on the different phases of Athenian imperialism, or on the whole of its development, we must begin by defining the essential features which he attributes to it in general. Thus, before plotting the curve in detail or discovering the formula which defines it, we must decide on a certain number of constants. This will amount to showing what is more specifically the province of the historian, before attempting to study the political reactions of the citizen or the theoretical analysis undertaken by the philosopher. This will be the aim of the first part of this book and here I shall not take account of the problem of the actual way the work was written. Or, rather, I shall study this problem only when I have to establish whether such and such an attitude is a permanent one. But generally speaking, the matter will have little to do with a possible change in Thucydides' attitude. The features considered in this part of the book represent the first encounter between the mind and the subject of its study, and define the more or less conscious attitude which Thucydides adopts towards his subject-matter. It will be less a question of analysing a particular passage which deals with imperialism, expresses an idea or reveals an intention, than of using information given *en passant* — for example, the use of one word rather than another, the omission of this or that fact, the choice of such and such an episode. Keeping Thucydides' specific remarks on imperialism in the different parts of his work until later, I shall here be concerned with the way in which he speaks of it in his work as a whole. Thus I shall establish both the importance which Athenian imperialism has in his History, and the way in which it is presented to the reader. And this should afford a first and very general approach to his personal judgment.

To establish these points, we need do little more than compare the way in which Thucydides presents the facts either with the evidence furnished by his contemporaries or with information obtained elsewhere. In the first case, we shall merely be comparing one mind with a number of others; in the second, we shall have to make a definite critique of the evidence provided by Thucydides, since it is only by doing this that we can determine how and to what extent his own personal opinions intervene. This does not mean that I shall be criticizing such an intervention or suggesting that Thucydides twists the facts to suit his purpose. For there is always enough difference between the complex events and their careful, critical interpretation by the historian to enable us to find traces of his personality in the very place where he seems to be giving the most faithful statement of facts.

CHAPTER ONE

THE PLACE OF ATHENIAN IMPERIALISM IN THUCYDIDES' WORK

THE importance given by Thucydides to Athenian imperialism depends as much on his own intellectual attitude as on the facts themselves. And it is obvious that, both in the composition of the separate episodes and in their general disposition, he was guided by certain ideas which tended to give a particular emphasis to this imperialism. But if there is one special place where his own interpretation of events should be more perceptible than in any other, it is the section in which he analyses the causes of the war. The actual military campaigns give the historian an objectively defined framework. The analysis of the causes of a war, on the other hand, implies a choice as to the kind of events which are to be mentioned, the time at which they should begin to be studied, and the importance to be attributed to particular historical characters. Thus, this part of the work should provide many clues for our research.

But for this very reason, the problem is a more delicate one and needs to be treated separately. Such a reliable means of discovering Thucydides' approach cannot be used to establish a permanent characteristic or a normal feature: if, really, this part of his work presupposes a high degree of personal judgment and intervention, it is then more noticeably dependent upon the date, or dates, at which it was written. The explanation of the causes of the war comes at the beginning of the work, and it can therefore be supposed that it was written first. But it is also a kind of introduction, and this may mean that it puts forward a general view which might have been revised at a later date.[1] Thus, for this section, we shall have to give some attention to the way in which the work was written.

Nevertheless, the study of this problem will only be intended to define the exact importance of a general characteristic present in the other parts of the work and all I shall do here is to show to what

[1] W. Jaeger (*Paideia*, I. p, 394 of the English translation) mentions the difference between the two editions of Leopold von Ranke's *History of Prussia* and adds: 'It was in the same way, then, that Thucydides, after the war ended, rehandled the beginning of his work which described the origins of the war.'

extent the same characteristic can also be found in this particularly important section.

I. THE CAUSES OF THE WAR

The most widespread tradition, that of the theatre and the man in the street, or of the political opposition, is that the cause of the war was the conflict about Megara. Since Pericles had insisted on maintaining the decree on Megarian trade which had aroused the indignation of Sparta, and had caused that city to send a solemn ultimatum, his opponents had profited from his insistence on this question to render him responsible for the outbreak of the war.

Aristophanes developed this theme in 421, in the *Acharnians*,[1] and in 425, in the *Peace*.[2] Andocides and Aeschines repeat it in texts which are so similar that both are obviously derived from an oligarchical pamphlet probably written towards the end of the Peloponnesian War.[3] Diodorus later repeats this allegation, apparently on the authority of Ephorus.[4] It occurs again in Plutarch.[5] And, at the time of Aelian, the idea that the Peloponnesian War had begun with the Megarian decree had become a commonplace: it was then considered as the best example of the way in which small issues give rise to great wars.[6] There was thus an easy way of explaining the outbreak of the war by insisting on the responsibility of Pericles and on the importance of the Megarian decree.[7]

[1] *Ach.*, 513-556. Müller-Strübing has shown that it would be wrong to interpret the passage too literally, but it nevertheless reveals a general intention; thus 530 ff.:

> Ἐντεῦθεν ὀργῇ Περικλέης οὑλύμπιος
> ἤστραπτ', ἐβρόντα, ξυνεκύκα τὴν Ἑλλάδα,
> ἐτίθει νόμους ὥσπερ σκόλια γεγραμμένους,
> ὡς χρὴ Μεγαρέας μήτε γῇ μήτ' ἐν ἀγορᾷ
> μήτ' ἐν θαλάττῃ μήτ' ἐν ἠπείρῳ μένειν.

[2] Pericles is presented as wanting war as a means of avoiding the punishment which fell on Pheidias; thus 608 ff.:

> πρὶν παθεῖν τι δεινὸν αὐτὸς ἐξέφλεξε τὴν πόλιν,
> ἢ 'μβαλὼν σπινθῆρα μικρὸν Μεγαρικοῦ ψηφίσματος
> ἐξεφύσησεν τοσοῦτον πόλεμον ὥστε τῷ καπνῷ
> πάντας Ἕλληνας δακρῦσαι, τούς τ' ἐκεῖ τούς τ' ἐνθάδε.

[3] Cf. Mathieu, *Survivances* . . . The first says (*Peace*, 8): πάλιν δὲ διὰ Μεγαρέας πολεμήσαντες . . . ; the second (II, 175): πάλιν δ' εἰς πόλεμον διὰ Μεγαρέας πεισθέντες καταστῆναι.

[4] Diodorus, XII, 38-41. Ephorus himself probably took this version from the same kind of text as the common source of both Andocides and Aeschines. Cf. M. A. Croiset, *Histoire de la Littérature grecque*, IV, p. 660; Mathieu, *Les idées. . . .*, p. 202.

[5] *Pericles*, 30 ff.   [6] *Aelian*, XII, 53.

[7] The echo of this idea can be found in Thucydides' eternal opponent: Beloch. Pericles, in his view, thought war necessary and decided to have it at that moment in order to strengthen his position at home (*Att. Pol. seit Perikles*, p. 22).

Thucydides, however, not only fails to describe the conflict to which this incident gave rise and limits himself to mentioning it as one among other incidents, but also, in Book I, he absolves Pericles from all blame by subordinating all the various incidents to one central cause which, in his view, made war inevitable. For him, these incidents make up a number of immediate causes which he calls αἰτίαι καὶ διαφοραί, or: grievances and disputes.[1] They take place during a period of approximately three years, and are contrasted with the real cause, the ἀληθεστάτη πρόφασις, which can be traced back fifty years before the outbreak of the actual war. And this cause depends entirely on the existence of Athenian imperialism, for the war can be explained by the fear which the Spartans had of the growth of Athenian power.

These two explanations are introduced side by side in I. 23. 5, and developed together in Book I. The narration of the αἰτίαι καὶ διαφοραί, which begins with the episodes of Corcyra and Potidaea, leads to a debate at the end of which the Lacedaemonians vote for war (I. 88). Thucydides then goes back to the ἀληθεστάτη πρόφασις, and, in a long parenthesis (often called the Pentecontaëtia) he traces the growth of Athenian power from the time of the Persian wars to the most recent incidents. He then resumes the description of these (I. 118. 3) and continues it to the end of the book.[2]

The very structure of Book I, then, insists on the ἀληθεστάτη πρόφασις, and thereby on Athenian imperialism.[3] But the question arises: was this structure adopted by Thucydides as soon as he began writing? Or, in other words, was the description of the ἀληθεστάτη πρόφασις, always included in the book, and was it always given in its present form?

The answer to the first of these questions is obviously 'Yes'. Even if we suppose that Book I contains some original material that was later re-written, there is no indication that the idea of ἀληθεστάτη πρόφασις was ever absent.

---

[1] I. 23. 5. Αἰτίαι must contain the idea of an accusation, or a thing incriminated; cf. ibid.: αἱ ἐς τὸ φανερὸν λεγόμεναι αἰτίαι. Hence the use of πρόφασις, apparently surprising, in the other part of the sentence.

[2] I. 146: αἰτίαι δὲ αὗται καὶ διαφοραὶ ἐγένοντο ἀμφοτέροις πρὸ τοῦ πολέμου.

[3] Athenian imperialism is the cause of the war: this in no way means that when Pericles wants war he is acting from imperialistic motives. The war is the result of an imperialistic development of Athenian power, not the expression of an actual imperialistic ambition. It is, therefore, even more remarkable that Thucydides should have been able to isolate the idea of Athenian imperialism with such clarity.

The main reason for considering this idea as a late addition is the fact that the Pentecontaëtia seems to have been written late.[1] Thucydides justifies the existence of his digression in I. 97. 2 by referring to Hellanicus' History, which, since it described the end of the Peloponnesian War, could scarcely have appeared earlier than 404.[2] Moreover, such a digression would seem of itself rather irrelevant to a ten years' war which had had little effect upon the political situation in Greece. On the other hand, its relevance becomes obvious if it is considered as part of the introduction to a long war which led to the fall of the Athenian empire. It is this fact which explains the importance assumed in the preceding chapters by the building of the walls which were to be destroyed in 404: and it may be that the expression used in I. 93. 5 (τὸ πάχος τοῦ τείχους, ὅπερ νῦν ἔτι δῆλόν ἐστι περὶ τὸν Πειραιᾶ) is a direct reference to this destruction.[3] Taken together, these reasons suggest that the Pentecontaëtia could not have been written before 404.

Some scholars have maintained that the whole idea of the ἀληθεστάτη πρόφασις also dates from after 404.

Repeating an idea of Eduard Meyer, they have assumed[4] that before 404 it would have been impossible to attribute the war to the growth of Athens. This could have been done only by someone who saw the whole series of events from a distance, and who, moreover, took a somewhat distorted view of them, since in fact the years immediately before the war had in no way marked a growth in Athenian power.

This is perhaps a rather categorical statement. If it is true that Athens had not acquired any new territory during this period, and had even undergone a certain number of setbacks since 450, it is nevertheless true that she had considerably increased her sovereign power. She had organized her empire, extended her prerogatives, and shaped the formidable instrument that her system of domination had become. Moreover, she had sailed to the Cimmerian Bosporus,

---

[1] The extent of the passage considered as late is the only point really discussed. Some scholars, like Cwiklinski and Wilamowitz, would consider as such the actual Pentecontaëtia (98-117). Others, whose opinion I rather prefer, the whole of the parenthesis (89-117).

[2] This clue is discussed by Ziegler (Der Ursprung der Exk. im. Thuk., Rh. M., 78, 1929, pp. 58-68). The sentence could, in fact, be a later addition.

[3] As to the place which the passage occupies in the book, it is perfectly satisfactory and, whatever Cwiklinski may have thought, in no way proves it to be a later addition.

[4] C.A.H., V, pp. 190 ff., cf. Ed. Meyer, Forsch., II, 313-314.

sent Athenian settlers to several places, founded colonies like Amphipolis, contracted alliances like those with Leontini and Rhegium,
and, finally, by putting down a rebellion like that of Samos, she had
increased her naval power and had reaffirmed her authority in a
manner as impressive as the most brilliant military victory. She had
perhaps ceased to extend the area of her power, but she was con-
solidating and strengthening it where it already existed. Thus Thucydides might well have considered, as early as 431, that these later
years were to be taken with those immediately preceding them as a
period of constant and continued progress.[1] Other authors, writing
even later but not having the same reasons for distorting the facts,
present this period in basically the same manner.[2]

This is by no means to say that the war was essentially a defensive
one as far as Sparta was concerned. In fact, there was a long-standing
rivalry between the two cities,[3] and the Spartans were alarmed not
for their immediate fate nor by any imminent aggression on the part
of the Athenians, but by the way in which Athens was slowly
drawing ahead in power and influence. This was the threat which
they had to parry. Without this consideration, it would not be possible
to explain why they should have chosen this particular moment to
attempt the destruction of Athenian power. The character of the
Spartans would scarcely have led them to commit aggression against
Athens, whose position, however one may judge it, was not weak
enough to offer an easy victory.

The idea of ἀληθεστάτη πρόφασις thus fits the facts, and consequently could be taken into consideration from the very beginning
of the war.

Moreover, if one considers Thucydides' work, it is clear that the
whole of Book I, including the parts which would seem to have been
written first, presupposes the existence of this idea of ἀληθεστάτη
πρόφασις.

This is first of all true of the sections dealing with the very distant

---

[1] Thucydides certainly says μεγάλους γιγνομένους (I. 23. 6), and not, as Weidner and
Steup propose: γεγενημένους (cf. Jacoby, in Zahn, n. 100); on the contrary, in I. 88 and
I. 118, he calls to mind a process of development which has already been completed. The
presence of different expressions in different passages is a proof of the very general
character which Thucydides assigns to this growth.

[2] Cf. Andocides, III, 7, and Aeschines, II, 174, who bring together in one unity
the construction of the southern Long Wall and the constitution of a reserve of a
thousand talents. On page 17, I have indicated the close relationship between the two
texts.

[3] Cf. Thuc. I. 23 and Pentecontaëtia, Herodotus VI, 98.

past. When Thucydides writes the history of sea-power in the Greek world, he obviously paves the way for the power of Athens; and when he presents side by side the two great forces which have come into being and which now share Greece between them,[1] he suggests the idea that the struggle between them goes much further back than any recent individual incident.

Similarly, when he relates the two incidents of Corcyra and of Potidaea, Thucydides does not fail first of all to underline the importance of the role played by Athenian imperialism, and secondly to insist that these incidents were only of secondary importance in causing the war.

In fact, all the different actors in the drama know from the very beginning that the war is going to take place: Corinth is already hostile to Athens, Sparta already fears her, and these feelings together bear the seeds of war within them. The Corcyraeans say so quite clearly in I. 33. 3.[2] The Athenians share this belief.[3] The Corinthians themselves do not deny the possibility of war, but simply say that it is 'not certain' (42. 2: ἐν ἀφανεῖ). Thus the important factor in determining the decisions to be taken is the idea of preparing for war. One must think of Corcyra's fleet (I. 33. 1; I. 44. 2); one must prepare to enter the war in the best possible conditions (I. 36. 3); one must take care to ensure Athens' safety in the near future (I. 36. 1). In all these details, the two speeches present the incident as a prelude to the war, not as its actual cause.

As to the Potidaean incident, it occupies less space and, since there are no speeches dealing with it, offers little scope for interpretation. But in itself this incident was even more closely linked with the rise of Athenian imperialism, since Potidaea was a dependent ally which paid the tribute and tried to abandon Athens; it was this fact alone that gave the affair any importance at all (cf. I. 57. 6; I. 66). Moreover, even there the incident is little more than a pretext for action, and the ambitions which it brings into play go far beyond the actual dispute itself. There is Perdiccas (I. 57. 4) and Potidaea (I. 58. 1), but also Corinth and the allies that she summons to Sparta: how could the Spartans be the only ones to remain indifferent towards the manœuvres of a city which was already arousing so much mistrust

---

[1] I. 18-19.

[2] τὸν δὲ πόλεμον, δι᾽ ὅνπερ χρήσιμοι ἂν εἶμεν, εἴ τις ὑμῶν μὴ οἴεται ἔσεσθαι, γνώμης ἁμαρτάνει καὶ οὐκ αἰσθάνεται τοὺς Λακεδαιμονίους φόβῳ τῷ ὑμετέρῳ πολεμησείοντας καὶ τοὺς Κορινθίους δυναμένους παρ᾽ αὐτοῖς καὶ ὑμῖν ἐχθροὺς ὄντας . . .

[3] I. 44. 2: ἐδόκει γὰρ ὁ πρὸς Πελοποννησίους πόλεμος καὶ ὡς ἔσεσθαι αὐτοῖς.

C

and resentment? These two incidents thus form part of a much wider problem — the problem discussed in the assembly at Sparta.

The description of the assembly certainly belongs to the ἀληθεστάτη πρόφασις, and the four speeches which it contains deal with the problem of Athenian imperialism as a whole rather than with the conflicts arising from any recent disputes. The Corinthians, indeed, denounce Athenian imperialism without referring to any of these disputes. For them its origin is to be found in the attitude adopted by Sparta immediately after the end of the wars against Persia. They recall the construction of the walls and the progressive submission to Athens of all her former allies; they point to the technique used by the Athenians in achieving their ends, and explain the character of the city. Their accusation is couched in very general terms, and in their reply the Athenians also try to justify their empire in very general terms: οὔτε ἀπεικότως ἔχομεν ἃ κεκτήμεθα, ἥ τε πόλις ἡμῶν ἀξία λόγου ἐστίν (73. 1). They likewise go back to the wars against Persia. After them, the two Spartans, Archidamus and Sthenelaïdas, pay no more attention than the previous speakers had done to contemporary affairs. And Sthenelaïdas then succeeds with his motion, refusing to let the power of Athens increase or to betray the allies: καὶ μήτε τοὺς Ἀθηναίους ἐᾶτε μείζους γίγνεσθαι μήτε τοὺς ξυμμάχους καταπροδιδῶμεν (I. 86). The problem discussed and settled is the one pointed out by the ἀληθεστάτη πρόφασις; the analysis of it is given by the facts mentioned in the Pentecontaëtia.

Finally, the last part of the book, made up of the Corinthians' speech and the last negotiations, also confirms the idea of the 'real cause'.

The speech made by the Corinthian delegates repeats the theme of a vast war of liberation. All the different parts of Greece, they say, are threatened by Athens (I. 120. 2), and all the cities will consequently be ready to join the Peloponnesians.[1] Here liberty must be restored, and there prevented from disappearing; the tyrant-city which rules over some and threatens others must be cast down ... Although the general tendency of this speech is to show that the war to be undertaken will be successful rather than to argue that it is necessary, its basic theme rests upon the idea that the reason for war is the threat which the whole process of Athenian imperialism constitutes for all Greek cities.

As to the final negotiations, they must of necessity be subordinated

---

[1] I. 123. 1: τὰ μὲν φόβῳ τὰ δὲ ὠφελίᾳ. The interpretation of ὠφελίᾳ by ἵνα ἐλευθερώθη is justified by II. 8. 5 as much as by the context.

to the ἀληθεστάτη πρόφασις. Even if they were not preceded – as in Thucydides – by the vote of the Peloponnesian League in favour of war (I. 125. 1) which reduces them to an empty comedy (I. 126. 1), they would still suggest the existence of the 'real cause'. In fact, the events are presented in such a way as to leave all discussion until the end, with the result that Pericles, speaking at the very last moment, can thus treat all the incidents as a whole, as a series of events in themselves of small importance but which reveal and express older and more fundamental attitudes.

I have already mentioned how this fact minimizes the importance of the Megarian dispute. The whole composition of the episodes is aimed at producing this effect, and Louis Bodin has underlined the masterly skill which Thucydides shows in avoiding any direct narration of this incident.[1] In I. 139, he indicates the principal clause of the decree, and even gives the name of its author by mentioning him as the person most opposed to its reversal. Nevertheless, he avoids considering the fact directly, or mentioning the role which Pericles plays in this precise instance.[2] The analysis is cleverly kept to the end, with the result that each of the incidents is shown to be secondary in importance to the deep hostility which gave rise to all of them.[3]

The same is true of the famous ultimatum on the independence of Greek states. Thucydides could obviously have given it more importance and linked it with the ἀληθεστάτη πρόφασις; but, as Momigliano has shown, this would have given it a meaning which it certainly did not have;[4] and by insisting overmuch on what was nothing more than a pretext, Thucydides would have disguised the fact that the role played by Athenian imperialism in causing the war was one which both preceded this particular dispute and remained independent of it. And this was the idea which the whole closing passage of Book I was intended to give, and which the concluding speech was meant to reinforce.

This speech can nevertheless be considered as departing from the

---

[1] *Autour du décret mégarien.*

[2] 'Pour lui', he writes, 'c'est toute cette politique qui est en cause [i.e.: Pericles' policy as a whole], et non l'attitude de Périclès dans tel ou tel conflit, fût-ce même dans ce différend mégarien autour duquel ses contemporains menaient si grand bruit.'

[3] Cf. I. 140. 2: Λακεδαιμόνιοι δὲ πρότερόν τε δῆλοι ἦσαν ἐπιβουλεύοντες ἡμῖν καὶ νῦν οὐχ ἥκιστα.

[4] *La comp. della Storia di Tucidide, Mem. della Reale Acc. delle Scienze di Torino*, ser. II, vol. 67, n⁰ 1, Class. di Sz. mor., stor. e fil., pp. 1-48. This interpretation contradicts that of Pasquali (*Stud. Ital.*, N. S., V, 1927-1928, pp. 299 ff.), who considers that when Thucydides wrote this speech he did not know about the ultimatum.

ἀληθεστάτη πρόφασις, for, while admitting the existence of a fundamental cause and a definite hostility, Pericles makes no mention of imperialism. He maintains that Athens must fight to defend her possessions, and that Sparta shows deliberate hostility; he does not explain, as in his speech in Book II, why this is so. But this should occasion no surprise,[1] for both by its theme and purpose, the speech in Book I is linked to an analysis of the forces involved, while that in Book II is more specifically an exhortation to battle. Because of this distinction, the speech in Book I does not, it is true, express the ἀληθεστάτη πρόφασις, but, by referring to a wider conflict — whose causes Pericles does not explain — it leaves an empty space into which the ἀληθεστάτη πρόφαις can be easily fitted.[2]

There is thus no part of Book I where the idea of ἀληθεστάτη πρόφασις does not occur in a more or less precise form. And it is impossible to believe that, in 404, Thucydides could have added the second cause to the first in a purely mechanical manner.

The only possibility is that, while re-writing the History, he slightly modified the importance and even the appearance of the theme. This second hypothesis involves a more detailed examination of the text, and an attempt to discriminate between early and later passages.

Schwartz introduced a fundamental difference between the early and the later passages. In his view, Thucydides showed in his first version of Book I how the hostility of the Corinthians finally overcame the more hesitant attitude of the Spartans, but in 404, reacting against the then triumphant opposition, he arrived at the idea of a deep and ancient hostility between Athens and Sparta, and of an inevitable conflict between the two cities. For him, the description of the different incidents and the two speeches of the Corinthians and of Archidamus in the assembly at Sparta belong to the first version: the speeches of the Athenians and of Sthenelaïdas, like the Pentecontaëtia, and like Pericles' funeral oration and his last speech in Book II, belong to the second. His thesis thus rests upon the idea of a fundamental difference in the assembly at Sparta between the group Corinthians-Archidamus on the one hand, and the group Athenians-Sthenelaïdas on the other.

[1] This is by no means to be regarded as a contradiction (as Zahn suggests).

[2] What Pericles says is that the war breaks out, not for any of the causes put forward, but for more fundamental reasons. As Jacoby has very well pointed out (Zahn, p. 7), it is Thucydides' own theory which is presented in this speech.

However, Pohlenz has shown that this idea must be discarded, and that the four speeches in the assembly at Sparta form a complete whole. But he was less satisfied by the relation existing between Archidamus' speech there and those made by the Corinthians at the last meeting and by Pericles at the end of the book. The old king seemed to him to have ruined the argument of his allies in advance, and to have taken all their originality from the arguments put forward by Pericles. Pohlenz thus came to think that the whole of the debate in the assembly at Sparta was a later addition, while the last two speeches, which many themes link together without regard to distance or time, represent the older version. In that case, the changes undergone by this section would fit into a less violent evolution than that established by Schwartz. At the end of the ten years' war, Thucydides, although fully aware of the fear which the development of the Athenian empire caused to Sparta, insisted mainly on the part played by Corinth. Then, at the end of the twenty-seven years' war, faced with the collapse of Athenian power, he tended to attribute greater importance to more fundamental causes.

In fact, even when it is reduced to these more modest proportions, the evolution in Thucydides' thought still seems greater than the texts would authorize. In my view, the revisions of Book I are neither as large nor as straightforward as Pohlenz, Schwartz, and other scholars believe. The different elements which make up Book I are interrelated rather than contradictory, and fit together like the pieces of a jigsaw puzzle.

This can be demonstrated by setting out from the elements attributed to the first version.[1]

Now, if there *was* a first version for this part of the work — or for the work as a whole — the two passages which most certainly belong to it are the description of the first two incidents (Corcyra, Potidaea) in Book I, and the description of the first years of the war in Book II.[2] This is a basic miminum which no scholar who has studied the way in which the work was written has called in question.[3]

---

[1] If one ancient passage involves another, the second must be ancient as well; such a mode of reasoning does not apply to late passages.

[2] Certain clues — none of which give absolute proof — have been put forward (thus II. 23. 3: ἣν νέμονται Ὠρώπιοι, Ἀθηναίων ὑπήκοοι, a remark which ceases to be true in 411; or II. 54. 3: ἣν . . . ξυμβῆ γενέσθαι λιμόν, a hypothesis which the λιμός of 404 makes useless). Supposing one admits the theory that the work was written in several stages, the passage must obviously have belonged to the early one.

[3] Some scholars have merely argued (as Cwiklinski did) that all the speeches, even those of the first episodes, were later additions. This fails to recognize the strong link in

But, then, the description of the Megarian incident has to be added to the account given of the earlier incidents, and this leads to the negotiations which fill the end of the book, up to the speech of Pericles which forms its logical conclusion. It is quite inconceivable that there should have been an original plan that did not include both the description of the negotiations and an intervention by the principal character in the drama, especially since he has been carefully held back from the very beginning of the book. It is therefore certain that if an original version existed, in one form or another, it must have included both the description of the negotiations and the speech. The only question that needs to be decided is the manner in which the events were then presented: was it the same as now or was it different? Indeed, scholars have wondered[1] if there may not have existed previously a definite account of the two last incidents, instead of the short allusions, which are all we have now: their impression was that the description in its present form could not be considered as the natural continuation of the Corcyraean and Potidaean incidents. Certainly there is nothing to prove that Thucydides did not think of presenting the events in a different way, and did not actually do so at one time.[2] But one fact is certain: we have already seen how the whole description of the final negotiations implies a deliberate silence on Thucydides' part as far as the Megarian dispute is concerned, and the idea which governs the composition of the whole is very closely connected with the ideas that dominate the first two episodes.[3] It is thus very probable that the final negotiations and the speech which rounds them off formed part of the original version and were re-written only in certain details.

The same conclusion is reached if we set out from the other starting-point which I have indicated, the beginning of Book II. As Rose

[1] Cf. Schwartz, ch. IX.

[2] Such a question belongs to what Jacoby (G.G.N., 1929) calls the 'metaphysics' of the Thucydides problem. Only the text should be considered, and it gives no indication that the account was ever different from its present form. When the inhabitants of Aegina are shown in II. 27. 1 as being responsible for the war οὐχ ἥκιστα, Thucydides is careful to point out that this is only a pretext (ἐπικαλέσαντες).

[3] From the point of view of the ideas put forward, there is in both cases reference to a deeper cause; and as regards the composition there is in both cases the desire to leave Pericles' intervention to the end.

Thucydides between the narration and the passages of reported speech, a link whose nature and importance have been very well defined by Louis Bodin. The speeches of the Corinthians and Corcyraeans at the beginning of Book I may have been re-written at a later date (although the reasons put forward by Droysen: Athen und der Westen, Exk. II, pp. 55-56, do not seem to be very convincing); but they were certainly not just 'added on'.

Zahn has very convincingly shown (pp. 54-65), this account simply shows the analyses of Book I being put into practice: it is the methodical realization of everything foreseen, commanded or feared by Pericles, exactly in the same way as the description of a battle, in the History, repeats the terms of the speech in which the general laid down his master plan. In fact, the whole of this account corresponds even more closely with the summary of Pericles' ideas given in the short speech reported in II. 13. This is more concrete than the speech in Book I, and contains a series of formulas whose application is systematically illustrated by the events narrated. Thus the following similarities can be noted:

II. 13. 2: τὰ ἐκ τῶν ἀγρῶν ἐσκομίζεσθαι = II. 14. 1: ἐσεκομίζοντο ἐκ τῶν ἀγρῶν ...

II. 13. 2: ἔς τε μάχην μὴ ἐπεξιέναι = II. 22. 1: πιστεύων δὲ ὀρθῶς γιγνώσκειν περὶ τοῦ μὴ ἐπεξιέναι.

II. 13. 2: ἀλλὰ τὴν πόλιν ἐσελθόντας φυλάσσειν = II. 24. 1: οἱ Ἀθηναῖοι φυλακὰς κατεστήσαντο κατὰ γῆν καὶ κατὰ θάλασσαν, ὥσπερ δὴ ἔμελλον διὰ παντὸς τοῦ πολέμου φυλάξειν.

Now, if the narrative presupposes the description given in II. 13,[1] this description presupposes, in an analysis similar to that provided by the speech in Book I.[2] There is, moreover, a direct reference (II. 13. 2: ἅπερ καὶ πρότερον; II. 13. 9: ἔλεγε δὲ καὶ ἄλλα οἷάπερ εἰώθει Περικλῆς) in the same way as the speech itself looked forward to II. 13 (I. 144. 2: ἀλλ᾽ ἐκεῖνα μὲν καὶ ἐν ἄλλῳ λόγῳ ἅμα τοῖς ἔργοις δηλωθήσεται).

Thus, using two different ways of approach, we reach the same conclusion: *if there was an original version of Book I, or of the whole work, then Pericles' first speech was included in it. It was perhaps not in the form in which we see it today, but it was at least a speech asking for war, analysing the forces brought into play, and describing the plan to be followed. In other words, it was essentially similar to the speech in the present version.*

Now this speech by Pericles, which concludes the final negotiations, cannot be conceived independently of the speech by the Corinthians which is, as it were, a preface to it. In fact the two speeches correspond

---

[1] Wilamowitz, *Hermes*, 35, 1900, pp. 556 ff., proves authoritatively the strong unity in this passage. Schwartz maintained that II. 13. 2-9 was reintroduced, as was II. 29-65. This suggestion would eliminate any account of the much discussed plan of Pericles, and make the conduct of the Athenians quite incomprehensible. The plan must be put forward, more or less as it actually is. Besides, there is nothing in the text to suggest the idea that the passage was very much re-written.

[2] The narration refers to certain points put forward only in the first speech; thus, the plan of attacks by sea in enemy country, foreseen in I. 143. 1, takes shape in II. 26. 1-2; cf. II. 30, etc. ...

to each other in their very structure, and although supposed to have been given at different places and at different times, are presented by Thucydides as antithetical.

The arguments put forward by the Corinthians to show the superiority of the Peloponnesian League are these: in the first place, the general qualities of the Peloponnesian forces (number, experience, discipline); then the possibility of fighting the Athenian fleet at sea, of being able to cause Athens' allies to desert her, or of being able to plant a fort in enemy country. Now these analyses form the framework for Pericles' speech, and the particular expressions used underline the dialectical relationship between the two texts. Pericles also begins by speaking of the general character of the Peloponnesian forces, and he shows how they are inferior to those of Athens because of the inevitable lack of money, mobility, and homogeneity.[1] After this analysis, he considers in succession two of the Corinthian solutions: ἡ ἐπιτείχισις[2] (cf. 122: ἐπιτειχισμὸς τῇ χώρᾳ); τὸ ναυτικόν (cf. 121. 3: ναυτικόν τε); the only thing lacking in his reply is thus the ξυμμάχων ἀπόστασις: this, however, is mentioned later, since it provides him with the warning at the end of his speech (143. 5: καὶ ἢν σφαλῶμεν, τὰ τῶν ξυμμάχων, ὅθεν ἰσχύομεν, προσαπόλλυται; cf. I. 122. 1: ξυμμάχων τε ἀπόστασις, μάλιστα παραίρεσις οὖσα τῶν προσόδων αἷς ἰσχύουσιν).[3] In addition to this, Pericles uses practically the same terms as the Corinthians when discussing details. This is especially true of the discussion about ναυτικόν: the Corinthians had considered two possibilities: either borrowing money to pervert the loyalty of the sailors in the Athenian fleet, or training sailors if the war lasted. Pericles deals with them in turn; ἀπὸ τῆς ὑπαρχούσης τε ἑκάστοις οὐσίας ἐξαρτυσόμεθα καὶ ἀπὸ τῶν ἐν Δελφοῖς καὶ Ὀλυμπίᾳ χρημάτων of I. 121. 3 is taken up again in the: εἴ τε καὶ κινήσαντες τῶν Ὀλυμπίασιν ἢ Δελφοῖς χρημάτων of I. 143. 1; ὑπολαβεῖν οἷοί τ' ἐσμὲν μισθῷ μείζονι τοὺς ξένους αὐτῶν ναυβάτας which follows, in the first speech, is taken up again in the μισθῷ μείζονι πειρῷντο ἡμῶν ὑπολαβεῖν τοὺς ξένους τῶν ναυτῶν which follows in the second. As to the second case, εἰ δ' ἀντίσχοιεν,

---

[1] Thus he repeats, with a different purpose, certain indications given by the Corinthians; for instance, I. 141. 5: σώμασί τε ἑτοιμότεροι οἱ αὐτουργοὶ τῶν ἀνθρώπων ἢ χρήμασι πολεμεῖν, cf. I. 121. 3: ἡ δὲ ἡμετέρα ἧσσον ἂν τοῦτο πάθοι, τοῖς σώμασι τὸ πλέον ἰσχύουσα ἢ τοῖς χρήμασιν.

[2] The article itself might prove that Pericles is replying to a specific suggestion.

[3] Cf. p. 115.

μελετήσομεν καὶ ἡμεῖς, discussed in I. 121. 4, it has simply been put, by Pericles, before the other:[1] τὸ δὲ τῆς θαλάσσης ἐπιστήμονας γενέσθαι οὐ ῥᾳδίως αὐτοῖς προσγενήσεται· οὐδὲ γὰρ ὑμεῖς μελετῶντες αὐτὸ εὐθὺς ἀπὸ τῶν Μηδικῶν ἐξείργασθέ πω· πῶς δὴ ἄνδρες γεωργοὶ καὶ οὐ θαλάσσιοι καὶ προσέτι οὐδὲ μελετῆσαι ἐασόμενοι ... ἄξιον ἄν τι δρῷεν; then: ἐν τῷ μὴ μελετῶντι ἀξυνετώτεροι ἔσονται ... and at last: τὸ δὲ ναυτικὸν ... οὐκ ἐνδέχεται, ὅταν τύχῃ, ἐκ παρέργου μελετᾶσθαι (142. 6-9). Without going into the nature of the arguments put forward, it is obvious that they are based on those of the Corinthians and are very closely linked to them. The concordances between the two speeches are too close and too decisive to allow them to be attributed to different dates — as far, of course, as the main parts of the texts are concerned. This has been generally recognized, with the result that we arrive at the following conclusion: *if there was an original version, or an original plan of the book, then the last speech of the Corinthians must be considered as having formed part of it.*

But once this group has been constituted, further conclusions are unavoidable. First of all, there seems to be an external link between the two Peloponnesian assemblies, for by a certain number of details, the second clearly refers back to the first.[2] It is, however, possible that these similarities are due to the fact that the passages in question were partially re-written, and this view has been put forward by Schwartz and Pohlenz.[3] What must be discovered is therefore whether the relationship between the two speeches that we have just discussed and the speech made by Archidamus in the first assembly — a speech whose subject-matter and themes are similar to those in the two others — implies that they were written at different times (as Pohlenz thinks) or (as Jacoby does[4]) at the same time. In my view, Jacoby's solution seems correct. By comparing the three speeches closely with one another we can in fact show that they are complementary and not contradictory, and, moreover, it can also be shown that the speech by Archidamus could not have been written or conceived after the two others.

The close relationship between the three speeches has been well established by Rose Zahn, who has shown how they do come

[1] On this different order, cf. p. 115, n. 1.

[2] I. 119: αὖθις δὲ τοὺς ξυμμάχους παρακαλέσαντες; ibid.: καὶ οἱ Κορίνθιοι ... παρόντες δὲ καὶ τότε; I. 120. 1: τοὺς μὲν Λακεδαιμονίους, ὦ ἄνδρες ξύμμαχοι, οὐκ ἄν ἔτι αἰτιασαίμεθα ..

[3] Schwartz: chapter VIII; Pohlenz: I, p. 114.

[4] In Zahn, p. 46.

together to form a whole (pp. 40-54). The only criticism that can
be made of her approach is that she did not carry it far enough, since
all the available details do in fact prove it to be true. When Pohlenz
states that Archidamus' speech ruins all the arguments put forward
by the Corinthians before they are even presented, he can prove his
thesis only by considering isolated passages. And, in dealing with
speeches constructed with the subtlety found in Thucydides, this is a
most serious failing. Of course, if one proceeds in this way, it becomes easy to prove the point: the Corinthians, Pohlenz says,
simply make the suggestion that Athens' allies should be induced to
revolt, without seeming to realize that Archidamus had just shown
that this was impossible since the Peloponnesian League did not have
a fleet (I. 81. 3). But Pohlenz himself seems to forget that the Corinthians have just explained exactly how they could obtain a fleet.
Similarly, the Corinthians calmly affirm that money will be raised
by a contribution (I. 121. 5). Do they not know, asks Pohlenz, that
Archidamus has already shown that because of their lack of resources,
the Peloponnesian League could not arrive at any result whatsoever
by this means (I. 80. 4)?[1] But here again it seems that Pohlenz
ignores the distinction made by the Corinthians between a long and
a short war; to provide for immediate needs they propose raising a
loan; in the case of a longer war, the idea of forced contribution,
which would thus become less sudden and less heavy, would easily
fall into place — as well as the idea of naval training, which Archidamus had criticized because of the length of time involved (80. 4).

As to Pericles' speech, it does in fact discuss certain ideas put
forward by Archidamus. Thus, to keep to the two main points
already mentioned, he repeats that the Peloponnesians have no
money (141. 3), and that they could not achieve any result by training
sailors (142. 6-8). But he does not repeat these ideas in the form in
which Archidamus has expressed them. For between Archidamus'
analysis and his, there has been the possible solution put forward by
the Corinthians, and it is this which Pericles now dismisses. Thus, as
the themes are repeated from one speech to another, they grow in
precision and accuracy, exactly as an idea takes shape in the course of
an actual dialogue. Pericles repeats that the Peloponnesians have no

---

[1] Ἑτοίμως refers both to what the Peloponnesians feel and to what they are actually
able to pay: the former is the result of the latter. In any case, the matter will become
easier with the passage of time. The Corinthians add another remark about this question of
readiness and feeling (I. 121. 5), which once again marks the fact that they are replying to
the causes for concern mentioned by the king.

money, but he does so in a passage setting out to dismiss the Corinthian solution by insisting on the inevitable inferiority of money
raised by contribution to that already lying in a public treasury. He
repeats that it would be of no use for the Peloponnesians to undertake
any form of naval training, but the time that this would require is by
no means the only objection to this idea: however much time they
have, they will never be able to rival the Athenians, since the difficulties which they will encounter as a result of already being at war will
make all their efforts useless.[1]

It can thus be shown that by the careful arrangement of their
arguments[2] these three speeches are complementary: taken together,
they form a single whole, constructed with equal subtlety and
rigour.[3]

In fact, Pohlenz's thesis was all the more disquieting because it
seemed such an obvious one. In his view, Thucydides wrote Archidamus' speech after the two others, carefully repeating all the different

[1] Between one speech and the next there are specific details which, together with a
new general idea, reinforce the argument. This can be seen about the suggestion that the
Peloponnesians might train sailors, or about the idea that they might be able to corrupt the
loyalty of foreign sailors employed by Athens. Some precise and concrete modes of
reasoning, which are entirely new in the discussion, are introduced at this point; cf. later,
note 3.

[2] Generally speaking, Pohlenz fails to take into account how very subtle Thucydidean
dialectic can be. Thus he expresses surprise (p. 110) that, in speeches which reply to each
other, there are terms which correspond in sections which are not parallel to one another
(for instance, about the πρόσοδοι from which Athens derives her strength: I. 81. 4 = I.
122. 1). This is very frequent in Thucydides' antithetical speeches: cf. Louis Bodin,
Diodote contre Cléon.

[3] A summary of the arguments put forward, even without going into the actual reasoning, shows how subtle these oppositions are. Archidamus talks of the Athenian superiority,
and enumerates the difficulties likely to be encountered by the Peloponnesian League:
they have no *fleet* (and *training* will take a long time); no *money* or *contributions*; no
means of inducing Athens' allies to *revolt*, because of the absence of a *fleet*; probability
that the war will be a *long one*.
The Corinthians indicate the superiority possessed by the Peloponnesian League; they
add to it that they will be able to provide a *fleet* (*money* will be provided by *loans*, and
they will thus *corrupt the loyalty* of the sailors employed by Athens: if they win a naval
victory, then the war will be a *short one*; and, if it lasts, they will get some *training* and
make a financial *contribution*); thus they will be able to induce Athens' allies to *revolt*
and will *plant a fort* in enemy country (ἐπιτειχίζεσθαι takes the place of δηοῦν).
As for Pericles, he indicates the inferiority of the Peloponnesian League, consisting
partly in the fact that the Peloponnesians have no *money* and must have recourse to
contribution, which is always less practical: this inferiority will be even more noticeable
since the war will be a *long one*; they will not be able to *plant a fort* in enemy country,
because they have no fleet; and they will not be able to acquire a *fleet*, because they will
not be in a position either to get *training* or to raise money by a *loan* and thus *corrupt the
loyalty* of sailors employed by Athens.

themes, and yet he did not realize that he was spoiling the general meaning! Such minute attention to detail cannot possibly be reconciled with such intellectual carelessness. And one cannot suppose either that Thucydides wrote Archidamus' speech with the intention of putting it in the place of the two others. All this long analysis of the rival forces is intended to explain and emphasize the plan put forward by Pericles — a plan which has to be put forward in the speech in Book I before it is shown being applied in Book II.

But if these close links between the three speeches imply that they were intended to form a coherent whole, they also prove that the speech by Archidamus, being the most simple and straightforward, could not have been written after the two others: it indicates the problems that the second two try to solve, establishes the facts that they assume to be generally known,[1] and finally lays down the basic themes of a discussion which becomes steadily more complex from one speech to the next. After the speech by Archidamus the themes are split up, and far more details are brought into play. It is thus natural to think that the three speeches were written at the same time, and that, *if there was a first version, then it already contained the essential points of Archidamus' speech, as well as the last two speeches of the book.* But Thucydides' work holds so closely together that this speech, again, seems to involve other parts of Book I.

First of all, and this is a minimum, it involves the speech made by the Corinthians at the first assembly.[2] Together, the two speeches form a pair that no scholar has ever thought of separating.[3] The very discussion which I have just quoted, and which has been shown to be linked by its details to the following speeches, represents the best possible reply to the Corinthians: οὐ δυνατόν is Archidamus' answer to the Corinthians.

In addition, Pohlenz[4] showed, in 1919, how impossible it was to separate, as Schwartz had done, the couple formed by the speeches of the Corinthians and of Archidamus, from the couple formed by the speeches of the Athenians and Sthenelaïdas, which is interwoven

[1] It is one of the reasons why Pericles can avoid dealing directly with the theme of Athenian superiority: cf. p. 114.

[2] The difference in tone between their two speeches can be explained quite easily: in the first assembly, they are not concerned with practical questions, and only want to have a decision taken about the whole matter (besides, their speech comes after a number of others which would have been more precise: cf. I. 67. 5); the second is different, since they now want approval for a particular plan of action.

[3] Cf. Bodin, *Mélanges Desrousseaux.*

[4] I, pp. 95-138.

with it.[1] This is something which, after the proofs put forward by Pohlenz, no longer needs demonstrating. And besides, whatever may have been the changes made in this part of the work, or whatever links there may be between the different speeches, the argument from probability is really sufficient in itself. As Pohlenz has pointed out, it is obvious that neither of the pairs which Schwartz dissevered is in fact conceivable without the other. One does not even need any precise research to prove this: can one really imagine that the Athenians-Sthenelaïdas pair could ever have been intended to take the place of the two speeches written for the first version? What would in that case be this curious Peloponnesian assembly in which the only speakers, practically, would be these Athenians, whose presence is already so surprising? What would be the function of this speech on the origins of Athenian imperialism, if this had not been mentioned before by any previous speaker? What significance could the few decisive words of the ephor have, if no indication had been given of the reasons for hesitation? If the second pair of speeches were written after the others, they were intended to complete and not to replace them; and, in fact, there is no valid reason for taking them out of the context and considering them together.

Moreover, there is every possibility that the speech by Sthenelaïdas always formed part of the debate, since it is this speech which explains the vote and brings it to a close; the pacifist note of the speech made by the old king would be a poor preparation for a vote in favour of war, and, if taken by itself, would be an incomplete and therefore inaccurate piece of historical evidence.[2]

As to the speech made by the Athenians, this must probably have been there in some form or another from the very beginning. By laying the blame on the policies pursued by Athens, the Corinthians certainly offered opportunity for such a speech. But it is difficult to say what form it might have taken. An Athenian speech in this Peloponnesian debate was somehow superfluous, and its themes could therefore be developed in whatever manner one liked. And

[1] On the relationship between the Athenians' speech and those of the other pair, cf. p. 266. Similarly, Sthenelaïdas, while putting all the Athenian arguments on one side together, replies to the analyses of Archidamus, directly (I. 86. 3).

[2] Sthenelaïdas' speech reveals that a desire for war existed in Sparta as well as in Corinth: this is something which Thucydides could be aware of from the very outbreak of the war, and the idea of an opposition between the two cities can already be found in Herodotus VI, 98 (a passage quoted by Pohlenz): the text comments upon the sufferings undergone by Greece at the time of Darius, Xerxes and Artaxerxes: τὰ μὲν ἀπὸ τῶν Περσέων αὐτῇ γενόμενα, τὰ δὲ ἀπ' αὐτῶν τῶν κορυφαίων περὶ τῆς ἀρχῆς πολεμεόντων.

in the actual speech, the reply to the accusations put forward is so far-reaching and so remote from the immediate subject of the debate, that it could well have been written, if not completely, then at least to a very great extent, at a different date. This could only be confirmed by studying the speech systematically; and the research would for the time being go beyond the immediate framework of this chapter;[1] but whatever part is considered as being a later addition, this would in no way change the explanation given for the outbreak of the war. The speech replies to the Corinthians by defending a policy which they had attacked. From the point of view of the general analysis, it perhaps makes the explanation clearer and more precise; but it does not alter it. And, without trying to discover the nature and extent of any modifications that might have been made in this speech, we are already able to conclude that neither the distinction suggested by Pohlenz nor those put forward by Schwartz fit Book I. Even if it has been extensively re-written and expanded, the ideas governing its composition were fixed from the very beginning in the form which they present today. Not only did the ἀληθεστάτη πρόφασις already exist in Thucydides' mind; it was already expressed by a planned arrangement of narrative and speeches which is very similar to the one we have today;[2] and it already showed the same mixture of Corinthian hatred on one hand, and Spartan timidity but increasing fear on the other. The whole of this structure belongs to Thucydides' first version — if, indeed, there was a first version of Thucydides' work.

This last hypothesis, which had appeared in the beginning of this research to be *a priori* the most reasonable and prudent one,[3] might in fact be considered as fitting in with the ideas discussed in the speeches. For without wishing to raise any precise issue of the dates to be attributed to the various sections of the work, one can point out that, in general,[4] all the arguments presented describe a war like the ten-year war. The speakers foresee neither the mad imprudence of the Athenians, nor the considerable role played by Persia, nor the

---

[1] This study will be made further on, in chapter I of Part III.

[2] This scheme is moreover very well planned, and seems to have been deliberate from the very beginning. For instance, there is: an Athenian discussion — a Peloponnesian discussion — a single speech on the Peloponnesian side — a single speech on the Athenian side.

[3] Setting out with such a hypothesis adds greater value to the conclusions we have been able to reach, as regards the unity of the book.

[4] Reservations must be made of possible additions, which will not be discussed here.

alliance with Syracuse, nor the changes of government. They envisage nothing more than a straightforward war of liberation, undertaken with the means immediately available, and go no further than considering the possibility or impossibility of raids in enemy country; yet, everything seems to be carefully weighed and foreseen: it would indeed look as if Thucydides wanted the last part of the war to come upon us as a surprise; and it may be that it came as a surprise to the historian himself.

The only important passages to remain independent in the construction of this part of the work are the speech made by the Athenians — at least in part — and the Pentecontaëtia. These passages are parenthetical and unattached; they are not indispensable to the rest of the work. Moreover, the Pentecontaëtia seems to have been written in a late period; and if there was an original version of the work, it must have been added to that version afterwards.[1]

Now it happens that these two passages reveal a similar tendency: without in any way modifying the ἀληθεστάτη πρόφασις, they form a commentary on Athenian imperialism and throw it into greater relief. The general construction of the book gives a clear and definite indication of the part which this imperialism plays, but these two passages study its history and characteristics for their own sake. It thus becomes possible to affirm that Thucydides distinguished the central role of Athenian imperialism from the very moment that he began to write his work, and also that if — as is probable — he did rewrite the beginning of his History after 404, one of his aims must have been to bring out the importance of this imperialism even more clearly.

There is nothing at all improbable in this, since it was precisely in its closing years that the war showed itself to be the supreme crisis in the history of the empire which had given it birth. The power of Athens was destroyed; and, as it drew to a close at the same time as the conflict itself, it became, quite naturally, the real subject of Thucydides' work. A description of this power became a necessary

[1] One might wonder at the appearance which this book would take without the Pentecontaëtia; but the two speeches by Nicias are closer to one another than those of the Corinthians would be; and the beginning of Book III, with the events of Plataea and Mytilene, contains a higher proportion of speeches than Book I would then include, even though Book I is essentially concerned with analysis. On the other hand, Eduard Meyer considers (in *Forsch.*, II, p. 280, n. 2) that, without the Pentecontaëtia, the most important element would be lacking: this seems rather an exaggeration; the addition is certainly good, but it is quite possible to imagine the book without it, or containing only shorter indications.

preface to the battle in which its fate was to be decided; and an analysis of its nature provided the theme for the great debate which was to be settled by the force of arms. The end of the empire focused people's attention on what it had been and gave rise to critical attacks on imperialism. Thucydides was thus able to insist more on this theme than he had originally done, and his task was so much the easier since he had always understood and indicated the part which it had played.

Such a conclusion assumes that nowhere in his work did Thucydides neglect the importance of Athenian imperialism, and presupposes also that, if he further developed its characteristics in later additions, this was nevertheless a natural continuation of the earlier passages.[1] In other words, it assumes that although the importance attributed to Athenian imperialism might vary from place to place, its role is nevertheless permanently indicated. And a study of the work as a whole provides evidence that this is indeed the case.

II. THE HISTORY OF THE WAR

At the same time as it explains the origins of the war, Athenian imperialism also plays an important part in its actual history. The analyses in Book I have already shown that her empire was the practical means which Athens intended to use during the war, the cause for complaint which her enemies were to put forward in order to acquire help, and the issue which both sides gave as constituting the main object of the war. This triple role recurs in every episode, and shows itself in all the speeches that are not exclusively military.

Book II begins the description of the war with a series of campaigns and various events which have nothing to do with imperialism except that they realize in practice the ideas expressed by Pericles. But the theme of imperialism nevertheless recurs spontaneously in these episodes, and shows the feelings which inspired both sides. For Athens' enemies, it is a basis for the idea of a war of liberation: Thucydides recalls this in II. 8. 4, and, in II. 72. 1, Archidamus makes

1 Above all, Thucydides may have considered it much more as an event in itself and less in its relationship with the war: a comparison between his aims in the Archaeology and in the Pentecontaëtia is a fairly clear indication of this. The first is concerned with the growth of Athenian power in so far as this explains the importance of the war, while the second is concerned with the wars because of the light which they throw on the growth of Athenian power. If the Pentecontaëtia is a later addition, the Archaeology might well belong, in spite of its maturity of method, to the first version (cf. in particular I. 10. 2).

it into the essential argument justifying the action against Plataea. On the other hand, even a speech such as that of Phormio, dealing with practical strategy, reminds the Athenians that the real question at issue is the rule over the sea (II. 89. 10). Nowhere is this idea better illustrated than in the last speech in which Pericles tries to justify his general policy (II. 60-65). Apart from his funeral oration, it is the only political speech in the book, and one of the most important in the whole work. What is more, it is a speech which stands by itself, which the actual description of events in no way made necessary, and to which Thucydides has added a long discussion of the man himself. These different characteristics give it a special place in the book, and it is noteworthy that the aim of this speech is to show that Athens' empire is at the same time the best means of winning the war and the principal reason why it should be fought. The first of these themes is developed in paragraph 62, where the principles of Periclean strategy are closely related to a genuine theory as to the possibilities offered by the Athenian rule over the sea. 'You think that your empire is confined to your allies, but I say that of the two divisions of the world accessible to man, the land and the sea, there is one of which you are absolute masters, and have, or may have the dominion to any extent which you please.' As to the second theme, paragraph 63 develops it in no less detail, when Pericles explains that Athens is, as it were, a prisoner of her own empire, and called upon to run the greatest risks because of its existence: 'And do not imagine that you are fighting about a simple issue, freedom or slavery; you have an empire to lose, and there is the danger to which the hatred of your imperial rule has exposed you. Neither can you resign your power . . .' Wishing to justify the war, Pericles is led on to justify the existence of the empire, showing that it is at the same time a necessary (63. 2) and an admirable thing (64. 3 to the end). Thus, standing out above the various events, this analysis puts the whole of the emphasis on Athenian imperialism.

In Book III, the theme is brought into closer connection with the narrative of events. In particular it dominates the two episodes of Mytilene and Plataea, on which Thucydides concentrated almost all his attention, since between them they take up more than half the book[1] and are analysed in a whole series of speeches. Of course these

---

[1] 61 paragraphs out of 116, that is to say, for Mytilene: 2-7; 8-20, 25-30; 35-51; for Plataea: 20-25; 52-69.

D

two episodes were bound to be treated, but they might well not have been given quite so much importance in comparison with the other episodes described. Diodorus, for example, bases his presentation of the same facts on an essentially geographical division, and these two episodes take up only one paragraph each.[1] Diodorus simply presents the basic facts, while the interest which Thucydides has in the problems raised by Athenian imperialism enables him to give them a living structure.

The Mytilenian affair raised the question of the desertion of Athens by her allies, and of their consequent repression. Each of these problems corresponds to one of the two acts in which the episode is treated. The speech made by the Mytilenians to the Lacedaemonians is part of the first act, and the two opposing speeches made at Athens by Cleon and Diodotus are part of the second.

The speech made by the Mytilenians (III. 9-15) contains first of all an attempt to justify their action, and it is Athenian imperialism which provides them with this. Thus they accuse Athens and describe the method she employs: Athens, they say, is enslaving Greece; and the term δουλοῦν recurs with typical insistence.[2] This imperialism begins little by little (by attacking the weakest) and hypocritically (by disguising itself with fine reasons) (10-11), and this Sparta ought to attack and cast down (13).When they come to the practical aspect of their analysis, they show how their desertion of the Athenian cause may serve a useful purpose; and we find a repetition of the terms defining sea-power, which dominated the discussion of Archidamus, Pericles and the Corinthians in Book I. The advantage put forward by the Mytilenians is that their action will allow the Peloponnesians to destroy the sources of income which create Athenian power,[3] and also to acquire a large fleet (13. 7). Here, once again, it is imperialism which explains both the undertaking itself and the means that it will employ.

When the promise obtained by the Mytilenians does not enable them to avoid being crushed, it is then the turn of Athens to make her views known. Thucydides describes her hesitations in a pointed debate between Cleon, a supporter of severity, and Diodotus, a

---

[1] Diodorus, XII, 55 and 56.

[2] III. 10. 3: ξύμμαχοι μέντοι ἐγενόμεθα οὐκ ἐπὶ καταδουλώσει τῶν Ἑλλήνων Ἀθηναίοις — 4: ἐπειδὴ δὲ ἑωρῶμεν αὐτοὺς τὴν μὲν τοῦ Μήδου ἔχθραν ἀνιέντας, τὴν δὲ τῶν ξυμμάχων δούλωσιν ἐπειγομένους . . . — 5: οἱ ξύμμαχοι ἐδουλώθησαν, πλὴν ἡμῶν καὶ Χίων.

[3] 13. 5-6: οὐ γὰρ ἐν τῇ Ἀττικῇ ἔσται ὁ πόλεμος, ὥς τις οἴεται, ἀλλὰ δι' ἣν ἡ Ἀττικὴ ὠφελεῖται· ἔστι δὲ τῶν χρημάτων ἀπὸ τῶν ξυμμάχων ἡ πρόσοδος.

supporter of moderation. For the first speaker, the problem is to preclude such desertions in the future, since they are fatal to the sources of Athenian income.[1] For the second, it is to prevent such desertions from becoming irreparable, which would be fatal to the sources of Athenian income.[2] Thus the first speaker argues in favour of making a striking example of Mytilene, whereas the second thinks Athens should show herself merciful on this occasion and take all possible precautions against a repetition. The whole debate is thus concerned with the attitude which Athens should adopt towards her subject peoples. At the same time it aims at defining the nature of her domination, since both speakers are led to explain to what extent this dominion is tyrannical (III. 37. 2) and unjust (III. 40. 4), or to what extent it can be accepted and maintained (III. 47. 2). Now such an exclusively Athenian discussion has only an indirect bearing on the war between the two cities; it is important only for someone whose attention is turned towards Athenian imperialism and who is trying to make its workings known.

The Plataean episode ought to be narrated from a completely different point of view, since the Athenians played no part in it. Nevertheless, Thucydides' treatment of it implies the same approach. The episode contains first of all a military section, which separates the two acts of the great Mytilenian drama (20-25), and later an important debate in which both the Plataeans and the Thebans take part (53-69). Against the noble appeal made by the Plataeans, their speech is an act of accusation which concerns Plataea only through Athens, and the question of Athenian imperialism thus becomes the centre of the affair. By remaining faithful to Athens, they maintain that Plataea has betrayed the rest of Greece, even more than if she had adopted the same attitude towards the Persians, whose methods were basically the same.[3] Thus, by the attitude she has adopted, Plataea has become guilty of all the crimes committed by Athens,[4] and it is, indirectly, against these crimes that the Thebans are protesting.[5] The

---

[1] III. 39. 8.   [2] III. 46. 2-3. On the concordances, cf. p. 157.
[3] 62. 2: τῇ μέντοι αὐτῇ ἰδέᾳ ὕστερον ἰόντων Ἀθηναίων . . .
[4] 64. 3: ἀπελίπετε γὰρ αὐτὴν (τὴν ξυνωμοσίαν) καὶ παραβάντες ξυγκατεδουλοῦσθε μᾶλλον Αἰγινήτας καὶ ἄλλους τινὰς τῶν ξυνωμοσάντων ἢ διεκωλύετε . . . 64. 4: μετὰ γὰρ Ἀθηναίων ἄδικον ὁδὸν ἰόντων ἐχωρήσατε.
[5] Certain minor arguments are to be found here which are used elsewhere against Athenian imperialism. Thus the Thebans refuse to accept the παλαιὰς ἀρετάς of Plataea, saying that guilty people who have acted correctly in the past deserve double punishment (διπλασίας ζημίας); Sthenelaïdas had expressed the same idea with reference to Athens (I. 86. 1: διπλασίας ζημίας).

presence of such an attack is even more remarkable since its actual historical role was by no means decisive. We know that the reasons put forward by the Thebans had no effect on the decisions taken by the Spartans, since Thucydides tells us that the latter were thinking only of their own interests (III. 68. 4). It may thus be possible to think that, beneath its apparent absence of function, the role of the Thebans' speech was precisely to connect the whole episode with the problem of imperialism. However that may be, we must note the fact that Thucydides did not let slip the opportunity of putting in a speech whose main theme was once again Athenian imperialism.

The other episodes in the book are not treated so fully. Apart from the Corcyraean episode (69-86), to which Thucydides attached a particular moral importance, there are only fairly simple military operations which are rapidly described. But the role played by Athenian imperialism is nevertheless noted when the occasion arises, for it is this which explains the steps taken by Sparta to liberate and by Athens to conquer. The first aspect is particularly noticeable in the case of the Ionian affair (31. 1), while the second shows itself for the first time in the episodes of Sicily and Melos. These were attempts whose causes[1] seemed independent of the war itself, but Thucydides is careful not to omit them because they betray a tendency which was shortly to become much more important.

In Book IV these aspects are analysed in much greater detail, and the interest is concentrated on four main centres: Pylos, Sicily, Boeotia and the Thracian coast. In the first three, the active character of imperialism is now very well marked; in the last, the idea of a war of liberation finally takes systematic form.

The affair of Pylos takes up the whole of the first third of the book.[2] In itself it had nothing to do with imperialism, since it was simply an episode of the war, and not even one which in any way depended on the possibilities which Athens drew from her domination. Nevertheless, by the way in which he treats it and by the speeches which he includes when describing it, Thucydides does link it up with imperialism; in his work, Pylos represents the unexpected success with which the Athenians ought to have been satisfied. There is only one speech, at the very centre of the description of the episode, and in it the Spartan ambassadors do nothing except warn Athens of the dangers

[1] Cf. III. 86. 4 and III. 91. 2.
[2] In actual fact the first 41 chapters (out of a total of 116), less chapters 7 and 24-26.

of ambition. They argue that Athens should not be tempted by this accidental success, that she should moderate her thirst for conquest and be prepared to share with Sparta the hegemony over Greece. In other words, she should bring her imperialism under control. And as if to show even more convincingly that these are not simply arguments put forward by ambassadors trying to make peace, Thucydides himself denounces this very ambition which the Spartan ambassadors wished to discourage: it appears both in Athens' refusal and in her subsequent conduct, for, if the Athenians acted as they did, it was, he says, because they had further ambitions (IV. 21. 2: τοῦ δὲ πλέονος ὠρέγοντο – IV. 41. 4: οἱ δὲ μειζόνων τε ὠρέγοντο). He consequently sees, in a military success followed by a particularly fortunate undertaking, an event due to chance followed by a political error. And he can do this only because he looks at the very principles involved in the action, by connecting it here again with that Athenian imperialism which he ferrets out and shows at the root of every enterprise.

The role played by Athenian imperialism in Sicily was more obvious. And, in fact, Thucydides gave more attention than was necessary both to the episode itself and to its interpretation. He not only links it up with the desire to acquire more, which the affair of Pylos had already revealed (IV. 65. 4: οὕτω τῇ γε παρούσῃ εὐτυχίᾳ χρώμενοι ἠξίουν σφίσι μηδὲν ἐναντιοῦσθαι) and brings out in this way the Athenian ambition which prevails in all the different episodes: he also feels the need to have it denounced by the Syracusan Hermocrates (59-65). Hermocrates declares that Athenian imperialism threatens the whole of Sicily, and several times repeats the idea with great insistence.[1] He quotes the conduct of Athens on other occasions as proof, and asks for the formation of a Sicilian alliance aimed at resisting this ambition. Now if this episode was necessarily related to Athenian imperialism, Thucydides was nevertheless not obliged to bring it out quite so clearly; in itself, the expedition was not particularly important, and it was shortly to reveal itself as having been little more than a curtain-raiser. Hermocrates himself was destined to play another role later on, and to make other speeches.[2] Finally, even if it

---

[1] IV. 60. 1: ἐπιβουλευομένην τὴν πᾶσαν Σικελίαν, ὡς ἐγὼ κρίνω, ὑπ' Ἀθηναίων – IV, 60. 2: ἄνδρας οἳ καὶ τοῖς μὴ ἐπικαλουμένοις αὐτοὶ ἐπιστρατεύουσι . . . εἰκός, ὅταν γνῶσιν ἡμᾶς τετρυχωμένους, καὶ πλέονί ποτε στόλῳ ἐλθόντας αὐτοὺς τάδε πάντα πειράσασθαι ὑπὸ σφᾶς ποιεῖσθαι – IV. 61. 3: τῶν ἐν τῇ Σικελίᾳ ἀγαθῶν ἐφιέμενοι.

[2] All the indications are that Thucydides knew about the great expedition when he wrote the Sicilian episode (cf. IV. 1. 2 and the passages quoted in the note above). There

be supposed that Thucydides did want to draw his reader's attention to the plan of Sicilian unity put forward by Hermocrates, Droysen points out that the arguments ought to be different from what they are[1] — which means at least that they could be. Droysen shows that Syracuse, the powerful city, ought to give guarantees to those cities which might be afraid of her, and, as a result draw near to Athens. If Hermocrates does not do this, and insists only on the danger of Athenian domination, it is because Thucydides' aim was to throw the whole light on this imperialism which, in his view, was the most important factor.

In addition, at the same time as they are denouncing Athenian imperialism, the Sicilian episode and the speech which it contains highlight the formation of a movement of resistance among those whose independence is being threatened by Athens; they show the beginning of a series of failures which will punish Athens for her excessive ambition. After Hermocrates has spoken, Book IV brings in one after the other, in similar roles, Pagondas the Boeotian, the champion of another independence movement, and, above all, Brasidas of Sparta, the liberator.

Pagondas intervenes in the Boeotian affair only by a short speech of encouragement. But we note once again that it is Athenian imperialism that he attacks, and Athenian imperialism that he uses as an argument to urge the army to fight. In order to show this more clearly, Thucydides has no hesitation in making Pagondas use the same words that we have seen repeated throughout the book: the imperialism of the affair of Pylos, the imperialism of the Sicilian affair are here repeated in textual form: ὅστις τὰ μὲν ἑαυτοῦ ἔχει, τοῦ πλείονος δὲ ὀρεγόμενος ἑκών τινι ἐπέρχεται (IV. 92. 2). Pagondas recalls that Athenian imperialism is a threat to everyone[2] and he offers proof of this, mentioning the situation in Euboea and that prevailing in the whole of Greece. In contrast, he provides a description of a non-imperialistic policy: τήν τε αὐτῶν ἀεὶ ἐλευθεροῦν μάχῃ

---

[1] *Athen und der Westen . . .* , Exk. I. pp. 50-54.

[2] It should be noted that the unity of this great drama which is carried over from one episode to another is marked by similarities in expression: πρὸς τούτους γε δὴ οἳ καὶ μὴ τοὺς ἐγγὺς ἀλλὰ καὶ τοὺς ἄπωθεν πειρῶνται δουλοῦσθαι of IV. 92. 4 echoes the ἄνδρας οἳ καὶ τοῖς μὴ ἐπικαλουμένοις αὐτοὶ ἐπιστρατεύουσιν of IV. 60. 2.

---

may have been some re-writing, but it is equally possible that Thucydides wrote his first version of this part of the work after the Sicilian expedition, and yet before 404. In any case, he certainly did not — as some scholars have thought in the past — add everything about Sicily in a later version.

καὶ τὴν ἄλλων μὴ δουλοῦσθαι ἀδίκως (IV. 92. 7). If, in so short a speech, Thucydides insisted on repeating such familiar ideas, it was surely to stress the fact that the same fundamental conflict, the same dominating factor and the same essential features recur everywhere: he did not want his reader to lose sight of them for a single moment.

But while Pagondas represents only the leader of a country which has been attacked and which is defending its independence as could be expected, Brasidas is alone in suggesting a systematic policy of liberation as an answer to Athenian imperialism. He is the first to use all his strength in an effort to persuade Athens' allies that they must desert her, to undermine her rule and to put a policy of anti-imperial-ism into practice. And it is obvious that Thucydides has given him a place of honour in his work, and has treated him in a particularly favoured way. After having brought out the role he played in Pylos (11. 4-12. 2), then at Megara (70-75), he waits until the begin-ning of his action in the Thraceward parts before concentrating the whole of his attention on him. This begins in paragraph 78 of Book IV, and ends only with his death, just before the peace of 421, in paragraph 11 of Book V. In the first pages of this whole series, Thucydides even goes so far as to comment on the role and influence of Brasidas in the light of subsequent events, which is something that he does elsewhere only for Pericles. Finally he gives him a speech – the speech to the Acanthians in IV. 85-88, whose main points Brasidas repeats on a number of other occasions[1] and which provides the key to his whole campaign. He presents himself as the liberator (85. 1): 'By sending me with this army, citizens of Acanthus, the Lacedaemonians have merely confirmed the motives which they gave as ours at the beginning of the war, that we should fight against Athens in order to liberate Greece.' He expects Athens' subjects to be Sparta's allies from the outset (85. 4), since not to be so is to refuse liberty for oneself and for other people (85. 5), to become an accomp-lice of Athens, and, as he says in his *epilogos*, to prevent Greece from seeing an end to her slavery (87. 3); whereas he is bringing each city independence, and this has been guaranteed by an oath (86. 1).[2]

These principles enable him to win over Acanthus (88), Amphi-

---

[1] Cf. at Torone, 114. 3: ἔλεξε τοῖς ἐν τῇ ᾿Ακάνθῳ παραπλήσια (Thucydides nevertheless feels that the message of this speech is so important that he repeats it in indirect speech); similarly at Scione, 120. 3: ἔλεγεν ἅ τε ἐν τῇ ᾿Ακάνθῳ καὶ Τορώνῃ; the idea is taken up yet again in the purely strategic speech which he makes at the time of the struggle against Cleon, in V. 9. 9.

[2] Thucydides recalls this last detail once again in 88. 1.

polis (102-108), Torone (110-117) — and thus bring Athens to decide
to accept an armistice.[1] During the period of the armistice itself,
these principles produce the spontaneous desertion of Scione, and
then of Mende (123). In spite of the attempts made by Cleon, and in
spite of Brasidas' own death, these desertions are sufficiently dangerous to constitute one of the reasons for which Athens accepts
peace.

Thus all these facts are centred on imperialism. Whether one sees
in it a duel between conquest and liberation (be it present conquest or
not and self-liberation or not), or a series of military operations determined by the character of the empire, the war is in every manner
dominated by the idea of imperialism.

What is more, the different roles which imperialism plays react on
one another so as to account for the course of events. In V. 14. 2,
Thucydides explains the acceptance of peace in the following way:
'They (the Athenians) were afraid too that their allies would be elated
at their disasters, and that more of them would revolt; they repented
that after the affair of Pylos, when they might honourably have done
so, they had not come to terms.'[2] Thus fear and remorse are linked
together in the minds of the Athenians, for they are afraid that they
might offer further opportunities to the liberation movement, and
sorry that they were not able to restrain their own ambition. But
these two feelings reinforce each other since it is precisely because
they did want more and more, precisely because they have advanced
too far along the path of empire, that they are now afraid of seeing
this empire reduced by the action of the liberating armies. The
influence which these different ideas have on one another and which
links them all together is what makes Athenian imperialism into the
real subject of Thucydides' work.

The interest which he constantly shows in imperialism thus joins
the different episodes together. And whatever date we may assign to
each individual section, it is obvious that such a permanent characteristic cannot be the result of a later evolution in his thought. As my
analysis of Book I has already shown, Thucydides approached his
work with a fairly clear idea of the role that Athenian imperialism
was going to play, and he indicated the importance of this role in
both the earlier and the later passages.

---

[1] 117. 1: νομίσαντες Ἀθηναῖοι μὲν οὐκ ἂν ἔτι τὸν Βρασίδαν σφῶν προσαποστῆσαι οὐδὲν
πρὶν παρασκευάσαιντο καθ' ἡσυχίαν. Cf. p. 45.

[2] There is no valid reason to think, as Steup did, that this sentence is suspect.

Nevertheless, without going into any detailed discussion, it may at least be noted that if, as is very probable, Thucydides did later rewrite certain passages which had been either planned or composed at an earlier date, all he can have done is to stress even more clearly the influence exercised by Athenian imperialism; and that is the very conclusion which we have already drawn from Book I.

Leaving aside, for the moment, the main and best organized episodes, in which traces of composition tend to disappear, I can offer one small fact, taken from the last episodes, as proof of this theory. We have already seen that Thucydides showed the greatest interest throughout the closing sections of Book IV in the character of Brasidas and the influence of his campaign of liberation. In this respect, the chapters of Book V which deal with the conclusion of the peace treaty sound a slightly different note. This difference, although slight in itself, has nevertheless appeared to some scholars, and in particular to Steup, as the proof that these chapters were not by the same author and had been added by Thucydides' 'editor'. In my view, this difference is merely an indication that the chapters were written at different dates.

In IV. 117, the armistice is explained, as far as the Athenians are concerned, by the fear of further desertions: νομίσαντες 'Αθηναῖοι μὲν οὐκ ἂν ἔτι τὸν Βρασίδαν σφῶν προσαποστῆσαι οὐδὲν πρὶν παρασκευάσαιντο καθ' ἡσυχίαν. In V. 15. 2, it is explained by the defeat of Delium: σφαλέντων δὲ αὐτῶν ἐπὶ τῷ Δηλίῳ παραχρῆμα οἱ Λακεδαιμόνιοι γνόντες νῦν μᾶλλον ἂν ἐνδεξαμένους ποιοῦνται τὴν ἐνιαύσιον ἐκεχειρίαν. This contradiction is no doubt less important than first appears, for the two facts are connected, and the defeat at Delium is one of the reasons which explain why Brasidas was so successful when dealing with extremely hopeful allies (IV. 108. 5: ἅμα δὲ τῶν 'Αθηναίων ἐν τοῖς Βοιωτοῖς νεωστὶ πεπληγμένων). Yet these two passages are obviously not written in quite the same spirit, since the fact which, in Book IV, is presented as being quite essential, is not even mentioned in Book V as providing a link between Delium and the armistice.

Similarly, in IV. 81, Thucydides gives a long commentary on the merits of Brasidas, while in V. 16. 1, he explains that Brasidas wanted the war to go on because of the glory and success which it brought him. Here again, the contradiction is not absolute, since in one case Thucydides is dealing with his actions and in another with his motives.[1] Moreover, there is nothing shameful in these motives, for their only defect is that they are rather selfish. Nevertheless, Thucydides' admiration is more marked in Book IV than in Book V, and this difference is similar to the one already mentioned.

Now all the indications are that the developments in Book IV were a later addition. In his commentary in IV. 81, Thucydides refers to the later part of the war and to the desertions which followed the failure of the Sicilian expedition: ἔς τε τὸν χρόνῳ ὕστερον μετὰ τὰ ἐκ Σικελίας πόλεμον. It is even possible that when he was describing the confidence which Brasidas could impart to the cities, Thucydides had in mind another and very different Lacedaemonian.[2] Lysander was indeed to profit from the actions of Brasidas, but he was also to betray the programme of liberation that Brasidas had supported, and in doing so to make Sparta just as unpopular in Greece[3] as his predecessor had made it popular. The implicit contrast between the two men would provide an excellent explanation for a renewed admiration based upon Thucydides' realization of the difference between them.

Similarly, in his commentary in IV. 108, Thucydides insists both upon the mistake made by the allies and on the extent of Athenian power as later manifested (ὅση ὕστερον διεφάνη): this would surely imply that he wrote the passage when he could see the events in perspective, for the same mistake is mentioned in Book VII (28. 3), and, although with a less obvious reference to the actual situation, in Book VIII (2. 2: μάλιστα δὲ οἱ τῶν Ἀθηναίων ὑπήκοοι ἕτοιμοι ἦσαν καὶ παρὰ δύναμιν αὐτῶν ἀφίστασθαι διὰ τὸ ὀργῶντες κρίνειν τὰ πράγματα καὶ μηδ᾽ ὑπολείπειν λόγον αὐτοῖς ὡς τό γ᾽ ἐπιὸν θέρος οἷοί τ᾽ ἔσονται περιγενέσθαι). On the whole, the extent of this mistake could only be appreciated when the long resistance put up by Athens during the last eight years of the war was taken into consideration.[4]

---

[1] In general, chapters V. 15-16 consider the motives of the different characters in a fairly selfish form (cf. the case of Nicias, particularly) but there is no text to indicate that this was not Thucydides' natural interpretation.

[2] πρῶτος γὰρ ἐξελθὼν καὶ δόξας εἶναι κατὰ πάντα ἀγαθὸς ἐλπίδα ἐγκατέλιπε βέβαιον ὡς καὶ οἱ ἄλλοι τοιοῦτοί εἰσιν.

[3] For the fact itself, cf. Xen., Hell., VI, 3, 7; and for the result, Diod., XIV, 33: Παυσανίας... φθονῶν μὲν τῷ Λυσάνδρῳ, θεωρῶν δὲ τὴν Σπάρτην ἀδοξοῦσαν παρὰ τοῖς Ἕλλησιν...

[4] It seems, moreover, for reasons which I shall discuss on pp. 150 and 229, that Thucydides made a point of insisting, after 404, on the resistance put up by Athens and on the resources that this supposed. It is one of the themes which he treats in his judgment on Pericles (II. 65), obviously written after 404.

In this case it could be admitted that the developments now under discussion could be the effect of re-writing, and there is perhaps a specific piece of material evidence for this. While the end of every year in this war is marked by the mention of the author's name (ὃν Θουκυδίδης ξυνέγραψεν), this is missing on two particular occasions: first of all in II. 47, just after the funeral oration which brings to an end the first year of the war, and again in IV. 116, just after the campaign by Brasidas which marks the end of the eighth year. Now most scholars are agreed that the funeral oration was a later addition, and it is possible that in both cases the signature could have disappeared in the process of re-writing.

If this were so, the desertions in the later part of the war and the contrast with Lysander would help in two ways to explain Thucydides' intention. Nevertheless, this intention can be really understood only if one sees the full significance of these desertions and the full importance of this contrast between the two policies by relating them to the question of Athenian imperialism and of the fate awaiting it. It is only when the war between Athens and Sparta is seen clearly as the crisis of this policy of imperialism that the intervention of Brasidas assumes real importance together with the consequences which it had and the different principles which later emerged in its place:[1] Thus, above all minor considerations, the end of Athenian imperialism is the main reason which brought about this re-writing.

And if it is true that Thucydides progressively underlined this central fact, it is even more understandable that, in spite of slight difficulties raised by points of detail, the unity of his work is all the more noticeable precisely because of the alterations which it has undergone.

The same tendency is visible in the second phase of the war, for if the events themselves were more obviously connected with Athenian imperialism, this is emphasized by the way in which Thucydides develops them.

The first indication of a personal judgment can be found in the very fact that he described this second phase, and considered the renewal of hostilities as merely a continuation of the previous war. After 404, he himself defends this view of the Peloponnesian War as a single whole, as an original and controversial interpretation of

[1] On the other hand, events like the defeat at Delium seemed then more accidental and less closely related with the fundamental problem.

events (V. 26. 2: καὶ τὴν διὰ μέσου ξύμβασιν εἴ τις μὴ ἀξιώσει πόλεμον νομίζειν, οὐκ ὀρθῶς δικαιώσει). And, in fact, even after Thucydides had finished his History, traces of the theory he was criticizing can be found in texts where, instead of the Peloponnesian War being treated as a whole, one finds the description of two wars, separated by the peace of Nicias.[1]

Now it is reasonable to maintain that it was because he linked each of these wars to the idea of Athenian imperialism that Thucydides had so clear a view of their essential unity. Everyone could see, as he saw himself, that the peace treaty was not being observed, and that hostilities had broken out again. What others did not see was that these hostilities formed part of the same conflict, between the same forces, and that the second war was merely the continuation of the first. Why, then, the difference? Thucydides' view is easy to understand: if the real question at the beginning of the conflict had been that of Athenian domination, then it was natural to carry on the story of this conflict right up to 404 when this question was finally settled.[2] If the peace of Nicias had been in fact only a *pis-aller* for Athenian imperialism, refused at the time of the victory of Pylos and reluctantly accepted later on, it was normal to consider it as merely a truce, abandoned, as soon as it was possible to do so, for the same reasons for which it had earlier been rejected. Finally, if the main inspiration for the actions undertaken over the last ten years had been Athenian ambition, it was normal to complete the description of the events in the framework of one single work by adding to them the one episode which resumed them all, an episode in which this ambition came to full fruition and then collapsed. For the Sicilian expedition was inspired by the same motives that had produced Cleon's actions; it came up against exactly the same type of resistance as had originally brought the Peloponnesian League into the war and

---

[1] Cf. Plato, *Menexenus* 242 e; Andocides, *Peace*, 9. Aischines, II, 176 (these two passages are moreover taken from one and the same source, cf. p. 17). The second war begins, according to these different authors, at different dates. Some (cf. *Menexenus*) make it include the Sicilian expedition, while Isocrates, on the other hand, makes it begin in 413, with the occupation of Decelea, since he writes (XVIII, 47-48): δέκα μὲν ἔτη συνεχῶς ὑμῖν Λακεδαιμονίων πολεμησάντων . . . ἐπειδὴ δ' οἱ τριάκοντα κατέστησαν; in this case, we need to count three wars, two against Sparta and one against Sicily. Although Diodorus accepts that all these wars are linked together (XII, 37, 2), he nevertheless thinks that they are more independent of one another than Thucydides does (for the distinction between the two 'Peloponnesian wars', see XII, 74, 6 and 75, 1; for the 'Sicilian War', XII, 84, 4: ἐπὶ τὴν ἀρχὴν τοῦ πολέμου τοῦ συστάντος Ἀθηναίοις καὶ Συρακοσίοις).

[2] V. 26. 1: μέχρι οὗ τήν τε ἀρχὴν κατέπαυσαν τῶν Ἀθηναίων Λακεδαιμόνιοι καὶ οἱ ξύμμαχοι καὶ τὰ μακρὰ τείχη καὶ τὸν Πειραιᾶ κατέλαβον.

caused, one after another, the desertion of Athens by Mytilene, the
policy of Sicilian unity, the defence of Boeotia and the campaign of
Brasidas. Although the meaning is uncertain, it is possible that
Thucydides indicates this by using a descriptive phrase which echoes
those which he used earlier, when talking, in VI. 24. 4, of: τὴν
ἄγαν τῶν πλειόνων ἐπιθυμίαν.[1] However, it was because in every
case he went back to their deep and permanent cause that the facts
thus presented themselves to him with such unity. And it will be
noted that the authors who do not recognize this unity also ignore
the role played by Athenian imperialism, for they speak of a first war
undertaken because of the Megarians, of another attributable to the
Argives, of a third undertaken on behalf of the people of Leontini.[2]
While Thucydides offers only one cause for war, these writers
suggest many and varied causes. That is why he saw one war where
others saw three. The idea which links the different episodes together
also provides the unity of the different wars. And, in fact, Thucydides
emphasizes this idea in the second part of his work in a manner that
the events alone in no way demanded.

Between the peace of Nicias and the Sicilian expedition one single
fact held his attention enough for him to present an actual debate
and indulge in a deep political analysis. And this fact is the only one
which, before the Sicilian expedition took place, reveals the increasingly obsessive need which Athens had for further conquests.[3] This
fact is the annexation of Melos in 416. The island was small, and the
enterprise had no intrinsic importance. But on this occasion Athens
had attacked a small country that was doing her no harm, and had
treated her in an unforgettable manner. Thus, although this action

---

[1] πλειόνων can also be considered as a masculine, meaning: the enthusiasm 'of the
majority'. Even then, the ἄγαν . . . ἐπιθυμίαν is characteristic.

[2] Cf. (1) Andocides, Peace, 8: πάλιν δὲ δ διὰ Μεγαρέας πολεμήσαντες = Aeschines, II, 175:
πάλιν δ᾽ εἰς πόλεμον διὰ Μεγαρέας πεισθέντες καταστῆναι; – (2) Andocides, Peace, 9:
πεισθέντες καὶ τότε ὑπ᾽ Ἀργείων = Aeschines, II, 176: πεισθέντες ὑπ᾽ Ἀργείων. It should
be noted that these two texts, both hostile to Athenian imperialism, do not denounce it;
similarly, although Thucydides explains the war by imperialism, he does not therefore
blame Pericles. People hostile to the war set out to prove that the causes for which it is
being fought are frivolous and not in the best interest of Athens; people in favour of it
try to show that they are important, and vital to her. – (3) Menexenus, 243 a: ὑπὲρ τῆς
Λεοντίνων ἐλευθερίας (the text in question is deliberately and crudely apologetic).

[3] The same cause is emphasized in the two episodes, but the fact that they are brought
together in this way has no special significance, and does not seem to be especially intended to show Hubris followed by Nemesis. On why Thucydides put this analysis at this
point in the book, cf. pp. 281 ff.

had only an indirect connection with the war itself, it was full of meaning from the point of view of Athenian imperialism. And it is in this spirit that Thucydides analyses it in the dialogue between the Athenian and Melian representatives which occupies the end of the book (V. 85-113). Once again, the question raised is that of Athenian imperialism: does Athens really need to conquer Melos? Is she not afraid that she may one day see this policy turn against her or end in failure? General principles are involved and the problem of imperialism is treated in all its possible aspects: in its relationship with justice (89-91), with the Gods (104-105), with Athens' own subjects (95-99), and with her enemies (105-111). So detailed a treatment indicates that Thucydides wanted to deal with the central question of Athenian imperialism, and it is obvious that the Melos incident is simply an opportunity to do this, and one which scarcely required such a thorough analysis.

Things were very different in the case of the Sicilian expedition, for this was and will always remain the imperialistic undertaking *par excellence*, and one which ended in a catastrophe startling enough to attract considerable attention. But even when these facts are admitted, it is indisputable that Thucydides emphasized the episode in a most striking manner in the two books which he devoted to it. Together with their separate introduction (a feature which has surprised certain readers) their considerable length (one hundred and ninety-two chapters for two and a half years) the importance of the political analyses which they contain (spread over seven important speeches in Book VI) the perfection of their form (a feature which strikes most readers and which struck Plutarch himself),[1] these chapters read like a model of care and finish in the whole of Thucydides' work.

And the main theme of all this is the crisis of Athenian imperialism. Every time that the opportunity arose, Thucydides brought out in the actual description of events the nature of the policy pursued by Athens,[2] that is to say of her imperialism; and all the analyses in Book VI are devoted to it.

The discussion of the events is presented in three acts. The Athenian point of view occupies the first antithetical speeches of Nicias and Alcibiades (9-24); the point of view of her adversaries takes up the

[1] *Nicias*, I, 1.
[2] Cf. VI. 1. 1; VI. 6. 1; see also p. 200, n. 1

second, which presents the argument between Hermocrates and Athenagoras (32-41); the two points of view are finally weighed one against the other in the neutral city of Camarina, which two speakers try to win over to their side: the Syracusan Hermocrates and the Athenian Euphemus (76-88), the latter having replaced Alcibiades, who has disappeared in the interval between the two acts. Alcibiades nevertheless reappears, but it is in Sparta that he then speaks (89-93).

In the whole of this discussion, all the speeches, without exception, are concerned with Athenian policy and aim solely at defining the risks that it is running.

This fact is obvious in the first group of speeches; moreover, we can note Thucydides' concern to treat the problem in a general and almost abstract manner. The opposition is between different principles. Nicias, the supporter of prudence, wishes to consolidate but not to expand the empire;[1] Alcibiades, on the other hand, defends the very principle of conquest, for this has enabled the empire to be established,[2] and the empire is a necessity for a city like Athens. Such a city is in danger of collapse if she ceases to expand, and she cannot decide by her own free will to limit the area of her dominion.[3] Thus the real question is less the expedition itself than the very mechanism of imperialism, and it is easy to recognize Thucydides' own intervention at this point.[4]

The same is true of the speeches made by the two Syracusans. Hermocrates repeats the accusation that he has already made in Book IV, arguing that the Athenians want to take over Sicily,[5] and that she must therefore unite against them. Fear will doubtless be a sufficiently powerful motive: πάντα γὰρ ὑπὸ δέους ξυνίσταται (33. 5), and it will even provide the Syracusans with allies, Carthage perhaps among them (34. 2). Thus, as Brasidas did, Hermocrates directs against Athenian ambition a coalition created by all the different resistance movements which it provokes, the only difference

---

[1] VI. 10. 5: μὴ . . . ἀρχῆς ἄλλης ὀρέγεσθαι πρὶν ἣν ἔχομεν βεβαιωσώμεθα.

[2] VI. 18. 2: τήν τε ἀρχὴν οὕτως ἐκτησάμεθα καὶ ἡμεῖς καὶ ὅσοι δὴ ἄλλοι ἦρξαν.

[3] VI. 18. 3: καὶ οὐκ ἔστιν ἡμῖν ταμιεύεσθαι ἐς ὅσον βουλόμεθα ἄρχειν, ἀλλὰ ἀνάγκη, ἐπειδήπερ ἐν τῷδε καθέσταμεν, τοῖς μὲν ἐπιβουλεύειν τοὺς δὲ μὴ ἀνιέναι, διὰ τὸ ἀρχθῆναι ἂν ὑφ' ἑτέρων αὐτοῖς κίνδυνον εἶναι εἰ μὴ αὐτοὶ ἄλλων ἄρχοιμεν.

[4] These two speeches are (like the others) reconstructed by Thucydides. In Diodorus XII, 83, 6 we find the summary of the speech that Nicias is presumed to have made. Although its general meaning is the same, its arguments are presented in a different way. It has, in particular, a long comparison with Carthage which corresponds to nothing in Thucydides, and which, precisely, has but an incidental value.

[5] VI. 33. 2: Σικελίας ἐπιθυμίᾳ.

being that he is dealing with people who are still independent. On the other hand, Athenagoras refuses to prepare for battle, because he cannot believe that Athens would be mad enough to launch herself into such an enterprise at this time. For the reader, warned by the previous chapters, this incredulity only emphasizes the ambition which Hermocrates has so justifiably denounced.

And as if the question needed even more emphasis, Hermocrates soon makes a third speech, in which he repeats the same accusations,[1] and shows in the condition of Athens' subjects the example of what must be avoided. Euphemus' reply then confirms that it is still Athenian imperialism as a whole which is on trial, since he begins by declaring (82. 1): ἀγάγκη καὶ περὶ τῆς ἀρχῆς εἰπεῖν ὡς εἰκότως ἔχομεν. Once again, he goes back to the wars against Persia. He also provides general explanations, speaking of the great rivalry between Athens and Sparta, the Dorian city, and of all the difficulties and hatreds which explain Athenian action. Imperialism is thus judged in as much detail from the outside as it has just been from the inside, so that the reader is able to consider the question in all its different aspects. And he sees, standing out above all the individual incidents, the clash between a force with which he is now perfectly familiar and the different movements of resistance that it has called into being.

These movements receive their final reinforcement in the help that Alcibiades brings to Sparta, for his last speech, which brings out more than any other the principles guiding Athens' policy, provides thereby the instrument that will enable her enemies to frustrate this policy. For the first time, in the closing section of the book, the Sicilian expedition takes its place as simply a part of a vast ambition, which is now visible in the most concrete of forms, and whose unlimited nature Alcibiades no longer wishes to disguise (90. 2): 'We sailed to Sicily hoping in the first place to conquer the Sicilian cities; then to proceed against the Hellenes of Italy; and lastly, to make an attempt on the Carthaginian dominions, and on Carthage itself. If all or most of these enterprises succeeded, we meant finally to attack Peloponnesus (. . .) Thus we hoped to crush you easily, and to rule over the Hellenic world' (or, more exactly, 'to extend our rule over the whole of the Greek world': (καὶ τοῦ ξύμπαντος Ἑλληνικοῦ

---

[1] VI. 76. 2. He declares that he will leave the accusation against Athens on one side (77. 1: ἀλλ' οὐ γὰρ δὴ τὴν τῶν Ἀθηναίων εὐκατηγόρητον οὖσαν πόλιν νῦν ἥκομεν ἀποφα-νοῦντες ἐν εἰδόσιν ὅσα ἀδικεῖ). Nevertheless, he does treat it indirectly in so far as he uses past history to encourage present resistance.

ἄρξειν). But against this plan of a Hellenic, and, as it were, a universal dominion, Alcibiades suggests to the Spartans a programme which will lead to the destruction of the whole of the Athenian empire: ἵνα . . . καὶ ᾿Αθηναίων τήν τε οὖσαν καὶ τὴν μέλλουσαν δύναμιν καθέλητε. The advice which he gives to bring this about is designed by the author as a prelude to the description of events in Book VII and to the disaster which brings it to an end.[1] Now these two themes, each of them presented in its most striking form, are surely not brought together by chance. Taken together, they show the risk which Athens is being made to run by her own ambition, and suggest the idea — already hinted at previously — that the undertaking of new conquests endangers those actually completed.

The value of these analyses lies precisely in this relation: the dangers and advantages of an imperialistic policy, the obstacles and possibilities which may await it, the arguments which can be put forward for or against it, all these different ideas are important because this final ambition will turn against Athens herself. Because of its own errors, imperialism will meet with a setback and this will reveal all its inherent defects. These become apparent immediately after the expedition.

The desertions take up the beginning of Book VIII. The Athenians expect them (1. 2), prepare for them (1. 3), the cities desert with enthusiasm (2. 1), the Euboeans, the Lesbians, the people of Chios and of Erythrae spontaneously appeal to Sparta (5). All take the same path (15. 1), the first encourage others to follow their example (19), and occasionally succeed (22. 2). There is no way of stopping this process, neither rewards, nor the granting of autonomy (12), nor a change of government (48, cf. 64-65).

But here Thucydides gives only the basic minimum of information, without speeches, without a noticeable choice among the episodes, without any kind of plan, and the book runs on, flat and monotonous, offering no outstanding feature as a starting-point for an analysis. This could be explained in the following way: although the desertions themselves were linked with the drama of imperialism, the practical negotiations and plans had become quite

---

[1] Cf. later pp. 205 ff., for the relationship between the account in Book VII and the analyses in Book VI. It will be noted that, in Books VI and VII as in Book II, Thucydides often reminds us in all the short speeches of how important are the issues at stake and the reason for action provided by Athenian imperialism (VI. 69. 3; VII. 56. 2; 66. 2; 68. 2).

E

independent of it. The description of the long and uncertain campaigns in Asia, in which the struggle, having become a matter of life and death for both sides, no longer offered any scope for the ideas of conquest or liberation,[1] would thus be quite naturally sacrificed by Thucydides, whereas he had given the Sicilian expedition the greatest attention and care. It is also quite possible that the condition of Book VIII can be explained by other considerations.[2] In any case, no matter what the relation between the two facts may be, it should be noted that the only part of the work in which the role of imperialism is not clearly defined is also the one in which Thucydides' own presence is the least perceptible. Book VIII is thus, so to speak, the exception that proves the 'rule' discovered in the other books.

If it is true that the idea of imperialism did indeed govern the fundamental structure of Thucydides' work during the whole of the second part of the war, it is obvious that the place which it occupies can in no way be dependent on later alterations and re-writings. It is very possible that the idea was given greater importance by subsequent additions or alterations[3] since it seems, in a general way, that this was one of the effects of Thucydides' revisions. But it is absolutely certain that this idea was present from the very beginning, and that it dominated his historical and intellectual attitude.

By interpreting all the different facts in the light of Athenian imperialism, Thucydides provides them with a definite unity, and, as we have seen, makes it visible in the close relationship which is established between the various episodes. This unity is also apparent in the succession of speeches dealing with imperialism. These are not only concerned with the same theme: they develop the same arguments, with all the enemies of imperialism on one side and all its supporters on the other. Thus the whole work is filled with the

[1] There might be some cause for surprise in the fact that Thucydides did not give greater emphasis to the alliances between Sparta and Persia which marked the end of the idea of liberation. Doubtless he did not find these alliances quite so scandalous as other thinkers did (see pp. 100-101).

[2] Cf. p. 225. The condition of Book VIII is the only argument in favour of the view that the work might have originally been written in a form in which the idea of Athenian imperialism did not play an important role. The analyses given of the other books seem to me to eliminate this hypothesis, and justify the idea that reasons derived from the events themselves were as important, here, as those depending upon the way the work was written. Nevertheless, Book VIII does still show that, as he clarified his work, Thucydides did bring out more and more the role of Athenian imperialism.

[3] The problem of the extent to which certain passages were re-written is a very tricky one in this part of the work; it cannot be discussed here.

ever-strengthening echo of their debate, as their two voices are heard from beginning to end, replying to each other in an eternal and dramatic conflict.

The first series is made up of numerous speeches which are not all equally important: the two speeches of the Corinthians at Sparta in Book I, the speech of Archidamus in Book II, the speeches of the Mytilenians and of the Thebans in Book III, Hermocrates' first speech and the speeches of Pagondas and Brasidas in Book IV, and finally the two speeches of Hermocrates in Book VI.

Two different types of speeches make up the second series: sometimes the orators are speaking abroad and defending the policy of Athens there (like the Athenians in Book I and Book V, or Euphemus in Book VI), and sometimes they are speaking in Athens itself, and, while discussing what policy ought to be pursued, are defending imperialist principles against the attacks made on them by other Athenians (this is the case with Pericles in Books I and II, Cleon in Book III and Alcibiades in Book VI).

In both series we can see the same attitudes repeated throughout: the same accusation on one side and the same defence on the other.

The accusation is a simple one, for it aims simply to show that Athens has imperialistic ambitions. Whether they are trying to make a people decide to go to war, to resist or to desert, or whether they are justifying it for having done one of these things, the different speakers never try to do anything but persuade their audience to acknowledge the fact, in order to emphasize Athenian ambition. Some do it quickly, with rapid affirmations, while others, who try to argue their case in more detail, refer to the conduct of Athens in the past and show how she has progressively established her rule; and any one particular case, chosen by the orator to fit the circumstances under which he is speaking, can be made to illustrate her intentions: thus, for the Corinthians of Book I, the important examples are those of Corcyra and of Potidaea, while the Mytilenians choose to speak of the previous members of the federation in general; Hermocrates in Book IV talks about the Chalcidians and Pagondas about Euboea. Each of the speakers states a certain number of probabilities: in I. 68. 4, the Corinthians say: οὐ γὰρ ἂν Κέρκυράν τε ὑπολαβόντες βίᾳ ἡμῶν εἶχον καὶ Ποτείδαιαν ἐπολιόρκουν. In III. 10. 6, the Mytilenians say: οὐ γὰρ εἰκὸς ἦν αὐτοὺς οὓς μὲν μεθ᾽ ἡμῶν ἐνσπόνδους ἐποιήσαντο καταστρέψασθαι, τοὺς δὲ ὑπολοίπους, εἴ ποτε ἄρα δυνηθεῖεν, μὴ δρᾶσαι τοῦτο. And in VI. 76. 2, Hermocrates says οὐ

γὰρ δὴ εὔλογον τὰς μὲν ἐκεῖ πόλεις ἀναστάτους ποιεῖν, τὰς δὲ ἐνθάδε
κατοικίζειν, καὶ Λεοντίνων μὲν Χαλκιδέων ὄντων κατὰ τὸ ξυγγενὲς
κήδεσθαι, Χαλκιδέας δὲ τοὺς ἐν Εὐβοίᾳ, ὧν οἵδε ἄποικοί εἰσι
δουλωσαμένους ἔχειν. Only in certain speeches is the analysis carried
further and made to bring out one characteristic rather than another.
But these characteristics themselves all contain the same principle, and
merely complete one another from one speech to the next. Athenian
rule, they say, has been established gradually (κατ' ὀλίγον, I. 69. 3),
by beginning with the weakest of the allies (καὶ τὰ κράτιστα ἐπί τε
τοὺς ὑποδεεστέρους πρώτους ξυνεπῆγον, III. 11. 3), by using high-
sounding pretexts (αἰτίαν εὐπρεπῆ ἐπενεγκόντες, VI. 76. 3, cf.
III. 11. 2). Thus from one end of the work to the other the same
imperialism is revealed in the same way and denounced under the
same form: the fact that it is never denounced or criticized in any
other way enables each speech to be brought back to the same single
theme, and makes the accusation even more telling.

This accusation is also reinforced by yet another circumstance:
none of the Athenian orators ever denies the character of their policy
in the speeches which they make in its defence. They only discuss
whether or not it is necessary; and to the perpetual cry 'they have
imperialistic ambitions', their reply is 'our situation forces us towards
imperialism'. Thus they contribute to create exactly the same effect
in the reader's mind as the speeches made by their opponents.

Like those in the first series, all the speeches in the second are
connected together by the presentation of parallel arguments. But this
fact could not be stressed so much as in the first series without risking a
serious misrepresentation of the truth. A man defending some
imperialist measure in Athens cannot speak in the same way as
another who is speaking at a different time about a different problem.
And when the Athenians are speaking abroad in order to defend the
policies of their own country, they must interpret the facts mentioned
by their opponents: so their arguments have to be more detailed and
more varied in their approach than those they are attacking.

It is therefore even more striking to see that by presenting very
different arguments under the same form, Thucydides has restored
their fundamental resemblance. Throughout the whole of his work,
one attitude is adopted by one set of speakers and is contrasted with a
single attitude presented by another set. Thus the Athenians declare
in Book I: ἐξ αὐτοῦ δὲ τοῦ ἔργου κατηναγκάσθημεν τὸ πρῶτον
προαγαγεῖν αὐτὴν ἐς τόδε (I. 75. 3), or: εὖ ἴσμεν μὴ ἂν ἧσσον ὑμᾶς

λυπηρούς γενομένους τοῖς ξυμμάχοις καὶ ἀναγκασθέντας ἂν ἢ ἄρχειν
ἐγκρατῶς ἢ αὐτούς κινδυνεύειν (I. 76. 1), or, finally, on a different
level: οὐδ᾽ ἡμεῖς θαυμαστὸν οὐδὲν πεποιήκαμεν οὐδ᾽ ἀπὸ τοῦ ἀνθρωπείου τρόπου, εἰ ἀρχήν τε διδομένην ἐδεξάμεθα καὶ ταύτην μὴ ἀνεῖμεν
ὑπὸ ⟨τριῶν⟩ τῶν μεγίστων νικηθέντες, τιμῆς καὶ δέους καὶ ὠφελίας,
οὐδ᾽ αὖ πρῶτοι τοῦ τοιούτου ὑπάρξαντες ἀλλ᾽ αἰεὶ καθεστῶτος τὸν
ἥσσω ὑπὸ τοῦ δυνατωτέρου κατείργεσθαι (I. 76. 2). Similarly,
Pericles declares in II. 63. 2: ἧς οὐδ᾽ ἐκστῆναι ἔτι ὑμῖν ἔστιν εἴ τις
καὶ τόδε ἐν τῷ παρόντι δεδιὼς ἀπραγμοσύνῃ ἀνδραγαθίζεται· ὡς
τυραννίδα γὰρ ἤδη ἔχετε αὐτήν· ἣν λαβεῖν μὲν ἄδικον δοκεῖ εἶναι,
ἀφεῖναι δὲ ἐπικίνδυνον. And Cleon also remarks, in III. 40. 4: εἰ γὰρ
οὗτοι ὀρθῶς ἀπέστησαν, ὑμεῖς ἂν οὐ χρεὼν ἄρχοιτε· εἰ δὲ δὴ καὶ οὐ
προσῆκον ὅμως ἀξιοῦτε τοῦτο δρᾶν, παρὰ τὸ εἰκός τοι καὶ τούσδε
ξυμφόρως δεῖ κολάζεσθαι ἢ παύεσθαι τῆς ἀρχῆς καὶ ἐκ τοῦ ἀκινδύνου
ἀνδραγαθίζεσθαι. Similarly, on another level, the Athenians in
Book V note (105. 2): ἡγούμεθα γὰρ τό τε θεῖον δόξῃ, τὸ ἀνθρώπ-
ειόν τε σαφῶς διὰ παντὸς ἀπὸ φύσεως ἀναγκαίας οὗ ἂν κρατῇ ἄρχειν
... εἰδότες καὶ ὑμᾶς ἂν καὶ ἄλλους ἐν τῇ αὐτῇ δυνάμει ἡμῖν γενομένους
δρῶντας ἂν ταὐτό. And Alcibiades states in VI. 18. 3: οὐκ ἔστιν
ἡμῖν ταμιεύεσθαι ἐς ὅσον βουλόμεθα ἄρχειν, ἀλλὰ ἀνάγκη, ἐπειδήπερ
ἐν τῷδε καθέσταμεν, τοῖς μὲν ἐπιβουλεύειν, τοὺς δὲ μὴ ἀνιέναι. And
Euphemus declares, in VI. 87. 2: φαμὲν γὰρ ἄρχειν μὲν τῶν ἐκεῖ ἵνα
μὴ ὑπακούωμεν ἄλλου, ἐλευθεροῦν δὲ τὰ ἐνθάδε ὅπως μὴ ὑπ᾽ αὐτῶν
βλαπτώμεθα, πολλὰ δ᾽ ἀναγκάζεσθαι πράσσειν διότι καὶ πολλὰ
φυλασσόμεθα.

Thus the nature of the arguments used on both sides, together with
their more or less complete repetition from one speech to the next,
finally brings out — by insisting on the continuity of the conflict
which it provokes — the essential fact of Athenian imperialism
which gives the work its whole meaning and purpose. Moreover,
this similarity between the arguments put forward, a similarity even
more noticeable because of its very artificiality, gives proof to the
results at which we had already arrived: Athenian imperialism
represents a permanent feature of the work, which may perhaps have
become more marked with the passage of time, but which remains
basically independent of the way in which the *History of the
Peloponnesian War* was written.

CHAPTER TWO

THE CHARACTERISTICS OF ATHENIAN IMPERIALISM IN THE WORK OF THUCYDIDES

THUCYDIDES nowhere studies the principles or the achievements of Athenian imperialism, but contents himself with describing a series of actions which show how it develops. Nevertheless he provides the elements for a systematic analysis of its nature by the relationship which he establishes between these actions, the explanations which he offers for them, and the speeches which he inserts in his work either to defend or attack them. Our task is thus to bring together a number of different texts in order to see what idea he intended his reader to have of Athenian ambition and Athenian dominion.

In both cases, the Pentecontaëtia, being more especially concerned with imperialism and more compact in its presentation of events, provides the first centre of interest. The features which guide Thucydides in his selection of actual incidents to discuss will be more easily noticeable in the Pentecontaëtia, for he will certainly have selected them more rigorously in this particular part of the work. Because it is more concise, the Pentecontaëtia will bring out more clearly the principles that direct his choice. Yet these principles will be of interest to us in so far as they recur again in other parts of the work. For they will then enable us to make out not the attitude governing a particular series of chapters, but a more fundamental disposition and Thucydides' first approach to the general fact of Athenian imperialism.

I. ATHENIAN AMBITION

Any complete analysis of Athenian imperialism must take place on several different levels. If we want to discover what characteristics Thucydides attributed to Athenian imperialism, we must ask how its political manifestation and its programme, the means of achieving its ends and its field of actions, its innermost nature and psychological inspiration are presented in his work. And if there are any questions which his work does not enable us to answer, this fact in itself will be an extremely interesting piece of information.

This is, indeed, what happens when we ask the first of our three questions.

In the work of Thucydides, Athenian imperialism is presented purely and simply as the practical policy pursued by Athens. There are no party political attitudes towards imperialism, nor any traditional political programmes to which speakers ever refer. Consequently there are no different forms which this imperialism tended to adopt under such and such a political party, and no different phases in the history of Athenian politics. There is just this one fact, as if there were only one permanent unchanging will — as if the whole of Athens were always imperialistic in its attitude, and always imperialistic in exactly the same way. This unity is particularly apparent in the Pentecontaëtia, and is never absent from the rest of the work.

From the moment when Themistocles originated the idea by suggesting that the Athenians should 'take hold' of the sea and thus inaugurating what later became the empire,[1] the movement appears to advance smoothly with no discussion and no further intervention by any particular individual. In the first fifty years of its expansion, one finds Athenian proper names only in the phrase 'under the command of', and even this is often missing.[2] Only one, unchanging subject, assures the continuity of this development: οἱ Ἀθηναῖοι, the Athenians. Isolated individuals seem to have been subordinated to this one great collective personage, and to have been merely the passive instruments of a will which remained external to them. No idea can be gathered of the struggles which must have divided Cimon, Pericles and Thucydides, son of Melesias, and it is equally impossible to suspect that there might have been a change in Athenian policy in 446. Athens' acts are mentioned, but her inner motives are never described.

This schematic view of events is naturally not allowed to continue when Thucydides begins to go into more detail and when, because the actions of Athens belong directly to his field of study, he begins to explain them, to comment on them or discuss them. But even

---

[1] I. 93. 4. On the meaning given here to the word ἀρχή, cf. later p. 119, n. 6

[2] This formula can be found four times for Cimon, once for Leocrates, once for Myronides, twice for Tolmides, three times for Pericles. Apart from that, Pericles is named four times: in I. 114. 1; 116. 3; 117. 2, but always in a strictly military role.

when he contrasts the differing views of two Athenians on imperialism — which only happens twice: in Book III (Diodotus and Cleon) and in Book VI (Nicias and Alcibiades) — or when he explains why such and such a measure was taken, even then he never seems to deal with definite programmes concerning imperialism. In the speeches which he puts into the mouths of his orators there is nothing to indicate that they are referring to a tradition. The position which they adopt seems to be explained by the immediate circumstances and to be valid only for them; and the problem under discussion always seems to be a new one, unrelated to any others. Although certain individuals do now play a role — and Thucydides indicates this only in particularly important cases — the difference between them is never a theoretical or systematic one. Consequently, the relationship between Pericles and Cleon or between Pericles and Diodotus is no better defined than that existing between Cimon and Pericles or between Cimon and Thucydides, son of Melesias.

Nevertheless, if we want to understand how Athenian politics worked, we must re-establish, as a background, a picture of the theoretical struggles which both explains the disputes over practice and gives meaning to the decisions which are finally taken. We must make our way into what is, for Thucydides, forbidden territory and look at this conflict which exists within the city among the different political personalities and programmes or the different political parties.

We then discover that the Athenians can be divided into three main groups according to the attitude they adopt towards imperialism. First, although in normal times they play only a very small role, there are the opponents of imperialism: it is these whom Pericles attacks in his final speech;[1] and they had doubtless always existed in Athens, forming a revolutionary opposition which put all its hopes on Sparta and admired no other city. One can see from the behaviour of the governments of 411 and 404 how little concern they had for the greatness of Athens.

Nevertheless, this was only a small minority, and the bulk of the Athenians did not share these ideas. In the same way as they served their city in her democratic institutions, they generally favoured her greatness and the extension of her power. Thus they were all 'imperialists', but limited their agreement to this very general programme and

[1] II. 63. 2: ἧς οὐδ᾽ ἐκστῆναι ἔτι ὑμῖν ἔστιν, εἴ τις καὶ τόδε ἐν τῷ παρόντι δεδιὼς ἀπραγμοσύνῃ ἀνδραγαθίζεται. Cf. p. 127.

were divided on how it should be pursued. From this there sprang two general tendencies, which can be called extreme and moderate imperialism.

These two tendencies can be distinguished by the attitude which people adopted towards Sparta. The extremists maintained that the power of Athens should supplant all others, including, naturally, the rival city of Sparta. (This was a vague hope at the beginning, but then became a veritable programme, since Alcibiades says in VI. 90. 3: τοῦ ξύμπαντος Ἑλληνικοῦ ἄρξειν.) Their aim was to crush Sparta by war, or else to reduce her power, little by little, by strengthening Athenian forces in spite of her and against her; for the extremists, the city walls, the treasure, the supremacy of the Athenian navy had only one purpose: to ensure the superiority of Athens in Greece. The moderates considered this rivalry between the two cities as equally unfortunate for them both, and for the rest of Greece. In their opinion, the fight against the barbarians formed a worthier object of Athenian expansion, and they considered that Athens should share the rule over the rest of Greece with Sparta, in a system that is sometimes referred to as 'dualist'. They considered that Athens was naturally destined to rule over the sea and Sparta over the land, and that they should simply take care always to remain united. In particular, since Athens was naturally the more active of the two cities, she should take care not to offend Sparta, which should remain her sister rather than her rival. The extremists constantly supported the 'Peloponnesian Wars', while the moderates recommended an alliance with Sparta and the colonization of the barbarian lands.

The idea of such an opposition within Athens itself makes the opening of the Pentecontaëtia immediately clear. Themistocles' influence marks a desire for absolute supremacy, and by constructing the walls round Athens he is deceiving and annoying Sparta. Thucydides is at least obliged to note this.[1] On the other hand, Cimon represents the attempt to reach an agreement with Sparta. Between the time of Themistocles' and Cimon's ostracism, Athens is at war only with the barbarians or with the subjects of Sparta who have rebelled against her (this happened in the affair of Ithome). When, as a result of this affair, relations with Sparta are broken off, Cimon suffers ostracism, and a period begins during which, under the direction of Myronides and of Tolmides, we find Athenian

----

[1] I. 92, cf. p. 119.

expeditions in Greece and even Athenian ships sailing round the Peloponnese (108. 5). Many failures are needed before Cimon is eventually recalled from exile. In fact, Thucydides does not mention the event; nevertheless, Cimon's name begins to appear again when, as if by chance, the policy of making war in Greece itself is abandoned: ʽΕλληνικοῦ μὲν πολέμου ἔσχον οἱ Ἀθηναῖοι (112. 1).

The mention of such a tradition would also have explained the disagreement which arose during the actual course of the war between Cleon and Nicias on the question of whether or not Athens should negotiate with Sparta. The speech which Thucydides puts into the mouth of the Spartan ambassadors needs to be understood in the light of this permanent difference of opinion.

This difference is equally noticeable elsewhere, namely in the field of pacific and, as it were, internal imperialism, and it is manifested in the attitude adopted by both parties towards the allies. In the same way that the extremists want Athens to rule over all peoples, in order that she may have the greatest possible power, they also want to make her authority absolute and centralized, and they sacrifice the interests of the allies to this particular aim. The moderates, on the other hand, want to limit Athenian domination and think of the interests of Greece as a whole; they admire Sparta and her confederation, and thus naturally try to prevent Athens from becoming tyrannical by protecting the rights of the allies and by making her authority keep the appearance of a generally accepted leadership. Both sides realize that any growth in Athenian power tends to create a dangerous lack of balance between the two cities, and this is one of the reasons why the extremists seek greater power for their city while the moderates oppose it.

Thucydides never thought of informing his reader of the existence of these different views, but they do nevertheless make the second part of the Pentecontaëtia much clearer. Cimon had adopted a very liberal attitude towards the allies, and although Pericles is obliged, after the death of Cimon, to give up any ambitious undertakings, he still does not abandon the idea of reinforcing Athenian rule: he invents a pacific form of imperialism. But soon we see again the moderates rising up against this system of conquering by peaceful means, of reorganizing the empire, of sending forth *cleruchies*, and of gradually whittling away the constitutional rights of the allied cities. The struggle breaks out when Pericles wants to use the federal treasure for the buildings on the Acropolis. Just as the moderate

Cimon had opposed the carrying of the war into the mainland of Greece, so Thucydides, son of Melesias, himself a moderate, tries to protest against the 'satellization' of the cities. His disgrace, in 443, is a triumph for the extremists exactly as the disgrace of Cimon was a triumph for them in 461.

By openly mentioning such a tradition, Thucydides would also have clarified a number of events in the war itself, and in particular the disagreement which arose in Book III between Cleon and Diodotus on the question of the punishment to be inflicted on Mytilene.

Finally, this opposition between the moderates and the extremists also occurs in the geographical direction which they each assigned to Athenian expansion. Two possible directions, East and West, existed from the very beginning. Those who envisaged only a war against the Persians naturally looked to the East. Those who wanted to rule over all the other Greek peoples, and hold Sparta and the other powers at bay by controlling the grain routes, looked towards the West. The East, and the Aegean sea, was the traditional area for the operation of Athenian ships; the area in which one could conceive of the existence of a number of cities grouped together by a common interest, and united as much by commercial relationships as by geographical proximity. The West presupposed different plans, less essential relationships with other cities, more serious dangers and, in short, a less justified form of expansion.

Since this Western policy, which in this instance was again that of Themistocles,[1] did not originally assume a military form, it is natural to find no mention of it in the Pentecontaëtia, and the description of the various facts does not suffer much because of this; but, although this tendency was to play an important role in the course of the Peloponnesian War, Thucydides does not comment upon it even there, and does not link it up with anything at all. Yet the opposition between the two different types of ambition would have brought out the importance of the Corcyraean and Sicilian affairs; and, above all, it would have illuminated the argument between Nicias and Alcibiades on the question of whether or not the expedition which fills Books VI and VII should be attempted.

But what is most important is that the opposition between the two forms of imperialism also corresponds to another political conflict, which gives it a clearer significance. To reach an understanding with

[1] Cf. p. 200.

Sparta means reaching an understanding with an oligarchy; to fight against Sparta means fighting as a democracy against an oligarchy. Consequently moderate imperialism is the policy of moderate democracy and extreme imperialism the policy of extreme democracy. From this point of view, the opposition between Cimon and Themistocles, or between Cimon and Pericles, is the same as the one which will occur later between Nicias and Cleon, for instance. Now this is something which Thucydides never even mentions. Certainly there is no definite order that can be attributed to these ideas, for politicians may seek an understanding with Sparta because they are sympathetic towards a conservative system of government, or they may wish for a conservative system of government because it is a barrier against an over-adventurous policy. They may want both because they are by nature reasonable and moderate, or because it is a family tradition, or because it is in their own interest; but the fact remains that these different motives do come together to form a definite political attitude. If it seems anachronistic to speak of political parties,[1] we can at least speak of certain political traditions. And it is important to note that Thucydides refuses to provide information on these topics, with the result that the facts he relates are often less easy to understand.

He clearly refrains from speaking about these political questions because he considers them irrelevant to his real subject, which is the history of the war between Athens and Sparta.[2] His silence can also be explained by the frequent tendency of the fifth century to treat cities as if they were real people. But even without these considerations, Thucydides' decision not to speak of these questions is perfectly justified in itself as a legitimate attempt to present things in a simplified and abstract form. By leaving entirely on one side the struggles between the different political parties concerning Athenian imperialism, and by attributing its existence solely to Athens herself, by eliminating all the variations which this imperialism underwent and by presenting it as the single development of one and the same idea, he goes beyond the mass of individual detail and arrives at one generalized form illustrated by the expression οἱ ᾿Αθηναῖοι. But, as he does so, he never misrepresents what really happened. He not only respects the facts and offers the necessary material to anyone who wishes to interpret them, but also in no way makes them unintelligible

---

[1] Cf. later p. 232 ff.
[2] Cf. later p. 97.

by refusing to provide this interpretation himself. For there is, in fact, only a difference of degree between the two forms of imperialism. Extreme when circumstances permit, moderate when there are more obstacles, Athenian ambition always tends by its very nature to have no limits. It tends to fight against Sparta,[1] to impose itself firmly on subject peoples, to extend the field of conquest to both East and West. This is the true imperialism, the only one which can really be described as such, and the degree of its intensity varies only in accordance with the possibilities open to it. This idea considerably reduces the importance of the variations which Athenian policy undergoes and of the discussions which govern its development. It is circumstances which decide whether Athenian imperialism shall be extremist or moderate, and the influence which the different groups or different individuals exert depends upon these conditions. The attitude adopted by the different parties is only a link between these conditions and the action to which they give rise, a link which is doubtless quite interesting to reconstitute and study, but which can be omitted without any essential loss.

The fact that Thucydides himself left it out indicates a personal decision, which he certainly had a perfect right to make, although one may doubt whether he was well-advised to make it.[2] In any case, it enables him to bring out a simple and coherent idea of Athenian ambition, contrasted with the resistance put up by the rest of Greece. It gives this ambition its soberest form, in the same way as the individual or antithetical speeches in which Thucydides immobilizes them gives sobriety to the long and sometimes confused debates in the assemblies.

The way in which this ambition works is brought out with the same sureness of touch, for although Thucydides never analyses it directly, he has many opportunities to mention it, either when

[1] This essential aspect of Athenian imperialism completely prevented the ancients from seeing that, if it had been successful in its aims, it would have unified Greece (Cf. Thibaudet, p. 425). It even prevented people of the fifth century from appreciating Athenian actions in respect to the barbarians (see below, p. 95).

[2] Very different opinions have been expressed on the value of Thucydides' attitude in not talking about the internal history of the city and the quarrels to which it gave rise. Eduard Meyer not only defended it, but gave it great praise (Forsch., p. 374-379). On the other hand, Müller-Strübing criticized it quite sharply (Th., p. 385-387). It is certainly an obstacle for someone looking to Thucydides' work — as we are obliged to do today — for a complete history of Athens and Greece in the second part of the fifth century. But we must not forget that Thucydides did not set out to write such a history.

describing the motives inspiring Athenian actions or in the arguments contained in the different speeches; and all the indications which he gives fit together perfectly. We learn that Athens is a maritime power, that her constant aim is control over the sea, that her field of action is the islands[1] and that the means she is using to achieve these aims is her fleet. She needs money to maintain this fleet, and her empire provides her with this. Thalassocracy is avowed as an already conscious and coherent system.

The idea is present from one end of the work to the other. In the Pentecontaëtia the origin of Athenian power appears with the audacious suggestion of Themistocles that Athens must 'take hold' of the sea: τῆς γὰρ δὴ θαλάσσης πρῶτος ἐτόλμησεν εἰπεῖν ὡς ἀνθεκτέα ἐστίν (I. 93. 4), and the only passage of analysis to be found in the Pentecontaëtia is made to explain how Athens improves her fleet at the expense of her allies (I. 99. 3). In the narration of events there is permanent reference to the general principle of sea-power: it is because Corcyra has a fleet that an alliance with her is important for Athens (I. 33. 1; I. 44. 2); and it is Athenian naval supremacy which is favourably or unfavourably discussed in the speeches in Book I. It is at the basis of the whole theory which Pericles puts forward in his first speech (μέγα γὰρ τὸ τῆς θαλάσσης κράτος, I. 143. 4), and its infinite character is expounded in his final speech (οἴεσθε μὲν ... τῶν ξυμμάχων μόνων ἄρχειν, ἐγὼ δὲ ἀποφαίνω δύο μερῶν τῶν ἐς χρῆσιν φανερῶν, γῆς καὶ θαλάσσης, τοῦ ἑτέρου ὑμᾶς παντὸς κυριωτάτους ὄντας, ἐφ' ὅσον τε νῦν νέμεσθε καὶ ἢν ἐπὶ πλέον βουληθῆτε, II. 62. 2).[2] This is why the islands played a leading role in the eyes of the Athenians, who gave them priority in defence (IV. 121. 2).

[1] There is certainly an obvious and inevitable link between ruling over the sea and having control over the islands. Thibaudet writes on p. 90: 'If navies serve to conquer and hold the islands, the mastery of the sea inevitably leads to the conquest of more and more islands. Today, all the world's largest islands (except those of Japan) and nearly all the small ones belong either to the British or to the Dutch naval empire (the Indian peninsula, attached to an impassable mountain chain ... , has for centuries behaved like an island). The Athenians were thus led to put forward the principle that all the Greek islands belonged to them; and, in the Sicilian War, all the Dorian and Ionian islanders had to take up arms on Athens' side. Among the people living on the islands bordering on the Peloponnese "the Cephallenians and the Corinthians (i.e. the Zacynthians)", Thucydides tells us, "were independent. But, as islanders, they were expected to accompany the Athenians because these were the masters of the sea" (VII. 57).' The text says, with a revelatory neuter adjective taken as a substantive: κατὰ δὲ τὸ νησιωτικὸν μᾶλλον κατειργόμενοι ὅτι θαλάσσης ἐκράτουν Ἀθηναῖοι.

[2] In actual fact, it is only a question here of ruling over the sea, not of controlling the islands (cf. later p. 123): similarly, in II. 89. 10, the question at stake is that of the freedom to sail.

This is why Athens could not allow them to defect (IV. 122. 5) or even to remain independent (V. 97).

The importance which this idea of Athenian sea-power (or thalassocracy) has for Thucydides can be seen in the fact that he cannot imagine any other form of imperialism either having existed or being possible for Athens in the future.

The introductory chapters, which are commonly referred to as the Archaeology, are a good illustration of the first point, for they are in fact nothing more than the history of the various people who ruled over the sea — Minos, Agamemnon, the tyrants of Corinth, Polycrates of Samos, Cyrus and Darius.[1] The dominion which they each exercised inevitably resembles the form of Athenian dominion, and is founded on the same three elements: a fleet, money, and the rule over the islands. Thucydides' insistence is particularly noticeable where more depends on personal interpretation. Thus, for Minos, he writes (I. 4): Μίνως γὰρ παλαίτατος ὧν ἀκοῇ ἴσμεν ναυτικὸν ἐκτήσατο καὶ τῆς νῦν Ἑλληνικῆς θαλάσσης ἐπὶ πλεῖστον ἐκράτησε καὶ τῶν Κυκλάδων νήσων ἦρξέ τε καὶ οἰκιστὴς πρῶτος τῶν πλείστων ἐγένετο; this empire, the prefiguration of the Athenian empire, even pays him a tribute (τοῦ τὰς προσόδους μᾶλλον ἰέναι αὐτῷ). Now, if the tradition according to which Minos was the first Greek to have ruled over the sea is a well-established one, it is nowhere presented with such certainty and detail as in Thucydides. By a contradiction which is worth noting, the critical and enlightened historian accepts as fact that which other, more credulous writers such as Herodotus and Diodorus dismiss as legendary.[2] And it looks as if the form

---

[1] The expressions of ναυτικόν and of νῆσοι are repeated in each case: Minos = παλαίτατος ὧν ἀκοῇ ἴσμεν ναυτικὸν ἐκτήσατο καὶ . . . τῶν Κυκλάδων νήσων ἦρξε (I. 4); Agamemnon = ναυτικῷ τε ἅμα ἐπὶ πλέον τῶν ἄλλων ἰσχύσας (I. 9. 4); and Thucydides quotes Homer: πολλῇσι νήσοισι καὶ Ἄργεϊ παντὶ ἀνάσσειν. With the rise of tyranny, Greece ναυτικά τε ἐξηρτύετο (I. 13. 1); Polycrates = ναυτικῷ ἰσχύων ἄλλας τε τῶν νήσων ὑπηκόους ἐποιήσατο (I. 13. 6). Similarly, fine navies are found in Sicily and Corcyra (I. 14. 2), and the people who have these become powerful by acquiring riches and dominions ἐπιπλέοντες γὰρ τὰς νήσους κατεστρέφοντο . . . Finally, Thucydides writes of Darius that: τῷ Φοινίκων ναυτικῷ κρατῶν καὶ τὰς νήσους (ἐδούλωσε) (I. 16).

[2] Herodotus considers that the first rule over the sea in historical times was that of Polycrates; that of Minos did not belong to the 'age of men' (III, 122): Πολυκράτης γάρ ἐστι πρῶτος τῶν ἡμεῖς ἴδμεν Ἑλλήνων ὃς θαλασσοκρατέειν ἐπενοήθη πάρεξ Μίνω τε τοῦ Κνωσσίου καὶ εἰ δή τις ἄλλος πρότερος τούτου ἦρξε τῆς θαλάσσης· τῆς δὲ ἀνθρωπηίης λεγομένης γενεῆς Πολυκράτης ἐστὶ πρῶτος, ἐλπίδας πολλὰς ἔχων Ἰωνίης τε καὶ νήσων ἄρξειν. Diodorus also places Minos among the legendary heroes (V, 78, 1: μετὰ δὲ τὰς τῶν θεῶν γενέσεις ὕστερον πολλαῖς γενεαῖς φασι γενέσθαι κατὰ τὴν Κρήτην ἥρωας οὐκ ὀλίγους ὧν ὑπάρχειν ἐπιφανεστάτους τοὺς περὶ Μίνω καὶ Ῥαδάμανθυν καὶ Σαρπηδόνα· τούτους γὰρ μυθολογοῦσιν ἐκ Διὸς γεγεννῆσθαι). The rule over the sea is certainly mentioned as one of

assumed by Athenian imperialism had brought the character of Minos to life, simply because he could be seen as a forerunner.[1]

Thus the whole of the Archaeology tends to give the impression that the only real empires which ever existed were those based upon sea-power. It is the sea which allows great expeditions to be made, while military conflicts on land can end only in a victory over a few neighbours.[2] It is a complete surprise when, at the end of the Archaeology, we suddenly meet the power of Sparta, and see the Spartans leading the rest of the Greeks because they are δυνάμει προύχοντες. Even though Thucydides then points out the different nature of the two dominions, that established by Sparta remains an isolated fact, independent of the main tradition which interests him.

He is even less able to consider that Athens, the Athens which rules over the seas, could ever think of establishing her rule on land. And yet this was sometimes a sufficiently strong temptation to exercise a certain influence over the sequence of events. Certainly the moderate imperialists never considered the possibility, for they thought that in the division of Greece into Athenian and Spartan areas of influence, Athens would naturally not rule over the land. Aristophanes knew this when he gave his advice to the Athenians in the *Peace* (507), saying: 'As for you, Athenians, if you really want to draw her out (i.e.: the peace), stand back a little *towards the sea.*' Yet, the opposition between action on land and action on the sea does not correspond absolutely with the opposition between extreme and moderate imperialism. If action on land is inevitably blamed by the representatives of moderate imperialism, it is by no means approved by all the extreme imperialists. Generally, they want to rule over the whole of Greece, but they want to do so by means of sea-power. They want to make war on Sparta, but they want to make it a war of

[1] Similarly Agamemnon comes in only because of the islands over which he ruled and for the fleet which this authority implied. The whole of his kingdom in the Peloponnese is less important in Thucydides' eyes than these islands whose value was so great for Athens in the fifth century.

[2] I. 15. 2. The fact that only the rule over the sea allows large and long-distance expeditions to be made is one of the frequent arguments in its favour ([Xenophon], *Constitution of Athens*, II, 4 and especially 5). On the relationship between the sea and imperialism, cf. later pp. 69-70.

Minos' achievements (κτήσασθαι δὲ καὶ δύναμιν ναυτικὴν μεγάλην καὶ τῶν τε νήσων τὰς πλείστας καταστρέψασθαι καὶ πρῶτον τῶν Ἑλλήνων θαλαττοκρατῆσαι), but in Diodorus it all remains fairly legendary. It is on the same plane as that of Rhadamanthys who acquires numerous islands and a large section of the Asiatic coast . . . because of the admiration which his justice evokes among men! Compared to texts such as these, the authority which Thucydides shows is extremely revelatory.

sea against land. Thus, for Athens, the question of action on land was only a tactical one and it concerns only the small group of those who wanted to unite both forms of action. Their view accounts for the different attempts made either before or during the war to gain a foothold in the Peloponnese, and in particular for the whole of the Argive policy of Alcibiades. Now Thucydides does not stop to explain this and scarcely seems to understand it.[1] The portrait which he gives of Alcibiades is that of a man whose political action develops without reason or system: we have to consult Plutarch to understand the motives behind Alcibiades' enterprises, and to see that he 'advised his fellow citizens not to loose their hold on the land' (*Alc.*, 15). The expression used: ἀντέχεσθαι τῆς γῆς, does, as Hatzfeld has pointed out,[2] stress in a rather remarkable way the difference that there is between this plan of action and that put forward by Themistocles: ἀντέχεσθαι τῆς θαλάσσης.

I must hasten to add that Thucydides' neglect of these tendencies deserves no serious criticism. By presenting Athenian imperialism and, indeed, all imperialisms, as inevitably maritime in nature, he was distorting no essential facts. Even for Alcibiades, territorial conquest was never anything but a secondary kind of action. It can never have represented for an Athenian anything but a distant aim which naval power could lead to, or else a means of making war that could be added to those provided by naval power but would always remain subordinate to them. Moreover, the conditions of political life in the ancient world are sufficient explanation in themselves of the reason why Greek imperialism remained essentially maritime. The rule over the sea did in fact offer possibilities not made available by the rule over land. Thucydides gives a brief indication of this as far as earlier periods are concerned (I. 15. 2), but the *Constitution of Athens* handed down under the name of Xenophon explains it very clearly. The people who depend on the sea for their trade (as do those who live in the Aegean Sea) are, for that very reason, easily held in check. Since they cannot bring together their forces, they cannot defend themselves against an enemy stronger than themselves (II, 2-3). On the other hand, the mastery of the sea, in practice,

---

[1] Cf. later p. 196.

[2] *Alcibiade*, p. 100. Following L. Robert (*Etudes épigraphiques et philologiques*, Bibl. Ec. Hautes Études, CCLXXII, pp. 296-307) he gives an excellent interpretation of the passage following this one. Plutarch mentions a sentence from the oath taken by the young men: this was deliberately distorted by Alcibiades who gives it the meaning that the Athenians considered all fertile and cultivated land as belonging to them.

F

enables a city to resist all attacks: since she is at home on the sea, she can harm others when and where she chooses without being exposed to the fear of reprisals (II, 4-5). It is thus understandable that the slightest superiority tends, when it is based upon the sea, to develop indefinitely and with complete impunity. This is doubtless the reason why Lysias, in his *Olympic Speech* (5), states it as an obvious fact that the empire belongs to the rulers of the sea: ἐπίστασθε δὲ ὅτι ἡ μὲν ἀρχὴ τῶν κρατούντων τῆς θαλάττης (ἐστί). Similarly, when Isocrates speaks of empire or imperialism he never envisages anything but what he calls ἡ ἀρχὴ τῆς θαλάττης or ἡ ἀρχὴ ἡ κατὰ θάλατταν;[1] he does not say that the Spartans changed their customs in 404 when they began to exercise their dominion, but when they began to rule over the sea (*On the Peace*, 101); the Spartans triumphed because of the courage which went with their hegemony on land, but ambition and pride came to them with 'that rule'[2] and it was this which made them think that they could do anything; consequently, for Isocrates, it is that rule over the sea which every ambitious nation tries to achieve (*On the Peace*, 110; 115). Imperialism in general, like that of Athens in particular, seems at that time to be necessarily looking towards the sea.

But if Thucydides here sacrificed an element that could be omitted, in favour of one that it was absolutely essential to include, the little interest which he has in land imperialism and the immense concern which he shows in questions related to the sea indicates the great importance which maritime imperialism had in his eyes. And he produces the same effect here as in the first case: the clearness of his general approach is reinforced by the sacrifice of detailed shades of meaning.

Moreover, Thucydides gives no other indication of the area of Athenian expansion, and does not discuss the reasons which, with the whole sea before them, make the fleets setting out from Piraeus sail in one direction rather than another. He does not tell us whether they were looking for corn routes, for countries to pillage, or for strategic points, and he never discusses whether there was a system in Athenian conquests. Just as he shows but one single will to power, which is that of Athens, so he provides it with but one single object, which is to rule over the sea.

---

[1] There seems to be almost no difference between the two expressions. Perhaps the expression ἡ ἀρχὴ τῆς θαλάττης describes the rule over the sea in an abstract way, while ἡ ἀρχὴ ἡ κατὰ θάλατταν would describe the more organized and systematic authority which it produces?

[2] *On the Peace*, 102: ταύτης τῆς ἀρχῆς; 105: τὴν ἀρχὴν ταύτην. But the text is doubtful.

But this last simplification can only be judged if one considers what was, according to him, the aim and purpose of Athenian imperialism.

Certain modern scholars, particularly Grundy, have criticized Thucydides for not having indicated the true aims of Athenian imperialism, which, in their opinion, are essentially economic: Athens was trying to protect her supply routes for grain and to provide food for her poorer classes. It is true that Thucydides brings out neither of these two ideas, and we have to explain his silence.

According to Grundy, Athens' conquests were intended to provide her with the grain that she herself lacked. Athenian imperialism was born of a simple struggle for life, and it remained marked by this origin even in its later development; for after the Athenians had made sure of their own grain supply, they had nothing else in mind but to prevent others from obtaining theirs.[1] This would explain the important role played in the history of Greece by certain rich grain-producing areas – the Black Sea, Egypt, Sicily and, finally, Euboea.

Thucydides only once mentions this concern for grain, when he is discussing the first attempts made to invade Sicily in III. 86. 4, but it is for him a motive which is closely connected with the war and unrelated to the desire for conquest itself: βουλόμενοι δὲ μήτε σῖτον ἐς τὴν Πελοπόννησον ἄγεσθαι αὐτόθεν, προπειράν τε ποιούμενοι εἰ σφίσι δυνατὰ εἴη τὰ ἐν τῇ Σικελίᾳ πράγματα ὑποχείρια γενέσθαι. Whenever he indicates the advantages to be gained from occupying a particular area, these are only connected with sea-power: Amphipolis, for example, can provide wood for making ships and money for the treasury.[2] Usually, however, he does not discuss this question.

This motive could nevertheless explain the Athenian attitude in quite a large number of cases. In the Pentecontaëtia, for example, it could explain the expedition to Egypt, which otherwise seems to have no significance; and in the description of the war itself it seems to have played an important role in the Athenian attempts against Melos and Sicily.[3] By the way in which he presents these two episodes, however, it is clear that Thucydides quite deliberately neglects it.

[1] Grundy, p. 187 (dealing with Pericles): 'It looks as if the intent of it was to dominate Greece by means of corn-supply.'

[2] When the Athenians lose Euboea, he simply notes that it was more useful to them than Attica (VIII. 96. 2: ἐξ ἧς πλείω ἢ τῆς 'Αττικῆς ὠφελοῦντο); but this is a very vague indication.

[3] One dominated the lines of communication between Sparta and Egypt, while the other was one of the largest grain reserves of Greece, one of the most important sources of grain for the Peloponnese.

In the case of Melos, the only motive for Athens' action is the fact that, unlike the others, the island was unwilling to submit (V. 84. 2). The only argument put forward by the Athenians is that the acceptance of their authority by Melos will add to their dominion and, by increasing their prestige, give them security (V. 97). Nothing could be more general.

As for Sicily, when Thucydides describes so thoroughly the great expedition, he does not even mention the economic motive which he had mentioned before as combining with Athenian ambition. He gives no more details than in the case of Melos about what the Athenians want to obtain there: he just says that they wish to gain control over Sicily (VI. 1) or are eager to exercise their authority in Sicily (VI. 6. 1). He once explains their reasons for wanting to do this in VI. 24, but these are in no way specially relevant to the particular case of Sicily: the Athenian motive is always the desire to 'obtain more': the old men hope for conquest, the young wish to travel, the crowd wants money, both now and to be distributed by the treasury in later times; but why exactly Sicily? The speech by Alcibiades provides us with no further information, since all he does is to show that Athens perpetually needs new fields to conquer. And when finally he reveals his master plan, in the speech which he makes in Sparta, it is clear that the conquest of Sicily was only intended, together with those of Italy and Carthage, to help in the final conquest of the Peloponnese. In this immense mobilization of resources, each country would have had to make its own particular contribution, and grain certainly figures amongst them, but as an element far less important than timber for the building of ships; Thucydides just says that it should produce no cause for alarm.[1]

Faced with so systematic a silence on the part of Thucydides, we must admit that somewhere a mistake is being made: either Thucydides, for some reason or other, is distorting the facts, or the explanation put forward by a number of modern historians does not fit the realities of the ancient world.

All the facts suggest that it is not Thucydides who is wrong. To begin with, Thucydides' silence is shared by all his contemporaries.

---

[1] VI. 90. 4: χρήματα δὲ καὶ σῖτον, ὥστε εὐπορώτερον γίγνεσθαί τι αὐτῶν, αὐτὰ τὰ προσγενόμενα ἐκεῖθεν χωρία ἔμελλε διαρκῆ ἄνευ τῆς ἐνθένδε προσόδου παρέξειν. The ending of the sentence is characteristic, for it shows that it is above all the first term, χρήματα, which Thucydides has in mind and which he considers important.

And the explanation that all Greek writers disliked dealing with economic factors is a rather facile one, particularly as Thucydides has no hesitation in talking about the treasury, and certainly does not neglect timber as he does grain. It is therefore more likely that the Greeks looked down on economic factors just as much in their everyday lives as in the history which they wrote; if they did not talk about them it was because they did not consider them to be supremely important. This is precisely the conclusion reached by a more detailed study of the facts carried out by Gernet. In his book on Athenian grain-supply in the fourth and fifth centuries B.C., he shows how unsystematic Athenian conquests were, for Athens grabs and extorts without ever trying to organize her food supplies: 'It was a question of acquiring riches', he writes, 'rather than regular food-supplies',[1] and his conclusion is that scholars who look upon the supply of grain as a problem which the Athenians tried to solve in a methodical manner are in for a disappointment. This is true even in a study of the conquest routes opened up and he adds: 'The decisive factor was the power of tradition, or of collective ideas modified under the more or less powerful pressure of circumstances, but to no extent the systematic desire to provide a supply of food.'[2]

It thus seems likely that Grundy, applying to the study of Athenian imperialism the conditions which he saw governing British imperialism in the nineteenth century, failed to recognize the difference brought about by place and time. The Greek city-state was more spontaneous and more illogical than the modern State, and, in the fifth century, the mastery of the Aegean Sea was a more self-sufficient aim than naval supremacy in the nineteenth and twentieth centuries. The mastery of the Aegean Sea allowed the Athenians to turn now in this and now in that direction, to stop enemy convoys and so on ... ; with a few ports placed here and there, it could be exercised with absolute freedom. But when world trade routes are to be considered, when there are great rivalries between several nations, when there are millions of men to supply with food, the situation is completely different.

Thus for a fifth-century Athenian, the rule over the sea is a sufficient end in itself, and by showing an interest only in the supplies of wood and money that were essential to maintain this rule,

[1] P. 357
[2] The relative neglect of the Cimmerian Bosporus provides him with the proof of this.

Thucydides presents Athenian imperialism as it really was. Athens certainly was eager to ensure her grain supplies, but this was neither the cause for her conquests nor the reason deciding the direction in which she chose to expand.

And yet, it remains true that however incidental such an aim may have been, the fact that Thucydides did not mention it is yet another proof of his desire to present as clear and simple a picture as possible. Through a perfectly legitimate silence he provides Athenian imperialism with a new unity by making it almost an abstract desire for conquest, a desire that can turn almost equally to any country bordering on the sea.

The most important way in which these countries could satisfy Athenian ambition was in the riches which they offered. We have just seen that, in Gernet's view, Athenian ambition was mainly financial: 'To reign, for the Athenians, meant living off foreign countries, taking their corn, hindering their trade in every possible manner, and taxing the product of whatever wealth they deigned to leave them.'[1] If this is true, then one of the links between imperialism and democracy becomes obvious,[2] since it was in the first instance the poorer classes who could profit economically from the different conquests.

[1] P. 383.

[2] In reality, there is a mutual relationship between the two principles, for the existence of the empire naturally causes power to fall into the hands of those who protect it, namely the sailors. Thus the time of foot and horse soldiers is over, like that of the farmers; and the movement of democratic reform which follows the disgrace of Cimon is, as Glotz points out (p. 142): 'The logical and necessary result of this fact: a state based on the cultivation of land was being transformed into an industrial and maritime trading nation.' The contemporary of Thucydides who wrote the *Constitution of Athens* was well aware of this, for from the very beginning of his work he shows that the democratic system of government (which he despises) is the logical one for a city like Athens which is at the head of a large empire: 'I will say first of all that there it is just that the poor and the ordinary people should get more than the nobles and the rich, for it is they who work the ships and gain power for the city. For it is the steersmen, the boatswains, the under-boatswains, the helmsmen and the ship-builders who, far more than the hoplites (πολῖται corrected to ὁπλῖται) the nobles and the rich, gain power for the city. Since this is the case, it is just that they should all take part in public offices, both by the lot-drawing now in use and by election, and that it should be possible for any one citizen to speak.' He finally notes that these conditions also explain the rights accorded even to slaves and metics. Isocrates mentions the same idea with equal clarity when he says (*Panath.*, 115-116) that the rule over the sea compelled the people of ancient times to adopt regrettably democratic measures: they knew that the rule over the sea developed ἔκ τε τῶν τεχνῶν τῶν περὶ τὰς ναῦς καὶ τῶν ἐλαύνειν αὐτὰς δυναμένων καὶ τῶν τὰ σφέτερα μὲν αὑτῶν ἀπολωλεκότων, ἐκ δὲ τῶν ἀλλοτρίων πορίζεσθαι τὸν βίον εἰθισμένων.

Now Thucydides gives no more attention to this feature of imperialism than he did to its other economic aspects. Apart from the rather vague reference in IV. 61. 3, in which Hermocrates (in order to inspire the Sicilians to rebellion) declares that the Athenians have come τῶν ἐν τῇ Σικελίᾳ ἀγαθῶν ἐφιέμενοι, Thucydides only once makes reference to this theme. Even then he does so when speaking of a definite measure — again the Sicilian expedition — and refers to it as an additional motive which influences only the crowd: the crowd, he says, would like to obtain money now and also to provide some means of doing so in the future: ὁ δὲ πολὺς ὅμιλος καὶ στρατιώτης ἔν τε τῷ παρόντι ἀργύριον οἴσειν καὶ προσκτήσεσθαι δύναμιν ὅθεν ἀίδιον μισθοφορὰν ὑπάρξειν (VI. 24. 3). Although this is only an indication given in passing, it is nevertheless easy to see that the conditions which Thucydides analyses here did play an important role in the history of Athenian imperialism, and this time we can find confirmation of it in the whole of the classical tradition.

As Thucydides notes in this rather summary fashion, these conditions explain both the liking for expeditions and for the conquests they achieve. The expeditions themselves enabled the people to be paid as soldiers,[1] and in Plutarch's view all the expeditions undertaken by Pericles can be explained by this consideration.[2] As to the conquests, they gave the same result in a number of different ways, since, as the *Constitution of Athens*[3] formally declares, every Athenian could grow rich on the goods of the allies. The simplest way of achieving this was through the tribute, and this had the first advantage of enabling the government to pay civil indemnities to the population.[4] In 425 the tribute was greatly increased, and at the same time the indemnity paid to the heliasts was increased from two to three obols. Pericles also conceived the idea of organizing a public works

[1] This is certainly one of the reasons why military expeditions are more popular with the ordinary people than with the rich. There is also another more permanent and more negative reason, which is that since the poor have fewer possessions to lose, they run fewer risks than the rich (*Constitution of Athens*, II, 14; Aristophanes, *Ecclesiazusae*, 197 ff.).

[2] *Pericles*, 11, 4. After the institution of public entertainments, these expeditions are the first act mentioned as being aimed at pleasing the people: 'He sent out sixty triremes every year, in which many citizens sailed for a period of eight months, being paid for their trouble and acquiring seafaring experience at the same time.'

[3] I, 15: τοῖς δὲ δημοτικοῖς δοκεῖ μεῖζον ἀγαθὸν εἶναι τὰ τῶν συμμάχων χρήματα ἕνα ἕκαστον ἔχειν Ἀθηναίων.

[4] This point seemed to be of the utmost importance; cf. Isocrates, *Panath.*, 116: 'when . . . they oblige them to pay taxes and a tribute in order to provide wages for the kind of people I said'.

programme, and Plutarch argues[1] that one of his main objectives was
to provide a living for a number of different categories of workmen
with money taken, as we have seen, from the federal treasury.
There were, in addition, various other methods of extracting money
from the allies and making them serve Athenian interests. The
Constitution of Athens, for example, describes them coming to
Athens in order to bring a suit before a court of law. Thus, at the
same time as they provided an income for the judges, they had to
pay 1 per cent tax when they entered Piraeus, they rented houses and
hired carriages, and offered work for the heralds: all the opportunities they provided were worth taking.[2] Now there is an immense
amount of contemporary evidence to show that denouncers were
highly skilled in increasing the number of opportunities for this kind
of profit. Neither did the Athenians stop there, but they also used
other even more radical methods: the original owners of land in the
conquered countries were — whatever the motive or pretext —
evicted, and the land given to working-class Athenians. For Plutarch,
this was one of the main reasons for sending the *cleruchies*.[3]

Thus, the practical consequences of ruling over different countries
do seem to have played a more important role than Thucydides
indicates: of course, that may be because these consequences belonged
partly to the realm of home policy, which we know that he did not
want to go into. But they did not belong wholly and exclusively to
the realm of home policy, and there is some cause for surprise in the
fact that, of all the numerous speeches made for or against Athenian
imperialism, not one mentions this particular aspect, either favourably
as a means of encouraging the people, or unfavourably as revealing
greed and demagogic methods. This silence can be justified only if,
once again, it forms part of a rational choice, and if Thucydides did
neglect these considerations because they really were of incidental
importance. This is precisely what I think they were.

It would be clearly absurd to maintain that economic considerations of this type played no role at all, and Thucydides himself, in the
sentence already quoted, gives a clearer summary than anyone else of
the two main advantages that conquests had for the Athenian people.

[1] *Pericles*, 12, 5: 'To those who had the youth and strength to take part in them, the
expeditions provided financial resources taken from state funds; wishing that the large
numbers of people who were not on the lists should be neither excluded from the profits
nor paid for doing nothing . . . '
[2] I, 16-17.
[3] *Pericles*, 11, 6, he sends them: ἐπανορθούμενος (δὲ) τὰς ἀπορίας τοῦ δήμου.

But in a more general way it seems quite certain that economic motives played a much smaller role in fifth-century Athens than they do in modern Europe. The city was not wholly disinterested in the question of financial profit, naturally, but this consideration inspired only a secondary and intermittent course of action. Many people adopted an imperialistic attitude without ever considering the financial aspect, and those who did think of filling the treasury intended merely to use the money for further conquests: wealth led to power, not power to wealth. Similarly Benjamin Constant, in his essay *De l'Esprit de Conquête et de l'Usurpation*, notes that this characteristic belongs to every type of the will to conquest before the modern age, pointing out that the custom of the Scandinavian heroes was to burn the treasures they had captured in order to compel themselves to undertake new ventures.[1]

Athenian imperialism did not go quite so far as this, and certainly kept some sense of reality. But it was by no means limited to the over-simplified idea of financial profit with which it has at times been associated, for another and more important motive is mentioned by all the authors who have dealt with this question, a purely psychological motive, which is the one on which Thucydides concentrates his attention.

When the Athenians 'want more', they certainly contemplate possession and are inspired by greed.[2] Nevertheless, this desire is rooted in psychological forces which remain independent of the straightforward idea of material gain. In Thucydides, this desire depends upon two basic emotions, the love of action and the need for power, and all his analyses are centred round these two themes.

The behaviour of the Athenians can be explained by the love of action, and Thucydides obviously chose to insist upon this. This is the idea brought out by the Corinthians in Book I in the parallel between the Athenians and the Lacedaemonians (I. 70). The Athenians, they say, are innovators (νεωτεροποιοί), as quick in thought as in action. They are also 'ready to hope' (εὐέλπιδες): the Corinthians use the word that Aristophanes was to make famous by making it into

---

[1] Chapter IV. According to Benjamin Constant this aspect of conquest would disappear in a civilization based on trade, and whose wars no longer offered any possibility of immediate military glory.

[2] The words used by Thucydides indicate real greed, e.g. ἐφίεσθαι (I. 128. 3; IV. 61. 2; IV. 87. 5; IV. 92. 7; VI. 6. 1; VI. 8. 4; VI. 11. 5; VI. 33. 4; VI. 85. 3; VIII. 46. 3) or ὀρέγεσθαι (IV. 21. 2; IV. 41. 4; VI. 10. 5).

the name of one of his characters; and Thucydides, in a most significant repetition, will use it to describe the Athenians on the day they sail out for the Sicilian expedition. As a result of this characteristic, the Athenians can never stop acquiring more, and can neither rest themselves nor allow other people to rest (μήτε αὐτοὺς ἔχειν ἡσυχίαν μήτε τοὺς ἄλλους ἀνθρώπους ἐᾶν). Nicias too shows his awareness of this disposition when, wishing to dissuade the Athenians from embarking on the Sicilian expedition, he considers the possibility of coming into conflict with τοὺς τρόπους τοὺς ὑμετέρους (VI. 9. 3). Euphemus, in Book VI, is even more definite; he says: τῆς ἡμετέρας πολυπραγμοσύνης καὶ τρόπου (VI. 87. 3). But what is even more important is the fact that even the chief supporters of imperialism do not deny the existence of this characteristic, and the agreement between the different texts is very well marked. Thus, in Book II, Pericles attacks ἀπραγμοσύνη[1] and Alcibiades, in Book VI, after having criticized the ἀπραγμοσύνη of Nicias (VI. 18. 6), reminds Athens of her tradition of πόλιν μὴ ἀπράγμονα, to which a policy of ἀπραγμοσύνη would be fatal (VI. 18. 7). The idea comes out very clearly from these different but confirmatory texts, and provides the first essential definition of the psychological characteristic which determines Athenian policy, explaining both why Athens has to turn to action, and why she has to go on, no particular action ever being able to fulfil her desire.

But this desire itself, all the same, feeds on something very specific. The unceasing activity of Athens is no doubt caused by the character of her inhabitants: because of it, each stage in the expansion of the city tends to become but one step towards new power and new conquests. Yet although the end of all this activity seems to be constantly receding, the Athenians are aware of its existence: what they want is, finally, the greatest possible power, and the domination over all other countries; and if we are to take as a sign the feeling to which the imperialist leaders chose to appeal,[2] this final aim is less

[1] The word occurs several times: II. 63. 2: ἀπραγμοσύνη; II. 63. 3: τὸ γὰρ ἀπραγμον; II. 64. 4: ὁ μὲν ἀπράγμων. Cf. later p. 127 for this. Pericles also notes in the Funeral Oration that the idea has no unfavourable connotations for an Athenian (II. 40. 2): μόνοι γὰρ τόν τε μηδὲν τῶνδε μετέχοντα οὐκ ἀπράγμονα ἀλλ' ἀχρεῖον νομίζομεν.

[2] These naturally stress only the noblest and most disinterested aspect of imperialism, and the evidence provided by their speeches must consequently be treated with a certain amount of care. One may nevertheless point out that, on the one hand, Thucydides often allows certain of these leaders to use rather crude language, and could therefore allow them to appeal to baser motives; and, on the other, that the speeches made by the opponents of imperialism in no way contradict the idea given of it by its supporters.

the desire to possess something than the ambition to exercise authority.

What in fact inspires the Athenians is the desire which they have for fame, renown and honours. In its highest form, their ambition aims at glory, in its lowest at the use of power. On the one hand we have Pericles, on the other the man in the street.

We see the desire for glory not only in the speeches of Pericles himself, but also in those of the other Athenian leaders. The appeal is to the ideas of τιμή,[1] of ὄνομα,[2] of θαυμάζεσθαι,[3] and to those of λαμπρότης, δόξα, μνήμη.[4] But we note that even there the aim is not always of a purely moral quality. In the same way as this 'respect' of all the Greeks, which the Spartans promise to Athenians (IV. 20. 4: τό γε ἄλλο Ἑλληνικὸν ἴστε ὅτι ὑποδεέστερον ὂν τὰ μέγιστα τιμήσει), the honour which, in Pericles' words, is a joy to each and every Athenian (II. 63. 1: τῷ τιμωμένῳ ἀπὸ τοῦ ἄρχειν ὧπερ ἅπαντες ἀγάλλεσθε) also provides something more immediately appreciable which is expressed by the plural of τὰς τιμάς.[5] We are here not far from the vanity denounced by the author of the Constitution of Athens when, having enumerated all the material advantages gained by obliging the allies to come to Athens for legal judgment, he mentions the psychological satisfactions that this also implied for the Athenians (I. 18); if the cases were not judged at Athens itself, only a few citizens would benefit from the respect of the allies (τοὺς ἐκπλέοντας Ἀθηναίων ἐτίμων ἂν μόνους); but, under the present system, the allies are forced to go out of their way to flatter the people, for it is they who will give judgment; the different parties have to greet people, shake hands with them, etc.... Such petty considerations, even assuming that they had some foundation in fact, would be clearly out of place in the history of a war; nevertheless they still express, while remaining on a purely individual level, the same delight in ruling that can be found on a national level in the pure ideal of Pericles.

The analysis can be carried even further, for the expressions used

---

[1] Cf. I. 75. 3; I. 76. 2; II. 63. 1.

[2] Cf. II. 64. 3: γνῶτε δὲ ὄνομα μέγιστον αὐτὴν ἔχουσαν ἐν ἅπασιν ἀνθρώποις; VII. 64. 2: τὸ μέγα ὄνομα τῶν Ἀθηνῶν.

[3] Cf. II. 41. 4: τοῖς τε νῦν καὶ τοῖς ἔπειτα θαυμασθησόμεθα; VII. 63. 3. ἐθαυμάζεσθε κατὰ τὴν Ἑλλάδα.

[4] They are all brought together in the different speeches of Pericles: cf. p. 129, and note there.

[5] The plural τιμαί is used twice with a strictly material sense, in V. 11. 1.

enable us to discover the secret root of this feeling. They show that
the act of ruling was really considered as the perfect expression of
both internal and external freedom, and, in fact, as a superior freedom.
The text of Thucydides which gives the clearest indication of this is
probably the remark that he makes in VIII. 68. 4. There, he notes the
difficulty encountered, a hundred years after the fall of the tyrants, in
abolishing the democratic system of government (internal liberty) in
a country 'which not only obeyed no one (external liberty), but had
even been accustomed, during more than half of this period, to
governing others' (highest expression of this liberty).

This explains the parallel which Thucydides likes to make between
independence and domination,[1] at the same time as it brings out the
full force of the superlative ἐλευθερωτάτη, which he uses on a number
of occasions when speaking of Athens, the city whose people
enjoyed, in addition to their democratic liberty, the complementary
pleasure of ruling over those around them.[2]

Thus all the different expressions used come together to clarify
the whole issue: Thucydides achieves exactly the same precision
when defining in a few words the nature of Athenian ambition
and the motives which inspire it as he does when defining its form
and the area over which it extends. In both cases he omits everything of
secondary importance and systematically repeats whatever is essential.

And this attempt at abstraction here again succeeds in bringing out
the most fundamental and consequently the most universal characteristic. Syracuse, for instance, seeks the same glory as Athens does
(ὑπό τε τῶν ἄλλων ἀνθρώπων καὶ ὑπὸ τῶν ἔπειτα πολὺ θαυμασθήσ-
εσθαι, VII. 56. 2) and Corinth acknowledges that what she expected
from a colony were marks of respect (I. 38. 2: ἐπὶ τῷ ἡγεμόνες τε
εἶναι καὶ τὰ εἰκότα θαυμάζεσθαι· αἱ γοῦν ἄλλαι ἀποικίαι τιμῶσιν
ἡμᾶς): in one form or another the satisfactions of vanity are equally
important for everybody,[3] and the analysis which Thucydides gives

---

[1] In III. 45. 6, Diodotus puts them both on the same plane as being the principal
motives for which cities go to war: περὶ μεγίστων τε ἐλευθερίας ἢ ἄλλων ἀρχῆς. In V. 69. 1.
the exhortation made to the Mantineans contrasts the good associated with sovereignty
with the evil connected with slavery: ὑπὲρ ἀρχῆς ἅμα καὶ δουλείας, τὴν μὲν μὴ πειρασα-
μένοις ἀφαιρεθῆναι, τῆς δὲ μὴ αὖθις πειρᾶσθαι.

[2] The excuse of the democratic regime, in Alcibiades' view, is to have made Athens
μεγίστη and ἐλευθερωτάτη (VI. 89. 6); and Nicias uses the same superlative in an expression
which goes with the idea of individual liberty: πατρίδος τε τῆς ἐλευθερωτάτης ὑπομιμν-
ῄσκων καὶ τῆς ἐν αὐτῇ ἀνεπιτάκτου πᾶσιν ἐς τὴν δίαιταν ἐξουσίας (VII. 69. 2).

[3] Naturally one cannot too often repeat the fact that these motives complete the
idea of material benefit but in no way exclude it.

of Athenian ambition thus takes on a wider and more general human value.

At the same time, however, this analysis provides in its very details a most exact reproduction of what he saw before him.[1] In particular the close association which he establishes between liberty and dominion is repeated, more or less consciously, in numerous other texts.[2] Thus we see Herodotus using quite a natural opposition when, speaking of Athenian foreign policy, he writes that 'instead of receiving orders from a master, they gave orders themselves to all other nations' (I, 210); the author of the *Constitution of Athens* associates the two ideas when speaking of home policy: ὁ γὰρ δῆμος οὐ βούλεται εὐνομουμένης τῆς πόλεως αὐτὸς δουλεύειν, ἀλλ᾽ ἐλεύθερος εἶναι καὶ ἄρχειν· τῆς δὲ κακονομίας αὐτῷ ὀλίγον μέλει (I. 8). Finally Lysias also brings the two notions together when he speaks of the double aim of driving both the barbarians and tyrants from Greece (Olymp., 3 and 6).[3]

The precise and definite way in which these two ideas are linked together reveals an aspect of classical imperialism which the modern reader at first finds difficulty in understanding. In modern times the relationship between liberty and authority is, for practical as well as for intellectual reasons, far less marked than it was in the ancient world. 'In the republics of classical antiquity', writes Benjamin

[1] We have already seen several texts, in particular those taken from the *Constitution of Athens*, which confirmed the general idea. It should be added that all the terms used in Thucydides' analysis also occur in later or contemporary works on Athenian imperialism, and make up a repertory of the subject. This is particularly clear in the case of Isocrates. In the treatise *On the Peace*, we may quote not only the central opposition between the notions of πολυπραγμοσύνη and ἡσυχία, which dominates paragraphs 26 to 56, but also expressions which are even more reminiscent of the analyses made by Thucydides. Thus when, like the Corinthians in Book I, he speaks of the evils ὧν αὐτοί τ᾽ ἔχομεν καὶ τοῖς ἄλλοις παρέχομεν (64), or when, repeating the expression used by Thucydides in Book IV, he says: ἀεὶ τοῦ πλείονος ὀρεγομένους (23). As to the aim pursued, he frequently defines it as the desire to 'seize that which belongs to other people', but the constant comparison which he makes with tyranny helps to define the nature of these 'seizures' more closely; they are pursued much more for their principle than for their object. As far as Thucydides' contemporaries are concerned, cf. later p. 134, note 2, for the likeness in feeling between the imperialistic theories of Pericles, such as Thucydides expresses them, and some passages in Euripides.

[2] There is, moreover, nothing particularly surprising in this, since these are indications which Thucydides gives almost in spite of himself, and which spring from his way of talking, which is that of a fifth-century Athenian. It is still true, however, that in a less fair-minded person, this could reveal more individual and partisan associations.

[3] As far as home policy is concerned, one can also note that, according to Aristotle (Pol., 1314 a, 5), the tyrant aims at being the only one to enjoy dignity and liberty (σεμνῷ-ἐλευθέρῳ).

Constant,[1] 'the smallness of the territory covered by the city gave
each citizen a much greater individual importance in political
matters . . . The advantage which the people derived from liberty, in
the opinion of the ancients, lay in the fact that they were personally
governing, which was a genuine advantage, satisfying both
vanity and convenience.' In our own times, liberty no longer leads to
the exercise of authority; under several influences (one of which may
have been Kant's) the notions of universality and reciprocity gradually helped to dissever the two ideas. Men realized that their own
liberty should be accompanied by that of other people. The French
Revolution, for instance, obeying philosophical doctrines rather than
spontaneous desires, began by liberating those whom the democratic
revolutions of Athens — acting under the influence of wholly individual and spontaneous motives — aimed at bringing under stronger
domination. The same difference constantly recurs between the
modern state and the city of the classical world, the gulf which
separates a large, complex body from a narrow group of men
inspired by intense individual passions. And, however schematic it
may be, the analysis offered by Thucydides contains sufficient
elements to explain this basic difference.

This preliminary investigation thus in no way leads us to criticize
the picture which Thucydides gives of Athenian imperialism or to
alter any of its features. It simply shows with what precision he
brings out the abstract form of imperialism by pruning it down to its
essentials. Nothing remains of the discussions between the different
political parties or of any false starts and incidental aims. There remains the clear picture of a national policy, based on sea-power and
aiming at the sheer satisfaction of domination; and this policy is
presented as a single and united force threatening Greece.

It is thus natural that we should feel no surprise when we note that
all the more suspect explanations of imperialism, which were never
anything but inferior excuses put forward by certain of its supporters
and a means whereby they disguised its true nature, should also be
absent from his work. This is the case with the theories which have
tried to present Athenian policy as resting on an alliance of Ionians
against Dorians, or of democracies against oligarchies.

[1] *De l'Esprit de Conquête...*, chapter VI. The texts of the *Constitution of Athens*
completely confirm this idea. We have already seen how, according to its author, the
empire satisfied the vanity of each individual citizen.

The theme of racial opposition (or alliance) was of course traditional at the time of the Peloponnesian War, and Thucydides certainly does not fail to introduce it, as a source of emotional appeal, in a large number of speeches. It is true that these are generally speeches made by Dorians, in which a thinly disguised contempt for the island race can usually be perceived.[1] Only Euphemus (because Hermocrates had suggested that Dorians should become united in Sicily) represents Athenian policy in Greece as a defence of Ionians against Dorians.[2] But neither of these two speakers pretends to give any real explanation for all Athenian actions; far from it. Indeed, in his speech in Book IV, Hermocrates insists that, on the whole, Athenian imperialism attacks all cities, regardless of race.[3] And Euphemus himself soon points out that only self-interest can govern the system of alliances and enmities adopted by a city at the head of an empire.[4] Moreover the list of allies drawn up by Thucydides just before the great battle of Syracuse is wholly inspired by his desire to show that racial opposition is insignificant by the side of the real relationship founded on self-interest; he indicates this in VII. 57. 1: οὐ κατὰ δίκην τι μᾶλλον οὐδὲ κατὰ ξυγγένειαν μετ' ἀλλήλων στάντες, ἀλλ' ὡς ἑκάστοις τῆς ξυντυχίας ἢ κατὰ τὸ ξυμφέρον ἢ ἀνάγκη ἔσχεν. And he recalls it again and again as he continues with his list.[5] Thus we are not here concerned with some purely secondary factor which Thucydides

---

[1] In I. 124. 1, the Corinthians do not define this exactly; they say: οὖσι Δωριεῦσι καὶ ὑπὸ Ἰώνων πολιορκουμένοις; but Brasidas says in V. 9. 1: καὶ ὅτι Δωριῆς μέλλετε Ἴωσι μάχεσθαι ὧν εἰώθατε κρείσσους εἶναι, Hermocrates, in VI. 77. 1: ὅτι οὐκ Ἴωνες τάδε εἰσὶν οὐδ' Ἑλλησπόντιοι καὶ νησιῶται οἳ δεσπότην ἢ Μῆδον ἢ ἕνα γέ τινα αἰεὶ μεταβάλλοντες δουλοῦνται, ἀλλὰ Δωριῆς ἐλεύθεροι, ἀπ' αὐτονόμου τῆς Πελοποννήσου τὴν Σικελίαν οἰκοῦντες, Gylippus, in VII. 5. 4: Πελοποννήσιοί τε ὄντες καὶ Δωριῆς Ἰώνων καὶ νησιωτῶν καὶ ξυγκλύδων ἀνθρώπων κρατήσαντες; and finally, for the Argives, cf. VIII. 25. 3: καταφρονήσαντες ὡς ἐπ' Ἴωνάς τε καὶ οὐ δεξομένους.

[2] VI. 82. 2: τὸ μὲν οὖν μέγιστον μαρτύριον αὐτὸς εἶπεν ὅτι οἱ Ἴωνες αἰεί ποτε πολέμιοι τοῖς Δωριεῦσίν εἰσιν· ἔχει δὲ καὶ οὕτως· ἡμεῖς γὰρ Ἴωνες ὄντες Πελοποννησίοις Δωριεῦσι, καὶ πλείοσιν οὖσι καὶ παροικοῦσιν, ἐσκεψάμεθα ὅτῳ τρόπῳ ἥκιστα [αὐτῶν] ὑπακουσόμεθα.

[3] IV. 61. 2: παρεστάναι δὲ μηδενὶ ὡς οἱ μὲν Δωριῆς ἡμῶν πολέμιοι τοῖς Ἀθηναίοις, τὸ δὲ Χαλκιδικὸν τῇ Ἰάδι ξυγγενείᾳ ἀσφαλές· οὐ γὰρ τοῖς ἔθνεσιν, ὅτι δίχα πέφυκε, τοῦ ἑτέρου ἔχθει ἐπίασιν, ἀλλὰ τῶν ἐν τῇ Σικελίᾳ ἀγαθῶν ἐφιέμενοι, ἃ κοινῇ κεκτήμεθα.

[4] VI. 85. 1: ἀνδρὶ δὲ τυράννῳ ἢ πόλει ἀρχὴν ἐχούσῃ οὐδὲν ἄλογον ὅ τι ξυμφέρον οὐδ' οἰκεῖον ὅ τι μὴ πιστόν· πρὸς ἕκαστα δὲ δεῖ ἢ ἐχθρὸν ἢ φίλον μετὰ καιροῦ γίγνεσθαι.

[5] In fact he does use an ethnic framework, but in each instance he points out how inadequate it is. Thus, in Athens' allies, in 57. 6: Ῥόδιοι δὲ καὶ Κυθήριοι Δωριῆς ἀμφότεροι . . . ; in 57. 7: Κερκυραῖοι δὲ οὐ μόνον Δωριῆς ἀλλὰ καὶ Κορίνθιοι σαφῶς ἐπὶ Κορινθίους τε καὶ Συρακοσίους . . . ; in 57. 9: Ἀργεῖοι μὲν οὐ τῆς ξυμμαχίας ἕνεκα μᾶλλον ἢ τῆς Λακεδαιμονίων τε ἔχθρας καὶ τῆς παραυτίκα ἕκαστοι ἰδίας ὠφελίας Δωριῆς ἐπὶ Δωριᾶς μετὰ Ἀθηναίων Ἰώνων ἠκολούθουν. We may add that the barbarians who join the list help to invalidate the idea that race can be considered as being in any way a determining factor.

would be justified in omitting, but with a wrong explanation that he mentions in order to dismiss it, bringing out at the same time the real reasons for the conflict between the two sides.

The same is true of the explanation offered by party opposition (or alliance). These two ideas have their place in Thucydides' work, and play a much more important part than questions of race. Not only does a man such as Diodotus mention the feelings of friendship (εὔνοια) 'shared by the democratic parties of every city towards Athens' (III. 47. 2), but Thucydides himself notes that it was everywhere the democratic leaders who appealed to Athens for help, while the leaders of oligarchies turned towards Sparta (III. 82. 1); this is, in fact, the summary of almost all the episodes in Book III. Thus this is a factor whose importance Thucydides himself underlines,[1] while at the same time pointing out that it was a fairly limited one. For he never presents it as being anything more for Athens than an instrument which she uses to facilitate her conquests,[2] but which in no way explains the principles which lead her to act. It is the natural tendency for democracies to unite which will help to bring about the predominance of Athens, not this predominance which will foster an ideal union of democracies. What is even more important is that this instrument is only valid within certain limits. Thucydides is most careful to insist that, like racial differences, political differences fade away before the fundamental motives which inspire the two sides: for Athens, the desire to rule, for the others, the desire to be independent. Brasidas, the liberator, is the first to present the idea of depriving Athens of this weapon, and for this reason he refuses to allow one political party to triumph over another in the cities he has liberated.[3] And soon the Athenians become unable to hold their subjects with the support of any political party, for the desire for independence overcomes all other differences. As Phrynichus says in VIII. 48. 5: οὐ γὰρ βουλήσεσθαι αὐτοὺς μετ' ὀλιγαρχίας ἢ δημοκρατίας

---

[1] In a general way he does consider that the question of internal government plays a part in international relations; for example it is a factor in the changes of alliance in Book V: the Mantineans come closer to Argos δημοκρατουμένην τε ὥσπερ καὶ αὐτοί (V. 29. 1); the Argives come nearer to Athens δημοκρατουμένην ὥσπερ καὶ αὐτοί (V. 44. 1); on the other hand the Boeotians remain loyal to Sparta νομίζοντες σφίσι τὴν 'Αργείων δημοκρατίαν' αὐτοῖς ὀλιγαρχουμένοις ἧσσον ξύμφορον εἶναι τῆς Λακεδαιμονίων πολιτείας (V. 31. 6).

[2] For instance, the Athenians are sorry that they attacked Syracuse, a democratic city like Athens, for they are unable to spread discontent and make friends there (VII. 55. 2).

[3] IV. 86. 4: οὐ γὰρ ξυστασιάσων ἥκω, οὐδὲ ἂν σαφῆ τὴν ἐλευθερίαν νομίζω ἐπιφέρειν, εἰ τὸ πάτριον παρεὶς τὸ πλέον τοῖς ὀλίγοις ἢ τὸ ἔλασσον τοῖς πᾶσι δουλώσαιμι.

δουλεύειν μᾶλλον ἢ μεθ' ὁποτέρου ἂν τύχωσι τούτων ἐλευθέρους εἶναι.

Thus the vital conflict produced in Greece by the development of Athenian imperialism causes all other problems to fade into the background. It is useless for Athenian imperialism to try to shelter behind these other problems: *eripitur persona, manet res*. Athens seeks only conquests and the cities think only of acquiring or defending their freedom. Every city is equally in danger, and equally eager to escape.

This abstract and almost universal characteristic once again shows itself, from one end of the work to the other, by the repetition of certain schematic phrases. The first recalls the twofold condition of the Greeks *vis-à-vis* Athenian imperialism (οἱ μέν ... οἱ δέ ...); the second evokes the threat which this imperialism represents for every Greek (κἂν ἐπὶ σφᾶς). Thus we see the following passages repeated with suggestive monotony:

I. 68. 3 (speech of the Corinthians): ὧν τοὺς μὲν δεδουλωμένους ὁρᾶτε, τοῖς δ' ἐπιβουλεύοντας αὐτούς.

I. 123. 1 (speech of the Corinthians): τῆς ἄλλης Ἑλλάδος ἁπάσης ξυναγωνιουμένης, τὰ μὲν φόβῳ, τὰ δὲ ὠφελίᾳ.

I. 124. 3 (speech of the Corinthians): καὶ τὴν καθεστηκυῖαν ἐν τῇ Ἑλλάδι πόλιν τύραννον ἡγησάμενοι ἐπὶ πᾶσιν ὁμοίως καθεστάναι, ὥστε τῶν μὲν ἤδη ἄρχειν, τῶν δὲ διανοεῖσθαι.

II. 8. 5 (remark by Thucydides): οἱ μὲν τῆς ἀρχῆς ἀπολυθῆναι βουλόμενοι, οἱ δὲ μὴ ἀρχθῶσι φοβούμενοι.

VI. 18. 3 (speech by Alcibiades): ἀνάγκη, ἐπειδήπερ ἐν τῷδε καθέσταμεν, τοῖς μὲν ἐπιβουλεύειν, τοὺς δὲ μὴ ἀνιέναι.

VII. 56. 2 (indication given by Thucydides of the aims pursued by the Syracusans): τοὺς μὲν ἐλευθεροῦσθαι, τοὺς δὲ φόβου ἀπολύεσθαι.

or, in the other case, we have:

I. 120. 2 (speech of the Corinthians): τοὺς δὲ τὴν μεσόγειαν μᾶλλον καὶ μὴ ἐν πόρῳ κατῳκημένους εἰδέναι χρή ..., προσδέχεσθαι δέ ποτε, εἰ τὰ κάτω πρόοιντο, κἂν μέχρι σφῶν τὸ δεινὸν προελθεῖν, καὶ περὶ αὐτῶν οὐχ ἧσσον νῦν βουλεύεσθαι.

V. 98 (remark of the Melians): ὅσοι γὰρ νῦν μηδετέροις ξυμμαχοῦσι, πῶς οὐ πολεμώσεσθε αὐτούς, ὅταν ἐς τάδε βλέψαντες ἡγήσωνταί ποτε ὑμᾶς καὶ ἐπὶ σφᾶς ἥξειν.

VI. 77. 2 (question asked by Hermocrates): καὶ οἰόμεθα τοῦ ἄπωθεν ξυνοίκου προαπολλυμένου οὐ καὶ ἐς αὐτόν τινα ἥξειν τὸ δεινόν ... ;

G

VIII. 2. 1 (remark by Thucydides): οἱ μὲν μηδετέρων ὄντες ξύμμαχοι
... νομίσαντες κἂν ἐπὶ σφᾶς ἕκαστοι ἐλθεῖν αὐτούς, εἰ τὰ ἐν τῇ
Σικελίᾳ κατώρθωσαν, ... μάλιστα δὲ οἱ τῶν Ἀθηναίων ὑπήκοοι
ἕτοῖμοι ἦσαν καὶ παρὰ δύναμιν αὐτῶν ἀφίστασθαι.

Both by the degree of insistence implied in the repetition of these
phrases and by the care with which Thucydides dismisses anything
which might hide the true nature of the conflict from the reader, he
brings out the full importance of Athenian ambition, with the result
that this force stands out in the clearly defined and unmistakable form
with which he has succeeded in endowing it.

II. THE NATURE OF ATHENIAN RULE

Just as we can bring together certain texts to reconstruct the picture
that Thucydides gives of Athenian ambition, so we can also see this
ambition at work and come to define the result of its action.

It obviously shows itself, first of all, under the form of a series of
military expeditions, aiming at conquest or repression: Thucydides
describes them all, not only those more or less directly connected
with the Peloponnesian War, but also those which took place before.
Thus, with the exception of chapter I. 99, the Pentecontaëtia is
nothing but a long list of military expeditions. Nevertheless, to
conquer is not to rule: it is only one of the various means to that end.[1]
And the establishment of authority, in itself, is just as important as
are the military expeditions: it has a powerful influence not only on
the actual history of imperialism but on the general judgment made of
it. It is therefore of interest to consider how Thucydides presented
this matter.

Thucydides made no attempt to hide the fact that Athenian rule
was both vigorous and unpopular. The whole of the Pentecontaëtia
is intended to explain how Athens transformed a confederation of
independent allies (I. 97) into a more or less strongly held empire
(I. 118: τήν τε ἀρχὴν ἐγκρατεστέραν κατεστήσαντο). Similarly, he
never misses the opportunity of reminding the reader of the hostility
which Athens always met with from her subjects.[2]

[1] Thucydides suggests it himself in I. 97. 1: τοσάδε ἐπῆλθον πολέμῳ τε καὶ διαχειρίσει
πραγμάτων μεταξὺ τοῦδε τοῦ πολέμου καὶ τοῦ Μηδικοῦ. But there is no sign of any further
development of this idea elsewhere.

[2] In addition to the texts already quoted, cf. I. 75. 4; I. 76. 1; II. 63. 1; II. 63. 2; III. 37. 2.

The vocabulary which he uses is yet another indication of this.

First of all, the imperceptible transformation of a confederation into an empire is accompanied by a distinction among the groups of words ἡγεῖσθαι, ξύμμαχος, ξυμμαχία,[1] and ἄρχειν, ἀρχόμενος, ἀρχή.[2] But what is most important is that in the case of peoples brought under the rule of Athens, either after they have tried to desert the alliance or after a direct military conquest, these words give way to others whose meaning is even clearer. Thucydides then normally says that they have become subjects (ὑπήκοοι) and that Athens has enslaved them (δουλοῦν). Although he can, when the occasion demands it, use words in their precise, official sense,[3] he here deliberately departs from the language used in the inscriptions[4] and even from that used by certain Athenians; and he has no hesitation in using exactly the same terms to speak of Athenian rule and of the rule of Polycrates of Samos, who also has 'subjects' (I. 13. 6), or of Cyrus (who 'enslaves' cities in I. 16).

It must be noted, however, that this frankness is not attained by neglecting any nuances, for these words are never used for allies who pay no tribute; these are sometimes classed as ἀρχόμενοι and assimilated to the ἀρχή,[5] but they are never called ὑπήκοοι;[6] as ξύμμαχοι

---

[1] One should add the word ξυμμαχίς, which is used like ἀρχή, to indicate the countries which come under Athenian rule as a whole, but which have no other features in common (cf. V. Martin, *La vie internationale dans la Grèce des cités au VIème et au Vème siècles*, Publ. de l'Inst. Univ. de H. E. Intern., Geneva, 1940, in the chapter called 'Incompatibilité de l'État-ville et de certaines formes d'impérialisme', particularly p. 331).

[2] The two series of expressions are never confused with each other. If Euphemus uses ἡγεμονία and ἀρχή side by side in VI. 82. 3, this is because he speaks as a skilful barrister (cf. p. 243). After a certain date, the first series is only used when things are looked upon from a purely military point of view.

[3] Cf. the distinction between the words ξύμμαχος and φίλος in III. 70. 2 and VI. 47 (they are found together in I. 58. 2 only because the actual conditions are found together), or the distinction between ξυμμαχία and ἐπιμαχία in I. 44. 1.

[4] One hardly ever finds the series of expressions ἀρχή, etc., in inscriptions (however, cf. in Thucydides' own text, V. 18. 7 and V. 47. 2). They obviously do not use the last and crudest series.

[5] See, however, III. 36. 2 (of the Mytilenians): οὐκ ἀρχόμενοι ὥσπερ οἱ ἄλλοι.

[6] The word ὑπήκοοι is, however, used on one occasion where it does not apply to those paying tribute; but this use is caused by the parallelism of the expressions and its meaning is made quite clear by what is added; it is in the list of allies, in VII. 57. 5: Μηθυμναῖοι μὲν ναυσὶ καὶ οὐ φόρῳ ὑπήκοοι, Τενέδιοι δὲ καὶ Αἴνιοι ὑποτελεῖς. As to the presence of people of Chios among the ὑπηκόων καὶ φόρου ὑποτελῶν (VII. 57. 4), with the reserve οὐχ ὑποτελεῖς ὄντες φόρου, it in any case presupposes, in the present state of the text, a fairly unprecise link. Now it is my view that the present reading is correct, and that the uncertainty regarding classification can be explained by the mixture of various classificatory systems.

αὐτόνομοι,[1] they are contrasted with the ξύμμαχοι φόρου ὑποτελεῖς or χρήματα φέροντες,[2] who alone deserve this title.[3]

Thus the language used by Thucydides, although straightforward, does not imply any emotional bias or confusion; his only aim is to present in clear and intelligible terms both the complex features of the picture which he had before his eyes, and the hypocritical form conveyed by official language. He thus once again shows the same concern for clarity, which has already been noted in connection with his description of Athenian ambition.[4]

Things are not quite the same, however, if we try to see what exactly each category involved and find out some more details about these general features.

The major difference between the two categories of subjects lies in the services demanded of them: some have to send military help, while others have to make a financial contribution. Thucydides explains very clearly that both these obligations date from the beginning of the federation (I. 96. 1: ἔταξαν ἅς τε ἔδει παρέχειν τῶν πόλεων χρήματα . . . καὶ ἅς ναῦς); he also explains why the first form of participation rapidly came to be more important than the second (I. 99).We must now study what information he provides about each of them.

The obligation to send military contingents is the most legitimate that can be imagined, and seems normal in any form of alliance. Even those who bought themselves out of the obligation to provide ships by paying the tribute still had, on occasion, to provide troops for use on land, and this comes out clearly from the remark in II. 9. 5: τούτων ναυτικὸν παρείχοντο Χῖοι, Λέσβιοι, Κερκυραῖοι, οἱ δ' ἄλλοι πεζὸν καὶ χρήματα. As far as this obligation is concerned,

---

[1] This autonomy does not amount to absolute independence (ἐλεύθεροί τε καὶ αὐτόνομοι); this difference explains both the pretensions of the Spartans before the war (cf. Nesselhauf, *Hermes*, 69) and the clause in V. 18. 5: τὰς δὲ πόλεις φερούσας τὸν φόρον τὸν ἐπ' Ἀριστείδου αὐτονόμους εἶναι. Here, once again, Thucydides' vocabulary is quite precise.

[2] For the use of the first expression, cf. I. 56. 2; I. 66; I. 80. 3; I. 83. 2; II. 9. 4; VII. 57. 5; for the second one: I. 93. 2.

[3] Cf. VII. 57. 4: τῶν μὲν ὑπηκόων καὶ φόρου ὑποτελῶν . . .

[4] It is for the same reason that he never uses, to describe the Athenian subjects, the famous word πόλεις, which Eupolis took as title to his comedy and which is constantly used by Aristophanes (cf. *Acharnians*, 192, 506, 636, 643; *Knights*, 802 etc.). It is an expression whose meaning is clear only when it is being used among Athenians, in the daily life of the city above which Thucydides constantly rises. The only occasion in which an expression seems similar is in VIII. 64. 5 (σωφροσύνην γὰρ λαβοῦσαι αἱ πόλεις) which nevertheless implies no special meaning to be attributed to the term.

Thucydides provides all the information that we might require: we know the exact number of all the naval contingents[1] and of most of the land forces,[2] sent by the allies on each occasion. It would be easy to make a whole list of these, which would show us how Athens made wide use of the resources offered by her empire (when the independent island of Melos was conquered, for example, there were more allied than Athenian hoplites engaged upon the task: V. 84. 1). Yet Thucydides makes no attempt to deduce any general ideas about the relationship of Athens to her empire from the lists of forces that he provides: he restricts himself to giving the history of the battle and saying how many troops were involved.

The obligation to pay tribute was also important in the actual history of the war; and although Thucydides often gives extremely valuable information about the payments made, he does so only in so far as the resources available to Athens are one of the elements likely to cause the scales of war to tip to one side rather than to the other.

The information which he provides is in fact as follows:

I. 96. 2: the tribute was received by Athenian magistrates, the Hellenotamiae; the first tribute was fixed at 460 talents, and the sum was deposited at Delos, where the allied meetings took place.

I. 99. 3: the allies who did not wish to take part in the military expeditions arranged to pay a fixed sum which made up their tribute and which corresponded to the amount of money they would have spent in fitting out ships.

II. 9. 5: when the Peloponnesian War began, all the allies except Chios, Lesbos and Corcyra paid tribute under this form.

II. 13: at the beginning of the war, Pericles reminds the Athenians that they receive the tribute annually, and that this sum amounts roughly to 600 talents, that they have a balance of 6000 talents on the Acropolis, and that the highest figure so far reached by this sum was 9700 talents, on which they had drawn for the buildings on the

[1] Cf. II. 25. 1: 50 ships from Corcyra; II. 56: 50 ships from Chios and Lesbos; III. 3. 4: 10 ships from Mytilene; IV. 13. 2: 4 ships from Chios; IV. 129. 3: 10 ships from Chios; V. 84. 1: 6 ships from Chios and 2 from Lesbos; VI. 43. 1: 34 ships from Chios and other places; VII. 20. 2: 5 ships from Chios.

[2] Athens had the right to summon them (προσκαλεῖν, III. 6. 1). On their participation in the different expeditions, the list drawn up by Busolt-Swoboda is incomplete; one must also quote: III. 75. 1; III. 88; IV. 28; IV. 42; IV. 53; IV. 54; IV. 75; IV. 129; V. 2; V. 84; VI. 43; VII. 17; VII. 20; VII. 57; VIII. 25; VIII. 69. Thucydides gives details of the number of land troops only in exceptional cases.

Acropolis, in particular for the Propylaea, and for the siege of Potidaea.

III. 19. 1: since the tribute proved insufficient to pay all the costs of the war, the Athenians themselves paid the εἰσφορά in 428, and sent twelve ἀργυρολόγους ναῦς to the allies.

V. 18. 5: the peace treaty of 421 lays it down that the towns handed back by Sparta will pay 'Aristides' tribute' (τὸν ἐπ' Ἀριστείδου).

VII. 28. 4: in 413, the costs of the war having become heavy, the Athenians fixed a tax of one-twentieth on all maritime transactions performed by their subjects, in the place of the φόρος.

I consider that this information is for the most part correct, even though two of the figures given above (that of 460 talents in I. 96 and that of 9700 talents in II. 13)[1] are hotly contested by many scholars. But there is nothing improbable about the first;[2] it may indicate the average tribute paid to Athens during the first period, in which case Thucydides has simply followed his normal habit of generalizing and simplifying. It may even be that this figure does represent the exact amount of money initially paid by allies still worried by the Persian menace.[3] As for the second, it does set a more difficult problem, but one which belongs to the realm of textual criticism: the scholiast of Aristophanes does in fact quote the passage in rather a different way,[4] and tradition offers no means of deciding

[1] I am not here speaking of the figure of 600 talents given in II. 13, which there is no reason to reject. Doubtless it is much higher that the average tribute noted for this period on the lists of Hellenotamiae. But Pericles is probably giving here the theoretical amount, and making no attempt to reduce it; and he probably includes in it the indemnity paid by Samos, which was perhaps 80 talents a year. In any case this indemnity was supposed to cover for Athens the expenses of the siege which were over 1300 talents.

[2] The following scholars in particular have rejected it: Kirchhoff (*Untersuchung über den Delischen Bund im ersten Decennium seines Bestehens, Hermes*, 11, p. 1), Adcock, *C.A.H.*, V. pp. 44-46, Busolt-Swoboda, pp. 1336-1360. In fact, for the period 454 to 415, which is fairly well known to us, the tribute varied between 410 talents (429-428) and 525 or even 495 (in 454-450); between 450 and 435 it never seems to have been more than 460 talents. There is consequently some cause for surprise that it should have reached this figure at a time when far fewer allies were paying tribute and when Athenian demands, according to the men of the next generation, were extremely moderate.

[3] This is the view of Steup, Cavaignac and Glotz. We must also note that the figures given by our list of tributes are always too low. There must certainly have been a considerable discrepancy between the amount paid 'on paper' and the amount really paid. The law of 425, at first sight astonishing by the enormous taxes which it imposes, and including certain cities which were inscribed only as a matter of pure form, is the obvious proof of this.

[4] Cf. schol. *Ploutos*, 1193. By a minute difference of textual reading, the sums become, instead of 9700 and 6000 talents, 6000 and 5700 talents.

between the two readings.[1] But even if we admit — as the evidence might seem to indicate[2] — that the figure given in Thucydides' text is incorrect, and that of the scholiast correct, it would seem more normal to attribute the mistake to one of Thucydides' copyists rather than to Thucydides himself. In fact there is nothing easier than to admit that the scribe, influenced by tradition, either made a mistake or introduced an inaccurate correction. But if, on the other hand, we admit that the error is Thucydides' own, we must suppose that the scholiast of Aristophanes deliberately introduced an extremely intelligent correction into the historical text that he was quoting, while at the same time giving no indication that he was doing so. Such an action would imply that he was both extraordinarily well informed and amazingly discrete.

But supposing there is no actual mistake in Thucydides' text, it must be admitted that the information which he offers is very incomplete: its only function is to explain what resources were available to Athens, and it gives no help in analysing how her rule had evolved and how it worked. Indeed, he omits all the facts which are most significant from this point of view.

In the Pentecontaëtia, for example, he makes no mention of the transference, in 454, of the treasury of Delos to Athens; he makes no mention of the triumph, in 443, of a policy which consisted of using the money contributed by the allies for other purposes than waging war; he makes no mention of the division of the allies into five districts, which took place at the same time and marked the beginning of an imperial mode of organization, or of the fusion of Athena's treasury with the federal treasury. Yet these different measures both marked and brought about the transformation of the allies into subjects.

He shows the same attitude of mind in the actual history of the war, although he had more space there to include additional information. In particular, while he devotes long sections of his discussion about Mytilene to dealing with the attitude of Cleon towards the allies, he never mentions the fact that in 425 Cleon had considerably increased the amount of tribute to be paid. This is nevertheless the

[1] Tradition speaks of 10,000 talents (Diod., XII, 40, 2; Isocr., *Antidosis*, 234), a figure which can either call into question the scholiast's text (Beloch's view) or, if it is exaggerated, explain the error of Thucydides' copyist (Cavaignac's view).
[2] By consulting inscriptions, traditions, and even Thucydides' text, one finds it difficult to arrive, for the sums taken from the reserve up to that point (end of the building on the Acropolis — beginning of the siege of Potidaea) at a figure of some 3700 talents.

information given to us by the inscription IG I² 63, from which we learn that the tribute was doubled or even trebled,[1] at least in principle. And even tradition tells us about this increase, although with a certain lack of precision.[2]

If Thucydides prefers not to mention this increase, it is clearly not because he is uninterested in financial affairs. These are of the greatest interest to him as long as they concern the war, and he then insists upon their importance.[3] But in so far as they concern the relationship of Athens with her allies he seems to deal with them as belonging to the realm of home policy, which, as we have already seen, he constantly neglects. Perhaps the history of the war lost something because of this, but it was nevertheless in order to deal more fully with the war itself that Thucydides sacrificed these other questions.

This explains why he remains extremely vague about any encroachments by Athens on the independence of her allies, whenever these did not directly increase her capacity for waging war. Yet it was by such encroachments that the condition of the allies was radically transformed, to such an extent that voices were raised in violent protest even within Athens herself.

If we consult Isocrates, we find in the *Panegyricus* and in the *Panathenaicus* the series of grievances normally associated with Athenian imperialism: Isocrates makes a list of them in order to examine them one after another. In the first text he lists the following items: excessively harsh repressions, as at Melos and Scione (100); the sending of *cleruchies* (107), the question of the law-suits (113); as to the various examples of disorders, revolution and brutality, the *Panegyricus* attributes them all to Sparta (114). In the *Panathenaicus*, the same grievances are mentioned: the question of the law-suits (66), that of the tribute (67), the excessively harsh repressions at Melos, Scione and Torone (62) and, finally, the suppression of autonomy (97), and the disorders, revolutions and brutalities of every kind (99). The

---

[1] The complete figure can be reconstituted as 960 talents (for Adcock, West, Tod, Cavaignac, Glotz, Mathieu) or 1460 (for Beloch, Busolt, Swoboda, Kolbe).

[2] Writers speak of a tribute of 1200 to 1300 talents for the peace of Nicias (Andocides, *Peace*, 9; Aeschines, II, 175). On the other hand [Andoc.], *Against Alc.*, 11, speaks of an increase doubling the tribute paid by each town, and Plutarch (*Arist.*, 24) speaks of a total of 1300 talents, representing three times the previous amount.

[3] Moreover, see I. 122. 1: τῶν προσόδων αἷς ἰσχύουσι — I. 143. 4: τὰ τῶν ξυμμάχων, ὅθεν ἰσχύομεν — III. 39. 8: τῆς ἐπετείας προσόδου, δι' ἣν ἰσχύομεν — III. 46. 3: προσόδου... ἰσχύομεν δὲ πρὸς τοὺς πολεμίους τῷδε.

contemporary texts, which are naturally less systematic, note the same points: the question of the law-suits is dealt with by the author of the *Constitution of Athens* (I, 16), and is often mentioned by Aristophanes;[1] the *Constitution of Athens* also speaks of the setting up of democratic regimes in the conquered cities, and Aristophanes, in an innocent play like the *Birds*, does not fail to bring before our eyes, among the other characters who come to disturb the peace of Nephelococcygia and represent all the vices of democracy, that redoubtable Inspector (1022 ff.) who is like the Eye of Athens, watching over a political life which has not yet even come to birth.

Now if we omit, from the list of all these grievances, the isolated acts of cruelty mentioned by Thucydides as being the final stage of certain military measures,[2] there still remains a series of peaceful encroachments to which he pays no attention at all.

In the realm of law, Athens progressively took over certain prerogatives,[3] and increased the number of actions she filed against people in the cities. Thucydides refers to this in the speech made by the Athenians in I, 77;[4] but he does so in order to draw a rather hasty conclusion as to the moderation shown by the Athenians in occasionally accepting the jurisdiction of the allies in law-suits for which there were legal conventions.[5] In fact this is only mentioned as an example and one on which Thucydides does not insist; for he soon comes round to identifying the Athenian attitude as a whole

[1] Cf. in particular the episode of the Sycophant in the *Birds*, 1410-1470 (similarly *Peace*, 639-647; *Knights*, 324-326).

[2] Scione = IV. 122. 6; Torone = V. 3. 4; Melos = V. 116. 4; finally, one could add Mytilene (a decision that was abrogated). It can even be said that Thucydides adds a genuine commentary to his account of these measures, since one (Mytilene) gives rise to a discussion with antithetical speeches, and the other (Melos) to a dialogue. Nevertheless these two episodes treat the problem only from the point of view of the Athenians and as a part in the general struggle. The dialogue is a debate on conquest, the two speeches a debate on repression: conquest and repression: imperialism, in Thucydides' work, is only shown as imperialism in arms.

[3] Cf. IG I² 39; I² 22; Antiphon, V, 47; and, among the studies on the question, H. Grant Robertson, *The Administration of Justice in the Athenian Empire* (*Univ. of Toronto Stud. Hist. and Econ.*, t. IV, no. 1, 1924) (cf. P. Cloché, *R.E.G.*, XXXVIII, 1925, pp. 123 ff.), Hans Weber, *Attisches Prozessrecht in den Attischen Seebundstaaten*, Paderborn, 1908 and particularly H. Lipsius, *Attisches Recht und Rechtverfahren*, III, 1915, pp. 969 ff.

[4] Καὶ ἐλασσούμενοι γὰρ ἐν ταῖς ξυμβολαίαις πρὸς τοὺς ξυμμάχους δίκαις καὶ παρ᾽ ἡμῖν αὐτοῖς ἐν τοῖς ὁμοίοις νόμοις ποιήσαντες τὰς κρίσεις φιλοδικεῖν δοκοῦμεν.

[5] My view, like that of Busolt-Swoboda, is that it is a question of law-suits like those alluded to in the decree on Phaselis, in 465 (IG I² 16), and which must take place κατὰ τὰς οὔσας ξυμβολάς; see also IG I² 60, for Mytilene, and Hesychius, ἀπὸ σ. δ. Thucydides seems to be contrasting the impartiality of Athenian courts with the partiality of allied courts.

with the general principle of a rule of law contrasted with open violence: once more, in this speech, we can see Thucydides' own tendency to take always the most general and abstract view of matters. And finally this isolated mention simply brings out how little importance Thucydides attached to these facts, which were then at the centre of so much political argument.

Politically, Athens set up democracy everywhere, and appointed her own delegates to watch over the way it worked. From the time of Aristeides, only Chios, Lesbos and Samos — if we believe Aristotle (*Constitution of the Athenians*, 24, 2) — had kept their own constitutions and magistrates, having merely φύλακες to keep them obedient. Now Thucydides, who indicates in I. 19 that the Lacedaemonians saw to it that only oligarchy should prevail among their allies, does not once[1] mention the Athenian attitude on this question.

Finally, as far as property is concerned, Athens had brutally affirmed her sovereignty by the system of *cleruchies*, that is to say by the establishment of Athenian settlers in imperial territory. Thucydides is careful to mention this custom whenever it is the result of one of the military expeditions that he describes,[2] but he pays no other attention to it. In the Pentecontaëtia, for example, he does not indicate how the gradual increase in measures of this kind has, under Pericles, become a real way of carrying out conquest by peaceful means. Even when he speaks of the actual circumstances, he never pays any attention to the principle of this institution in itself; the indication which he gives of its existence is not developed in any way, and the establishment of a *cleruchy* is merely treated as the conclusion of an open struggle, not as an episode in the development of a particular policy.

The consequence of this is that his work bears no resemblance to the analyses given by political writers setting out to judge the nature of Athenian rule: he seems to be uninterested in its methods[3] and indifferent towards its faults.

The same thing is naturally true as far as the merits of Athenian

[1] He merely quotes, in VIII. 64-65, a voyage aimed at overthrowing democratic governments everywhere from which one may suppose that they did already exist.

[2] Thus I. 98. 2; I. 114. 3; II. 70. 4; III. 50. 2; IV. 102. 3.

[3] There are many speeches about Athenian ambition, but not one about Athenian rule, even coming from subject peoples like the Mytilenians. There is only the speech of the Athenians in Book I which contains a paragraph showing that Athenian rule is moderate; even then, the speech sticks to general terms; and it stands apart from the texts surrounding it (cf. pp. 256-257).

rule are concerned. If Thucydides does not show how Athens came little by little to govern her subjects with an unbearably despotic rule, he gives no indication, either directly or in a speech, of the benefits which Athens brought to them. These advantages are nevertheless clearly visible, and once again we see how different texts and different accounts all come together to underline to what extent Thucydides is uninterested in these advantages. Once again, it is Isocrates who gives the most precise information. In the *Panegyricus* (103-106), he recalls that Athens gave the allies unity and concord, that she endowed them with that democratic regime under which she was glad to govern herself, and that for seventy years the allies lived free from tyranny, independent of barbarians, at harmony among themselves and in peace with all men. In the *Panathenaicus* (53-62), he again says that Athens gave the cities the same constitution as had provided her so many satisfactions, and that her dominion lasted for sixty-five years, during which the barbarians had to keep quiet. Similarly, in the *Epitaphios* of Lysias (55-58), we read that for seventy years the rule of Athens has enabled her subjects to live in harmony among themselves, to enjoy democratic regimes, and to see the Great King give up his ambitions: no fleet from Asia has dared to sail against the countries of Greece, no tyrant has established his dominion on Greek territory, and no Greek city has been conquered by the barbarians. Finally Lycurgus also points out (*Against Leocrates*, 72) that for ninety years[1] Athenian rule has maintained the independence of the Greeks, even of those who lived in Asia.

Certainly such a notion could scarcely be appreciated before the fourth century: then, on the one hand, the comparison with the Spartan rule of 404 could bring out the importance of the advantages that had now been lost, and, on the other, acts could be considered from the point of view of the results to which they gave rise rather than of the motives which inspired them (for if the result of Athenian rule was to hold the barbarians at bay,[2] this was not the ambition which inspired Athens, whose primary aim was to establish her own rule over the other Greek cities).[3] Nevertheless, if Thucydides had wanted to take into consideration the achievements of Athenian rule, then he would have noticed the benefits brought about by the

---

[1] Taylor proposes the correction of ἐνενήκοντα by ἑβδομήκοντα; cf. the texts quoted above.

[2] Moreover, see p. 100, about Thucydides' position as regards Greeks and barbarians.

[3] Cf. II. 64. 3 and VI. 90. 3.

effort towards unification that this rule represented. In fact, he never
takes these achievements into account, either to praise or to blame
them, and is as ignorant of how Athens assured ἐλευθερία to the
Greeks as he is of how she deprived them of their αὐτονομία.

When Athens brings Greece under her rule, he sees this fact only as
an increase in the amount of strength now available to Athens. He is
indifferent towards this empire, towards the way it is organized and
towards the spirit that animates it: what counts for him is the army,
the treasury, the experience that Athens has gained in acquiring the
empire. This is the frame of mind in which he concludes the Pentecontaëtia, in I. 118. 2: ἐν οἷς οἱ Ἀθηναῖοι τήν τε ἀρχὴν ἐγκρατεστέραν
κατεστήσαντο καὶ αὐτοὶ ἐπὶ μέγα ἐχώρησαν δυνάμεως.[1] The rule of
Athens is only an instrument for Athenian ambition, and the ἀρχή
becomes a δύναμις, impressively turned towards the outside world.
By leaving everying which concerns Athenian rule itself carefully
in the background, Thucydides thus once again brings out the
clearest possible picture of this eternally active force: Athenian
ambition.

Thus, in the same way as he defined the nature of Athenian
ambition by emphasizing certain factors and neglecting others, so
Thucydides uses the same technique to describe the type of rule set
up by Athens. But although his technique is the same in both cases,
the results that it gives show considerable differences.

The essential feature of his presentation of Athenian ambition lay
in a tendency towards simplification and generalization which
remained compatible with accuracy. All the essential facts were
reported, without any excursions into the realm of different programmes, false starts and incidental explanations. Thucydides
followed the same method here as he does everywhere, omitting
minor incidents, proper names, figures and anecdotes, but exploiting
these omissions and thereby reaching a form of truth, belonging to
the domain of reason and appealing directly to her.[2]

The same characteristic can be found in the passages dealing with
Athenian rule, as, for example, in the description of its former
organization or in the brief summary of later modifications. If this

---

[1] See also the ending of the Archaeology in I. 19: καὶ ἐγένετο αὐτοῖς ἐς τόνδε τὸν πόλεμον
ἡ ἰδία παρασκευὴ μείζων ἢ ὡς τὰ κράτιστά ποτε μετὰ ἀκραιφνοῦς τῆς ξυμμαχίας ἤνθησαν.

[2] Cf. the excellent definition given by Thibaudet: 'The example of Thucydides shows
that history can be made to unite two apparently contradictory characteristics: the
greatest accuracy in the realm of detail, and the greatest generality.'

quality is less noticeable, it is because another tendency has come to assume greater importance.

This tendency consists of taking into consideration only the war itself and the action that it involved.

As far as Athenian ambition was concerned, this tendency only reinforced Thucydides' general concern with what was essential, and the two tendencies combined so as to divert his attention from the home politics of the city. The same thing is not true of what he says about the nature of Athenian rule, for, here, a whole aspect of reality is sacrificed, and Thucydides condemns himself to giving only an incomplete account of Athenian imperialism.

Of course it may be argued that the war was his main subject. It was. And the very choice of this subject is in itself interesting. But the strict and exclusive way in which he chose to treat it remains even more remarkable. A modern historian, writing the history of a war, would begin by describing the two antagonists: Thucydides, on the other hand, is interested only in the actual clash. Challenging the epic while reacting against its methods, he retains in his emulation something of its spirit. Like the author of an epic, he seems to consider that only a great struggle is worthy of attention and capable of true greatness, and that the only theme for history is a warlike action. What he is writing is, in a way, an anti-epic.

This is why imperialism is depicted with the greatest clarity and emphasis when it leads to war and battles, but is neglected in its purely political forms.

CONCLUSION

THE POINT OF VIEW ADOPTED BY THUCYDIDES IN HIS JUDGMENT ON ATHENIAN IMPERIALISM

ATHENIAN imperialism would thus appear to be the object of Thucydides' main attention and concern, but a theme which is presented in a deliberately abstract and sometimes incomplete form. Now each one of the characteristics which Thucydides either rightly or wrongly leaves in the background constitutes an element absent from his final judgment, and each omission can be explained by reference to an intellectual attitude whose effect makes itself felt in every aspect of the subject he is studying. By bringing out the importance of Athenian ambition, Thucydides certainly recognizes the extent to which Athens herself is responsible for the events which he describes. By refusing to concern himself with the nature of Athenian rule, he shows himself relatively unaware of the wrongs she has committed. It is this which already distinguishes his judgment both from that of certain of Athens' critics and from that of some of her supporters.

In a more definite manner, however, the omissions detectable in his description of Athenian imperialism can help us to see in advance what kind of judgment he is likely to make; or, rather, they can show us how to begin by setting aside certain associations which might be thought to have influenced this judgment.

We thus start by eliminating such ideas as might link imperialism with any one of a whole range of notions, beginning with the most moral abstract sentiment, and passing by intermediate ideals such as that of Panhellenism, to end with partisan theories of this or that political group.

Purely moral considerations play no part at all in Thucydides' judgment of Athenian imperialism. While he himself undoubtedly attributes the greatest importance to the idea of justice and to all general moral factors — as is clearly shown by his analysis of the disorders in Greece in III. 82 — it is equally obvious that he has no intention at all of judging imperialism by these standards. If this

98

were not the case, he would certainly not have failed to deal with the 'crimes' committed by Athens, and would not have included so many speeches in which the critics of imperialism denounced its existence but did not list the wrongs committed in its name. These critics certainly say that Athens is guilty (ἀδικεῖ), but they do so without ever referring to any specifically moral concept; the guilt with which they are concerned is purely political, and takes the form of aggression and broken treaties. The existence of this guilt should arouse resistance, but it finally is a mere statement of fact, and a very plain one. Everyone, indeed, admits the 'unjust' character of imperialism as something that does not even deserve discussion, and Thucydides indicates this from the very beginning when he writes in I. 98. 4: πρώτη τε αὕτη πόλις ξυμμαχὶς παρὰ τὸ καθεστηκὸς ἐδουλώθη. The imperialists themselves never think of denying this circumstance.[1] They simply see it as being normal and fully justifiable by reference to usual practice. They accept the fact that they are pursuing an unjust policy in the same way as a tyrant accepts the fact that he is using an unjust authority, and they do so because they are dealing with a political and not with a moral question. Thucydides himself seems to have admitted their point of view, since the opponents of imperialism are shown as agreeing with its supporters on this particular issue, and frequently expressing the conqueror's point of view. The Corinthians, for example, think that the Spartans are responsible for what has happened because they have not succeeded in preventing it,[2] and Hermocrates argues that if anyone is to be blamed it is those who surrender, since the imperialistic ambitions which inspire Athens are a natural part of man's nature.[3] Similarly, when in Athens itself Diodotus criticizes the excesses of which Cleon is being guilty, and puts forward a more moderate policy, he is very careful to point out that he has no intention of bringing morality into politics.[4] Everyone considers imperialism as an established fact which is unjust and therefore regrettable, but although it is condemned on moral grounds the condemnation remains in the background. Thucydides does not

---

[1] Cf. I. 76. 2; II. 63. 2; III. 40. 4; V. 89; VI. 85. 1.

[2] Cf. I. 69. 1: οὐ γὰρ ὁ δουλωσάμενος ἀλλ' ὁ δυνάμενος μὲν παῦσαι, περιορῶν δὲ ἀληθέστερον αὐτὸ δρᾷ, εἴπερ καὶ τὴν ἀξίωσιν τῆς ἀρετῆς ὡς ἐλευθερῶν τὴν Ἑλλάδα φέρεται.

[3] IV. 61. 5: καὶ τοὺς μὲν Ἀθηναίους ταῦτα πλεονεκτεῖν τε καὶ προνοεῖσθαι πολλὴ ξυγγνώμη, καὶ οὐ τοῖς ἄρχειν βουλομένοις μέμφομαι, ἀλλὰ τοῖς ὑπακούειν ἑτοιμοτέροις οὖσιν· πέφυκε γὰρ τὸ ἀνθρώπειον διὰ παντὸς ἄρχειν μὲν τοῦ εἴκοντος, φυλάσσεσθαι δὲ τὸ ἐπιόν.

[4] III. 47. 5: καὶ τὸ Κλέωνος τὸ αὐτὸ δίκαιον καὶ ξύμφορον τῆς τιμωρίας οὐχ εὑρίσκεται ἐν αὐτῷ δυνατὸν ὂν ἅμα γίγνεσθαι.

make his orators treat this moral question as being of primary importance, and he himself was certainly not very concerned with it, since his narration follows the same principles as the speeches which form part of it. The Pentecontaëtia, among other passages, explains the development of Athenian imperialism in a dispassionate manner, treating it just as a fact, with a typically objective impartiality.[1] For Thucydides, the injustice shown by Athens is to be considered by the side of the different but parallel injustice shown by Sparta. He seems to admit that, in general, both men and cities act according to their own interest,[2] and that any discussion about human or political relationships should be based on this assumption. Since, in his view, imperialism was an essentially political phenomenon, the judgment which he passes on it is likewise an essentially political one.[3]

Neither does he, within this purely political framework, accord any great importance to the feeling of unity among the Greeks themselves. Grundy declared that Thucydides criticizes Athenian imperialism because he is indignant at 'the idea of Greeks ruling over other Greeks'.[4] But if this were the case, Thucydides would give much greater prominence both to the fact that Athenian imperialism violated the very aims of the confederation, and to the fact that it destroyed the independence of the allied cities; moreover, he would insist far more than he does on the difference between the moderate and extreme forms of imperialism. If he does not do this it is because such a distinction would imply an intense awareness on his own part of the opposition between Greeks and barbarians, and such a distinction is in fact quite foreign to him.

He never uses the idea of the general kinship between Greeks, either to criticize the form taken by Athenian imperialism, or, on the other hand, to praise Athens as being the protector of all Greek peoples. He even refrains — unlike other writers[5] — from making any

---

[1] Cf. Lange, pp. 629-630.   [2] Cf. later p. 256.

[3] This does not prevent his analysis from reaching a moral level, but the moral concepts that he uses will form part of an attempt at an objective investigation of the nature of Athenian imperialism, rather than part of an attempt at an immediate moral judgment.

[4] Grundy, p. 32. It must, moreover, be noticed that the example which he quotes to support his thesis is that of I. 98. 4, which I have already mentioned, and in this passage Thucydides insists rather on the non-observance of treaties than on the harm done to Greek independence.

[5] The first manifestation of a Panhellenic feeling can be found in Herodotus (cf. especially VIII, 144). In fifth-century Athens, this idea was linked first and foremost with a criticism of aggressive imperialism, as bringing Athens into conflict with Sparta.

distinction between his treatment of Greeks and barbarians; for instance, in Book VIII, he shows no indignation at the alliance between Sparta and the Great King,[1] nor had he shown any interest in the negotiations entered into at the beginning of the war;[2] he readily mentions Greeks and barbarians together (as in I. 82. 1), and insists that they are to be found side by side in the list of allies in VII. 57.

Moreover, in a passage which betrays a certain emotion on his own part, he endows Pericles with a particular pride in the thought that — to quote Grundy — the rule of Athens is a 'rule of Greeks over Greeks': Ἑλλήνων τε ὅτι Ἕλληνες πλείστων δὴ ἤρξαμεν (II. 64. 3): the fact that civilized and normally independent people accept the authority of Athens is probably, in his view, an even greater cause for pride.

Thus, in his judgment of Athenian imperialism, Thucydides adopts the point of view of Athens herself and not that of Greece. It may be that both Greece as a whole and the general principles of morality may suffer from this imperialism, but Thucydides is no more concerned with the danger to Greece than with the threat to morality. He considers this policy of conquest only in so far as it affects the city, and judges it only from this point of view.

However, we have still not sufficiently narrowed down our terms of reference. In deciding which factors influence Thucydides' view of events, we must also eliminate any idea of an association between

---

[1] This action did, nevertheless, provoke great indignation (the very opposition of Lichas in VIII. 43. 3 is sufficient indication); the fact that Sparta then abandoned a policy of 'liberation' made the action even more provocative.

[2] Cf. I. 82. 1 and II. 67. 1. In both cases it is a question of attempts made by Sparta, but they are mentioned purely by the way, and it was certainly not patriotic scruples, as Glotz would have us believe (p. 159) that prevented Thucydides from talking about the peace of Callias or about the treaty between Athens and Persia in 424. We must look for an explanation of this rather in the general principles indicated at the beginning of chapter II, in the first part of this book.

There is a very clear echo of this in Aristophanes, in particular in plays such as the *Peace* or *Lysistrata* (cf. on this point: W. Meredith Hugill, *Panhellenism in Aristophanes*, University of Chicago Press, 1936). The few plays by Euripides which, like *Iphigenia in Aulis*, bear the mark of Panhellenism could have been written at a time when the author despaired of victory. The final development of these doctrines can be found in the fourth century, with Gorgias, Lysias, and above all Isocrates. For a view of the movement as a whole, see the interesting analysis of J. H. Süssmann, *Die Grundzüge der panhellenischen Idee in V und IV Jahrhundert v. Chr.*, Diss. In. Zürich, 1921, and especially: Mathieu, *Les idées . . . (III: L'Unité hellénique avant Isocrate*, pp. 17-28); Cf. also later in this study p. 178.

H

imperialism and a particular political system or particular political party. Because he criticizes the excesses of democracy, or attacks democratic politicians like Cleon,[1] and because he praises the regime set up by Theramenes,[2] some people have seen him as one of the 'reactionaries' offended by both democracy and imperialism.[3] This is too hasty a judgment. It is certain that Thucydides had no liking for extreme democracy, but people of very differing shades of opinion agreed in criticizing some of its more glaring excesses, and one did not need to be inspired by any party political zeal to attack them. Moreover, apart from this one isolated point, it is difficult to place Thucydides in any very definite political party. If he approved of the regime set up by Theramenes, he also had great admiration for that set up by Pericles since, as he says, it was democratic in name but in fact gave power to one man (II. 65. 9). He even, in passing, defended the regime set up by the tyrants (VI. 54), while real 'moderates', people who belonged to Theramenes' party, admired neither Pericles nor the tyrants. In particular, they had none of Thucydides' great enthusiasm for the achievements and person of Pericles, but went back to Solon and Clisthenes.[4] Here at least there is no similarity between them and Thucydides.[5]

But the most important reason why Thucydides makes no attempt to judge events from the point of view of any one political party is that he refuses to see any primary connection between home and foreign policy. Had this not been the case, he would not have neglected all the features which linked imperialism to Athenian political life in general. If he deliberately ignored the conflict between different political doctrines and the link between democracy

---

[1] III. 36. 6; IV. 28. 5; cf. his scorn for the mob: II. 65. 4; IV. 28. 3; IV. 65. 3-4, etc.

[2] VIII. 97. 2: καὶ οὐχ ἥκιστα δὴ τὸν πρῶτον χρόνον ἐπί γ' ἐμοῦ Ἀθηναῖοι φαίνονται εὖ πολιτεύσαντες· μετρία γὰρ ἥ τε ἐς τοὺς ὀλίγους καὶ τοὺς πολλοὺς ξύγκρασις ἐγένετο. — Τὸν πρῶτον χρόνον ἐπί γ' ἐμοῦ can only be understood as it is in Classen and Herbst: 'For the first time in my life'; the example of VII. 87. 1 (τοὺς πρώτους χρόνους) mentioned by Lange is very different.

[3] The author of the Life goes much further; he declares in paragraph 4 that the whole work can be explained by the resentment that Thucydides felt against those responsible for sending him into exile. For this reason, the author argues that he is writing in a partisan spirit: διὰ τοῦτο δοκεῖ πολλὰ χαρίζεσθαι μὲν Λακεδαιμονίοις, κατηγορεῖν δὲ Ἀθηναίων τυραννίδα καὶ πλεονεξίαν. Presented in this manner, the argument is just plain stupid, but nevertheless shows what temptation an inattentive observer might undergo.

[4] This indeed is what Isocrates still does, cf. Mathieu, Les idées . . ., pp. 22 and 138.

[5] This is particularly admitted by Eduard Meyer (Forsch., II, p. 403); Thucydides more generally represents — as Beloch does very well to point out (Att. Pol., p. 20, note 1) — the view of the monied and land-owning classes favourable to Pericles.

and imperialism, it was because he considered home and foreign policy as belonging to separate spheres of action. Thus, in his subtle and thorough study entitled *Thukydides und die Parteien*, Lange finally isolates Thucydides from the known political groups and, in his analysis of the historian's ideas, distinguishes foreign policy from home policy and social questions. In Thucydides' view, imperialism belonged to the realm of foreign policy, and he allowed no other considerations to enter into his study of it.

The task that he assigned himself thus consisted of judging a particular policy from one practical point of view, considering no one but Athens and nothing but foreign relations. And it is precisely because he imposes such strict limits upon his field of study, precisely because he shows himself completely unprejudiced and unbiased in his approach, that his judgment is so extraordinarily subtle and has given rise to so much disagreement as to its real nature. For him, each new set of circumstances presents a completely new problem, and the measures taken to solve it can never be praised or blamed on *a priori* grounds. Only the immediate circumstances matter, and only one standard can be used in judging the measures adopted, namely, their suitability to each particular case. Thucydides loves the power of Athens and can find moving terms in which to praise it; he admires those who contribute to it, but can also blame those who try to increase it in a clumsy, untimely or excessive manner. Thus his final judgment can only be understood by bringing together a whole series of different opinions that he expresses on isolated occasions.

Since these opinions are connected with a number of particular instances, the relationship between them is not always quite clear. Thus Thucydides reproves the lack of moderation shown by Cleon, but also makes Pericles declare that Athens has almost unlimited resources at her disposal. He criticizes the imprudence of Alcibiades, but also remarks that the Sicilian expedition was even more mismanaged than ill-conceived, and that, in any case, people were very wrong to minimize the extent of Athenian power. He lends practically the same words to Pericles and Cleon, or to Pericles and Alcibiades; and yet his general opinion changes as he moves from one to the other. Certain cities, in certain circumstances, are praised for having observed the virtue of moderation; with other cities, in different circumstances, boldness seems to receive more approval.

There is no fixed, ready-made and absolute principle: everything depends upon the time, the place and the circumstances.

Thus the very objectivity which Thucydides shows in his judgments indicates the nature of the task that we have to perform. Since he chose to consider each Athenian action in its particular context, so we must do the same; we must consider each episode by itself, taking into consideration as we do so the question of the date at which it was written. By discovering what relationship links these different episodes together, we shall be able to see what kind of overall judgment Thucydides makes on the value of Athenian imperialism.

Part Two

The successive forms assumed by Athenian imperialism

INTRODUCTION

FROM the very moment that we try to form an exact idea of what kind of political judgment Thucydides made of Athenian imperialism, we find ourselves confronted with the problem of how the work was written. Each episode, then, presents us with a double task: we have first to bring out the nature of the judgment implicit in Thucydides' narration of the events concerned, and secondly to discover when the narration was composed and the judgment given.

The first task is a fairly easy one, since the way in which Thucydides constructs each episode indicates how he judges the particular events. However impartial he may be — and in my view he has no rival in this field — he still organizes each episode in such a way as to bring out its general meaning. He does not merely reproduce facts, but carefully thinks out how best to choose and interpret them for the reader. The reality which he thus presents is something which has been, as it were, filtered through his own mind, and which thus reflects his own opinion. This opinion is expressed mainly through the speeches which he reports and through the links which they have with the rest of the narration.

The second part of our task — that of determining when a particular passage was written — will be more difficult. It is never easy to assign a definite date to any literary text, and in the case of Thucydides the problem is even more complicated since Thucydides, writing as a historian, is judging an object which is itself changing with the passage of time. Thus there are two possible explanations for any changes that we may notice in Thucydides' views on Athenian imperialism: it may be, in the first place, that this imperialism has in fact undergone certain changes which have altered its nature; or it may be that Thucydides' own attitude may have changed, and that the difference is a purely subjective one. An effort has to be made to choose between these two possible explanations, and the choice itself is an important one since it will determine what meaning should be attributed to the text.

This double task will have to be performed throughout the whole work, and should really deal with all the different texts about Athenian imperialism. In fact, however, if we want to draw a precise distinction between the successive aspects assumed by Athenian imperialism, it will be safer to consider only the speeches and episodes which bring out the direct influence of one particular leader. Pericles, Cleon and Alcibiades: these are the men who represent, one after the other, Athenian imperialism, and whose policy we shall study in the following chapters. Pericles dominates Books I and II, Cleon Books III and IV, and, finally, Alcibiades Books V, VI and VII, without mentioning Book VIII. Nicias comes in as Cleon's and Alcibiades' opponent, but does not play a very important role in the events themselves.

We must add to these names those of their predecessors, Themistocles and Cimon, whom Thucydides discusses without having actually known them. The way in which he judges them depends upon the ideas which he derived from his own experience but is no direct part of this experience. Thus these men will have to be considered in our study, although not with the same importance as the others.

On the other hand, we must put temporarily on one side any instances where Thucydides is analysing not a particular decision taken by one man, but a policy that can be said to be 'Athenian'. This is the case when he introduces Athenians speaking abroad in defence of their country's policy. Thucydides is not then describing purely individual acts, for he generally refers to these Athenians not by their proper names, but simply as 'the Athenians' (so in Book I and Book V). This is a clear indication that he intends their speeches to be taken as expressing the *logos* of the city, a *logos* which is quite independent of party strife, individual opinion or private convenience. In texts of this nature, imperialism is considered in a general and theoretical manner, and this implies that we should accord them a different place in our analysis. They will therefore be left aside for the present, since we shall try to distinguish, in spite of apparent resemblances in words, a series of different policies and successive judgments.

Our task presupposes an attempt to reproduce a living experience and we have an invaluable instrument at our disposal: this is the evidence provided, almost year by year, by the contemporary theatre. More particularly, the plays of Euripides and Aristophanes are constantly dominated by political preoccupations, and reflect an experience which exactly paralleled Thucydides' own. Thanks to them, we do know what the reactions of at least many Athenians were, and we do know what men were thinking and saying. Even when Thucydides had left Athens, he certainly remained in contact with Athenians. From this city in which everything was discussed, in which the same problems, thought out in the street, elaborated in the course of innumerable private conversations, found their expression in a wide variety of different works, news would still reach the ears of Thucydides the historian. Moreover, the attitude from which he set out to judge events was similar to that of his fellow citizens. And so it is in the light of the evidence provided by contemporary sources that we can reconstitute his general point of view.

CHAPTER ONE

PERICLES

As far as imperialism is concerned, Pericles played a most important role, but before the Peloponnesian War began; and it is therefore not discussed in Thucydides' work. While, in fact, Pericles led the democratic party and directed Athenian policy in general for the thirty-two years between 461 and 429, Thucydides can only discuss in any detail his influence during the last two of these years, at a time when imperialist aims were necessarily subordinated to the immediate needs of the war.

This fact could suggest that the portrait given of Pericles in Thucydides' work is a rather incomplete one. Initially the opponent of Cimon, and later of the son of Melesias, Pericles dominated all the different aspects assumed by imperialism after the departure of Cimon into exile. The Egyptian expedition, the attempts at a Panhellenic policy, the organization of the empire to serve the profit of Athens, the use of the tribute-money for building the monuments on the Acropolis, the increasing number of *cleruchies*, the examples given to the rest of Greece by the repression of the rebellions in Euboea and in Samos — all these belong to the different phases of his influence. It was on account of them that he was attacked[1] and for these enterprises that he was presented both as the man who 'insulted Greece',[2] and to whom men handed over 'both the tributes paid by the cities and the cities themselves'.[3] Not one of these features of his character and career is to be found in Thucydides.

Nevertheless, Thucydides did express an opinion on the whole of

[1] The crisis of Euboea and that of Samos do seem to have aroused violent opposition. A fragment of a lost comedy (*adesp.*, 41 K), quoted by Plutarch (*Per.*, 7, 8), and that Bergk (*Rel. Com. Att.*, 330 ff.) attributes to Telecleides, accuses Pericles of having given the people an unlimited amount of liberty, so that they refuse to obey, but 'tear Euboea apart and trample the islands under foot'. Aristophanes repeats this idea in 423 in the *Clouds* (211-213) and in 422 in the *Wasps* (715, and see Müller-Strübing, pp. 75-105). Finally Xenophon (*Hell.*, II, 2, 3) indicates that people still remembered this reproach in 404. The same thing is true for the crisis of Samos, and it is in this light that we must understand the anecdote which makes Elpinice say that Cimon did not send excellent citizens to their death to crush 'an allied town whose people were of our blood' (Plut., *Per.*, 28, 6).

[2] Plut., *Per.*, 12, 2.

[3] Telecleides (42 K), quoted by Plutarch (*Per.*, 16, 2.).

this period, using as he did so a precise formula which can be found in the general judgment in II. 65. He writes, in fact: ὅσον τε γὰρ χρόνον προύστη τῆς πόλεως ἐν τῇ εἰρήνῃ, μετρίως ἐξηγεῖτο καὶ ἀσφαλῶς διεφύλαξεν αὐτήν, καὶ ἐγένετο ἐπ᾽ αὐτοῦ μεγίστη (65. 5). The way in which he combines power (μεγίστη) with moderation and prudence (μετρίως – ἀσφαλῶς) indicates complete and absolute approval on his part of the policy carried out by Pericles. Even though this approval remains vague, it does at least allow us to set on one side any reservations which might tend to limit the extent of the more detailed judgment which he makes concerning the actual period of the war: on the contrary, it confirms this judgment and, at the same time, is justified by it.

In fact, the two years of Pericles' leadership with which Thucydides does deal give him the opportunity of putting forward a complete theory of imperialism such as Pericles conceived it. Since an imperialistic policy plays a decisive role in the outbreak of war, and since Pericles is, *par excellence*, the man of thought who never acts without intellectual reasons for doing so,[1] Thucydides was naturally led to make a complete analysis of his ideas on this subject.

These ideas find their expression first and foremost in the two political speeches which he gives to Pericles, when he makes him intervene for the first time at the end of Book I, and, for the last time, in Book II, just before the general praise which he gives to his life. We must add to these two speeches the Funeral Oration inserted in Book II, and which treats similar ideas, only in a different tone. But although Pericles' own views on imperialism are expressed in these three speeches, it is from their relationship with the rest of the work that we can discover the point of view of Thucydides himself. Thus we shall be repeatedly led to compare these speeches with other passages, in order to discover what was the real point of allowing Pericles to express such and such an idea, and further, in order to define the meaning which should be attributed to it.

The first of Pericles' three speeches takes up the end of Book I (140-145), and marks the close of the period of preliminary negotiations. Although the speech forms part of a debate dealing with the recent demands put forward by Sparta, it nevertheless departs from this subject to deal with the war in general. Pericles shows first of all

[1] II. 40. 2: οὐ τοὺς λόγους τοῖς ἔργοις βλάβην ἡγούμενοι, ἀλλὰ μὴ προδιδαχθῆναι μᾶλλον λόγῳ πρότερον ἢ ἐπὶ ἃ δεῖ ἔργῳ ἐλθεῖν. On this feature of Pericles, cf. Schadewaldt, *Das Vermächtnis des P.*, *Die Antike*, VIII, 1932, pp. 32-33.

that the war is necessary, and then, by analysing the forces confronting one another, he shows that Athens will win.

The first part is much shorter than the second, and depends essentially on a question of fact: Sparta, Pericles says, has borne a grudge against Athens for a long time now,[1] and the proof of this can be found in the fact that she now refuses the peaceful settlement that Athens has offered her. Thus the Megarian decree and the other points raised by Sparta are mere pretexts, and it is in fact Athenian sovereignty which is being threatened.[2]

This rapid statement is very probably an accurate account of Pericles' ideas on the question and of the type of arguments that he put forward. He had for long believed war to be necessary, as we know, and Plutarch seems to be reporting the very words that he used when he makes him say that 'he could already see war striding from the Peloponnese'.[3]

It is also clear that Thucydides completely shares Pericles' ideas, since the whole structure of Book I tends to dismiss the idea that the war could have been caused by the Megarian problem, and to prove, on the contrary, that 'the real cause' lay in the attitude of Sparta towards the power of Athens.[4]

This general intention, visible in the over-all construction of Book I, also involves a number of more detailed points of resemblance: thus the reader accepts the truth of what Pericles says because of what Thucydides has already told him. He knows, in fact, that Athens has mentioned the possibility of a peaceful settlement to be decided by arbitration (I. 78. 4; 85. 2) but that Sthenelaïdas has demanded immediate and energetic action (I. 86. 3); that the Peloponnesian assembly has voted in favour of settling the dispute by war (I. 125. 1), and that the final negotiations were an attempt by Sparta to gain time while simultaneously strengthening her grounds for complaint (I. 126. 1: ὅπως σφίσιν ὅτι μεγίστη πρόφασις εἴη τοῦ πολεμεῖν ἦν μή τι ἐσακούωσιν). Thus the narration prepares the ground for the speech, and supports its arguments before they have

---

[1] I. 140. 2: Λακεδαιμόνιοι δὲ πρότερόν τε δῆλοι ἦσαν ἐπιβουλεύοντες ἡμῖν καὶ νῦν οὐχ ἥκιστα.

[2] I. 141. 1: αὐτόθεν δὴ διανοήθητε ἢ ὑπακούειν πρίν τι βλαβῆναι, ἢ εἰ πολεμήσομεν, ὥσπερ ἔμοιγε ἄμεινον δοκεῖ εἶναι, καὶ ἐπὶ μεγάλῃ καὶ ἐπὶ βραχείᾳ ὁμοίως προφάσει μὴ εἴξοντες μηδὲ ξὺν φόβῳ ἕξοντες ἃ κεκτήμεθα.

[3] Plut., Per., 8, 7: τὸ τὸν πόλεμον ἤδη φάναι καθορᾶν ἀπὸ Πελοποννήσου προσφερόμενον. Eduard Meyer (Forsch., II, p. 324) thinks that this remark can be dated as far back as 435-434. In any case, it does belong to an earlier period than the speech here under discussion.

[4] Cf. pp. 20-24.

even been put forward. It leads the reader to accept Pericles' view
that the immediate conflict has more distant origins, and that
Athens must choose between war and surrender.

It will be noticed, moreover, that Pericles wastes no time in
rejecting the possibility of surrender, devoting only a few earnest but
banal commonplaces to it.[1] He admits, in fact, that anyone who sees
the situation as it really is will realize that war is the only solution.
Similarly, Thucydides himself never actually says anywhere that the
war occurs because Athens would not give way, and for him, as for
Pericles, her attitude of defiance is a foregone conclusion. Thus he
separates himself, along with Pericles, from those citizens who
wanted to reach an understanding with Sparta at the price of a few
concessions. His view of the situation was very different from theirs,
and included an intense awareness of the need for Athens to retain her
sovereignty, even, if necessary, in an aggressive manner.[2]

It is impossible, however, to describe this attitude in any detail at
the moment, since, unlike the speech which we shall be studying
from Book II, Pericles' first speech is conceived neither as a reply to
the arguments of these citizens nor as part of a debate on Athenian
policy, but as a reply to the Corinthians, intended to form part of the
analysis of forces which is to be found in Book I.

This explains why the first part of this speech should be entirely
subordinated to the second.[3]

This second part itself bears signs of a certain lack of symmetry
between the two sections that compose it. The first deals with the

---

[1] These are, rapidly sketched in, the main themes of Athenian power, and, as it were, the
'slogans' of imperialism: no surrender — keep one's own possessions without fear —
accept no orders from others (141. 1) and (in 144. 1): secure the greatest honour — develop
Athenian power by a heroism worthy of the great ancestors who fought against the
Persians. These themes are taken up again elsewhere: see later, p. 129 and note 2.

[2] According to Wilamowitz (*A.u.A.*, II, 101), Pericles was already thinking, as early
as 462, of the idea of an Athenian rule over the whole of Greece and he was inspired by
it when he tried to make the Athenians declare war. Eduard Meyer discusses this idea
(*Forsch.*, II, p. 305, note 1); in his view, Pericles is without ambition, and if he does allow
himself to be dragged into this war (which he wishes to fight in a defensive manner) it is
simply because he considers it as inevitable. The truth would seem to lie between the two
extremes. If Pericles does not want to set up Athenian rule, he certainly wants to strengthen
and maintain it; and in order to achieve this aim, he views the war as neither opportune
nor inevitable, but simply as a necessary and adequate measure.

[3] And certainly, if the analysis of the chances of success does not explain the entry into
the war, it is nevertheless an excellent argument justifying it: moreover, it is a necessary,
conventional and traditional argument. Cf. on this point, Zahn, p. 8, note 7, where the
indication given by Anaximenes 2, p. 25, 1 H is quoted.

resources available to Sparta, and shows that they are insufficient (141. 2 - 143. 3); the second is concerned with what Athens can do if she wishes to win the war (143. 3 - 144).[1] This second section, however, is much shorter than the first, and instead of containing an analysis as the first does, takes the form of advice and exhortation.

This structure can be explained by the main idea which the passage contains. The dominant theme is that the Spartans can do nothing against Athens, who, being mistress of the sea, is almost invulnerable. It is this which constitutes her superiority, which is based essentially on a negative factor: the powerlessness of Sparta. Once this has been proved, all that needs to be shown is that Athens herself can act (the idea is easily expressed in a single sentence).[2] We then see not only the advantage itself, but also its meaning and reasons, since it is linked to this very invulnerability, which must be exploited to the greatest possible extent (the idea involves the advice). Thus the plan of the section simply reflects the political ideas inspiring it.

In order to show the powerlessness of the Peloponnesians, Pericles refutes the solutions put forward by the Corinthians, solutions which were themselves part of a reply to the doubts expressed by Archidamus.[3] He deals with the suggestions one by one, in a detailed fashion, reproducing the terms originally used, and shows them all to be inadequate. In general,[4] he insists, the Peloponnesians will

---

[1] All this still fits the division indicated by Anaximenes 2, p. 25, 20 H: τὰ μὲν τῶν ἐναντίων ταπεινοῦντες, τὰ δὲ ἡμέτερα ταῖς αὐξήσεσι μεγάλα καθεστῶντες.

[2] Jacoby (in Zahn, p. 20) explains the brevity of this second part by the fact that Thucydides is keeping certain arguments back for II. 13 (as he himself says he will in I. 144. 2 without any fear of destroying the illusion by doing this). However, this method would be a very curious one if these arguments were of such a type that they could form part of the speech in Book I. In fact, II. 13 gives some very definite information which is quite different from the theoretical and intellectual analysis of this speech, and which under no circumstances could have been used as a contrast to the first part. It would be more correct to assume that the development aimed at proving the superiority of Athens is not included because it would simply be the converse of the first part, which proved the inferiority of Sparta (cf. Plato, *Phaedrus*, 241 e). But this explanation is itself only partially valid (cf. I. 143. 3: τὰ δὲ ἡμέτερα τούτων τε ὧνπερ ἐκείνοις ἐμεμψάμην ἀπηλλάχθαι καὶ ἄλλα οὐκ ἀπὸ τοῦ ἴσου μεγάλα ἔχειν), and it does not bring out sufficiently the nature of Athenian superiority. In fact, Pericles demonstrates that Sparta is not *inferior* to Athens but *powerless* against her; all he needs to do is to show that Athens can *act* (by landings in enemy country), and her superiority is immediately established, in the form of the precise and negative demonstration, which indicates the course of action to be pursued.

[3] Cf. pp. 30-31 and note 3 on p. 31.

[4] The general development on the Peloponnesian army is made up of one movement, from 141. 3 to 142. 2; then two precise solutions are examined: ἡ ἐπιτείχισις and τὸ ναυτικόν.

suffer from the absence of accumulated wealth and of a central organization – the first of these being more important than the second. Because of these drawbacks, the Peloponnesians will be unable to undertake large-scale expeditions on either land or sea, to prolong the war, and to seize quickly any favourable opportunity. And it is clear that Athens will be able to do all this, for the organization of the federal treasury will make it possible for her.

Pursuing his argument in more detail, Pericles observes that the Peloponnesians will not reach any result by trying to build up a navy or to plant a fort in Attica. As regards the latter possibility, Athens' sea-power will make it ineffective, for she will always retain complete freedom of action because of her fleet (142. 4: οὐ μέντοι ἱκανόν γε ἔσται ἐπιτειχίζειν τε κωλύειν ἡμᾶς πλεύσαντας ἐς τὴν ἐκείνων, καί, ἧπερ ἰσχύομεν, ταῖς ναυσὶν ἀμύνεσθαι). And there is no reason, either, to fear any navy that the Peloponnesians could try to build up, for they will be denied the opportunity to practise, and will not be able to bribe enough sailors to desert the Athenian navy and join theirs.[1] So the Athenian navy will protect her against both these dangers.

Thus all attempts by the Peloponnesians to harm Athens will come to grief because of the two factors on which Athenian superiority depends: the federal treasury and the mastery of the sea provided by her navy – that is to say the two factors which Thucydides himself considers to be the basic essentials of any strong power.

The originality of the speech, however, lies less in the fact that it points this out than in the conclusions which Pericles deduces from it.

Since Athens can undertake effective action against Sparta by landings in enemy country, whereas Sparta cannot undertake anything effective against Athens either on land or on sea, the Athenians must let the Spartans do what they want without interference,

---

[1] It will be observed that the Athenian advantage always comes back to the fact that Athens has a navy, and sea-power in itself carries a guarantee of its own duration. In fact, the Peloponnesians will not be able to gain experience on the sea because Athens, *being mistress of the seas*, will prevent this (142. 7: καὶ προσέτι οὐδὲ μελετῆσαι ἐασόμενοι διὰ τὸ ὑφ' ἡμῶν πολλαῖς ναυσὶν αἰεὶ ἐφορμεῖσθαι; 8: πολλαῖς δὲ εἰργόμενοι ἡσυχάσουσι); and they will not be able to bribe the foreign sailors to leave the Athenian fleet because Athens, *being mistress of the seas*, offers them a more certain guarantee (143. 2: καὶ ἐπὶ τῷ κινδύνῳ οὐδεὶς ἂν δέξαιτο τῶν ξένων τήν τε αὐτοῦ φεύγειν καὶ μετὰ τῆς ἥσσονος ἅμα ἐλπίδος ὀλίγων ἡμερῶν ἕνεκα μεγάλου μισθοῦ δόσεως ἐκείνοις ξυναγωνίζεσθαι). These two arguments are only incidental, but they nevertheless bring out the systematic nature of Thucydides' thought and composition.

remembering that nothing can really be dangerous, and not worrying about the vulnerable territory of Attica. They must strive towards achieving the perfect condition that would be theirs if Athens were an island: they must protect the city, defend the sea, but not allow themselves to be drawn into a costly and useless struggle to defend the land. They must allow the Spartans to pillage Attica and, if they dared to do so, pillage it themselves in order to demonstrate to the Spartans how indifferent they are towards it. Pericles' strategy thus emerges clearly from the analysis which he gives of the situation; it rests entirely on the principle of thalassocracy, conceived as a sufficient and wholly satisfactory weapon: sea-power can achieve victory over the land.[1]

The only condition demanded by this plan is prudence; and this is the meaning of the reservation made in 144. 1: Athens must not, by extending her empire, run into unnecessary dangers (ἦν ἐθέλητε ἀρχήν τε μὴ ἐπικτᾶσθαι ἅμα πολεμοῦντες καὶ κινδύνους αὐθαιρέτους μὴ προστίθεσθαι). After the rest of the speech has insisted upon the unshakeable power of Athens, this final condition sets a limit to the development of imperialism. The combination of both defines a very thorough system and a clear political attitude.

It seems, moreover, that this political attitude can be recognized both as an authentic indication of Pericles' ideas, and as the expression of a policy which Thucydides himself considered a valid one.

The analysis attributed to Pericles corresponds not only to his general views, but also to the arguments that he must have put forward. The Ἀθηναίων Πολιτεία attributed to Xenophon, and written about the beginning of the war, is proof of this. In order to show to what extent the Athenian democratic regime is consistent (even in its worst features), the author gives a good third of his work to explaining the advantages of the ἀρχή; these depend first and foremost on the idea that the masters of the sea *can do* a thousand things that those who are superior on land *cannot do*;[2] amongst others, they

---

[1] The term 'defensive war' used by Eduard Meyer (*Forsch.*, II, p. 305) is not quite correct, since it neglects the considerable possibilities that passivity on land still left open to the Athenians.

[2] II, 4: οἷόν τ' ἐστὶ ... τέμνειν τὴν γῆν (παραπλεῖν γὰρ ἔξεστιν),

II, 5: οἷόν τε ἀποπλεῦσαι (τοῖς δὲ κατὰ γῆν οὐχ οἷόν τε),

II, 11: τὸν δὲ πλοῦτον μόνοι οἷοί τ' εἰσὶν ἔχειν,

II, 13: ἔτι δὲ πρὸς τούτοις παρὰ πᾶσαν ἤπειρόν ἐστιν ἢ ἀκτὴ προύχουσα ἢ νῆσος προκειμένη ἢ στενόπορόν τι ὥστε ἔξεστιν ἐνταῦθα ἐφορμοῦσι τοῖς τῆς θαλάττης ἄρχουσι λωβᾶσθαι τοὺς τὴν ἤπειρον οἰκοῦντας ...

can harm their enemies without fear of retaliation (II, 4-5). In short, direct sentences, the whole of this section of the work merely comments on the idea of Athenian superiority such as Pericles explains it in this speech. The parallel is so exact that we can find the very same words used in both texts to express the idea that Athens should try to achieve the perfect situation that would be hers if she actually were an island.

Pericles (I. 143. 5): εἰ γὰρ ἦμεν νησιῶται, τίνες ἂν ἀληπτότεροι ἦσαν; καὶ νῦν χρὴ ὅτι ἐγγύτατα τούτου διανοηθέντας τὴν μὲν γῆν καὶ οἰκίας ἀφεῖναι, τῆς δὲ θαλάσσης καὶ πόλεως φυλακὴν ἔχειν.

[Xenophon] (II, 14-16): ἑνὸς δὲ ἐνδεεῖς εἰσιν· εἰ γὰρ νῆσον οἰκοῦντες θαλασσοκράτορες ἦσαν Ἀθηναῖοι, ὑπῆρχεν ἂν αὐτοῖς ποιεῖν μὲν κακῶς, εἰ ἐβούλοντο, πάσχειν δὲ μηδέν ... ἐπειδὴ οὖν ἐξ ἀρχῆς οὐκ ἔτυχον οἰκήσαντες νῆσον, νῦν τάδε ποιοῦσιν· τὴν μὲν οὐσίαν ταῖς νήσοις παρατίθενται, πιστεύοντες τῇ ἀρχῇ τῇ κατὰ θάλατταν, τὴν δὲ Ἀττικὴν γῆν περιορῶσι τεμνομένην, γιγνώσκοντες ὅτι εἰ αὐτὴν ἐλεήσουσιν, ἑτέρων ἀγαθῶν μειζόνων στερήσονται.

Attempts have been made to explain so perfect an agreement by supposing that both texts referred to a speech actually made by Pericles.[1] However that may be, the agreement does prove that Thucydides puts forward the theory in exactly the manner that was normal at the beginning of the war, and exactly as the Athenians of that time conceived it.

In a less certain, and, moreover, a less decisive field, it is perhaps not irrelevant to recall a remark that Plutarch attributes expressly to Pericles, and which also echoes the phrases used in this speech:

Pericles in Thucydides (I. 143. 5): οὐ γὰρ τάδε τοὺς ἄνδρας, ἀλλ' οἱ ἄνδρες ταῦτα κτῶνται.

Pericles in Plutarch (Per., 33, 5): ὡς δένδρα μὲν τμηθέντα καὶ κοπέντα φύεται ταχέως, ἀνδρῶν δὲ διαφθαρέντων αὖθις τυχεῖν οὐ ῥάδιόν ἐστι.

The second antithesis differs too much from the first for it to be considered merely as a commentary that either Plutarch or another writer before him had made upon it. And although there can be no certainty about this, it is possible to consider the quotation as reflecting certain words actually pronounced by Pericles.

As to the reservation in paragraph 144, it obviously seems 'too

---

[1] Cf. ed. Kalinka of the treatise, p. 233.

I

good to be true'. Did Pericles really tell the Athenians that they would
win as long as they made no attempt to achieve conquests during the
war and ran no unnecessary risks? and then, after years of war,
Athens was ruined precisely by an attempt to conquer Sicily? There
is nevertheless nothing impossible about it. We know, in fact, that
during the first years of the war certain Athenians did look fondly on
the idea of conquering not only Sicily but other places as well.[1] We
also know through Plutarch that Pericles stood out against these day-
dreams.[2] Without going so far as to share Droysen's view that
Pericles opposed the alliance with Corcyra which, as we know,
implied a certain preoccupation with Sicily,[3] we can nevertheless
admit that Pericles looked with some apprehension at the aspirations
of some of his fellow citizens, and that he disapproved all the more
strongly of them because they went against the logic of his
system.

Therefore, although the phrasing and structure of this speech are
of course Thucydides' own reconstruction, and were chosen by him
to fit into the general plan of the whole section, it is highly probable
that in writing it he borrowed from one or more of Pericles' actual
speeches, and limited his own contribution to bringing out certain
of the arguments, to prepare thereby a reply to the speech made by
the Corinthians and a preface to his own narrative of events.
It is certainly Pericles' opinion that he is both expressing and
approving.

For he approves of this very plan, admits this precise reservation,
is himself devoted to this same Athenian power, and inspired with
the same confidence in the force of reason. There can be no
doubt about this. And he makes it quite clear in his judgment

[1] See Droysen, and, later, pp. 200-201.

[2] Plut., *Alc.*, 17, 1; *Per*, 20-21: the countries mentioned there are Egypt, the possession
of the Great King on the coast, Sicily, Tyrrhenia and Carthage.

[3] Droysen bases himself essentially on the fact that, according to Plutarch (*Per.*, 29)
Pericles was asked to send more troops to Corcyra. Thucydides does not explain the
dispatch of the second expedition by any party consideration, and this may be because of
his care not to become involved in the details of home politics. But in any case Thucydides
puts forward excellent intellectual reasons to explain the decision concerning Corcyra
and would thus seem to approve of it. It is therefore unlikely that this decision was
forced on Pericles (whom Thucydides admires) by a pressure group representing extreme
imperialism (which Thucydides constantly condemns). Eduard Meyer (*Forsch.*, II, 325)
even considers that Pericles, having long since realized that war was necessary, insists
because of that, on having an alliance with Corcyra. One could imagine, in that case, that
he came up against opposition of the type represented later on by Nicias in the case of
Sicily, opposition taking the form of: 'Then that is not enough.'

in II. 65; for the words that he uses all insist upon the same idea: Pericles had calculated aright, had correctly understood, had been right to say . . . ; he had formed a true estimate of Athenian power,[1] and his plan of action was the best one.[2]

Moreover, does not the whole theory attributed to Pericles form the basis of Thucydides' own analysis? Is it not the same which inspires the Archaeology?[3] Does he not make Themistocles the prototype of Pericles?[4] Does he not praise him for having the same qualities?[5] Does he not show him as the first to use a policy which, while deceiving Sparta, aims at ensuring the complete security of Athens by using city walls, a fleet and an empire?[6] Both the admiration which Thucydides shows for Themistocles and the way he expresses it prepare the way for his admiration for Pericles and confirm it.

His work thus appears as wholly dominated by Pericles' ideas; and the speech in Book I, which no one is shown as contradicting and which every circumstance serves to corroborate, thus occupies a very exceptional position in the preliminary discussions: it stands there as a clear demonstration of the ideas which he considered most import-

---

[1] II. 65. 5: προγνοὺς τὴν δύναμιν — 6: ἡ πρόνοια αὐτοῦ ἡ ἐς τὸν πόλεμον — 7: ὁ μὲν γὰρ . . . ἔφη περιέσεσθαι — 13: ἀφ' ὧν αὐτὸς προέγνω πάνυ ἂν ῥᾳδίως περιγενέσθαι τὴν πόλιν Πελοποννησίων αὐτῶν ἐν τῷ πολέμῳ.

[2] II. 65. 7: ὁ μὲν γὰρ ἡσυχάζοντάς τε καὶ τὸ ναυτικὸν θεραπεύοντας καὶ ἀρχὴν μὴ ἐπικτω-μένους ἐν τῷ πολέμῳ μηδὲ τῇ πόλει κινδυνεύοντας ἔφη περιέσεσθαι. Οἱ δὲ ταῦτά τε πάντα ἐς τοὐναντίον ἔπραξαν.

[3] Cf. p. 67.

[4] See Jacoby, in Zahn, p. 5, who calls him: 'den grossen Vorgänger und Wegbereiter des Perikles'. As far as the building of the walls is concerned, this fact is generally admitted (cf. in particular Plato, *Gorgias*, 455 e).

[5] I. 138. 3: οἰκείᾳ γὰρ ξυνέσει καὶ οὔτε προμαθὼν ἐς αὐτὴν οὐδὲν οὔτ' ἐπιμαθών, τῶν τε παραχρῆμα δι' ἐλαχίστης βουλῆς κράτιστος γνώμων καὶ τῶν μελλόντων ἐπὶ πλεῖστον τοῦ γενησομένου ἄριστος εἰκαστής, καὶ ἃ μὲν μετὰ χεῖρας ἔχοι καὶ ἐξηγήσασθαι οἷός τε, ὧν δ' ἄπειρος εἴη κρῖναι ἱκανῶς οὐκ ἀπήλλακτο, τό τε ἄμεινον ἢ χεῖρον ἐν τῷ ἀφανεῖ ἔτι προεώρα μάλιστα — Cf. II. 65. 5-6: ὁ δὲ φαίνεται καὶ ἐν τούτῳ προγνοὺς τὴν δύναμιν . . . ἐπὶ πλέον ἔτι ἐγνώσθη ἡ πρόνοια αὐτοῦ and I. 139. 4: ἀνὴρ . . . λέγειν τε καὶ πράσσειν δυνατώτατος.

[6] Cf. I. 93. 3-4: νομίζων τό τε χωρίον καλὸν εἶναι, λιμένας ἔχον τρεῖς αὐτοφυεῖς, καὶ αὐτοὺς ναυτικοὺς γεγενημένους μέγα προφέρειν ἐς τὸ κτήσασθαι δύναμιν (τῆς γὰρ δὴ θαλάσσης πρῶτος ἐτόλμησεν εἰπεῖν ὡς ἀνθεκτέα ἐστί), καὶ τὴν ἀρχὴν εὐθὺς ξυγκατεσκεύαζεν. The role of initiator and prophet is underlined by the words πρῶτος ἐτόλμησεν; the idea of domination is evoked with so much precision by the expression κτήσασθαι δύναμιν, that it is difficult to understand why, in τὴν ἀρχήν, the great majority of editors have thought that it was a question of building fortifications and not, as I myself would admit like the older editors, of the beginnings of Athenian power. Cf. also the importance attributed to Themistocles in the building of the first large Athenian fleet, in the Archaeo-logy: I. 14. 2.

ant. It thus provides us with a firm and well-established point of departure.

The narration of events in Book II corresponds to this analysis and shows it to have been true, in exactly the same way as the description of a battle, in the historian's work, confirms the forecasts of the speeches which precede it. Thucydides returns to his analysis only twice, and on both occasions he insists upon the unity of the ideas expressed: in II. 13. 2, by παρήνει δὲ καὶ περὶ τῶν παρόντων ἅπερ καὶ πρότερον, and in II. 61. 2 by καὶ ἐγὼ μὲν ὁ αὐτός εἰμι καὶ οὐκ ἐξίσταμαι. But while in the first case Thucydides only recalls the plan of Book I in a few brief phrases, and then completes it by some purely practical details on the nature of Athenian resources, he really deals again with the same ideas in the last speech, and more fully than he had done in Book I. This last speech must therefore be considered beside the first one, and it is for this reason that I shall examine it before dealing with the Funeral Oration, which stands more apart from it.

Its contents, from our point of view, will be even more important because of the indication which they will give of the reason for its insertion there. For if public despair justified and perhaps demanded such a defence of Pericles' policy and the repetition of the same arguments as he had put forward in his first speech, Thucydides himself was by no means obliged to reproduce a speech whose practical results did not justify its inclusion. He nevertheless did so, and by putting it in his work, alone, without any debate or discussion, and just before the praise of Pericles in II. 65, presenting it almost as his political testament, he seems to have been particularly anxious to attract his readers' attention to certain aspects of Pericles' political ideas considered for their own sake.

The speech is divided into two parts: in the first (60-61), Pericles gives a personal justification for the policy he has followed; in the second (62-63) he offers encouragement to the Athenians. These two sections correspond to the main ideas put forward in the first speech: Pericles' policy can in fact be justified only if the war was necessary; and the Athenians can be encouraged only by the idea that they will win.

But the first section tells us nothing new, since Pericles deliberately refuses to deal once again with the motives for which the Athenians have gone to war. He proceeds by general ideas, beginning by contrasting the prosperity of the state with that of the individual and thus asking the Athenians to continue the struggle for the sake of the city, and to give up the resentment which they feel against him. Then, dealing directly with the idea of this resentment, he shows the Athenians that they rightly saw in him a man possessed of all the qualities necessary to a statesman when they voted in favour of going to war, and that it is illogical to bear a grudge against him now. For him, it is only the Athenians who have changed, and he blames them for it by once again bringing in the idea of a fight for the salvation of the city:[1] he now even supports this idea, as if in a peroration, by all the moral and emotional themes with which the theme is associated.

In the whole of his speech the reasons for going to war are recalled only once, when the vote in favour of war is mentioned, and they are contained in a phrase which is an excellent summing up of the dilemma of Book I: εἰ δ' ἀναγκαῖον ἦν ἢ εἴξαντας εὐθὺς τοῖς πέλας ὑπακοῦσαι ἢ κινδυνεύσαντας περιγενέσθαι (II. 61. 1). This is simply a parenthesis, just a reference in a passage which is itself subordinated by γὰρ to an argument with wider general implications. Such a mode of arguing confirms the ideas expressed in the first speech more completely than a repetition of them would have done, but it adds nothing new.

The same is true neither of the second passage, nor of the *epilogos* which must be added to it. There, Pericles takes up the question again (62. 1: δηλώσω δὲ καὶ τόδε, ὅ μοι δοκεῖτε οὔτ' αὐτοὶ πώποτ' ἐνθυμηθῆναι . . . οὔτ' ἐγὼ ἐν τοῖς πρὶν λόγοις).

This second development is divided into three successive parts. In the first, Pericles repeats his analysis of sea-power, this time revealing the true nature of Athenian ἀρχή (62. 1-62. 3). This analysis brings out a

---

[1] The two general developments end in similar phrases expressing what must be done: II. 60. 4: πῶς οὐ χρὴ πάντας ἀμύνειν αὐτῇ καὶ μὴ ὅ νῦν ὑμεῖς δρᾶτε . . . τοῦ κοινοῦ τῆς σωτηρίας ἀφίεσθε, καὶ ἐμέ τε . . . καὶ ὑμᾶς αὐτοὺς δι' αἰτίαν ἔχετε.

II. 61. 4: χρεών . . . ὑφίστασθαι καὶ . . . μὴ ἀφανίζειν . . . ἀπαλγήσαντας δὲ τὰ ἴδια τοῦ κοινοῦ τῆς σωτηρίας ἀντιλαμβάνεσθαι.

In the first case the formula follows on a series of abstract arguments and refers to Athens by ὅ νῦν ὑμεῖς δρᾶτε; in the second, it is introduced in order to contrast (by ὅμως δέ, 61. 4) with the Athenian attitude already analysed after the sentence of 61. 1-2: καὶ ἐγὼ μὲν ὁ αὐτός εἰμι καὶ οὐκ ἐξίσταμαι, ὑμεῖς δὲ μεταβάλλετε. This composition recalls the speech of Nicias in VI. 11, when he shows that this is not the right moment for the conquest of Sicily and that this conquest is not really possible. A first development leads to the statement of what must be done (ὥστε χρή, in VI. 10. 5); a second and more precise development starts again with καίτοι, and the analysis of Athenian behaviour brings new mention of what must be done, coming in contrast (χρὴ δέ in 11. 6).

lesson as to the correct action to be undertaken – that already announced in the first speech; and we can find in this section, in the form of a series of infinitives, the statement of this same plan, accompanied by the various moral and emotional ideas connected with the subject[1] (62. 3: οὐδ' εἰκὸς χαλεπῶς φέρειν — μᾶλλον ἢ οὐ ... ὀλιγωρῆσαι — καὶ γνῶναι — τῶν τε πατέρων μὴ ... φανῆναι — ἰέναι δὲ). Then, after a general maxim which seems to conclude this long lesson, there is another piece of advice (a new εἰκός), which is joined by τε to the first (63. 1: τῆς τε πόλεως ὑμᾶς εἰκός ... βοηθεῖν — καὶ μὴ φεύγειν — μηδὲ νομίσαι[2]): this final piece of advice concerns the obligations created by the existence of the empire. It thus introduces the analysis of a point which is not mentioned in the first speech, and which deals with the risk of vengeance to which Athens' imperial rule has exposed her (63. 1-64).

Similarly the *epilogos*, in the midst of the advice expected, includes, at the very centre of its argument, a passage dealing with the glory of ruling over the empire (64. 3-6).

Thus the speech contains in fact three pieces of analysis, all of which are new and deal with the empire. This time it is no longer merely a question of the strategic possibilities which it creates, and it is no longer looked upon simply as providing mastery over the sea. While the first speech mentioned only τὸ τῆς θαλάσσης κράτος, and used the word ἀρχή only in the piece of negative advice ἀρχήν τε μὴ ἐπικτᾶσθαι, the last speech, in each of the three passages indicated, uses the words ἀρχή and ἄρχειν.[3] The first speech was concerned with the

---

[1] Cf. later p. 129.

[2] One recognizes here the same series of ideas: positive action – negative action – intellectual attitude, which the first εἰκός already introduced:

$$\begin{cases} \text{χαλεπῶς φέρειν} - \text{ὀλιγωρῆσαι} - \text{γνῶναι} \\ \text{βοηθεῖν} \qquad - \text{φεύγειν} \quad - \text{νομίσαι} \end{cases}$$

For the first εἰκός, a moral supplement is added to this group, by τε (τῶν τε πατέρων μὴ χείρους κατὰ πάντα φανῆναι ... ἰέναι δέ): the second, on the contrary, leads to a real analysis: ἧς οὐδ' ἐκστῆναι ...

After each of these two movements, a general reflection is introduced by γάρ:

$$\begin{cases} \text{αὔχημα μὲν γάρ} ... (62. 4) \\ \text{τὸ γὰρ ἄπραγμον} ... (63. 3) \end{cases}$$

These different features show that the last piece of advice (the second εἰκός) is not just linked up to the others but is parallel to them; if the others do emerge from the analysis made at the beginning of paragraph 62, this second εἰκός introduces a different analysis which is independent of it. The form of exhortation serves as transition from one to the other, but without subordinating the second to the first.

[3] $\begin{cases} \text{II. 62. 1: μεγέθους πέρι ἐς τὴν } \underline{\text{ἀρχήν}} \\ \quad ... \text{ 2: οἴεσθε μὲν γὰρ τῶν ξυμμάχων μόνων } \underline{\text{ἄρχειν}} \end{cases}$

war, while the last one is concerned with the empire. It reverts to the question of the empire all the time, and therefore embodies a study of its main features or aspects one after another: it deals with the possibilities that the empire offers, with its necessary implications and with its splendour.

It was on the possibilities offered to Athens by her empire that the first speech principally insisted; but while it dealt with these only in so far as they concerned the war against Sparta, the analysis in Book II deals with the permanent advantages which her empire gives to Athens[1] and with the general range of her power.

This power extends over the whole of the sea, and Attica is of little importance by the side of this vast domain. Athens is at home everywhere on the high seas. In thus according to her no longer a zone of influence but a whole element (62. 2: δύο μερῶν τῶν ἐς χρῆσιν φανερῶν, γῆς καὶ θαλάσσης, τοῦ ἑτέρου ὑμᾶς παντὸς κυριωτάτους ὄντας) and by offering it as an unlimited possibility for extending her authority (62. 2: ἐφ' ὅσον τε νῦν νέμεσθε καὶ ἢν ἐπὶ πλέον βουληθῆτε), Pericles is expressing a new idea. It would nevertheless be wrong to assume that he thereby intends to encourage the Athenians to undertake new conquests. He speaks only of the sea, of people sailing on it (62. 2: πλέοντας ὑμᾶς): he really means the water itself. There is no question of seizing islands, coasts or ports. This may indeed be necessary, but the point remains incidental and is not discussed here. His ideas thus still follow, as they did in the first speech, the principle of spheres of influence laid down in 446, according to which Athens renounced any attempt to extend her influence on land. But this principle did not, in Pericles' eyes, imply any real restriction for Athens, since the system of sea-power, such

---

[1] The construction used in II. 62. 1: ὑπάρχον ὑμῖν μεγέθους πέρι ἐς τὴν ἀρχήν, in which ἐς τὴν ἀρχήν must be directly attached to ὑπάρχον, clearly has the effect of laying great emphasis on the word. In general, the translators of Thucydides do not seem to have taken very much account of this. The precise meaning is: 'the strength that you have, as regards the importance, *for* your rule'; ἐς clearly indicates that this rule is here an aim treated as an end in itself, not as a circumstance. This conclusion is a further confirmation of the characteristic already mentioned above.

⎧ II. 63. 1: τῷ τιμωμένῳ ἀπὸ τοῦ ἄρχειν
⎨ . . . . ἀλλὰ καὶ ἀρχῆς στερήσεως καὶ κινδύνου ὦν ἐν τῇ ἀρχῇ ἀπήχθεσθε.
⎩ . . . . 3: οὐδὲ ἐν ἀρχούσῃ πόλει ξυμφέρει
⎧ II. 64. 3: Ἑλλήνων τε ὅτι Ἕλληνες πλείστων δὴ ἤρξαμεν
⎨ . . . . 5: ὅσοι ἕτεροι ἑτέρων ἠξίωσαν ἄρχειν

as he conceived it and such as he now fully describes it, had in its very essence something complete and self-sufficient.

Thus the development of the second speech does not in the least contradict the theory of the first.[1] In fact, it even provides the key for a better understanding of it, and expresses the same ideas, only in greater depth and on a different plane. The first speech gave advice: neglect Attica. The Athenians had neglected Attica, and now thought that they had lost everything. The second speech thus explains why Attica is unimportant. The first speech said: this is the strength that you have against your enemies; the second: this is why you have this strength. The first speech gave the theory on which Pericles' strategy depended; the second analyses the very notion on which this theory is based. This notion explains both the intellectual rigour and the feeling of pride with which this theory is put forward.

Because of the possibilities that it offers, the ἀρχή should thus stimulate the zeal of the Athenians, because it means they are the strongest. It should also inspire them to action in yet another way, if they understand what is now at stake and what risks they are running. It is this which explains the presence of the second main passage in the speech, dealing with the obligations created by the empire; it introduces a previously unfamiliar idea[2] by which Athenian rule is considered in a new light.

Here this rule becomes a dead weight, a threat, something which it is dangerous to abandon. Athens has, in fact, subjects who hate her, and is thus, like the tyrant, exposed to a particular risk. This prevents her from simply renouncing her imperialism, and giving way to Sparta:[3] it forces her, on the contrary, to continue to act and to be

---

[1] Thucydides has been careful to indicate this by using similar sets of words:

I. 143. 5: τήν τε ὀλόφυρσιν μὴ οἰκιῶν καὶ γῆς ποιεῖσθαι.

II. 62. 3: οὐ κατὰ τὴν τῶν οἰκιῶν καὶ γῆς χρείαν.

[2] He did not exactly say in the first speech that the Athenians had to fight in order to keep the delights of power, but such an idea was somehow implicit. What he certainly did not say was that the Athenians would expose themselves to particular dangers by the loss of their empire. Once this is regarded as valid, surrender becomes not only undesirable but even impossible. This fits in well with the fact that the first idea is passed over so rapidly here, and omitted in Book I: the second idea now makes it unnecessary.

[3] Athens cannot prevent her surrender from slipping into death. The ἀπολέσειαν of 63. 3 is extremely precise. It is thus a mistake to admit, as scholars usually do, that ἀσφαλῶς δουλεύειν depends only on ἐν ὑπηκόῳ (ξυμφέρει), and is the equivalent of ὥστε δουλεύειν. This construction would be quite extraordinary and completely out of keeping with Thucydides' normal usage; on the contrary, one often finds the word ξυμφέρειν with an infinitive as its subject, either directly expressed or understood. In fact, the mere idea of any submission to Sparta is expressed by Pericles through the words δούλωσιν (I. 141. 1), δουλείας

firm. This is a theory which no longer takes into consideration the simple fact of thalassocracy, but which deals with the empire itself; it is no longer a single element, the sea, which is in question, but the peoples and cities who are the subjects of Athens.

Pericles defines the relationship between Athens and her subjects in the clearest possible manner by the word tyranny (63. 2: ὡς τυραννίδα γὰρ ἤδη ἔχετε αὐτήν). He has no hesitation in speaking of hatred (ἀπήχθεσθε). In the *epilogos*, he will speak of being detested, and odious (μισεῖσθαι καὶ λυπηροὺς εἶναι). Moreover, such a state of affairs arouses no indignation on his part, for he considers it as normal (64. 5: πᾶσι μὲν ὑπῆρξεν), and uses it as a quite ordinary factor in his argument. This realistic attitude is indeed worthy of attention, for when we consider that some people, like Diodotus in Book III, attempted to base the solidity of the empire on the εὔνοια of the allies (III. 47. 2), it may appear strange that the virtuous, idealistic and moderate Pericles should reveal such cynicism.

Yet there is nothing at all improbable about this.

In the other speeches which Thucydides attributes to Pericles, there is nothing at all to contradict this idea,[1] and indeed contemporary evidence indicates that such a way of speaking was neither revolutionary nor extraordinary in the mouth of a statesman.

The pseudo-Xenophon, who is certainly not making any attempt to be original, assumes as obvious the fact that there is no rule without hatred (I. 14: γιγνώσκοντες ὅτι μισεῖσθαι μὲν ἀνάγκη τὸν ἄρχοντα ὑπὸ τοῦ ἀρχομένου).[2]

[1] Even if Pericles seems to say in II. 61. 4, that hostility is linked with the blameworthy aspects of imperialism (ἐν ἴσῳ γὰρ οἱ ἄνθρωποι δικαιοῦσι τῆς τε ὑπαρχούσης δόξης αἰτιᾶσθαι ὅστις μαλακίᾳ ἐλλείπει, καὶ τῆς μὴ προσηκούσης μισεῖν τὸν θρασύτητι ὀρεγόμενον) we can clearly base nothing on such a passage which, using a classic rhetorical device, merely sets off two extremes one against the other. By interpreting this idea literally, Pericles would appear as a real opponent of imperialism (τῆς μὴ προσηκούσης is the argument of the Melians in V. 95; and, as regards the words, for θρασύτητι see p. 326, and for ὀρεγόμενον p. 77, note 2).

About some ideas in the Funeral Oration which would seem to differ from the theory now under consideration, see later p. 138.

[2] Kalinka admits, it is true, that the relationship between ἄρχων and ἀρχόμενος is here being considered within the city. This is far from certain; in any case, whatever interpretation may be adopted, the idea is very close to the one with which we are here concerned (cf. Frisch: pp. 218-219).

(II. 63. 1): δουλεύειν, here, expresses the same idea. We must thus interpret the passage as meaning: it is not when she gives orders to others, but when she herself obeys, that a city can accept a security resting on slavery. The idea recalls the statement made in II. 63. 1: μηδὲ νομίσαι περὶ ἑνὸς μόνου δουλείας ἀντ' ἐλευθερίας ἀγωνίζεσθαι. In both cases, the δουλεία appears as a lesser evil.

Aristophanes insists on several occasions on the despotic quality of Athenian rule,[1] and, in a typical parallel, he even uses the same comparison as that of Pericles, remarking in the *Knights*, in 424, in a text supposedly celebrating the delights of the imperialists:

$$(1114)\quad\text{'Ω Δῆμε, καλήν γ' ἔχεις}$$
ἀρχήν, ὅτε πάντες ἄν-
θρωποι δεδίασί σ' ὥσ-
περ ἄνδρα τύραννον.

Finally, if we may suppose that it comes from an older source, we can add to these texts the passage in which Plutarch, discussing the building of the monuments on the Acropolis, puts the same remark into the mouth of Pericles' opponents: καὶ δοκεῖ δεινὴν ὕβριν ἡ Ἑλλὰς ὑβρίζεσθαι καὶ τυραννεῖσθαι περιφανῶς . . . (Plut., *Per.*, 12, 2).[2]

The objection may be made that in all three cases we are listening to the enemies of imperialism, who resemble the Corinthians in Thucydides, remarking in I. 122. 3: τύραννον δὲ ἐῶμεν ἐγκαθεστάναι πόλιν; it may also be that, in the first two, we are listening to ideas expressed later on in the war (as when Cleon says, in III. 37. 2: οὐ σκοποῦντες ὅτι τυραννίδα ἔχετε τὴν ἀρχήν, or when Euphemus says, in VI. 85. 1: ἀνδρὶ δὲ τυράννῳ ἢ πόλει ἀρχὴν ἐχούσῃ οὐδὲν ἄλογον ὅ τι ξυμφέρον οὐδ' οἰκεῖον ὅ τι μὴ πιστόν). It may be maintained that nothing in all this takes us back to Pericles. Yet although none of these texts actually allows us to attribute this way of speaking to him, their very similarity does give us some justification.

For each one of these texts is notable for its very banality and lack of pretension. The word and the idea are slipped in as though they were mere commonplaces, the most natural thing in the world. Besides, how many facts already seemed to justify them at the time![3] And it would have been all the more difficult for Pericles to be ignorant of this state of affairs, since a large number of both his peaceful and military actions were aimed at preventing the desertion of Athens by her allies.

His language, in fact, is more normal than it would seem at first; for there is no need to attach the slightest emotive significance to the terms which he uses. These terms only fitted the accuracy of his

---

[1] In the *Babylonians*, he was already comparing subjects to slaves at the mill.

[2] The uncertainty as to its source would not make the passage very decisive if it were the only one of its kind. As it is, however, it forms part of a whole bundle of evidence.

[3] Later, the image became a habitual one (cf. Isocrates, *Peace*, 89, 115; *Antidosis*, 64, etc.).

political analysis, and he naturally has no hesitation in qualifying as
'tyrannical'[1] a power exercised by one sovereign and resting on force
rather than on accepted law.[2] He says nothing which departs in any
way from a 'dictionary' definition of tyranny, and he simply makes,
as Euphemus does, a plain and obvious parallel between authority
exercised at home and authority exercised abroad. He just refers to
clearly defined notions, and once again deduces the type of action to
be undertaken from the nature of Athenian rule.

This realistic cast of thought, then, is but another sign showing the
logical and systematic nature of the analysis, and this is the final
characteristic which agrees with what we know about Pericles' ideas.

The argumentation to which it gives rise also fits the circumstances.
Pericles is arguing against the ἀπράγμονες, the people hostile to the
empire, who, through fear, would have liked to act in a virtuous
manner. He is disproving the ideas of those who thought that Athens
could give up her empire. Now it is quite certain that Pericles did
have to argue with people who held these views. By her final ultimatum and by her frequently repeated statements, Sparta had
managed to give the war the appearance of being a war of liberation,
and had thus provided her supporters with an easy argument to
justify their severity towards Athens. From the very beginning it had
been the empire that this opposition had been criticizing when it
objected to the building of the Long Walls,[3] to the putting down of
revolts such as that of Euboea − in short, to everything which
might annoy Sparta. Now in 429 the influence of this opposition was
(leaving out the year 411) at its peak; for it had just succeeded in
having envoys sent to Sparta (II. 59. 2). The way in which Pericles

[1] It is even easier for him to do this since, for someone in the ancient world, the idea of
power was linked very easily with the idea of liberty; cf. pp. 80-81.

[2] Cf. Aristotle, *Pol.*, 1295 a, 19: 'This tyranny is necessarily absolute monarchy which,
with no responsibility towards anyone, and exercised only in the tyrant's interest, governs
men who are as good as he and better, with no thought for the interests of the subjects.
Thus this monarchy exists in spite of them, for there is not a single free man who would
willingly endure such a power'; and 1285 a, 27: 'one (the king), legitimately and without
constraint, the other (the tyrant) against the will of the citizens: the bodyguard of the
former is furnished by the citizens, that of the latter is used against them'. Similarly
Isocrates distinguished the 'confederation' (ἡγεμονία) from the 'tyrannical' power
(τυρσννίς, τυρσννικὴ ἀρχή) or the regime based on force (δυναστεία, *Peace*, 142). He uses
the word ἄρχειν to describe the power exercised in the interest of the governed, and the
word τυρσννεῖν to describe that which aims at satisfying selfish ambitions (*Peace*, 91);
as he writes about it with the insistence of a reformer, the emotive distinction between the
two words is much more clearly marked in his works than in most others.

[3] Thucydides points out very precisely that the opposition did not hesitate to reach an
understanding with Sparta to try to defeat the project (I. 107. 4).

presents his arguments is thus equally probable in its purpose and in
its content.

And Thucydides certainly identifies himself with this argument
of Pericles just as much as he did with the preceding one. He seems
to have criticized the opposition and thought — as Pericles suggests
here—that it was acting under the impulse of fears that were groundless.[1] Besides, where political analysis is concerned, no one could be
as keen as he is on realism; and he has himself several times insisted
upon the hostility which her subjects generally felt for Athens. It can
thus be justifiably argued that here, once again, his ideas coincide with
those of Pericles,[2] especially since he has presented them here, as
before, without any debate or objection, and with enough logical
clarity as to seem capable of carrying conviction.

The realism of the second passage dealing with the ἀρχή is moreover somewhat corrected by the idealism of the third passage, which
deals with the appeal of domination.

This idealism makes itself felt in the *epilogos*. This is made up of
two parts, each of which contains a negative exhortation and each of
which ends with a general moral maxim. The first part corresponds
to Pericles' attempt to offer a personal justification for his own attitude,
the second to his defence of an active policy. The development with
which we shall now be concerned serves as a very natural transition
between the two.[3]

Like the development in paragraph 63, it is directed against the
enemies of imperialism, against those who would have Athens give
up her actual policy. But instead of replying to them by showing the
danger of the solution which they propose, it insists on the beauty of
the opposite solution. The two developments thus stand to each other
in the relationship ἀναγκαῖον — καλόν.

In this apologia for imperialism, Pericles celebrates the renown and
fame of Athens (ὄνομα μέγιστον . . . ἔχουσαν — δύναμιν μεγίστην . . .

---

[1] II. 65. 1-2, cf. II. 63. 2.

[2] Thucydides may well have not always approved of these ideas, but he certainly
approves of them here. See later, pp. 164 ff.

[3] The *epilogos* is composed according to a dual construction. Both developments begin
with the words ὑμεῖς δέ (which can also be found, for example, in the speech of Diodotus
in III. 48. 1). They are linked together by a development introduced by the formula
γνῶτε δέ (which can also be found introducing another transitional development, in the
speech made by the Spartans at Pylos, in IV. 18. 1: it there links together two groups
whose parallelism is underlined by the repetition of the relative ὅ . . . in the same way that
we here have the repetition of the introductory phrase ὑμεῖς δέ . . .).

κεκτημένην, II. 64. 3), but insists on the spiritual and idealistic character which belongs to these achievements. The renown of Athens rests upon her highmindedness and generosity; her power seems to be important only for the memory which it will leave, and which will make her an object of envy for all peoples who love action.[1] The hostility which Athens is encountering is here recalled, and Pericles evokes it in the words μισεῖσθαι, λυπηρούς εἶναι, ἐπίφθονον, μῖσος; but he contrasts with them the words μεγίστοις, λαμπρότης, δόξα, giving to the first ones only a passing significance (ἐν τῷ παρόντι — οὐκ ἐπὶ πολύ), and to the others an eternal importance (αἰείμνηστος καταλείπεται). The present development thus completes what was said before and in no way offers a contradiction to it.

This development, moreover, is not absolutely new, and the ideal which it defines inspired all the more emotive themes which provided the conclusion for each of Pericles' arguments.[2] The expression given to this ideal in this passage simply takes it on to a more elevated plane.

We find first of all, in the expression of this ideal, the general difference already noted between Pericles' first and second speeches. Thus, in the first, it is a question of not giving way *to the Peloponnesians*, and of leaving an undiminished power *to our descendants*; in the second, it is a question of not giving way *to circumstances*, and of leaving an unperishable memory *to posterity*.[3]

At the same time, within the speech itself, the analysis of the

[1] δρᾶν τι takes up τοῦ δραστηρίου again (63. 3); on the other hand ὁ μὲν ἀπράγμων echoes the ἀπραγμοσύνη of 63. 2 and the τὸ γὰρ ἄπραγμον of 63. 3. The two passages are closely linked together.

[2] There are five principal passages in which these themes can be found: the perorations of the two parts of the first speech (I. 141. 1 and 144. 3), the perorations of the first part, of the middle of the second part, and of the whole, in the last speech (II. 61. 4, 63. 3 and 64. 3). The ideas missing here are those which deal with the resistance of the Athenians: they must not obey (I. 141. 1: ὑπακούειν — II. 62. 3: ὑπακούσασι); they would thereby risk losing what they already have (I. 141. 1: μηδὲ ξὺν φόβῳ ἔξοντες ἃ κεκτήμεθα — II. 62. 3: τὰ προκεκτημένα φιλεῖ ἐλασσοῦσθαι); they must keep up with their ancestors (I. 144. 4: οἱ γοῦν πατέρες ἡμῶν ... II. 62. 3: τῶν δὲ πατέρων μή ... χείρους φανῆναι — I. 144. 4: ὧν οὐ χρὴ λείπεσθαι — II. 61. 4: τῆς τε ὑπαρχούσης δόξης ὅστις μαλακίᾳ ἐλλείπει. On the contrary, the most general terms reappear with the greatest emphasis; thus the greatness of the end pursued: II. 64. 5: ὅστις δὲ ἐπὶ μεγίστοις τὸ ἐπίφθονον λαμβάνει, cf. I. 144. 3: ἔκ τε τῶν μεγίστων κινδύνων ὅτι ... μέγισται τιμαὶ περιγίγνονται; or the idea of glory: II. 64. 6: δόξα, cf. II. 61. 4: δόξης.

[3] The transposition is marked in the expressions used:
⎰ I. 140. 1 (cf. 141. 1): μὴ εἴκειν Πελοποννησίοις.
⎱ II. 64. 3: ταῖς ξυμφοραῖς μὴ εἴκειν.
⎰ I. 144. 3: καὶ τοῖς ἐπιγιγνομένοις πειρᾶσθαι αὐτὰ μὴ ἐλάσσω παραδοῦναι.
⎱ II. 64. 3: ἐς ἀΐδιον τοῖς ἐπιγιγνομένοις ... μνήμη καταλελείψεται.

epilogos, separated from any practical question, constitutes a kind of summit. It thus represents a statement of principle, which summarizes all the different detailed exhortations.

The way in which these considerations fit into imperialistic theories, like their general agreement with the policy producing the new temples on the Acropolis,[1] already enables us to assume that, like the previous passages, they are a faithful echo of the main arguments put forward by Pericles. But these same reasons, to which we can add the exceptionally high level of the analysis, do offer us some justification for thinking that Thucydides has reproduced them here in order to defend this very policy, and to vindicate it not only against the attacks made upon it by contemporaries, but before the general judgment of history. Such a passage shows him taking up a position against the enemies of imperialism, while at the same time differentiating himself from certain imperialists who, as seems to have been the case with Cleon, lacked faith and inspiration.

It indeed looks as if, by the three analyses, which are soon followed by his praise of Pericles, Thucydides was trying to explain one system of ideas concerning imperialism, which ran the risk of being misunderstood, and trying to defend its various features – its rigorous clarity, its realism and its fervent idealism – against the criticisms made of it by the pacifists.

However, the value of the final passage of this second speech, like the relationship linking these different ideas together, can be fully appreciated only after it has been compared with another text. In the same way as the first of these passages referred back to the speech in Book I, so the third contains in germ the spirit of the Funeral Oration, and can be fully understood only when compared to the leading themes in this speech.

In appearance at least, the Funeral Oration is not a speech about Athenian rule, since after briefly mentioning the conquests which established this rule, Pericles says that he is going to leave this subject on one side in order to concentrate upon the political and moral qualities of Athens. He deals with foreign policy only in two places (40. 4 and 41. 2-4), and only the second of these passages is devoted

[1] It may even be noted, when considering these constructions, that Plutarch quotes a speech of Pericles for which Thucydides did not provide him with a model, and the expression which he records corresponds very closely to those found here. He says in fact (*Per.*, 12, 4):ἀφ' ὧν δόξα μὲν γενομένων ἀίδιος, εὐπορία δὲ γιγνομένων ἑτοίμη παρέσται. Cf. later for this point, pp. 133 ff.

to dealing with the Athenian power, which it is intended to celebrate.

But by the position which it has in the speech, this passage throws new light upon Pericles' ideas, for this power is considered only as the result (and, on this occasion, the proof) of the Athenian merits which have been analysed in the speech as a whole. This power owes its existence to the principles on which Athens acts, to her political habits and to her way of life in general; it follows from what might be called her spiritual superiority. This is what Pericles says at the very beginning (II. 36. 4: ἀπὸ δὲ οἵας ἐπιτηδεύσεως ἤλθομεν ἐπ' αὐτὰ καὶ μεθ' οἵας πολιτείας καὶ τρόπων ἐξ οἵων μεγάλα ἐγένετο, ταῦτα δηλώσας πρῶτον εἶμι καὶ ἐπὶ τὸν τῶνδε ἔπαινον). He repeats the idea at the close (II. 41. 2: καὶ ὡς οὐ λόγων ἐν τῷ παρόντι κόμπος τάδε μᾶλλον ἢ ἔργων ἐστὶν ἀλήθεια, αὐτὴ ἡ δύναμις τῆς πόλεως, ἣν ἀπὸ τῶνδε τῶν τρόπων ἐκτησάμεθα, σημαίνει). In this respect, the whole analysis is indeed part of a theory on imperialism.[1]

When we take into consideration some of the extremely realistic passages in his speeches, the manner in which Pericles links these two themes together is rather surprising, and it is difficult to understand how the moral superiority of Athens can justify her rule, if this does take the form of a tyranny.[2]

The justification he gives, however, is not quite so simple, and he does not present his argument exactly in this form. He mentions the qualities that have contributed towards the greatness of Athens in II. 43. 1; they are courage, clearsightedness, and, in action, concern for honour (ἐνθυμουμένους ὅτι τολμῶντες καὶ γιγνώσκοντες τὰ δέοντα καὶ ἐν τοῖς ἔργοις αἰσχυνόμενοι ἄνδρες αὐτὰ ἐκτήσαντο). But these qualities are in turn the result of a certain form of civilization, with certain moral and political values, which brings them to birth and fosters them.[3] Pericles thus in no way does what Isocrates does in the

---

[1] It is this which constitutes the originality of the speech. It is banal to demonstrate the superiority of Athens (Pericles does so with expressions that can be found also in Lysias; for example, expressions like, in 37: παράδειγμα; in 39: διαφέρομεν; in 40: μόνοι γάρ — διαφερόντως γάρ — ὃ τοῖς ἄλλοις . . . — ἐνηντιώμεθα τοῖς πολλοῖς — μόνοι οὐ . . . ; 41: μόνη γάρ . . . ; in 42: μὴ περὶ ἴσου . . . καὶ οἷς τῶνδε μηδὲν ὑπάρχει).

[2] The merits of Athens could perhaps be made to fit in with the notion of the 'tyrant-city', but they could not provide an actual explanation. On the 'rights' of Athens to her empire, cf. later p. 248.

[3] On the one hand Pericles considers that this civilization gives birth to certain practical qualities (cf. 40. 2-5); on the other, the contemplation of the greatness of their country inspires men to use these qualities in her service (cf. 43. 1). This is why he can finally discuss all the features for which Athens is ἀξία θαυμάζεσθαι.

Panegyricus:[1] justify the imperialistic ambitions of Athens by her cultural superiority; or, if he does so, it is only indirectly and by suggestion. He strives rather to show, at the root of this empire, the particular greatness of the sovereign city that built it.

It is in the same spirit that we must understand the remark made by Pericles in his passage on Athenian power, when he declares (II. 40. 2) that the subjects of Athens have no reason to complain that they are forced to obey unworthy masters. In context, the meaning of the sentence is quite clear: Pericles is talking about the power of Athens, and it is this power alone which justifies the authority which she exercises;[2] it must simply be remembered that this power itself depends on all the various qualities which render it possible.

The present theme is thus no more in contradiction to the realistic arguments of the final speech than was, in the final speech itself, the *epilogos*, to which this theme is closely related.[3] In the same way as Athenian supremacy is presented in the *epilogos* as a valuable ideal because of the glory it gives, it is here presented as a valuable ideal because of the qualities on which it depends. And the ideal remains the same throughout: indeed, it is these qualities which deserve and achieve glory.

The ideal here defined as a whole was certainly that of Pericles himself. He was always trying to establish the superiority of Athens in every possible domain and to add to her splendour.[4] And as to the manner in which the reflection proceeds, it is by no means surprising in a pupil of Anaxagoras, accustomed to giving pride of place to the νοῦς.[5]

---

[1] Cf. Mathieu, *Isocrate et Thucydide*, and later on in this study, p. 248.

[2] Ἄξιος must not be taken solely in a moral sense; cf. p. 248 with the note, and note 1 on p. 255.

[3] The expressions in II. 41. 4: τοῖς τε νῦν καὶ τοῖς ἔπειτα θαυμασθησόμεθα; II. 43. 2 οὐκ ἐν ᾧ κεῖνται μᾶλλον ἀλλ' ἐν ᾧ ἡ δόξα αὐτῶν παρὰ τῷ ἐντυχόντι αἰεὶ καὶ λόγου καὶ ἔργου καιρῷ αἰείμνηστος καταλείπεται; II. 43. 3: ἄγραφος μνήμη παρ' ἑκάστῳ τῆς γνώμης μᾶλλον ἢ τοῦ ἔργου ἐνδιαιτᾶται, must all be placed by the side of II. 64. 5: ἡ δὲ παραυτίκα τε λαμπρότης καὶ ἐς τὸ ἔπειτα δόξα αἰείμνηστος καταλείπεται and II. 64. 3: ἧς ἐς ἀΐδιον . . . μνήμη καταλελείψεται.

[4] The idea of dominion in the artistic field had inspired his building programme; that of dominion in religious matters his attempt to give more importance to Eleusis; that of political dominion his efforts at Panhellenic enterprises. It is thus more than probable that he should have tried to emphasize, by his words as well as his actions, the very nature of this superiority, which had so much importance for him.

[5] Certain ideas can in fact be found here, which it is possible to attribute to Pericles. For instance, Eduard Meyer (*Forsch.*, II, V, p. 398) relates the idea concerning unwritten laws (II. 37. 3) to the evidence provided by [Lysias], *Against Andoc.*, Περικλέα ποτέ φασι παραινέσαι ὑμῖν περὶ τῶν ἀσεβούντων μὴ μόνον χρῆσθαι τοῖς γεγραμμένοις νόμοις περὶ αὐτῶν ἀλλὰ καὶ τοῖς ἀγράφοις καθ' οὓς Εὐμολπίδαι ἐξηγοῦνται (10).

All the other available evidence also invites us to consider such an expression of Athenian patriotism as something normal during the first years of the war, and Euripides offers extremely convincing proof of this. In almost all the plays dating from the War of Archidamus,[1] he also exalts the characteristic features of the Athenians.[2] This explains the role of Aegeus in *Medea*, of Demophon in the *Heracleidae*, and above all that of Theseus, who appears as the faithful and sensible friend in *Heracles*,[3] as the protector of the oppressed in the *Suppliants*, almost certainly as the admirable hero in the lost play entitled *Theseus*, as the person who arranges everything in *Alope*: in all that, he seems to be the very incarnation of Athens. And since I have already quoted two lost tragedies, a particular place must be set aside for *Erechtheus* where the king sacrificed his daughter to his country, and such a sacrifice was praised when made to a country such as his. All these tragedies have an obviously patriotic message, and Lycurgus points this out when discussing *Erechtheus*.[4] Euripides himself says, in this play, that the superiority of Athens creates an argument in favour of patriotism;[5] he also indicates, in the *Dictys* in 431, that it is shameful to praise another country at the expense of one's own.[6]

[1] I cannot here discuss the problems concerned with the correct date to be attributed to each tragedy, for this would involve far too lengthy a digression. It is simply a question of showing that Thucydides did not write his analysis in the light of subsequent events. I shall thus not discuss any tragedy which might have been written after the Sicilian expedition, and it is my belief that I have discussed none written after the peace of Nicias. As to the one which is of most interest here, that is to say the *Heracleidae*, it is my view — shared by most philologists — that it dates from the first years of the war, namely from between 430 and 427.

[2] As Weil very well notes, in his thesis, p. 6, there is nothing at all in the plays of Aeschylus or Sophocles which corresponds to this patriotism. The fact that the war is now taking place is not sufficient reason for the difference: the fact that Athenian imperialism had fully developed when Euripides wrote his plays might also provide some explanation.

[3] Euripides tells us, in this tragedy, that Theseus owes his virtues to his country (1405). And as regards the *Heracleidae*, the episode itself is one of the traditional themes in any praise of Athens (Lysias, *Epit.*, 11; Plato, *Menexenus*, 239 b; Isocrates, *Paneg.*, 56-60; *Philippus*, 34; *Archid.*, 42; *Panath.*, 194; Demosthenes, *On the crown*, 186; [Demosthenes] *Epit.*, 8.

[4] *Against Leocrates*, 100; Euripides is writing in order to offer the Athenians an example and inculcate in them the love of their country; cf. II. 43. 1: τὴν τῆς πόλεως δύναμιν καθ' ἡμέραν ἔργῳ θεωμένους καὶ ἐραστὰς γιγνομένους αὐτῆς.

[5] Fragment 362 N, 5:

πρῶτα μὲν πόλιν
οὐκ ἄν τιν' ἄλλην τῆσδε βελτίω λαβεῖν.

[6] Fragment 349 N:

Εἰ δ' ἦσθα μὴ κάκιστος, οὔποτ' ἂν πάτραν
τὴν σὴν ἀτίζων τήνδ' ἂν εὐλόγεις πόλιν,
ὡς ἔν γ' ἐμοὶ κρίνοιτ' ἂν οὐ καλῶς φρονεῖν
ὅστις πατρῴας γῆς ἀτιμάζων ὅρους
ἄλλην ἐπαινεῖ καὶ τρόποισιν ἥδεται.

K

The intention, the general trend of argument, and the adversary are thus identical, whether we consider the tragedies of Euripides or the Funeral Oration put into Pericles' mouth by Thucydides. The detail of the themes is also the same.

In his introduction, Pericles states that the inhabitants of Attica have not changed: this is the presentation of the theme of autochthonism in a rational form; and similarly Euripides says in the *Heracleidae* (line 69): δαρὸν οἰκοῦντες χρόνον.

Pericles begins his real praise of Athens when he speaks of her democratic regime, and an echo of his ideas can be found in the words uttered by Theseus in the *Suppliants* (404 ff.); like Pericles, he insists on the principle of equality between rich and poor:

οὐ γὰρ ἄρχεται
ἑνὸς πρὸς ἀνδρός, ἀλλ' ἐλευθέρα πόλις.
Δῆμος δ' ἀνάσσει διαδοχαῖσιν ἐν μέρει
ἐνιαυσίαισιν, οὐχὶ τῷ πλούτῳ διδοὺς
τὸ πλεῖστον, ἀλλὰ χὠ πένης ἔχων ἴσον.

Pericles then celebrates different qualities possessed by Athens such as her culture and her habit of deliberating before taking action. In the *Heracleidae*, Euripides calls Athens the city of poetry and the city of beautiful choirs (359); and Demophon or Theseus are presented a being first and foremost rational and enlightened men.

Pericles then speaks of the courage of Athens, of her liking fo action, and of the way in which she faces danger. He passes quickly over these ideas, but they occur again in several places (in particula in his final speech), and are especially emphasized in the closing section of the Funeral Oration.[1] Now all the tragedies of Euripides

---

[1] II. 43. 1: ἀτολμοτέραν δὲ μηδὲν ἀξιοῦν τὴν ἐς τοὺς πολεμίους διάνοιαν ἔχειν . .
ἐνθυμουμένους ὅτι τολμῶντες καὶ γιγνώσκοντες τὰ δέοντα καὶ ἐν τῷ ἔργῳ αἰσχυνόμενο
ἄνδρες αὐτὰ ἐκτήσαντο.

[2] A large number of passages can be noted in which Euripides relates the notions o *toil* and *dangers* to that of the *glory* which stems from them. These ideas have often sur vived even where the tragedy as a whole has been lost:

Erechtheus (f. 366 N):
ἐκ τῶν πόνων τοι τἀγάθ' αὔξεται βροτοῖς
ὁ δ' ἡδὺς αἰὼν ἡ κακή τ' ἀτολμία (or: ἀνανδρία?)
οὔτ' οἶκον οὔτε βίοτον οὐδὲν ὠφελεῖ.

Andromeda (f. 147 N):
εὔκλειαν ἔλαβον οὐκ ἄνευ πολλῶν πόνων

Licymnius (f. 477 N):
πόνος γάρ, ὡς λέγουσιν, εὐκλείας πατήρ.

express a similar ideal, though not always with the same insistence.[1] Moreover, Euripides himself also recognizes the fact that this ideal finds its exact expression in the city of Athens, whose guiding principle is thus expressed by Theseus in the *Suppliants* (576):

Herald: Πράσσειν σὺ πόλλ' εἴωθας ἤ τε σὴ πόλις.

Theseus: Τοιγὰρ πονοῦσα πολλὰ πόλλ' εὐδαιμονεῖ.

[1] The only apparent exceptions are the *Ion* and the *Antiope*, where different ideas are expressed; but it must be noted that the problem in the *Ion* is a purely individual one, and that, in the *Antiope*, the Athenian ideal is merely shared out between two brothers, one of whom represents action and the other intellectual superiority. In any case, the ideal that we have just described is mainly expressed in the first plays (like *Philoctetes*) in the 'Athenian plays' (like the *Erechtheus*), and, finally, in the play of *Archelaus*, in which it seems that Euripides finds outside Athens, as Thucydides himself will do, when returning to an Athens henceforth strange and foreign to him, new faith in an old ideal.

Archelaus, f. 239 N:

Νεανίαν γὰρ ἄνδρα χρὴ τολμᾶν ἀεί.

Οὐδεὶς γὰρ ὢν ῥάθυμος εὐκλεὴς ἀνήρ,

ἀλλ' οἱ πόνοι τίκτουσι τὴν εὐδοξίαν (or, cf. Nauck: εὐανδρίαν)

240 N:

οὐκ ἔστιν ὅστις, ἡδέος ζήλῳ βίου,

εὔκλειαν εἰσεκτήσατ', ἀλλὰ χρὴ πονεῖν

241 N:

ὁ δ' ἡδὺς αἰὼν ἡ κακή τ' ἀνανδρία

οὔτ' οἶκον οὔτε πόλιν ἀνορθώσειεν ἄν.

242 N:

τίς δ' ἄμοχθος εὐκλεής;

238 N:

σὺν μυρίοισι τὰ καλὰ γίγνεται πόνοις

Telephus 719 N:

μοχθεῖν ἀνάγκη τοὺς θέλοντας εὐτυχεῖν

Temenidae 745 N:

τολμᾶν δὲ χρεών· ὁ γὰρ ἐν καιρῷ

μόχθος πολλὴν εὐδαιμονίαν

τίκτει θνητοῖσι τελευτῶν.

Incert. Fab., f. 1038 N:

σὺν τοῖσι δεινοῖς αὔξεται κλέος βροτοῖς.

But the most significant passage in this respect is to be found at the beginning of Euripides' *Philoctetes*, of which three fragments (785, 786, 787 N), made more precise by the two commentaries of Dio (*Orat.*, 52 and 59) are indeed quite clear: Ulysses begins by wondering if he is not mad, when he could live a quiet life (ἀπραγμόνως ζῆν), to go and plunge into difficulties (cf. Dio: ἐν πράγμασι καὶ κινδύνοις — πλείω τῶν ἄλλων πονεῖν). He then explains his conduct by remarking that people who act as he is doing are honoured (τιμῶμεν, cf. Dio: θαυμάζομεν); he concludes by deciding to obey φιλοτιμία and declares (f. 787 N):

ὀκνῶ δὲ μόχθων τῶν πρὶν ἐκχέαι χάριν

καὶ τοὺς παρόντας οὐκ ἀπωθοῦμαι πόνους.

Exactly the same relationship between the *toil and dangers* on one hand and *glory* on the other can be found in Thucydides (cf. I. 144. 3; II. 63. 1; II. 64. 3, and also I. 70. 7): this is a kind of motto of Athenian patriotism.

Closely linked to this principle is the generosity of Athens. Pericles says (40. 4) that she alone makes friends by conferring and not receiving favours, and that she alone helps others not for reasons of self-interest but because of the confidence characteristic of freedom. Similarly, in the *Heracleidae* (329), Euripides says:

> Ἀεί ποθ' ἥδε γαῖα τοῖς ἀμηχάνοις
> σὺν τῷ δικαίῳ βούλεται προσωφελεῖν.
> Τοιγὰρ πόνους δὴ μυρίους ὑπὲρ φίλων
> ἤνεγκε, καὶ νῦν τόνδ' ἀγῶν' ὁρῶ πέλας.

What, indeed, is missing? Is it the word μόνοι used by Pericles? But verse 306 provides even that, at the very end of the line:

> οἳ τοσῆσδ' οἰκουμένης
> Ἑλληνίδος γῆς τῶνδε προύστησαν μόνοι.

Or is it the reason for this help, the 'confidence characteristic of freedom'? But verse 198 declares that, if this help were not forth-coming, one would not be able to recognize 'freedom-loving Athens'; and the some idea recurs in line 245.

Thus, both in the general ideas and in the detail of the argumenta-tion,[1] almost all the views put into Pericles' mouth by Thucydides are repeated by Euripides. What this proves, in addition to an un-deniable similarity of intellectual outlook, is the complete normality of such a speech as the one made by Pericles. It seems to express the exact tradition of contemporary patriotism, which was incarnated by Pericles himself.

But, at the same time, when we try to discover whether the ideas in this speech correspond to those of Thucydides, it seems once again that his views and those of Pericles mingle together inseparably.

The tradition reported in the biography of Euripides and attribut-ing to Thucydides the epitaph in which Athens is called 'the Greece of Greece' is at least a proof that, for the people of the ancient world,

---

[1] Other detailed comparisons with the Funeral Oration or with the last speech could be quoted. Thus the discretion which is such an excellent thing in woman: II. 45. 2 = *Hera-cleidae*, 476; on the importance of public happiness for the individual: II. 60. 2 = *Erech-theus*, 362 N, 40; on the limits of pacifism: II. 61. 1 = *Heracleidae*, 371 ff.; on the necessity for courageously enduring what is sent to us by the Gods: II. 64. 2 = *Heracleidae*, 619 *Aeolus*, f. 37 N; *Dictys*, 340 N, 6 (Cf. also Sophocles, *Philoctetes*, 1316).

Thucydides was considered as sharing feelings and ideas closely corresponding to those of the Funeral Oration. And Thucydides' work itself is there to show that they were right. Indeed as in the case of the final speech — and, even more so, in that of the Funeral Oration — the very presence of the analysis is an argument in favour of such an interpretation: it is clear that the Funeral Oration had nothing at all to do with the course of the war; the ceremony of which it forms part took place every year, and the ideas expressed by Pericles are not intended as a reply to any speech previously made or even to any general opposition within the city. Moreover, Thucydides develops these ideas in terms which, in Greek, always indicate positive qualities; abandoning the normal habits of orators, he also gives these ideas an elevation of tone and an intensity of analysis which are very different from those which Pericles could in fact have reached when speaking before the people. These characteristics indicate that Thucydides himself wanted to describe, for its own sake and in all its splendour, the ideal of the man for whom he showed elsewhere so intense an admiration.[1]

It is thus clear that the Funeral Oration was written as a highly sympathetic expression of Pericles' ideas. What is more important, however, is the fact that nothing at all in the detail of the argumentation departs from what Thucydides himself could honestly celebrate. In a realistic writer as quick to perceive both the faults of democracy and the wholly selfish motives inspiring any political undertaking abroad, such a circumstance is worth noting; it implies a kind of collaboration between the historian and the orator.

Thucydides is a severe judge of contemporary democracy;[2] but it is nevertheless noticeable that when he praises democracy in the Funeral Oration, he does so by referring only to the most general principles of the Athenian constitution. He evokes it as it stands in

[1] Classen (Introd., XX) sees in this speech 'den Ausdruck seiner eigenen Liebe und Bewunderung für diese höchsten Geistesgüter' and speaks of 'einer tief innerlichen Erfahrung des Schriftstellers'. Lange (p. 624) says that the Funeral Oration does reproduce Pericles' ideas, but that only a historian who shared them could reproduce these ideas 'mit innersten Theilnahme'; and he points out how indicative the very presence of the Funeral Oration is from this point of view. Eduard Meyer (Forsch., II, 397) is also compelled to admit Thucydides' approval and sympathy; but he argues that it should be interpreted as a sign of the impartiality of Thucydides who, although himself hostile to democracy, is nevertheless sufficiently capable of putting himself in the frame of mind of a democrat and of being moved by memories of the past. But this, I think, would be a curious lack of consistency in a mind like Thucydides'.

[2] See p. 102.

contrast to the other regimes in Greece, and speaks of it in terms appropriate to any time after Cleisthenes — in terms appropriate, in fact, to that 'constitution of the ancestors' used by the reactionaries as a stick with which to beat contemporary democracy. In the same way as he praises Pericles — in II. 65 — by insisting on his personal and moderate role rather than on the frequently highly democratic laws which he had had voted, so also, in his praise of democracy in the Funeral Oration, Thucydides avoids talking about its actual laws,[1] concentrating rather on the general spirit which inspires it. The terms used in both cases are similar, and refer to the same ideal.[2] It is thus not very important if the actual state of affairs was not quite as admirable as the description given of it; and Pericles may have been just as conscious as Thucydides himself of the imperfections of the system; all he is doing here is defining, in the realm of home policy, the ideal which characterized Athens and which she was striving to achieve.

The same is true of what is said about her activities abroad. Thucydides never gives a disinterested explanation for any action performed by Athens, and yet we read in the Funeral Oration, in 40. 4: οὐ γὰρ πάσχοντες εὖ ἀλλὰ δρῶντες κτώμεθα τοὺς φίλους . . . καὶ μόνοι οὐ τοῦ ξυμφέροντος μᾶλλον λογισμῷ ἢ τῆς ἐλευθερίας τῷ πιστῷ ἀδεῶς τινα ὠφελοῦμεν. It may be argued that this is nothing more than a cliché which formed part of any traditional praise of Athens, and which Thucydides reproduced without personally agreeing with it. However, if the idea is given its exact meaning, such an interpretation is no longer possible. The remark forms part of a more general development dealing with the activity of Athens and with her energy and vigour, characteristics certainly attributed to her by Thucydides. If he shows her as inspired by selfish motives, these motives finally coincide with the concern for her glory, and this distinguishes her very clearly from a narrowly calculating city like

---

[1] The idea of the μισθός could well have formed part of this development.

[2] II. 37. 1: κατὰ δὲ τὴν ἀξίωσιν = II. 65. 8: δυνατὸς ὢν τῷ τε ἀξιώματι . . . and next: ἐπ᾽ ἀξιώσει.

II. 37. 2: ἐλευθέρως δὲ τά τε πρὸς τὸ κοινὸν πολιτεύομεν = II. 65. 8: κατεῖχε τὸ πλῆθος ἐλευθέρως.

II. 37. 2: οὐ δι᾽ ὀργῆς ἔχοντες = II. 65. 8: ἔχων . . . καὶ πρὸς ὀργήν τι ἀντειπεῖν.

These ideas may be different, but they appeal to the same notions, with the same positive or negative associations: they all belong, as the Germans would say, to the same 'Weltanschauung'.

Sparta. In this sense, his remark can easily be justified. The word ξυμφέρον, rejected by Pericles, doubtless contains, like the rest of the speech, a polemical intention, and echoes a large number of remarks which, throughout the work, insist upon the selfishness of Sparta; for instance, the dialogue contained in Book V, between the Athenians and the Melians, uses it twice to describe the actions of Sparta, and contrasts it with the more Athenian ideas of action and risk.[1] Now this is exactly what the Funeral Oration means, and the particular expressions used are proof of it: for Pericles does not, in the traditional manner, contrast the idea of justice with the 'self-interest' which Athens does not pursue; he does not say that Athens acts τῷ δικαίῳ but: τῆς ἐλευθερίας τῷ πιστῷ. He thus respects the particular nature of Athens and that feeling for liberty which we have already seen fitting in perfectly with the idea of imperialism.[2] By the side of the practical defects of which he is just as aware as anyone else, Pericles once again picks out, this time in a different context, the ideal which distinguished Athens and which she was striving to achieve.

The composition of the panegyric thus implies no reservations on the part of Thucydides; it transcends party divisions, and retains only those general features to which Thucydides, the enemy of the ἀπράγμονες, could not fail to be attached.

The very trend of the ideas in the Funeral Oration fits in with Thucydides' own views, and the moral values on which Pericles bases the power of Athens can be considered as the ones whose disappearance will bring about her fall. Thucydides does in fact explain this fall, in II. 65, by referring to the way in which the political system and the patriotic ideal of Athens were turned away from their true nature. This agreement between the two passages even seems to indicate that they are linked together by a common apologetic intention.

The Funeral Oration can thus be interpreted as a double defence. First of all, it defends Athenian rule, and is characterized by a strong anti-Spartan feeling which inspires all its open or implicit comparisons. It is also characterized by an enthusiasm which enables Thucydides to bring out all the ideals implicit in the real political situation;

[1] V. 105. 4: ἐπιφανέστατα ὧν ἴσμεν τὰ μὲν ἡδέα καλὰ νομίζουσι, τὰ δὲ ξυμφέροντα δίκαια — 107: οὔκουν οἴεσθε τὸ ξυμφέρον μὲν μετὰ ἀσφαλείας εἶναι, τὸ δὲ δίκαιον καὶ καλὸν μετὰ κινδύνου δρᾶσθαι· ὃ Λακεδαιμόνιοι ἥκιστα ὡς ἐπὶ τὸ πολὺ τολμῶσιν. — Thucydides himself often insists upon the selfishness revealed by Sparta, see p. 278.

[2] See pp. 80-81.

and in this respect it is a reply to the friends and supporters of Sparta who attacked the imperialistic policy of Athens. Secondly, it is a defence of Pericles, and by the very fact that it is attributed to him, it is a reply to those same friends of Sparta who took pleasure in attacking his motives,[1] while at the same time it serves to distinguish his imperialism from that of his successors.[2]

It shares this aim with Pericles' final speech, and in both of them Thucydides is defending both a principle and a man against the ἀπράγμονες. He shows that Athenian rule was possible, coherent and admirable, while at the same time he also shows Pericles as pursuing a logical plan, acting with full awareness of the situation, and inspired by the highest ideals. The Funeral Oration insists more on the ideal of the system, and the final speech more upon the qualities of the man, but this is a difference which springs from the nature of the two speeches and in no way prevents them from being complementary.

These three texts, taken together, thus make up a completely unified whole, presenting one single system of ideas, which it is easy for us to define.

Pericles' attitude, based on a number of rigorous analyses and on sincerely held feelings, takes on a very precise form. It must be first and foremost defined by what may be called its positive elements: by his love for Athenian power, his determination to assert it against Sparta, his awareness of the obligations and necessities which it involves and his decision to accept them, Pericles comes out as the continuer of the imperialist tradition and the opponent of the ἀπράγμονες. He is immediately recognizable as the previous enemy of Cimon,[3] and as the man whom the comic writers never ceased to abuse. Nevertheless, this picture must be completed by what may be called the negative aspect of his ideas, and this has a two-fold form: his concern is only for the sea, and he advises the Athenians to be prudent. He is recognizable here as the colleague of Nicias,[4] as the

---

[1] His political opponents naturally explained both his home and foreign policy by despicable personal or party ambitions; all the different traditions collected by Plutarch, and from which he did not always manage to free himself, agree on this point. Cf. H. A. Holden, Plutarch: *Per.*, Macmillan, Introd., p. xxxviii.

[2] See p. 289.

[3] Cf. Aristotle, *Constitution of Athens*, 27. 1; Plut., *Per.*, 28, 4-7 (on the intervention of Elpinice at the time of Samos) and 10, 4: οἰκείως γὰρ εἶχον οἱ Λακεδαιμόνιοι πρὸς αὐτόν (Cimon), ὥσπερ ἀπήχθοντο τῷ Περικλεῖ καὶ τοῖς ἄλλοις δημαγωγοῖς.

[4] Plut., *Nicias*, 2, 2.

man who knew how to refuse imprudent battles and resist over-ambitious conquest,[1] the man against whom Cleon entered politics.[2] He is thus shown as maintaining a balance between audacity and moderation.[3] But the speeches in Book II show clearly that, in this picture, the positive elements are more important than the negative ones.[4] For the difference between sea and land does not imply a limit to be placed on Athenian power;[5] and his advice to be prudent is only a question of circumstances. There is nothing, therefore, very striking in this negative element. The one reason for bringing it out and for commenting on it in II. 65 is the contrast which it provides between Pericles and his successors. His imperialism may have been moderate in some of its application: its aims were not moderate, nor the principles inspiring it.

It is this imperialism which Thucydides defends in all the passages of his work which deal with it.

But if it is possible to combine together the different analyses that Pericles gives of imperialism, and, thereby, to bring out a coherent and faithful record of his ideas on the subject, it is perhaps not quite legitimate to do the same for Thucydides himself. He can very well have conceived from the very beginning the general plan of this section, and accepted as a whole the general system that he was studying, but he can also have written it in successive phases, each of which corresponded to a particular stage in his own experience and to a different purpose: his thought, then, is built up by these different intentions; and these in turn are inseparable from the date at which he was writing. We are thus led to consider, for each of the passages

---

[1] On the opposition against Pericles on this matter, see Plut., *Per.*, 33, 6; 8. Traces of this opposition can still be found in Isocrates, *Peace*, 77: ὥστε μηδὲ πρὸ τῶν τειχῶν τολμᾶν ἐπεξιέναι τοῖς πολεμίοις (cf. Mathieu, *Les Idées* . . . , pp. 22 and 127). Thucydides' authority and the arguments he puts forward have had the general tendency of making most modern authors adopt Pericles' plan as the most obviously suitable one; see nevertheless Beloch, *Att. Pol.*, p. 24.

[2] Cf. Plut., *Per.*, 33, 7, quoting a fragment of Hermippus (*Moirai*, 46, 7 K).

[3] This balance itself must have satisfied Thucydides' intellectual demands: it can be compared with the balance between ἀνδρεία and σωφροσύνη, which will later be established by Plato (*Pol.*, 306e-309e). See also here, pp. 330 ff.

[4] See Lange, p. 624: if Thucydides' ideas were exactly the same as those of Nicias, he would not have introduced the Funeral Oration, with its great praise for democratic Athens.

[5] See p. 123. It is this which explains how he can say in the Funeral Oration (II. 41. 4): πᾶσαν μὲν θάλασσαν καὶ γῆν ἐσβατὸν τῇ ἡμετέρᾳ τόλμῃ καταναγκάσαντες γενέσθαι. The sea is sufficient, but as a means; the remark made here, which has nothing at all to do with strategy, implies no contradiction with the idea of sea-power; but it discloses an enthusiasm which shows how important this is in Pericles' eyes.

which we have been dealing with, the problem of the time when they were composed.

The problem presents itself in a different way for each of the three passages under consideration.

If we look back at the study made of the causes of the war in the first part of this book, we can see that, if there was a primitive version, then both the first speech of Pericles and the narration of events which follows it and illustrates its principal themes must have formed part of this version, in a form fairly similar to the present one.

This is not to say that these passages were not rewritten, for there does not seem to be any single section in Thucydides' work which does not bear more or less extensive traces of late composition or revision. But if really the speech belongs to what can be called the original plan, then we should accept as having been written late only passages which provide sure evidence of it, leaving on one side all the more doubtful ones.

There are, for some scholars, signs of late composition in Pericles' first speech. They are to be found in passages dealing with the evaluation of the forces on each side, and they are based upon definite circumstances. Archidamus, the Corinthians and Pericles reckon with possible developments, many of which were in fact realized in the facts. Now, when these possibilities bear on concrete instances, one might suppose that Thucydides is following his usual method of closely relating speeches to the narration of events, and that he mentioned the possibilities only when later events showed their relevance and importance. This is so in four particular cases.

The first is the possibility of *attracting sailors away from the Athenian fleet by offering them higher pay* (I. 121. 3; I. 141. 1). This, we know through Xenophon,[1] was part of the programme put forward by Lysander. But several reservations must be made in this particular case: first of all, in Xenophon, the idea is not presented as being an original one peculiar to Lysander. It is the putting into practice of the idea rather than the idea itself which is mentioned by Xenophon, and it is possible (and even probable) that consideration was given to this device from the very beginning of the Peloponnesian War. On the other hand, Pohlenz points out (I, p. 112) that Thucydides would not present Pericles as being so simply confident that this could not

---

[1] *Hell.*, I, 5, 4: διδάσκοντες ὅτι ἂν οὗτος ὁ μισθὸς γένηται, οἱ τῶν Ἀθηναίων ναῦται ἀπολείψουσι τὰς ναῦς καὶ μείω χρήματα ἀναλώσει: see Plutarch, *Lysander*, 4.

come about, and would not allow him to mention such an argument if events had already shown him to be wrong: in other words, that Thucydides could not have written this after 408.[1] I would go even further and maintain that the text itself, in this or rather these passages, implies that Thucydides did not have these later events in mind, and that he was therefore probably not aware of them. In both cases, the method envisaged as a way of obtaining money is very precise – a loan from Delphi or from Olympia. We are a long way from Lysander. Is it reasonable to believe that Thucydides, reintroducing ideas intended to prepare the way for these facts *after* they had taken place, would have gone to the trouble of presenting the ideas in a manner unsuited to them? There was certainly some question both of obtaining this loan and of attempting to offer higher wages to Athenian sailors from the very beginning of the war, whether or not the Peloponnesians actually tried to put this plan into practice. Neither part of the plan actually came to anything, and yet Thucydides does examine them because they determined the conditions under which the struggle took place. As to the war of Lysander, it is quite irrelevant here, and the comparison is merely a result of the fact that the same conditions prevailed in both cases. Far from supporting the contention that this passage is a later addition, this indication would, in my view, justify attributing it to an early version.

The second possibility to be examined is that of *planting forts in enemy country* (I. 122. 1; I. 142. 3). The word ἐπιτειχισμός (just as ἐπιτείχισις) is in fact used only once, in the Peloponnesian War, to refer to an actual enterprise and that is when it describes the fortification of Decelea by the Spartans in 413. We find it used, however, to refer to a *project* just before the peace of Nicias, in a passage already pointed out by Pohlenz (I, p. 111) and R. Zahn (p. 67); it is V. 17. 2: περιαγγελλομένη κατὰ πόλεις ὡς ⟨ἐς⟩ ἐπιτειχισμόν, ὅπως οἱ Ἀθηναῖοι μᾶλλον ἐσακούοιεν. This proves that people had not waited for Alcibiades in order to think of a manœuvre which was, after all, a fairly obvious one, which Athens herself was to apply at Pylos,[2] and which, probably, the Spartans delayed so long in putting into practice for no other reason than their lack of energy. Also, we might once again wonder if Thucydides would really have waited to

---

[1] Rose Zahn, p. 67, points out that δεινὸν ἂν ἦν does not completely exclude the possibility of such an enterprise. But she seems to forget the arguments which follow this remark and which help to show that this danger cannot arise.

[2] Athens also tried to use it against Boeotia by fortifying Delium.

see the project carried out successfully before making Pericles argue, in a passage designed to prove his clearsightedness, that it was doomed to failure.

The third possibility to be discussed is that of a *long war*. Pericles indicates it by the expression: χρονίων πολέμων, and by the threat: ἄλλως τε κἂν παρὰ δόξαν, ὅπερ εἰκός, ὁ πόλεμος αὐτοῖς μηκύνηται (141. 5). Archidamus had been even more precise in mentioning the danger of handing the war on to the next generation (I. 81. 6).[1] But this consideration seems as normal as the two others, and consequently just as unconvincing in any attempt to prove a late date of composition. It is the people who possess both money and a fleet who are counting on a long war. The other side wants a 'blitzkrieg' — μιᾷ τε νίκη ναυμαχίας is the phrase used by the Corinthians. It was thus almost inevitable that the question should have been discussed. Moreover, a ten years' war which, at the end of ten years, still seemed likely to break out again, is certainly a long war; and it is in Book III. 89. 1, after five years of war, that we see Archidamus handing the war on to his son. It is just possible that the expression which he uses indicates that the passage has been rewritten, but I do not think so. As to the expression used by Pericles, it could not possibly suggest a later addition.[2]

There remains the famous piece of advice in which Pericles urges the Athenians to: ἀρχήν τε μὴ ἐπικτᾶσθαι ἅμα πολεμοῦντες καὶ κινδύνους αὐθαιρέτους μὴ προστίθεσθαι (I. 144. 1) and it is this which raises the most difficult problem.[3] It is certain that Pericles did give this advice, if not on this particular occasion then at least in one or another or perhaps in several of his speeches. Moreover, Thucydides

---

[1] The Corinthians, on the other hand, hope for a short war (I. 121. 4).

[2] Moreover, if it is admitted that we have, in this analysis of forces and this exposition of Pericles' plan (for the two are too closely linked together to be separated) a late development (and this must be admitted once one considers that any particular argument is of a late date, because of the subtlety in the construction and the close links between the different arguments put forward by Archidamus, the Corinthians and Pericles), then one arrives at the idea suggested by R. Zahn, according to which Pericles' speech belongs to an early version in the part which deals with the necessity of war, and to a later version in the whole of its second part. But since it is precisely this second part, with the plan of action which concludes it, that is so closely linked to the narration of events in Book II, this solution seems to me quite improbable. Therefore, if it is not accepted that the passages which we have just studied belong to the early version, we must give up looking for anything which might correspond to it and adopt the unitarian views of Eduard Meyer. I have indicated in the text why this solution did not seem to me satisfactory.

[3] As regards the way the idea is presented, everything seems most normal and satisfactory. Zahn (note 84) compares IV. 10. 2: ἢν ἐθέλωμέν γε μεῖναι καὶ μή ...

would not have praised him in II. 65 for an attitude which he did not in fact have. It is thus wrong to assert – as R. Zahn does (p. 30) – that this sentence is amazing at that time, and that it can be understood only after the Sicilian expedition has taken place. What should be noted is the presence of this sentence in a speech reported by Thucydides; for Thucydides does not reproduce everything that Pericles says, and when he does so it is with a particular purpose and in order to refer to a particular event. Now, in chapter II. 65, Pericles' advice is certainly made to bear upon the Sicilian expedition.[1] Thus, either Thucydides is repeating a piece of advice which he had himself put into his work without suspecting the extent of its importance,[2] or he inserted this piece of advice only after 415 – as is suggested by Pohlenz (but it must be recalled that, even in Pohlenz's view, this does not necessarily imply that it was inserted after 404). The final answer must inevitably vary with the personal opinion of every scholar. In any case, if it is admitted that the passage was rewritten, it is clear that this is no proof of an evolution in Thucydides' ideas – and, given the nature of the indications with which we are here concerned, there is nothing surprising about this. Even if one supposes that Thucydides should have added this piece of advice – which forms part of the 'negative element' in Pericles' imperialism – as a later addition in his text, he can only have done so in order to justify the 'positive element' by defining its exact bearing – that is to say in order to defend against later criticism the man whose views he had already exalted against contemporary attacks.

This is the only piece of rewriting that can, in fact, be detected, and even this evidence is rather inconclusive. I do not mean, of course, that there was no other revision or alteration in the actual details, that such and such a word, or sentence, or even idea, was not added after the first version had been composed. Who could tell? But it is sufficient here to be able to affirm that, on the whole, the theory of Athenian sea-power, as it is put forward in Pericles' first speech, existed both in its present general structure and in its main argumentation in what we have agreed to call the primitive or original version.

---

[1] See moreover I. 144. 1: μᾶλλον γὰρ πεφόβημαι τὰς οἰκείας ἡμῶν ἁμαρτίας . . . and II. 65. 11: ἐξ ὧν ἄλλα τε πολλά, ὡς ἐν μεγάλῃ πόλει καὶ ἀρχὴν ἐχούσῃ, ἡμαρτήθη καὶ ὁ ἐς Σικελίαν πλοῦς . . .

[2] It can be noted (Pohlenz, I. p. 111, n. 1) that the last element in II. 65. 7 (τῇ πόλει κινδυνεύειν) runs more like VI. 10. 5 than like I. 144. 1, which would suggest that I. 144. 1 was not written in relation with the actual words of II. 65. 7. But I do not believe there is much to be drawn from remarks of this nature.

The problem presents itself in rather a different form as far as the Funeral Oration is concerned, for it can be easily taken out of a context with which it has but few direct links. If Pericles' first speech could be considered as a later addition only in the places where it bore signs of having been rewritten, it is on the contrary quite possible for the Funeral Oration to belong, as a whole, to a later period.[1]

This is the solution most generally adopted by philologists, and it is the one which, for lack of more precise indications, the general meaning of the text invites us to adopt.

For if the ideas are certainly those of Pericles, and could normally have been expressed in the course of the war of Archidamus, the manner in which they are put forward and their presence in Thucydides' work are difficult to explain in any early version.

The themes, as we have seen, are presented in this speech in extremely general terms, and the tone is always exceptionally elevated. As different from the normal funeral orations as from most of the speeches in Thucydides' work, the Funeral Oration is devoted exclusively to celebrating the true nature of Athenian civilization. And there is no doubt that it was Thucydides himself who chose to limit its subject-matter in this manner, he who chose to make this elevated and detailed analysis and he who chose to insert this praise in his work. What function does this analysis and praise perform there? One can find nothing to relate it to, nothing which it would explain. Indeed, Thucydides is not setting out to contrast Athens with Sparta in their actual history and development, but to defend the glory and ideals of Athens against the glory and ideals of Sparta. It is thus natural enough to assume that he would do this at a time when Athens is being scorned and spurned, when Sparta is in fashion and when her friends have every reason to attack Athens: that is to say, after the defeat of 404.

Moreover, the purity which excludes even the echo of any political

[1] This does not of course mean that Thucydides did not very cleverly reintroduce it at the best possible place. I am speaking, as I was doing earlier, of revisions carried out by Thucydides himself, which could not have the incoherent quality of the modifications which Schwarz would discover. Eduard Meyer (*Forsch.*, II, p. 395) declares that the analysis could not be left out ('unerlasslich') and that it completes those in Book I (in the speeches of the Corinthians and of Archidamus). It is nevertheless obvious that this analysis is of a different type and belongs to a different plane. Pohlenz (I, p. 202) has clearly shown that the complement to those two speeches is in fact to be found in the speech made by the Athenians in Book I. The Funeral Oration is moreover not unrelated to the ideas put forward there (see p. 271); but it is not related to any element of the early plan in such a close relationship that this would demand and imply its presence in it.

quarrels from the Funeral Oration is also more easily explained once it is assumed that the speech was written after these quarrels had faded away and the very reality of Athenian greatness had become a thing of the past.

By its particular subject, the Funeral Oration could, when spoken by Pericles, towards the beginning of the war, have a genuine meaning: as a part of Thucydides' History, it has one only after 404 (and it is a slightly different one).

We could therefore admit that, after the defeat, Thucydides inserted into his work this long and moving passage which is entirely devoted, without any apparent necessity, to the glory of Athens and of Pericles, and which reveals complete support for the more positive and living ideals incarnate in the great statesman. If the empire of Athens and a reasonable concern for her greatness had ever been dear to Thucydides, it would appear that they were even dearer, by reaction, at a time when they only remained as a memory exposed to all kinds of criticism.[1]

If this is so, it allows us to delimit and narrow the significance of the revision which Thucydides, as we have seen, may — or may not — have carried out as regards the first speech of Pericles: this revision involved no fundamental change in Thucydides' attitude.

The problem presented by Pericles' last speech is different again.

In one way, this speech forms part of the 'original' narration of events. It is concerned with a movement of discontent which is caused on the one hand to a very great extent by the plague (II. 64. 1) — and Thucydides would clearly not have waited twenty years before discussing this plague and bringing out its importance — and which, on the other hand, is foreseen in the first speech[2] — and we have already seen that this speech forms part of the original plan. We

---

[1] Scholars who have maintained that the Funeral Oration was a later addition by Thucydides have generally considered that he meant to convey the idea of a strong opposition between the culture of Athens and that of Sparta: the desire to bring out such an idea would imply a spirit of hostility towards Sparta, which is characteristic of the warlike and imperialistic party. However, the real subject of the Funeral Oration is not so much the idea of an opposition between the cultures of Sparta and Athens as of the superiority of Athenian culture. This is why there is nothing in the whole work which corresponds to this speech, and it is in this way that its analysis differs from that put forward in Book I.

[2] I. 140. 1: καίπερ εἰδὼς τοὺς ἀνθρώπους οὐ τῇ αὐτῇ ὀργῇ ἀναπειθομένους τε πολεμεῖν καὶ ἐν τῷ ἔργῳ πράσσοντας, πρὸς δὲ τὰς ξυμφορὰς καὶ τὰς γνώμας τρεπομένους. Cf. II. 60. 1: καὶ προσδεχομένῳ μοι τὰ τῆς ὀργῆς ὑμῶν ἔς με γεγένηται ... καὶ ἐκκλησίαν τούτου ἕνεκα ξυνήγαγον, ὅπως ... μέμψωμαι εἴ τι μὴ ὀρθῶς ... ταῖς ξυμφοραῖς εἴκετε.

must add that this discontent revealed itself in particular events,[1] and that a historian could in no way ignore it.[2] It is thus rather improbable that, in the 'original' version, Pericles should not have been called upon at least once to justify a policy for which he fought on so many occasions. It is equally improbable that his death should not have been recorded, while those of Cleon, Nicias and Antiphon are, and that not a single word should have been said in praise of him, since in VII. 86 Thucydides praises Nicias, whom he admired much less and who had less need to be defended.

But if we may suppose that the 'original' version contained both a speech by Pericles and a passage in praise of Pericles, there is nothing at all to prove that they are the ones to be found in the present text. The final speech is less closely linked to immediate events than was the first, and has none of its close formal links with the context.[3] On the other hand, we know that the main features of the praise in II. 65, which deals with later events, 404 included, was necessarily written after that date. The praise and the speech both form, however, a perfectly homogeneous unit: the praise is the normal conclusion of the speech,[4] and the speech itself seems to be, as we have already seen, a completely consistent whole.

It is thus possible that the speech, or certain parts of it, should have been written earlier, but in that case we must admit that it was Thucydides himself who did the rewriting and that the 'later' revision was carried out in complete harmony with the spirit inspiring the 'original' version.

It will be no easy task to detect such revisions, and we are therefore compelled to try to find out whether the different parts of the speech

---

[1] The speech is placed a little before this discontent has any practical result (cf. II. 65. 3) so that the debate is concerned only with the principle of the war.

[2] The ξύλλογος in which it was made had in itself no importance, and the speech was, in a way, without consequences (Ed. Meyer, Forsch., II, 390): but the problem raised was certainly a very important one. On the contrary, the Funeral Oration could not appear as a historical event.

[3] The links between the first and last speeches do not imply that they formed part of the same plan.

[4] The personal justification in II. 60. 5 (οὐδενὸς ἥσσων οἴομαι εἶναι γνῶναί τε τὰ δέοντα καὶ ἑρμηνεῦσαι ταῦτα, φιλόπολίς τε καὶ χρημάτων κρείσσων) corresponds roughly to the praise in II. 65. 8 (δυνατὸς ὢν τῷ τε ἀξιώματι καὶ τῇ γνώμῃ χρημάτων τε διαφανῶς ἀδωρότατος γενόμενος). But the similarity is not overwhelming, and one would find several examples just as convincing in the first speech or in the indirect speech in II. 13. It is more important to note that II. 59. 3 corresponds closely, on the one hand to the plan of the speech, and on the other to the beginning of II. 65, and that finally the whole of the praise and of the speech seem inspired by the same apologetic zeal.

contain in themselves any clues which might enable us to date them. Some passages provide more information than others, or, if one prefers, offer less doubtful hypotheses.

One passage in particular seems to reflect recent events, and it is the very one which has already been seen as coming close to the spirit of the Funeral Oration. In this passage Pericles, seeking to encourage the Athenians, suddenly evokes the end of their empire in a passage explaining its greatness (II. 64. 3): ἦν καὶ νῦν ὑπενδῶμέν ποτε (πάντα γὰρ πέφυκε καὶ ἐλασσοῦσθαι). The memory of this greatness, he explains, will then still remain: μνήμη καταλελείψεται Ἑλλήνων τε ὅτι Ἕλληνες πλείστων δὴ ἤρξαμεν καὶ πολέμοις μεγίστοις ἀντέσχομεν πρός τε ξύμπαντας καὶ καθ' ἑκάστους, πόλιν τε τοῖς πᾶσιν εὐπορωτάτην καὶ μεγίστην ᾠκήσαμεν. This is quite a remarkable starting-point; for if one suggests that the Athenians should imagine what will remain after their empire has disappeared, that is certainly a very strange way of encouraging them to act. To be sure, it is characteristic of Pericles' ideas, wherever we find them in Thucydides' work, to envisage the Athenian empire *sub specie aeternitatis*; but only this particular passage and the Funeral Oration neglect its material and perishable value quite to this extent. It would thus seem that the actual disappearance of the empire plays some part here. Moreover, this passage has the same elevated tone and the same emotion as the Funeral Oration, and it is difficult not to explain it each time by a feeling of regret for things that have passed away. It is thus fairly probable that, like the Funeral Oration, this passage was written after 404.[1]

However, this passage does not necessarily involve the rest of the speech with it, although it does seem reasonable to link it with the development of paragraph 63 which is similarly but more precisely aimed at the ἀπράγμονες.

The object of this paragraph can be used as a guide in dating it, for it aims at defending the very principle of the empire against the criticisms put forward by the opposition. Now it was in 404 that the question of imperialism was posed in its most acute form, and it was then that the triumphant ἀπράγμονες finally dared to multiply the attacks which it had now become easy for them to make. That is why Schwartz, following Eduard Meyer,[2] could consider that the party

[1] The passage is in a very satisfactory place in the present *epilogos*, but this does not prove that Thucydides did not make up the *epilogos* out of early and later elements. The double form of the *epilogos* might favour such a hypothesis.

[2] *Forsch.*, II, 393.

L

at whom the speech was directed was not the opponent of 429 but was rather the theoretician of 404.

We have seen that some reservations need to be made and that Pericles could very easily have uttered the arguments which Thucydides puts into his mouth. But we have also seen that Thucydides had made a point of reproducing these arguments, with a clearly apologetic intention and an insistence which do not fit in very well with the tone of the first speech. It is thus more reasonable to think that, if he found he had to lay the stress on such a plea, it was because, at the moment when he was writing, the accusations against imperialism had acquired importance, because it was easy to condemn it and needful to defend it. This was not the case in 429 and even less in 420, but it was the case in 404. The friends of Sparta, in their moment of triumph, did not refrain from blaming, very severely, both the man and the idea. Ignoring the distinction made by Thucydides in his judgment of II. 65, they treated Pericles as representing war, imperialism and democracy. For the Athenians, as we have seen, there was no strong distinction between these three ideas; and the accusation of having begun the war was a very heavy charge against him. The oligarchic pamphlet already mentioned has not come down to us,[1] but we have Plato's word for the existence of such opinions. In the *Gorgias*, Socrates refers to a particular rumour when he says: 'I have for my own part heard that Pericles made the Athenians lazy, cowardly, over-talkative and greedy for money by beginning to pay them for carrying out public functions'; and Callicles gives the origin of this rumour when he says: 'it is our lovers of Sparta with their bruised ears who told you that' (515e).[2] In so far as they are a reply to a series of attacks made on Pericles and on Athenian rule, the arguments in this speech may correspond to those put forward by Pericles in 429, but they assumed their full importance in Thucydides' eyes only in 404.

This is confirmed by the detail of the development; it is so close to the form which events took in 404 that it allows no doubt to remain. When Pericles speaks of the desire for vengeance which is felt by subject peoples, when he refers to this vengeance as something worse than slavery itself — and this can only mean death — he is

---

[1] We at least know (cf. p. 17) that it insisted upon the gratuity of the war.

[2] Plato himself does not fail to name Pericles on several occasions as one of the people responsible for the imperialistic policies pursued by Athens (see in particular *Gorgias*, 515e–516b): cf. p. 364.

dealing with a possibility which was to be tragically confirmed by reality: it could be seen when the conquerors debated whether or not Athens would continue to exist and when her former allies made the fiercest of attacks against her (Isocrates says so: *On the Peace*, 78; 105).[1]

What is even more striking, because it is less relevant to the main ideas under discussion, is Pericles' suggestion that the ἀπράγμονες might set up a state of their own. The idea itself is rather a surprising one, and it does not fit in very well with Pericles' general reasoning. For what is it, in his view, which makes surrender impossible? As we have just seen, it is the empire (κινδύνου ὅν ἐν τῇ ἀρχῇ ἀπήχθεσθε), and this is certainly the conclusion that will be put forward almost immediately: οὐδὲ ἐν ἀρχούσῃ πόλει ξυμφέρει . . . But what about a group of ἀπράγμονες, dwelling apart with no longer any empire? The argument, then, would not hold. We must therefore admit that in the remark about them, we move away from the main idea in order to condemn their policy in a more general way. And we can look upon this parenthesis as a kind of intrusion of reality into a logical development, perhaps even as a reference to the installation of the oligarchs at Eleusis.[2]

Once again, the indication is not wholly decisive: these coincidences may be the effect of chance, and the reference may be quite different.[3]

We must note, however, that there are a number of probabilities which all come together here, and that both the tone and subject-matter of the passage are more easily explained if it is assumed to have been written after 404. It is then fairly probable, at least, that like the closing part of the speech, it was written after that date.

The rest of the speech is not so heavily marked by the influence of events. Certainly, the empire has, from beginning to end, an importance which it did not have in the first speech,[4] and when it deals with Athenian sea-power Pericles' final speech is very different both from the style of the first speech and from that used in the 'Αθηναίων

---

[1] Cf. later p. 276.

[2] See Aristotle, *Constitution of Athens*, 39, 1: τοὺς βουλομένους 'Αθηναίων τῶν ἐν ἄστει μεινάντων ἐξοικεῖν ἔχειν 'Ελευσῖνα ἐπιτίμους ὄντας καὶ κυρίους καὶ αὐτοκράτορας ἑαυτῶν καὶ τὰ αὑτῶν καρπουμένους.

[3] Marchant considers that this passage deliberately departs, for ironic intentions, from any historical reality: according to him, Pericles is expressing the idea that if the ἀπράγμονες want to see their ideas carried out, they would be better advised to go elsewhere.

[4] Cf. p. 122, n. 3.

Πολιτεία or in contemporary documents.[1] But such facts in themselves prove nothing, since we have already seen that there is nevertheless a general unity between these different texts; moreover, there is no proof that Thucydides needed twenty-five years to bring out or to wish to emphasize ideas which, in fine, are nothing but the natural development of those put forward in the first speech.[2]

It is thus impossible to say whether Thucydides conceived and wrote the whole of this speech after 404, or whether he merely used the more or less extensive passages that he had written of an 'original' speech;[3] what is certain is that the speech as we have it looks like a unit, belonging to a late section, and repeating with greater insistence the themes and ideas present in the 'original' passages.

Does the way in which he expresses them at a later date provide any indication of an evolution in Thucydides' own thought? This may possibly be the case, and Thucydides may, after 404, have used arguments to support Pericles that he would not have used earlier. An attempt has been made to prove this by comparing paragraph 63 with the discussion on Mytilene in Book III. Cleon, in fact, is blamed by Thucydides, but is made to use the same words as Pericles: οὐκ ἐπικινδύνως ἡγεῖσθε ἐς ὑμᾶς καὶ οὐκ ἐς τὴν τῶν ξυμμάχων χάριν μαλακίζεσθαι, οὐ σκοποῦντες ὅτι τυραννίδα ἔχετε τὴν ἀρχὴν καὶ πρὸς ἐπιβουλεύοντας αὐτοὺς καὶ ἄκοντας ἀρχομένους (III. 37. 2). On the other hand Diodotus, his opponent, insists on the friendship which the democratic party in every Greek city feels towards Athens. Is there not a contradiction here in Thucydides' own ideas? The question must be asked, for the development in paragraph 63 is absolutely new, and if there is nothing in the first speech to contradict it, there is nothing to prepare for it either. Basing himself upon this fact, Schwartz has maintained that Thucydides did not yet hold these realistic ideas when he wrote the first version of his work, and that he

[1] It is doubtless this which generally causes a later date to be attributed to this passage (Zahn, p. 61: 'Dass dieser Teil in Per. 3 dem letzten Plan zugehört wird von niemand bezweifelt'). This is nevertheless not real proof.

[2] Schadewaldt's theory, according to which Thucydides wrote speeches that were objectively accurate in his first manner and rose to a much wider subjective liberty in his second manner is by no means proven. And in any case we must be careful of coming too hastily to the conclusion: 'such and such a passage is so remarkable that it must have been written after 404', in the same way that we ought to be careful not to say too often: 'such and such a passage is so weak that it was clearly not written by Thucydides'.

[3] It is this final hypothesis that I would accept, as being the least costly in the conditions indicated on p. 148; but it would be quite hopeless to try to form an idea of the extent of these revisions.

made Cleon express them in order that he might be refuted, whereas after 404 he would reject any tendency to moralize at the very moment when everybody else was doing so.

I would hasten to add that such a complete and carefully emphasized change of attitude is more than merely surprising. It has already been noted how, throughout the whole of his work, Thucydides tended to accept the idea of the hostility felt for Athens by her subjects, which Pericles puts forward. Only a detailed study of the debate between Cleon and Diodotus will, in the next chapter, enable us to see what value there is in this comparison, which Schwartz seems to have interpreted incorrectly, and to decide whether or not Thucydides is contradicting himself. At the same time, such a study will provide us with a certain amount of new external evidence on the probable date at which our speech was written.

It seems that all these discussions produce doubt and uncertainty more than definite results. Nevertheless, these doubts and uncertainties are themselves results of a sort, which we can use both in discussing the problem of when the work was written and in discovering Thucydides' attitude to Athenian imperialism. They are at least as important as the few definite facts that we have been able to acquire.

The problem of how and when the work was written is, certainly, not much nearer to being solved. If certain passages are now seen as having been written after 404, it seems that most of them could have been written at any time between 430 and 404. It would certainly be more satisfying to be able to say, as Schwartz did: this passage was written at such and such a date, that passage at another; Thucydides changed his mind for this or that reason; his editor made this or that mistake. But these clear distinctions will not stand up to a critical analysis. As Book I, setting out the causes of the war, and certainly written at various dates, presents itself in fact as a complete, unified and consistent whole, so also the different passages about Pericles, which were also certainly written at various times, all form a united whole in which the different speeches each have their own individual function to perform and fit in with one another without undue repetition. This is no proof at all that they were all written at the same time, but it shows that Thucydides, when revising his History, worked in a more subtle and profound manner than some of the non-unitarian scholars have been prepared to admit. There may have been frequent and successive alterations, but we know nothing about them. Thus, even if we accept the hypothesis that the work was composed and written over a long period of years, we must not look for clear-cut solutions. Furthermore, as we have already said, since the days of Ullrich and his theory that there are two strata in the composition of the work, non-unitarian scholars have had to admit that the truth was much more complex than he fancied. Their only mistake was perhaps that they did not act according to this conclusion but kept on looking for more and more dates of composition and more and more different elements in texts which were apparently coherent units. Now, it is clearly useless to carry on with such methods of research, and the doubtful nature of the result which one scholar reaches only to be refuted by one of his fellows is a proof of this. We must not forget that when we are trying to discover the date of composition of a tragedy or a comedy, we are at least sure that there is a solution, even if we are not certain of finding it. In the case of a work which, like that of Thucydides, has been fused into a complete whole, the problem of finding the date at which every single passage was written — a problem we have to examine if we want to find out the right way in which the passage should be read — does not necessarily admit of an exact answer, for the reality itself is not quite so simple. It is therefore expedient to call a halt when confronted by so carefully finished a result that the process leaves no traces.

But the very possibility that Thucydides' work should have been so perfectly fused into a whole is important because of what it tells us about his ideas, since it implies that he must have remained faithful to the same basic attitude. He repeats themes already treated, only to deal with them in a more complete and satisfying manner, and brings back his early heroes, only to insist upon their virtues.[1]

Finally, even places where, instead of the hard unbroken surface of the Thucydidean construction, we detected here and there the impact of the events of 404 — namely, in the praise in II. 65, in the closing passages of the final speech, and in the Funeral Oration (whatever may be in fact the date at which all the other passages were written)[2] — we have ascertained that Pericles and his ideals are defended with

---

[1] Such a result would enable us to dismiss here and now the ambitious question of the composition, were it not still possible that our historian, although in general faithful to the same ideal, nevertheless did change his mind on certain points or accept new ideas.

[2] The most important thing is to distinguish the passages which seem to result from late preoccupations from those which, planned or prepared earlier, *could have been* written before, and which do not bear the intellectual mark of the period at which they acquired the form in which we read them today, cf. p. 348.

more fervour than ever. Now, the insistence and apologetic character of these passages can also be explained by the fidelity of Thucydides to his original ideas, since he only feels the need to be more assertive when others become more aggressive. The very changes either in the work itself or in the tone of the writing and even in the intensity of his conviction can only have resulted from an absolute fidelity to the past.

The experience of the years following Pericles' death may also have helped. It may have stimulated this fidelity and made it more warmly partisan. For Thucydides condemns these years in the most absolute manner. And, by bringing out the motives for this condemnation, we can perhaps find out more precisely why Thucydides had so whole-hearted an admiration for Pericles.

CHAPTER TWO

CLEON

AFTER the death of Pericles, the man with the greatest influence over the people was Cleon, son of Cleainetus (III. 36. 6; IV. 21. 3). There is no possible doubt about what Thucydides thought of him. He is a man of violence (III. 36. 6),[1] he uses deceit and calumny in the pursuit of his own interests (IV. 27. 4); wise men are glad at the idea of his possible death (IV. 28. 5); he supports war because it enables him to do evil and spread calumny freely (V. 16. 1). These condemnations of the man imply a condemnation of the policy he pursued.

This policy plays a part in three episodes in Thucydides' work: in the affair of Mytilene, Cleon makes a speech to which Diodotus replies; in the affair of Pylos, he inspires the Athenian decision about the possibility of a truce which is supported in a speech made by the Spartans; he finally plays a part in the Thracian campaign in which he was killed, but this episode is subjected to no political analysis by Thucydides, and is consequently of less direct concern to us than the first two, in which two very important questions concerning Athenian imperialism are discussed: that of maintaining subject peoples in obedience and that of knowing at what point the ambitions of Athens must stop.

I. The Defection of Mytilene

From the Athenian point of view, the defection of Mytilene set an important general problem concerning the methods of imperialism, and it is this that Thucydides treats in the great debate between Cleon and Diodotus. Their two speeches represent the two possible solutions open to the ruler, and the two principles that can be applied in his relationship with his subjects. As to the description of

---

1 Βιαιότατος τῶν πολιτῶν. This feature corresponds to a characteristic disposition on the part of Cleon: cf. Diod., XII, 55, 8: ὠμὸς τὸν τρόπον καὶ βίαιος, and Hermippus (46, 7 K) αἴθωνι Κλέωνι. But it is also obviously a criticism if one goes by standard Greek ethics: cf. Homer, Od., VI, 120; VIII, 575, repeated in Plato, Gorgias, 516 c.

the military operations and the speech made by the Mytilenians,[1] they merely set the stage for the central debate.

Before examining the main arguments, it may be noted that the different speakers are in agreement about the conditions which define Athenian sea-power. It is thus easy to explain the presence in the three speeches made by the Mytilenians, by Cleon and by Diodotus, of elements with which we are now well acquainted; they are, here, as they were with Pericles, the fleet, the islands, the taxes.[2] The presence of these familiar themes underlines once again how clearly Thucydides himself conceived the system of Athenian rule, but it tells us little about the individual opinions of the two speakers.

What divides them is that, within the framework of the same system, one supports severity and the other moderation. Diodotus wants to make the subject people trust Athens; Cleon wants them to be afraid of her.

It is obvious that Thucydides himself sides with Diodotus and disapproves of Cleon. The Athenians have decided on the mass execution of the Mytilenian population, and Thucydides tells us that they did so 'under the influence of anger' (36. 2); he insists on the extreme nature of this measure (οὐ μόνον . . . ἀλλὰ καί); in his view, it is based merely on 'allegations' (ἐπικαλοῦντες) and as soon as it is

---

[1] This account and these speeches have a certain number of links with the two speeches in the debate, and in particular with Cleon's. The Mytilenians prove that their defection was *just*, and Cleon that repression is *just*. In directly opposed expressions, the Mytilenians and Cleon bring in the idea of *precedents*; for the Mytilenians, these precedents encouraged rebellion (10. 6: παραδείγμασι τοῖς προγενομένοις χρώμενοι; 11. 6: παραδείγμασι χρώμενοι τοῖς ἐς τοὺς ἄλλους); for Cleon, these precedents ought to have encouraged the Mytilenians to obey (39. 3: παράδειγμα δὲ αὐτοῖς οὔτε αἱ τῶν πέλας ξυμφοραὶ ἐγένοντο). He also uses after them, but against them, the idea of the difference of treatment accorded to Mytilene (11. 2, cf. 39. 2). But these similarities remain fairly external, and the structure of the speeches enables us to consider the debate in Athens as independent from the Mytilenian attack.

[2] If the defection of Mytilene is so important, it is because Mytilene has a *fleet*, which is eminently precious for Athens (III. 11. 4), and would be no less precious for Sparta (13. 7); it is also because Mytilene is an *island*, possessing both a fleet and ramparts, and belongs naturally to the Athenian empire, from which no one could detach her against her own will (III. 39. 2). But even apart from all these circumstances, any defection is important because it is likely to bring others in its path (13. 7) and because each defection will mean that Athens will be deprived of the tribute which is vital to her, 13. 6: δι' ἣν ἡ Ἀττικὴ ὠφελεῖται· ἔστι δὲ τῶν χρημάτων ἀπὸ τῶν ξυμμάχων ἡ πρόσοδος; 39. 8: καὶ τυχόντες μὲν πόλιν ἐφθαρμένην παραλαβόντες τῆς ἐπετείας προσόδου, δι' ἣν ἰσχύομεν, τὸ λοιπὸν στερήσεσθε; 46. 3: καὶ ἢν ἕλωμεν πόλιν ἐφθαρμένην παραλαβεῖν καὶ τῆς προσόδου τὸ λοιπὸν ἀπ' αὐτῆς στέρεσθαι· ἰσχύομεν δὲ πρὸς τοὺς πολεμίους τῷδε. These expressions are an echo of the phrase used by Pericles in II. 13. 2: λέγων τὴν ἰσχὺν αὐτοῖς ἀπὸ τούτων εἶναι τῶν χρημάτων τῆς προσόδου.

considered carefully the decision appears 'grave and cruel' (ὠμὸν καὶ μέγα). Moreover the facts, as they are presented to the reader, confirm these indications: in the case of Mytilene, the decision was rescinded and nothing happened; but it was applied at Scione (Thucydides tells us that this was once again on Cleon's advice), and, soon afterwards, Mende also deserted Athens (IV. 122-123). Both in his narration of the immediate events and in his analysis of the more far-reaching effects of such excessive severity, Thucydides thus defines his attitude towards Cleon's proposal and condemns it.

This condemnation is also quite clear in the composition of the debate; for this composition brings out the superiority of the arguments put forward by Diodotus.

Each of the two speeches contains a theoretical part, dealing with the very principle of reconsidering a vote, and a practical part, concerned with the correct punishment to be applied to Mytilene.

In the theoretical part, Diodotus defends the rights of intelligence. Rejecting Cleon's argument that a tyrannical power must stand firm, he demands that any power, whatever it may be, must occasionally stop to think. His thesis is that of εὐβουλία,[1] and he asks for the greatest liberty of debate. In this, Pericles would have agreed with him.[2]

As to the action envisaged, both orators give closely parallel discussions.

Cleon analyses the wrongs committed by the Mytilenians, together with everything that makes these wrongs more serious. He shows that only the excessive amount of liberty that they have been

---

[1] Cleon takes the conditions imposed on the ἀρχή as his starting-point (37. 1), while Diodotus bases himself on the rules of εὐβουλία (42. 1). The symmetry of ideas is underlined by symmetrical expressions in places which do not correspond to one another; thus we have:

40. 2: μηδὲ τρισὶ τοῖς ἀξυμφορωτάτοις τῇ ἀρχῇ, οἴκτῳ καὶ ἡδονῇ λόγων καὶ ἐπιεικείᾳ, ἁμαρτάνειν.

42. 1: νομίζω δὲ δύο τὰ ἐναντιώτατα εὐβουλίᾳ εἶναι, τάχος τε καὶ ὀργήν. See also, in Diodotus, the frequent use of the expressions εὐβουλία, βουλεύειν, εὖ βουλεύεσθαι, which are very rare in Cleon. Diodotus, in fact, is illustrating a theme of traditional wisdom, cf. *Iph. Aul.*, 388: εἰ δ' ἐγὼ γνοὺς πρόσθεν οὐκ εὖ μετελέθην εὐβουλίᾳ, | μαίνομαι;

[2] III. 42. 2: τούς τε λόγους ὅστις διαμάχεται μὴ διδασκάλους τῶν πραγμάτων γίγνεσθαι ἢ ἀξύνετός ἐστιν ἢ ἰδίᾳ τι αὐτῷ διαφέρει = II. 40. 2: οὐ τοὺς λόγους τοῖς ἔργοις βλάβην ἡγούμενοι ἀλλὰ μὴ προδιδαχθῆναι μᾶλλον λόγῳ πρότερον ἢ ἐπὶ ἃ δεῖ ἔργῳ ἐλθεῖν. Like Pericles, Diodotus fights against the imprudent anger of the people. It will be noticed that Cleon leaves something to anger (38. 1) and declares that he mistrusts the ξυνετωτέροις (37. 3): Diodotus attacks ὀργή (42. 1) and defends ξύνεσις against the ἀξυνέτους (42. 2; 42. 3). Ξύνεσις is in Thucydides' view the finest of all qualities, that one that he attributes to Themistocles (1. 74. 1; 138. 3).

allowed has encouraged them to the point when they became guilty
of hubris,[1] and he therefore proposes that they be punished in a way
that will leave future rebels in no doubt as to the fate awaiting them.
He adds to this analysis a consideration (σκέψασθε, 39. 7) showing that
indulgence would bring about a vast increase in the number of
similar defections, and consequently a two-fold decrease in revenue
for Athens. He concludes that a policy of severity is consonant with
right, with self-interest, and with the demands of the empire.

Diodotus replies by analysing the uselessness of punishment in
general, which has never yet held back a man tempted by hubris;
and he therefore proposes that Athens should adopt a merciful
attitude, allowing the criminals to surrender. He adds to this analysis
two considerations (σκέψασθε, 46. 2; σκέψασθε, 47. 1); the first
consideration shows that severity would only bring about more
obstinacy on the part of any deserting city, and consequently a two-
fold decrease in revenue; the second shows that if Athens adopted a
policy of severity, she would lose the support of the democratic
party in other cities. And he concludes that self-interest demands
that the Athenians should not exercise all their rights, but should
adopt a moderate attitude, which would favour the maintenance of
the empire.

The parallel between the plans of the two speeches brings out the
rigorous nature of Diodotus' reply; for everything – analysis and
considerations – is more precise in his speech than in Cleon's. In the
analysis itself, Cleon merely mentioned Mytilenian hubris, while
Diodotus discusses the nature and consequences of hubris in general.
In the considerations, Cleon deals simply with the possibility of
future desertions,[2] while Diodotus (who, as his analysis shows,

---

[1] Scholars have wondered about the use of the expressions ἀπροσδόκητος and δι'
ἐλαχίστου, which are not particularly suited to the case of Mytilene; but the reflection is
a general one (like the analysis by Diodotus which corresponds to it), and these terms
belong to the traditional description of hubris (cf. p. 324). The case of the Mytilenians
comes near to it in that one might say that, being autonomous, they enjoyed 'exceptional
honours' (39. 2: αὐτόνομοί τε οἰκοῦντες καὶ τιμώμενοι ἐς τὰ πρῶτα ὑπὸ ἡμῶν; 39. 4: παρὰ
δόξαν; 39. 5: διαφερόντως τῶν ἄλλων ὑφ' ἡμῶν τετιμῆσθαι; cf., in the speech of the Mytilenians, 12. 1: δεδιότες ἐθεράπευον).

[2] He considers elsewhere (39. 6 and 40. 1) the two circumstances on which Diodotus'
arguments are based, but he takes only a partial view of them, and uses them only for
judicial arguments. First, Mytilene would not have been so inoffensive, had she not been
stopped: therefore she deserves to be punished. Secondly, the people, initially, rallied to the
oligarchs: therefore, they deserve to be punished. Both by the point of view from which
he sets out and by his analysis of the conditions, Diodotus offers a better reasoning than
Cleon.

considers them inevitable) judges them in relation to two specific circumstances, ignored by Cleon but mentioned in the narration of events (27. 2-3): the fact that Mytilene was easily reconquered, and the fact that the people soon changed their minds in favour of Athens.

At the same time, by the way in which he refuses to concern himself with anything that is not the interest of Athens, Diodotus avoids the *a priori* attacks made by Cleon against anyone whose plea for mercy shows him to be a traitor.

The two speeches were thus composed by Thucydides in such a way that the systematic contrast between them, although rather improbable in an actual debate, brought out the wisdom of one solution compared with the folly of the other. We cannot discover what resemblance there was between the ideas expressed in Thucydides and those put forward in real life by Cleon and his opponent.[1] But if Thucydides made a point of bringing this unknown opponent into the full glare of the light of history, it was because he wanted to use him in order to condemn certain ideas and show the validity of others.

The general principles adopted by Cleon fit into a clearly defined system. He considers that the empire is a tyranny: the subjects are full of hatred and ready to rebel; their obedience can be explained not by feelings of friendship but merely by the force of Athens (III. 37. 2); their interests are opposed to those of Athens (III. 38. 1); they want to massacre the Athenians (39. 2; 40. 5); they can be kept under only by terror (39. 7); they are enemies of Athens and nothing that she can do will change this (40. 3). It is for these reasons that the only attitude to be adopted towards them is one based on force: all the allies must be made to obey (39. 5), and they must be punished severely if they rebel. Severity is justified in the case of Mytilene, but even if it were not justified it would still be necessary: thus the Athenians must either adopt this policy or give up their empire and be virtuous without danger (ἐκ τοῦ ἀκινδύνου ἀνδραγαθίζεσθαι).

This implies a certain way of looking at the empire and a certain way of administering it. Where does Diodotus differ from these? That is a more difficult question to answer. There are certainly a number of indications which might suggest that he has a different view of the empire itself. The very thesis which he puts forward presupposes that

---

[1] Diodotus is unknown apart from the speech which he makes in this debate, but I do not believe his name to be a fictitious one.

force cannot be the only basis for Athenian rule, since it is not by making people afraid that one can make them obey. Rather than rely on force, he wants to use two specific factors, namely the possibility of repentance (46. 1) and the friendly disposition of the people (47. 2): both presuppose the existence of good-will towards Athens; one can therefore say that he tends to see in the ἀρχή the traces of the ξυμμαχία. Moreover, he has no hesitation in calling the Mytilenians 'free' men.[1]

But the existence of such a difference of opinion between these two men would in fact involve some difficulties, since, in the rest of his work, Thucydides seems to have shared the view of the empire as a tyranny put forward by Cleon.[2] Even though he is aware of the opposition between the people on the one hand and the ὀλίγοι on the other, and although he knows how useful this can be for Athens, he still presents it only as a secondary factor, and insists much more on the opposition between rulers and subjects. Even here, in this episode, he seems to approve in advance of the view put forward by Cleon, when he makes the Mytilenians say that they followed the Athenians only through fear (III. 12. 1: δέει δὲ τὸ πλέον ἢ φιλίᾳ κατεχόμενοι ξύμμαχοι ἦμεν).

But this very fact encourages us to look more closely at the few indications given by Diodotus' speech; and, if we do, we see that, although he does not base his argument upon it, Diodotus really shares Cleon's view about the empire. He wants to rely on the friend-liness of the *demos*, but this is because the *demos* is the only ally that Athens has left: ὃ μόνον ἡμῖν ἔτι ξύμμαχόν ἐστι (47. 4); moreover, he knows that subjects obey only through force (βίᾳ) and that defections are normal (εἰκότως, 46. 5): the hostility which, as subjects, they feel for Athens is not dealt with directly, but it is nevertheless assumed as implicit. At the same time as he tries to keep the supporters of the tyrant city faithful, Diodotus does not deny that the city is a tyrant.

---

[1] The expressions ἐλεύθερον καὶ βίᾳ ἀρχόμενον, in 46. 5, and τοὺς ἐλευθέρους, in 46. 6, tend to present the defection as 'normal' (46. 5: εἰκότως πρὸς αὐτονομίαν ἀποστάντα). In fact, both ἐλεύθερος and πρὸς αὐτονομίαν distorts the strict legal position, for in law the Mytilenians are αὐτόνομοι and want to be ἐλεύθεροι καὶ αὐτόνομοι. The expressions used by Diodotus, by bringing out the fact that certain pretensions of the cities are well founded, invite the Athenians to be moderate. It is moreover difficult to say whether in this context ἐλευθέρους means all the subjects of Athens and their natural quality of free men, or the Mytilenians in particular and the relative liberty which they enjoyed within the Athenian empire. In my view, the first interpretation fits more easily into the rest of the argumenta-tion.

[2] See pp. 84-85.

And his ideas on this subject, which coincide with those of Thucydides himself, are from this point of view as logical and consistent as the analysis of the pseudo-Xenophon. This writer knows how inevitable is the hatred that subjects feel for their rulers;[1] he explains why Athens has no need to be afraid of her allies in the islands, — which suggests they would otherwise be dangerous (II, 2-3), and among the cities on the mainland, he declares that the larger ones obey through fear and the others through need; but he can also recognize that Athens profits from the support of the popular party: τὸ κάκιστον ἐν ἑκάστῃ ἐστὶ πόλει εὔνουν τῷ δήμῳ· οἱ γὰρ ὁμοῖοι τοῖς ὁμοίοις εὔνοοί εἰσιν (III, 10).[2] The ideas of the moderate Diodotus are no more revolutionary than this. He knows what the empire is like and has no intention of changing the way in which it is organized — unlike Aristophanes who, in the Lysistrata, wants the cities to be recognized as independent members of one body who will be assimilated rather than subjected to rule.[3] Diodotus proposes nothing like this. He agrees with Cleon as far as general facts are concerned: where he differs from him is in the way this empire should be administered.

What is peculiar to him is that, at the same time as he recognizes the hostility which Athenian rule everywhere encounters, he tries to preserve whatever may counterbalance this hostility. He refuses to deduce from an already bad situation a principle for deciding future action which would make this situation even worse. He does not consider that the fact of ruling by force implies a brutal and unreflecting use of it. His ideas, like those of Thucydides, tend to prevent Athens from moving further in a direction which he deplores. But he realizes that she is indeed in a very difficult position.

Once they are reduced to these more exact limits, his ideas remain independent of the problems raised in the other parts of Thucydides' work, and it is for this reason that it is difficult to place them in the

---

[1] See p. 125.

[2] In this very general form, the reflection is a commonplace in the fifth and fourth centuries. Cf. Kalinka's edition, where a certain number of examples are quoted, see also Euripides, Bellerophon, 298 N.

[3] 582: καὶ νὴ Δία τάς γε πόλεις ὁπόσαι τῆς γῆς τῆσδ᾽ εἰσὶν ἄποικοι,
διαγιγνώσκειν ὅτι ταῦθ᾽ ἡμῖν ὥσπερ τὰ κατάγματα κεῖται
χωρὶς ἕκαστον· κᾆτ᾽ ἀπὸ τούτων πάντων τὸ κάταγμα λαβόντας
δεῦρο ξυνάγειν καὶ ξυναθροίζειν εἰς ἓν κἄπειτα ποῆσαι
τολύπην μεγάλην κᾆτ᾽ ἐκ ταύτης τῷ δήμῳ χλαῖναν ὑφῆναι.

Beloch (Att. Pol. seit Per., p. 67) thinks that this was the only policy capable of saving Athens. Thucydides does not seem ever to have considered its possibility.

Athenian political tradition. It is nevertheless reasonable to assume
that a former supporter of Pericles should have approved of them.
The repression of the revolt of Histiaea by Pericles, however impressive it might have been, did not include the slaughter of the inhabitants. In the debate itself, Cleon is certainly presented as putting forward a more rigorous policy than the one previously followed, and
Diodotus twice contrasts the present state of affairs with what would
happen if a more severe policy were adopted.[1] Diodotus himself, of
course, is also innovating in a way, for he claims that he is putting
forward a policy which will be more successful than the one which
has shown itself to be inadequate on this occasion;[2] but this innova-
tion tends practically to restore maxims which are not new in themselves,[3] and, as far as its principle is concerned, it follows the ideas
expressed by Pericles. Of the two men taking part in this debate,
Cleon wishes to whip up the instincts of the people and exaggerate
Athenian habits, while Diodotus wishes to correct these habits by
reason and to teach the people prudence. By choosing to support
the attitude of Diodotus, Thucydides is judging events in exactly the
same way as he did in the first two books when he defended the
equally prudent policy of Pericles and his equally severe warnings.

However, there is a curious observation to be added to this
conclusion: it is that, in the detail of the argumentation, it is the words
put into Cleon's mouth that echo those used by Pericles.

[1] νῦν μέν . . . ἐκείνως δέ . . . (46. 2).

[2] This policy is in fact contrasted with the solutions that are now being applied; so in
46. 5: οὗ νῦν τοὐναντίον δρῶντες; the νῦν does not apply only to the case of Mytilene, as is
shown by the extreme generality of the proposition which immediately follows it: ἤν
τινα ἐλεύθερον . . . , χαλεπῶς οἰόμεθα χρῆναι τιμωρεῖσθαι. Louis Bodin has provided a
perfect analysis of this apparent contradiction in his article *Diodote contre Cléon*, pointing
out that while Diodotus wishes to keep the principle of being moderate towards the allied
cities, he also wishes to modify it since it has not proved sufficient to prevent defections.

[3] Bodin writes (p. 48, n. 2): 'Diodotus thus recommends a change in the policy adopted
towards the allies. He must have already done this in the preceding assembly, thereby
calling previous decisions into question.' And this would, in Bodin's view, account for
the passage in which Cleon says that laws should be kept. But it seems to me that the actual
words of the text do not allow such an interpretation: Thucydides, writing for his readers,
had a duty to be clear and could not leave them to guess such an important circumstance.
It seems, on the contrary, that the development on the ἀκινήτοις νόμοις, in keeping with
the authoritarian tone of the whole passage, aims at demanding that the prevailing rules
should always be followed, whatever their value might be. What Cleon says in 37. 3:
χείροσι νόμοις ἀκινήτοις χρωμένη πόλις κρείσσων ἢ καλῶς ἔχουσιν ἀκύροις ought to be
placed by the side of Alcibiades' remark in VI. 18. 7: ἀσφαλέστατα τούτους οἰκεῖν οἱ ἂν
τοῖς παροῦσιν ἤθεσι καὶ νόμοις, ἢν καὶ χείρω ᾖ, ἥκιστα διαφόρως πολιτεύωσιν. In neither
case is it a question of laws in the strict sense of the word.

The most immediately similar are clearly those used to define the empire. Thus in II. 63. 2: ὡς τυραννίδα γὰρ ἤδη ἔχετε αὐτήν, ἣν λαβεῖν μὲν ἄδικον δοκεῖ εἶναι, ἀφεῖναι δὲ ἐπικίνδυνον, and in III. 37. 2: οὐκ ἐπικινδύνως ἡγεῖσθε ἐς ὑμᾶς καὶ οὐκ ἐς τὴν τῶν ξυμμάχων χάριν μαλακίζεσθαι, οὐ σκοποῦντες ὅτι τυραννίδα ἔχετε τὴν ἀρχὴν καὶ πρὸς ἐπιβουλεύοντας αὐτοὺς καὶ ἄκοντας ἀρχομένους.[1]

But the echo between these two speeches is also repeated in less important remarks. When Cleon declares himself faithful to one point of view (38. 1): ἐγὼ μὲν οὖν ὁ αὐτός εἰμι τῇ γνώμῃ, Pericles had said (II. 61. 2): καὶ ἐγὼ μὲν ὁ αὐτός εἰμι καὶ οὐκ ἐξίσταμαι.[2] When Cleon is ironical at the expense of those who would practise virtue far away from all danger (40. 4): παύεσθαι τῆς ἀρχῆς καὶ ἐκ τοῦ ἀκινδύνου ἀνδραγαθίζεσθαι, Pericles had said (II. 63. 2): εἴ τις καὶ τόδε ... δεδιὼς ἀπραγμοσύνη ἀνδραγαθίζεται.[3] The fact that the verb ἀνδραγαθίζεσθαι is found at the classical epoch only in these two texts makes the similarity even more significant.

When we consider that Thucydides condemns Cleon but approves of Pericles, these concordances present something of a problem. Two different explanations have been put forward, but neither of them seems to correspond to the characteristics noted in the debate.

The first explanation is that of Schwartz. In his view, Pericles and Cleon presented similar ideas, but Thucydides approved of them in the first place and blamed them in the second. Thus the verbal similarities between the two texts are accidental and not intentional: they come from the similarity of the ideas put forward and betray a change in Thucydides' own attitude.

But one can wonder whether the idea of this change can be reconciled with the text of the debate. Have we not seen that Diodotus does not differ from Cleon in so far as both speakers deal with the real

---

[1] We have here a similarity of thought which continues even when there are no precise verbal parallels; thus both men have equal fear as regards the allies (III. 40. 5: ἃ εἰκὸς ἦν αὐτοὺς ποιῆσαι κρατήσαντας ὑμῶν = II. 63. 1: κινδύνου ὢν ἐν τῇ ἀρχῇ ἀπήχθεσθε.

[2] See also I. 140. 1: τῆς μὲν γνώμης, ὦ Ἀθηναῖοι, αἰεὶ τῆς αὐτῆς ἔχομαι.

[3] Cleon is here ironically suggesting a solution which Pericles had declared to be impossible (see p. 127). Now the group of words in which he puts it forward breaks the regular design of the sentence; but it is wrong to see in this, as Steup does, a proof that the passage was to be revised and corrected. Cleon should in fact consider two possibilities: for if Athenian rule is unjustified, this consideration can either stop or not stop Athens from acting as she does. However, being a true realist, Cleon considers only the second possibility as something serious (εἰ δὲ δὴ καὶ οὐ προσῆκον ὅμως ἀξιοῦτε τοῦτο δρᾶν): the first is rejected in a subordinate clause: ἢ παύεσθαι ('or, if not, stop . . . '). The very lack of symmetry in the sentence forms part of its meaning.

nature of the empire, or with the view of it as a tyranny? Is there anything to suggest that this view is here being criticized? Because, on the
whole, Thucydides seems to disapprove of Cleon's speech and to
approve of those of Pericles, Schwartz has rather hastily concluded
that the themes which both speakers have in common are blamed in
one place and approved of in the other. This is not a legitimate
inference, nor can it be proved that the similarities in question imply
a change of mind on the part of Thucydides.

Now the second explanation assumes that these similarities are
quite deliberate and that, if they stress what the two men have in
common, it is in order to make the comparison clearer. For the
parallel — and this is the main fact — soon comes to an end. Cleon is
only copying some of Pericles' words, and, by underlining the
apparent similarities between the two, Thucydides only intends to
point out the difference between them more clearly. Cleon, in fact,
repeats Pericles' views on the empire, but does so in order to deduce
a glorification of force which Pericles had not recommended; where
Pericles wanted 'not to give up', Cleon wishes to 'punish severely'.
Similarly, what is perseverance in one case is sheer obstinacy in the
other. It is this idea that both Adcock and Pohlenz express when one
speaks of a *reductio ad absurdum* of the imperialist policy of Pericles,[1]
and the other of a caricature of this policy.[2]

However, the satirical intention which these scholars attribute to
Thucydides fits in no better with the actual characteristics of the
debate than did the first explanation. Did Thucydides really want us
to understand that, although the general view about the empire was
that of Pericles the conclusions drawn by the two men were in fact
different? Then why did he not use the very structure of the debate to
make that distinction quite clear? Diodotus, it is true, is not discussing
the idea of the tyrant city, but — and this is a remarkable feature —
we had to pay some attention before we could be sure of it: the
speech does not say it in so many words and is obviously not intended to point it out. Now is it not rather odd, if Thucydides had
wanted us to see where Cleon was wrong and where he differed
from Pericles, that he should not have been careful to show the exact
distinction? Is it not surprising that he should have so systematically

---

[1] *C.A.H.*, V, p. 217.
[2] I, p. 129. See also Zahn, p. 65: 'so macht er damit aufs wirksamte den Abstand der
beiden Männer voreinander fühlbar, bei denen sich in denselben Worten eine völlig
verschiedene Geistesart und Gesinnung ausspricht.'

M

underlined the similarities and yet not used the debate itself to show where the difference lay?

When we have made the necessary effort of analysis, we see that Schwartz is wrong. But the very fact that this analysis is necessary proves the inadequacy of the other view.

Moreover, these similarities are neither of the type nor of the importance to indicate that they are very significant. The ἐγὼ μὲν οὖν ὁ αὐτός εἰμι is quite a simple phrase, which in both cases is closely related to the circumstances under which the speech was made. The use of ἀνδραγαθίζεσθαι indicates neither a genuine similarity nor a real contrast. Cleon, like Pericles, is hostile towards the opponents of imperialism; he uses only irony but Pericles adds argument. Yet what conclusion can be drawn from this as to Thucydides' real intentions? Would it not be more natural to think that, in spite of the fact that we have no other examples of this use of the word, it was frequently employed by imperialists to describe their opponents? Cleon may have actually used it, and he may in reality have taken it from Pericles, and Thucydides may have been aware of it, but there is no reason to think that he had any deep motive in repeating the same expression. The idea of the empire as a tyranny provides no more really convincing evidence, for if, as we have already seen, it was by no means revolutionary when used by Pericles, why should it not be found in the mouth of other speakers? If Euphemus and the Corinthians talk like Pericles, then why should not Cleon?

In fact such similarities express a state of affairs which is obvious to all imperialists; they can serve to define and confront the two successive leaders of Athenian imperialism. Consequently, Thucydides cannot reproduce any of their speeches without leading us to use elements of this nature both to contrast and compare them and he may have enjoyed the opportunity. Yet such points of comparison as he does provide are not sufficiently emphasized, and cannot imply that the whole debate was meant to provide a contrast.[1]

Thus, from one text to the other, there is neither a complete

---

[1] Classen considers that Cleon is deliberately imitating Pericles but draws no conclusion as to why Thucydides makes him do this. His explanation is thus more prudent than that of other scholars, but at the same time it loses some of its meaning: if one does not take into consideration the strictly verbal resemblances like ἀνδραγαθίζεσθαι, ἐγὼ μὲν ὁ αὐτός εἰμι (which belong specifically to Thucydides' work, since this is not a textual reproduction of speeches actually made), the relationship between the two speeches is reduced to a very simple idea which is almost inherent in any theory of imperialism, and which implies no 'imitation' at all in the strict sense of the word.

change of attitude nor a systematic coherence. Both texts exist, without contradicting each other but without necessarily referring to each other in more than some details.

However, this very independence is worth noting. By failing to give a clear indication, in the actual composition of the debate, of what was right and what was wrong, Thucydides in no way considered that he was running the risk of discrediting certain ideas that he had praised elsewhere, or of confusing notions that he had elsewhere distinguished from one another. He paid no attention at all to this possibility. He was concerned with other things and with other aspects of the problem. For a writer who elsewhere shows such conviction and such concern for coherence, the fact is rather surprising.

We shall doubtless conclude that it was normal for an admirer of Pericles to show the superiority of Diodotus over Cleon; but also that it was not absolutely normal for the author of Pericles' last speech to prove this superiority by the debate we are now discussing, unless his thoughts were, in both cases, turned towards different objectives.

It is on this question that a study of the dating of the passage might throw some light.

Certain scholars have maintained that this section contains signs of having been written late. They include, in addition to Eduard Meyer, both R. Zahn and Pohlenz, and they base their arguments upon the subject-matter of the debate. In its concern with the chances of survival for the Athenian empire, this debate is said to form part of a vast collection of speeches which all deal with events from a fairly detached standpoint and which all study the problem of Athenian imperialism. The debate on Mytilene is said to have its place in this series between Pericles' last speech and the dialogue between the Athenians and the Melians. By criticizing Cleon's views, the analysis is thus said to contain a judgment comparable to that of Isocrates at the end of the *Antidosis*, in which he curses the sycophants who ruined everything by their harsh treatment of the allies. Moreover this analysis is said to have provided Thucydides with the opportunity to bring out the close relationship between the question of the allies and the conduct of hostilities, a relationship whose full importance he could only have realized towards the last part of the war.[1]

---

[1] This theory can also be based upon the τότε of 36. 6: τῷ τε δήμῳ παρὰ πολὺ ἐν τῷ τότε πιθανώτατος. But I shall not take such an argument into consideration: Thucy-

Although apparently satisfactory, this solution is not very probable or very suited to the actual characteristics of the text.

It will be noted, first of all, that in both speeches, it is impossible to suppose that we can find traces of revision or alteration: the construction of the debate is much too subtle and much too precise for anything to be removed. But then, the episode of Mytilene in general also forms another whole whose unity cannot be called in question and which can scarcely have been added at a later date: by all the different facts which it brings into play (certain of which are absolutely essential in the narration of events, like the invasion of Attica and the actual defection of Mytilene), the episode is a corner stone of this part of the work. Now this part contains a number of passages which rule out the idea of its being entirely a late composition. If there ever was an original version, then it included the explanations about the earthquakes in III. 89; it must therefore also have contained the narration of events which takes up the beginning of Book III. The debate, which forms part of this narration, would thus also form part of this original version.

The way in which the debate is composed confirms this hypothesis, for it does not really fulfil the function assigned to it by the scholars whose theory we are now discussing. The debate is concerned not with imperialism itself but with its methods, or rather with the particular method that it ought to adopt towards defections. The contrast between the two speeches is on the very question of what action should be taken. Moreover, even when we consider only this precise question, the debate reveals more dialectical subtlety than historical insistence. The problem is thoroughly dealt with, but the two theories are simply contrasted with each other: they are not analysed for their own sake, with all the arguments for or against, and their implications. It is this which explains why the themes developed are of a rather general nature.[1] For the most part, one can recognize in passing a number of ideas which are commonplaces in the fifth century, and which therefore cannot be taken as characteristic of the problem under discussion: the danger which Athens runs

[1] Sometimes, on the other hand, these themes are so closely linked to the case of Mytilene that they could not be valid for any other. (39. 1-2).

dides is writing for eternity, and he is transforming present-day events into history; even if he had written on the day after the debate, would he have written νῦν? — Obviously not. And in any case, a τότε is easily added.

because of eloquent orators is a mere banality, for, in the very year in which the revolt of Mytilene took place, the theme appeared in the *Hippolytus* of Euripides;[1] the whole of the section on the utility of punishment (which, in Plato, is linked with the problem of whether or not virtue can be taught) seems to have been a favourite subject with the sophists;[2] similarly, when Cleon attacks the Athenians for their instability, he is so unoriginal that he is, for once, in agreement with Aristophanes.[3] Since both speeches reflect such familiar ideas, it can be said that, while gaining in dialectical power, they forfeit some of their value as history. They take up contrary positions on a particular problem, but do not put forward any political theories in relation to it.

If one admits, *a priori*, a difference between the speeches written at the same time as the main narrative and those which Thucydides, having a definite problem in mind, introduced later in order to emphasize an important idea; and if one also admits that such speeches would naturally be characterized both by their concern with a single theme and by their wider general significance,[4] it must be noted that the debate on Mytilene, far from having any of the features proper to the second class, seems rather to belong to the first.

The episode of Mytilene is the drama of the rebellious city, and as such is naturally contrasted with that of Plataea, the faithful city. These two episodes are as it were set off one against the other in Book III, and they give rise to contradictory debates concerned with the particular problems that they create.

In both cases the event is one whose effect was certainly considerable and whose importance was immediately perceived. We have already seen, in fact, that the ξυμμάχων ἀπόστασις had certainly been considered from the very beginning as one of the possible means of acting against Athens. The revolt of Mytilene provided the first rather

---

[1] 487: καλοὶ λίαν λόγοι. Cf. *Hecuba*, 132.

[2] See especially Plato, *Protagoras*, 324b, and compare with Euripides *Iph. Aul.*, 558 ff., *Suppl.*, 913; *Hecuba*, 595 ff. In Euripides the discussions often do not fit very well into the context (*Hecuba*, 603), which underlines the fact that they are justified essentially by a kind of intellectual fashion.

[3] In the parabasis of the *Acharnians*, Aristophanes makes fun of the quickness with which the Athenians change their minds: 630 = ταχυβούλοις, and later: μεταβούλοις.

[4] The speeches reintroduced later into the work tend to develop the wider implications of the subject, since they are written with a more general experience in mind, but they also tend to be more directly relevant to it, since they are written for a particular purpose. The difference established by Pohlenz, and after him by Schadewaldt, between the original speeches, which showed less freedom, and the late ones, which were more free, is but another expression of this obvious circumstance.

dramatic realization of this project. Sparta had not played a very big part in this affair, and Brasidas was to do much better. Even supposing — which seems to me very unlikely — that Cleon's contemporaries should have been able, after Mytilene, to doubt the seriousness of this question, they could certainly not have kept on doing so after what happened in Thrace.[1] Even supposing that the events accompanying the ephemeral condemnation and the subsequent pardon of Mytilene should have passed unnoticed at the time,[2] this certainly could not still have been the case after the massacre at Scione. Besides the Ἀθηναίων Πολιτεία of the Pseudo-Xenophon is sufficient proof of the importance, even of the gravity, of the danger which the problem of the κάθεξις τῆς ἀρχῆς presented for Athens from the very beginning of the war.[3]

It thus appears more normal to consider the debate on Mytilene, and the episode in general, as belonging to the 'earlier' version of the work.

This hypothesis, by giving the episode and the debate a date different from that of Pericles' last speech and the judgment in II. 65, explains both certain differences in detail between these texts and the more general differences of inspiration which have been noted above.

For instance, it does seem that Pericles' words fit in with a reality with which the speakers in the debate do not seem to be acquainted. Both Pericles and Cleon mention the threat which the hatred felt by her subjects, who wish to kill their former masters, causes to hang over Athens; but, in Cleon's speech, this idea is accompanied by a particular explanation (III. 40. 5): he explains the violence which the Mytilenians would have shown, if their revolt had been successful, by saying that they would have feared reprisals: τὸν κίνδυνον ὑφορώμενοι τοῦ ὑπολειπομένου ἐχθροῦ· ὁ γὰρ μὴ ξὺν ἀνάγκῃ τ

---

[1] Even if the sections dealing with Brasidas are of a late date (cf. pp. 45-46), there is no question of his importance ever being passed over.

[2] Aristophanes, although he never misses an opportunity to attack Cleon's behaviour and particularly where his relationship with the allies is concerned, makes so little mention of the episode at present under discussion that, in the Knights, he chooses to illustrate the δωροδοκία of Cleon by showing him as having received bribes from the Mytilenians. (The figure of 40 minae mentioned in line 835 excludes any possibility of a reference to the debate we are now discussing; cf. Müller-Strübing, p. 361.) But this silence is not very convincing proof, for comedy is concerned only with the most striking events, and cannot perhaps take account of a proposition which came to nothing.

[3] In this respect, the debate about Mytilene is merely a continuation of the analysis of forces made in Book I.

παθὼν χαλεπώτερος διαφυγὼν τοῦ ἀπὸ τῆς ἴσης ἐχθροῦ. Now this explanation has no longer any meaning after the disaster of 404, and Pericles in fact omits it in order to speak only of the hatred felt for Athens by her subjects. Both Pericles and Cleon mention those who would like to act virtuously, but while Cleon speaks of them with an ironical contempt, which would no longer be possible in 404, Pericles feels the need to argue with them. In both cases, the different circumstances under which the speeches were written might explain the slight divergence in the arguments put forward.

These different circumstances explain even more clearly the different direction taken by the ideas of each speaker, and enable us to mark off another section of the path followed by Thucydides.

While in his judgment in II. 65 Thucydides seems particularly concerned to underline the difference between Pericles and his successors, he here makes no effort at all to mark the contrast between Pericles and Cleon. In fact he even allows the uninformed reader to confuse some of the ideas of Cleon with those of Pericles. The explanation is that between the composition of the debate on Mytilene and the judgment in II. 65, there was an interval: the contrast which had previously seemed unimportant turned out to be essential, and the attacks of the opposition, now triumphant, called for precise justification.

In the same manner, while Thucydides, in the speech which precedes II. 65, apparently wants to put forward a general defence of imperialism, in the debate on Mytilene he considers imperialism as an established fact and recommends, on the contrary, the greatest moderation. The reason again is that between the writing of the two passages, the most dangerous adversary and the most urgent problem have changed. The collapse of the empire and the success of the opposition explain this change of emphasis; they justify Thucydides' neglect of the discussions between imperialists (which have now become out of date), and his concentration on the principle of imperialism itself (which has now become of the utmost importance): his opinions have not altered, but his preoccupations are no longer the same.

The extent of this slight change of emphasis can, however, be more accurately indicated when we have seen what judgment he makes of the episode of Pylos, and have been able to compare it with his views on Mytilene.

II. The Affair of Pylos

The affair of Pylos takes place, in Thucydides, in two distinct acts,
and Cleon is directly concerned only in the second.[2] However, even
though his role in the first act remains strictly negative, it is nevertheless of the greatest political consequence, for it is he who causes the
Spartan peace proposals to be rejected.[3] This decision is sufficiently
important in Thucydides' eyes to justify the presence of a speech
made by the Spartans and of a new presentation of Cleon himself.[4]

This refusal of peace interests us in the same way as does the acceptance of war; and, by the motives which Thucydides attributes to this
rejection, it very closely concerns the question of Athenian imperialism.

Now, it is presented in a way which leaves no doubt at all as to
Thucydides' own opinion of it. Carried out by means of bad faith and
devoid of any justification, it is presented quite obviously as being an
act completely contrary to political wisdom. And Thucydides does
not fail to recall, at the time of the peace of Nicias (V. 41. 1 and
V. 15. 2), that the Athenians, who let a good opportunity go by,
then regretted their mistake.[5]

We can go even further, and say that Thucydides' own view of the
question is visible in the speech which he puts into the mouth of the
Spartans.

The very presence of this speech implies an intention on Thucydides' part, and it is obvious that he intends to use it in order to convey

---

[1] One has in fact a series of chapters allocated in the following manner.

I. { 8-14 : in Pylos / 15-22 : in Athens / 23 : in Pylos }   II. { 26 : in Pylos / 27-28 : in Athens / 29-41 : in Pylos }

[2] He plays the part of a buffoon: his success can be explained by a mere stroke of luck
and by the efficiency of Demosthenes. In order to make quite sure that his reader is under
no mistake about this, Thucydides makes a point of giving a direct judgment on his
proposition: 39. 3: καίπερ μανιώδης οὖσα.

[3] He just managed to obtain the approval of the people (Philochorus, fr. 105); but his
role, as in the case of Mytilene, is to encourage the people to follow its own impulse, cf.
p. 203.

[4] There are also two presentations of Pericles (I. 127. 3 and I. 139. 4), and two presentations of Alcibiades (V. 43. 2 and VI. 15. 2). In these cases, the first presentation is necessary
in order to make the passage clear while the second stresses the decisive intervention of the
character in question and throws all the light on it.

[5] Their regret is nevertheless more over the subsequent embassies: μετὰ τὰ ἐν Πύλῳ,
V. 14. 2, might leave some doubt, but μετὰ τὴν ἅλωσιν, in V. 15. 2, dismisses all possibility
of hesitation. The proposals to make peace which the Athenians regret not having
accepted are those in IV. 41. 3-4 which are not dealt with in any speech in Thucydides:
they were made at the time of Athens' greatest prosperity. On the reasons for Thucydides'
choice cf. later p. 177.

the lesson of the events. The Spartans are here given a speech while the Athenians, when they undertake a similar action, are not, as Dionysius of Halicarnassus points out,[1] treated in the same way. Thus the embassy which the Spartans send has a particular meaning and serves to bring out a particular idea. Moreover, they are given a speech to ask for peace, while Cleon, who refuses their request, is not treated in the same way. The idea must therefore be brought out by means of this one speech. Forgetful once again of the rules of εὐβουλία, and acting once again through passion or personal ambition rather than through reason, Cleon does not really represent a particular thesis; he has no more λόγος to express than had the adversaries of Pericles. Then, as now, the speaker to whom no one replies is the spokesman of wisdom.

When the Spartans put forward the reasons which should have persuaded the Athenians to make peace, we can thus assume that Thucydides is more or less giving his own judgment of the situation.

This is confirmed by the relationship which he establishes between what the Spartans say and what the narrative tells.

In the first part of their speech (17. 4-19), the Spartans analyse the unwisdom of refusing peace: it would mean yielding – as one so commonly does – to the temptation of hubris, which consists of basing excessive hopes on a success due to mere good fortune (IV. 17. 4): ὑμῖν γὰρ εὐτυχίαν τὴν παροῦσαν ἔξεστι καλῶς θέσθαι, ἔχουσι μὲν ὧν κρατεῖτε, προσλαβοῦσι δὲ τιμὴν καὶ δόξαν, καὶ μὴ παθεῖν ὅπερ οἱ ἀήθως τι ἀγαθὸν λαμβάνοντες τῶν ἀνθρώπων· αἰεὶ γὰρ τοῦ πλέονος ἐλπίδι ὀρέγονται διὰ τὸ καὶ τὰ παρόντα ἀδοκήτως εὐτυχῆσαι. Their analysis is based upon the two terms of good luck[2] and immoderate hopes.

---

[1] Dionysius of Halicarnassus shows an unparalleled failure to understand the principles on which Thucydides' work is based; he thus proceeds to pick out carefully as 'defects' in Thucydides all the passages in which, in order to make his different intentions clear, Thucydides moved away from a mechanical reproduction of the facts. In his *On Thucydides*, chapter XIV, he is quite indignant because, of the two embassies sent to ask for peace, the first, that of the Athenians, is dealt with in an off-hand manner in II. 59, without any information being given about the names of the ambassadors or the kind of speeches they made (φαύλως δέ πως καὶ ῥαθύμως, ὡς περὶ μικρῶν καὶ ἀδόξων πραγμάτων ταῦτα εἴρηκε) while the other embassy, that of the Spartans, is dealt with in detail. Such an unequal treatment is unjustifiable in his view, and he cannot explain why Thucydides should have chosen to concern himself with the embassy from Sparta: οὐκ ἔχω συμβαλεῖν κατὰ τί τὴν Λακωνικὴν προέκρινε τῆς Ἀττικῆς μᾶλλον (XV).

[2] They insist in a general way on the important role played by chance; cf. 18. 3: καὶ τὸ τῆς τύχης οἴεσθαι αἰεὶ μεθ' ὑμῶν ἔσεσθαι; 18. 4: ὡς ἂν αἱ τύχαι αὐτῶν ἡγήσωνται – ἐν τῷ εὐτυχεῖν; 18. 5: νομισθῆναι τύχῃ καὶ τὰ νῦν προχωρήσαντα κρατῆσαι.

Now Thucydides himself uses the same words and his account of events emphasizes two ideas: the Athenians have been lucky and they have not been able to moderate their desires.

They were lucky in the first battle at Pylos. Certainly the clearsightedness shown by Demosthenes, who keeps a strict control over events, does play a large part in the success of the enterprise, and this fact is made obvious by the verbal similarities between his speech and the actual description of the battle.[1] But Thucydides makes a point of remarking that chance also had a part to play: it was chance that produced the bad weather which held up the fleet and gave the soldiers the desire to fortify the place (3. 1: κατὰ τύχην χειμὼν ἐπιγενόμενος); it was chance that a festival prevented the Spartans from intervening (5. 1: οἱ δὲ ἑορτήν τινα ἔτυχον ἄγοντες); it was chance that the two Messenian ships which Demosthenes was able to use arrived (9. 1: οἳ ἔτυχον παραγενόμενοι); and it was chance again that the harbour mouths were not closed up (13. 4: οὔτε, ἃ διενοήθησαν, φάρξαι τοὺς ἔσπλους ἔτυχον ποιήσαντες); finally, the first Athenian success is presented as being due to good fortune (14. 3: τῇ παρούσῃ τύχῃ ὡς ἐπὶ πλεῖστον ἐπεξελθεῖν).

And, then, this stroke of luck exalts Athens: from this moment Thucydides insists several times on the fact that she wants more and more again; if she rejects the Spartan proposals, it is because she is inflamed with the desire to get more (21. 2: τοῦ δὲ πλέονος ὠρέγοντο);[2]

---

[1] One can easily verify this by referring to two essential factors among those which he indicates: the difficulty of landing on the shore and, as a consequence, the need to fight in small groups. One has, in fact:

{ Demosthenes: τοῦ τε γὰρ χωρίου τὸ δυσέμβατον (10. 3).
{ narration: ἀδύνατοι δ' ἦσαν ἀποβῆναι (12. 2).

{ Demosthenes: κατ' ὀλίγον γὰρ μαχεῖται, καίπερ πολὺ ὄν, ἀπορίᾳ τῆς προσορμίσεως (10. 4).
{ narration: οἱ δὲ κατ' ὀλίγας ναῦς διελόμενοι διότι οὐκ ἦν πλείοσι προσσχεῖν (11. 3).

[2] This motive is certainly that of the Athenians, and Cleon intervenes only to encourage them. Some writers have considered that he also was inspired by imperial ambition: the answer to the problem depends on the way in which one reads the analysis of his motives in V. 16. 1 and interprets it. If one keeps to the text of the manuscripts, there are two possible meanings: both Cleon and Brasidas sought to establish the supremacy *of* their own city (Lange, Müller-Strübing); or, according to Bekker and Bothe, their own supremacy *in* their city. If one eliminates ἡγεμονίαν, the sentence becomes more normal: τότε δή then marks the beginning of the *apodosis*, and this part of the sentence no longer refers to the motives of the two supporters of war; one reads: τὰ μάλιστ' αὐτήν (= εἰρήνην) and the clause then deals with the two supporters of peace (Stahl, Hude, Steup). This last explanation is much more satisfactory. In any case, it is rather difficult to see how the word ἡγεμονία could represent the aim of imperial ambitions.

if she rejects them again in 41. 4, it is because she is inflamed again with desire of getting more (οἱ δὲ μειζόνων τε ὠρέγοντο); if she condemns commanders who have not achieved anything in Sicily, it is because the unexpected successes which she has enjoyed have greatly increased her hopes;[1] and here Thucydides intervenes in his own name in order to analyse (and blame) the attitude of the Athenians (IV. 65. 4: οὕτω τῇ γε παρούσῃ εὐτυχίᾳ χρώμενοι ἠξίουν σφίσι μηδὲν ἐναντιοῦσθαι, ἀλλὰ καὶ τὰ δυνατὰ ἐν ἴσῳ καὶ τὰ ἀπορώτερα μεγάλῃ τε ὁμοίως καὶ ἐνδεεστέρᾳ παρασκευῇ κατεργάζεσθαι· αἰτία δ' ἦν ἡ παρὰ λόγον τῶν πλειόνων εὐπραγία αὐτοῖς ὑποτιθεῖσα ἰσχὺν τῆς ἐλπίδος); finally, when he recalls this refusal of a peaceful settlement in Book V, he cannot prevent himself from once again explaining the reasons that brought it about (V. 14. 1: οὐκ ἔχοντες τὴν ἐλπίδα τῆς ῥώμης πιστὴν ἔτι, ἧπερ οὐ προσεδέχοντο πρότερον τὰς σπονδὰς δοκοῦντες τῇ παρούσῃ εὐτυχίᾳ καθυπέρτεροι γενήσεσθαι). In both these two texts just quoted, the link between the prosperity brought about by good fortune and the desire to have more is made quite explicit by Thucydides, just as in the speech by the Spartans in Book IV.

The arguments put forward by the Spartans thus seem to have been constructed in close relationship with the narration of events, and to translate Thucydides' own ideas. Of course, in making the Spartans speak in this manner, Thucydides in no way departed from the arguments that they could in fact have put forward, and it is certainly very much in keeping with Spartan tradition to preach the virtues of moderation.[2] However, by the very authority of its tone, this speech reveals its real function: Thucydides himself recognizes that there is something unusual about the speech (17. 2: παρὰ τὸ εἰωθός), and, in spite of the precautions which the Spartans take, in 17. 3, it is rather striking to see the vanquished reminding the victors of the principles of political wisdom (τοῦ καλῶς βουλεύσασθαι);[3] however much they may say that the Athenians know all this already, their excuse is not

---

[1] This action seems to be independent of the affair at Pylos, but Thucydides links it up with the same ideas, cf. p. 41.

[2] In Book I, Archidamus insists upon the σωφροσύνη ἔμφρων of his country (I. 84. 2: μόνοι γὰρ δι' αὐτὸ εὐπραγίαις τε οὐκ ἐξυβρίζομεν ...); and Thucydides himself declares, in VIII. 24. 4: Χῖοι γὰρ μόνοι μετὰ Λακεδαιμονίους ὧν ἐγὼ ᾐσθόμην ηὐδαιμόνησάν τε ἅμα καὶ ἐσωφρόνησαν, καὶ ὅσῳ ἐπεδίδου ἡ πόλις αὐτῶν ἐπὶ τὸ μεῖζον, τόσῳ καὶ ἐκοσμοῦντο ἐχυρώτερον.

[3] There is noticeable similarity between the aim of Diodotus and of the Spartan ambassadors; also, the same criticism seems to be implied as regards Cleon.

really valid:[1] their remarks are less suited to Spartan ambassadors than to one of those men whom Thucydides, in IV. 28. 5, calls: οἱ σώφρονες τῶν ἀνθρώπων or, if one prefers, to Thucydides himself; and the whole of this first, negative part of the speech, can be considered as putting forward his own ideas.

He contrasts it, in the second part of the speech, with the programme of restricted ambition which Athens ought to have kept to. There, the speakers do in fact show what advantages a peace treaty signed at that moment would have: even if Athens were to enjoy further successes by pursuing the war, she would nevertheless find some profit in putting an end to hostilities; for what the Spartans are now offering her is something more than peace: it is a general friendly and happy relationship (19. 1: εἰρήνην καὶ ξυμμαχίαν καὶ ἄλλην φιλίαν πολλὴν καὶ οἰκειότητα ἐς ἀλλήλους); they show that the present hostility[2] between the two peoples would be made worse by further Athenian successes, insist on the advantages to be found in a genuine peaceful understanding between the two peoples,[3] and conclude by recalling the authority which they could both enjoy in Greece (20. 4: ἡμῶν γὰρ καὶ ὑμῶν ταὐτὰ λεγόντων τό γε ἄλλο Ἑλληνικὸν ἴστε ὅτι ὑποδεέστερον ὂν τὰ μέγιστα τιμήσει).

Here once again the Spartan ambassadors are fulfilling their own role, and it is even highly probable that the proposals which they put forward to the Athenians were expressed in a spirit comparable to the one which we find here; this at least is what Aristophanes would seem to suggest, when he too refers, several years later, to the possibility of Athens and Sparta 'after having reached agreement, ruling over Greece together'.[4] But the ideas expressed still remain those of Thucydides himself, and they indicate what meaning he intended to be attributed to the episode. It is precisely because the possibility did then exist of achieving a lasting peace that he blames the folly of the Athenians: Athens could then have reached an

---

[1] The complete formula is rather striking: ὑπόμνησιν τοῦ καλῶς βουλεύσασθαι πρὸς εἰδότας ἡγησάμενοι. It is even more noticeable in that it is different from the traditional formula about μακρηγορεῖν ἐν εἰδόσι, which is generally used for deliberate omission; thus in II. 36. 4; IV. 59. 2; VI. 77. 1. The untimely insistence of the Spartan ambassadors is thus openly admitted.

[2] It is a question of the *feeling* which divides the two peoples (ἔχθρα): see 19. 2; 20. 1.

[3] The expression used in 20. 4 (καὶ ἐν τούτῳ τὰ ἐνόντα ἀγαθὰ σκοπεῖτε ὅσα εἰκὸς εἶναι) leads one to expect an enumeration (which is, moreover, normal in the *epilogos*: cf. IV. 64. 5): now all the advantages are in fact to be found in this single programme, whose importance thus comes out more clearly.

[4] For this piece of evidence, see later p. 187.

understanding with Sparta and shared dominion over Greece with her. That is why Thucydides gave a speech to the members of the first embassy and not the second or third; the first embassy came before Cleon's success, whereas the two others followed it; now, the easiest and most common attitude would consist of regretting one's failure to come to terms at the moment of greatest prosperity, and it is this attitude which the Athenians adopt in V. 14. 2 and V. 15. 2. Thucydides, however, blames the Athenians for not having come to terms before this, at the time most suited for the creation of a lasting peace.

This intention also has its echo in the actual narration of events. After having refused to make peace, Athens does not undergo the defeats with which she was threatened, but achieves an unexpected victory, and then, some years later, negotiates an agreement. But, in Thucydides' view, she is then starting negotiations too late, at a time when reconciliation is no longer possible and when a lasting peace cannot be established. Nicias himself, the very author of the peace treaty, states this in terms which recall those used by the Spartans (VI. 10. 2: καὶ οἴεσθε ἴσως τὰς γενομένας ὑμῖν σπονδὰς ἔχειν τι βέβαιον); he explains that Sparta will use the first opportunity to make trouble for Athens, since, for her, peace has been concluded in humiliating conditions, after a series of reverses (οἶς πρῶτον μὲν διὰ ξυμφορῶν ἡ ξύμβασις καὶ ἐκ τοῦ αἰσχίονος ἢ ἡμῖν κατ᾽ ἀνάγκην ἐγένετο). Athenagoras also is aware of this same situation, and recalls how precarious peace is (VI. 36. 4: τὸν ἐκεῖ πόλεμον μήπω βεβαίως καταλελυμένους).

By the light which it throws on later events, the second part of the speech made by the Peloponnesians thus expresses Thucydides' own opinion even more precisely than does the first.

Now, the programme put forward in this second part of this speech is one with which we are quite familiar: it is the programme of Cimon, that of limited imperialism, that of the Panhellenic theories. For if one agrees to call 'Panhellenic' any policy which creates the unity of Greece in opposition to the barbarians, or at least by excluding them, then it is only by a temporary accident that this word can be made to fit the policy followed for a time by Pericles, grouping all the Greeks together in enterprises which were always centred upon Athens. Sparta also had her part to play, and the Athenians had either to fight against her (which was the programme of real Athenian imperialism, and led the Greeks to fight amongst themselves), or else reach an understanding with her in order to achieve Greek unity. This had already been hoped for by Athenians like Cimon, and later on Callicratidas in Sparta and Callistratus in Athens were to hope for the same thing.[1] This policy is often expressed by metaphors taken from the most ordinary 'pairs': Plutarch quotes the remark by Cimon which made a particularly deep impression on the Athenians: Cimon had asked them not to leave Greece lame in one leg, and not to deprive the city of her 'yoked partner'.[2] Leptines also mentions the idea that Greece must not be left 'with only one eye'.[3] In general, such theories take 'Greece' as their centre, and are based either upon a fairly clear feeling of Greek unity and brotherhood (such as are expressed in Herodotus VIII, 144) or upon a fairly clear feeling of the difference between Greeks and barbarians. It is this, for example, which decides Callicratidas, who said that the Greeks were extremely unfortunate in having to pay court to the barbarians in order to obtain money and even declared that 'if he got home safe and sound he would do his utmost to bring about a settlement between the Athenians and the Spartans'.[4] Now Thucydides does not himself insist upon this point, first of all because his ideas do not involve any Panhellenic theory,[5] and secondly because the circumstances which he is describing do not involve it either. In his work, the theory is put forward in the form of a political agreement concerning only Athens and Sparta;[6] in this respect, it can be compared with the remarks made to the Spartans by the Athenian Callistratus, in the *Hellenica*, VI, 3, 14-17. If Athens and Sparta were united, explains Callistratus, they would no longer need to fear anyone: no one would dare attack them on sea because of Athens or on land because of Sparta; by limiting their respective ambitions they could thus, working together, attain a new power: οὕτω γὰρ ἡμεῖς τ' ἂν δι' ὑμᾶς καὶ ὑμεῖς δι' ἡμᾶς ἔτι μείζους ἢ τὸν παρελθόντα χρόνον ἐν τῇ Ἑλλάδι ἀναστρεφοίμεθα.[7] The parallel between this text and that of Thucydides is

---

[1] See later, note 7.

[2] Plutarch, *Cimon*, 16, 10: μήτε τὴν Ἑλλάδα χωλήν, μήτε τὴν πόλιν ἑτερόζυγα περιϊδεῖν γεγενημένην.

[3] Aristotle, *Rhet.*, 1411 a, 5.   [4] Xenophon, *Hell.*, I, 6, 7.

[5] See p. 100.

[6] 'The Greeks' are mentioned, and what they will gain is mentioned also, but the development immediately moves towards a consideration of the point of view of their leaders. Neither their happiness nor their unity is taken into consideration, but only the possibility of their submission.

[7] See Cloché, *La Politique de l'Athénien Callistratos*, R.E.A., 1923, p. 18. These are, he says, 'ideas of Cimon'.

sufficient to indicate the unity of the political tradition to which both are referring.

It is this tradition that Thucydides was following when he composed the speech of the Spartan ambassadors.

Such a position seems completely opposed to the imperialistic and anti-Spartan ideas that he expressed when talking about Pericles. Here, once again, this opposition can be explained either by a difference in the political circumstances (that is to say an objective difference) or by a difference in the ideas by which Thucydides is inspired (that is to say a subjective difference). And, as in the previous cases, these two interpretations have both been suggested.

Eduard Meyer devotes a brilliant analysis[1] to showing that the action of Cleon and the democrats is, in the whole of this section of the work, completely opposed to the tradition of Pericles. The very affair of Pylos itself, which represents an attacking policy, is completely contrary to the defensive strategy of Pericles. And if Pericles wanted war, it was in his eyes exclusively a defensive one; he had himself drawn up the treaty of partition of 446 according to which Athens retained the sea and gave up the land: he would therefore have been perfectly willing to conclude a lasting peace with Sparta in 425.

Pohlenz, in contrast, sees a purely subjective difference, originating in a modification of Thucydides' own ideas. This modification would not, it is true, be concerned with the respective advantages of peace and war: as Pericles declares, there are no grounds for hesitation if one really has the choice;[2] it is solely a question of whether this choice does exist. Holding the view that the episode of Pylos was written early, Pohlenz maintains[3] that Thucydides had not started out with the idea of the inevitability of the conflict between Athens and Sparta: 'After Pylos, and even after the peace of Nicias, we can be sure that he considered an agreement between the two great powers and a sharing of spheres of influence to be possible.' Having changed his mind later on, under the influence of events and as a result of this war to the death which came about between the two cities, Thucydides then added, in a different spirit, the passages on ἀληθεστάτη πρόφασις which express the impossibility for the two powers to

---

[1] *Forsch.*, II, pp. 333-362.
[2] II. 61. 1: οἷς μὲν αἵρεσις γεγένηται τἆλλα εὐτυχοῦσι, πολλὴ ἄνοια πολεμῆσαι.
[3] I, p. 106.

exist face to face. It is then that, still according to Pohlenz, Thucydides began to insist upon the depth of the opposition between Athens and Sparta, an opposition of which he was not previously fully aware.

Eduard Meyer considers the facts whereas Pohlenz considers the work; but both their arguments are correct.

It is indeed impossible not to admit, with Eduard Meyer, that it was normal for Thucydides to wish for peace and to think it possible in 425, while still remaining faithful to the tradition of Pericles and still remaining aware of the causes which had made war necessary.

A man who supported war in 431, who did not want to yield in 429 when the situation was unfavourable and when Sparta had not really been harmed, could very well wish to seek an alliance with her when she had been sufficiently affected by the war to offer serious guarantees. It is the same political sense, as we have already seen, which leads Pericles to speak out against peace, and the Spartans to speak in its favour.

Similarly, even if the impression given in Book I is that war was the inevitable result of the presence of two cities that were equally powerful but powerful in different ways, and of which one had to conquer the other, this by no means indicates that these circumstances could not have been changed by a war. Moreover, it is through fidelity to Pericles' policy that Thucydides insists upon the inevitable nature of the conflict; and if we can accept that circumstances allowed him to wish for peace later on, while at the same time remaining faithful to his original ideas, it is equally obvious that circumstances enabled him, and even obliged him, to consider the conflict as having then been settled.

It thus appears that, according to the facts, there is no contradiction between the two judgments of Thucydides. What explains the mistakes made by certain scholars on this point is the fact that neither of the two men who represented Athenian policy after the death of Pericles, that is to say Cleon the man of war, and Nicias the man of peace, was the true representative of the Periclean tradition.

Nicias can, in a way, be considered as faithful to it, and Allen B. West (*Pericles' Political Heirs*), has no hesitation in declaring that in almost every one of his ideas and actions, Nicias shows himself to be the disciple of Pericles, a democrat and a conservative like his master. In this case, Cleon would represent the contrary tradition, and stand as the opponent of Pericles. There is no lack of ancient evidence to support this interpretation: Hermippus says that Cleon attacked Pericles (Plut., *Per.*, 33, 8.); Idomeneus that he accused him publicly (ibid., 35, 5)[1] and thereby alienated a section of the *demos*. On the other hand, there are writers who declare that Cleon was the only person to remain faithful to the tradition of the great statesman, and Müller-Strübing declares unhesitatingly that Cleon is the only leader to have carried on Pericles' ideas and his war policy.[2] In this case it is Nicias who would represent the contrary tradition and stand as the opponent of Pericles: Plutarch does in fact say that his supporters were the πλούσιοι καὶ γνώριμοι,[3] the men who were opposed to all imperialism and to all wars, and who indeed often contrasted Pericles, as the author of war, with Nicias, the author of peace.[4]

The fact is that the tradition of Pericles is, as it were, shared out between the two men. But if neither of them conforms exactly to it, we can nevertheless say that the imprudence shown by Cleon carries him further away from the Periclean tradition than do the excessive caution and moderation of Nicias — that the rash demagogue is further from it than the conservative general. Therefore, by putting himself on the side of Nicias and by supporting his policy, although without ever giving him the complete and whole-hearted support which he reserved for Pericles,[5] Thucydides did remain faithful to his original ideas.

The approval which he bestows upon Pericles and the blame which he allocates to Cleon are thus part of a coherent and consistent attitude. And he seems to have, as it were, consecrated this unity in his own ideas in the judgment in II. 65, where he evokes the successors of Pericles in a formula which is particularly well suited to

---

[1] I should think with Müller-Strübing (*Ar. und die hist. Krit.*, p. 573 n.) that Idomeneus is not right here against Theophrastus (who names Simmias), or Heracleides Ponticus (who names Lacratidas); but one can at least agree with Beloch (*Att. Pol.*, Exk. II, p. 332) that Cleon willingly encouraged the attacks against Pericles, attacks in which the *demos*, according to Thucydides himself, took part.

[2] Pp. 390-396 ('der einzige Staatsmann der den Gedanken des Perikles gefasst hatte und dessen Kriegspolitik fortsetzte').

[3] Plutarch, *Nicias*, 2, 2.

[4] Ibid., 9, 9.

[5] Thucydides is constantly sympathetic towards Nicias; cf. Lange, p. 651 and the judgment in VII. 86. 5. In the episode itself, one can see how he differs from those who tried to criticize Nicias for his 'desertion' (cf. Plut., *Nic.*, 8, 2). Nevertheless, Thucydides readily acknowledges his weaknesses (VII. 50. 4), and nowhere devotes an important passage of analysis to him; Nicias makes only one political speech, against the Sicilian expedition, and then without success.

N

the diptych Mytilene-Pylos, since he says: οἱ δὲ . . . κακῶς ἔς τε σφᾶς αὐτοὺς καὶ τοὺς ξυμμάχους ἐπολίτευσαν.

But if the choice here made by Thucydides implies no actual contradiction, we can nevertheless point out that, when he expresses it, he does not mention that the circumstances have changed: he, in fact, refers to principles of action which seem to differ from those to which he referred in at least some of the passages dealing with Pericles.

Making sure of the future and keeping quiet are already maxims somewhat removed from those which he attributes to Pericles. In Book V, the motives attributed to Nicias seem in fact to be the systematic denial of Pericles' ideas; one has:

— II. 63. 1: μὴ φεύγειν τοὺς πόνους; V. 16. 1: πόνων πεπαῦσθαι.

— I. 144. 3: ἔκ τε τῶν μεγίστων κινδύνων ὅτι καὶ πόλει καὶ ἰδιώτῃ μέγισται τιμαὶ περιγίγνονται; V. 16. 1: νομίζων ἐκ τοῦ ἀκινδύνου τοῦτο ξυμβαίνειν.

In Book VI, Alcibiades even speaks of the ἀπραγμοσύνη of Nicias (18. 6). Now, the opposition is less clearly marked in Book IV, but it is nevertheless disquieting. Also, the Spartan ambassadors ask for more than peace or prudence: they want closer understanding; they want an alliance; and the two traditions of Cimon and Themistocles are too clearly distinguished as regards the past to be mingled so easily in some form of happy unity; if Thucydides' ideal was always one of sharing and mutual understanding, then why this admiration for Themistocles and this silence about Cimon? Why this need to go so far back into the past to discover the causes of a conflict which can be so easily resolved? Why such insistence, in the Funeral Oration, on exalting Athens at the expense of Sparta? One is thus brought back to the other interpretation and to the ideas expressed by Pohlenz.

My own conclusion will be that it was normal for a supporter of Pericles to show himself favourable to peace in 425, and to blame the hubris shown by the excessive ambition of the democratic party; but that it is nevertheless surprising that a man who was such an enthusiastic advocate of Pericles' imperialism and who had insisted so much on the gravity of the present conflict, should draw from the episode the lessons contained in the speech of the Spartan ambassadors and in the general narration of events.

This twin conclusion is confirmed by a far from negligible source of information, that is to say by the theatre.

This does in fact reveal that at the time of Pylos there was a very clear movement in favour of peace: both the former opponents of Pericles, like Aristophanes, and his former supporters, like Euripides, were associated with it. Only one, however, seems to have linked this possibility of peace with the idea of a reconciliation and real drawing together of the two countries, and that is Aristophanes, the former opponent of Pericles.

Scholars usually date from the years around 422 the *Poleis* of Eupolis, a play which is a defence of the allies and consequently an attack on the excesses of imperialism. Eupolis does not seem to have shown himself a very keen supporter of the policy of Cimon, for the latter — from a strictly private point of view, it is true — is not very well treated, at least in the fragment 208 K; but Eupolis, on the other hand, reproaches Athens as Thucydides does with having more luck than wisdom (205 K):

ὦ πόλις πόλις
ὡς εὐτυχὴς εἶ μᾶλλον ἢ καλῶς φρονεῖς.

It is easy to recognize the essential words of the first part of the speech made by the Spartan ambassadors.

The same thing is found in Euripides. Here it is difficult to ascertain anything definite, because of the disputed date of many of his plays; however, during the last years of Archidamus' war, we do find in his plays, by the side of themes representing the patriotic ideal, a desire for peace that was not known until that time and which even seems to contradict the teaching of certain other plays like the *Heracleidae*.[1]

In *Hecuba*, for example, a play which is more or less contemporaneous with the affair of Pylos, we do find preoccupations which are fairly similar to those of Thucydides. There, in fact, repeated with much more insistence and indignation than in the *Hippolytus*, we find the theme of the glib democrat (130 ff.). We also find, repeated on a number of occasions, the idea that men should mistrust prosperity; thus in verse 283:

οὐδ᾽ εὐτυχοῦντας εὖ δοκεῖν πράξειν ἀεί.

or in verse 956:

οὐκ ἔστιν οὐδὲν πιστόν, οὔτ᾽ εὐδοξία
οὔτ᾽ αὖ καλῶς πράσσοντα μὴ πράξειν κακῶς.

[1] See pp. 133 ff.

Even if these themes are commonplaces in Greek wisdom and consequently in tragedy, the fact remains that the subject chosen by the
author entails ideas of this type and that they consequently reveal a
trend of thought. Finally, and most important, one finds the idea that
there is no difference between peoples and that the enemy also
suffers from the war:

> ... by Eurotas is moan,
> Where with tears for their homes' undoing
> The maidens Laconian groan,
> Where rendeth her tresses hoary
> The mother for sons that are dead,
> And her cheeks with woe-furrows are gory
> And her fingers are red

(lines 650 ff., transl. A. S. Way, in the Loeb Library); such an
indication is new in Euripides, and points a moral different from the
one preached in the great patriotic plays studied in the preceding
chapter.

In the *Cresphontes*, which also seems to date from shortly after
425, and to have been written, in any case, before 421 (it is quoted in
the *Georgoi* of Aristophanes, which itself contains allusions to
Pylos), we find the great tirade on peace (the very one of which
Aristophanes reproduces the opening passage); and this tirade is all
the more noteworthy since it does not seem to be made necessary by
the subject,[1] and is nevertheless developed in great detail (462 N):

> Εἰρήνα βαθύπλουτε καὶ
> καλλίστα μακάρων θεῶν,
> ζῆλός μοι σέθεν, ὡς χρονίζεις.[2]

---

[1] Its presence in the play is generally explained by an allusion to civil wars which would
have brought about the death of Cresphontes before the play begins.

[2] In what follows, Euripides seems to insist upon the expectation of peace:

> Δέδοικα δὲ μὴ πρὶν πόνοις
> ὑπερβάλῃ με γῆρας
> πρὶν σὰν χαρίεσσαν προσιδεῖν ὥραν
> καὶ καλλιχόρους ἀοιδὰς
> φιλοστεφάνους τε κώμους.
> Ἴθι μοι, πότνια, πόλιν,
> τὰν δ' ἐχθρὰν στάσιν εἶργ' ἀπ' οἴ-
> κων τὰν μαινομέναν τ' ἔριν
> θηκτῷ τερπομέναν σιδάρῳ.

Finally, although it is not possible to assign a definite date to it, one can also mention another play which seems to have been written in the last years of Archidamus' war, and which has already been quoted: the *Suppliants*. One might at first doubt whether it could offer evidence comparable to that of the other two, for it belongs to the 'patriotic' plays, concludes by celebrating the alliance with Argos, which was, according to Aristophanes, part of Cleon's programme,[1] and contains a violent and famous attack against Sparta: ὠμὴ καὶ πεποίκιλται τρόπους (187). These themes, however, could be explained by reference to particular circumstances which cannot be studied in this book, and it is nevertheless true that, on the whole, the play is dominated by the twin themes of moderation and peace. In fact it contains expressions which are almost identical with those used by the Spartan ambassadors, expressions which recommend wisdom, which blame those who cannot bear themselves aright in prosperity (124: εὐτυχοῦντες οὐκ ἐπίστανται φέρειν), which recall how variable good fortune is (269-270), and warn of the dangers involved in hope, as it encourages men to excess (479). Yet, the appeal for peace is even more remarkable. Apart from occasional references (cf. 747), there are two great speeches which, by their insistence and their general nature, seem to go beyond the context of the tragedy and address the Athenians directly. The first (in line 485) protests against the 'fury for spears' which seems to have taken hold of Greece. The second (in line 949) is directly addressed to mortals in general, and asks them to stop fighting one another:

> Helpless mortals!
> Why do ye get you spears and deal out death
> To fellow-men?
> Stay, from such toils forbear,
> And peaceful mid the peaceful ward your towns

(transl. A. S. Way, in the Loeb Library).[2]

These different texts, some of which may be questioned as regards

---

[1] See p. 193, n. 2.

[2] These themes, of course, are a result of the subject; but the choice of this subject is itself characteristic. Many of Euripides' tragedies have no comparable development: for instance *Ion*, *Iphigenia in Tauris*, the *Phoenician Women*, *Iphigenia in Aulis*, or many others, not to mention the early plays that have already been considered. Apart from a single mention in *Orestes* (1682), only the *Trojan Women* and *Helen* bear the same note — two tragedies following, one the sack of Melos, and the other the disaster in Sicily.

their date and others as regards their general significance, do nevertheless show, by their similarity with the ideas expressed in IV. 17-20, that Euripides, who was earlier in agreement with Thucydides in praising the ideal of Pericles, is in agreement with him once again in wishing for peace.

As for Aristophanes, he expresses his agreement in the actual details of his text.

In the *Knights*, in 424, he shows constant agreement with the opinion put forward by Thucydides: he too criticizes the military role played by Cleon and attributes all his success to Demosthenes;[1] he too regrets that Athens did not accept peace proposals, for in lines 668-673, we see the democrat refuse peace for the sake of a few anchovies, and in lines 792-820 the pork-butcher reproaches the Paphlagonian for having driven away the embassy led by Archeptolemus:

> and that is the reason, no doubt,
> Why the peace which, unsought, Archeptolemus brought,
> you were quick from the city to scout,
> And as for the embassies coming to treat
> you spanked them and chivied them out.

(transl. B. B. Rogers, in the Loeb Library).[2]

The Paphlagonian then replies to this criticism with what is in fact a programme of unlimited imperialism, for he answers: ἵνα γ' Ἑλλήνων ἄρξῃ πάντων.

In the *Peace*, in 421, regret is again expressed that peace was not concluded at the time of Pylos. It is Peace herself who complains (665):

> She says that after that affair in Pylus,
> She came, unbidden, with a chest of treaties,
> And thrice you blackballed her in full assembly.

(transl. B. B. Rogers, in the Loeb Library).

---

[1] The servant representing Demosthenes says (54):

Καὶ πρώην γ' ἐμοῦ
μᾶζαν μεμαχότος ἐν Πύλῳ Λακωνικήν,
πανουργότατά πως παραδραμὼν ὑφαρπάσας
αὐτὸς παρέθηκε τὴν ὑπ' ἐμοῦ μεμαγμένην·

(cf. 392: τὸ ἀλλότριον ἀμῶν θέρος). Even if this allusion is aimed more at the self-satisfied attitude of Cleon after his success, it still tends to restore the merit to Demosthenes and thus to confirm (in spite of Eduard Meyer) the judgment of Thucydides.

[2] 796: αἳ τὰς σπονδὰς προκαλοῦνται, cf. Thucydides IV. 19. 1.

Trygeus then replies that it was indeed a mistake but that
it must be excused, the people's minds having been, at the
time, ἐν τοῖς σκύτεσιν. Cleon's responsibility is thus clearly
indicated.

And, just as clearly, this peace which ought to have been concluded, fits into a definite political programme which Trygeus puts
forward in line 1082:

$$\text{ἐξὸν σπεισαμένοις κοινῇ τῆς Ἑλλάδος ἄρχειν.}$$

The evidence provided by both Euripides and Aristophanes thus
confirms the indications of the text itself, as regards the basic unity
which links the different judgments of Thucydides together, and the
difference of aim which nevertheless separates the text of Book IV
from that of Book II.[1]

We must therefore try to discover whether the date at which it was
written can explain this difference satisfactorily.

The very meaning of the episode, as it is presented in Thucydides,
is for Eduard Meyer proof that it was written 'late'.

Indeed, Thucydides does not only express pacifist ideas: he is not
Dicaeopolis. What he insists on is the moment, the opportunity: he
declares it to be unique and irreplaceable. The Spartans say, in fact, in
IV. 20. 1: ἡμῖν δὲ καλῶς εἴπερ ποτὲ ἔχει ἀμφοτέροις ἡ ξυναλλαγή.
Later, on the contrary, the moment will have passed. Such a judgment,
which brings the future into account, does look as if it was
made in the light of subsequent events. For Thucydides to have
shown so much care in demonstrating what a mistake was made at
Pylos, he must have been able to see the peace of Nicias as a false
peace, soon revealing the existence of this 'inevitable hostility' which
could in fact have been avoided, but which did cause the war to
break out again. After the peace, after the alliance, after the political
revival which made the allies of Sparta think that the two cities were
going to unite in order to enslave others (V. 29. 3), he must have
seen the agreement come to an end and it must have been clear that

---

[1] *At no time* can one find in Euripides ideas comparable to those put forward by
Aristophanes, and, in this case, by Thucydides. There is not the slightest reason to think
that Jocasta weeping over her two sons, in the *Phoenician Women*, represents Greece
suffering from the sight of two rival cities tearing each other to pieces (H. Weil, *Etudes
sur le drame antique*, 1897, pp. 164-165).

the opportunity had been missed.[1] It is this idea which the episode is designed to bring out,[2] and it implies that Thucydides is writing fairly late, and with a very clear idea of the unity of the war.

The reasoning is extremely sound, and if certain Athenians, or even Spartans, did at the time put forward ideas similar to those mentioned in Book IV, it is highly probable that Thucydides only retained, expressed and underlined them in the light of the greater significance given to them by later events.

We may add that the clues, however slight and inconclusive they may be by themselves, tend to support this conclusion. There are really two such clues: the first in the episode itself, the second in a passage clearly linked with it.

The first consists of a remark made in IV. 12. 3,[3] which says that 'at that time' (ἐν τῷ τότε), the Spartans were most famous for their army and for their strength on land, and the Athenians for their navy and for their sea-power. By this phrase, the time of Pylos, indicated by τότε,[4] is contrasted with another time at which these conditions are no longer true. Now these conditions had, at the time of Pylos, been obvious for years, and did not therefore really deserve a mention: Sparta acquired sea-power only after the situation had changed very considerably, and after the Sicilian expedition had taken place. It was on the advice of Alcibiades that Sparta began to concern herself with the sea (Isocrates, *Philippus*, 60); but if, immediately after the Sicilian expedition, the Athenians fear that an enemy fleet may arrive, it is still a Syracusan fleet (VIII. 1. 2). On the other hand we know through Xenophon that in 406 Lysander could be considered as master of the sea.[5] In order to bring this about, the great ship-building programme of 410 had been necessary (Xenoph., *Hell.*, I, 1, 24-25) as well as the additional Persian money of 407 (I, 5, 7); we are thus forced to admit that the phrase in question

---

[1] On this point Thucydides does after all differ from Aristophanes, who, carried along by his own partisan enthusiasm, still thinks reconciliation possible in 411, in *Lysistrata*. See Croiset (*Aristoph. et les partis politiques à Athènes*, 230-233).

[2] In fact there seems to be a close link, in Thucydides' ideas, between Pylos and the events in Sicily (VII. 18. 2; VII. 71. 7; VII. 86. 3): it may be that the events in Sicily enabled him to understand the episode of Pylos retrospectively.

[3] On this clue, cf. Meyer, *Forsch.*, II, p. 277 and H. Patzer's list of clues.

[4] But here. the indication is not constituted by the word τότε (see p. 167, n. 1); it is provided by the whole of the sentence, whose presence here implies an allusion.

[5] Xen.. *Hell.*, I, 6, 2: ἔλεγε τῷ Καλλικρατίδᾳ ὅτι θαλαττοκράτωρ τε παραδιδοίη κα ναυμαχίᾳ νενικηκώς — Plutarch, *Lysander*, 6: ἐμαρτύρατο πρὸς αὐτὸν ὅτι θαλαττοκρατοῦ τὸ ναυτικὸν παραδίδωσιν — ibid., 9: ἐπέδειξε τῷ πεζῷ παρόντι τὴν τοῦ ναυτικοῦ ῥώμην ὡ πλέων ᾗ βούλοιτο κρατῶν τῆς θαλάττης.

must have been written after 407. Was it added to an earlier version? This is possible, but not very likely since there was not much point in adding it at all.

The same thing is true of another clue, which does not belong to the episode itself but which nevertheless deserves examination: it forms part of the account of the troubles in Corcyra which comes immediately after the affair of Pylos (and, moreover, it follows on from some chapters closely interwoven with this affair): in IV. 48. 5, Thucydides states that the troubles of Corcyra came to an end 'at least for this war' (ὅσα γε κατὰ τὸν πόλεμον τόνδε). Now we know through Diodorus XIII, 48, in a passage whose accuracy is not open to any serious doubt, that there were disorders in 410 and then again in 374. Ullrich draws the following conclusion: either Thucydides, at the time of writing this episode, did not know about these new troubles (a hypothesis that the restriction itself, with the γε which underlines it, seems to me to dismiss straight away), or he does not mean by the expression 'this war' the twenty-seven year war, and has not yet therefore the idea of the unity of the Peloponnesian War which he puts forward in Book V. This passage, and those around it, would thus belong to the 'early' version. This is open to discussion, and in fact my own view is that if Thucydides does mean the war of Archidamus when he talks about 'this war', this is not necessarily a proof that he has not yet thought of the unity of the Peloponnesian War.[1] But one thing is certain, in my view, and that is that Thucydides is here referring to an event which is accurately dated as being after 410, and that consequently he must be writing after this date.[2]

---

[1] He could very well mean by this the war of Archidamus by opposition to the war of Decelea, even if he considers these two wars are only two parts of a single whole. He certainly says in V. 24. 2, in a passage which is not suspect from this point of view: ταῦτα δὲ τὰ δέκα ἔτη ὁ πρῶτος πόλεμος ξυνεχῶς γενόμενος γέγραπται. Finally, examples of this type abound in the account of the Sicilian expedition, and, in my view, this is solely because this expedition serves as a transition and a link between the different elements which make up the Peloponnesian War. Thus we have, in VI. 1. 1: καὶ ὅτι οὐ πολλῷ τινι ὑποδεέστερον πόλεμον ἀνῃροῦντο ἢ τὸν πρὸς τοὺς Πελοποννησίους, in VI. 6. 2: ὥστε τὴν γενομένην ἐπὶ Λάχητος καὶ τοῦ προτέρου πολέμου [Λεοντίνων] οἱ Ἐγεσταῖοι ξυμμαχίαν ἀναμιμνῄσκοντες, in VII. 18. 2: ἐν γὰρ τῷ προτέρῳ πολέμῳ . . . , in VII. 27. 2: τὸν ἐκ τῆς Δεκελείας πόλεμον, and in VII. 28. 3: ὅτι δύο πολέμους ἅμα εἶχον.

[2] This is the view of Cwiklinski and more recently of H. Patzer (p. 104). Leske, faced with the possible ambiguity of this indication and with the difficulties raised in the field of historical criticism concerning the text of Diodorus, considers that it should be ignored. In my view, such severity is excessive.

Other indications can be found in the rest of Book IV.[1] They all point in the same direction and there are no contradictory ones.[2] None of them would be particularly convincing, were it not a question simply of confirming probabilities based on common sense and on the actual text of Thucydides. Taken altogether, the evidence does form a whole which allows us to agree with Eduard Meyer that the episode was written *after the events in Sicily and as a part of the twenty-seven year war.*

Now, does this mean that the passage was written 'late'? If one understands, by 'late', after 404, such a conclusion is certainly rather hasty.

As far as the beginning of the work is concerned, it is possible to distinguish two strata: the first an 'early' one, probably written before anybody could know what the full extent of the war would be, and the second a 'late' one, made up of passages rewritten after the end of the war, that is to say after 404. But the further one goes, the more difficult it becomes to distinguish one stratum from the other. Thucydides had perhaps not finished writing the history of the Archidamus' war when he realized the tremendous scale his subject was assuming, and he perhaps did not wait for 404 before he went on with his work: he can thus have continued writing at a fairly advanced date, with a very clear idea in his mind of the unity of the war and with the knowledge of a large number of subsequent events, and yet still have been writing before 404, so that his account owed nothing to post-war preoccupations.

In fact this is what does seem to have happened as far as the whole of this part of his work is concerned. The difference already noted, in the first part of this thesis, between the passages in Book IV and

[1] This, without mentioning either the sections concerned with the events in Sicily, which seem very clearly to have been written with the great expedition in mind, or those concerned with Brasidas, for both could be due to rewriting. We must limit ourselves to details whose reintroduction seems more surprising, like the passage in IV. 74. 4, in which Thucydides says that the government set up at Megara after a rebellion by a small number of men lasted longer than any other government set up in this way. Such a sentence clearly presupposes that the events happened some time ago, and it does not seem important enough to have justified a late addition.

[2] I am here neglecting the argument based on the geographical difficulties raised by Thucydides' account. (He does not seem to know about the existence of the lagoon of Osmýn Agá and he presents the second entrance to the harbour as much narrower than it really is) some scholars infer from these difficulties that he had not yet made the voyage in the Peloponnese mentioned in V. 26. Such arguments, which Grundy tried to build up into a method, are always extraordinarily subjective. In the present case, reference can be made to the good refutation by Gomme (*Essays*, pp. 125 ff.).

those in Book V concerning Brasidas and the peace of Nicias proves
at least that there was not, even for the period immediately close to
the peace, one single definitive version, composed after 404. Whatever
may have been its date, there was, for this period in general, an
'early' version.

And in the actual episode itself, there is nothing which reveals any
further rewriting after 404.

The mistake made at the time of Pylos, which was to seem more
important with the renewal of hostilities and the increased gravity of
the conflict, must on the contrary have become rather less noticeable
in contrast with the more serious mistakes disclosed in the next
part of the war: in chapter II. 65, Thucydides picks out the mistake of
the Sicilian expedition, and insists on it, without making any allusion
to the previous one, made when peace was refused at the time of
Pylos.

Similarly, the impulse to which Athens then surrendered must
have seemed less of an imprudence as her strength was more clearly
revealed. In IV. 108, Thucydides does say: ὅση ὕστερον διεφάνη; and,
in II. 65, he actually insists on this power. Now such notions could
only minimize the idea of the good luck from which the Athenians
benefited in this episode.

Finally, the very idea of a division in the spheres of influence
seems to have become a little obsolete as the conflict appeared more
obviously to be a deadly one. As we have already seen, it seems
entirely absent from the passages of Thucydides which are most
directly influenced by the events and preoccupations of 404.

We thus arrive at the two following conclusions: on the one hand,
the episode certainly seems to have been written after the events in
Sicily, and probably also after 410 and even 407. But on the other
hand, it *owes nothing to the preoccupations of 404*,[1] *and it would seem
rather to correspond to an intellectual attitude prevailing before that date.*

Should we therefore conclude from this that the episode was
written between 407 and 404? By its very claim to accuracy, such a
conclusion would be somewhat presumptuous; and there is another
one which fits in better with these facts.

Everything can be explained if once we admit — what is highly

---

[1] There is no reason to see an allusion to the final disaster in the words in 18. 5: καὶ
μήποτε ὕστερον, ἢν ἄρα μὴ πειθόμενοι σφαλῆτε, ἃ πολλὰ ἐνδέχεται, νομισθῆναι τύχῃ καὶ
τὰ νῦν προχωρήσαντα κρατῆσαι. This disaster is too far removed from the circumstances
here under consideration and the participle μὴ πειθόμενοι would scarcely apply to it.

probable — that under one form or another (notes, plans, projects, isolated pieces of narration), the historical research and elaboration were completed before the actual version which we now possess was written. This version could thus have been written late (perhaps even after 404), but it had been thought out, conceived and prepared early (perhaps even immediately after the events had taken place), and the actual writing, in its general form, followed this early conception.

The composition, then, can be termed 'early' in a purely intellectual sense, for it conforms to a previous scheme, and differs in that respect from the passages deliberately introduced into the work after 404 owing to new preoccupations.

This conclusion explains the slight difference that we have noticed between the ideas expressed here and those in the passages of Book II dealing with Pericles.

Here once again we see that Thucydides, faithful to his original ideal, made a point of defending it, during the war, against the excesses of the demagogues for whom war and imperialism served only to flatter the ambitions of the people. Against these excesses, he put forward the principles of moderation and prudence. Then, as we have seen, the collapse of imperialism itself simply made him change the general trend of his plea. It revived in him, by reaction, ideas that were totally opposed to the possibility of reaching an understanding with the enemy. As a result of it, what had previously seemed to him like wisdom now only represented — and his attitude is easy to understand — an impossible course and a betrayal of former ideals.

In the two episodes of Mytilene and Pylos, as we have seen, Thucydides expresses the same veiled disapproval on the excesses of imperialism. It must be added that this spirit of censure accounts for everything else that Thucydides says — or does not say — about Cleon. His campaign in Thrace is narrated not without a certain derision,[1] and the defeat to which it leads is made terribly clear in Thucydides' work. Now it may be that this campaign did have less purely negative results than Thucydides gives us to understand,[2] and it was in any case aimed at that Thracian coast which had such an essential part to

[1] Both H. Delbrück (*Die Strategie des Per.*, p. 212) and Steup note the irony of V. 10. 9: ὡς τὸ πρῶτον οὐ διενοεῖτο μένειν, εὐθὺς φεύγων.

[2] According to Meritt and West (*A.J.A.*, 1925, pp. 59-69: *Cleon's Amphipolitan campaign and the assessment list of 421*), the act concerning the tributes IG I² 64 indicates that this campaign was much more successful than Thucydides suggests in restoring Athenian prestige.

play in the system of Athenian imperialism.[1] What was wrong with it, in Thucydides' eyes, was probably that it came at a time when the armistice could have been transformed into peace (cf. IV. 119. 13).

It is for a similar reason that Thucydides completely omitted to mention another line of activity which Cleon seems to have adopted in foreign policy. We know in fact by line 465 of the *Knights* that Cleon was openly working for the alliance with Argos:[2] although Thucydides recognizes in V. 14. 1 that this is a possibility which the Spartans fear, and though it may even appear as one of the decisive arguments that the war party might put forward,[3] Thucydides does not take it into consideration. Once again he leaves on one side anything which could encourage the Athenians in their ambition and turn them away from concluding peace.

The unity noticeable in the whole of this part of the work confirms what we have already seen of the consistency of Thucydides' ideas. It enables us to arrive at the following results on the two questions of the composition of the work and Thucydides' own ideas.

As far as the problem of when the work was written is concerned, these results give rise only to a new realization of our utter inability to find a complete solution. If it is true that even for the passages which, in the author's mind, referred to the twenty-seven years war, there existed what can be called an 'early' version — although these passages were perhaps not written until a fairly late date — then the distinction between 'early and 'late' passages loses much of its precision; it therefore most frequently becomes impossible (and useless into the bargain) to ascribe a precise date to the writing of any passage. The only passages which really are different from the others are those inspired by the events of 404, for which an earlier version either never existed or was destroyed.

But the fact that we have to give up this part of our quest gives us once again some definite information about the development of Thucydides' own ideas. We have in fact been able to see that the judgment made by Thucydides on this occasion agrees with the one which he made on the earlier episodes. This judgment seems to

---

[1] It is there that Nicias, in Book VI, asks that an intervention be made, rather than in Sicily (VI. 10. 5).

[2] οὔκουν μ' ἐν Ἄργει οἷα πράττεις λανθάνει,
     πρόφασιν μὲν Ἀργείους φίλους ἡμῖν ποεῖ, . . .

[3] It was in fact known that the treaty between Sparta and Argos was coming to an end. See Gilbert, *Beiträge* . . . , 189 ff.

express coherent views which fit in with the historian's own immediate experience, although he seems to be expressing them late. This implies that his ideas developed in exactly the same manner from 430 to 404. Only the events of 404 would thus have brought about some change of attitude whose nature is entirely explained by the circumstances. This change is in no way a denial of his earlier views – and this is why the passages of 'early' inspiration have been retained in the work, even though it was revised after 404 – but it did nevertheless call for commentaries whose tone makes them stand out from the other passages.

This distinction remained rather obscure when we could compare amongst themselves only passages which were concerned with Pericles and which were linked together by a unity both of subject-matter and ideas: it comes out fully as soon as we bring into play the evidence provided by a different experience, which then affords a point of comparison.

These conclusions presume that, when he was writing about Sicily for example, Thucydides' attitude was still the same as it had been when he was discussing Cleon, but that it changed after 404. This should be borne out by an examination of the parts dealing with Alcibiades, and by a study of the date at which they were written.

CHAPTER THREE

ALCIBIADES

WITH the intervention of Alcibiades,[1] the imperialistic policy of Athens manifests itself in its purest form with the Sicilian expedition. And it is noteworthy that Thucydides has given pride of place to the description of this expedition, devoting two whole books of highly polished narration to it.

Before considering the central ideas in his analysis of it, however, we must stop to consider another field[2] in which Alcibiades played a part, and examine the policy of alliance with Argos, which takes up most of Book V: this policy led to a renewal of the struggle against Sparta,[3] and for that very reason, it was an imperialistic one.[4]

The conquest of Melos, on the other hand, although directly connected with the history of Athenian imperialism, cannot be considered here, since Thucydides has attributed the responsibility for it not to Alcibiades but to Athens herself.

I. The Policy of Alliance with Argos

In the case of Cleon, Thucydides could pass over the attempts to form an alliance with Argos, since they were nothing more than

---

[1] In Thucydides, Alcibiades follows straight on from Cleon. Hyperbolus, who plays such an important role in the comedies of the period (cf. especially *Acharnians*, 846; *Knights*, 1304, 1363; *Clouds*, 876, 1065; *Peace*, 681, 921; *Frogs*, 570; Cratinus, fr. 262 K) appears in Thucydides only in Book VIII in an allusion made to the ostracism of this wicked man' (VIII. 73. 3). Thucydides does in fact omit consideration of all questions of some politics, and it so happens that although Hyperbolus did put forward dreams of conquest, he did not exercise any influence on the actual foreign policy of Athens.

[2] Alcibiades also has a part to play after the Sicilian disaster, but it is less definite and less directly linked with imperialism.

[3] The supporters of this policy are 'those who wanted to break the peace' (43. 1; 61. 2). And although in fact it is a little exaggerated to admit, as Plutarch does (*Parallel between Alcibiade and C. Marius*, 41, 2) that, by tricking the Spartan ambassadors, as Alcibiades does in Thucydides V. 45, he 'broke the peace', he did at least obtain the inscription on a stele of the fact that the treaty was not observed, and succeeded in having reprisals taken against Sparta (56. 3).

[4] See, in the exhortation to the Athenians, 69. 1, the words: τήν τε ἀρχὴν βεβαιοτέραν αἱ μείζω ἕξουσι. Hatzfeld (*Alcibiade*, pp. 82, 96) insists on the idea that in opposing peace when it was made, Alcibiades was in no way inspired by imperialistic ambitions, and that the alliance with Argos, just after, had an exclusively defensive character; but what Hatzfeld himself says a little later about Alcibiades' imperialism greatly limits the extent of these reservations. They are in any case in contradiction with the text of Thucydides.

projects. He is nevertheless compelled to record them when dealing
with Alcibiades' time, since they then become a reality and play a
decisive role in the relationship between Athens and Sparta. His
account of them, however, gives only the bare minimum of information, and is always couched in a tone of disapproval.

He who is usually so clear and so anxious to explain everything
completely neglects a large number of elements which would help
to bring out the meaning of events. We cannot see what aim Athens
is pursuing when she sends expeditions but does so in such a way
that they generally arrive after the action has taken place.[1] It is
difficult to see what role is played by Alcibiades, who intervenes as
general in 52. 2, as an ambassador in 61. 2, and who simply happens
to be there by accident in 76. 3.[2] There are even a certain number of
missing links in the chain of events, for we probably have to presuppose, at the outset, certain transactions prior to Alcibiades'
intervention in 43. 3; and we probably have to presuppose, in order
to explain the sudden outburst of energy which seizes the Argive
demos at the end (82), an Athenian action which is mentioned simply
in passing, when Thucydides is dealing with purely material achievements.[3]

A number of explanations might be put forward for these circumstances,[4] but they nevertheless seem to be essentially due to the
contempt which Thucydides has for this policy. It can be noted, in
fact, that he leaves on one side everything that might justify it. On
the other hand, he specifies the motives which lead Alcibiades to
follow it by a parataxis emphasizing his personal ambition: 43. 2 =
ᾧ ἐδόκει μὲν καὶ ἄμεινον εἶναι πρὸς τοὺς Ἀργείους μᾶλλον χωρεῖν
οὐ μέντοι ἀλλὰ καὶ φρονήματι φιλονικῶν ἠναντιοῦτο . . . Each Greek
particle underlines the fact that it is not the interest of Athens which
is here being considered. He is equally expansive on the means used
by Alcibiades, and according to him,[5] these were no more admirable:
the detailed account which we find in 45-46 is that of a genuine piece

---

[1] 55. 3; 75. 5.

[2] ἔτυχε γὰρ καὶ ὁ Ἀλκιβιάδης παρών.

[3] Compare Thucydides 82.6 (καὶ ἐκ τῶν Ἀθηνῶν αὐτοῖς ἦλθον τέκτονες καὶ λιθουργοὶ
and Plutarch (*Alcibiades*, 15), whose account of the events (in spite of Hatzfeld, *Alcibiade*,
p. 120, n. 4) seems convincing.

[4] Refusal on Thucydides' part to interest himself in the city's internal politics, unfinished
state of the work.

[5] Plutarch (*Parallel between Alcibiades and C. Marius*, 41, 2) relates the anecdote as
being Thucydides' own (ὡς Θουκυδίδης ἱστόρηκε); doubts have even been expressed as to
its reliability.

of sharp practice.[1] This scorn and this severity were not, however, the only possible attitude.

The text itself can provide arguments in favour of the policy adopted. When Alcibiades puts forward the warlike intentions of Sparta as a motive for his attitude, Thucydides cannot deny that these exist, however much he tries to invalidate Alcibiades' remarks by the intention which he attributes to them. In 43. 3 Alcibiades declares that the Spartans are not to be trusted, but that their only object is to crush the Argives and then attack the Athenians when they are isolated. Now Thucydides himself had already indicated, in 36. 1, that there was a war party at Sparta, which sought an alliance with Argos in order to fight Athens more easily.[2]

Even the results of this policy can also provide a justification for it.[3] Although pursued rather irregularly and incoherently by Athens, it did have very unfortunate consequences for Sparta, which are mentioned by Thucydides himself, only in passing and without any insistence.[4] Even the defeat of Mantinea could not restore the situation (VI. 16. 6; 89. 3), and Sparta must have been seriously affected not to make any move when the Athenians attacked Melos. Apart from these results, the alliance itself was to remain precious for Athens;[5] only the Argive and Mantinean contingents represented a

---

[1] Themistocles' device in I. 90. 3 is a patriotic stratagem which only takes in the foreigner; that used by Alcibiades, on the contrary, by violating the conditions under which the people deliberated, is more reminiscent of the means used by Cleon in IV. 21-22. It might be added that, according to Hatzfeld (*Alcibiade*, pp. 89-93), Thucydides is here giving an incorrect account of the action of Alcibiades: the truth would be, according to that view, that Alcibiades, far from having confused the negotiations, made the Spartans confess the emptiness of their alleged 'full-powers'.

[2] Thucydides provides, in passing, another reason for the rapprochement between Athens, Argos and Mantinea: it is that they share the same political regime (V. 44. 1, cf. V. 29. 1).

[3] Eduard Meyer (*Forsch.*, II, 354) agrees with Thucydides in condemning the policy of alliance with Argos: the war of 460-450 had, he says, shown what it was worth. But the argument is not valid. On the other hand Beloch (*Att. Pol. seit Per.* X, p. 24) considers that it constituted the only means of defeating Sparta, and even condemns the strategy of Pericles for not having taken it into account. Busolt describes Alcibiades' military campaign (V. 52) as an unprecedented success (*Griech. Gesch.*, III², p. 1232). Bender also insists on the value of this policy, and notes (p. 63, n. 167) that an attack from Argos would have reduced Sparta to fearing the worst.

[4] V. 57. 1: Λακεδαιμόνιοι, ὡς αὐτοῖς οἵ τε Ἐπιδαύριοι ξύμμαχοι ὄντες ἐταλαιπώρουν καὶ τἆλλα ἐν τῇ Πελοποννήσῳ τὰ μὲν ἀφειστήκει τὰ δ' οὐ καλῶς εἶχε . . . and, similarly, 63. 2: ἐπειδὴ δὲ καὶ περὶ Ὀρχομενοῦ ἠγγέλλετο ἑαλωκέναι, πολλῷ δὴ μᾶλλον ἐχαλέπαινον.

[5] But here again Thucydides shows little insistence: he twice explains the Argive intervention in Sicily by motives which in no way bring in Alcibiades' action, and which are of doubtful value (VI. 69. 3 and VII. 57. 9).

O

contribution from outside the empire to the Sicilian expedition; their presence earned Alcibiades the favour of the people (VI. 29. 3), at the same time as it caused his enemies to be cautious in their plans when they were determined to ruin him (VI. 61. 5); Nicias, in his exhortation in VI. 68. 2, also reserves a special place for them.[1] All these advantages, which one finds scattered about haphazardly in Thucydides, provide arguments for the defenders of Alcibiades,[2] and show them to have been right in spite of what he wants us to believe.

In fact, if one refers to Athenian tradition, it is clear that the policy of alliance with Argos had a number of reliable precedents. It linked up with the policy followed by Themistocles, since Thucydides himself indicates that, after his ostracism, the latter sought refuge in Argos (I. 135. 3); it was probably under his influence that the unification of the Argolid was achieved, and that democratic governments, the signs of Athenian influence, began to appear in Argos and Mantinea. Cimon, on the other hand, drew closer to Sparta. As soon as he fell, Athens turned towards Argos for alliance (I. 102. 4: εὐθύς): then began a period of intervention in the Peloponnese, in the course of which can be placed the alliance with Megara (I. 103. 4), the building of the walls from Megara to Nisaea and the watch kept on them; from all this arose a war — already a Peloponnesian war. But in 451, when Cimon had returned, Argos signed with Sparta the thirty-year peace, which was to keep her out of the whole Archidamian war, and removed any possibility for Athenian action in this direction until 421.[3]

As this peace was coming to an end, the problem presented itself anew; and all those who considered Sparta to be a natural rival for the Athenians would of course look upon Argos as their foremost potential ally.

In fact Euripides, who has been our witness up to now, seems, in spite of his peaceful ideas, to have seen the situation in this light. This is apparent in two of his plays, of which one could have been written a few years earlier and the other a few years later than the peace of Nicias; namely the *Suppliants* and *Ion*.[4]

---

[1] VI. 68. 2: ὅπου γὰρ Ἀργεῖοι καὶ Μαντινῆς καὶ Ἀθηναῖοι καὶ νησιωτῶν οἱ πρῶτοί ἐσμεν . . .

[2] Isocrates, XVI, 15: καὶ ὅτι διακοσίους ὁπλίτας ἔχων τὰς μεγίστας πόλεις τῶν ἐν Πελοποννήσῳ Λακεδαιμονίων μὲν ἀπέστησεν, ὑμῖν δὲ συμμάχους ἐποίησεν.

[3] It is nevertheless not impossible that Pericles or Nicias should have thought of exerting pressure on Argos (cf. Glotz, p. 648).

[4] Attempts have been made, in the *Suppliants*, to see allusions to Alcibiades every time Euripides talks about young men: Weil shows convincingly (in his thesis, p. 19) that these

The first of these two plays, as we have seen, bears the marks of a pacifist attitude; but the alliance with Argos, solemnly sworn at the end, seems to establish Athens' right to a future alliance. This twin preoccupation, which seems to inspire the play, can be explained by the twin desire to finish the war, but to finish it with glory and to guarantee the future.

In *Ion*, the modifications to the legend have long since been noted; Ion, in Euripides, becomes the son of Apollo himself (and not of Xuthus), and Dorus becomes his half-brother (who has no divine blood), instead of his father's brother. This way of presenting the legend, which is neither that of Hesiod, nor of Herodotus, nor of Aristotle, nor even of Euripides himself in *Aeolus* or *Melanippe Philosophos*, corresponds, like so many versions of mythological legends, to practical considerations: it ratifies the rights of Athens in the Peloponnese.

Once again, then, it seems to be the imperial tradition which Thucydides is here discarding.

It is nevertheless possible to understand how he can have done this without betraying his previous ideal, and two circumstances can be mentioned to explain his attitude.

First of all, the policy of alliance with Argos was a war policy, whereas we have already seen in the previous chapters that Thucydides now wished for peace, without thereby denying his earlier ideas. Imperialism is in fact indirectly responsible for that spirit of vengeance which is prompting the actions of Sparta: it ought not to be allowed to have a direct effect on Athens herself and drive her towards war.[1]

Moreover, the very methods of this policy implied action on the continent, which departed from the system of sea-power laid down by Pericles.

Since the policy followed by Athens diverged from the tradition of Pericles in two essentials, Thucydides, always a supporter of that tradition, was justified in treating it as he did. It should merely be

---

[1] There is here a double criticism of imperialism whose effect is to reduce the clarity of the book. For in order to support this criticism, Thucydides is obliged to show both Athens and Sparta as responsible for the break. It is probably this double intention which explains the rather exceptional fact that he attributes the steps he mentions not to cities but to political parties.

---

so-called allusions do not even contain a definite opinion. Similarly, for an earlier epoch, we must agree with Weil in dismissing Hartung's suggestion that the *Helen* is an allusion to Alcibiades, innocent and in exile like the heroine herself, and thus an attempt to have him recalled.

noted that in doing so, he was following the most negative part of the Periclean heritage, and advocating prudence and moderation of the strictest kind. Here again, he has moved away from some of those with whom he was formerly in agreement: he has followed the Pericles of the first speech, rather than the Themistocles of Book I or the Pericles of the last speech.

Only the lack of firm and neat formulations in all these passages could impair the value of the information they provide, and prevent us from drawing very definite conclusions from them. This leads us to keep this information as a point of comparison: and to contrast the confused picture of the Alcibiades who is despised in Book V with the vigorous portrait of the Alcibiades who dominates Books VI and VII.

II. THE SICILIAN EXPEDITION

With the Sicilian expedition, Athens launches out on the path of conquest. As Thucydides notes on several occasions, it is the actual possession and domination of Sicily that she is striving to attain.[1] This, moreover, can be considered as being only a first stage, since after Sicily she aims to conquer Carthage, then to turn back to Sparta and secure dominion over the whole of Greece. This last stage of the plan is revealed only later, in the speech of Alcibiades at Sparta.

Thucydides could not fail to condemn these aims.

The final disaster was in itself sufficient invitation to him to do so, and, in any case, nothing was more opposed to the traditions to which he was attached. In so far as it was a 'western' policy, a concern with Sicily could certainly claim to be the tradition of Themistocles:[2] two of his daughters bore the highly significant names of Sybaris and Italia (Plut., *Them.*, 32, 2); Herodotus tells us (VIII, 62), of his demands on Siris; he seems to have fought against Hiero (Plut., *Them.*, 25), and to have thought of seeking refuge in Sicily; in any case, he began by seeking refuge in Corcyra, whose 'benefactor'

---

[1] VI. 6. 1: ἐφιέμενοι μὲν τῇ ἀληθεστάτῃ προφάσει τῆς πάσης ἄρξαι; similarly, IV. 60. 1: ἐπιβουλευομένην, ὡς ἐγὼ κρίνω, τὴν πᾶσαν Σικελίαν ὑπ' Ἀθηναίων. VI. 10. 5: ἀρχῆς ἄλλης ὀρέγεσθαι, cf. VI. 18. 3; VI. 20. 2; VI. 33. 2: πρόφασιν μὲν Ἐγεσταίων ξυμμαχίᾳ καὶ Λεοντίνων κατοικίσει, τὸ δὲ ἀληθὲς Σικελίας ἐπιθυμίᾳ. Thucydides thus discards the pretext that can be provided by the Leontines. This pretext is nevertheless in the Menexenus, 243 a (ὑπὲρ τῆς Λεοντίνων ἐλευθερίας) which proves that the Athenians still used to put it forward.

[2] See H. Droysen, *Athen und der Westen vor der Sicilischen Expedition.*

Thucydides tells us he was (I. 136). It is thus certain that Themistocles was keenly interested in the western regions, which for Cimon seem to have had no interest at all. But he never intended to conquer Sicily by a military expedition.

The same is true of Pericles: he is interested in the west:[1] in 454, an Athenian fleet seems to have appeared in western waters and Egesta and Halicyae asked for an alliance with her; in 445, treaties are signed with Leontinoi and Rhegium, and also in 445, the colony of Thurii is founded; in 433 the treaties of 445 are renewed; the very alliance with Corcyra, with which Thucydides begins his history, was concluded partly because the island is situated on the route to Italy and Sicily. It is thus quite certain that Pericles never neglected the west, which Nicias seems to have been more or less prepared to abandon.[2] But not only did Pericles not try to conquer Sicily by a military expedition: he even opposed with the greatest vigour, as Plutarch tells us, the idea of this conquest which already existed in his day,[3] and with which are linked the names of Cleon, Hyperbolus and Alcibiades. Although Alcibiades represents the imperialist party against Nicias, it is thus legitimate for someone who was an admirer of Themistocles and Pericles, and a devoted admirer of Athenian greatness, to see in this plan only a mistake and an extremely regrettable attitude.

If we do not find any clearer confirmation for this in the theatre, the reason is that the expedition rapidly assumed the character of a defensive struggle, and, once it had started, the most elementary patriotism demanded that the whole city should wish for its success. That is why Euripides,[4] in his *Electra* (probably in 413), shows the

---

[1] On the events of 454, see Diodorus, XI, 86; IG I², 20; Beloch, II², 1st part, p. 202, n. 4; Hackforth, *C.A.H.*, V, 159; Glotz, pp. 153-154. On the treaties of 445: IG I², 51 and 52; Bauer, *Klio* XV, 1917, 188 ff.; Beloch, II², 1st part, p. 202, n. 5; *C.A.H.*, V, pp. 162 ff.; Glotz, p. 173. Droysen saw only Pericles' resistance, and was thus led to give an incorrect interpretation of the alliance with Corcyra; on the other hand, Nissen probably gives it too great a significance.

[2] His attitude in 423 seems to prove it; cf. Beloch, *Att. Pol. seit Per.*, p. 58, and note 3.

[3] On the previous existence of the great design, see Plutarch, *Per.*, 20, 3-4; *Nic.*, 12, 2; *Alc.*, 17, 2 and Aristophanes, *Knights*, 174, 1303. Thucydides, following his usual habit, mentions it only when it begins to enter into the realm of reality. In this respect, there is in Book IV a sudden and unexpected change: the Athenians send troops in III. 115. 4, in the hope of finishing off this war and acquiring a little experience, and they are inconsolable, in IV. 65, when they see these troops come back without having conquered Sicily. The success at Pylos explains this different tone, but also, perhaps, the influence of later events, which was absent from the passages in the first books.

[4] The *Trojan Women*, performed in March 415, expresses a certain disapproval of all wars of aggression. But the play was prepared and written before the vote to send the

Dioscuri endeavouring (because they cherish what is pious and just) to help a fleet off Sicily (1347-1348); and Aristophanes himself, in the *Birds* (in 414), identifies himself with the fight against Sparta and Corinth (814, 1012, 1280 and 969). But then, Nicias too, in all the speeches which he makes as a general, is passionate in assuming the mission that he had wanted to refuse, and he finds the right words to encourage the soldiers.[1] The attitude of these authors, who are writing in the midst of the action and directly addressing the people, is easy to understand: it does not allow us to judge beforehand what opinion they had on the expedition. It nevertheless seems possible that the whole of the imperialistic policy of that time (Argos, Melos, Sicily) did present to everyone's eyes a marked contrast with that of Pericles. This, in any case, is what comes out of the fragments 100 and 117 K of the *Demoi* of Eupolis, a play which was written about that period; it is, in fact, Pericles who is evoked, and contrasted, with the greatest regret, with the imprudent young leaders of the present time.[2]

It is thus not surprising to see with what insistence Thucydides underlines everything that made the Sicilian expedition an error, as he calls it in II. 65. In the very first sentence of Book VI, he indicates the excessive character of Athenian ambition.[3] As in the case of Pylos and Mytilene, the error can be explained by the very motives which he attributes to the decision: these are, in fact, just as contrary

---

[1] When he asks them to defend their city now in danger, he naturally comes to speak in Periclean accents (VII. 61-64; 69. 2; 77). In particular, he urges them not to give way to circumstances (61. 2); he reminds them of the virtues of their ancestors (69. 2), and of the fact that their city is 'the freest of all' (ibid.); he also asks them to restore its 'great power' (77. 7).

[2] Nicias has an important role in the play, and Pericles appears as one of those whom he summons from the underworld in order to ask their opinion. The fragment 94 K contains praise for the eloquence of Pericles, the fragment 100 K calls upon him with a respect full of regret:

Καὶ μηκέτ', ὦναξ Μιλτιάδη καὶ Περίκλεες,
ἐάσατ' ἄρχειν μειράκια βινούμενα
ἐν τοῖν σφυροῖν ἕλκοντα τὴν στρατηγίαν.

The fragment 117 K similarly recalls the wisdom of former statesmen (ὥστ' ἀσφαλῶς ἐπράττομεν, cf. Thucydides, II. 65. 5: ἀσφαλῶς διεφύλαξεν αὐτήν).

[3] VI. 1. 1: ἄπειροι οἱ πολλοὶ ὄντες τοῦ μεγέθους τῆς νήσου. As in the affair of Mytilene and in that of Pylos, the remorse felt by the Athenians underlines the extent of the mistake made: VII. 55. 1: πολὺ δὲ μείζων ἔτι τῆς στρατείας ὁ μετάμελος.

---

expedition had taken place. Thus, it may be a condemnation of the sacking of Melos (as Gilbert Murray, for instance, has often indicated), but only later readers can connect it with the Sicilian expedition. See, moreover, here, p. 281.

to εὐβουλία as were the ὀργή of Mytilene or the ἐλπίς of Pylos; they
are very close to the latter, since, although each class of citizens is
actuated by its own particular desires — the old wish for conquest, the
young wish to travel, the people want money now and state payments in the future — these passions mingle to form one single
desire and hope. Like Cleon, Alcibiades leads the people only in the
direction in which they want to go, and Thucydides uses for him in
Book VI the same verb ἐνῆγε that he used for Cleon in Book IV.[1]
Nicias, on the contrary, represents εὐβουλία: he speaks because the
city seems to him to have decided unwisely (οὐκ ὀρθῶς βεβουλεῦσθαι).

These different pieces of information are sufficient indication that
Athens has made a mistake, but they do not tell us exactly what this
mistake is. This is reserved for the antilogy which opposes Nicias
to Alcibiades.

Like the two speeches of Diodotus and Cleon in Book III, these
correspond to each other point for point.

In his introduction Nicias justifies both his intervention in the
debate and the whole of his political career: he recalls in passing that
Athens is about to throw away present advantages in order to attain
an uncertain and distant good (ἑτοίμοις — ἀφανῶν καὶ μελλόντων):
such a contrast is traditional in Greek ethical thought, and is often
repeated by Thucydides.[2]

In his introduction Alcibiades justifies both his intervention in the
debate and his way of life in general;[3] he recalls that those who try to
stand out from the common run of men are hated while they are
alive (λυπηρούς), but that, after their death, everyone claims to be
related to them, and that they bring glory to their city: a similar
contrast could already be found in the expression of Pericles' own
ideals.

In the first part of his speech, Nicias shows the disadvantages of the
expedition as far as Greece proper is concerned (ἐνθάδε): at the first
Athenian failure, the rest of the Greeks will join the Sicilians; it
would thus be far better to consolidate the empire rather than extend
it. He shows then the disadvantages of the expedition on account of
Sicily itself (ἐκεῖ): even if the Athenians are victorious, they will not

---

[1] Compare VI. 15. 2: ἐνῆγε δὲ προθυμότατα τὴν στρατείαν Ἀλκιβιάδης ὁ Κλεινίου and
IV. 21. 3: μάλιστα δὲ αὐτοὺς ἐνῆγε Κλέων ὁ Κλεαινέτου.

[2] See p. 293 and note 2.

[3] This is attacked by Nicias in the last part of his speech.

be able to maintain their dominion there; on the other hand, if Syracuse became the mistress of the island, she would not be likely to come and attack Athens, whereas she might, otherwise, come and help the cities of Greece proper, and will certainly do it if ever the Athenian intervention meets with any failure. Nicias finally concludes this part of his speech by general considerations concerning the necessity of continuing the struggle against Sparta;[1] and he attributes the ambition of the Athenians to that unfortunate elation which follows an unexpected success: ὅπερ νῦν ὑμεῖς, ὦ Ἀθηναῖοι, ἐς Λακεδαιμονίους καὶ τοὺς ξυμμάχους πεπόνθατε· διὰ τὸ παρὰ γνώμην αὐτῶν πρὸς ἃ ἐφοβεῖσθε τὸ πρῶτον περιγεγενῆσθαι καταφρονήσαντες ἤδη καὶ Σικελίας ἐφίεσθε (11. 5). Here, one recognizes once again the wise advice given at the time of Pylos. Similarly, when in the same passage Nicias contrasts τύχη with γνώμη, he is merely repeating the great lesson that we have found in the preceding episodes.

In the first part of his speech, which runs parallel to the first part of Nicias', Alcibiades demonstrates the possibility of success by considering the state of Sicily (ἐκεῖ).[2] The island, he says, is lacking in unity and will therefore allow itself to be divided. As to the state of Greece proper (ἐνθάδε), it does not constitute an obstacle: the Athenians' ancestors gained the empire in spite of the hostility of Persia, and as far as Sparta is concerned, she can do nothing against Athens. Alcibiades finally concludes this part by general considerations on imperialism, and he links his policy with that of the Athenians' forefathers, showing that, for Athens, the very existence of the empire makes progress necessary and inaction dangerous (18. 2). Athens has enemies and she runs dangers that others do not run: his teaching is here very similar to that of Pericles in his last speech, for both the vocabulary and the arguments put forward are the same.

Finally, in the last section of his speech, Nicias launches a personal attack on Alcibiades and his way of life; he blames the young in general and encourages the older men not to be ashamed of being thought cowards if they vote against the war. He is thus brought back to the general considerations put forward in the first part of his speech: he asks the older men not to give way to the desperate

---

[1] The parallelism between the two speeches underlines the difference in the two positions. While Alcibiades concludes this part by talking about imperialism, Nicias concludes it by talking about the war against Sparta: each speaker follows the idea which matters most to him.

[2] This chiasmus is the only difference in the parallel construction of the two speeches. Each speaker begins by the aspect of the question which is most favourable to him.

craving of the young for things out of their reach (μηδ' ὅπερ ἂν
αὐτοὶ πάθοιεν, δυσέρωτας εἶναι τῶν ἀπόντων), and he contrasts the
dangers of ἐπιθυμία with the virtues of πρόνοια.

In his final section, which parallels that of Nicias, Alcibiades
attacks Nicias' ἀπραγμοσύνη and the distinction which the latter
made between young and old. He also repeats the ideas expressed
in his own first section: the example of the ancestors, the dangers of
doing nothing, and, above all, the impossibility for a city which is
active by nature ever to become inactive without perishing.

Another speech by Nicias then joins this diptych, a speech which is
closely associated with the other two, and in which he discusses
factors absent from his first speech. He had shown the risks involved
in failure,[1] but, then, Alcibiades had shown the possibility of success:
he now proceeds to demonstrate the possibility of failure, by a series
of practical considerations on the situation.

The arguments of the two speakers are thus put forward in a
closely integrated form. In fact, there is every reason to think that
they reproduce the ideas and opinions actually put forward by
Nicias and Alcibiades,[2] but this form was one that Thucydides himself chose, and the contrasts and oppositions in the debate are his own
work.

What we must now try to discover is whether this reconstitution of
the debate by Thucydides was inspired by the desire to bring out
certain ideas about Athenian imperialism, and what these ideas were.

Only one part of the debate provides the possibility of judging
who is supposed to be right, and why: it is the section concerned with
the practical problems of the Sicilian expedition. The narrative of
Books VI and VII, at the same time as it confirms on the whole the

---

[1] In his first speech, he considers only two possibilities, abstention or failure; 10. 2:
ἡσυχαζόντων μὲν ὑμῶν — σφαλέντων δέ που; 11. 4: εἰ μὴ ἀφικοίμεθα — εἰ δὲ σφαλεῖμέν τι.
The possibility of success is mentioned only in passing, and in a very discouraging way, in
11. 1: εἰ καὶ κρατήσαιμεν.

[2] On this point, cf. the excellent argument which Hatzfeld (*Alcibiade*, pp. 150 ff.) puts
forward against de Sanctis. In fact, even for a supplementary theme like the opposition
between youth and age, it is possible that the debate reproduces a real theme of the discussion between the two men. In the *Demoi* of Eupolis, a contemporary play in which, as
we have seen, Nicias has an important role, the attack against Alcibiades is presented in a
very specific manner and concentrates essentially on his being a 'young whipper-snapper':
ἐάσατ' ἄρχειν μειράκια βινούμενα; cf. 310 K that Meineke attributes to the *Demoi*:

καὶ λέγουσί γε
τὰ μειράκια προϊστάμενα τοῖς ἀνδράσιν.

general thesis put forward by Nicias, should also allow us to see in some detail to what extent the facts are meant to fit his analysis and contradict the other one.

It is, indeed, clear not only that the facts in general confirm the accuracy of Nicias' forecast, but that his ideas, which are also formulated by the two Syracusans, Hermocrates and Athenagoras, constitute themes deliberately repeated throughout Book VI, the result being an analysis of forces comparable to that of Book I, but made up, on this occasion, of confirmatory evidence coming from different sources.

This is particularly clear in the passages concerned with Sicily itself.

Sicily, Nicias points out, is a large and distant country.[1] It is all very well for Alcibiades to say that its inhabitants lack unity and weapons, Nicias easily replies that they can be neither won over nor really defeated. As far as defeat is concerned, he mentions among other difficulties created by the distance between Sicily and Athens, the absence of supplies and the lack of cavalry; and he uses this analysis to bring out the great danger that would accompany any reverse in enemy country.

All he says on that matter is shown to be true by what happens later: the Sicilian towns refuse to be won over,[2] and, on the contrary, form themselves into an alliance. This is what Hermocrates had hoped for in his speech in Book IV, and what he had insisted on in his speech in Book VI.[3] Since Athenagoras here agrees, there is a definite link between the three opposite speakers. Thus we have:

Nicias (21. 1): ἄλλως τε καὶ εἰ ξυστῶσιν αἱ πόλεις φοβηθεῖσαι.

Hermocrates (33. 4-5): μᾶλλον γὰρ ἐθελήσουσιν ἐκπλαγέντες ἡμῖν ξυμμαχεῖν· πάντα γὰρ ὑπὸ δέους ξυνίσταται.

Athenagoras (37. 2): ἐν πάσῃ πολεμίᾳ Σικελίᾳ (ξυστήσεται γάρ).

---

[1] II. I: διὰ πολλοῦ γε καὶ πολλῶν ὄντων.

[2] Compare VI. 20. 2: μεγάλας καὶ οὔθ' ὑπηκόους ἀλλήλων οὐδὲ δεομένας μεταβολῆς, ἣ ἂν ἐκ βιαίου τις δουλείας ἄσμενος ἐς ῥᾴω μετάστασιν χωροίη ... and VII. 55. 2: πόλεσι ... ὁμοιοτρόποις ἐπελθόντες, δημοκρατουμέναις τε, ὥσπερ καὶ αὐτοί, καὶ ναῦς καὶ ἵππους καὶ μεγέθη ἐχούσαις, οὐ δυνάμενοι ἐπενεγκεῖν οὔτ' ἐκ πολιτείας τι μεταβολῆς τὸ διάφορον αὐτοῖς, ᾧ προσῆγον ἄν, οὔτ' ἐκ παρασκευῆς πολλῷ κρείσσονος ...

[3] He counts on fear to create this union, and immediately proposes sending ambassadors everywhere; this will be done, with the results that are known. Practically all the cities in Sicily join with Syracuse; cf. VII. 33. 2: σχεδὸν γάρ τι ἤδη πᾶσα ἡ Σικελία πλὴν 'Ακραγαντίνων (οὗτοι δ' οὐδὲ μεθ' ἑτέρων ἦσαν), οἱ δ' ἄλλοι ἐπὶ τοὺς 'Αθηναίους μετὰ τῶν Συρακοσίων οἱ πρότερον περιορώμενοι ξυστάντες ἐβοήθουν.

On the other hand, the cities are equally impossible to defeat, and the reasons for this are expressed in a series of terms which are also underlined by close verbal similarities. Thus we have:

Nicias (21. 2): πολύ τε ἀπὸ τῆς ἡμετέρας αὐτῶν μέλλομεν πλεῖν.

Hermocrates (33. 5): πολὺ ἀπὸ τῆς ἑαυτῶν ἀπάραντες.

Nicias (22): ἵνα καὶ τὰ ἐπιτήδεια ῥᾷον ἐσκομιζώμεθα ... ἵνα ἤν που ὑπὸ ἀπλοίας ἀπολαμβανώμεθα ἔχῃ ἡ στρατιὰ τὰ ἐπιτήδεια.

Hermocrates (33. 5): δι' ἀπορίαν τῶν ἐπιτηδείων.

Nicias (21. 1): μὴ ὑπὸ ἱππέων πολλῶν εἴργεσθαι τῆς γῆς, ἄλλως τε καὶ εἰ ... μὴ ἀντιπαράσχωσιν ἡμῖν φίλοι τινὲς γενόμενοι ἄλλοι ἢ Ἐγεσταῖοι ᾧ ἀμυνούμεθα ἱππικόν.

Athenagoras (37. 1): οἷς γ ἐπίσταμαι οὔθ' ἵππους ἀκολουθήσοντας, οὐδ' αὐτόθεν πορισθησομένους εἰ μὴ ὀλίγους τινὰς παρὰ Ἐγεσταίων.

And, as to the fate of this army defeated deep in enemy country, we know that Nicias had foreseen it only too accurately.

His arguments thus form part of an analysis which Thucydides himself presents as valid, while Alcibiades, on the other hand, is mistaken. The same thing is true for the passages concerned with Greece proper, and here we come nearer to the basic argument of the two speeches. The whole of Nicias' analysis, in his first speech, does in fact come down to this double idea: Sparta will go and help Syracuse, and Syracuse in turn will help Sparta. Here again the speeches made in Syracuse and the events that occur confirm the accuracy of his forecast.[1]

Does this, however, mean to say that Alcibiades is mistaken? In fact, Thucydides does not make him express any argument (apart from an analysis of the impotence of the Spartans in face of Athenian sea-power, which Pericles himself would not have disowned); but, instead, he allows him to express a reservation, to which the rest of the work gives added significance. Alcibiades says, indeed, that Sparta will not come to the help of Syracuse ἢν ὑμεῖς ὀρθῶς βουλεύησθε (17. 6). Now, what made possible the Spartan intervention in Sicily was, apart from the strategic errors committed by Nicias,[2] the presence at Sparta of Alcibiades himself, an Alcibiades whom

---

[1] Athenagoras says in 36. 4: οὐ γὰρ αὐτοὺς εἰκὸς Πελοποννησίους τε ὑπολιπόντας καὶ τὸν ἐκεῖ πόλεμον μήπω βεβαίως καταλελυμένους ἐπ' ἄλλον πόλεμον οὐκ ἐλάσσω ἑκόντας ἐλθεῖν, ἐπεὶ ἔγωγε ἀγαπᾶν οἴομαι αὐτοὺς ὅτι οὐχ ἡμεῖς ἐπ' ἐκείνους ἐρχόμεθα, πόλεις τοσαῦται καὶ οὕτω μεγάλαι.

[2] See VII. 42. 3.

Athens had had the folly to condemn. It is certainly on this explanation that Thucydides insists most strongly, indicating it directly in VI. 15. 3,[1] and going into great detail about the political manœuvres and intrigues of Alcibiades' enemies in chapters 27-30 and 53-61.[2] Indeed, he considers this last episode to be sufficiently characteristic to justify the introduction of a long parenthesis on the tyrannicides.[3] Finally, one of the keystones in the construction of the book is the speech which he gives to Alcibiades at Sparta (89-93): it is this which gives perfect expression to the two ideas originally suggested by Hermocrates and the Corinthians,[4] and which provides them with the two-edged weapon that was to give them victory: the idea of sending Gylippus and of fortifying Decelea.

✳ Without the arrival of Gylippus, Syracuse might have fallen – it might, indeed, have fallen immediately if Nicias had not waited before taking action (VII. 42. 3). And Thucydides is careful to present the arrival of Gylippus as a sensational event: everything is going in Athens' favour, Syracuse is beginning to despair (VI. 103. 2) – then Gylippus arrives (104)! It is at the very moment when Syracuse is going to ask for terms, when the assembly is just about to meet, that Gongylus arrives with the good news. The dramatic effect brought out by the actual narration of events is made even more conspicuous by the direct commentary which Thucydides himself gives in VII. 2. 4: παρὰ τοσοῦτον μὲν Συράκουσαι ἦλθον κινδύνου.[5]

The second plan was realized in a less dramatic fashion, but was equally fatal to Athens; and this again is proved by the direct commentary which Thucydides gives in VII. 28. Yet, even then, Athens still seemed able to hold out, which was a surprise to everyone: Thucydides recalls this in VII. 42. 2, showing how near Athens had been to winning.

---

[1] After a severe portrait of Alcibiades, Thucydides adds: ὅπερ καὶ καθεῖλεν ὕστερον τὴν τῶν 'Αθηναίων πόλιν οὐχ ἥκιστα, and he then explains that the Athenians turned away from him, although κράτιστα διαθέντι τὰ τοῦ πολέμου (see later, p. 214 and p. 223).

[2] And he clearly takes sides against them: they are acting through jealousy (28. 2), with trickery (29. 3); good people are arrested on the word of wicked ones (53. 2); there is no proof for the whole business (60-61).

[3] This is linked to the main idea only as a footnote might be, but it tells us about the direction of Thucydides' ideas. The fact that its presence can be justified only by deep reasons, but which are not immediately obvious, makes it impossible to agree with Schwartz that it was added by an unintelligent editor: the rule of the *lectio difficilior* is valid for this type of problem.

[4] See Bodin, *Alcibiade interprète* . . .

[5] Nicias himself remains hopeful for a long time: in VII. 49. 1, he is the only one who wants to stay in Syracuse, because of some favourable information that he has.

Thus, if Alcibiades, by proposing the Sicilian expedition, had led Athens to take a wrong decision, Athens herself, by the policy which she later followed — and in particular by sending Alcibiades into exile — [1] failed even more seriously to follow the principles of εὐβουλία and committed an even worse mistake.[2]

Indeed, one cannot insist too strongly on the absolute coherence to be found between the account of the expedition such as it is presented in the whole of Books VI and VII, and the judgment made of it by Thucydides in II. 65. There, as we know, Thucydides distinguishes two reasons why the expedition was a mistake, and these correspond to the two ideas which we have followed out in the narrative of events: 'Such weakness in a great and imperial city led to many errors, of which the greatest was the Sicilian expedition; the mistake was not so much (οὐ τοσοῦτον) a miscalculation about the enemy's power as (ὅσον) a mistake of the people who, instead of consulting for the interest of the expedition that they had sent out, were occupied in intriguing against one another for the leadership of the democracy, and not only grew remiss in the management of the army, but became embroiled, for the first time, in civil strife.' In both the judgment and the narrative, two different responsibilities are mentioned, and that of the politicians is even greater than that of the imperialists.[3]

This responsibility on the part of the politicians makes the problem a little more complicated and makes Thucydides' judgment of it more subtle.[4] Nevertheless it does not change the meaning of the antilogy. The reservation made by Alcibiades indicates the possibility of a mistake for which it provides no remedy, and does not wipe out his own mistake.[5]

---

[1] It should in fact be noted that this lack of political wisdom on the part of Athens is not only marked by the exile of Alcibiades: Thucydides often refers to it, for instance when Nicias is forced to give to his letter a tone of desperate insistence (VII. 11 ff.), or when he considers how angry the Athenians will be if a retreat takes place (VII. 48. 3-4).

[2] Hatzfeld (*Alcibiade*, pp. 199-200) does not consider this judgment by Thucydides to be valid. If it is not an obvious one, then it is all the more important for us.

[3] In certain cases, in Thucydides, οὐ τοσοῦτον . . . ὅσον is more or less the equivalent of οὐκ . . . ἀλλά (I. 9. 1); but this is not most frequently the case (cf. I. 11. 1; II. 87. 4; V. 95; VIII. 45. 2). That is why we changed some words in Jowett's translation, quoted here for all the rest of the sentence.

[4] It even has some bearing on the analysis of the forces, since some people have supposed that Alcibiades would have succeeded in exploiting, as he wanted to, the possible disagreements between the Sicilian cities; cf. Thibaudet, p. 96.

[5] Alcibiades' speech does contain some indications which could have made the final issue less disastrous: he certainly says that if things do not go well, all the Athenians will have to do is to come back with the fleet. Now if this had been done when it was still possible,

All that we can say is this: if, in the antilogy, Nicias appears as the spokesman of wisdom, the antilogy itself expresses only one aspect of the problem, only one of the two terms — and that the less important — of Thucydides' judgment. Once this is assumed, it is possible to maintain that Thucydides is entirely favourable to the argument in the first speech.

Now, as far as theory is concerned, this first speech seems once again to be further away from the Periclean tradition than does the second. It is, in fact, easy to show the relationship between Nicias' and Pericles' prudence. But it is even easier to show what close links there are between Alcibiades' speech and the last speech of Pericles.

Not only does he, like Pericles, though in a different field, support and defend an unpopularity which is and will be compensated for by glory, but he also expresses very similar ideas about imperialism. Like Pericles, and like the 'Fighters-of-Marathon' of Aristophanes, Alcibiades declares himself the follower of the great tradition of the Persian wars and of the Fifty Years;[1] like Pericles, he invokes the example of all those who have ever ruled over any empire,[2] and finally, again like Pericles, he speaks of the danger threatening Athens because of the hostility which everyone feels towards her, and which obliges her to pursue her imperialistic policies indefinitely.[3]

However, the two sets of arguments differ as much as the two policies.

In the same way as the principle of 'glorious unpopularity' changes its meaning as it moves from the realm of foreign policy to that of private life,[4] so do the ideas of imperialism, as they pass from a policy of firmness to one of conquest. Where Pericles declares that Athens

---

[1] Compare Pericles, II. 62. 3: τῶν τε πατέρων . . . and Alcibiades, VI. 17. 7: οἱ γὰρ πατέρες ἡμῶν . . . , or VI. 18. 6: ὥσπερ καὶ οἱ πατέρες ἡμῶν.

[2] Compare Pericles, II. 64. 5: ὅσοι ἕτεροι ἑτέρων ἠξίωσαν ἄρχειν, and Alcibiades, VI. 18. 2: ὅσοι δὴ ἄλλοι ἦρξαν.

[3] Compare Pericles, II. 63. 2: ἧς οὐδ' ἐκστῆναι ἔτι ὑμῖν ἔστιν . . . ὡς τυραννίδα γὰρ ἤδη ἔχετε αὐτήν, ἣν λαβεῖν μὲν ἄδικον δοκεῖ εἶναι, ἀφεῖναι δὲ ἐπικίνδυνον, and Alcibiades, VI. 18. 3. καὶ οὐκ ἔστιν ἡμῖν ταμιεύεσθαι ἐς ὅσον βουλόμεθα ἄρχειν, ἀλλὰ ἀνάγκη, ἐπειδήπερ ἐν τῷδε καθέσταμεν, τοῖς μὲν ἐπιβουλεύειν, τοὺς δὲ μὴ ἀνιέναι, διὰ τὸ ἀρχθῆναι ἂν ὑφ' ἑτέρων αὐτοῖς κίνδυνον εἶναι εἰ μὴ αὐτοὶ ἄλλων ἄρχοιμεν.

[4] For Thucydides, there is a considerable difference between the two problems: in the realm of foreign policy, he uses no standards other than those of enlightened self-interest; but as far as private life is concerned, he deplores any tendency towards a decline in morality (see, in particular, III. 82).

---

the expedition would merely have been a reversal with no further consequences. There is therefore much less folly in his words than in Athens' actions. He is nevertheless wrong, and even this reversal with no further consequences should have been avoided.

must not give up (ἐκστῆναι). Alcibiades refuses to reckon with any limits (ταμιεύεσθαι ἐς ὅσον βουλόμεθα ἄρχειν): what must be done is to contrive action against some, without losing hold of the others (τοῖς μὲν ἐπιβουλεύειν, τοὺς δὲ μὴ ἀνιέναι). Both statesmen fight against the ἀπράγμονες, and present apparently similar reasons for doing so; but the two arguments differ in meaning; and, contrary to what we saw when comparing Cleon to Pericles, the very expressions used by Thucydides mark the exact point at which the two policies begin to diverge.

At the same time, they show where Alcibiades' programme is mistaken, or, at least, might be.

For even if the argument established by Alcibiades were valid in principle, it is not — as is that of Pericles — an argument with only one possible application. In the antology of Book VI, the debate centres round a specific question: should the Athenians go and make war against Sicily or should they not? Alcibiades says: we are forced to go to Sicily because we must either make conquests or find ourselves in danger. But there is nothing to prove that this danger might come from Sicily, or that it is against Sicily that Athens must go to war: Nicias can even insist on the common interest which links together two such 'tyrant-cities' as Athens and Syracuse.[1] 'Not to give up' is a precise law, but 'to intervene' an uncertain and therefore dangerous principle. Athens, while attempting to apply this principle, did not keep in mind her most formidable enemy and her greatest risk: unable to arrive at a correct estimate of the means at her disposal, she thus fell into error.

By this distinction between the two policies, the analysis made in the second case completes that made in the first: they can be brought together and thus disclose the unity and logical connection between these wise and then unwise measures.

We must therefore ask ourselves whether these similarities are or are not deliberate, whether the speeches by Pericles and Alcibiades are written to illustrate each other, and fairly freely arranged with the intention of bringing out a certain relationship between the two policies, or whether they express facts and opinions independent one

---

[1] The idea of a Syracusan threat to Athens was not an absurd one. The Egestaeans declare in 6. 2: ἀλλά τε πολλά . . . καὶ κεφάλαιον εἰ Συρακόσιοι Λεοντίνους τε ἀναστήσαντες . . . τὴν ἐκείνων δύναμιν ξυγκαθέλωσιν, and, similarly, Athenagoras says in 36. 4: ἐπεὶ ἔγωγε ἀγαπᾶν οἴομαι αὐτοὺς ὅτι οὐχ ἡμεῖς ἐπ' ἐκείνους ἐρχόμεθα. But these rather prejudiced remarks carry little weight when placed by the side of what happened both before and after the expedition.

from another, whose similarity becomes apparent only afterwards, as a kind of additional and independent verification.

Now if the particular phrase with which we were just concerned is capable, by the echoes it arouses, of making us lean towards the first interpretation, the same thing is not true of the context as a whole, in which this phrase is to be found. There, nothing recalls Pericles, either by contrast or by similarity: the whole thought process and the whole climate are different.

The idea of the obligations which are peculiar to Athens and which push her on to the path of conquest is in fact both followed and preceded by purely psychological considerations which, since they are repeated at the end of the speech (18. 6-7), are likely to represent the most important part of Alcibiades' argument. The idea which they express is that the city, if inactive, would, like anything else, wear itself out;[1] if it prefers inactivity, then it should change its whole way of life;[2] and everyone should remain faithful to his own way of life, whatever that may be.[3]

Unlike Pericles, Alcibiades thus bases his argument on a general consideration and not on a particular fact peculiar to the Athenian empire. He comes near to Pericles only in a short part of one sentence, the meaning of which is in fact weakened by the less definite ideas with which it stands tightly interwoven.

Moreover, the reasoning itself is presented in a less rigorous form. What Alcibiades fears is not massacre or death, this something 'worse than slavery' which was evoked in Book II; it is, on the contrary, something which Pericles did not think it was possible even to stop to consider: the danger of falling under the rule of somebody else (ὑφ' ἑτέρων); and even then, he presents it as a risk which Athens might avoid, since, like Cleon in III. 40. 4, he considers the possibility of Athens changing her manner of life, of giving up. Obviously, this is not a possibility that he seriously envisages, but he does present it as one solution: where Pericles showed that there was only one way that Athens could follow, Alcibiades, like Cleon, puts forward an alternative (18. 3: εἰ μὴ καὶ τὰ ἐπιτηδεύματα ἐς τὸ ὁμοῖον μεταλήψεσθε).

---

[1] 18. 2: περὶ αὐτῆς ἂν ταύτης μᾶλλον κινδυνεύοιμεν, and, with more precision, 18. 6: τρίψεσθαί τε αὐτὴν περὶ αὐτήν, ὥσπερ καὶ ἄλλο τι.

[2] 18. 3: καὶ οὐκ ἐκ τοῦ αὐτοῦ ἐπισκεπτέον ὑμῖν τοῖς ἄλλοις τὸ ἥσυχον, εἰ μὴ καὶ τὸ ἐπιτηδεύματα ἐς τὸ ὁμοῖον μεταλήψεσθε.

[3] 18. 7: παράπαν τε γιγνώσκω πόλιν μὴ ἀπράγμονα τάχιστ' ἄν μοι δοκεῖν ἀπραγμοσύνης μεταβολῇ διαφθαρῆναι, καὶ τῶν ἀνθρώπων ἀσφαλέστατα τούτους οἰκεῖν οἳ ἂν τοῖς παροῦσιν ἤθεσι καὶ νόμοις, ἢν καὶ χείρω ᾖ, ἥκιστα διαφόρως πολιτεύωσιν.

All these circumstances indicate that, taking the speech as a whole, there is no deliberate attempt to contrast Alcibiades' ideas with those of Pericles.

If we add that this 'way of life' of Athens is here evoked in slightly derogatory terms, reminiscent rather of the harsh tone of Cleon than of the ardour of the Funeral Oration,[1] and that, in addition, the speech made by Nicias is very similar to the lesson of Book IV, it must be admitted that the agreement between the different elements in Thucydides' ideas does not seem here to have been brought out by a deliberate and systematic intention. It is possible that one of the sentences in Alcibiades' speech was deliberately connected with the last speech of Pericles (whether the former suggested the latter or the other way round), but the antilogy itself was constructed according to an intention which remained independent of this speech. There are indeed connections, but no primary and peremptory relation.

This shows all the more clearly the complete consistency of Thucydides' ideas: the practical analysis of the situation, and the narrative of events to which it provides the key, exactly fit the judgment of II. 65 — and the theoretical part of the analysis exactly fits the ideas expressed in Pericles' last speech.

In order to trace the development of Thucydides' ideas, we need to establish whether this consistency comes from the fact that these passages were written at the same date, or whether, before the later passages (like the judgment of II. 65 and Pericles' last speech) were written, Thucydides' ideas had already assumed the form that they present here.[2] This involves raising, for the Sicilian books, the question of the composition of the work.

The elements which might be used to solve this problem are the following.

In any case, the account of the Sicilian expedition was written late: this is obvious as soon as one takes into account the lapse of time necessary for Thucydides to make a general judgment of the events that he is presenting, and also to gather and arrange information

---

[1] See p. 163, note 3, for the similarity which exists, as regards both the ideas and the expression used, between III. 37. 3 and VI. 18. 7.

[2] There is no difference of general tendency which could enable us to link the antilogy and the Sicilian books as a whole with what I have called the early chain; but it is possible that the extremely obvious character of the judgment to be made on the expedition would have made it less easy for differences to show themselves than in the books analysed hitherto.

P

about the different circumstances. More precisely, certain passages could not have been written before a period round about 404, and can thus be used as clues. To mention only those which are fairly certain,[1] one might quote the three following:

– in VII. 87. 5, Thucydides says of the Sicilian expedition: ξυνέβη τε ἔργον τοῦτο ['Ελληνικὸν] τῶν κατὰ τὸν πόλεμον τόνδε μέγιστον γενέσθαι. This remark takes us beyond 404.

– in VII. 57. 2, he speaks of the inhabitants of Aegina: οἳ τότε Αἴγιναν εἶχον. This indication takes us beyond 405.

– in VI. 15. 3, speaking of the jealousy aroused by the life of Alcibiades, he remarks: ὅπερ καὶ καθεῖλεν ὕστερον τὴν τῶν 'Αθηναίων πόλιν οὐχ ἥκιστα. It does seem that we must see in this καθεῖλεν, as Schadewaldt does, an allusion to the final disaster.[2]

On the other hand, there is no reliable indication which might enable us to fix the date before which these books were written.[3] These are the elements which one must start with to solve the problem.

By themselves, they are insufficient. Three interpretations of them are possible, and three have been put forward.

First of all, one may consider that the whole narrative is early, and even that it was written before Thucydides saw the unity of the Peloponnesian War. This is Ćwikliński's theory: he, in fact, considers the account of the expedition to be a monograph,[4] inserted afterwards. In this interpretation, the passages which are found to be

---

[1] I am deliberately omitting the clues which have been suggested, but which do not seem definitive (such as VI. 17. 5: the anachronism of ἐν τῷδε τῷ πολέμῳ).

[2] See later p. 223.

[3] In VI. 62. 2 and in VII. 58. 2, Thucydides uses the present tense in order to speak of Himera, which was destroyed in 409. This indication, first noted by Ziegler, has been developed by Pohlenz, but Patzer, p. 31, n. 67, has very convincingly refuted the argument by showing that geographical information always seems to be given by Thucydides in the present tense, without this implying any definite temporal significance; in I. 56. 2, Thucydides says of the Potidaeans: οἳ οἰκοῦσιν ἐπὶ τῷ ἰσθμῷ τῆς Παλλήνης, which only remained true until 430-429 (see Patzer, p. 14).

[4] He bases his argument on a number of considerations. First of all, Thucydides, in these books, talks about the Sicilian expedition as if it were a separate war. On this point, see p. 189, n. 1. Moreover, these books include an archaeological preface; they sometimes repeat facts which were already mentioned in the first books (VI. 1. 2, cf. IV. 24. 4-5; VI. 15, cf. V. 43. 2; VI. 31. 2, cf. I. 56. 1, etc.), the principal repetition being that dealing with the Peisistratidae; the passages which seem to show signs of revision all concern Greece proper (thus the speech of Alcibiades at Sparta, the catalogue of allies, chapter VII. 28 on the φιλονικία of Athens, VI. 93, VI. 105 and VII. 1, VII. 9). I shall not refute these arguments in detail, but shall simply present my own interpretation of these facts when the time comes.

late date from the revision which had to take place at the time of insertion.

It is also possible to consider that the account was written early, that is to say before 404, but that it was nevertheless written with the twenty-seven year war in mind. This is the theory put forward by Schwartz, and in this case the passages which appear to be later additions are due to revisions. For Schwartz, these revisions are partly the work of an editor piecing together as best he can the successive fragments left by Thucydides.

Finally, one can maintain that the whole narrative is late, and that it was written after the final defeat and occupation of Athens. This theory is put forward by Schadewaldt, who considers that Thucydides saw the full meaning of the episode only in the light of the great disaster, and that he described it when the link between the Sicilian expedition and the events of 404 appeared to him in all its force.

The first interpretation has scarcely any supporters now, and should in my view be completely abandoned. The arguments on which it is based are not convincing, and there are many facts which contradict it. It is extremely difficult to admit the notion that all the passages dealing with Greece proper — among which is the speech of Alcibiades at Sparta[1] — were added afterwards in a narrative which otherwise was left untouched. Even if this could be done, the hypothesis would still be improbable, for surely the condemnation which Thucydides makes of the expedition is that the war with Sparta is still going on. This idea comes into Nicias' speech (VI. 10), as well as into that of Athenagoras (VI. 36. 4), and it is implicit throughout the narrative. Moreover, it is impossible that Thucydides should not have waited for the expedition to be over before writing its history, and it is highly unlikely that he could have seen the Spartans fortifying Decelea without at the same time conceiving the idea of the unity of the war: what other fact could have better brought this home to him? Finally, if one considers the rest of the History, the same idea becomes apparent, for it is extremely difficult to admit that all the references to Sicily — references which are carefully spaced out, and of which some are indispensable to the account of the war — should have been inserted after the work was completed. The opposite is more likely to be the case, for these indications show, from the very beginning, the link between the events which take place in Sicily and those which concern Greece proper, and suggest that it was normal

[1] See later, p. 220.

to link the great expedition with the Peloponnesian War in exactly the same way.

If we reject Ćwikliński's theory, two possibilities still remain to be considered: that of Schwartz, which applies the non-unitarian views to the Sicilian books, and that of Schadewaldt, who considers them as a single unit written late.

Schadewaldt's interpretation depends on the meaning which, in his view, Thucydides attributes to the expedition.

Is Schadewaldt right in maintaining that the idea of the final disaster is necessary to justify both the perfect finish of the narrative and the general meaning of the Sicilian books? There is no *a priori* reason for thinking so. By the enormous losses which it involved, the expedition immediately appeared, taken quite by itself, to be an unprecedented occurrence; the allied risings which immediately followed it are a proof that this was an impression shared by the whole of Greece. And when Nicias insists, in VII. 61. 1 or in VII. 64. 2,[1] on the seriousness of what is at stake, he is certainly doing no more than expressing the feelings of all those who took part in the expedition. Why, therefore, should we suppose that Thucydides waited ten years before deciding that the expedition deserved special treatment because of the irreparable harm which it had done to Athens?

Certainly, when he analyses the reasons for the disaster which over-took the Sicilian expedition, Thucydides brings out the first symptoms of that evil that was to be fatal to Athens in the course of the Ionian War, namely the untimely interference of internal political conflicts which brought all effective external action to an end. Now this factor, on which he insists, as we have seen, in the judgment of II. 65, is actually brought out in Books VI and VII. But why should it have been necessary for him to wait for the last years of the war before realizing its importance? That this was in no way the case is shown once again by the theatre, and more particularly by Aristophanes.

---

[1] Thucydides' own insistence is fairly explicable by the circumstances of the narrative; this insistence is very well marked, which is why it seems particularly unfortunate to delete, in the first passage, as Stahl and Hude do, the words οὐχ ἧσσον ἢ τοῖς πολεμίοις: they underline the extraordinary nature of the situation, since it is the invader himself who is fighting for the salvation of his own country. It will also be noted that this indication of what is at stake is here placed at the beginning of the speech, whereas it is normally a theme of the *epilogos* (thus II. 89. 10; IV. 63. 2; VI. 80. 4-5).

In the *Birds*, in 414, we already find numerous allusions to the internal strife from which the city is suffering;[1] and a joke like that of lines 1071 ff., which, rather foolishly, raises again the affair of the tyrannicides,[2] is sufficient to assure us that Thucydides was right when he mentioned the general attention given at that time — sometimes in a very abusive way — to such events. This justifies the presence in the Sicilian books of the famous parenthesis on the tyrannicides, whose inclusion Schwartz so strongly criticizes.

In *Lysistrata*, in 411, things are even clearer; there are a very large number of allusions to tyranny, to the sons of Peisistratus, and to their murder;[3] in lines 1150 ff. Aristophanes justifies Thucydides' observation in VI. 53. 3 by telling how the Spartans put an end to the tyranny of Hippias. And in the same play there is a long and very important passage asking the Athenians to cure the internal condition of the city by eliminating certain citizens and allowing more reliable elements to take their place.[4] So the evil of civil strife from which Athens suffered was already noticeable, and the subject of normal comment, in 411.

In the *Frogs*, in 405, the need for reforms on the home front is more clearly stated than ever; but the very comparison between the themes of this play and those of the two preceding ones shows the continuity of Aristophanes' judgment, and confirms that what we had in the *Birds* and *Lysistrata* was a very general judgment, which did not depend on everyday life and problems. Here, the idea is given full importance;[5] the good citizens appear like old pieces of gold when set beside others, and it is the whole of the Athens of the present day which is contrasted with the Athens of the past. In this last period of the Peloponnesian War, attacks against individuals are replaced in Aristophanes by more fundamental criticisms of policy,[6] exactly at the same time as in Thucydides we begin to find the idea of a deep-seated reason for all the ills from which Athens is suffering. If, therefore, it is true that such an idea came to be perceived even more clearly as the years went by and these ills became more

---

[1] Cf. 124, 147, etc.

[2] ἤν τε τῶν τυράννων τίς τινα|τῶν τεθνηκότων ἀποκτείνῃ.

[3] See 619, 630, 665, 1150 ff.

[4] 574 ff.

[5] See 359 ff., 686-705, 716-737, 1008-1088.

[6] See Croiset, *Aristophane et les partis à Athènes*: 'Behind the action of the individual, he could see more general and more profound causes which his play tended to bring to light.'

grave, it is also true that it could well have appeared as early as 414, and certainly before 404: proof of both these affirmations can be found in the plays of Aristophanes. Thus the very foundation of Schadewaldt's theory begins to give way.

There are certainly late passages in the account of the expedition, and passages which, as has already been admitted, refer to the disaster of 404. There may be many more than has been stated.[1] But there is no proof that these passages were not added later to a narrative which had already been composed, since, as we have seen, there is no proof that the narrative as a whole necessarily refers to these events.

Is it, on the other hand, possible to prove that these passages were added later? To do this, we should need to establish that they do not fit normally into the narrative and thus discover which are the uneven joints. Now, it would be very strange if Thucydides had revised his text so unskilfully that all the later additions were easily detectable. Nevertheless, if it could be proved that passages of this kind do exist, we should at the same time have proved that the narrative in which they were inserted was written earlier, and that consequently the account of the expedition was not written all at once after 404.

Two attempts have been made to detect these passages, first by Ćwikliński and later, in more detail, by Schwartz. The latter even finds such clumsy insertions in the text that he attributes them to a mistaken editor, holding that they are unworthy of Thucydides himself.

Now, among the passages noted by Ćwikliński and Schwartz (if we omit the passages on tyrannicides, which only Schwartz mentions and which I have already discussed), the first does in fact contain one of the clues that have been noted as indicating a date after 405: it is the 'catalogue' of allies, with the reference to the inhabitants of Aegina; the second is the one noted as certainly indicating a late date of composition, and is the speech of Alcibiades at Sparta; and the third, although containing in itself no clue as to the date at which it

---

[1] I have taken into account only those indications which seem sure. There are many other passages which have not been noted up to now, and which are not in themselves conclusive, but which could be very well explained on the assumption that, when Thucydides wrote them, he had the final disaster in mind. For example, when the Syracusans foresee that their victory will deal a fatal blow at Athens (VII. 56. 2), or when Nicias speaks in the past tense, and with so much emotion, of the Athenian empire (VII. 63. 3: ἐθαυμάζεσθε κατὰ τὴν Ἑλλάδα).

was written, can, as we shall see, be explained particularly well if it is assumed that it was written after 404. It is thus interesting to see whether it is true that these passages could not have been written at the same time as the context from which they are taken, and in order to be included where we read them now.[1]

The list of allies seems to be the least convincing of the passages. The essential argument put forward by Ćwikliński and Schwartz is provided by the first sentence. Both scholars are, in fact, surprised that the Sicilians, in order to prove their merit, mention in VII. 56. 3, the number of their own allies as well as the number of the Athenian allies. This surprise reveals a faulty understanding of the passage; the pride of the Syracusans comes less from the merit which they will show in winning the battle than from the very importance of this battle. The double list is thus justified, and it underlines, as in Homer or Herodotus, the importance of the forthcoming victory. We should therefore have no reason to be surprised either at the τοσοίδε of 57. 1, or at the repetition of the idea after this parenthesis in 59. 2. The meaning attributed to it by Schwartz — the destruction of ethnic groupings by the war — is in fact only a second meaning: perhaps it is even meant to be subordinate to the first, and Thucydides, by noting on each occasion the destruction of earlier groupings, might be intending to indicate that the present conflict is so serious that none of the traditional links has been able to prevail against it. However that may be, the reasons put forward are not sufficient to prove that the passage was inserted by an editor; they do not even prove that it was not written at the same time as the context in which it is found.[2]

The problem raised by Alcibiades' speech at Sparta is rather more difficult. Scholars who see in it a passage written after the rest of Book VI note some surprising facts both before and after it takes place: before, Alcibiades suddenly appears in an unexpected manner, and the role which he plays in relation to the Syracusans and the Corinthians is not very well defined; afterwards, one finds a certain confusion in the results: in particular, we are told that the Spartans

[1] These of course are two different questions.

[2] The other particular clues which have been offered are of secondary importance and do not deserve discussion. They could only be added to some better and more significant indication; this is true, for instance, of VII. 59. 1 (mentioned by Cwiklinski) where Thucydides says that no more reinforcements will arrive, something we already know. These different remarks show in both critics a lack of understanding, which almost seems to be systematic, and which it is useless to try to correct on each individual point.

I will recall, moreover, that I shall make no attempt here to prove that their conclusions are incorrect, but merely that their arguments are insufficient.

'are thinking' about fortifying Decelea, which does not mean anything, since they have not yet put their plan into operation. What is even more important is that, as Schwartz notes, the role which Alcibiades plays in relation to Decelea seems, according to VII. 18. 1, to be quite a subordinate one. It can thus be argued that the speech which he makes at Sparta represents a new idea of the influence which he exercised, and one which is lacking in the rest of the narrative, since Thucydides did not realize how great this influence was until he had already completed his account of the Sicilian expedition. It was only later, according to this view, that Thucydides considered Alcibiades as the man whose genius prepared and foresaw everything.

There is nothing conclusive about these different remarks. They do not take sufficient account either of Thucydides' method of writing history or of the meaning and composition of Books VI and VII.

I have already indicated earlier that this speech plays a definite part in the composition of these books, for it provides the double programme that explains the final outcome of the struggle. In the progressive definition of this programme, the role played by this speech in relation to that of the Syracusans and Corinthians is perfectly clear. And as to the device of presenting together, for the purpose of analysis, the two different parts of this programme, which will be realized only one after the other, and of using a more or less skilful sentence so as to postpone one of them until later, we have already seen a very clear example of this in the case of Pericles' first speech (I. 144. 2).

It is therefore possible that Thucydides did not, at the beginning, give so clearly marked a role to Alcibiades, and that he did not originally put into his mouth the speech which we read in the present version of the History; but the way in which the events of Book VI are presented does not enable us to state that this is definitely the case.[1] If the passage is a later addition, then it was brought in by Thucydides in the course of a careful revision of his text, which took full account of all he had written before.

The final passage that must be discussed is that of the persistence and determination of the Athenians in carrying on the war which are described in VII. 28, in the context of the decision to send back the Thracian mercenaries. Schwartz considers that paragraphs 27 and 28

---

[1] This is what both Bodin and – although he thus contradicts his earlier opinion – Wilamowitz, have shown (see *Hermes*, 60).

are made up of three passages written by Thucydides and put together at that point in the book by the editor, but that none of
them has anything to do with the decision to send back the Thracian
contingents. Ćwikliński criticizes only a particular section of the
passage, that contained in 28. 3.

The arguments put forward by Schwartz to prove that the analysis
of the financial difficulties of Athens could not have been originally
intended to occupy the place that it does, are as follows: first of all,
the analysis is placed by Thucydides at a time when the occupation of
Decelea has only just begun, and yet he speaks of it as something which
has been going on for a long time;[1] secondly, he begins by giving this
occupation as the main cause of Athens' difficulties, and then, soon
afterwards, begins to explain them by different reasons.

These two arguments are in no way conclusive: the only thing
which they indicate is Thucydides' own intervention in the composition of his work. As in many other cases, he has here brought
together, at a place which he himself has chosen, a number of
different facts spaced out over a period of time or concerning various
questions.[2]

What is more serious is that, as Ćwikliński had already pointed out
before Schwartz, the two parts of the passage dealing with Athens'
financial difficulties do not fit well together. The immediate reason
for this digression is the decision to send back the Thracian mercenaries; thus, what is being discussed is Athens' poverty, and the
exhaustion revealed by her inability to keep up the struggle at the
necessary intensity. However, what paragraph 28. 3 insists on is her
unquenchable determination, and the astonishment felt by the whole
of Greece at her apparently inexhaustible power. By a detour in
Thucydides' thought, the φιλονικία of Athens does not, in this
passage, appear as a defect which explains the unfavourable situation
in which she now finds herself, but as the means which enables her
to resist. No one has brought this out more successfully than Bartoletti.[3] For him, the φιλονικία of Athens is here not a symptom of the
deep crisis affecting the very soul of the city, but the strength that

---

[1] 27. 3: κατὰ διαδοχήν; 28. 2: καὶ θέρους καὶ χειμῶνος.

[2] The same is true for Schwartz's final argument: according to him, the measure
concerning the duty on imports and exports in 28. 4, is first of all explained by Decelea,
and then otherwise. But it is obvious that a complete explanation will always bring in
both reasons (Decelea — war expenditure): the remark at the end leaves the first explanation on one side because it has already been developed.

[3] *Studi Italiani di Filologia Classica*, XIV, 3, 1937, pp. 227-235.

enables her to overcome the situation. In fact the idea of φιλονικία is soon replaced by the words δύναμις and τόλμα, the very ones which were dear to Pericles himself; and the amazement felt by Greece at this power and audacity is exactly that insisted on in the judgment of II. 65. It must be added that this δύναμις made itself felt above all in the last years of the war, and Thucydides indicates this both in his judgment in II. 65 and in allusions like that of IV. 108. 4: ὅση ὕστερον διεφάνη. Thus Bartoletti considered that this development about φιλονικία represented a late idea of Thucydides, and was intended as a reply to those who, after Athens had been defeated, attacked the leaders who had begun the war by saying that it was doomed to failure from the very start.[1]

However, even if there is no real contradiction between the different sections of this passage, even if we do not need to invoke either the intervention of an editor or a hasty piece of rewriting by Thucydides in order to explain them, and even if there is no real proof that the passage has been misplaced or was written at a different period from its context, the fact remains that the ideas follow on in a way which the context itself does not lead us to expect. The link between them is not wholly satisfactory.[2]

The study of these different passages thus gives rise to two conclusions, one of which is certain and the other uncertain. What is certain is that we must give up any attempt to follow Schwartz in trying to find, in Books VI and VII, evidence of clumsy additions and contradictions which presuppose the intervention of an editor. The different chapters which he criticizes were certainly written by Thucydides, and intended by him to be put where they now are. But at the same time it is possible that the difficulties which Ćwikliński already noted, before Schwartz, are traces of revisions carried out by Thucydides himself on his own text. Once this is assumed, it

---

[1] This φιλονικία of Athens is here presented without hostility or severity: in this respect, it should be contrasted with the parallel passage in Isocrates (Peace, 84): εἰς τοῦτο γὰρ κατέστησαν τῶν μὲν οἰκείων ἀμελείας, τῶν δ'ἀλλοτρίων ἐπιθυμίας, ὥστε Λακεδαιμονίων εἰσβεβληκότων εἰς τὴν χώραν καὶ τοῦ τείχους ἤδη τοῦ Δεκελειᾶσιν ἐστηκότος, εἰς Σικελίαν τριήρεις ἐπλήρουν, καὶ οὐκ ἠσχύνοντο τὴν μὲν πατρίδα τεμνομένην καὶ πορθουμένην περιορῶντες, ἐπὶ δὲ τοὺς οὐδὲν πώποτ' εἰς ἡμᾶς ἐξαμαρτόντας στρατιὰν ἐκπέμποντες, ἀλλ' εἰς τοῦτ' ἀφροσύνης ἦλθον, ὥστε τῶν προαστείων τῶν οἰκείων οὐ κρατοῦντες, Ἰταλίας καὶ Σικελίας καὶ Καρχηδόνος ἄρξειν προσεδόκησαν.

[2] Bartoletti, having (against Schadewaldt) restored the correct value of the ideas put forward, admits (against Schwartz) that the passage constitutes a whole. But he is thus obliged to translate καί (in καὶ ἐς φιλονικίαν καθέστασαν τοιαύτην . . .) by 'and yet' (eppure), which is rather hard.

becomes possible to explain the uncertain nature of the clues with which we are faced: this would be the result of the effort made by Thucydides to hide the traces of his own revisions.

These traces would only show in the form of a slight difference of aim or inspiration.

From this point of view, we must add to the passages already considered that of VI. 15, in which Thucydides, after an unflattering portrait of Alcibiades, adds that the Athenians ruined their state by depriving themselves of his services. Here again, the two indications can be reconciled; yet the one does not really prepare us for the other. And, here again, we have one of the passages certainly written at a late date.

There would be nothing improbable in the idea that these passages, which are both late and a little unexpected, should correspond to additions made when the text had been already prepared or written. This seems the more likely when one considers their nature: each of them, without exception, represents an intervention of the historian, a parenthesis and a commentary, in which he interrupts his narrative in order to place his experience at the disposal of the reader.[1]

For that purpose, Thucydides appears to have used two kinds of remarks:[2] the first kind insisted on the importance of the internal disputes which, by depriving Athens of her best general, contributed greatly to her defeat (examples of this are in VI. 15 and VI. 89-93);[3] the second kind tended to insist on the power of Athens and on the amazing character of her resistance (as, for example, VII. 28).

In that case, it would seem that there existed, in some form or other, an 'early' version of the Sicilian books, which was rather severe towards Alcibiades and Athenian imperialism; that this version was revised by Thucydides, in some way or other, with the intention

---

[1] This is true for all the passages criticized by Schwartz, even when his criticism is entirely unjustified, as in the case of the parenthesis on the tyrannicides. This simple observation should have put scholars on their guard against the ideas that he put forward, and made it clear that they were based on a failure to understand the way Thucydides wrote. What Schwartz finds 'badly linked up with the rest' are always the passages which Thucydides introduces into his narrative as a commentary on the events recorded.

[2] If there were passages that were rewritten, they probably were much more numerous than those mentioned here. I can only deal with those which are visible, because of the use they show Thucydides to be making of his later experience.

[3] We have already seen that Alcibiades' speech is a corner stone in the composition of the Sicilian books. If there are reasons for thinking that it was written later than certain parts of the narrative, it could only have been inserted in the course of a careful and extensive revision. It is in any case certain that it was not simply added there, as Cwiklinski and Schwartz considered.

of stressing other responsibilities and of defending those who had
banked on the power of Athens. It would indeed look as if the balance
had then become unequal between the two different kinds of
explanation – which is exactly what is suggested in II. 65, with the
subordination expressed by the words οὐ τοσοῦτον . . . ὅσον.

This seems to be confirmed, indirectly, by Books V and VIII. At
least, they can be used as a proof that there probably was an 'early'
version for the last part of the work.

This does not mean that I acknowledge more noticeable traces of
insufficiently integrated revisions in these books than in Books VI and
VII. Attempts have been made to establish this by using, on the one
hand certain inconsistencies between Thucydides' narrative and the
text of the treaties (as, for example, by Kirchhoff, Wilamowitz and
Schwartz), and on the other the difficulties raised by the second
prooimion (as by Schwartz). Such attempts always originate in a
failure to understand the intentions of Thucydides as a historian, and
the principles on which he bases his presentation of events. This has
been shown by Pohlenz as far as the second *prooimion* is concerned,
and by Eduard Meyer and Momigliano in relation to the texts of the
treaties. Their arguments can be considered as definitive.

But even though they cannot be so easily dealt with, Books V
and VIII do nevertheless present, on the whole, a rather hasty and
summary character, which we might almost refer to as provisional, and
which would suggest that they could be a first version which has not
been very thoroughly revised.

We have seen that the meaning of Book V is not altogether clear.
Moreover, it contains no speeches, no allusion to later events, no clue
indicating late composition.[1] It can also be noted that it is made up
exclusively of information coming from Peloponnesian sources:
it is Sparta's armies with whose numbers, movements and feelings
Thucydides is acquainted.

Now these features can also be found in Book VIII, where they are
even more marked than in Book V. Book VIII contains no allusion
to later circumstances;[2] the meaning of events is not very well brought

[1] Book V is here considered from the second *prooimion* to the beginning of the
Melian dialogue: these two passages were written late, but they are in fact independent of
their context.

[2] As Eduard Meyer has shown, the account of the revolution of the Four Hundred is
by no means a proof that Thucydides did not have sufficient information; it does not,
however, suppose that Thucydides knows of the revolution of 404. Theramenes appears
in exactly the same light in the narrative of Book VIII as in the *Frogs* of Aristophanes

out; and the composition is often rather clumsy: the same facts are
repeated several times, generally with some difference or variation,[1]
and events are not presented in a clear sequence. This has been
perfectly well illustrated in all the studies made of Book VIII.
Moreover, even though the political judgments made do not flatly
contradict the late passages about Pericles, they nevertheless differ
perceptibly from them and are closer to the less nationalistic spirit
of the earlier parts. This can be seen in the approval given to the
regime set up by Theramenes,[2] or in the praise given to Spartan
moderation.[3]

Without necessarily wishing to maintain that the excellence of the
Sicilian books can be explained by the amount of revision devoted to

[1] These doublets were noted, before Schwartz, by Holzapfel, Prenzel and Wilamowitz.
In fact, apart from the very doubtful case of VIII. 82-86, Thucydides only repeats himself
deliberately because he is going back in time in order to examine a new aspect of reality
(the repetition is introduced in 45 by ἐν δὲ τούτῳ καὶ ἔτι πρότερον, and in 63 by: ὑπὸ γὰρ
τοῦτον τὸν χρόνον καὶ ἔτι πρότερον). But this is accompanied by some real awkwardness.
To take the first case as an example (29-45 = 45-55), one can detect a certain inconsistency
in the account of events: in 36, the pay is still quite sufficient; in 45, it is not even three
obols; in this same paragraph, Hermocrates' opposition is explained by reasons different
from those given in 29; similarly, in 44. 1, the Peloponnesians go to Rhodes as a result of
their disagreement with Tissaphernes, while according to 52 they are already there when
it takes place. Finally, although it seems to be a question of the same attempt in 42 and 55,
it has neither the same motive nor the same success. Whether we are here concerned with
only one or with several different events, the confusion is undeniable.

Besides, when Thucydides goes back into the past in order to explain the home politics
of Athens or the role of Alcibiades, it is normal that he should make use of sources of
information coming from Athens or from Alcibiades, while in the sections devoted
to military operations he is sure to use also Peloponnesian sources of information.
This is by no means extraordinary or surprising, and Holzapfel is wrong in explaining
the existence of these doublets by the purely mechanical interplay of the sources of
information.

[2] VIII. 97. 2. This judgment does not, as Momigliano thinks, contradict those in which
Thucydides is less severe on democracy. Lange gives a very good explanation of the unity
of his thought on this question: in his desire for a regime which combines democracy and
oligarchy, in his awareness of the wrongs of the oligarchical party in the domain of
Athenian patriotism, in his admiration for the superior qualities of Pericles, Thucydides
is always consistent with his own views. But the tone adopted here and that used in the
Funeral Oration imply that Thucydides is writing with a different aim in mind.

[3] VIII. 24. 4. Here again, it is a quality which no one has ever thought of denying to
Sparta; but the admiration implied in this unnecessary remark indicates a frame of mind
closer to that in the speech on Pylos than to that in the Funeral Oration.

(541, 967). One might wonder if, when Thucydides speaks in a general way of the
oligarchies born of democracies (89. 3), he is referring to that of 404 as well as to that of
411; but if one takes into account Thucydides' liking for generalization and abstraction,
this appears in no way certain.

them,[1] it may be suggested that Books V and VIII are nearer to the 'early' version, and that Thucydides also devoted less revision to these passages which, originally, he had composed with less care.

Proof for this can be found in the fact that what seems to have characterized the spirit in which the revision of the Sicilian books was made also seems to be what distinguishes them, as far as their ideas are concerned, from Books V and VIII.

Certainly the idea that the Athenians ought not, for sterile political dissensions, to have deprived themselves of the leadership of Alcibiades is still there in Book VIII: those who were responsible for this happening are πονηροί, who bring all the misfortune on to the city.[2] But their responsibility is lessened by the fact that Alcibiades himself no longer plays so immense a role.

If one studies the part which he plays in the course of the History, it will be noted that one of the aspects of his character is expressed in exactly the same way in Books V, VI and VIII. Thus his successive interventions at Athens or with Tissaphernes are explained on each of the three occasions by the juxtaposition of a theoretical motive and a more important one of personal ambition:

V. 43. 2: ᾧ ἐδόκει μὲν καὶ ἄμεινον εἶναι πρὸς τοὺς ᾿Αργείους
            μᾶλλον χωρεῖν
            οὐ μέντοι ἀλλὰ καὶ φρονήματι φιλονικῶν ἠναντιοῦτο,
            ὅτι . . .

VI. 15. 2: βουλόμενος τῷ τε Νικίᾳ ἐναντιοῦσθαι
            καὶ μάλιστα . . . ἐλπίζων Σικελίαν τε δι᾿ αὐτοῦ καὶ
            Καρχηδόνα λήψεσθαι[3]

VIII. 47. 1: ἅμα μὲν τῷ Τισσαφέρνει . . . ἄριστα εἶναι νομίζων
              ἅμα δὲ τὴν ἑαυτοῦ κάθοδον ἐς τὴν πατρίδα ἐπιθεραπεύων

---

[1] It can doubtless be explained by artistic and intellectual motives. And, as regards the disorder of Book V (which has, in my view, often been exaggerated), it is probably more explicable by the nature of the subject than by the way in which the book was written. It will be noted that the account of the battle of Mantinea, the only interesting episode for a theoretician of strategy like Thucydides, provides an excellent narrative section: see Eduard Meyer, *Forsch.*, II, p. 366: 'er hat nicht anders erzählen wollen'.

[2] VIII. 47. 2 should be placed by the side of VI. 89. 5. Cf. the intervention of Peisander in VIII. 53. 2-3, and the action of the regime of Theramenes (praised by Thucydides) in VIII. 97. 2.

[3] The second motive here does take the form of a self-interested piece of calculation, but it at least implies the idea that the result could be reached, which means a certain assimilation between Alcibiades' own interests and those of Athens.

Also, the office of proxenus is evoked in similar terms in Books V and VI.[1]

In Book VI, however, another aspect of his character becomes apparent, the one which we saw appear in a rather unexpected fashion in the second part of the portrait of VI. 15, when Thucydides says, to describe his action: κράτιστα διαθέντι τὰ τοῦ πολέμου,[2] or in his speech at Sparta, in which he is shown to have such control over events. This aspect is not at all clear in Books V and VIII. Thucydides despises Alcibiades' policy of alliance with Argos,[3] and when, in VIII. 86. 4, Alcibiades dissuades the Athenians at Samos from sailing to Piraeus, this service, however great it may be, is in Thucydides' view the first that Alcibiades has done his country.[4] Nevertheless, Book VIII certainly offered a number of opportunities for insisting on Alcibiades' influence; instead of doing so, however, Thucydides tries to minimize and deny its very existence. The Alcibiades to whom the Spartans listen with such docility in Book VI, has only the most obscure and indirect action upon them in Book VIII: he influences them because of his family ties (unmentioned in Book VI), and through the intermediary of Endius.[5] What is even more important is that twice (in VIII. 56 and 88) Thucydides, against all appearances, presents the influence of Alcibiades on Tissaphernes as much less important than the latter maintains it to be. If Alcibiades appears as the only person capable of saving Athens, this is presented as the result of an almost fortuitous set of circumstances, and he is never described as the well-defined and powerful character whom we find in Book VI.

Just as in the sections dealing with Pericles, it thus happens that the

---

[1] VI. 89. 2 = V. 43. 2.

[2] Hatzfeld (*Alcibiade*, p. 199, n. 2) rightly underlines the aorist, which applies not to his military activity in general, but to what he had done for the Sicilian expedition. It is nevertheless quite possible, and even probable, that this judgment, although concerning his activity at that time, was in some way influenced by the qualities which he was to show later.

[3] Hatzfeld (*Alcibiade*, pp. 89-93) explains the severity shown towards Alcibiades in Book V by the idea that it was written late, that is to say 'at a time when it was generally agreed that Sparta could not have been wrong and Alcibiades could not have been right'. Such a conclusion, which is generally in accordance with the theory of de Sanctis on the evolution of Thucydides' ideas, does not, as we have seen, apply to Thucydides' text as a whole.

[4] In VIII. 86. 4, I adopt the text of B: καὶ ἐδόκει 'Α. πρῶτον τότε (with Classen, against Schwartz, Stahl, Hude, and others). The position of the word is in fact an invitation to do this, as is the unaccustomed way in which πρῶτος would be used, should it be adopted here.

[5] VIII. 6. 3 and VIII. 12. 2.

differences in emphasis are easier to grasp when showing in two different books[1] than in different passages of the same book, which are near to one another.

These differences can be used to establish a certain number of conclusions about the way in which the History was written and about the development of Thucydides' ideas on Athenian imperialism.

The conclusions about the way in which the work was written are, once again, extremely uncertain. For it seems that an original version did exist for the second part of the work as a whole, but it remains impossible to say definitely what relationship there is between this version and what we have called later revisions. It is impossible to say whether this version consisted of detailed notes which were put into their present form after 404, or whether it was a version actually written out in full and then partly revised. It is impossible to assign a date to this early version,[2] impossible to number these revisions or indicate their length. In short, it is impossible to try to reconstruct a kind of 'Ur-Thukydides'.

However, as before, these revisions are easier to interpret than to define; and though we cannot detect them with any precision, we can guess fairly well their nature and purpose. And what we find out confirms our former hypothesis as to the development of Thucydides' ideas.

These revisions never reveal a real change in Thucydides' ideas or a reversal of an earlier opinion. Thus, from this point of view, the agreement brought out in the first part of this chapter comes from the firmness of his thought and from his fidelity to his own ideas.

---

[1] There are yet more features by which the Sicilian books differ from those around them in the same way as 'late' passages do from 'early' ones. We have already seen how little favour Book VIII shows for democracy, whereas, on the contrary, in Alcibiades' speech at Sparta, where circumstances demand a phrase attacking democracy (which is in fact there), Thucydides does give space to a praise of this regime which links up with that of II. 65, since he makes Alcibiades say that under democracy the city was: μεγίστη ... καὶ ἐλευθερωτάτη (VI. 89. 6).

[2] The 'earlier version', for this part of the work, must nevertheless be attributed to a period only shortly before 404. Common sense alone is sufficient proof of this, and one could also quote certain more detailed indications, such as, in VIII. 97. 2, the τοῦτοι πρῶτον ἀνήνεγκε τὴν πόλιν, which seems an allusion to the recovery of Athens later carried out by Alcibiades. But these arguments all remain rather vain if it is admitted, as I would suggest, that the version which we possess was written late, that it reproduced more or less faithfully the original version, but can also differ from it in adding minor remarks to the former text.

The 'early' version fits in with the 'late' judgment; the way in which Alcibiades' imperialism is described and judged, at an 'early' time, fits in with the way that of Pericles is described and judged after 404. This unity in Thucydides' judgment may have been deliberately underlined, in one place, by a similarity of verbal expressions, but it did nevertheless exist earlier.

However, in the analyses whose value he still continued to recognize, it seems that Thucydides finally decided to emphasize certain points, like the importance of the internal conflicts which led to the sending of Alcibiades into exile, or the reserves of power that were to be shown by Athens.

This intention can be explained in both cases.

First of all, the importance of these internal conflicts necessarily appeared greater to him (as it did to Aristophanes) when they became more and more serious; similarly, the power shown by Athens was seen to be progressively more amazing as the years went by, and as Athens continued to resist.

But what is most important is that in this post-war period of defeat, in which, as we have seen, and as may easily be understood, Thucydides' patriotism especially asserts itself, it is normal for him to have insisted on the two ideas which tended to lessen the importance of Sparta's triumph and to justify Pericles. By insisting on the importance of the internal dissensions and the ability to resist shown by the Athenians, Thucydides is defending at the same time both Pericles and Athens herself. He defends the latter exactly as the speech in *Menexenus* (243) will do: attacked by the Greeks, filled with ingratitude, she resisted, we are told, magnificently: οὖ δὴ καὶ ἐκφανὴς ἐγένετο ἡ τῆς πόλεως ῥώμη τε καὶ ἀρετή; when she was thought to be ready to surrender and already defeated, she nevertheless won, in spite of the enormous difficulties from which she was suffering, the battle of Arginusae: morally speaking, she can even be said to have won the war, since it was only the internal dissensions which brought about her ruin: τῇ δ᾽ ἡμετέρᾳ αὐτῶν διαφορᾷ ἐκρατήθημεν, οὐχ ὑπὸ τῶν ἄλλων· ἀήττητοι γὰρ ἔτι καὶ νῦν ὑπό γε ἐκείνων ἐσμέν, ἡμεῖς δὲ αὐτοὶ ἡμᾶς αὐτοὺς καὶ ἐνικήσαμεν καὶ ἡττήθημεν (243 d).

While remaining faithful to his earlier opinions, Thucydides is thus even truer to his earlier faith.

Q

CONCLUSION

THEMISTOCLES AND CIMON

IT can be seen, from his various opinions on the events that he himself lived through, that Thucydides was a moderate imperialist. If we go back from these events and study those of the past, it would be natural to find that his judgment of earlier happenings was dominated by the same ideas.

If this were the case, Thucydides would be expected to insist primarily on the personality of Cimon: unlike Cleon, Cimon adopted a policy of reason and moderation towards the allies, and thus set himself apart from the other Athenian leaders;[1] unlike Cleon, Cimon sought an alliance with Sparta, and thus opposed the policy of Themistocles;[2] as Nicias wished to do, when speaking against Alcibiades, Cimon concentrated on the Thracian coast;[3] like Nicias, Pericles, and Thucydides the historian, Cimon served the greatness of Athens, but did so while remaining moderate.[4] To these reasons should be added the fact that, in some way or other, Thucydides was certainly related to the family of Miltiades and of Cimon.[5]

However, Thucydides' main admiration is reserved not for Cimon

[1] Plutarch, Cimon, 11: οἱ μὲν ἄλλοι στρατηγοὶ τῶν Ἀθηναίων ... Κίμων δὲ τὴν ἐναντίαν ὁδὸν ἐν τῇ στρατηγίᾳ πορευόμενος βίαν μὲν οὐδενὶ τῶν Ἑλλήνων προσῆγε.

[2] See Glotz, pp. 122 and 128; Judeich, Hermes, LVIII (1923), pp. 9 ff.

[3] The first Athenian conquest, the first act of Cimon, is in the Pentecontaëtia none other than the taking of Eion (cf. the expeditions in Chersonese, Plut., Cimon, 14. 1).

[4] It is this which explains that Plutarch, when defining the policy followed by Cimon should use expressions very similar to those found in Thucydides, in particular when he describes (and criticizes) the attitude of the Athenians: Plut., Cimon, 18. 1: γενομένη δ' εἰρήνης ὁρῶν τοὺς Ἀθηναίους ἡσυχίαν ἄγειν μὴ δυναμένους ἀλλὰ κινεῖσθαι καὶ αὐξάνεσθαι ταῖς στρατείαις βουλομένους (cf. Thuc., I. 70. 9).

[5] The name of his father, Olorus, is that of the king of Thrace whose daughter Hegesipyle became the wife of Miltiades (Herodotus, VI, 39; 41; Plut., Cim., 4) and who bore him a son Cimon. The Life by Marcellinus also gives a Hegesipyle as Thucydides' mother According to the Souda, Thucydides is connected to Miltiades on his mother's side, and to Olorus king of Thrace by his father. Similarly the other Thucydides, the son of Melesias, was related by marriage to Cimon (Arist., Const. of Athens, 28, cf. Plut., Per. 11. 1: Kirchner, 7268); according to some (Cavaignac), he was his brother-in-law, and according to others (Beloch) his son-in-law. Finally, Thucydides' cenotaph is said to have been set up among the Miltiades family graves. The fact that he was related to them is thus certain, but exactly how is more obscure. Cavaignac gives a genealogical table in which both Thucydides' grandmothers are daughters of Miltiades, and where his grandfather is Thucydides son of Melesias. This conclusion is nevertheless a little disquieting.

but for Themistocles, and the portrait which he gives of Pericles resembles not that of Cimon but that of Themistocles.[1]

The role played by Cimon is reduced to nothing. In the whole of the Pentecontaëtia his name appears only five times, each time in a genitive absolute with no commentary. In a telescoping of time rare in Thucydides, the fifteen years during which he presided over the destiny of Athens take up only five paragraphs.

Plutarch, in a very precise passage, expressly attributes to Cimon the great step that was to transform the Delian Confederacy into an empire by making the allies pay tribute instead of sending military contingents. Thucydides tells us, rather obscurely, that the allies 'had a definite sum of money fixed for their regular contribution'[2] and does not bring Cimon's name into it.

The most widely discussed action of Cimon was the intervention against the Helots of Ithome: in his discussion of this event, Thucydides mentions only the military role played by Cimon, and speaks of the anger of the Athenians without mentioning the most important evidence of this anger, which was Cimon's ostracism. Neither does he mention the fact that he was recalled before the full period of time had elapsed, however solemn or even important this recall may have been.

On the other hand, everything which might go against Cimon's policy is carefully noted by Thucydides, as, for example, the secret promise made to the inhabitants of Thasos by the Spartans – a promise which no one could check,[3] and which he may perhaps have taken from Cimon's political enemies. By mentioning this in paragraph 101. 2, just before the Athenian intervention on Sparta's side, he shows this intervention to be doomed to failure and ridicule.

On the contrary, when we come to consider Themistocles, we see that everything is chosen, developed and presented in order to glorify him.

Independently of the narrative itself, an excursus is inserted with the purpose of freeing him from any suspicion of pro-Persian sentiments. The study made by Louis Bodin[4] shows how the whole

[1] Pericles can belong to the two series: in the double list (rather a simple-minded one) drawn up by Aristotle (*Const. of Athens*, 28) there is no one to counterbalance Pericles after the death of the son of Melesias; for a few years he unites the two, as it were.

[2] I. 99. 3.

[3] See the criticisms of de Sanctis (*Atthis*, p. 404): for him, this is merely an argument that the instigators of the rebellion put forward at Thasos.

[4] *Phanias d'Erèse.*

composition of the episode, and in particular the use made of the letter, tends to give the facts an interpretation favourable to Themistocles. The first betrayal is mentioned as being merely a fictitious excuse (and Thucydides insists on this by a parenthesis in I. 137. 4), while the later promises are put into the background, glossed over by another explanation which is more to Themistocles' honour (I. 138. 2). The whole passage ends with the famous praise of Themistocles, rivalled in the History only by the praise accorded to Pericles, and which emphasizes, by all the terms which it uses, his political genius.[1]

The parenthesis itself in which the Fifty Years are studied contains two very distinct sections; the first stands out from the main description of the Fifty Years by the fact that it is as rich in details as the excursus which has just been noted: the reason is that once again the hero is Themistocles. Both the explanations and the concrete instances offered by Thucydides are so numerous, and the dramatic quality of the account is so carefully planned, that because of these very features the account of Themistocles' role has appeared suspect. Whatever the historical value of the passage may be, it is certain that Thucydides takes great pleasure in describing Themistocles' projects, both where the wall of Athens (91. 5-7) and the wall of Piraeus (93. 3 and 6) are concerned. In this final instance, Thucydides brings out the twin concept on which Themistocles' policy depends, the idea of an essentially maritime empire and of the need to base the defence of Athens on the sea. One immediately recognizes the model which Pericles will follow.

Thus, by the very way in which he treats these two characters Thucydides reveals a definite choice between them, and this choice is, at first sight at least, rather a surprising one.

However, all it really does is to confirm the validity of the results we have already obtained: it fits in with the rest of Thucydides' ideas, at the same time as it shows, inside these ideas, a 'later' tendency.

There was, in fact, nothing to prevent Thucydides from admiring Themistocles, who was certainly a very highly regarded person, and Thucydides' opinions, on the whole, were not so exclusive as to forbid him to do this.

We must not, in this respect, lose sight of the fact that Athenian 'political parties' had nothing of the clear and fixed distinctions

[1] See p. 119, n. 5.

which characterize our own.[1] Themistocles, it is true, opposed Cimon and Aristeides, but he supported Miltiades in his court case, and Aristeides supported Themistocles over the business of the walls. Similarly, later writers are quite prepared to give exactly the same praise to all the great men who contributed to the fame of Athens,[2] and among these Themistocles is most often mentioned as the great man *par excellence*: Aristophanes himself has no hesitation in praising his work, outside any purely party considerations, as that of a great patriot.[3]

Now it is certainly in this spirit that Thucydides praises him, and he in no way presents him as having anything in common with people like Cleon and Alcibiades. Nowhere does he suggest that the extreme elements of the imperialist party might try to justify their policies by his example. In the construction of the Long Walls, he attributes his plan to the desire to fight against the barbarians; and this explanation (which is of such a kind that no one, not even Cimon, could have rejected the principle inspiring it) is even more noteworthy since it is not wholly reliable,[4] and is presented by Thucydides himself merely as a hypothesis.[5]

Since, on the other hand, Thucydides places limits on Athenian imperialism only in the name of circumstances,[6] we are justified in concluding that there is no contradiction between the portrait which

[1] See the article of P. Cloché, *R.E.A.*, 1928, 269-279: *La politique des Alcméonides de 507 à 482 av. J-C*. The study is conceived in a largely negative vein, contrasting the hypotheses of Busolt, Beloch, Walker and de Sanctis in such a way as to bring out on what fragile grounds they are based.

[2] One thus finds brought together, as great men: in Lysias (*Against Nicom.*, 28): Solon, Themistocles, Pericles; in Plato (*Meno*, 93-94): Themistocles, Aristeides, Pericles, Thucydides; in Plato again (*Gorgias*, 515 ff.): Miltiades, Themistocles, Cimon, Pericles; in Isocrates (*Antidosis*, 232-234): Solon, Cleisthenes, Themistocles, Pericles; in Aeschines (*in Ctesiph.*, 181): Aristeides, Themistocles, Miltiades; or (*in Tim.*, 25); Pericles, Themistocles, Aristeides; or again (*in Ctesiph.*, 257-258): Solon and Aristeides; finally, in a fragment already quoted of the *Demoi* of Eupolis (100 K): Miltiades and Pericles.

[3] See *Knights*, 813-820: he filled up the city after he had found it empty; moreover, he gave it Piraeus as an additional dish for its lunch, and, taking none of its fish away, he served it others.

[4] The very discontent of the Spartans would be enough to prove that this was not the only meaning of his policy.

[5] I. 93. 7: ταῖς γὰρ ναυσὶ μάλιστα προσέκειτο, ἰδὼν ὡς ἐμοὶ δοκεῖ τῆς βασίλεως στρατιᾶς τὴν κατὰ θάλασσαν ἔφοδον εὐπορωτέραν τῆς κατὰ γῆν οὖσαν.

[6] Pericles advises the Athenians to avoid conquests *for the time being* (ἅμα πολεμοῦντες); in the episode of Pylos the Spartans, who express Thucydides' own point of view, say that peace should be made because *it is the right moment* (εἴπερ ποτέ); moreover Nicias, who also expresses Thucydides' opinion, blames the Sicilian expedition because *it is not the right moment* (οὔτε ἐν καιρῷ σπεύδετε).

he draws of this ideal Themistocles and the unprejudiced restrictions which we find in other cases.

But it will once again be noted that although such praise would not have been out of place at any time in Thucydides' experience, it comes most naturally — like the relative silence about Cimon — at the time of the 'late' passages, after 404. At that time, when he exalts the grandeur of Athens in the Funeral Oration and defends Pericles by showing the merits of his plan, it is more than ever satisfying to find him singing the praises of the man who was at the birth of this greatness and who laid the foundations for this plan.

And it is a fact that the passages devoted to Themistocles do seem to present clues which suggest that they were written after 404. An indication has already been given earlier[1] as far as the building of the walls is concerned, and it is easily understandable that the passage in question should have been inspired by the destruction of these walls; in 404, Thucydides is not the only one to evoke the great figure of Themistocles.[2] As to the episode of his exile, it should be noted that this, like the passage dealing with Pausanias, was written in order to fit in with the Pentecontaëtia: the narrative picks up again where the Pentecontaëtia had come to an end, and uses exactly the same terms.[3] Finally, there seem to be two factors in Thucydides' preoccupations after 404 which explain the presence of this digression. First of all, as far as Pausanias is concerned, the comparison with Lysander is so obvious[4] that it would be strange if Thucydides had not deliberately suggested it: the conclusion of such a comparison even seems to have been provided by Thucydides himself in I. 77. 6: καὶ προσέτι εἴς ἕκαστος ἐξιὼν οὔτε τούτοις χρῆται, οὔθ' οἷς ἡ ἄλλη Ἑλλὰς νομίζει Secondly, as regards the contrast between the two leaders who were as Thucydides says, λαμπροτάτους γενομένους τῶν καθ' ἑαυτούς Ἑλλήνων (138. 6), does it not represent, in a particular diptych, the

---

[1] See p. 19.

[2] The contrast with Theramenes, who was responsible for the destruction of the walls, was a classical one: Lysias, *Against Erat.*, 63; Plutarch, *Lys.*, 14.

[3] 95. 5-6: ἀπολύεται μὴ ἀδικεῖν . . . καὶ ἐκεῖνον μὲν οὐκέτι ἐκπέμπουσιν ἄρχοντα, Δόρκιν δέ . . . Cf. 128. 3: ἐπειδὴ Παυσανίας ὁ Λακεδαιμόνιος . . . ἀπελύθη μὴ ἀδικεῖν, δημοσίᾳ μὲν οὐκέτι ἐξεπέμφθη, ἰδίᾳ δὲ αὑτός . . .

[4] Both lost their former moderation while enjoying the customs of Asia, were recalled by the 'skytale', returned to Sparta, and were betrayed by their correspondence with the king (or with the satrap). And when Thucydides insists on the excessive and impious honour that Pausanias has arrogated to himself in the inscription on the tripod at Delphi one thinks of the bronze statue of Lysander, which, Plutarch tells us, was set up in the temple itself.

contrast between Athens and Sparta which Thucydides makes a point of indicating in the Funeral Oration?

This last field of investigation thus confirms the validity of the results at which we had already arrived.

In the emphasis which he gives, at different times, to the mistakes of certain leaders and to the merit of others, Thucydides always makes a very clear distinction between Pericles and his successors. It is this which explains the place in his work of the one general judgment that he ever made, and it is this judgment which enables us to place him in relation to the rest of his contemporaries. For as the evils of imperialism became more marked, some took fright earlier and some later.

By refusing to admire even the first measures carried out by Alcibiades, Thucydides does not go so far as Euripides; by nourishing a whole-hearted admiration for Pericles, he goes further than Aristophanes and most of the other writers of fifth-century comedy. He addresses to Cleon the reproaches which the playwrights direct at Pericles. Each of these writers regrets a more or less remote past[1] which never ceases to fade into the distance.

The reason for this is that the real cause of the evils from which Athens suffers is not to be found in any one of these political leaders but in the city itself;[2] it is not one single politician who is ambitious, but the Athenians in general: it is of them that Thucydides says that they 'wanted more'.

We thus come to the subject-matter of the third part of this book: the study of Athenian imperialism from the point of view of its unity and of its continuous development.

---

[1] The past tends to be confused with the ideal state. Isocrates uses the same words to describe the beginnings of the Delian league (*Paneg.*, 80: σωτῆρες ἀλλὰ μὴ λυμεῶνες ἀποκαλεῖσθαι ...), and to evoke the confederation of the future (*Peace*, 141: σωτῆρας ἀλλὰ μὴ λυμεῶνας ... κληθῆναι).

[2] This circumstance explains an apparent contradiction in the judgment of Isocrates on Pericles. In general, he makes the division where Thucydides makes it, and reserves his warmest praise for Pericles (*Antid.*, 234-235); on the other hand, in *Peace*, 126, he seems to make serious reservations: Καίτοι Περικλῆς ... παραλαβὼν τὴν πόλιν χεῖρον μὲν φρονοῦσαν ἢ πρὶν κατασχεῖν τὴν ἀρχήν, ἔτι δ' ἀνεκτῶς πολιτευομένην. But the reason is that here it is a question not of Pericles himself but of the city, and Isocrates knew (if only by Thucydides) that Pericles had been able to resist it.

Part Three

The Unity of Athenian Imperialism

INTRODUCTION

ONCE it has been established that imperialistic ambition is something created by the Athenian people themselves, and that it consequently remains the same through the different decisions denoting the influence of such and such a leader and such and such a programme, it should be possible to study the policy which stemmed from this ambition, from the Persian wars to Aegos Potamoi, as a single development for which Athens in general is to be held responsible.

As soon as one begins to study this aspect of the problem, it is no longer a question of cricizing the policy of one man but of criticizing that of Athens herself; one is no longer judging a particular plan of political action, but imperialism as a whole. It is this which forms the real subject matter of the debates in which the Athenians take part, in the speeches made at Sparta in Book I, and in the Melian dialogue in Book V. In both cases, we see anonymous Athenians speaking in the name of Athens, and defending the whole of her policy against the arguments put forward by representatives of another city. In appearance at least, the speech of Euphemus in Book VI is also a speech of this type, for it also is a defence of Athenian policy against an attack made on it by one of Athens' enemies. If, as we shall see, the function which this speech fulfils sets it somewhat apart from those of Book I and Book V, it can nevertheless be compared with them.

In order to discover to what extent these speeches can tell us something about Thucydides' own ideas, we shall have to ask the same questions about them that we have asked about the texts already studied, attempting to discover in what frame of mind Thucydides wrote them and at what time. The only difference will be that these questions will now be asked under slightly different conditions.

To begin with, we shall have fewer elements that we can use in order to bring out Thucydides' own opinions: the speeches with which we shall now be concerned will not be limited by a particular episode, and will therefore not be made easier to interpret by their context. We shall not now be able to use the narrative, and to compare the speaker's ideas with corresponding facts: the only evidence that we shall be able to use is that provided by the Pentecontaëtia, but this was not — unlike the narrative in the ordinary episodes — written in connection with the speeches.

For the same reason, it will be more difficult to come to a definite conclusion about the date of any particular passage. Because of their general nature, these speeches will not necessarily express ideas linked with the circumstance in which they are supposed to be delivered, and, just as they occupy a separate part in the general narrative, so they also stand apart from their context in any study of the composition of the History. At the same time as we are faced with a wider number of possible solutions, we shall also have fewer elements at our disposal enabling us to choose between them: there will be no possibility of making a definite check by an indication from what comes before or after, and no opportunity for using evidence provided by the theatre: the theatre deals with immediate problems, and with men and issues of the day; if it is a question of mature judgments or passages of general analysis, then it is with Isocrates and Plato that Thucydides must be compared; and this will in no way help us to solve the problems raised by the composition of the work, since these men began to express their opinions only after Thucydides had fallen silent. As long as it is a question of political discussions, Thucydides has contemporaries; as far as meditation and theory are concerned, he has only successors.

However, by the very fact that the texts with which we are now going to be concerned are more independent of their immediate context and less closely linked to the order in which events took place, they allow of a much greater liberty on Thucydides' part and therefore offer fresh possibilities of analysis. Since they are presented anonymously, they do not need to be as close to the actual words of the speakers as do the other speeches. When one is relating what Pericles or Archidamus said, there is a certain obligation to respect them and to reproduce their speeches fairly accurately. But when one is reporting the speeches of people unknown, the same limits do not apply. Similarly, since they are dealing with a whole collection of facts, these speeches allow, and even demand, a more personal interpretation. When one is reporting a speech dealing with a specific measure, one cannot, unless prompted by very strong motives, bring in arguments based on or inspired by later events. But it is almost impossible not to do this when one is judging something continuous which attains its final form only at a time when, in fact, all the voices called to life by the historian have fallen silent for ever. In a case of this nature, it would therefore be natural to find more personal intervention in the texts under discussion; we should come across more clearly formulated opinions and more frequent references to events going beyond the immediate facts. That is to say, finally, that what we should expect to find are words which themselves reveal both the preoccupations inspiring them and the time at which they were written.

If these two texts — the speech of the Athenians at Sparta and the Melian dialogue — are thus different in their historical tenor from those which we have already studied, they nevertheless contribute to the expression of the same ideas; and, in this fervent follower of the principles of εὐβουλία, they certainly stem from the same intellectual attitude. Thucydides, in fact, is not the kind of man who judges acts or individuals without reference to a general idea, and neither does he judge the successive aspects assumed by Athenian imperialism without at the same time referring back to a general appreciation of imperial policy as a whole, resting on a solid philosophical basis. Therefore, the information that these two texts will provide will not only complete our earlier conclusions: it will both confirm and, one might even say, explain them.

CHAPTER ONE

THE DEFENCE OF ATHENIAN IMPERIALISM
AT THE ASSEMBLY AT SPARTA

THE Corinthians, in the assembly at Sparta in Book I, denounce
the very existence of Athenian imperialism, which, they say,
has enslaved some and threatens all others, which leaves no one
at rest and which, with an infallible logic, develops its principle of
annexation. The Athenians then try to justify this imperialism:
δηλῶσαι ὡς οὔτε ἀπεικότως ἔχομεν ἃ κεκτήμεθα, ἥ τε πόλις ἡμῶν
ἀξία λόγου ἐστίν (I. 73. 1). To do so, they begin by explaining how
they obtained the leadership because of their conduct at the time of
the Persian wars (73. 2-74); they then proceed to explain the reasons
which have led them to extend their authority from that time onwards (75-76. 2), and they argue that, after all, the authority which
they exercise remains essentially moderate (76. 2-78). Thus, what
they are justifying is a whole policy of ruling over other people, in
its continuous development and unity.

But if it is important to indicate that the subject for discussion is
general in nature, it is equally important to note that Thucydides'
manner in treating it is itself quite general and abstract. This becomes apparent as soon as one considers the way in which the
Athenian reply is presented.

First of all, this reply is delivered by no definite person. This
anonymity does not only mean that we should have learned nothing
if the name of the speakers had been given to us, for in Book VI
Euphemus is neither a famous man nor an outstanding personality;
it is rather that by opposing 'the Athenians' to 'the Corinthians' —
or, later on, to 'the Melians' — Thucydides is showing that what
he intends to express is the very *logos* of the city. We are not
hearing the views of this or that Athenian: it is the voice of Athens
herself which is speaking. And this fact immediately gives the debate
a much wider significance.

Moreover, these Athenians have no reason to speak at this juncture,
for what are they doing in this Peloponnesian parliament? What
authority do they have to undertake so general a justification of

Athenian policy? Even if – which is somehow difficult to believe – they did actually speak on that day and in those terms, why should Thucydides reproduce a speech which brought out no results? The reason is, of course, that this justification has for him a definite value of its own.

The very tenor of the speech confirms this, for, as Sthenelaïdas points out in I. 86. 1, the Athenians give no reply to the accusations made against them, and do not prove that they have not acted unjustly towards Sparta's allies. There is a lack of relationship between the debate as a whole and the Athenians' reply, for this rises above the immediate subject matter and stands out from it, precisely because it treats the problems of imperialism in the abstract; it takes account neither of the speakers who have criticized Athens nor of the aim which Athenian speakers in such an assembly might be expected to pursue; it neglects the politicians present in Sparta in order to speak directly to the future reader of Thucydides' History.[1]

Thus, everything fits together to suggest that Thucydides' intention was to use this opportunity, at the very beginning of his work, in order to deal with the question of Athenian imperialism, considered for its own sake.

This comes out particularly clearly when one compares this speech with that of Euphemus in Book VI.

Euphemus is replying to attacks by Hermocrates, which are remarkably reminiscent of those made by the Corinthians in Book I, since they denounce in exactly the same way the inexorable advance of Athenian domination. Like the Athenians in Book I, Euphemus thus endeavours to justify the very existence of Athens' empire (VI. 82. 1): ἀνάγκη καὶ περὶ τῆς ἀρχῆς εἰπεῖν ὡς εἰκότως ἔχομεν, the words are almost exactly those used in Book I; and the arguments which he uses are often similar. Both speeches repeat the two different arguments about the Persian wars and about Athens' need to act as she did. The difference lies, however, in the fact that Book VI introduces a particular individual speaking; his speech is the indispensable reply to that of Hermocrates; in the whole of the second, and by far the most important part of his speech, Euphemus is talking about future events in Sicily, and his only purpose is to keep Camarina in the Athenian alliance. On the whole, his arguments are those needed on that particular day by that particular situation, and it is for this reason that he explains Athenian policy essentially by the fear which

[1] See Zahn, pp. 43-50.

Athens had of the hostile Dorian city of Sparta: as we have already seen,[1] the theme of racial conflict is foreign to Thucydides' ideas in general, and one which is absent from the Pentecontaëtia in particular; as for the hostility of Sparta towards Athens, it began to exist for Thucydides (under the form of a suspicion of Athens' motives) only when Athens began to lay the foundations for her rule (I. 102). Such arguments might therefore convince the Camarinaeans, but Thucydides' reader can only appreciate them as being the ones most likely to be put forward by the Athenians in a vital diplomatic campaign. Thus, Euphemus is making a speech wholly different in nature and intention from that made by the Athenians in Book I, which goes far beyond the immediate subject matter of the debate, and does not have any influence on Sthenelaïdas, but appeals solely to the reader of the History.

If this is the case, it is not unreasonable to assume that each one of the arguments expressed corresponds to one of Thucydides' own opinions or intentions, and to try to bring out its meaning independently of the debate in which the speech was made.

I. THUCYDIDES AND THE ATHENIAN DEFENCE

A. *The Persian wars and Athenian Hegemony*

The speech contains a passage which deals with the Persian wars and stresses their importance. This indeed was a classic theme for anyone wishing to praise or defend Athens; it is found in all the Funeral Orations, except that of Pericles, where it would have been merely a repetition. Even here, when the Athenians start talking about their conduct in the Persian wars, they begin by apologizing for repeating things that everybody knows: by thus underlining the well-known character of this theme, they merely succeed in emphasizing it even further.

They first of all introduce it with solemnity (I. 73. 4: φαμὲν γὰρ Μαραθῶνί τε μόνοι προκινδυνεῦσαι . . .); after speaking briefly of Marathon, they give more details about Salamis: the three elements by which Athens contributed to the defeat of the Persians are first mentioned rapidly (she had the most numerous ships, the most able general, the most courageous determination), and are then repeated in the same order, each of them giving rise to longer commentaries.

---

[1] See above, p. 83.

Finally, the Athenians reach their conclusion, which is still presented with the same solemnity (I. 74. 3: ὥστε φαμέν . . .): they exalt the service which they then rendered Greece and the Peloponnese by showing themselves braver than other people. In their view, it is exactly this which should place Athens above the attacks made on her because of her empire.

This affirmation of the merits of Athens raises a question of fact, and the conclusions which the Athenians draw from these merits raise a question of right. In both cases, if we wish to discover the spirit in which Thucydides wrote the passage, we must compare it with texts that are parallel to it.

As far as the narrative is concerned, it is clear that the analysis put forward by the Athenians conforms to the best Athenian tradition, and also to what Thucydides himself could have said about Athens' role in the Persian wars. The speech made by Euphemus in Book VI is evidence of this, and it confirms the text of Book I by the very features which make it different, since these are explained, in the case of Euphemus, by the actual circumstances in which he is speaking. It is immediately apparent that while Euphemus is putting forward a plea, the Athenians in Book I are offering a serious analysis.

As far as Marathon is concerned, the matter is quickly settled: Euphemus puts this episode aside, but this does not mean that the indication given by the Athenians in Book I is not valid. They recall that at Marathon Athens acted alone. One might certainly feel a little surprise here that there is no mention of the Plataeans, but this is fairly general in Athenian tradition. The word μόνοι is moreover repeated insistently by Herodotus (IX, 27: οἵτινες μοῦνοι Ἑλλήνων δὴ μουνομαχήσαντες τῷ Πέρσῃ; VII, 10: εἰ στρατιήν γε τοσαύτην σὺν Δάτι καὶ Ἀρταφρένεϊ ἐλθοῦσαν ἐς τὴν Ἀττικὴν χώρην μοῦνοι Ἀθηναῖοι διέφθειραν); so that it is by no means surprising that later speakers should have seized hold of it.[1] Such an over-simplification was normal and Thucydides repeats it on his own account when he writes, in I. 18. 1: ἡ ἐν Μαραθῶνι μάχη Μήδων πρὸς Ἀθηναίους. The Athenians are thus mentioning a widely admitted and true fact.

As far as Salamis is concerned, Euphemus' analysis echoes that of the Athenians, but he brings out only two of the three factors that they mention: ναυτικὸν πλεῖστον (cf. ἀριθμόν τε νεῶν πλεῖστον) —

---

[1] Cf. Lysias, Epitaphios, 20: μόνοι γὰρ ὑπὲρ ἁπάσης τῆς Ἑλλάδος — Lycurgus, Against Leocrates, 70: ἐγκαταλειπόμενοι δὲ οἱ πρόγονοι ὑπὸ πάντων τῶν Ἑλλήνων . . .

R

προθυμίαν ἀπροφάσιστον¹ (cf. προθυμίαν ἀοκνοτάτην) — The third is lacking, and it is precisely the one to which Thucydides was most deeply attached, since it depended on the genius of Themistocles and the intelligence of Athens, on the two factors whose praises he most likes to express. Moreover, the importance of the role played by Themistocles, which is confirmed by everything which we know about the battle, appears prominently in many Greek orators.² Once again it is because of the circumstances under which his speech was made that Euphemus, concerned solely with persuading the Camarinaeans to remain on Athens' side, fails to speak of it. As to the two other factors, they are confirmed by the speeches of all the orators,³ and, as far as the number of ships is concerned, by all the historical information that we possess.⁴

Thus, when the Athenians describe the service which they rendered to the whole of Greece, they are clearly doing nothing more than stating the truth.

Certain texts, which at first sight appear to suggest the opposite, do in fact confirm this idea. The first are not of great interest to us; they are the allusions — themselves rather exceptional — by which the enemies of Athens try to minimize the importance of her victories and attribute the defeat of the barbarians to their own mistakes. This tendency can be found in the Corinthians (I. 69. 5: τὸν βάρβαρον αὐτὸν περὶ αὑτῷ τὰ πλείω σφαλέντα), and even, though it is far less marked, in the speech of Hermocrates at Syracuse (VI. 33. 6: τοῦ

---

¹ The change of adjective is not due to chance: on the first occasion, the Athenians say ἀοκνοτάτην (later: τολμηροτάτην) because they are contrasting their city with Sparta, which is always criticized for its hesitation; on the second occasion, Euphemus says ἀπροφάσιστον because he is defending Athens against Hermocrates' accusation that it is always seeking pretexts (VI. 76. 1: προφάσει μέν . . .).

² One reads in the *Epitaphios* of Lysias, 42: 'The Athenians provided the greatest and noblest contribution for saving Greece, that is to say Themistocles as a general . . . , ships that were more numerous than all those of the allies taken together, and soldiers most experienced.' The praise of Themistocles is itself reminiscent of the words used by Thucydides, since it is said of him that he is: ἱκανώτατος εἰπεῖν καὶ γνῶναι καὶ πρᾶξαι (cf. Thucydides, I. 138. 3). Similarly, in the *Panathenaicus* of Isocrates, we find the points brought out by Thucydides: Isocrates has just recalled the courage shown by the Athenians in leaving their city and taking to the ships, and then shows their superiority from two points of view: they provided more ships and a more remarkable general, to wit Themistocles; he calls him: τὸν ὁμολογουμένως ἅπασιν αἴτιον εἶναι δόξαντα καὶ τοῦ τὴν ναυμαχίαν γενέσθαι κατὰ τρόπον καὶ τῶν ἄλλων ἁπάντων τῶν ἐν ἐκείνῳ τῷ χρόνῳ κατορθωθέντων (*Panath.*, 51).

³ Cf. note above.

⁴ On the number of ships, see Herodotus, VIII, 47-48 (180 out of a total of 378, according to him).

Μήδου παρὰ λόγον πολλὰ σφαλέντος ἐπὶ τῷ ὀνόματι ὡς ἐπὶ ᾿Αθήνας ᾔει ηὐξήθησαν); this interpretation, however, is rare, even among those who are trying to disparage Athens:[1] in the two passages where it is found it can be explained by the polemical intentions of the speaker, and is clearly nothing more than an opinion put forward by an advocate arguing his case. When one considers that it would be normal for her enemies to try to reduce the importance of a role that Athens herself might be expected to exaggerate, the caution which they show in doing so indicates that it was more difficult for them to present such a view than it was for the Athenians to present the opposite one.

Euphemus, on the other hand, replying to a remark by Hermocrates in VI. 76. 4, seems to suggest that we might have more serious reservations to make. In fact, he dismisses all Athenian self-praises about Marathon as useless arguments, since he maintains that it is impossible for Athens to justify her empire by maintaining that she alone conquered the Persians or that she sacrificed herself for the liberty of the people over whom she now rules: these, he says, would be just high-sounding phrases (VI. 83. 2), since what Athens did was to follow her own interest. But this very reservation shows that Euphemus does not consider the whole of the argument under discussion as completely ruined by the vanity which he denounces. In particular, the reservations which he expresses do not affect the speech made in Book I, but serve rather to confirm it. The Athenians, in fact, do not say that they alone *won the victory over the Persians* (Μαραθῶνί τε μόνοι προκινδυνεῦσαι is not the same as τὸν βάρβαρον μόνοι καθελόντες), nor do they say that they fought in order *to free enslaved peoples* (ἐπ᾿ ὠφελίᾳ ἐκινδυνεύετο ἧς τοῦ μὲν ἔργου μέρος μετέσχετε is not the same as ἐπ᾿ ἐλευθερίᾳ τῇ τῶνδε μᾶλλον ἢ τῶν ξυμπάντων τε καὶ τῇ ἡμετέρᾳ αὐτῶν κινδυνεύσαντες).[2] The words used in Book I express a moderate opinion, half way between the severity of Hermocrates, who maintains that he can see imperialist ambitions in all Athenian actions, and the exaggerations of the orators who never cease glorifying Athenian generosity.

Thus the speech in Book I, while containing more fervour and enthusiasm than that of Euphemus, takes care not to distort the truth

[1] There are no other examples in Thucydides. Sthenelaïdas, in I. 86. 1, provides an example of the opposite view.

[2] It is moreover quite obvious that Euphemus cannot be saying this to criticize the argument he has just used (cf. ἄξιοί τε ὄντες ἅμα ἄρχομεν in 83. 1, and εἰκότως ἄρχομεν in the introduction).

and become an empty piece of eloquence. It represents everything which a sympathetic view can accord to Athens, but nothing that goes beyond this; and, like Pericles' Funeral Oration, it represents definite facts in terms which Thucydides himself would not have disowned.

The value of these facts as arguments justifying Athenian rule can raise more doubts.

It should, however, be noted first of all that the principle on which this argument is based is not in itself particularly surprising, and that the mind easily associates[1] the ideas of superiority and leadership. As far as Athens is concerned, it is for this reason that, in the Funeral Oration, the military value of the city, considered in general, is made to justify its rule. Pericles himself affirms: οὔτε τῷ ὑπηκόῳ κατάμεμψιν (ἔχει) ὡς οὐχ ὑπὸ ἀξίων ἄρχεται (II. 41. 3), and, in Isocrates' view, the fact that Athens is the first among cities because of her monuments and buildings also makes her worthy to rule (Antidosis, 234: ἄρχειν ἀξίαν). Now Athens was never more obviously the first among cities than in the Persian wars, and Marathon already provided the Athenians of Herodotus with the opportunity to claim pride of place (IX, 27, 6: ἀλλὰ καὶ ἀπὸ τοῦ ἐν Μαραθῶνι ἔργου ἀξιοί εἰμεν τοῦτο τὸ γέρας ἔχειν; cf. 7: ἆρ' οὐ δίκαιοί εἰμεν ἔχειν ταύτην τὴν τάξιν ἀπὸ τούτου μούνου τοῦ ἔργου). Similarly, according to Lycurgus (Against Leocrates, 70), Marathon justifies the predominance of Athens over the rest of Greece, and according to Isocrates, the behaviour of Athens during the Persian wars is one of the reasons which entitle her to claim a new hegemony.

Now it should be noted that the text of the Athenians' speech in Book I does not push their claims so far. The speech uses the idea of moral superiority (προθυμίας ἕνεκα τῆς τότε καὶ γνώμης ξυνέσεως) in order to demand first place from a general point of view (ἀρχῆς γε ἧς ἔχομεν μὴ οὕτως ἄγαν ἐπιφθόνως διακεῖσθαι). Here again, 'to deserve not to be too sharply criticized for one's empire' is not the same as 'to deserve obtaining the empire' or even 'to deserve obtaining the hegemony'.[2] This vagueness, which is not

---

[1] The words ἄξιοι or εἰκότως refer in fact to this practical domain: cf. later p. 255. Aristotle raises this principle (of superiority accounting for leadership) to a universally valid rule (Pol., 1288 a, 15).

[2] A little later on, in I. 76. 2, they repeat the word ἄξιοι in the exact sense of 'worthy of power' (ἄξιοί τε ἅμα νομίζοντες εἶναι καὶ ὑμῖν δοκοῦντες). The difference lies in the fact that it is now no longer only a question of Athenian heroism at Marathon or Salamis. The realism of the speech, moreover, reduces this judgment to a mere corollary.

unskilful,[1] makes the argument more convincing, and where it departs from the views put forward by other speakers it is in order to correct them.

Moreover, how could one pretend that Athens is asking for too much? She is asking only for what she has actually been given; and she certainly seemed worthy of the hegemony, since the others immediately entrusted her with it. The historical account of the beginnings of her empire is introduced by γάρ, and provides evidence for the pride of the Athenians; it evokes a *consensus*, whose existence Thucydides himself admits in the Pentecontaëtia (I. 96. 1: ἑκόντων τῶν ξυμμάχων).[2] Thus the claims of the Athenians agree with the strictest realism.[3] All they do is express a perfectly proper pride in a thoroughly respectable manner.

There is, however, a text which seems to constitute an objection to this conclusion — the dialogue between the Athenians and the Melians. Like Euphemus at Camarina, but for different reasons, the Athenians at Melos do not allow themselves to use the argument of the Persian wars which, in their view, rests only on empty words: ἡμεῖς τοίνυν οὔτε αὐτοὶ μετ' ὀνομάτων καλῶν, ὡς ἢ δικαίως τὸν Μῆδον καταλύσαντες ἄρχομεν ἢ ἀδικούμενοι νῦν ἐπεξερ-χόμεθα, λόγων μῆκος ἄπιστον παρέξομεν, οὔθ' ὑμᾶς ἀξιοῦμεν ἢ ὅτι... ἢ ὡς... λέγοντας οἴεσθαι πείσειν (V. 89). Here, it is no longer a question of exaggeration as with Euphemus, but of the very value of the argument. Clearly, the argument which the Athenians at Melos are discarding is more definite and therefore more open to disagreement than the one used by the Athenians at Sparta, but this is a very slight difference; and, in fact, the speakers in Book V completely refuse, in the rest of the dialogue, to take any argument of this kind into consideration: what in the case of Euphemus was a correction is indeed a complete refusal at Melos, so that there is no doubt about the full extent of the contradiction.

Yet we must consider the basis of this refusal to use the argument of the Persian wars in the Melian dialogue. If one replaces it in its context, it will be noted that the Athenians dismiss this argument only because they dismiss any argument founded on the idea of

[1] It enables them to extend their conclusion so that it covers Athens' present empire; thus, as they go beyond the stage of hegemony while apparently refusing to do so, they finally demand at the same time both more and less.

[2] See also the speech of the Mytilenians (III. 10. 12).

[3] See later, p. 256, note 1.

justice:[1] the two arguments which they do not allow the Melians to use might similarly have no effect, and nevertheless have a certain value in themselves. It is quite possible that the Athenians at Melos no longer wished to consider anything which gave them rights, and that they felt the sharp contrast between their past glory and their present behaviour, and even that this behaviour did lead them towards an attitude of brutal political realism; however, this does not of itself render the argument of the Persian wars invalid; and the contrast between the Athenians of Book I and the Athenians of Book V is a subject which goes beyond the scope of this chapter.

This may be either a subjective or an objective difference, being either the result of a change in Thucydides' attitude or a change in the position of Athens: in order to discover this, we shall have to find out in what frame of mind Thucydides wrote the Melian dialogue, and at what date the two passages were written. It seems in any case impossible to believe that Thucydides should not, at least at the time of writing them, have felt some kind of sympathy for these apparently useless 'fine words' of Book I, which he chose to be at the same time so moderate and so fervent. They did constitute a defence of Athens, perhaps an inadequate one, but nevertheless a defence that he thought worthy of being retained, and they corrected the unpleasant idea of a tyrant city by the concept of a pure and glorious sovereignty.

The Athenians, however, still had to prove that Athens had not fallen from grace in realizing this sovereignty under the form of the ἀρχή.

B. From Authority to Empire

In order to show that since the Persian wars they had continued to behave rightly, the Athenians do not hesitate to tackle the grave and essential problem of how their authority became an empire. They make a formal distinction between the two things, and in this respect act differently from Euphemus, who seems to consider Athenian rule as a unity realized at a blow.[2] The Athenians at Sparta, on the other

---

[1] That is why, like Euphemus, they then insist, in presenting the argument, on the very notion which they want to dismiss altogether: where the Athenians in Book I and Euphemus in Book VI say εἰκότως, the Athenians at Melos say δικαίως. They thus underline the idea of a definite right based on justice, which deliberately distorts the argument such as it is presented elsewhere.

[2] The excuse put forward by Euphemus when speaking of the Persian wars is the same one put forward by the Athenians when speaking of the evolution of their empire (VI. 83. 2: πᾶσι δὲ ἀνεπίφθονον τὴν προσήκουσαν σωτηρίαν ἐκπορίζεσθαι = I. 75. 5:

hand, base themselves on the distinction established by Thucydides himself in the Pentecontaëtia between the Delian Confederacy, at the beginning, and the empire at the end.

They explain how the first became the second by using the familiar argument put forward by all guilty people: they were not responsible. They begin by showing that the establishment and maintenance of the empire were necessary: (75. 3: κατηναγκάσθημεν — 76. 1: ἀναγκασθέντας ἄν — 76. 2: νικηθέντες). Their conduct, they suggest, was determined by circumstances which made them obey (ὑπό) certain feelings; these feelings are, as it were, the means through which the actual circumstances become compulsory for Athens. Their influence develops according to chronological order, and the portrait given of Athenian imperialism depends to some extent on the way in which this order is interpreted. Some scholars, like Classen, have maintained that Thucydides was making a distinction between two periods by τὸ πρῶτον and καὶ οὐκ . . . ἔτι. But if there is something correct in this distinction, it nevertheless remains of secondary importance. Thucydides distinguishes essentially three feelings which act successively on the Athenians: fear, honour and self-interest (μάλιστα μέν — ἔπειτα καί — ὕστερον καί): they correspond to the three stages in the formation of the empire; but, at the same time, this period of formation is contrasted with the maintenance of the empire by the distinction: κατηναγκάσθημεν τὸ πρῶτον προαγαγεῖν . . . — οὐκ ἀσφαλὲς ἔτι ἐδόκει . . . ἀνέντας κινδυνεύειν. The two systems are independent and correspond to different ideas, but there is nevertheless a relationship between them: if one is developing the empire this necessarily presupposes that one is also maintaining it, and, similarly, in order to maintain it the Athenians are obliged to develop it; this is why Thucydides can repeat the three terms of honour,[1] fear and self-interest in 76. 2 under the general heading of μὴ ἀνεῖμεν, which then sums up the Athenian attitude in general. If he earlier distinguishes the two problems of acquiring and keeping the empire, it is in order to draw attention to the danger which

---

[1] τιμῆς is repeated at the beginning as the most noble term and the one most fitted to excuse Athens; this fact emphasizes, however, that the different factors indicated by the Athenians as following on one after the other do not replace one another but all add up together. It is this which explains why in 75. 3 one finds μάλιστα μέν instead of the πρῶτον μέν demanded by a strictly chronological point of view.

πᾶσι δὲ ἀνεπίφθονον τὰ ξυμφέροντα τῶν μεγίστων περὶ κινδύνων εὖ τίθεσθαι). This simple fact is sufficient to show that the Athenians in Book I are not less realistic but simply more precise.

Athens must now take into account, and which is set apart from the rest by the element οὐκ ... ἔτι. This element dominates the whole of the final period, and Thucydides subordinates all other necessities to it without, however, at the same time dismissing them completely. This intellectual concern which contrasts 'before' and 'after', in order to emphasize the last point more effectively, thus partially destroys the succession provided for by the chronological framework.

This final idea which he thus detaches from the others is the same one on which Pericles insists in II. 63. 2: ἧς οὐδ' ἐκστῆναι ἔτι ὑμῖν ἔστιν ... ὡς τυραννίδα γὰρ ἤδη ἔχετε αὐτήν, ἣν λαβεῖν μὲν ἄδικον δοκεῖ εἶναι, ἀφεῖναι δὲ ἐπικίνδυνον. — Ἐκστῆναι, ἀφεῖναι — ἀνιέναι, these various verbs of similar meaning all bring out the same impossibility; and this last part of the analysis can be immediately seen as conforming to Pericles', and consequently to Thucydides', own ideas. The only difference is that the idea is here made to cover the whole development of Athenian imperialism. From the very beginning, the hostility of Athens' subjects is shown as something obvious;[1] and, from the very beginning, the mistrust felt for Athens by Sparta adds to a danger which could still be relatively small by itself;[2] then, having started that way, the situation is constantly getting worse, since every act whereby Athens demonstrates her authority necessarily increases the enmity felt for her, and consequently the danger which she runs. The text of the Athenians thus explains how the situation described by Pericles has come about; it explains the concatenation which governs the conduct of Athens, and it raises the condition imposed on her to the status of a genuine evolutionary law. This is what is confirmed by the example: ὑμεῖς γοῦν; since everyone acts in his own interest, and since the interest of a people that rules must lead to empire, any other city placed in the same position as Athens would have yielded to the same necessities, and would have been led, as she was, from authority to empire.[3]

[1] Compare I. 75. 4: τοῖς πολλοῖς ἀπηχθημένους and I. 76. 1: εἰ τότε ... ἀπήχθεσθε ἐν τῇ ἡγεμονίᾳ with II. 63. 1: ἐν τῇ ἀρχῇ ἀπήχθεσθε. No explanation is needed in any of these passages, cf. pp. 125-126 and 313-314.

[2] This mistrust is confirmed, in the very expressions used, by the account given in the Pentecontaëtia (I. 92; I. 102. 4). The idea of hostilities existing outside the empire also appears in the statement of the law found in Alcibiades' speech in VI. 18. 2-3.

[3] I. 76. 1: εἰ τότε ὑπομείναντες διὰ παντὸς ἀπήχθεσθε ἐν τῇ ἡγεμονίᾳ, ὥσπερ ἡμεῖς, εὖ ἴσμεν μὴ ἂν ἧσσον ὑμᾶς λυπηροὺς γενομένους τοῖς ξυμμάχοις, καὶ ἀναγκασθέντας ἂν ἢ ἄρχειν ἐγκρατῶς ἢ αὐτοὺς κινδυνεύειν. Λυπηρός indicates someone who is *disliked* and who *acts harshly* (cf. in English words like 'unpleasant' or 'odious'). The two meanings, which are linked together logically, often exist side by side; the context simply indicates the

This wider general significance in no way calls into question the value of the original analysis, which is merely receiving here its logical complement.

There is now only one gap to be filled, and that is the initial period, where the consent of the governed changes first of all to hostility or to mistrust, and where the ruler takes the first, decisive steps, on the road that will lead to empire. It is to this period that the analysis which the Athenians make of the three feelings inspiring them can be said to correspond. This is the only time, in the whole of Thucydides' work, that the feelings of Athens receive an explanation,[1] and the Pentecontaëtia provides no means of checking its validity; for it describes the practical system which enables Athens' power to grow, but never gives the initial reason why this should happen.[2] These three feelings, however, are not wholly unfamiliar to us.

Two of them, fear and self-interest, are fairly near to the law of security which we have just examined: the fear of the Persians, the fear of Sparta, the fear of rebellion, the need of food-supplies — all these already represent the same preoccupation in a more or less inevitable form. Authority, under the guise of a natural and normal desire rather than of an unavoidable compulsion, is already dictating its laws to the future masters of the empire.

As to the third feeling, to which the Athenians give first place in their conclusion, it could indicate the vainest of reasons, were it not

[1] In a way, they are explained in all the indignant analyses made by the opponents of imperialism, and in all the enthusiastic appeals of its supporters; but in these cases it is never a direct or complete analysis.

[2] Chapter I. 99 even tends to hide the explanation of the cause by insisting on the incidental responsibilities brought out by the process of events. In this respect, one may quote the remark of G. K. Chesterton: 'If I set a house on fire, it is quite true that it may illuminate many other people's weaknesses as well as my own. It may be that the master of the house was burned because he was drunk; it may be that the mistress of the house was burned because she was stingy, and perished arguing about the expense of a fire-escape. It is nevertheless broadly true that they were both burned because I set fire to their house' (*The Barbarism of Berlin*, Cassell, 1914, pp. 7-8). It seems that the speech of the Athenians, as it considers this problem which had been left on one side in the Pentecontaëtia, provides a natural complement to the Pentecontaëtia. See later p. 271.

dominant notion. That of the agent predominates in VI. 18. 1, where it is a judgment on somebody's behaviour; that of the patient in I. 99. 1, where it is a comment on somebody's feelings; similarly in II. 64. 5. Here, the presence of ἀπήχθεσθε in the subordinate clause indicates that it is the notion of the agent which predominates, without which the idea would be an unnecessary repetition: on the other hand, the reasoning process is quite satisfactory if the Athenians explain that there is a necessary link between unpopularity and severity, so that one inevitably arrives at the dilemma: rule or be in danger.

that by the word τιμή it is closely linked to the ideal of Pericles, of which it forms an essential part.[1] While it is found in no other justification of the empire, it is here characteristic of a patriotism whose vibrant note could already be heard in the passage on the Persian wars. It is associated with the other two terms, in exactly the same way as, for Pericles, the ideal of glory was linked to the notion of necessity. And one can say that, on the whole, the analysis of the Athenians proceeds from the same spirit as Pericles' last speech, with this sole difference that it presents as two realities linked together in their chronological development the twin features which Pericles' speech exhibited in a single, instantaneous view, a cross-section as it were. It transforms Pericles' ideas into a theory, and gives them a temporal significance.

These different characteristics thus make Athenian action normal and right, if not praiseworthy: οὐδὲ θαυμαστὸν οὐδέν . . . οὐδ' ἀπὸ τοῦ ἀνθρωπείου τρόπου; and this conclusion shows the same moderation already found in the first part. The Athenians justify themselves only in so far as all men are acknowledged to have certain weaknesses and faults, or feelings which are more or less generous and noble in themselves. This moderation in the praise which the Athenians accord themselves is the final characteristic whereby this speech can be seen to reflect Thucydides' own point of view.

This notion of relativity is also to be found in the second justification, which is linked to the first by οὐδ' αὖ, and comes in both as a conclusion and as a transition. This justification consists of the argument that an authority which is unjust is nevertheless a normal and justifiable thing in itself: the weaker has always been kept down by the stronger (αἰεὶ καθεστῶτος τὸν ἥσσω ὑπὸ τοῦ δυνατωτέρου κατείργεσθαι), and no argument based on justice has ever changed this (τῷ δικαίῳ λόγῳ . . . ὃν οὐδείς πω παρατυχὸν ἰσχύϊ τι κτήσασθαι προθεὶς τοῦ μὴ πλέον ἔχειν ἀπετράπετο); and it is only because they are being hypocritical that the Spartans are now trying to use the argument of justice.

At first sight, this justification seems to contradict the first one which the Athenians put forward: while they began by excusing the authority which they exercised by the circumstances which had led them to assume it, they now suddenly assert that imperial rule is a normal condition whatever be the particular circumstances. In

[1] See pp. 128 ff.

so far as this second explanation is considered as self-sufficient, it seems to destroy much of the value of the first one.

But the role attributed to the argument, in the development of the ideas in the speech, allows us to dismiss this objection. Both arguments are based on the idea of human nature, and are summed up in I. 76. 3 by the words: χρησάμενοι τῇ ἀνθρωπείᾳ φύσει ὥστε ἑτέρων ἄρχειν; they are thus similar to a certain extent, but whereas the first deals with the feelings which have inspired Athens, the second is concerned with the actual fact of empire; one is concerned with a particular case, the other with a general principle, one with something that has come about gradually, the other with the final situation and result. We can thus appreciate why the second excuse, which belongs to a different type of consideration, should be presented only as a confirmation and an additional proof. It is essential to see this in order to appreciate the value of the argument.

Now, the ideas expressed by the Athenians seem to involve a whole series of moral judgments: the rule of the strong over the weak presented as the natural condition of society, justice considered as an empty word — such ideas presume the abolition of any notion of morality. But it must be noted that Athens has no intention of conforming her actions to these ideas, and that she is not, here, explaining her own behaviour.

Athens, in fact, does not give up the idea of acting morally, and, on the contrary, maintains that she differs from other states, since her empire is not merely the product of brute force. This idea is expressed within the passage itself, by a marked parallelism between two notions: οὐδ' αὖ πρῶτοι ... ὑπάρξαντες — ἄξιοί τε ἅμα νομίζοντες εἶναι καὶ ὑμῖν δοκοῦντες μεχρὶ οὗ τὰ ξυμφέροντα λογιζόμενοι τῷ δικαίῳ λόγῳ νῦν χρῆσθε: ἄξιος, deliberately repeated, represents a balance between justice and reality,[1] and it is this balance which Athens pretends to be characteristic of her behaviour. But the most important thing to note is that the whole development is in fact leading to a praise of Athenian moderation: in the passage which now

---

[1] Ἄξιος can in Greek indicate pure justice; but in this speech we have seen that a distinction needs to be made: one can *deserve* the empire for qualities which have nothing at all to do with morality, and this right is one that rests on a generally accepted opinion rather than on a moral principle. Since it thus belongs to the realm of practical morality, it is not contrasted with realism as δίκαιος is; it represents an agreement between both realms, an agreement which the Peloponnesians suddenly destroy by a distinction made in bad faith: the Athenians are not defending reality against justice: they are simply asking that they should still be allowed to reconcile them.

follows, Athens is shown as transcending this idea of human nature which, in the first passage, served as an excuse for all human actions; she does not behave as others would easily do if they were in her place, but still takes justice into account in what she does: ἐπαινεῖσθαί τε ἄξιοι, οἵτινες χρησάμενοι τῇ ἀνθρωπείᾳ φύσει ὥστε ἑτέρων ἄρχειν, δικαιότεροι ἢ κατὰ τὴν ὑπάρχουσαν δύναμιν γένωνται. Thucydides' Athenians thus only use the idea of the reign of power first as a confirmation and then as a comparison, and this idea is a turn-table that enables them to pass from the excuses put forward for Athens to a praise of her moderation. Here again, they differ from the speakers in the Melian dialogue, in the same way as they already have been seen to differ from them in their manner of using the argument of the Persian wars.

Thus limited by the context in which it is found, this passage only indicates that the Athenians have a realistic way of looking at things,[1] which does not, however, influence their behaviour. Now, this kind of realism is typical of Thucydides himself. He is distinguished from more credulous historians[2] by the fact that he never tries to explain events otherwise than by the self-interest of the parties concerned. He puts the most lucid maxims in the mouth of the most admirable people,[3] and in the very passage where he seems to give the greatest importance to morality, that is to say in the great analysis occasioned by his comments on the Corcyraean massacres in III. 82, he deplores a corruption about which he has absolutely no illusions: not only does he describe it with a bitter clairvoyance, but he is also well aware that all the horrors which he describes will occur again, because such is human nature (καὶ αἰεὶ ἐσόμενα ἕως ἂν ἡ αὐτὴ φύσις ἀνθρώπων ᾖ). The realism shown by the Athenians, a realism based on an intelligent

---

[1] The realism of their ideas is also noticeable in the way in which they put forward their arguments. The Athenians refrain from drawing conclusions themselves, but base themselves on actual judgments made by other people. When they say that they deserve to be allowed to rule, the immediate confirmation for this is that they were asked to. When they recall that they remained worthy of this rule, they add, first, that they themselves believed this to be so, but add immediately that the Lacedaemonians believed it also (καὶ ὑμῖν δοκοῦντες). It is this which explains the care taken in the last part of the speech to account for the opinion of Athens' subjects.

[2] From a thousand possible examples, let us make a comparison between Thucydides and Diodorus reporting the same event:

Thucydides III. 75. 3: ὁ δὲ δῆμος, δείσας μή τι νεωτερίσωσιν, ἀνίστησί τε αὐτοὺς πείσας καὶ διακομίζει ἐς τὴν πρὸ τοῦ Ἡραίου νῆσον.

Diodorus XII. 57. 4: οἱ δὲ Κερκυραῖοι, διὰ τὴν πρὸς τοὺς θεοὺς εὐσέβειαν τῆς μὲν τιμωρίας αὐτοὺς ἀπέλυσαν, ἐκ τῆς πόλεως δὲ ἐξέπεμψαν.

[3] Like Hermocrates (for example, in IV. 61. 5).

understanding of events and involving no loss of ideals, does not differ from that of Thucydides in his judgment on the Corcyraean massacres. It supports Athens' pride in the same way as the argument of political necessity supported Pericles' ideal in his last speech. And it is reasonable to think that if Thucydides had here spoken in his own name, he would not, for this part at least, have expressed himself differently from the Athenians in Book I.

The idea of Athenian moderation is the natural conclusion of the passage which has just been considered and which was concerned with realistic considerations. These afford a basis for the argument, and are constantly repeated.[1] The reason for this is that the idea of absolute power drawn from the right of the strongest provides the Athenians with a foil to bring out their own viewpoint. They show, in effect, that their power is distinguished from that of a tyrant precisely by its moderation, and that it is this very moderation which causes their empire to arouse criticism to which a more absolute one would not give rise.

This paradox is developed in a passage of analysis and followed by a corollary; both these are linked together by an example, and the whole passage is completed by another example, this time a hypothetical one.

For greater precision, the analysis limits itself to a single point taken as an example — Athenian legal practices. In choosing this example, the Athenians are replying to a criticism which the Corinthians had not made, and in which they were not at all interested; but outside this actual debate, this criticism was constantly put forward by the opponents of imperialism. The Athenians thus bring into the discussion a question that was not immediately relevant, but which deserved to be treated by anyone who was putting forward a serious explanation of the problems raised by Athenian imperialism; their φιλοδικεῖν δοκοῦμεν takes us to another audience and to other adversaries.

However, the choice of this example is not unimportant from the point of view of the main argument. For if the Athenians take the opportunity to speak only of their most moderate customs, it is

---

[1] 77. 3: ἐκείνως δὲ οὐδ' ἂν αὐτοὶ ἀντέλεγον ὡς οὐ χρεὼν τὸν ἥσσω τῷ κρατοῦντι ὑποχωρεῖν. Similarly, in what follows, it is assumed that men look upon rule based on force as normal and do not protest against it; thus 77. 4: ἀδικούμενοί τε, ὡς ἔοικεν, οἱ ἄνθρωποι μᾶλλον ὀργίζονται ἢ βιαζόμενοι.

essentially the existence of a judicial procedure, under whatever form, which illustrates the difference between their empire and one based solely on force. The very idea of judicial procedure does in fact assume relationships other than those based on force: βιάʒεσθαι γὰρ οἷς ἂν ἐξῇ δικάʒεσθαι οὐδὲν προσδέονται. Nevertheless the existence of privileges, defined within a legal framework, is more annoying than violence, which allows no recourse: ἀδικούμενοί τε, ὡς ἔοικεν, οἱ ἄνθρωποι μᾶλλον ὀργίʒονται ἢ βιαʒόμενοι. If men are angry with Athens, it is because they have forgotten that she could condemn without even taking the trouble to judge the case.

The better to appreciate the nature of this argument, it can be compared with that proposed by Isocrates in the same case. Isocrates does not reason, and certainly not in the abstract; he adduces facts, and compares the attitude of Athens with that of Sparta: thus, in the *Panegyricus* (113), we have: 'They dare to speak of lawsuits, who have in three months *killed without trial* more people than our city has *put on trial* during the whole period of her empire'; or in the *Panathenaïcus* (66): 'Who is stupid enough not to find the reply that the Spartans have *killed without trial* more Greeks than, since the foundation of our city, we have *brought up for trial in court*?' The principle on which the comparison is based is exactly the same as in Thucydides, and Isocrates' texts bring a sort of confirmation to the arguments put forward by the Athenians. Nevertheless, there are two differences between the Athenians and Isocrates.

First of all, the Athenians are arguing in the abstract and Isocrates is using particular cases. Doubtless this difference is partly a result of the fact that Thucydides, or rather the Athenians, did not yet have so precise an example at their disposal as Isocrates did,[1] but this is certainly not the main reason. Even if he had been able to, Thucydides would not have quoted a concrete instance. Facts, with him, are subordinated to ideas, and rather than contrast two particular states he goes back to the basic difference between two orders and two sets of principles. He is not so much concerned to answer the criticism about court cases as to suggest a theory of Athenian imperialism which shows its relationship to justice and power. The first difference thus brings out the intellectual method of Thucydides.

But at the same time, by the very fact that the Athenians compare

---

[1] They did, however, have the example of Persia, which is mentioned later, but then only in passing and in order to illustrate an argument which goes much further than any example.

themselves not to such and such a people who committed such and such a crime, but to the abstract essence of tyranny based on power — a tyranny which it would have been normal for them to exercise — they show both more insolence and more realism in justifying themselves. They present the idea of such a tyranny as natural, and they accept it intellectually: it provides the real background for the moderation they profess. And this second difference can also be explained by the difference in character between Thucydides and Isocrates, for it corresponds to the lucidity of the first and the occasionally vain optimism of the second. In both cases we find the distinguishing characteristic of Thucydides, and it is as if this argument — which is not really addressed to the Corinthians — ought not really to be attributed to the Athenians either, but to Thucydides himself.

The Athenian justification was moreover all the more acceptable because it was a more realistic, and, consequently, a more relative one. By accepting as natural the comparison which their enemies usually made between their empire and that of the Persians,[1] the Athenians were giving themselves the freest of free hands in presenting their arguments.

This comparison nevertheless raises a difficulty and thus draws a corollary after it. The authority of Athens, in spite of everything which has just been said, seems heavy compared to what has gone before. Why? Because the present always seems heavier to bear than the past.

Scholars have often put forward a mistaken interpretation of the function of this new development. The previous analysis, they say, has justified the ἀδοξία of Athens by her moderation. That another explanation should now be put forward is possible (though a little surprising), but it must be recognized that this will contradict the previous one. The rule which it tries to establish was surely valid in the Persians' time, and their authority must have seemed heavy as well, even more so than that of Athens; thus the argument justifies nothing, and is, on the contrary, rather alarming. This has been argued by Classen, Conradt, Steup and other philologists. Some, with Conradt, have argued that the whole passage, from εἰκότως to ὑπηκόοις is a gloss, and should be omitted; others, like Steup, have

---

[1] See I. 69. 5; VI. 77. 1.

argued that the whole of this last part of the paragraph is simply a projected version which Thucydides in no way intended to include in this context.

No more superficial interpretation could be put forward. If we read the text we shall see that the question is not the purely idle one of: why does our empire seem harsh when that of the Persians did not? What the Athenians are talking about is what people think now; and the problem under consideration is this: why does our empire seem harsh when compared to the very much harsher one exercised by Persia? Why are people not more conscious of the progress that has been achieved? Why are they not grateful to us? And Thucydides replies: the past always seems less hard to bear than the present, and the wrongs of Athens make men forget the wrongs of Persia; similarly, the wrongs of Sparta will make them forget those of Athens. Between these two examples the idea comes out with all its force, and concludes the demonstration with a resounding Q.E.D.

The very structure of the sentences underlines the homogeneity of the argument: the two successive examples introduced by γοῦν and by γὰρ οὖν parallel those of the preceding paragraph; in 77. 6 as in 76. 4 we find the same device of the hypothetical example, and in both cases the repetition of the ἄν; the accurate interplay of the four alternating comparisons even presupposes, whatever Steup may say in his *Anhang*,[1] a construction carefully prepared in advance. The last comparison is the most precise of all; it takes account of the Spartan character, and is both a threat and a warning. For that very reason, it was well chosen to conclude the speech.

There may be difficulties in the composition of this speech, and it may be difficult to justify the analysis made of it; but this would in no way be the result of any incoherence. For, starting with the passage on the Persian wars the developments come one after the other, each completing and confirming its predecessor; and only the rigorous links between the different ideas can prevent us from discovering the clear-cut divisions which such a speech would presuppose in our own day.[2] Here, the composition of the speech seems

---

[1] The examples in no way overlap: the first and the third are concerned with the past, first with Sparta and then with other cities; the second and fourth, on the other hand, are purely hypothetical; in the second example, Athens' probable successor is anonymous and purely fictitious; in the fourth, the successor is supposed to be Sparta, after her having triumphed over Athens.

[2] Cf. Schadewaldt, *Die Antike*, VIII, 1932, p. 31.

to correspond from beginning to end to the same basic idea and the same inspiration.[1]

The character of each of the arguments as well as that of the speech itself invite us to attribute this inspiration to Thucydides himself.

We should doubtless be wrong, however, in looking at this speech, as we should be wrong in looking at the Funeral Oration, as an expression of personal faith on the part of Thucydides. He makes his speakers say τὰ δέοντα, and consequently reveals only one aspect of reality. This instability of Athens, this desire for more which the Corinthians denounce did obviously exist, and Thucydides himself refers to the fact sufficiently often in his own work for there to be no doubt at all about it. But he indicates it as he would a particular failing, and it in no way prevents him, for example, from praising the achievements of Pericles. Athens — he thought — did have something else apart from this unfortunate and reprehensible characteristic: now, it is on this that he is here insisting. Since he thus brings out, freely and in a manner satisfactory in itself, the different circumstances which can be held to justify Athens, there are reasons for thinking that at that time in his life and at that point in his work he thought it suitable that these circumstances should be recalled, when other men might perhaps run the risk of forgetting them.

However that may be, it is certainly to him that we should attribute, if not the actual detail of the arguments which could be demanded by the thesis itself, then at least the general tendencies revealed when these arguments are stated. There are two such tendencies which stand out in a particularly decisive fashion.

The first combines patriotic enthusiasm and fidelity to a tradition. In addition to the specific arguments which celebrate the great achievements of Athens or her admirable moderation, these feelings are marked in the emotional warmth which characterizes these passages: this was certainly shown, as far as the first passage was concerned, by the contrast with the speech of Euphemus. With a due sense of proportion, we can compare the accents of this speech with those of the *Panegyricus* of Isocrates, or the *Panathenaïcus*, which both emphasize the glory of Athens and dismiss the criticisms made of her empire. Another point of comparison is that, in both these

---

[1] On the whole, one can at least bring out a simple progression which makes the reply to the criticism it has provoked follow on after the justification of the empire. This order is repeated by Isocrates in the *Panegyricus*, cf. Bodin, *Isocrate et Thucydide*.

texts, patriotic ardour is accompanied by a strong anti-Spartan feeling: in the account of the Persian wars it shows itself in allusions to Sparta's cowardice, and in the second part in allusions to Sparta's earlier rule and to her possible future authority. This polemical intention is, in Bodin's view, brought out by what he calls the 'insidious γοῦν'[1] of the Athenians. As in the Funeral Oration, this feeling combines with the patriotic ardour of the Athenians and gives this ardour a particular flavour.

By the side of this, however, the speech reveals a precise under-standing of the nature of authority. The Athenians, it says, are up against something from which they cannot get free: this is stated in the argumentation (κατηναγκάσθημεν), but it is also suggested by the general structure of the text. What else can be the significance of the oft-repeated examples (ὑμεῖς γοῦν, ἄλλους γὰν οὖν, ὑπὸ γοῦν τοῦ Μήδου, ὑμεῖς γὰν οὖν) except to insist on the abstract nature of the problem of imperialism, and to suggest that Athens is being com-pelled to follow a destiny which escapes her but from which she cannot escape? Here, once again, a comparison can be made between Thucydides and Isocrates; thus, in *On the Peace*, Isocrates speaks against imperialism and shows it as provoking everyone's hostility and developing like a genuine illness in the cities which give way to it.[2] A more hesitant thinker than Thucydides, Isocrates has indeed developed the two ideas we have just distinguished, but as two separate themes, aimed at answering different purposes at different times; Isocrates never brought them together in this moving objectivity which constitutes one of the reasons for Thucydides' greatness.

If the defence put forward by the Athenians at Sparta thus corre-sponds to one of Thucydides' attitudes, and if in fact it represents what he thought he had to say at a certain moment to justify Athenian imperialism — or, rather, the authority of Athens — we must try to identify this moment in order to see the kind of criticism he meant to refute.

II. THE DATE AT WHICH THE SPEECH WAS COMPOSED

One point immediately emerges for anyone studying this speech: it contains at least certain elements indicating that it was written 'late', that is to say after 404, as is shown by the example which con-cludes the second part, the famous ὑμεῖς γὰν οὖν.

[1] *Isocrate et Thucydide, Mélanges Glotz*, p. 97.
[2] See pp. 319-320.

It is already quite remarkable that, in a speech intended to frighten Sparta, the Athenians should put forward the then very unlikely hypothesis that Athens should one day lose her empire to Sparta.[1] This hypothesis could, it is true, be explained by the development of the argument. But the way the example is stated shows logic itself suffering from this excessive intrusion of reality. Only the beginning closely follows the train of thought: the present, says the text, always seems harder to bear than the past, so that the fear men have of Athens and the enthusiasm which they show for Sparta are both linked to the existence of Athenian rule; were this rule to disappear, then these two feelings would go with it, and the attitude of the Greeks towards these two cities would be completely reversed. All this is completely logical, but Thucydides suddenly adds to this almost abstract beginning the consideration of a particular set of circumstances — introduced by the future indicative εἴπερ . . . γνώσεσθε — , actually a particular attitude of the Spartans that would provoke the hostility of the Greeks. In so far as the explanation given takes this attitude into account, it constitutes a departure from abstract reasoning and from the very principle on which the Athenians' argument is based; and it weakens it to the same extent. Now we can explain the circumstance which intrudes into the logical pattern of the argument, since it is an exact portrayal of what happened after 404. Sparta then destroyed the power of Athens (καθελόντες ἡμᾶς) and ruled over the cities (ἄρξαιτε). She thus immediately lost popularity with them (τὴν εὔνοιαν . . . (ἄν) . . . μεταβάλοιτε), and her ephemeral authority was, it would seem, more disliked than had been that of Athens. Events followed exactly the same course as they had after the Persian wars (οἷα καὶ τότε πρὸς τὸν Μῆδον): deserting the jealous traditions of his fatherland,[2] Lysander repeated the mistakes of Pausanias; he rapidly abandoned Spartan customs, causing concern to Sparta as well as annoyance to the allies, and was, like Pausanias, recalled by the ephors in order to be judged.

Certainly, the Spartans had long been afraid of a new Pausanias (I. 95. 7), but that does not explain the general significance which the

---

[1] At that time, the war did not seem to involve such radical consequences; and even the loss of her empire by Athens did not seem necessarily to involve her being replaced as ruler over the Greeks by Sparta at the end of the war presented as one of liberation.

[2] This closed and secret quality of Sparta (indicated by ἄμεικτος) is contrasted with the welcoming liberty of Athens. This is a quality exalted in Pericles' Funeral Oration, to which we have already attributed a late date: it is not insignificant to find this contrast here and to be able to link it with the events which followed 404.

Athenians give to their remarks. This can only be explained if we assume that the new Pausanias has already appeared in the person of Lysander. We have seen elsewhere that in speaking of Pausanias, Thucydides seems to be following the idea of this comparison,[1] in the same way as in his description of Brasidas he seemed to be depicting the person who was an exception to this rule.[2] This idea of an almost relentless repetition of the same mistakes explains the assurance of the εἷς ἕκαστος ἐξιών.

Moreover, the Athenian phrase describing the attitude adopted by the Spartan generals towards the allied cities deserves to be retained; and it seems that in these 'customs' which are neither those of Sparta nor those of Greece, we must see an allusion to the regime set up by the Spartans in the captured cities. The nature of this regime would explain the words chosen by Thucydides, which at first sight seem obscure. In fact, the criticism which the Athenians here suggest strangely coincides with what Isocrates, in particular, has to say about the famous decarchies, this regime, as he calls it: οὔθ' ὁμοίαν τῇ παρ' αὐτοῖς οὔτε ταῖς ἄλλοθί που γεγενημέναις.[3] Isocrates, who is describing what actually happened, is too close to Thucydides, who is supposed merely to be foreseeing it, for the latter's predictions not to have been based *ex eventu*.[4] In this case, these few lines at least were written after 404.

However, if we examine the rest of the speech, no other clue is visible.[5] The simplest solution would thus be to assume that the whole of it was written after 404. This is also supported by a study of the plan and composition of the speech.

If it is true that more than any other speech this one is dominated by a continuous inner movement, which links each section very closely to its neighbours, it is also more satisfying to think that it was written all at the same time. The very sentence which we have just seen to have been written late is itself part of the skilful interplay of examples which extends throughout the second part of the speech; it is difficult to see how this unity of ideas and these formal relation-

---

[1] See above, p. 234

[2] Cf. IV. 81. 3: πρῶτος γὰρ ἐξελθὼν καὶ δόξας εἶναι κατὰ πάντα ἀγαθὸς ἐλπίδα ἐγκατέλιπε βέβαιον ὡς καὶ οἱ ἄλλοι τοιοῦτοί εἰσιν. This is certainly a passage written late, since it mentions events coming after the Sicilian expedition.

[3] *Panath.*, 54.

[4] Cf. Bodin, *Isocrate et Thucydide*, p. 99.

[5] The omission of the Plataeans in respect of Marathon can be very well explained by other than chronological considerations. See above, p. 245.

ships could have been obtained by putting together elements composed at different times.[1]

Thus everything would seem to indicate, if one considers the speech by itself, that it was all written late.

This conclusion is less easily accepted, however, if we look at the context in which the speech is placed.

We have already established,[2] in fact, that if there was an earlier version, then the great debate at Sparta, of which the speech of the Athenians forms part, was included in it; or rather, that the three speeches of the Corinthians, of Archidamus and of Sthenelaïdas, between which the speech of the Athenians is inserted, appeared in this version. We must therefore try to see whether this speech could have been put there later, after the three others had been written.

Now it is difficult to believe that this speech should not have always existed, in some form or other, at the same time as the others. It is not irrelevant to the rest of the debate, for its purpose is to answer the general criticism put forward by the Corinthians, and it produces the solution suggested by Archidamus. And since the speech of the Corinthians indicates both the wrongs committed by Athens and those of Sparta, it is natural that both should be given the opportunity to reply. On the other hand, the speech of the Athenians tends to dismiss any point of view based strictly on justice, and the reply which Sthenelaïdas makes, and which at the beginning is directed immediately at the Athenians, is inspired from start to finish by an opposition to such an attitude, and consequently presupposes its existence and expression. It thus seems that by omitting the speech of the Athenians from the debate, one would be omitting a useful and even essential element.

This double relationship between the Athenians' speech and the rest of the debate is probable on *a priori* grounds, and is also indicated by the detail of the expressions used. This is what Pohlenz has very

---

[1] It must be added that there are numerous repetitions of similar expressions which serve to rivet the different elements of a particular development together, or which link one development to another. Thus we have:

$\left\{\begin{array}{l} 75. \ 1: \ \mu\grave{\eta} \ o\H{u}\tau\omega\varsigma \ \mathring{\alpha}\gamma\alpha\nu \ \mathring{\epsilon}\pi\iota\varphi\theta\acute{o}\nu\omega\varsigma \ \delta\iota\alpha\kappa\epsilon\~{\iota}\sigma\theta\alpha\iota \\ 75. \ 5: \ \pi\~{\alpha}\sigma\grave{\iota} \ \delta\grave{\epsilon} \ \mathring{\alpha}\nu\epsilon\pi\acute{\iota}\varphi\theta\text{o}\nu\text{o}\nu \ \tau\grave{\alpha} \ \xi\upsilon\mu\varphi\acute{\epsilon}\rho\text{o}\nu\tau\alpha \ \tau\~{\omega}\nu \ \mu\epsilon\gamma\acute{\iota}\sigma\tau\omega\nu \ \pi\epsilon\rho\grave{\iota} \ \kappa\iota\nu\delta\acute{\upsilon}\nu\omega\nu \ \epsilon\H{u} \ \tau\acute{\iota}\theta\epsilon\sigma\theta\alpha\iota \end{array}\right.$

$\left\{\begin{array}{l} 75. \ 3: \ \mu\acute{\alpha}\lambda\iota\sigma\tau\alpha \ \mu\grave{\epsilon}\nu \ \mathring{\upsilon}\pi\grave{o} \ \delta\acute{\epsilon}\text{o}\upsilon\varsigma, \ \mathring{\epsilon}\pi\epsilon\iota\tau\alpha \ \kappa\alpha\grave{\iota} \ \tau\iota\mu\~{\eta}\varsigma, \ \mathring{\upsilon}\sigma\tau\epsilon\rho\text{o}\nu \ \kappa\alpha\grave{\iota} \ \mathring{\omega}\varphi\epsilon\lambda\acute{\iota}\alpha\varsigma \\ 76. \ 2: \ \mathring{\upsilon}\pi\grave{o} \ \tau\~{\omega}\nu \ \mu\epsilon\gamma\acute{\iota}\sigma\tau\omega\nu \ \nu\iota\kappa\eta\theta\acute{\epsilon}\nu\tau\epsilon\varsigma, \ \tau\iota\mu\~{\eta}\varsigma \ \kappa\alpha\grave{\iota} \ \delta\acute{\epsilon}\text{o}\upsilon\varsigma \ \kappa\alpha\grave{\iota} \ \mathring{\omega}\varphi\epsilon\lambda\acute{\iota}\alpha\varsigma \end{array}\right.$

Although they do not constitute decisive objections against the idea of possible revisions, they do nevertheless make it especially difficult to discover where these are.

[2] See pp. 32 ff.

well shown,[1] and the passage that follows reproduces the essential points of his analysis.

First of all, the portrait of Athens presented by the Athenians in their speech is a direct reply to the one made by the Corinthians (I. 70. 1: περὶ ὧν οὐκ αἰσθάνεσθαι ἡμῖν γε δοκεῖτε οὐδ᾽ ἐκλογίσασθαι πώποτε πρὸς οἵους ὑμῖν ᾽Αθηναίους ὄντας καὶ ὅσον ὑμῶν καὶ ὡς πᾶν διαφέροντας ὁ ἀγὼν ἔσται = I. 73. 3: δηλώσεως (ἕνεκα) πρὸς οἵαν ὑμῖν πόλιν μὴ εὖ βουλευομένοις ὁ ἀγὼν καταστήσεται). The idea of the boldness of the Athenians, used in a hostile spirit by the Corinthians (I. 70. 3: καὶ παρὰ δύναμιν τολμηταὶ καὶ παρὰ γνώμην κινδυνευταί) is repeated by the Athenians but transformed into a compliment (I. 74. 1: προθυμίαν ἀοκνοτάτην − cf. 2: προθυμίαν δὲ καὶ πολὺ τολμηροτάτην; ibid.: ἠξιώσαμεν . . . κινδυνεῦσαι; − 3: ἡμεῖς δὲ . . . ὑπὲρ τῆς ἐν βραχείᾳ ἐλπίδι οὔσης κινδυνεύοντες, ξυνεσώσαμεν ὑμᾶς τε τὸ μέρος καὶ ἡμᾶς αὐτούς). Similarly, the conclusions of both sets of speakers correspond closely to each other by their contrasting themes (I. 71. 4: βοηθήσατε κατὰ τάχος, cf. I. 78. 1: βουλεύεσθε οὖν βραδέως).

Moreover, Pohlenz has indicated that the speech of the Athenians constitutes with those of Archidamus and Sthenelaïdas a single unit, with closely associated ideas and expressions. By distinguishing between young and old in the assembly (72. 1), the Athenians seem to prepare the later conflict between the two Lacedaemonians dissimilar in age; by offering to settle difficulties by peaceful negotiation (78. 4) they provide Archidamus with a very specific argument (85. 2).

These links are far too close for us to accept the idea of Thucydides having slipped this fourth speech in afterwards, since this would have required too much care and attention: Thucydides would have scarcely been able either to take everything he had already written so carefully into account or to correct it in accordance with what he was adding; when the links between the different speeches are so close, it seems reasonable to say that if Book I always included an account of the debate at Sparta, similarly the debate in Sparta never existed without a speech by the Athenians, a speech which may perhaps have been rewritten and revised, but fragments of whose original version are still present in the text that we now possess.

If this is so, it is perhaps not impossible to discover traces of the

[1] I, 102.

earlier version of this speech. Such attempts at reconstruction are always extremely hypothetical, and should be presented only with the greatest care. However, in this particular case, there are two features which deserve to be noted.

The first is that the actual subject-matter of the speech which we now possess does not completely coincide with the subject announced in advance. The themes indicated in the exordium are obviously too general and imprecise for us to be able to say with any certainty whether they are actually dealt with in the speech. Moreover, even if Thucydides did in fact re-write the speech, he would not have left too obvious a contradiction. But it just so happens that, in this instance, the subject is announced in two different texts, one being the introduction which precedes the speech, and the other the exordium which begins it, and these texts can serve as a commentary on each other. Thus, by comparing the introduction with the exordium, and then with the actual content of the speech, the difference becomes immediately obvious.

The exordium repeats the introduction almost word for word:

72. 1: τῶν μὲν ἐγκλημάτων πέρι μηδὲν ἀπολογησομένους ὧν αἱ πόλεις ἐνεκάλουν,	73. 1: οὐ τοῖς ἐγκλήμασι τῶν πόλεων ἀντεροῦντες
— δηλῶσαι δὲ περὶ τοῦ παντὸς ὡς οὐ ταχέως αὐτοῖς βουλευτέον εἴη.	ἀλλ' ὅπως μὴ ῥᾳδίως περὶ μεγάλων πραγμάτων τοῖς ξυμμάχοις πειθόμενοι χεῖρον βουλεύσησθε,
— καὶ ἅμα τὴν σφετέραν πόλιν ἐβούλοντο σημῆναι ὅση εἴη δύναμιν καὶ <u>ὑπόμνησιν ποιήσασθαι τοῖς τε πρεσβυτέροις ὧν ᾔδεσαν καὶ τοῖς νεωτέροις ἐξήγησιν ὧν ἄπειροι ἦσαν.</u>	καὶ ἅμα βουλόμενοι περὶ τοῦ παντὸς λόγου τοῦ ἐς ἡμᾶς καθεστῶτος <u>δηλῶσαι ὡς οὔτε ἀπεικότως ἔχομεν ἃ κεκτήμεθα, ἥ τε πόλις ἡμῶν ἀξία λόγου ἐστίν.</u>

At the end of these two texts, in the propositions underlined, there might seem to exist a difference in intention: where the introduction speaks in terms of power and tries to inspire fear, the exordium — one could say — tries to explain and obtain approval, as, in fact, does the speech itself.

But this difference is only apparent, and it can be shown that in reality the two texts of the introduction and the exordium coincide. Are not the early actions of which the introduction speaks (ὑπόμνησιν ποιήσασθαι ...) intended to justify the authority of Athens (οὔτε ἀπεικότως ...)? Does not the extent of Athens power (ὅση εἴη δύναμιν) correspond to the idea that Athenian is a city 'not to be despised' (ἀξία λόγου)? The two themes are thus the same, from one text to the other, and it is only the order in which they are presented which is different. The slight vagueness that might be found in the exordium when it is taken by itself disappears as soon as it is placed by the side of the introduction, with which it corresponds exactly.

We can thereby see that the justification announced in the exordium was intended to take up only one part of the speech, that this justification was going to be made up of an account of past events with which the young men would not have been acquainted, and finally that it was to be accompanied by another passage dealing with the extent of Athenian power.

The justification is then easy to identify, and can be found in the passage about the Persian wars. This fits in perfectly well both with the text of the introduction and with the exordium. The few words by which it begins are very close to the introduction, and show the same concern to recall the greatness of Athens; and the aim is as much to intimidate the Spartans as to free Athens from the accusations made against her: I. 73. 3 = ῥηθήσεται δὲ οὐ παραιτήσεως μᾶλλον ἕνεκα ἢ μαρτυρίου καὶ δηλώσεως πρὸς οἵαν ὑμῖν πόλιν μὴ εὖ βουλευομένοις ὁ ἀγὼν καταστήσεται. The conclusion is exactly the same as the one which announces the exordium, and deals with the legitimate character of Athenian rule: I. 75. 1 = ἆρ' ἄξιοί ἐσμεν, ὦ Λακεδαιμόνιοι, καὶ προθυμίας ἕνεκα τῆς τότε καὶ γνώμης ξυνέσεως ἀρχῆς γε ἧς ἔχομεν μὴ οὕτως ἄγαν ἐπιφθόνως διακεῖσθαι.

On the other hand, the other section announced does not coincide with the second part of the speech.[1] The whole section which is concerned with the passage from authority to empire, and which tries to find excuses for Athenian conduct in the general behaviour of humanity, goes beyond the framework foreseen in the introduction and exordium, and implies a different aim. As for the theme actually

[1] It is not at all necessary for the *plan* of the speech to be announced in the exordium and it even seems that Thucydides (like most of the Greek orators in general) was no acquainted with such a custom. It is still customary, however, when two ideas are announced, that they should indeed be brought out either in successive sections, whatever their order may be, or together if they present similar meanings. This is not the case here

announced — that of the extent of Athenian power — it makes absolutely no appearance.

This contrast is further underlined by the nature of the *epilogos*, which coincides, in fact, not with the speech that we now have but with the speech announced in advance. It is the logical conclusion of a speech whose aim has been to frighten Sparta by showing her with how powerful a city she was about to enter into conflict; in fact, the speech concludes with a warning: 78. 1 = βουλεύεσθε οὖν βραδέως ὡς οὐ περὶ βραχέων καὶ μὴ ἀλλοτρίαις γνώμαις καὶ ἐγκλήμασι πεισθέντες οἰκεῖον πόνον πρόσθησθε. Since the Athenians have just shown that their reputation for harshness is unjustified, this conclusion is somewhat out of place, whereas if the speech had shown that Athens was 'a city not to be despised', then it would have been wholly in keeping with its general tenor.

It thus seems that the exordium, the argument based on the Persian wars, and the *epilogos* do coincide and fit into the function intended to be fulfilled by the earlier version of the speech, whereas the second part, dealing with Athenian rule in more detail, would seem to be wholly or partly the result of later revisions or additions.

This conclusion is confirmed by an analysis of the detail of the speech. If in fact we look at the comparisons made by Pohlenz which prove that the speech formed part of the general plan of the debate at Sparta, it is worth noting that all the examples he quotes, *without any exception*, are taken from the introduction, the exordium, the passage on the Persian wars and the *epilogos*;[1] none is taken from the very important part which deals with Athenian rule. It would thus seem that this part alone is independent of the rest of the debate; and it is precisely because it goes beyond the limits of the discussion that it could not be foreseen as a normal theme of the speech.

Finally, it is within this part alone that the unity of composition is indicated by precise verbal correspondences.

It may still be possible that, even when he was writing this part of the speech, Thucydides made use of fairly long extracts from his early version: we cannot know anything about this. All we can say is that, on the whole, we seem to have here, as in Pericles' last speech, an early version revised at a later date. It will, moreover, be noted that in both cases Thucydides has sealed up the joints very carefully, but that as the passage gradually goes further beyond its context, it reveals itself to the reader, and finally betrays its secret as it escapes

[1] See above, p. 266.

from the fiction of the past. Thus, in both cases, the place of the 'late' clue seems easy to understand.

Without wishing to carry what are inevitably hypothetical conclusions too far, it is nevertheless possible to bring out the following points as regards Thucydides' ideas on Athenian imperialism.

The first part of the Athenians' speech, which is closely linked to the rest of the debate and which is more valid as an appeal for sympathy than as a decisive argument, probably belonged to an 'early' version. At that time, it represented the finest part of the Athenian cause, and corrected the picture of Athens as a city which was a source of annoyance to its neighbours. The fact that this theme is treated at this point in the work justifies its omission from the Funeral Oration. However that may be, and whether the passage was or was not written at an 'early' date, it represents in any case something to which Thucydides remained faithful at a late period, and which he thought deserved to be expressed. If he did not write it then, he at least kept it, and included it in the version of the speech which we now have without it being in any way out of place. There is nothing surprising in this if we consider that at the time when Athenian power had been cast down and was being everywhere reviled, Thucydides would have wanted to present the most radiant vision of its grandeur, as we have already seen him do in the Funeral Oration. It was certainly not at a time when reactionary forces were at last triumphant, when they were free to talk and strong in arguments with which to denounce Athenian imperialism, that Thucydides was going to consider such a memory unnecessary or out of place.[1]

As to the second part of the speech, it certainly seems to have been conceived after 404. It deals more precisely with the problem of Athenian rule, and does not hide the fact that there are criticisms which can be made. It replies to these criticisms by an argumentation which is unambitious as far as its claims are concerned, but which contains a closely knit analysis. The composition of this second part fits in with everything that we can suppose to have been in Thucydides' mind at that time.

[1] The mention of the Persian wars comes even more naturally at that time since it offers a natural contrast with the idea of the disaster which has overtaken Athens and with the idea of the relentlessness shown towards her by the rest of the Greeks. Thus in the *Menexenus* (244 c): τάς τε ναῦς περιελόμενοι, αἵ ποτ' ἐκείνους ἔσωσαν, καὶ τείχη καθελόντες ἀνθ' ὧν ἡμεῖς τἀκείνων ἐκωλύσαμεν πεσεῖν. This memory seemed so valid at that time that it was then considered to have caused Athens to be spared (Xenophon, *Hell.*, II, 2, 20).

By the fact that it constitutes a more rigorous and systematic analysis of the formation of the Athenian empire, this part of the speech is linked with the ideas by which, after 404, Thucydides brings out the features of Athenian imperialism and gives it an even greater importance at the very beginning of his History. We have placed the writing of the Pentecontaëtia after 404; now, we have seen that chapter 75 comes to complete the narrative and give it a new and additional dimension.

Similarly, by the indication which it gives of a more clearly marked polemical and apologetic intention, this part of the speech also fits in with the ideas by which Thucydides reacts against the opponents of imperialism. Their criticisms are here discussed directly, and the contrast with Sparta openly admitted, as it is in the Funeral Oration. If it is true, as Bodin has written,[1] that 'the Apology can be considered as completing the Epitaphios, and as completing it systematically by virtue of a kind of plan worked out in Thucydides' mind', then we can say that these three texts concerned with Athenian Imperialism (the Pentecontaëtia, the speech of the Athenians and the Funeral Oration) seem to come together to form a large single unit, linked together both by its plan and by the preoccupations inspiring it, and conceived by Thucydides after 404.

Finally, it is only in this part of the speech that the second characteristic of this defence of Athenian imperialism makes itself felt, that is to say this objective realism which, while fully recognizing the more unfortunate aspects of Athenian imperialism, excuses them only by relating them to the needs inseparable from any imperialism. Certainly, Thucydides could not mention Athenian rule, even to defend it, without taking into consideration the problems that it created; he less than anyone else could ignore these problems, since he had shown himself so severe towards Cleon or Alcibiades and so ready to agree with the critics of imperialism. But, at the same time, it would clearly have been easier for him to consider them as part of an almost abstract account of the evolution of any imperialism once Athenian imperialism had run its course and he had seen this course repeated by Sparta.

This characteristic was already present in the kind of bold lucidity to which Pericles' last speech bore witness; but this lucidity is even more obvious here, and by the very generality of its subject matter, the speech of the Athenians indicates more fully than

[1] *Isocrate et Thucydide*, p. 94.

others one of the essential directions taken by Thucydides' ideas after 404.

Thucydides is here dealing with a whole line of political development which no longer belongs to the present and which no longer involves any choice; it is shown as made up of good and bad elements which are indissolubly linked together by the very necessity of their development. Thucydides takes note of this development and explains it; and, in his impartial, theoretician's mind, the particular case brings out the general law. This scientific detachment, on which Thucydides' impartiality is based, enables him to understand, and consequently to justify, without prejudice and without illusions. The defence of Athenian imperialism thus rests upon a profoundly realistic attitude. And, at the same time, as the analysis rises to consider the very nature of Athenian imperialism as a particular experience given to the scientist to study, so the philosophical ideas begin to appear. Realism becomes a moral attitude, and, as the facts stand out in their eternal essence, we begin to see, beyond the individuals whose acts are described, the naked principles of justice and force, of might and right.

Thus the speech of the Athenians is related to those we have already studied not by the more or less favourable attitude towards imperialism which inspires it, but by the degree of generality and objectivity achieved by the analysis which it gives. When intelligence thus widens the field of the historian's vision, the partisan gives way to the observer and opinion to experience.[1]

The experience which we here find set out is by very nature pessimistic: Athens acknowledges that she has been carried away, and tries to justify herself by proving that this was inevitable. Nevertheless, in this speech of the Athenians, such pessimism is present only in a very attenuated form, and is still linked to an intense awareness of the greatness and generosity of Athens.

This balance is destroyed in the dialogue between the Athenians and the Melians, and we shall have to find out the reason for such a difference.

---

[1] Jaeger, whose slightest hints generally contain so much truth, writes in *Paideia* (I, p. 396 of the English translation): 'They are Thucydides' own ideas, and he could not have worked them out till after the fall of Athens, when he reached the painful height of his political experience.'

CHAPTER TWO

THE MELIAN DIALOGUE

UNLIKE the speech of the Athenians in Book I, the subject of the Melian dialogue is not, at least in appearance, imperialism in general. The negotiations have a precise and definite aim, which is to obtain the surrender of the island.

There are nevertheless a number of characteristics already contained in the speech of the Athenians in Book I, whose repetition in the Melian dialogue would seem to indicate that Thucydides wanted to give this a wider and more general significance than its immediate framework would suppose.

The first and most obvious of these characteristics is the anonymity of the speakers in both cases. We do not now know who suggested that this expedition should be made, nor what were the dominating factors leading Athens to undertake it. Plutarch indicates Alcibiades as having supported the project of massacring its inhabitants,[1] but then it is merely a question of the 'punishment' of Melos. And we must not forget that Nicias was in command of the first expedition against this island (III. 91. 1). Whoever may have made the actual suggestion, Thucydides attributes to the whole city of Athens the responsibility for the expedition by making οἱ Ἀθηναῖοι justify it.

By itself, this indication is by no means conclusive, and it becomes really significant only if one compares the place which the dialogue occupies in Thucydides' work with the occasion that gave rise to it. The taking of Melos was, in itself, a relatively insignificant incident which did not have any great influence on the course of the war. It assumes its real importance only if it is looked upon as particularly characteristic of a whole policy, and if one sees, in this imperialistic act, the general features of imperialism.

Now the very nature of the arguments put forward indicates that

---

[1] *Alc.*, 16, 6: τὴν πλείστην αἰτίαν ἔσχε τῷ ψηφίσματι συνειπών. This text does not even prove that Alcibiades was the author of the decree: συνειπών in fact marks the contrary. In [Andocides], *In Alc.*, 22, it is he who makes the proposition, but it is one which does not include massacre: γνώμην ἀποφηνάμενος ἐξανδραποδίζεσθαι.

Thucydides wanted to give this analysis a significance wider than any other. They are indeed of a highly improbable tenor, and the dialogue itself is as much Thucydides' own work as one of Plato's dialogues is one of his works. Can we really imagine a group of ambassadors carrying on this closely knit discussion in a manner unknown to Greek diplomacy or, for that matter, to diplomacy in general? Can we really imagine them talking about justice and the Gods? Can we really imagine the Melians warning the Athenians, advising them to offer precedents for clemency and causing to rise up before them the figure of a new Brasidas? This way of arguing indicates Thucydides' own intervention and his desire to give his own treatment of the question of imperialism as a whole.

Thanks to the dialogue form, the only one in the whole of the History, the particular and the general mingle together. This form enables maieutics to take the place of formal demonstration, so that the complete pattern Thucydides has in mind is revealed little by little, in all its aspects down to its deepest foundations. Instead of using general maxims in order to bring out the continuous parallel between a particular example and the universal rule, Thucydides seems to be concerned only with the particular, but by examining thoroughly the whole range of conditions and consequences it discloses, he brings out a system of universal value. No circumstance or consideration is mentioned here that does not find its place in this system, with the final result that, although built up around the immediate example of Melos, it is equally valid for all the other manifestations of Athenian policy. In the course of the discussion, we reach heights unknown in the rest of the work; the speakers examine the role of courage, of hope, of the Gods, and the very principles of human action and endeavour: indeed this debate, dealing with the case of Melos, runs like a metaphysical discussion — the reason being that this attack is here envisaged not in the accidents of its manifestation but in the eternal principle inspiring it.

Thus, we can say that the Melian dialogue rises above the particular incident of Melos in the same way as the speech of the Athenians rises above the debate at Sparta. Thucydides seems to have used the opportunity presented to him in order to analyse in the widest possible fashion a general policy that could be attributed to Athens as a whole.

This policy is obviously that of imperialism in its conquering phase.

I. THE DATE OF COMPOSITION

If this dialogue occupies this extremely important place in Thucydides' ideas, then it is especially important to discover at what time it was written. However, by the very fact that it is linked with Thucydides' own intentions rather than with the demands of the narrative, and since it can be explained throughout as the development of a single thesis, it seems normal to try to infer a general date of composition from the nature of these intentions, and also to be more prepared to give detailed clues a decisive value as concerns the whole.

Now information of both types fits together, and the presence of certain details, like the presence of the dialogue as a whole, can be more satisfactorily explained if one assumes that it was written after 404.

As in the speech in Book I, and even more in this dialogue, the characters made to speak by Thucydides show a strange foreknowledge of the events which marked the end of the war.

The Melians know that the neutral cities will abandon Athens. This, certainly, happened before 404, but it is an initial indication, and the words used are too close to those found in the narrative for us to see the dialogue as written 'under the immediate impact of events'; one has, in fact:

V. 98: ὅσοι γὰρ νῦν μηδετέροις ξυμμαχοῦσι, πῶς οὐ πολεμώσεσθε αὐτούς, ὅταν ἐς τάδε βλέψαντες ἡγήσωνταί ποτε ὑμᾶς καὶ ἐπὶ σφᾶς ἥξειν;

VIII. 2. 1: οἱ μὲν μηδετέρων ὄντες ξύμμαχοι ὡς ἤν τις καὶ μὴ παρακαλῇ σφᾶς οὐκ ἀποστατέον ἔτι τοῦ πολέμου εἴη, ἀλλ' ἐθελοντὶ ἰτέον ἐπὶ τοὺς Ἀθηναίους, νομίσαντες κἂν ἐπὶ σφᾶς ἕκαστοι ἐλθεῖν αὐτοὺς εἰ τὰ ἐν τῇ Σικελίᾳ κατώρθωσαν.

They also foresee that Athens will be defeated, and allude to this idea in paragraph 90 (σφαλέντες). Yet they are speaking at the very time that Athenian power is at its height, when there is a lull in the war with Sparta, and when they themselves are just about to be crushed. Their remark is an astonishing one, and they show no less boldness in the forecast in paragraph 110 when they say what Sparta could do to Athens and bring up the idea of a new campaign to win over Athens' allies, like the one that will be made so easily after the failure of the Sicilian expedition.

There is, moreover, an even more precise reference, for the speakers apparently know that after her defeat Athens will be saved only by her rival. When the discussion has rather strangely moved in the direction of a possible defeat of Athens, the Athenians declare that they are in no way afraid of the prospect that their empire may collapse. It is not, they say, ruling states like Sparta which are dangerous for their vanquished enemies, but former subjects who may rise up and conquer their masters. Events confirmed the validity of the Athenians' remarks, for Xenophon writes in the Hellenica (II, 2, 19, quoted in C. L. Brownson's translation, Loeb Library): 'When they arrived, the ephors called an assembly, at which the Corinthians and Thebans in particular, though many other Greeks agreed with them, opposed making a treaty with the Athenians and favoured destroying their city. The Lacedaemonians, however, said that they would not enslave a Greek city which had done great service amid the greatest perils that had befallen Greece ... ' Xenophon particularly denounces the Corinthians and the Thebans, but the former allies, or subjects, of Athens supported them or at least were generally considered to have done it. Isocrates recalls this several times, and in the most definite manner, in his treatise On the Peace: [1] 78 = Λακεδαιμονίων ... εὐνουστέρων ἐτύχομεν ἢ τῶν πρότεροι ἡμῖν συμμάχων ὄντων – 105: ἡμεῖς τε γὰρ μισθέντες ὑπὸ τῶι συμμάχων καὶ περὶ ἀνδραποδισμοῦ κινδυνεύσαντες ὑπὸ Λακεδαιμονίωι ἐσώθημεν. Thus, Isocrates expresses himself no differently after the event than the Athenians of Thucydides had done beforehand.

Was it so normal a thing to be able to foresee this? Certainly the idea expressed in this passage coincides with a number of reflections that could have been made before 404: the Pseudo-Xenophon hints that Athens is afraid only of her allies (II, 1 = καὶ νομίζουσι τὸ ὁπλιτικὸν ἀρκεῖν εἰ τῶν συμμάχων κρείττονές εἰσιν). But the comparison here enables us to measure the difference, which is a considerable one: the Pseudo-Xenophon is considering the possibility of war and Thucydides the prospect of defeat. Athens certainly fears her subjects, but why should she be more afraid of being defeated by them than by a city which already has authority over others? This is a new idea, which is not immediately explicable. Is it because a ruling city would be reluctant to give her own subjects an example of vengeance? This is Arnold's view, and the idea would thus be

---

[1] This is what Momigliano does not seem to take into account. He puts forward the objection that the danger came not from Athens' subjects but from those of Sparta. To be quite accurate, the Athenians at Melos consider a rising that would not be either suggested or guided by anybody else: αὐτοὶ ἐπιθέμενοι; what happened in 404 at least gives weight to that hypothesis and is much in favour of what the Athenians say.

similar to the one expressed by Nicias in Book VI (11. 3): οὐκ εἰκὸς ἀρχὴν ἐπὶ ἀρχὴν στρατεῦσαι. But the situation here is not the same, and Sparta, who was then head of a confederation, had nothing to fear from such an example. Is it, then, because a powerful city wants to leave its rivals face to face with other rivals? This is the view of Grundy and Curtius, and it certainly fits the facts.[1] It does not, however, fit our text, for the idea of a counterweight has nothing to do with the idea of ruling and subject cities. The correct explanation is certainly the one which brings all these different ideas together by contrasting an emotional and passionate war with one obeying coldly political reasons. Subjects are inspired by hatred; empires by political considerations. Cities which already rule over others try to defeat their enemies, not to destroy them. This is a principle which the Athenians recognize as valid in their own case: ἡμεῖς δὲ μὴ διαφθεί-ραντες ὑμᾶς κερδαίνοιμεν ἄν; and it is also the principle in whose name Diodotus tried to save Mytilene. On the other hand, when Athens fears her subjects, she fears that their hatred will make itself felt in the vengeance that they extort, and she is afraid of something worse than slavery: Cleon makes an allusion to it in III. 40. 5, and Pericles states it with no ambiguity in what is probably a 'late' part of his speech (II. 63. 3).[2] Here, the same idea is merely presented, in its very brevity, with much more conciseness; one might even say with too much conciseness. It can be added that before 404, Sparta the liberator could not be so obviously called a city ἄρχουσα ἄλλων. Thus, the whole analysis doubtless fits in with the rest of Thucydides' ideas, but it goes beyond them and seems the result of a specific experience.

Therefore, the Athenian reply departs somewhat from the question at issue and is not immediately clear. If, however, we assume that its function is to bring to bear in advance on the general theory of Athenian imperialism a final experience which did not take place until after 404, then both its existence and its general tenor are fully justified.

This proof could be sufficient in itself, but there are other themes which also fit better into the idea of a late date of composition, and which thus confirm the validity of this result.

---

[1] Glotz, p. 758; cf. in addition the evidence of Polyaenus, I, 45, 5. It will be noted that it is precisely against the opposition of Thebes and Corinth that Sparta manages to have Athens spared.

[2] See p. 125.

If to attribute an ἀρχή to Sparta is to show a foreknowledge of that city's future, perhaps the Athenians' insistence on its egoism also shows an awareness of events to come. In paragraph 105, they sum up the attitude of Sparta by saying that more than any other city she identifies what is pleasant with what is honourable, and what is most expedient to her with what is just. In paragraph 107, they show her as refusing to run risks for the sake of justice and honour, and preferring the safer way of looking after her own interests. In paragraph 109, they show her as being concerned with the strength of her allies rather than with the justice of their cause before going to their aid. These last two remarks are simply illustrations of the first, and express exactly the same idea. Now the Athenians are not speaking at random. Indeed, Sparta did not intervene to save Melos, and Thucydides knew this, but we may wonder if this was sufficient reason for him to give so general and positive a note to the ideas expressed in this passage.

Egoism and hypocrisy are among the criticisms made of the virtuous city;[1] in Thucydides, in particular, the Athenians recall that Sparta came into the war against the Persians only in her own interest (I. 74. 3: ἐπειδὴ ἐδείσατε ὑπὲρ ὑμῶν); she was known to be dilatory in going to the help of cities who rebelled against Athens (III. 13. 7: τὴν αἰτίαν ... ἣν εἴχετε μὴ βοηθεῖν τοῖς ἀφισταμένοις); she paid more attention to her own interests than to the voice of her allies (I. 88: οὐ τοσοῦτον τῶν ξυμμάχων πεισθέντες τοῖς λόγοις ὅσον φοβούμενοι τοὺς Ἀθηναίους μὴ ἐπὶ μεῖзον δυνηθῶσιν); and she was not afraid to use very underhand methods to get rid of the helots (IV. 80. 3-4). In other writers than Thucydides, we find that hypocrisy is the great reproach which Athenian patriotism has to make against Sparta.[2]

But if this defect was the one most frequently criticized in the case of Sparta, we still have to explain why the criticism should here be made with such universality and such certainty. All the examples quoted above show first and foremost the realistic attitude of Thucydides; they indicate that Sparta was somewhat slow off the

---

[1] On the different forms of selfishness of Sparta and Athens, see Lange, pp. 635-636.

[2] One often finds cautious references to this in Aristophanes (Ach., 308; Peace, 1068), and more open condemnations by Euripides in the Suppliants (187): ὠμὴ καὶ πεποίκιλται τρόπους or in the famous tirade of the Andromache (445): Σπάρτης ἔνοικοι, δόλια βουλευτήρια, | ψευδῶν ἄνακτες. Herodotus also indicates the hypocritical character of Sparta when he writes (IX, 54) that the Athenians εἶχον ἀτρέμας σφέας αὐτοὺς ἵνα ἐτάχθησαν, ἐπιστάμενοι τὰ Λακεδαιμονίων φρονήματα ὡς ἄλλα φρονεόντων καὶ ἄλλα λεγόντων.

mark, a failing seized upon by her critics; but there is a wide gap between these individual indications and the sweeping statement of the Athenians in this dialogue. This difference must be one that can be explained by circumstances, and we can therefore ask when it was that it was most apparent that Sparta used fine words to justify her own self-seeking attitude.

A certain number of incidents are available before 404, of which the most important is Plataea. And, in fact, by the speech which he puts into the mouth of the Plataeans in Book III, Thucydides brings out everything which should have stopped Sparta from behaving as she did but which failed to do so; he insists on the ideas of egoism and hypocrisy in the warning in III. 56. 3: εἰ γὰρ τῷ αὐτίκα χρησίμῳ ὑμῶν τε καὶ ἐκείνων [πολεμίῳ] τὸ δίκαιον λήψεσθε, τοῦ μὲν ὀρθοῦ φανεῖσθε οὐκ ἀληθεῖς κριταὶ ὄντες, τὸ δὲ ξυμφέρον μᾶλλον θεραπεύοντες. He himself notes a little lower down that when the Spartans make demands based on justice, they are in fact only trying to keep the Thebans on their side (III. 68. 1, cf. III. 68. 4). And in fact the memory of Plataea remained as one of the great arguments of anti-Spartan propaganda in the fourth century,[1] exactly as Thucydides had foreseen in III. 58. 2: βραχὺ γὰρ τὸ τὰ ἡμέτερα σώματα διαφθεῖραι, ἐπίπονον δὲ τὴν δύσκλειαν αὐτοῦ ἀφανίσαι.

The second fact to be mentioned is the peace of Nicias, and the apparent betrayal of her allies which it involves on the part of Sparta. It is at that moment that she is most criticized (V. 28. 2), that men think she is working not in order to protect the Peloponnesians but to enslave them (V. 27. 2), and are afraid that she may even join forces with Athens against her former allies (V. 29. 3). This, it is true, is only a false alarm, but the disappointment felt at her conduct left its trace in many people's minds.

It would thus not have been impossible for the Athenians to say what they did in 416. However, if one assumes that the remark was written only after 404, it can be explained even more satisfactorily: at that time other events occurred which illustrated this tendency of the Spartans and brought it into the full light of day, thus providing her enemies with much more valuable ammunition to use against her in this propaganda war. It was then that the Sparta of Lysander revealed itself, and we know through the anecdotes of Plutarch — however exaggerated they may be — what were the maxims that he followed: trickery, political realism, the end justifying the means. In

[1] See Isocrates, *Panath.*, 92.

her acts, this new Sparta made herself known by the regime of decarchies and by the violation of all the promises she had made. Although Dercylidas and Agesilas will try to revive the former programme of Brasidas,[1] Sparta nevertheless gave, at the decisive moment, an image of herself which ruined the whole value of her triumph in the eyes of later history. If, once again, we quote Isocrates, we can recall that in the *Panegyricus* it is this period which he chooses to put Sparta to shame (110, 113); he can then, in conclusion, declare that the end of the Athenian empire coincided with the beginning of all the misfortunes of Greece (119), and reproach the Spartans with the contradiction between what they said in the beginning and what they did later, between their promises and their achievements.[2] Xenophon makes the Thebans express the same criticism (*Hellenica*, III, 5, 12-13): the Lacedaemonians have deceived their own allies by becoming their rulers; they have deceived Athens' allies by bringing them a double slavery in the place of freedom, and they have even deceived the king of Asia.[3]

Finally, the *Lacedaemonian Constitution* of Xenophon bears witness to the same change in the way in which Sparta can now be judged. Xenophon, in fact, insists constantly on the change which has come over this city, making her neglect virtue and become a danger to the rest of Greece.[4] The reason for this is that the Lacedaemonians have now become a ruling people themselves, and have entered into the category of ἄρχοντες ἄλλων, with realistic ideas and brutal acts.

What before could be only insinuated and suggested can now be openly proclaimed, as by the Athenians at Melos.

---

[1] Compare the words of Brasidas, recalling the principle of a war of liberation, and proclaiming his intention to respect the independence of the cities (Thuc., IV. 85. 1-2; 86. 1), with the demands of these leaders as regards the Asian cities (Xenophon, *Hell.*, III, 1, 20; III, 2, 20; III, 4, 5.)

[2] *Paneg.*, 122: Isocrates says that one must μέμψασθαι δὲ Λακεδαιμονίους ὅτι τὴν μὲν ἀρχὴν εἰς τὸν πόλεμον κατέστησαν ὡς ἐλευθερώσοντες τοὺς Ἕλληνας, ἐπὶ δὲ τελευτῆς οὕτω πολλοὺς αὐτῶν ἐκδότους ἐποίησαν, καὶ τῆς μὲν ἡμετέρας πόλεως τοὺς Ἴωνας ἀπέστησαν ἐξ ἧς ἀπῴκησαν, καὶ δι' ἣν πολλάκις ἐσώθησαν, τοῖς δὲ βαρβάροις αὐτοὺς ἐξέδοσαν, ὧν ἀκόντων τὴν χώραν ἔχουσι καὶ πρὸς οὓς οὐδὲ πώποτ' ἐπαύσαντο πολεμοῦντες, — καὶ τότε μὲν ἠγανάκτουν ὅθ' ἡμεῖς νομίμως ἐπάρχειν τινῶν ἠξιοῦμεν, νῦν δ' εἰς τοιαύτην δουλείαν καθεστώτων οὐδὲν φροντίζουσιν αὐτῶν.

[3] See also in the *Hellenica* the feelings which show themselves when, in Athens, the town party has to give way: Sparta seems to be breaking faith again, this time with her Athenian supporters; and orators like Thrasybulus have an easy task in denouncing this (cf. II, 4, 41).

[4] See XIV, 2: πρότερον μέν . . . — 3: πρόσθεν μέν — νῦν δέ — 5: ἦν μὲν ὅτε — νῦν δέ — 6: πρότερον μέν — νῦν δέ.

At the same time, this indication guides us in our search for Thucydides' own intentions. At certain points in his work, he seems to be insisting rather on Sparta's merits, and to be implicitly blaming Athens by recalling how wise her rival is showing herself. In Book VIII, for example, where traces of an earlier and probably provisional version are most easy to detect, we find a quite unnecessary passage of praise for this moderation, which has enabled Sparta always to remain wise in prosperity (VIII. 24. 4). This is also the idea of Sparta which runs through the speech made by her ambassadors in Book IV, and which inspires the speech of Archidamus in Book I — two texts which seem to have been always part of the work. On the other hand, the passages which have definitely seemed to have been written 'late', like Pericles' Funeral Oration and the speech of the Athenians in Book I, reveal a strong anti-Spartan feeling and in a number of details recall the views expressed in this dialogue.[1] At that time Thucydides had two reasons to be severe towards Sparta, since she had begun to follow evil ways at the very moment that her supporters were loudest in her praise. It is thus at this 'late' date that the indication in the dialogue is most easily explained both as far as its general contents and its presence in the work are concerned.

The actual writing of the dialogue also seems most easily explained if it is attributed to a later date.

Beloch[2] and Momigliano both considered that Thucydides needed to be writing under the immediate influence of events in order to pay so much attention to what happened at Melos. We have already seen that the actual detail of the arguments put forward in the dialogue makes this idea rather improbable; but this is not the only objection. In 416, the war could be considered to be over: it is unlikely that Thucydides, who never seems to have written up events day by day, should have happened to do this for a period which he did not yet know would definitely form part of his subject. Finally, it does not seem as though the attack on Melos caused such a very great stir at the time. Certainly, one can find in Euripides' *Trojan Women*, performed in 415, a feeling of condemnation for the cruelty of all conquerors. But this feeling remains very general,[3] and we must not

---

[1] The Athenians in Book I make a specific allusion to the decarchies (I. 77. 6); they underline the hypocrisy displayed by Sparta (I. 76. 2).

[2] II², 2nd part, p. 14.

[3] Cf. p. 201, note 4.

neglect the fact that in the complete trilogy the play was preceded by the *Alexander*, showing the wrongs committed by the Trojans before those committed by the Greeks, and thus limiting the significance of these.

In any case, apart from this rather vague indication, there is nothing to show that the attack on Melos had then a very great effect on people's minds. In Aristophanes' *Birds*, performed in 413, the expression 'Melian hunger' (186: λιμὸς Μήλιος) seems to be used in its proverbial sense, which would indicate notoriety but not indignation. Elsewhere, there is nothing.

The contrast with 404, at the time of the great reaction against imperialism, is extremely striking. Then, the people remember Melos, and Xenophon indicates this with the greatest precision when he writes (*Hell.*, II, 2, 3, quoted in the Loeb translation): 'And during that night no one slept, all mourning, not for the lost alone, but far more for their own selves, thinking that they would suffer such treatment as they had visited upon the Melians, colonists of the Lacedaemonians, after reducing them by siege, and upon the Histiaeans and Scionaeans and Toronaeans and Aeginetans and many other Greek peoples.' Melos heads the list, and it alone is held to deserve explanation. And this explanation is all the more noteworthy since, by its colourless nature, it in no way justifies the Athenians' remorse: it simply recalls what Melos was for those who happen not to know. And this would seem to indicate that the introduction of the idea of Melos ought not to be attributed to Xenophon himself, for otherwise he would have given in his comment on the event a clearer sign of what his intention was. On the other hand, the very mention of Melos cannot be explained either by a wave of indignation which, born in 416, left a scar of shame on Athens: otherwise, Xenophon would not have thought of adding a comment at all. It would thus seem that the event acquired this importance only afterwards, when the opponents of imperialism seized hold of it for their own use.

This is confirmed by the speeches of Isocrates, for they are obviously intended to reply to a very specific attack on the subject of Melos. Thus, we read in the *Panegyricus*, paragraph 100: τινὲς ἡμῶν κατηγοροῦσιν, ὡς ἐπειδὴ τὴν ἀρχὴν τῆς θαλάττης παρελάβομεν πολλῶν κακῶν αἴτιοι τοῖς Ἕλλησι κατέστημεν, καὶ τόν τε Μηλίων ἀνδραποδισμὸν καὶ τὸν Σκιωναίων ὄλεθρον ἐν τούτοις τοῖς λόγοις

ἡμῖν προφέρουσιν; or, in paragraph 110: τολμῶσι κατηγορεῖν οἱ . . .
(καὶ) τὰς μὲν Μηλίων ὀδυρόμενοι συμφοράς, περὶ δὲ τοὺς αὐτῶν
πολίτας ἀνήκεστα τολμήσαντες ἐξαμαρτεῖν; or in the *Panathenaicus*, 63:
οἶμαι δὲ τοὺς ἀηδῶς ἀκούοντας τῶν λόγων τούτων τοῖς μὲν εἰρημένοις
οὐδὲν ἀντερεῖν, . . . κατηγορεῖν δὲ τῆς πόλεως ἡμῶν ἐπιχειρήσειν,
ὅπερ ἀεὶ ποιεῖν εἰώθασι, καὶ διεξιέναι τὰς δυσχερεστάτας τῶν πράξεων
τῶν ἐπὶ τῆς ἀρχῆς τῆς κατὰ θάλατταν γεγενημένων . . . καὶ μάλιστα
διατρίψειν περὶ τὰ Μηλίων πάθη καὶ Σκιωναίων καὶ Τορωναίων . . . ;
or in paragraph 89: τοῖς γὰρ ὀνειδίζουσιν ἡμῶν τῇ πόλει τὰς Μηλίων
καὶ τὰς τῶν τοιούτων πολιχνίων συμφορὰς ἀντέλεγον . . .[1] Pericles'
speech had replied to criticisms made of imperialism; here, there is so
much precision that one can really evoke the idea of a text written
against imperialism. Moreover, the other attacks to which Isocrates is
replying in the *Panegyricus* and the *Panathenaicus* are repeated with
so much similarity in both texts[2] that this by itself would suggest the
existence of a specific original, which we can call the Oligarchical
Pamphlet.

Wilamowitz has in effect assumed[3] the existence of a pamphlet of
pro-Spartan inspiration attacking Athens for the wrongs committed
by the Delian Confederacy. Mathieu has very convincingly shown
there are traces of this in two strangely similar passages of Andocides
and Aeschines,[4] and he has studied its influence in the fourth century.
It is Bodin's view that at the same time as the relevant sections of the
Panegyricus can be considered as a reply to this pamphlet, so also can
certain passages in Pericles' Funeral Oration or in the speech of the
Athenians in Book I.[5] The existence of such a pamphlet seems indeed
to have left traces on all sides, and the only question we have to ask
is whether there was not one but several pamphlets of this kind. By
an apparent contradiction, we have seen that it was at the very
moment when Sparta's defects were most in evidence that she was
most highly praised, and that it was when she was giving most

[1] The names of Melos and Scione will later remain the slogan of those who wish to
criticize Athens. They can be found in Arrianus (I, 95): ἡ Μήλου καὶ ἡ Σκιώνης ἅλωσις,
νησιωτικά τε πολίσματα ἦν, καὶ τοῖς δράσασιν αἰσχύνην μᾶλλον τε προσέβαλεν ἢ ἐς τὸ
ξύμπαν Ἑλληνικὸν μέγαν τὸν παράλογον παρέσχε; also in Procopius of Gaza (Boisson,
Anecd., II, p. 86): σιωπῶ τοὺς σοφωτάτους Ἀθηναίους, ὅπως Μηλίους καὶ Σκιωναίους
διέθηκαν.

[2] See the way he speaks of the legal cases judged at Athens (*Paneg.*, 113 = *Panath.*, 66).

[3] *Aristoteles und Athen*, II, 388-389.

[4] *Revue de philologie*, 1914, XXXVIII, pp. 189-194. The passages are Andocides,
Peace, 3-7 and of Aeschines, II, 172-176. Cf. here, p. 17.

[5] *Isocrate et Thucydide*, pp. 101-102.

ammunition to her enemies that her supporters were loudest in glorifying her achievements: both circumstances can be explained by her power. Anyhow, and whatever the number and date of such pamphlets, their arguments were certainly similar, and we have every right to assume that one of the most frequent arguments used was the example of Melos.

It is natural to think that it was when the discussion of the 'Melian question' was beginning that Thucydides decided to devote to it the sole dialogue in his work and the most far-reaching piece of analysis.[1] This imperialistic act, now so widely criticized, had then become the symptom under which he studied imperialism, and the very symbol of every policy of conquest and aggression.

By assuming this, we can explain a peculiarity about the dialogue which cannot fail to be surprising.

Thucydides treats the attack on Melos as the perfect example of unjustified and scandalous aggression. Was he right to do so? This is not at all certain. There certainly was a scandal in the Melian affair, but this in no way consisted of the actual expedition: the scandal lay in the 'punishment', the cruel decision which condemned all men capable of bearing arms to death and sent all the women and children into slavery. This is what the Melian affair had in common with what happened at Scione, and what was judged completely unacceptable. As for the aggression itself, nothing was more innocent, and Thucydides gives it a vital significance which it perhaps only half deserves. We have seen that Nicias was in command of the first expedition against Melos (III. 91. 1), and Beloch thinks it was he who suggested the second.[2] Melos, as an island and one of the Cyclades, was in fact

---

[1] Hatzfeld (*Alcibiade*, pp. 124-126) does not bring the two circumstances together: 'If Thucydides wished to emphasize the importance of the event, it was because with the taking of Melos all the islands of the Aegean sea were for the first time united under Athenian rule, because the Athenian empire had never been either so large or, apparently, so firmly established, because the years that followed were to bring Athens only failure and disaster, and because this was a good opportunity, for a historian writing at a time when he could judge events with a certain perspective, to sum up and define the nature of this imperialism which had led to the ephemeral triumph of today and was going to end in the disasters of tomorrow.' Such an explanation does in fact remain possible, but it also presupposes that the Melian dialogue was written fairly late, and in this case it is difficult to see how the existence of a 'Melian question' should not have played some part in Thucydides' decision.

[2] *Att. Pol.*, 57: 'The conquest of Melos, which Nicias had in vain tried to achieve for already ten years...' Cf. Hatzfeld, *Alcibiade*, p. 215: 'Everything indicates that this decision seemed natural to everyone, and that it was approved of by Nicias as well as by Alcibiades, I would even say by Nicias more than by Alcibiades...'

part of the area which Pericles himself recognized as belonging to the Athenian sphere of influence. To invade Melos was to follow the advice of Aristophanes in the *Peace* (507), where he tells the Athenians to 'go back a little towards the sea'. To invade Melos, which had once been attacked in vain, and had been included on the list of the cities paying tribute to Athens,[1] was to obey the advice given by Nicias in his speech in Book VI (VI. 10. 5), in which he told the Athenians to strengthen the existing empire, where Athens was not sufficiently obeyed, instead of going off to Sicily. Finally, to invade Melos, the nearest of the Cyclades, was to follow the advice Nicias had given in the same speech (VI. 11. 7) when he had warned the Athenians to defend themselves against Sparta. An invasion of Melos meant a return to the policy of small, piecemeal attacks that were annoying to Sparta, and which Pericles himself had not disdained. Thus, by itself, the enterprise seems to have been a most moderate one: it was one of those acts which could be criticized for its timing rather than blamed for the principle inspiring it.

And, in fact, this seems to have been Thucydides' own attitude to the first expedition: he mentions it in passing without any word to suggest that he considers it reprehensible.[2] And yet the conditions were exactly the same in both cases.[3]

Consequently, in the Melian affair, it was the 'punishment' alone which aroused a scandal — and yet it is the aggression alone which is here dealt with by Thucydides.

Such a change of emphasis is obviously not very surprising in itself, and one finds a hint of it in Xenophon whose indication (Μηλίους τε Λακεδαιμονίων ἀποίκους ὄντας κρατήσαντες πολιορκίᾳ) exactly designates the subject treated by Thucydides; and it was natural that, in a discussion of the question, people should bring

---

[1] IG, I², 63, l. 5. The inscription gives the lists for 425. Hatzfeld thinks that it is a calculation made in advance by the τάκται; this solution is in fact the only probable one — it does not exclude the existence of a kind of precedent.

[2] In Book V, even in the simple statement of the fact, he mentions the circumstances which put Athens in the wrong, which he omits in III. 91. 2; as, for example, the fact that the Melians are colonists of Sparta, and that they wished to remain neutral (V. 84. 2).

[3] One could, at a stretch, argue against the second expedition that it took place in what was supposed to be a period of peace, but Thucydides was better aware than anyone else that this 'peace' was in fact nothing of the sort. On the other hand, one can argue in its favour that the first expedition provided a precedent, and consequently a justification. On the whole, the only thing which really distinguished the second expedition from the first, and could give rise to an indignation which the first had not caused, was the treatment inflicted on the island by the Athenians after they had been victorious, a treatment often recalled by the enemies of imperialism after Athens' own defeat.

forward, together with the cruelty of the 'punishment', the unjustified nature of the conquest, which in fact made things still worse.[1]
But if this change of emphasis is normal in the course of an intellectual
discussion dealing with the question of imperialism after the events
concerning it have all taken place, it would seem much less probable
in a work supposed to be the direct product of an emotional reaction
and to have been written 'under the immediate impact of events'.

By explaining the origin of the dialogue in this manner, we can also
account for the general significance which we have already
accorded to it: Thucydides seems to have written it after 404,[2] in
order to study the policy of conquest as a whole, in relation to certain
criticisms that had recently been made of it.

This study takes place on two levels. Although the moral considerations which complete the passages of political analysis are
constantly mingled with them, and contribute to give them a wider
and more abstract character, we can nevertheless separate them in
order to make our present task easier. They in fact deserve to be
considered apart from the purely political discussion, for these can
be compared with a number of others in the work itself, while the
moral considerations have a unique position in being the only ones of
their kind in Thucydides' History.

II. POLITICAL ANALYSIS IN THE MELIAN DIALOGUE

The dialogue can be conveniently divided into three sections. A
preliminary section contains a discussion of the fundamental moral
thesis of the relationship between justice and force. Then, in paragraph 91, the Athenians put forward their political thesis, asserting
that it is in the interest of both cities for the Melians to surrender without a struggle: then, up to paragraph 100, they try to prove, against
the objections put forward by the Melians, that they must obtain the

---

[1] It was certainly this idea of the unjustified and unprofitable nature of the conquest
which Isocrates retained when, speaking of Timotheus, he wrote (*Antidosis*, 113):
τεττάρων καὶ εἴκοσι πόλεων κυρίους ὑμᾶς ἐποίησεν, ἐλάττω δαπανήσας ὧν οἱ πατέρες
ἡμῶν εἰς τὴν Μηλίων πολιορκίαν ἀνήλωσαν. Isocrates is acquainted with the traditional
criticism, and it is not by accident that he here uses the example of Melos; yet he insists no
more than Thucydides on the cruelty displayed by the Athenians.

[2] Eduard Meyer, basing himself on paragraphs 90-91, naturally arrives at the same
conclusions about the date of the dialogue (*Forsch.*, II, 364). I shall not here take into
consideration the objection of Grundy, p. 495, who sees the dialogue form as representing
an early and provisional version of the text, which was later to be replaced by two speeches.
Nothing is more inconsistent with the actual features of the dialogue, or, for that matter,
with common sense.

surrender of the island; and from paragraph 101 onwards that the Melians can have no hope of success. This corresponds to saying, in the first place that Athens needs to conquer and, in the second, that she can do so.

The first of these two statements is the more interesting of the two; although it is immediately applied to Melos, it is not based on particular circumstances, except for *a fortiori* arguments, and can consequently be valid for any other country; it thus provides a very precise definition of the activity of imperialism in its conquering phase. Moreover, even the conditions peculiar to Melos (97: ἄλλως τε καί) finally serve to make the general system of this imperialism more precise. This section thus enables us to define its nature.

The analysis which it contains is based on one single idea: the fear which Athens has of the hostility of her subjects. In order to keep them at bay, she needs to show her strength, and in order to do this she can allow no one to flout her authority. Conquest thus becomes a measure of ἀσφάλεια (97).

This idea of her subjects' hostility towards her also came into the preliminary section, since Athens there explained that if she were defeated she would have more to fear from her former subjects than from a city like Sparta.[1] It recurs constantly in the political part of the dialogue: in paragraph 95 the Athenians want to destroy Melos in order to impress their subjects with their strength; in paragraph 97, they admit that it is normal that there should be a struggle between Athens and her subjects, and that authority should be always hated and always unjustifiable; in paragraph 99, they make it clear that the people of whom they are really afraid are islanders who might want to defend their liberty and all those who would like to cast off the bonds of empire: τοὺς ἤδη τῆς ἀρχῆς τῷ ἀναγκαίῳ παροξυνομένους.

[1] Certain commentators have even tried to go further and give the proposition ἔστι δὲ οὐ πρὸς Λακεδαιμονίους ἡμῖν ὁ ἀγών (91. 1) a strong, general meaning. Bloomfield interprets it as: 'Now our great struggle and danger is not as respects the Lacedaemonians.' This gives too much importance to the idea of the fear felt by Athens as regards the hostility of her subjects. The text is dealing with the behaviour of an adversary having won the war, not of one who can be defeated; from this last point of view, Sparta naturally remains the great enemy. — In fact, the sentence is simpler than this; it does not even have the meaning attributed to it by Steup: 'übrigens befinden wir uns gar nicht im Kriege mit den Lakk.', an interpretation which takes account neither of the use of the word ἀγών nor of the position of οὐ, and which, moreover, is almost meaningless. The real meaning, on the contrary, is: we are at war with Sparta; right then, we will deal with her; but for the time being that is not the point. ('We are not contending now with the Spartans'). That is the normal meaning of the expression, the one which it has, for example, in VI. 11. 7, or even, without leaving the dialogue, in paragraph 101.

This idea is also at the basis of Pericles', Cleon's and Alcibiades' political views, and we have also seen it playing its part in the speech of the Athenians in Book I. But nowhere is it expressed so absolutely and with such insistence as here.

The situation in which Athens is placed makes a trial of strength, a δυνάμεως παράδειγμα, essential. No neutrality is possible: her subjects know that Athens would only respect it through fear, and they would immediately draw their own conclusions. Athens has inspired her subjects with such hostile feelings, and has given such a fearful idea of her policy, that she is henceforth obliged to conquer without reason or repose. It is a kind of vicious circle in which the conqueror, threatened by his very conquests, is compelled to go forward in spite of himself.

This argument, which can be called the argument of safety, recurs in all the speeches made by Athenians in Thucydides, but under different forms: and although it is always a question of acting by force, this action can take different forms in different cases. Pericles asks the Athenians 'not to let go'; Cleon demands punishment for rebels and traitors; Alcibiades wants counter measures against possible threats; and the Athenians in Book I bring these different ideas together by integrating them in the actual development of imperialism. Now the Athenians in Book V have this in common with those of Book I; they also foresee constantly repeated and renewed action, and thus presuppose a genuine evolutionary law. But — and this is the difference — exactly as Alcibiades' principles differ from those of Pericles, so the evolutionary law that the Athenians define has now become somewhat abstract, and each enterprise taken separately acquires a strikingly gratuitous quality. The actions that they envisage are valid only as pure examples,[1] chosen almost arbitrarily, and which may very well obey the rule, but in an unsatisfactory way.[2] Their undertaking no longer tries to find its own justification: it just answers the demands of a purely external necessity. When it reaches this point, the imperialistic motto condemns what it sets out to defend: it advocates a policy which has no place for rational deliberation, but

---

[1] The idea of παράδειγμα can already be found in Cleon; but there it is a guilty person who is treated so as to provide an example, and the warning is direct. The principle is thus more acceptable. As for Alcibiades, he justifies the idea of aggression in the same way as do the Athenians at Melos, but by an argument which justifies it in a more direct manner: he is attacking the possible enemy, and he does not refer to the idea of παράδειγμα.

[2] By this, the dialogue is to the speech of the Athenians what Alcibiades' speech is to that of Pericles.

which is the blind observance of necessity: *non ire ille vult, sed non potest stare.*

The ideas thus fit in perfectly well with those of the speeches we have already studied; [1] however, the argument is presented in a form as general as that of Book I, but in a much more brutal way.

This brutality is marked by yet another difference, which lies not so much in what the Athenians say as in what they do not say. Certainly, the argument based on ἀσφάλεια has changed its meaning; but what is most important is that this is all that remains of imperialism, and Athens seems to be governed by it alone.

We can naturally assume in the dialogue the existence of imperialist feelings: the Athenians find obvious pleasure or advantage in ruling and in extending their authority; but this is only an additional and subordinate reason, which they mention solely in passing (97: ἐξὼ καὶ τοῦ πλειόνων ἄρξαι); and this feeling itself is only imperial ambition in its most vulgar form; the expression used by Thucydides recalls the phrase so frequently repeated to indicate the blind and excessive nature of Athenian desires: πλείονος ὠρέγοντο; Thucydides may perhaps have introduced this indication merely to awake an echo of this phrase and thus vouch for its validity. In any case, in so far as this feeling is the only one mentioned here, and in this form into the bargain, the Melian dialogue differs from the other texts dealing with Athenian imperialism.

Neither the concern for glory so dear to Pericles, nor the idea of Athens' merit, nor the idea of progress and activity preached by Alcibiades find their place here. They were, perhaps, irrelevant to the discussion, but had he so wished, Thucydides could have brought them in or at least have hinted at them. Yet, they are rigorously excluded, as they are in the speeches of Cleon and Euphemus.

If we consider that the feeling mentioned by Alcibiades is nothing more than the idea of strength in a more exalted and dynamic form and has nothing spiritual about it, we can assume that this difference is an objective one by which Thucydides distinguishes the imperialism of Athens at her greatest from the ambition to which the city gives

---

[1] The realm in which imperialism is to exercise itself is also the one that we have found everywhere else, and it is this which is indicated by the passage devoted to the actual condition of Melos. It is, say the Athenians, all the more necessary to conquer Melos since it has more reasons to be conquered; among these is the fact that it is an island. Similarly, when the Athenians distinguish between the different categories of subjects according to the dangers to which they can give rise, islanders are put on one side and given pride of place.

way when she has lost control of both her appetites and her destiny
Of the three factors inspiring the Athenians in Book I — τιμή
δέος, ὠφελία — the first, which plays so great a role in Pericles
disappears in the whole of the rest of the work; it recurs only in the
purely patriotic speeches of a moderate like Nicias. The greatness o
Athens no longer counts, and its importance diminishes as that o
necessity and security grows. Of the two sources of imperialism — to
paraphrase Bergson — only one remains: the urge to greater glory
has gone, and the compulsion of base necessity taken its place.[1]

Between this imperialism and its victims, the choice is obvious, as
far as sympathy is concerned.

The Melians are presented as having a very vivid sense of their
independence (100); they act justly (104) and courageously (113): all
these features are compliments for Thucydides when he can apply
them to Athens. Similarly, he takes care to secure the reader's
sympathy for the Melians by frequently recalling the cruel situation
in which they are placed,[2] and the fact that they have right on their
side.[3] Moreover, Athenian brutality will inevitably be severely
criticized by a man who so deeply regrets the decline of morality in
Greece, or recalls with respect the ἀρετή of Nicias. This point is
obvious.

But it is not only a question of sympathy, and we may wonder
whether, in the strictly political domain, Thucydides does not show
the Athenians to be right. Is their policy likely to be beneficial to
them? Can they crush Melos without risk to themselves? This is what
the second part of the dialogue tries more particularly to find out,
and it thus gives Thucydides' own opinion more than the earlier part
does.

Since the arguments are all based on practical considerations, it is
only from this point of view that a judgment can be made. The
brutality shown by the conquerors should not be allowed to intervene
in the series of arguments justifying their policy: it is precisely because

[1] The disinterested attitude and the generosity of Pericles' declaration in the Funeral
Oration: καὶ μόνοι οὐ τοῦ ξυμφέροντος μᾶλλον λογισμῷ ἢ τῆς ἐλευθερίας τῷ πιστῷ ἀδεῶς
τινα ὠφελοῦμεν (II. 40. 5) are completely opposed to the principles on which the Athenians
in Book V base their actions. The time for generosity is over.

[2] 88: ἐν τῷ τοιῷδε καθεστῶτας; 92: ἡμῶν δουλεῦσαι (the term δουλεύειν, as in 100 and 86,
contrasts with the expressions ἄρξαι or ὑπακοῦσαι used by the Athenians); 93: πρὸ τοῦ τὰ
δεινότατα πάσχειν; 104: χαλεπὸν μὲν καὶ ἡμεῖς, εὖ ἴστε, νομίζομεν πρὸς δύναμίν τε τὴν
ὑμετέραν καὶ τὴν τύχην, εἰ μὴ ἀπὸ τοῦ ἴσου ἔσται, ἀγωνίζεσθαι.

[3] See in particular 90; 94; 96; 98; 104.

:hey have not made a sufficiently clear distinction between Thucy-
lides' opinions and his feelings that certain commentators have given
lifferent and contradictory interpretations of this dialogue.

From a rational and political point of view, one fact stands out
mmediately: the Melians were wrong to resist. Melos was conquered,
or Athens was by far the stronger.[1] Melos was wrong to trust to
10pe and chance (102): even without the confirmation provided by
what actually happened in this case, this is an idea which belongs to
:he best traditions of Greek wisdom, as Thucydides assumes in his
wn account. It was the great Pericles himself who said that intelligence places no trust in hope: ἐλπίδι τε ἧσσον πιστεύει ἧς ἐν τῷ
ἀπόρῳ ἡ ἰσχύς (II. 62. 5); it was the wise Diodotus who showed what
ɑ fatal role hope can play when it puts its trust in chance: by analysing
this mistake in politics, he seems to criticize in advance the method of
reasoning adopted by the Melians, and to provide a model for the
Athenian reply (III. 45. 5): 'Desire and hope are never wanting, the
one leading, the other following, the one devising the enterprise,
the other suggesting that fortune will be kind; and they do immense
harm'; he even explains how chance provides folly with one of its
best arguments: 'Fortune too assists the illusion, for she often presents
herself unexpectedly, and induces states as well as individuals to run
into peril, however inadequate their means; and states even more
than individuals, because they are throwing for a higher stake, freedom or empire, and because when a man has a whole people acting
with him, he magnifies himself out of all reason.' Similarly, it is the
intelligent Hermocrates who recalls how little relationship there is
between hope and reality: οὐδὲ ἰσχὺς βέβαιον διότι καὶ εὔελπι
(IV. 62. 4); finally Thucydides himself shows this disastrous influence
of hope, both in the case of Athenian imperialism, as in IV. 65. 4:
αἰτία δ' ἦν ἡ παρὰ λόγον τῶν πλειόνων εὐπραγία αὐτοῖς
ὑποτιθεῖσα ἰσχὺν τῆς ἐλπίδος, and in that of hasty desertions, as in
IV. 108. 4: εἰωθότες οἱ ἄνθρωποι οὗ μὲν ἐπιθυμοῦσιν ἐλπίδι ἀπερι-
σκέπτῳ διδόναι. Very many more examples could be given, and we
must not forget that the basic principle of Pericles' wisdom is to
attribute everything not to τύχη but to γνώμη; and expressed in this
way, it coincides with the most facile commonplaces. Thucydides'

---

[1] The traditional estimates give the strength of the Athenian army as 3020 men, and the
population of the island would, it is thought, consist of about 500 men capable of bearing
arms and, at the most, 3000 free citizens. And it is still only a question of the number of
Athenians *actually there*.

contemporaries, like Antiphon (Diels, fr. 58), or Euripides (*Aegeus*
fr. 6 Ddt = *Auge*, 273 N, *Suppl.*, 479) merely repeat a notion dear
to poets and philosophers, and which one finds among others, in an
oracle quoted by Herodotus (VIII, 77), in Democritus (Diels, fr. 176
58; 292), in Theognis (637), in Pindar (*Ol.*, XII, 5), in Hesiod (*Works*
498): all these texts, like those already noted in Thucydides, confirm
the truth of what the Athenians say. The fact that at the end of the
same paragraph one sees the words μαντικήν and χρησμούς by the
side of the word ἐλπίς makes it even clearer that Thucydides considered the Athenian view to be a principle of wisdom: the indication
was not essential here, and it evokes ideas which were very popular
in the positivist atmosphere of the fifth century. The examples from
Euripides are too numerous for any individual one to need quoting
and Thucydides himself does not fail to indicate whenever the
opportunity presents itself the vain and often dangerous character of
oracles (II. 54; V. 26. 3; VII. 50. 4; VIII. 1).

The same is true of the other sources of help mentioned by the
Melians, that is to say the Gods and the Spartans.

The Gods did not come to the help of Melos, and it was vain to
count on them. Without trying to find out what Thucydides'
opinion was on religious matters, it is obvious that the idea of divine
providence helping the pious through the medium of chance is
quite foreign to his very realistic attitude, which had certainly been
influenced, although we cannot say to what extent, by the materialis-
tic ideas of Leucippus and Democritus. Fortune exists for him only
under the form of blind chance, and the most unfortunate of men
are by no means the most guilty. The fate of the pious Nicias (VII.
86. 5) is a proof of this, and we might even say that the irony which
Thucydides shows in Book V towards the poor Lacedaemonians,
always held back by some religious festival or other, is not unworthy
of the Athenians who speak at Melos. He leaves such optimistic
arguments to the Melians, who can do nothing, or to Nicias, when
he is going to make his last despairing effort (VII. 77. 3): that is to
say, to people who have nothing else to fall back on, and who thus
betray their weakness.

As for Sparta, she was of this world, but to Melos she was no more
help than the Gods. Slow and selfish as we know her to have been,
she put into practice none of the plans of action envisaged by the
Melians, not even the last, the risk of which the Athenians had
accepted, and which consisted of going to make war on Athens and

her allies on their own ground; when she did so, it was too late, in a way which no longer concerned Melos, and which cannot here be considered: Melos had by then learnt at her own expense that the Athenians were right when they said that Athens could not be intimidated.[1]

As a conclusion to her dialectical triumph, Athens obviously has the last word at the end of the dialogue, and can play the part of a political sage. The Athenians first bring the dialogue to a conclusion by criticizing the arguments used by the Melians; then, in paragraphs 112-113, the two peoples sum up their respective positions. Because they have no other arguments at their disposal, the Melians repeat those which have already been shown to be useless by the Athenians, and which they themselves have already once abandoned. The Athenians comment for a second time on the attitude shown by the Melians, in a passage entirely centred on the contrast between reality and illusion. All the words marking uncertainty and folly are brought together on one side of the argument in a condemnation which forms something like a digest of Greek wisdom.[2]

We can add that the Athenian superiority in practical considerations is echoed in the very structure of the dialogue: from one end to the other it is the Melians who put forward the ideas — here a statement of hope, there an objection — but it is always they who invent; the Athenians, on the other hand, reply, and they have a reply to everything, so that the Melians are constantly non-suited and sent off to find another argument. This is, indeed, one of the features of the dialogue which most contribute to give this impression of an over-

---

[1] The punctuation, faulty in almost all editions, seems to be the thing which needs modifying at the beginning of paragraph 111; by correcting it, we reach the following meaning: from these means of action something could take place for you when you have already been yourselves through the experience (πεπειραμένοις καὶ ὑμῖν), and you would not then be unaware (precisely because of this experience) that...

[2] One has: for the Athenians: for the Melians:

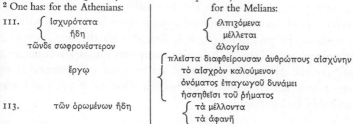

μέλλειν, which occurs twice, indicates a criticism; it is the motto of the prudent man — 'a bird in the hand is worth two in the bush'. Thucydides will apply the same terms to Athenian imprudence, when the roles have changed in the Sicilian expedition: ἐπὶ μεγίστῃ ἐλπίδι τῶν μελλόντων πρὸς τὰ ὑπάρχοντα (VI. 31. 6).

U

whelming power against which resistance is useless: in fact, the more
attempts that are made to find a defect in it, the more invincible does
this power appear, and the demonstration of the futility of Melian
resistance acquires an almost mathematical certainty.

However, there is one chink in the armour-plated construction of
the Athenian argument and it leaves one point unsettled: if Melos
herself was conquered — and with what cruelty — Athens also
finished the war disastrously. In their own best interest, the Melians
ought to have surrendered; but this does not mean that Athens could
pursue such a policy of conquest with impunity. It involved a risk,
and although this lay beyond the immediate circumstances of this
particular enterprise, it was none the less real for all that. This risk is
mentioned three times, and each time a door seems to open on a
catastrophic future. In the very first exchanges, the Melians, like the
Spartans in Book IV, put forward the possibility of an Athenian
defeat: σφαλέντες ἄν; then, in paragraph 98, they argue that the logic
of the policy followed by the Athenians will convert all neutrals into
their enemies; and finally, they suggest the idea of a new Brasidas, who
will come and attack Athens on her own territory and on the territory of her allies.[1] On each occasion the Athenians admit that this
danger exists but are quite willing to accept it. On the first occasion,
they only discuss how serious such a defeat might be; on the second,
they mention only the people of whom they would be most afraid;
and on the third and last occasion they simply reply by a threat.
Now these three indications are all the more important since each
one of them occurs at a turning point in the discussion. The first ends
what we have called the preliminary section, the second the first
political section, and the third the second political section.

The most important indication is the one to be found at the end of
the first political section: in the two others, an Athenian defeat is
envisaged only as an unexplained hypothesis or as a vague possibility;
in contrast, in paragraph 98, it is linked with the very system of
Athenian imperialism. If Athenian conquests can never come to an
end, say the Melians, then surely her enemies will increase at the
same rate as her conquests? This is both what did happen and what
inevitably had to happen.

---

[1] This passage has been corrected in a number of different ways. I adopt the reading
ἢ τῆς οἰκειοτέρας ξυμμαχίδος τε γῆς ὁ πόνος ὑμῖν ἔσται. It is easy to explain how a καί
should have been introduced after τε, especially since ξυμμαχίς is more often used as a
noun than as an adjective.

Melos may well be showing great imprudence in putting up a futile resistance, but this does not mean that Athens is right to act as she does, even from a political point of view. By blindly following a principle whose individual applications are open to doubt, she is spoiling the future, and all perhaps to no purpose. In this way, Thucydides suggests that the brutally imperialistic policy described by the Athenians in the Melian dialogue carries within it the seeds of its own destruction.

If the empire really obliges Athens to be constantly showing her strength in order to keep her subjects obedient, and if this continual show of strength perpetually increases the number of her enemies, then the remedy is simply making the situation worse; by giving rise to more numerous and sharper enmities, it is making the trial of strength at one and the same time more necessary and more dangerous.[1]

Benjamin Constant, in a chapter entitled: *Inevitable end of the triumphs of a conquering nation*,[2] writes: 'This nation would become the object of universal detestation. She would be threatened by the opinions, the vows and the hatred of all men, and sooner or later these would all explode and destroy her.' Already the Romans were comparing the conqueror to a stone carried away by its own weight: *quibus eundi finis est jacuisse.*

Thucydides presents a much less absolute view of events; he does not talk about necessity, and this is already an important difference. He certainly thinks that Athens could have been saved, and perhaps even that she should have been. But he is at least aware of the danger, and of the causes that produce it.

This is, as far as we are concerned, a new aspect of his ideas.

Thus, in the dialogue we are studying, there is not only a breaking off of sympathy towards imperialism on the part of Thucydides, but also a different political judgment. On the one hand, imperialism is no longer justified except by a law in virtue of which both its faults and excesses are linked to the logic of its development; and, on the other, it runs the risk of being condemned in practice, since this constant progression leads to a point beyond which one can see looming up the prospect of disaster. These two criticisms coincide,

---

[1] The seriousness of the situation is a result of the combination of these two factors cf. p. 329.

[2] *De l'Esprit de Conquête et de l'Usurpation*, chapter XIV. Cf. the remark of Montesquieu (*L'Esprit des Lois*, VII): 'À mesure que le pouvoir devient immense, la sécurité diminue.'

moreover, since it is the blindness of Athenian actions which might one day bring about a fatal lack of balance between the growth of her power and the growth of her unpopularity, and thus leave Athens at the mercy of a single mistake.

By the feelings which inspire the dialogue and by the political analysis which it contains, Thucydides' opinion stands out as exceptionally severe. This severity may correspond to an objective difference in the behaviour of Athens, and it is obvious that Thucydides himself is trying to suggest the idea of a difference between the various phases of imperialism.

In the days of the ancestors and of Pericles, imperialism was distinguished by a considerable degree of idealism. Both Pericles and the Athenians in Book I could well be acutely aware of the conditions of imperialism, of its unpopularity and consequently of the tyranny which it involved. They nevertheless had a glowing idea of Athenian greatness and tradition, an idea which was accompanied by a respect for justice and moderation. It is with this form of imperialism that Thucydides sympathized. The feeling of independence which belongs to Melos had in fact characterized Pericles, while the Athenians in Book I had laid claim to the justice on which the Melians try to base their arguments. Courage, above all, had been the great merit of the city which had stood up to the Persians, just as it is now courage that makes the Melians act as they do. The qualities which had made Thucydides admire imperialism when it was based on them render it hateful to him when they are neglected, to be replaced only by the desire for more and by the alleged obligation of maintaining authority.

Moreover, in the very analysis of the needs that she had to obey, Athens had never before admitted so absolute a rule nor one that was so universal in its application. It had never been a question of Athens going ahead with her eyes shut as it is here. This is why the evolutionary law, so far, had no reason to foresee her fall. It is only with the appearance of this idea of an almost mechanical progression that we also encounter the idea of a destiny that will one day bring the empire to an end.

Thucydides thus judges a form of imperialism which is merely the caricature of its former self. Placed by the side of that in Book I, his analysis in the Melian dialogue provides a diptych, whose two elements we must presume to be linked together by the evolution deplored in II. 65.

But although Thucydides deliberately applies this analysis to a period when Athenian imperialism had lost its ideals and when authority, perverted from its true function, was accumulating mistakes, he is nevertheless talking about the very nature of imperialism. He is describing what remains when everything that can make it acceptable but which is not an integral part has been taken away; in short, he is telling us what imperialism runs the risk of being and what it tends to become. There then remain only the desire for more and the conditions inseparable from any policy of conquest. This is what can be found in all forms of imperialism, whenever they appear and in whatever garb they cloak themselves.

Benjamin Constant, in his work *De l'Esprit de Conquête et de l'Usurpation* attempts to define what, in his view, are the characteristics of conquest in modern Europe, where war no longer provides either individual glory or practical benefit. But by the very fact that he is considering conquest as stripped of everything which might decorate or embellish it, his analysis coincides exactly with that of Thucydides in the Melian dialogue,[1] and assumes, like it, a universal value.

If it is true that the Melian dialogue is concerned not only with the period which is no longer that of early imperialism but with what we might call its 'basic essence', it may be to this circumstance that we must attribute a part of the excessively brutal realism of the Athenians.[2] The arguments they put forward are improbable in that they give unnecessary offence and blacken a policy which could have other excuses; the reason for this is that the speakers are merely instruments used by Thucydides to bring out his final interpretation. The arguments which these Athenians use hardly serve to justify them and scarcely to paint them as they were. They go beyond the Athenians of 416 and reach the very basis of imperialism, with the fixed intention of explaining the laws which govern its development. In a way, the dialogue is only more pessimistic than the other analyses in Thucydides' work because it goes further, and reaches the level of a philosophical inquiry.

---

[1] Benjamin Constant does not, however, seem to have been acquainted with Thucydides. The examples which he quotes are those of Cambyses, Alexander, the Romans, Attila, but never once Athenian imperialism. He belonged to a generation whose intellectual formation was based essentially on Roman history.

[2] This realism is here even more marked than that of Cleon or Euphemus. The reason is that Thucydides is not studying the psychology of one leader or of the masses, but is seeking out the more or less conscious essence of a policy.

III. The Moral Theory

If one stops to examine the nature of the relationship which is established between two cities as a result of military events, it seems obvious that this rests solely on force. It is thus natural that the analysis of Athenian foreign policy should lead, as it does here, to a theory of force considered as the natural basis of human relationships. The analysis of the Athenians in Book I already referred to it when they said: οὐδ᾽ αὖ πρῶτοι τοῦ τοιούτου ὑπάρξαντες, ἀλλ᾽ αἰεὶ καθεστῶτος τὸν ἥσσω ὑπὸ τοῦ δυνατωτέρου κατείργεσθαι. In the dialogue between the Athenians and the Melians, this idea rises to the height of a complete theory of the world and of morality.

The basic principle of this theory is expressed in paragraph 89: the Athenians dismiss any argument based on justice because, they say, this can play a part only when two equally strong adversaries stand face to face and are under an equal pressure; [1] when there is a weaker and a stronger, the relationship between them is determined by the immediate and practical circumstances of the case. This is the fundamental idea underlying all the arguments put forward by the Athenians: their subjects know that they only refrain from conquering when they are not strong enough; the Melians must give way to people stronger than they are; nothing can prevent the strong from ruling. On this last point, the Athenians' theory coincides with the pragmatic aspect of Greek ethical thought. It goes beyond it, however, when they come to discuss the possibility suggested by the Melians that help may come from providence: not only do the Athenians deny that the idea of providence has any reality at all, but by the very words which they use they place knowledge of everything divine on the level of mere opinion (δόξῃ). Only human actions can be known, and since they are seen to obey the rule of force it is legitimate to infer that the Gods themselves are also subject to it. This denial of providence on the part of the Athenians is thus only one of the aspects of the law that they stated at the very beginning, and which they now express in an even more assertive form: καὶ ἡμεῖς οὔτε θέντες τὸν νόμον οὔτε κειμένῳ πρῶτοι χρησάμενοι, ὄντα δὲ παραλαβόντες καὶ ἐσόμενον ἐς αἰεὶ καταλείψοντες χρώμεθα αὐτῷ, εἰδότες καὶ ὑμᾶς ἂν καὶ ἄλλους ἐν τῇ αὐτῇ δυνάμει ἡμῖν γενομέ-

---

[1] Without a shadow of a doubt, we must give to ἀνάγκη in the expression ἀπ᾽ ἴσης ἀνάγκης the practical meaning that it normally has in Thucydides (cf. III. 82. 2: πίπτειν ἐς ἀνάγκην). Here, we are dealing with a practical remark: men act by force when they have it, and talk of justice only when they cannot act by force.

νους δρῶντας ἂν ταὐτό. The words they use recall those of the
Athenians in Book I, but presume a universality which was there
limited to the domain of political necessity: in Book I, the idea of an
ethical law was mentioned only to provide an incidental justification
for Athenian rule; it did not offer an explanation for all possible undertakings. This shows the difference that there is between the two
texts, for that of the Melian dialogue leaves no further place for the
luxury of justice that the Athenians in Book I could still aspire to.
Instead, it makes force the one factor determining all human relationships.

This general thesis, which here assumes a philosophical form,
should be compared with similar expressions of belief which appear
in more specifically philosophical texts. Plato, in particular, discusses
it on two occasions, in the *Gorgias* and in the *Republic*. In the *Gorgias*,
it is linked with the distinction between nature (φύσις) and law
(νόμος). Law, says Callicles, is created by the weak in order to protect
their personal interest; in the realm of nature, on the other hand, the
superior should prevail over the inferior: δίκαιόν ἐστι τὸν ἀμείνω τοῦ
χείρονος πλέον ἔχειν καὶ τὸν δυνατώτερον τοῦ ἀδυνατωτέρου (483 d);
in the animal as in the human kingdom, the rule of the strong over
the weak is a universally admitted principle: οὕτω τὸ δίκαιον κέκριται
τὸν κρείττω τοῦ ἥττονος ἄρχειν καὶ πλέον ἔχειν. Similarly, in the
Republic (338 c), Thrasymachus defines justice as the interest of the
stronger: φημὶ γὰρ ἐγὼ εἶναι τὸ δίκαιον οὐκ ἄλλο τι ἢ τὸ τοῦ κρείτ-
τονος ξυμφέρον. These two texts are very close to that of Thucydides,
and the only difference between them lies in the more or less empirical notion presented of justice. The Athenians in Thucydides do not
deny that the idea of justice can have a certain validity: they only
point out that the cases to which it can apply are very limited.
Callicles goes much further when he admits not that the rule of the
stronger *overcomes* justice but that it *is* just. Finally, Thrasymachus
defines justice as the interest of the stronger, and thus completely
identifies the idea of right with that of might.[1] We have thus a sort of

---

[1] Barker (*Greek Political Theory*, 2nd edition, 1925, p. 72), without studying very
closely the thesis put forward in this dialogue, makes an excellent distinction between the
ideas of Callicles and Thrasymachus. He compares the first with Nietzsche, and shows that
he was less a destroyer of morality than a revolutionary in morals: he rejected the morality
of the herd in order to put the morality of the masters in its place, recognizing that natural
law does exist although arguing that it is based on force. Thrasymachus, on the other
hand, by pushing empiricism to its logical conclusions, is in Barker's view closer to
Hobbes than to Nietzsche.

regular progression; but the difference between Thucydides on the one hand and the two Platonic texts on the other is particularly noticeable: in their greater preoccupation with action, his Athenians show the enterprises of the strong not so much as being lawful but as being successful and habitual. He is concerned only with the way men behave, and his Athenians do not need the encouragement of a general philosophical system: they make no attempt to discover whether their action is lawful or not; it must be lawful, since everybody acts as they do. They are thus more realistic than the philosophers, at the same time as the ideas which they put forward are less revolutionary.[1]

However, the undeniable similarity between the remarks made by the Athenians in the Melian dialogue and the ideas put forward by these two philosophers in Plato has led certain scholars to argue that Thucydides was here making them express the doctrine of the sophists. Callicles is presented as a sophist,[2] Thrasymachus certainly was one,[3] and the *Lives* of Thucydides make him the pupil now of Antiphon, now of Gorgias and Prodicus. Moreover, it is certain that both his style and his manner of presenting an argument show a very deep influence of their teaching. It would thus seem reasonable to argue that he has here put forward their system; this thesis was first argued by Nestle.[4]

If it can be established that this system existed, under the form of a precise doctrine, in a particular circle of thinkers, and if it can also be shown that Thucydides deliberately reproduced it as such,[5] then

[1] Because he did not notice this distinction, Nietzsche slightly distorted Thucydides' ideas in order to bring them closer to his own when he wrote (in *Human, all too Human*, I, 92): 'Justice (equity) originates among men of roughly equal power, as Thucydides so well saw (in the terrifying dialogue between the Athenian envoys and the Melians).' 'Originates' is not quite correct; what he should have said was 'is valid' or 'is applied'.

[2] As we know, the problem of his existence has not been completely cleared up: it may be asked whether he is not brought in here because Plato needed to carry Gorgias' thesis to its third stage; Grote (*Plato*, II, XXII) points out that the character seems to have been just as disparaging towards the sophists as towards the philosophers. See Barker, *Greek Pol. Theory*, p. 71; Burnet, *Greek Philosophy*, p. 121; Ad. Menzel, *Kallikles. Eine Studie zur Geschichte der Lehre der Stärkeren*, 1922, 101 pp.; J. Humbert, *Polycratès, l'accusateur de Socrate et le Gorgias*, Paris, 1930.

[3] Provided our Thrasymachus was indeed the sophist of Chalcedon. Gomperz has cast doubt on this (*Sophistik und Rhetorik*, pp. 51-56).

[4] *Thukydides und die Sophistik, N. Jhb.*, 1914, pp. 648-685.

[5] I am not questioning the role played by certain sophists in spreading ideas of this type, nor the influence which they had on Thucydides. I am merely trying to discover whether this influence is definite enough to enable us to qualify and define the ideas here expressed by the Athenians.

we shall have acquired a most valuable piece of information about his aims and intentions.

But there is a first objection that must immediately be taken into account, namely, that since Grote and Gomperz, it can be considered as definitely proved that the sophists did not have a doctrine as such.[1]

As far as the ideas here under discussion are concerned, it is in any case quite obvious that not all the sophists shared this complete rejection of moral principles: Protagoras limits his relativistic outlook to the realm of knowledge, and is a teacher of virtue (ἀρετῆς διδάσκαλος, see Plato, *Protagoras*, 349 a); Hippias also preaches virtue in his *Troikon*, and, in order to advocate righteousness, Prodicus composed the fable of Heracles having to choose between vice and virtue. Finally, the anonymous text in Iamblichus castigates πλεονεξία. We are thus a long way from the Athenians in Book V.

What evidence therefore remains? A certain number of comparisons and parallels.[2]

There remains the fact that in his *Helen*, Gorgias uses a form of words which is fairly close to that of Thucydides, since he writes: πέφυκε γὰρ οὐ τὸ κρεῖσσον ὑπὸ τοῦ ἥσσονος κωλύεσθαι, ἀλλὰ τὸ ἥσσον ὑπὸ τοῦ κρείσσονος ἄρχεσθαι καὶ ἄγεσθαι.[3] But if there is an echo from one text to the other, the remark of Gorgias cannot, when replaced in its context, be linked with a genuine doctrine: an attempt is being made to show that Helen is innocent because she yielded to the will of a God, and because the Gods are in every way superior to men. This is a mere lawyer's trick, and a banal attempt to exploit a commonplace; it in no way constitutes a moral theory. Another indication is provided by Thrasymachus, who tries to prove that the

---

[1] See Grote, *A History of Greece* (1862), part II, ch. LXVII, and *Plato and the other companions of Socrates*, London, 1865, vol. II, ch. 22, and vol. III, ch. 38; Gomperz, *Griechische Denker*, 3rd ed., 1911, I, ch. V, and *Sophistik und Rhetorik — Das Bildungsideal des εὖ λέγειν in seinem Verhältnis zur Philosophie des V. Iahrhunderts*, Teubner, 1912, 292 pp. in-8. See also Diès, *Autour de Platon*, Paris, 1927, I, pp. 84 ff. Those who discuss their conclusions, like Pohlenz, *Aus Platos Werdezeit*, Berlin, 1913, pp. 193 ff. or Ad. Menzel, *Kallikles*, App. IV, attack only the purely formal character accorded to the teaching of the sophists by Gomperz, but do not try to give a single doctrine to the different sophists. (Even Nestle, in an article entitled *Politik und Aufklärung*, N. Jhb., 1909, pp. 1-22, shows the variations of opinion among the sophists on political matters, which obviously invalidates the conclusions of the article quoted above.)

[2] The distinction between law and nature seems to have been one of the sophists' favourites themes. (Cf. Hippias of Elis in *Protagoras*, 337 c-d, and Antiphon, *Pap. Ox.*, XI, 1364); but it seems that the discovery of this should be attributed not to them but to Archelaus, a disciple of Anaxagoras and the master of Socrates (cf. Diogenes Laertius, II, 16-17, and Barker, p. 53).

[3] *Helen*, 6.

Gods are not concerned about men, for otherwise they would not neglect the greatest human good which is justice: ὁρῶμεν γὰρ τοὺς ἀνθρώπους ταύτῃ μὴ χρωμένους.[1] But if the idea is similar in tone to the remarks made by our Athenians, it still does not have the dimensions of a theory: it is simply a facile remark made by a moralist.[2] Finally Antiphon, reducing law to a convention, notes that the individual has an interest in observing it only when he is in the presence of witnesses.[3] This comparison is, in my view, the only one that really deserves keeping. But it will be noted that it is part of a purely theoretical discussion of the nature of law of which the conclusion is missing,[4] and that other texts by Antiphon did preach order and self-control.[5]

These comparisons thus reveal the existence of a certain state of mind, but it is by no means certain that this had crystallized into an actual doctrine which was expressed by one particular group of people.

Plato himself seems to indicate that this was not the case when he suggests that these ideas were fashionable, were in the air, and that they were 'modern'. Thus, in the *Republic*, we read that the sophists simply take what is in the air and repeat it in their teaching (492 a; 493 a); in the *Gorgias*, Callicles' thesis is described as 'what everyone thinks but dares not say' (492 d); and there are similar ideas about which people are less timid, for when Callicles and Polus praise the life of the tyrant, Socrates declares that he has heard practically everybody saying the same things (καὶ τῶν ἄλλων ὀλίγου πάντων τῶν ἐν τῇ πόλει, 511 b).

There are many echoes which support this remark by Socrates, in the theatre in particular. Without even mentioning the rather brutal materialism of the *Cyclop*, we have, for example, the tirade in the *Phoenician Women*, in which Eteocles celebrates the virtues of tyranny, and approves of injustice when it helps to achieve it (525); we also have the tirade in *Bellerophon*, which notes that tyrants are

[1] Diels, fr. 8.

[2] It should be added that Thrasymachus, who seems to have been one of the most revolutionary of the sophists in these matters, could not, as Blass remarks, have influenced Thucydides, who had left Athens too early.

[3] *Pap. Ox.*, XI, 1364.

[4] Only the first fragment has been restored. The discussion is linked with the one found, for Hippias, in Xenophon, *Mem.*, IV, 4, 14, or, for Protagoras, in Plato, *Theaetetus*, 167 c: this discussion does not seem to have been particularly associated with very revolutionary ideas on morality.

[5] See particularly Diels, fr. 58; 59.

never punished, and that cities are more praised for their might than for their merits (fr. 288 N); we have the statement, very similar to one in our text, which is provided by fragment 263 of *Archelaus*:

οἱ γὰρ ἥσσονες
τοῖς κρείσσοσιν φιλοῦσι δουλεύειν βροτῶν.

Another example is that of the young Pheidippides, in the *Clouds*, and of the Unjust Reasoning which boasts of having triumphed, in spite of being the weaker, because it took up position against laws and justice (1039):

ὅτι πρώτιστος ἐπενόησα
καὶ τοῖς νόμοις καὶ ταῖς δίκαις τἀναντί᾿ ἀντιλέξαι.

Sophists, friends of the sophists, free thinkers; there is certainly a relationship, but it is a very wide and very general one.[1] And it in no way justifies us in saying that Thucydides intends to present this or that doctrine belonging to such and such a group of men.

It can be added that such an identification would be all the more surprising since sophist ways of thought seem to have been most popular in circles hostile to democracy, and, consequently, to imperialism. It is Antiphon who represents the influence of Gorgias, and Theramenes that of Prodicus; in Thucydides, Cleon shows himself hostile towards the sophists and opposes them by praising ἀμαθία. And in a similar way Athenian democracy, when it has causes for being afraid, puts on more trials for impiety.

It is thus difficult to believe that the ideas expressed in the Melian dialogue were intended to refer to doctrines actually preached elsewhere. It is much more true to say that they are here directly suggested by the political reality which Thucydides is analysing.

Moreover, we may even wonder whether it was not this very political reality which gave birth to these ideas, not only for Thucydides himself but also in a more general fashion. This would explain the apparent contradiction which lies in the fact that, of two opposite groups of people, the same principles seem to prompt now the former's action and now the latter's ideas. Nestle (*Politik und Aufklärung*, p. 18) insists on the fact that the *demos*, which condemns everyone with new ideas, nevertheless applies these theories much more readily than anyone else: it is on these ideas, he says, that

[1] The same thing is true as far as complementary themes and ideas are concerned: if Prodicus, Thrasymachus and Protagoras showed themselves somewhat reserved as far as religion was concerned, the names of Diagoras, Clinias, Hippon and Xenophanes prove that impiety was not a characteristic shared only by the sophists.

are based the notion of πόλις τύραννος, the behaviour of the sycophants, the proposed punishment of Mytilene, the Sicilian expedition
and, above all, the conquest of Melos. But presented in this form, the
assertion seems a little absurd, and it is much more likely that the
opposite is true: Athenian policy does not *apply* these ideas; it
inspires them. And it is not the philosophers who suggest them to
Thucydides; it is political facts, and above all others the great fact of
Athenian imperialism, which suggest them both to him and to the
philosophers.

The ideas of tyranny and domination (which are only two aspects
of the same idea, since both τυραννίς and τυραννεῖν are also used for
rule over other peoples) seem in fact to have played an important part
in the formation of Greek materialism.

Tyranny and domination provide the example of might triumphant and unpunished, and thus offer an argument[1] at the same time
as a temptation. In the case of domination, where no laws exist, this
argument seems so strong that it once carried away even the wise
Isocrates: it is better, he then said, to do evil rather than to endure it,
and 'to rule over others without this being just (μὴ δικαίως) rather
than avoid this reproach by obeying the Spartans unjustly (ἀδίκως)'
(*Panath.*, 117). Thus it is really the sight of tyranny which awakes in
the spectator a tyrant's soul; it is imperialism which makes men admit
intellectually that might is right.[2]

It will be noted, moreover, that in the whole of Thucydides' work
we only twice come across ideas similar to the ones with which we
are now concerned, and that in both cases they arise from a consideration of Athenian imperialism. The first occasion is in the speech of

---

[1] See the role played, in the tirade of the *Bellerophon*, by the idea that there are strong
but impious towns which rule over pious but weak ones (288 N, 10):

πόλεις τε μικρὰς οἶδα τιμώσας θεοὺς
αἳ μειζόνων κλύουσι δυσσεβεστέρων
λόγχης ἀριθμῷ πλείονος κρατούμεναι.

Facts of this nature are often mentioned, with even more precision, to illustrate the idea of
injustice: cf. Xenophon, *Mem.*, II, 1, 13 (where the conversation is about the conduct of
individuals): 'Or do you not see people gathering in the harvests and the fruits of the trees
that others have sown and planted, and using all the methods of siege against those that
are weaker and refuse to obey, until they persuade them to prefer slavery to fighting a war
against the stronger?' The very terms seem to evoke the example of Melos. The rule,
moreover, is valid for all times: cf. Constant, *De l'Esprit de Conquête et de l'Usurpation*,
XIII: 'Il faut en convenir, chez un peuple éclairé, le despotisme est l'argument le plus fort
contre l'existence d'une providence.' (See also *Gorgias*, 483 e.)

[2] It goes without saying that from that point onwards the progression is all the more
rapid since there is reciprocal action: cf. Plato, *Laws*, X, 889-890.

the Athenians at Sparta, when they declare: οὐδ' αὖ πρῶτοι τοῦ τοιούτου ὑπάρξαντες, ἀλλ' αἰεὶ καθεστῶτος τὸν ἥσσω ὑπὸ τοῦ δυνατωτέρου κατείργεσθαι (I. 76. 2); the second time is in the speech of an enemy of Athens, Hermocrates:[1] πέφυκε δὲ τὸ ἀνθρώπειον διὰ παντὸς ἄρχειν μὲν τοῦ εἴκοντος, φυλάσσεσθαι δὲ τὸ ἐπιόν (IV. 61. 5).[2] Such is the view of life implied by the spectacle of Athenian imperialism.

Thus, it may be that the Melian dialogue owes to the sophists the dogmatic and almost metaphysical nature of its assertions; but it owes its general inspiration only to the subject matter which it treats, and if this inspiration leads here to very abstract and extreme remarks, this is mainly because the analysis itself goes very deep into political reality.

Similarly, the objections which the Melians put forward against these views are also taken from reality. They do not try to defend justice for its own sake — which could have no influence on the Athenians. Instead, they try to show what advantages can be drawn from justice and moderation: if one should fail, they say, it is a good thing to have shown other people not to demand all that they would be entitled to (90).[3] Or, later on, they warn the Athenians that failure lies in wait for the powerful man if others decide to ally themselves against him (98). This is an argument that we find repeated in Plato, when Socrates replies to Callicles that, in the realm of nature, the many acting together are more powerful than the individual alone: οἱ πολλοὶ τοῦ ἑνὸς κρείττους εἰσὶν κατὰ φύσιν (Gorgias, 488 d); but, there again, the philosophical argument seems to be prompted by historical facts; for the Melians' reply is much more the statement of events that were soon to take place than the expression of a theoretical and more or less traditional objection.[4] The language of the historical and the philosophical texts largely differs, but the idea is the same; and Isocrates provides good evidence for this, since in his treatise On the Peace he uses an argument which is exactly half-way between the practical analysis of the Melians and the

[1] Hermocrates is talking about Athenian imperialism, and one might add that he belongs himself to an imperialistic city; if he is so ready to excuse the ἄρχειν βουλόμενοι, it may be because he belongs to their category.

[2] Hermocrates is here more concerned with resistance than with aggression; that is why he says τοῦ εἴκοντος instead of τοῦ ἥσσονος, and adds a second idea which does not concern the Athenians: φυλάσσεσθαι δὲ τὸ ἐπιόν; but it is the same view of the world as submitted to the rule of force which the Athenians express in the next book.

[3] Thucydides seems to have shared this argument in favour of justice: cf. III. 84. 3.

[4] See above, p. 275.

abstract reasoning of Plato. He is pointing out that although taken individually the cities are weaker than Athens, they are stronger than she is if they join together, and he writes (134): μιᾶς μὲν ἑκάστης τῶν πόλεων κρείττους ἐσμέν, ἁπασῶν δ' ἥττους. The philosophical refutation thus coincides exactly with the political objection, and we see once again how the two areas of thought exactly overlap, each explaining the same truth in its own different realm.

This should throw some light upon Thucydides' intentions in writing the dialogue. Barker, thinking that he is reproducing the analyses of the sophists, writes that in the passages such as the dialogue between the Athenians and the Melians, Thucydides is probably expressing the attitude of oligarchical circles towards the power of democracy in Athens and the power of Athens in the empire. This is not so; he shows the Athenians carried along by a principle which was presupposed by the very existence of their empire; and it is not even obvious that in dealing with the moral theory he intends to criticize Athens. His Athenians are often right, and Thucydides knew that justice is not likely to be very effective between the strong and the weak;[1] he knew that men normally talk of justice only when they cannot act by force, and his Hermocrates is thus afraid that the Camarinaeans may appeal to the principles of justice through cowardice (VI. 79. 1); finally, even if Thucydides himself finds it unpleasant, blameworthy and even dangerous for men to follow human nature in this way and to accept the results of this absence of moral values as wholeheartedly as they do, we have seen that, in practice at least, the maxims to which this absence gives rise are generally valid. Such is also the case with the Athenians' views on hope, the Gods and other peoples. The general thesis that they put forward is revolutionary, but their incidental arguments represent a kind of practical wisdom which Thucydides himself shares and which is adopted by all Greek thinkers. Both the main thesis and these incidental arguments are based on the same premiss, and the only really noteworthy point about the Athenians is that they develop the implications of this premiss with complete logic. Thus, if Thucydides shows an instinctive disapproval of them, one feels that he would very likely share Benjamin Constant's view and speak of a 'race which

[1] There are many texts which presume a similar notion of human relationships even among the weak, if they are clearsighted enough. It is because of this idea that the Mytilenians expect to be conquered in their turn, and they consider such a possibility as normal and likely (III. 11. 1). The only difference lies in the fact that the weak use such ideas only for prevision, whereas the strong justify thereby their action.

willingly degenerating, has no *illusion* to bear it up, and no *error* to excuse it'.[1] Thus it is more human nature than Athenian imperialism that he is condemning, and this dialogue expresses his general philosophical pessimism rather than a severe judgment of Athens in political matters.

Thus to explain rather than to judge denotes a superior form of impartiality. Werner Jaeger saw this very well when he wrote in *Paideia* that this perception which Thucydides had of immanent necessity enabled him to attain perfect objectivity. It is therefore perhaps not an accident if the analysis in Book V, which goes further than all the others contained in his work and discloses the highest kind of impartiality, should be the only dialogue included in it. As a result of the maieutics made possible by the dialogue form, each set of ideas is studied in greater detail, and their coherence is brought out by the close-knit discussion which this form involves; and if finally each side maintains its position, this is no surprise, as the reader is soon made to acknowledge, behind the individual figures of the Athenians and Melians, the eternal principles of might and right. The conflict between these two principles is, in Thucydides' view, as impossible to resolve as the one which separates the two peoples; in both cases, only action can bring it to an end.

Far from condemning the political thesis with which they are connected, the moral theories which the dialogue contains are merely the logical consequence of the impartiality shown by Thucydides in judging it: thus both sets of ideas join together and confirm each other. And if this deep understanding which, of its own accord, ripens into impartiality, was seen in the last chapter as coming more naturally at a time when the events had long since taken place, that is in the 'late' passages of the work, then this episode which carries this impartiality to its highest point, seems more than any other to bear the proof of late composition.

It is on this impartiality of Thucydides' judgment in general that we should insist if we wish to understand the whole meaning of the dialogue. This characteristic becomes quite obvious if, once again, we compare Thucydides with Isocrates in the latter's defence of Athens against the reproach regarding Melos. In the *Panegyricus* he tries to exonerate Athens by including Melos among the cities that were not allied to her and which 'had made war on her' (τῶν πολεμησάντων

[1] *De l'Esprit de Conquête . . .* , XIII.

ἡμῖν); and he argues that no one can rule unless he is prepared to punish the guilty (τοὺς ἐξαμαρτάνοντας!) (*Paneg.*, 102). In the *Panathenaicus* he replies to the same criticism by saying that Athens' victims were miserable and unimportant little islands which cannot really justify so great an outcry (περὶ νησύδρια τοιαῦτα καὶ τηλικαῦτα τὸ μέγεθος ἐξαμαρτεῖν, ἃ οἱ πολλοὶ τῶν Ἑλλήνων οὐδ' ἴσασιν in *Panath.*, 70; cf. 89: τοιούτων πολιχνίων). Such arguments are detestable, for they try in vain to minimize the wanton and serious character of the act committed by Athens. Therefore, Isocrates succeeds in exonerating Athens only by making counter-accusations, and by insisting on the crimes committed by Sparta (*Panath.*, 70; 89).

Thucydides proceeds in just the opposite manner. Where Isocrates speaks only of the immediate circumstances and tries to minimize the act in question, Thucydides generalizes as much as he can, and tries to show the Athenian action as something of considerable importance. By doing this, he concentrates so much on the principle involved that he heightens both what was said for and what was said against Athens.

First of all, what could be said against her: this is where he naturally differs most widely from Isocrates. The latter considers only the 'punishment', while Thucydides leaves this on one side, and looks less at the cruelty shown on this particular occasion than at the need for permanent conquest which causes it. For Thucydides, it is all part of the same phenomenon, two different aspects of the same process (the cruelty shown by Athens increases as her empire grows more unpopular,[1] for it is inseparable from the policy of 'making a show of strength'). Thus he takes what could have been considered as an accident and sees it as part of the general nature of imperialism. Similarly, when Isocrates examines this punishment, he tries to hide the two features — its importance and its wholly unjustified and gratuitous character — on which Thucydides most insists: in the History, the importance of the measure is emphasized by the fact of its discussion in the only dialogue which the work contains, while its

---

[1] In 430, as Thucydides tells us (II. 70), the Athenians contented themselves with banishing the Potidaeans; as early as 427, Cleon speaks of putting all the men of Mytilene to death (III. 36): this is what was done at Scione and then at Melos. The way in which Thucydides explains the aggression also explains this constant increase in cruelty. We must notice, however, that the Spartans had shown the same cruelty towards Plataea, and that it was tending to become the norm (see Colin, *R.E.G.*, LI, 1938, p. 310). The Thracians are murderous barbarians because, in addition to killing the men, they also slaughter the women and children (VII. 29); this, at least, is just not done.

illegitimate and gratuitous nature shows itself in the insolent way by which the Athenians justify their action. Finally, Isocrates pleads extenuating circumstances, while Thucydides neglects all circumstances and goes back to a universal principle. Thus, by turning his back on all these subterfuges, he seems to condemn the Athenian action at Melos irrevocably.

Yet, even while he condemns it, Thucydides also puts forward a much stronger defence than Isocrates, and this is once again because of the high degree of abstraction to which he rises. Isocrates, in effect, argues here — as he does when answering the reproach about trials — that other people have committed much worse crimes; Thucydides, going back to the general cause, explains that these crimes form part of the general nature of imperialism. The same argument which seemed to be turning against Athens now comes to her defence, for, as Thucydides reaches this level of impartiality, the two opposite views about Athens' action meet and join together, this action now being seen not under a particular angle showing only one side of it, but in the very principle which inspires it.

This same impartiality which thus links excuses with accusations also brings out this great desire for unity to which all Thucydides' ideas seem to bear witness. Just as a certain number of late passages which were studied in the second part of this book established a comparison between Pericles and his successors, and underlined the fact that it was logical to condemn the latter but not the former, so Thucydides' approach to imperialism in general is intended to show, through a system of interlocking analyses, how the situation of Athenian imperialism was determined by one unchanging principle, and how this progressively led Athens, in the most logical manner possible, to think and act in ways that were equally deplorable. The repetition of the same arguments in different passages merely confirms this desire to bring both good and evil together in the same sequence of events, and to show what causes this succession to take place.

In order to understand the whole of Thucydides' ideas on this subject we must try to define more clearly the nature of this concatenation. The Athenians speak of necessity, and Thucydides seems to be trying to bring out a kind of automatic process which dragged imperialism from conquest to conquest and finally to defeat. Nevertheless, in equally late passages of his work, Thucydides also insists, when he is talking about Pericles, on the beauty of Athenian imperialism, and on the possibilities of Athenian victory. It seems therefore

X

that this necessity began by showing itself only as a temptation (in fact, this accounts for the difference between the two passages of analysis that we have just studied). Through the mistakes made by Cleon and Alcibiades, the forces holding Athens back on the fatal slope gradually disappear, until the only thing which remains is the almost mechanical pressure of imperialism, like an evil force gradually controlling everything. How did this mechanism work? How, and to what extent, could it have been brought under control? To find an answer to these questions is to define the 'still point of the turning world' at which Thucydides' ideas on Athenian imperialism show themselves in their perfect unity.

CHAPTER THREE

THE THEORY OF ATHENIAN IMPERIALISM

THUCYDIDES' ideas on Athenian imperialism, considered as a whole, are not expressed only in the two texts that have just been studied. In the rest of the work, everything which we saw was repeated from one speech to another and from one analysis to another already defined the unity of this imperialism and the reasons for the constant forward movement of Athens. These different texts, linked one with another, will allow us finally to describe, in all its precision, the whole system which, for Thucydides, lies behind the development of Athenian imperialism.

The very possibility that we can bring out such a system pre-supposes a very great tendency towards abstraction on the part of Thucydides, by which he constantly rises from the particular to the general.

As a historian, he obviously indicates all the different circum-stances which have facilitated the rise of Athens, but these remain subordinate to other explanations. In I. 99 he indicates that Athens' subjects were in some way responsible for what happened, since by agreeing to pay tribute instead of providing military contin-gents, they gave Athens greater strength and thereby afforded the means by which to compel them to obedience. But here Thucydides is merely showing how it worked out and explaining a particular stage in the process, in the same way as he does when he shows the consequences that followed a triumph like that of Pylos or the influence of a man like Alcibiades. All this is subsidiary to the great force of Athenian ambition, and attracts less of his attention.

The personality of Athens as a city, in so far as it can account for this ambition, has already more importance.

At the very beginning of the work, the Corinthians draw a parallel between Sparta and Athens, and the famous passage (I. 70), is obviously written with great care; there, in order to explain the policy of Athens, the speakers define the 'nature' of the Athenians (πεφυκέναι ἐπὶ τῷ . . .). It is in fact their character, their natural disposition, to be quick to act and to hope, never weary and never

at rest. And indeed, in the whole of the analysis of Athenian πολυπραγμοσύνη such as it develops in the rest of the work, we find this
idea brought out again and again. It is the character of the Athenians
that Nicias attacks, both in their home and their foreign policy
(VI. 9. 3: τοὺς τρόπους τοὺς ὑμετέρους; cf. VII. 14. 4: τὰς
φύσεις ὑμῶν and VII. 48. 4: τὰς Ἀθηναίων φύσεις). Similarly, it is the
character (τρόπον) of the Athenians that Euphemus considers to be
the essential factor. And, to turn to those who praise Athens, it is her
τρόποι which are exalted by Pericles in the Funeral Oration (II. 36. 4)
and her ἤθη of which Alcibiades reminds her (VI. 18. 7) when both
statesmen want her to keep her quality of πόλιν μὴ ἀπράγμονα.
Imperialism thus seems to spring naturally from the character of the
Athenians, as water from a fountain. They are like the Persian kings
of Herodotus; they are not like the Spartans who are so difficult to
persuade whenever action is required, or like Pagondas the Boeotian,
whose ideal does not imply increasing the boundaries of his state:
τήν τε αὐτῶν αἰεὶ ἐλευθεροῦν καὶ τὴν ἄλλων μη δουλοῦσθαι ἀδίκως
(IV. 92. 7). Thus, throughout his work, Thucydides expresses,
recalls or suggests the existence of a motive belonging to the character
of Athens and the Athenians, and which could be sufficient to explain
her imperialism.

Yet, in his work, this cause is far from excluding more general
ones. Certainly, the character of the Athenians enables them to
acquire their empire,[1] but it then does little more than encourage
them to follow the direction created by circumstances. This combination of general and particular causes accounts for the two kinds of
arguments which we have often seen mentioned side by side — the
beauty of Athenian tradition and the practical necessity of maintaining the empire, or the hope of victory and the need to carry on the
struggle. Therefore, when Pericles puts forward one of the laws of
imperialism by saying πᾶσι μὲν ὑπῆρξε δὴ ὅσοι ἕτεροι ἑτέρων ἠξίωσαν
ἄρχειν (II. 64. 5), we can say that the 'nature' of the Athenians explains
first of all why they happen to come under this category (they indeed
wanted the empire), and then why they fall so willingly under the
law which lies in wait for them. But — and this is the essential point —
this law still remains highly general, and in the final analysis Athenian
imperialism is only the perfect example of a common experience
whose nature is governed by universal laws. Athens was rushing
head first towards her own destiny, but the fact that she willingly

[1] It is represented by the factor τιμή in the analysis of the Athenians in Book I.

accepted it in no way transformed it into an optional one. And it was this destiny, belonging to a type likely to repeat itself in future ages, that most attracted the eminently scientific intelligence of Thucydides.

There are different laws defining it, some of which are put forward in order to exonerate imperialism and some in order to condemn it.

Athens acts: the reason, she says, is that she is hated by her subjects, and, as can be expected in such a case, is thus compelled to show her strength. She justifies herself by invoking a political law.

Athens acts: the reason, her critics say, is that she is drunk with power, and, as can be expected in such a case, allows herself to be carried to excess. Her enemies condemn her by invoking a psychological law.

Athens acts: the reason, the passages of deepest analysis in Thucydides tell us, is that she is strong, and, as can be expected in such a case, uses her strength to rule over others. These texts explain her actions in the name of a philosophical law.

The Athenians speak of an obligation (ἀναγκασθέντας ἂν I. 76. 1; ἀνάγκη VI. 18. 3), her enemies and critics of a very frequent accident (παθεῖν ὅπερ οἱ ἀήθως τι ἀγαθὸν λαμβάνοντες τῶν ἀνθρώπων IV. 17. 4; ὅπερ ἂν αὐτοὶ πάθοιεν VI. 13. 1), the more general texts of a phenomenon which constantly recurs under certain conditions (αἰεὶ καθεστῶτος I. 76. 2; οὔτε θέντες τὸν νόμον οὔτε κειμένῳ πρῶτοι χρησάμενοι, ὄντα δὲ παραλαβόντες καὶ ἐσόμενον ἐς αἰεὶ καταλείψοντες V. 105). This implies that these three laws each correspond to a different type of reality, and influence Athens in a different way. The first two nevertheless have this in common: they make up a dialogue in which the problem of Athenian political wisdom is debated, a problem despised by the third law because of its higher preoccupations.

I. Political Necessity

The political law consists in fact of two different assertions: men who have an empire are hated — consequently they are forced to maintain this empire by a policy of strength. These two assertions are not, however, both equally obvious.

The hatred felt for Athens by her subjects is stated as a simple fact in certain passages (II. 63. 2: ὡς τυραννίδα... ἤδη ἔχετε αὐτήν — III. 37. 2: οὐ σκοποῦντες ὅτι τυραννίδα ἔχετε τὴν ἀρχὴν καὶ πρὸς ἐπιβουλεύοντας αὐτοὺς καὶ ἄκοντας ἀρχομένους); but it is a state of affairs which has always accompanied any sort of rule (II. 64. 5: πᾶσι μὲν ὑπῆρξε). In fact, it appears obvious and inevitable; Cleon, speaking of Athens' subjects, says: τοὺς οὔτ' ἀντοικτιοῦντας, ἐξ ἀνάγκης τε καθεστῶτας αἰεὶ πολεμίους (III. 40. 3). One might even think that Pericles is using an artifice when he presents as a truth based on experience something which is in fact an obvious truth based on logic. The Pseudo-Xenophon, in any case, presents the fact as a kind of axiom: ὅτι μισεῖσθαι μὲν ἀνάγκη τὸν ἄρχοντα ὑπὸ τοῦ ἀρχομένου (I, 14), and it can be found under a similar though less precise form in various contemporary texts, like the λυπρὰ γὰρ τὰ κρείσσονα of the *Ion* (597).

This hatred provoked by power can present itself at different stages. It can either be the latent hatred of subjects (like that mentioned by Pericles or Cleon) or, in a wider application, the hatred of those who fear they might soon be conquered and are ready for action (VI. 87. 2: διότι καὶ πολλὰ φυλασσόμεθα), or even already active (VI. 18. 2: τὸν γὰρ προύχοντα οὐ μόνον ἐπιόντα τις ἀμύνεται, ἀλλὰ καὶ ὅπως μὴ ἔπεισι προκαταλαμβάνει): these last two forms can be considered as additional, and, as the Melians indicate in V. 98, they make themselves felt only towards the end. Now, these different forms of hatred increase all the time in number and intensity but the important thing is that hatred inevitably existed from the very beginning.

Now this indeed appears to be inevitable, at least if one gives to the word ἄρχειν a strong sense, that of exercising absolute power based on force, that of τυραννεῖν. – Κατ' εὔνοιαν ἡγεῖσθαι is possible,[1] but precisely because it is then a question of 'hegemony' and not of domination or empire. This is what makes the statement an obvious one: it is as obvious as a definition can be, when stating what a thing is; for hatred is indeed inevitable if one considers a form of rule which has not been willingly accepted.[2]

Now Athenian rule was not willingly accepted, and Thucydides clearly says so. While still remaining aware of the support provided for Athens by the democratic parties of the different cities, and know-

---

[1] Alcibiades offers it as an ideal future to the Spartans (VI. 92. 5: αὐτοί τε ἀσφαλῶς οἰκῆτε καὶ τῆς ἁπάσης Ἑλλάδος ἑκούσης καὶ οὐ βίᾳ κατ' εὔνοιαν δὲ ἡγήσησθε); doubtless this is a figment of his imagination rather than a reality. However, since the Peloponnesian Confederation did not involve the same opposition between masters and subjects, and consequently gave rise to less hatred, the hypothesis was a more possible one.

[2] See Aristotle, *Pol.*, 1295 a, 23.

ing that Athens should have exploited her popularity with them,[1] he never, as we have seen, makes the conflict between democracy and oligarchy more important than the opposition between masters and subjects.[2] In order to form a genuine democratic alliance, Athens would have needed to go back to the ancient ξυμμαχία; but already too much hatred stood in her path: her tendency towards tyranny could be slowed down, as Diodotus saw, but not reversed. Because Athens had one day passed from authority to empire (through fear, ambition and self-interest as the Athenians in Book I explain) she is now obliged to accept that this empire should be a tyranny and an object of hatred.

Because of the hatred sown by rule, this rule itself involves a danger: if they are able to, the subjects will want to avenge themselves,[3] and the tyrant people have no choice between a terrible fate and the maintenance by force of an increasingly tyrannical power.

In the same way as the Persians of Herodotus do not for one moment consider that they can remain independent if they cease to rule,[4] so the Athenians are trapped between the vengeance of their former subjects and the need to continue ruling. But what for the Persians was a condition which they only half-consciously recognized becomes for the Athenians a definite situation of which they can give a rational analysis.

[1] Cf. the intervention of Diodotus, and here pp. 161-162. There were in fact cities which remained faithful to Athens, as Plataea or even, within Lesbos itself, Methymna; there were examples of betrayal in favour of Athens as well as against her; for instance Anactorium, and Megara, not to mention the negotiations about Boeotia (IV. 76). Even when Brasidas the liberator arrives, he is often welcomed only reluctantly, and either for reasons of practical interest, or because of particular circumstances.

[2] Cf. pp. 84-85. Practically, the opposition between democracy and oligarchy is mainly to be perceived up to Brasidas: afterwards, the contrast between masters and subjects leaves no room for anything else. It is also possible that the passages concerning the final period of the war, having been written later, should also bear the mark of Thucydides' own attitude and owe to this circumstance their more exclusive concern with this problem.

[3] The idea of this *danger* recurs everywhere; I. 75. 4: οὐκ ἀσφαλὲς ἔτι ἐδόκει εἶναι τοῖς πολλοῖς ἀπηχθημένους . . . ἀνέντας κινδυνεύειν – II. 63. 1: καὶ κινδύνου ὂν ἐν τῇ ἀρχῇ ἀπήχθεσθε – II. 63. 2: ἀφεῖναι δὲ ἐπικίνδυνον – V. 97: καὶ τὸ ἀσφαλὲς ἡμῖν διὰ τὸ καταστραφῆναι ἂν παράσχοιτε – VI. 18. 3: διὰ τὸ ἀρχθῆναι ἂν ὑφ' ἑτέρων αὐτοῖς κίνδυνον εἶναι εἰ μὴ αὐτοὶ ἄλλων ἄρχοιμεν.

[4] We see Cyrus warning the Persians to be prepared to receive rather than to give orders (IX, 122, 4: ὡς οὐκέτι ἄρξοντας ἀλλ' ἀρξομένους) and the Persians preferring to keep their empire rather than fall into slavery (ἄρχειν τε εἵλοντο λυπρὴν οἰκέοντες μᾶλλον ἢ πεδιάδα σπείροντες ἄλλοισι δουλεύειν).

In the same way as the hostility met by the imperialists can assume different forms, so the law which they must obey can also vary. First of all, it is a question of 'not letting go'; but as soon as one says 'don't let go', one is also saying 'move forward', since hatred exists, and is growing and threatening Athens. In the speech in Book I, the two ideas of προαγαγεῖν and of μὴ ἀνιέναι intermingle. One also has to follow the movement imposed by the necessity to rule if an ally rebels (and one has Cleon), if one is afraid of being attacked (and one has Alcibiades), or if one fears rebellions and judges the moment propitious to show one's strength (and one has the affair of Melos). The political law, as expressed above, finally justifies all the different policies adopted by imperialism.

In principle, the idea on which this law is based is a valid one: it simply says that since Athens is at the head of an empire which depends on force, then she must use force. This is no dubious pretext, but a serious reason. Thucydides sometimes mentions it himself, as when he explains the Athenian decision to send a new fleet in the direction of the Peloponnese (III. 16. 1): αἰσθόμενοι δὲ αὐτοὺς οἱ Ἀθηναῖοι διὰ κατάγνωσιν ἀσθενείας σφῶν παρασκευαζομένους, δηλῶσαι βουλομένους ὅτι οὐκ ὀρθῶς ἐγνώκασιν, ἀλλ' οἷοί τέ εἰσι . . .[1]

The argument is valid, but this does not necessarily mean that the measures taken are always good. Political wisdom ought to show the Athenians to what extent and on what occasions it is in their own best interest to use force. As Diodotus and then the Melians point out, they must avoid making the situation worse unnecessarily; and as Nicias insists, Athens must avoid running the risk of failing in one of her enterprises.

However, since each show of force makes the situation worse, it becomes increasingly difficult to observe the principles of political wisdom. Thus we arrive at the point where we could draw a graph defining the probable development of imperialism and state a sort of evolutionary law. Applied to the past, this law reveals itself in the speech of the Athenians in Book I, and applied to the future in the Melian dialogue. However, Thucydides himself never puts this law forward in a definite and rigorous form: the Melians do not talk about necessity but simply mention what might happen, while the Athenians in Book I do not talk about a constant and regular evolution but simply mention what actually happened in the past.

---

[1] This argument provides a good definition of the Athenian idea of ἀσφάλεια; this, as a result of the prevailing conditions, is exactly the opposite of what it is for Sparta.

Now if Thucydides does not state definitely the existence of a law governing the development of imperialism, it is because he does not acknowledge its existence, and the analysis which we have just given of it shows why: the law as it exists does not deprive the people who act of their liberty; the master-slave relationship may define the conditions under which action takes place, but it does not determine the actual action itself; and Thucydides himself shows far too lucid an understanding of events to accept such a simple-minded historical determinism. The empire must be maintained by force: agreed; but this can be done without making the situation worse, if one uses force when and where one should: Athens could have done this if she had remained faithful to the example given by Pericles. Thus the conditions imposed upon Athens submit her to a permanent and permanently increasing temptation which threatens to drag her into a probably fatal evolution if she yields to it; but in his attempt to lay the foundations for a science of politics, Thucydides is careful to establish a very thorough and methodical distinction between what is inevitable and what is only probable.

It should be added that, within the implied evolution itself, the fall of the imperial power is less probable than the worsening conditions of its rule. In the case of Athens in particular, it was only after the cumulative and joint effect of a large number of repeated mistakes that her power was destroyed. Thucydides insists on a number of occasions on this power, whose extent had never been sufficiently recognized (II. 65; IV. 108; VII. 28); Athens not only ought to have won, but until the very last day she could have won. Thus the political necessity arising from the conditions under which a country maintains her rule over others is absolute, but the evolution which may result thereby is only probable, and the final issue of events is only a risk which the ruler runs.[1]

At the same time as this attitude of Thucydides leaves room for his sympathy for imperialism and his admiration for Pericles, it also characterizes the steadfast quality of his analyses and the lucidity with

---

[1] In this respect, this evolutionary law becomes comparable to another one which also deals with the behaviour of a city in possession of an empire. Nicias states the existence of his when he affirms that it is improbable that one tyrant city should attack another: οὐκ εἰκὸς ἀρχὴν ἐπὶ ἀρχὴν στρατεῦσαι (VI. 11. 3), for it would be afraid of offering an example that might later be turned against itself. Later on, Alcibiades applies the same principle to relationships between Sparta and Tissaphernes (VIII. 46. 3): it is improbable, he says, that Sparta should destroy one empire and then respect the existence of another one. The existence of an empire supposes on both sides a particular attitude, but one which, in the final analysis, is only an εἰκός.

which he conducts them. Thucydides takes the situation to pieces
shows exactly what demands and dangers there were, but does no
eliminate the role played by man; he brings out all the abstrac
and universal implications that can be found in a particular object o
event, but he also knows that part of it remains particular and he care
fully refrains from any undue generalizing. Thibaudet himsel
seems to have sometimes underestimated this extreme caution o
Thucydides: vividly impressed by the power of Thucydidear
analysis, he did not always notice the precise limits which wer
placed upon it. Therefore, he speaks of the 'Euclidean elements o
history'; but history cannot be geometry and would lose its value i
any attempt were made to bring the two disciplines closer together.[1]

This is immediately proved by the comparison between Thucydides and those of his immediate successors who expressed idea
similar to his own.

We first of all find an indication of this in Xenophon; but Xenophon does not go as far as Thucydides, and it appears in his work ir
what is perhaps a tendentious argument put forward by an orator,
and not in a systematic analysis. The Thebans, trying to persuade th
Athenians to act, say to them (*Hellenica*, III, 5, 10): 'As to you
desire, Athenians, to recover the empire that you once possessed, w
are all acquainted with it; how will you achieve your ambition, in al
probability, except by coming to the help of those who are being
unjustly treated by the Lacedaemonians?': the fact that the Lacedaemonians now have the empire is rather a drawback, and puts them
in danger: ὅτι δὲ πολλῶν ἄρχουσι μὴ φοβηθῆτε, ἀλλὰ πολὺ μᾶλλο

---

[1] Thibaudet thus writes, on p. 71: 'In the whole of Thucydides, there is perhaps no word
which bears a greater weight of historical truth and which opens a wider perspective o
κτῆμα εἰς ἀεί than the remark which he puts into Alcibiades' mouth as he sets off for th
Sicilian expedition: we are not free to limit our will to rule as suits our own convenience.
However, this remark of Alcibiades cannot exactly be attributed to Thucydides. Similarly
when Thibaudet writes, p. 72: 'The occupation of India forced England to settle at th
Cape of Good Hope, then in Cyprus, then in Egypt, then in Persia, and perhaps, tomorrow, it will force her to go to Constantinople and to Revel. There is here a kind o
political ἀνάγκη which replaces the theological ἀνάγκη of Herodotus. War is inevitabl
because the suspicion which people have of this expansion of the greatest maritime powe
is also inevitable, because both this suspicion and the barrier set up at what it thinks to b
the most favourable moment by the strongest military state are also inevitable'; finally,
Thibaudet points out this idea of ἀνάγκη in the expression ἀναγκάσαι ἐς τὸ πολεμεῖι
(I. 23), without taking note of the fact that this is a purely local necessity, and rather a
particular obligation than a general law. However, he himself did point out, in a note
added in 1922, that this is solely a historical necessity which is analogous to psychologica
and moral necessity, and one which in no way excludes the factor of human liberty. For
his own part, Thucydides never neglected this fact.

διὰ τοῦτο θαρρεῖτε, ἐνθυμούμενοι ὅτι καὶ ὑμεῖς, ὅτε πλείστων ἤρχετε, τότε πλείστους ἐχθροὺς ἐκέκτητε; and the Thebans add: 'it was only s long as they did not know to whom to address themselves if they eft you that your subjects disguised their hatred: but once the Spartans put themselves at their head, then they showed their real eelings towards you'. In this text, as in that of Thucydides, the idea of a possible repetition of events because of a similarity of conditions s carefully marked. But Xenophon sees only one aspect of the influence which these conditions have: he shows how hatred, and consequently danger, is formed; he does not see what political evolution will result from this as far as the tyrant city is concerned, nor what necessary or probable progress of events will stem from it. For him, this hatred leads directly to rebellion, without passing through the intermediary stage of provoking an extension of the original authority: the law which he establishes is simple, rather hastily made and rather facile, and is all the less reliable since it rests on a rougher analysis. One might perhaps attribute this inferiority of Xenophon's ideas to the circumstances in which the speech is sup-posed to be delivered, since the Thebans had no reason to mention an increase of the imperialistic spirit here. Nevertheless, it is more likely that this over-simplified view of events corresponded to Xenophon's own ideas on the subject, since the person who has treated these matters in the most detail, that is to say Isocrates, has not carried his analysis much further.

It is in the speech which is intended to criticize imperialism, the speech *On the Peace*, that he expresses ideas similar to those we are here studying. He also has understood that the empire constitutes a danger, and he wants to show the Athenians that imperialism is not profitable (74 ff.: οὐ συμφέρει). The first example which he offers to prove his thesis is that of the former Athenian imperialism: Athens made her-self detested: ἀπηχθάνοντο τοῖς Ἕλλησι (79), οὕτω γὰρ ἀκριβῶς εὕρισκον ἐξ ὧν ἄνθρωποι μάλιστ' ἂν μισηθεῖεν (82). She soon began to neglect her real interests in order to obey imperialism, setting out to conquer Sicily when the Spartans were at Decelea, and dreaming of becoming mistress of Italy, Sicily and Carthage when she had ceased to be mistress of Attica (84; 85). This is why the Athenians, having acted as tyrants, have met the fate of tyrants. The ἀρχή corrupted them and thus led them to disaster.

Sparta then provides Isocrates with a second example: scarcely had she acquired the empire than she began to neglect laws and morality.

She thus made herself detested, and was consequently defeated. The beginning of her misfortunes must be placed at the time when she took over the empire of the sea (101).[1] The influence of empire is indeed so great that these two cities, whose political customs were different and yet equally satisfactory, no longer differed from each other once they began to rule: everything happened as if they had both been struck down by the same illness, which inevitably led them to their ruin as it corrupted them (104).

The word νόσος shows the same desire to present abstract explanations in Isocrates as in Thucydides, and the two texts are often very close together in inspiration. Nevertheless, there is a very deep difference between them.

Like Xenophon, Isocrates insists much more than Thucydides on the idea of an inevitable catastrophe. Both authors establish an almost automatic movement pushing the two states regularly to and fro, as each of them is inevitably led from empire to defeat,[2] while their subjects go inevitably from one feeling to another and from one extreme to another.[3] This idea involves a severity towards imperialism which was not shared by Thucydides. In his treatise On the Peace, Isocrates condemns everything which goes beyond mere confederation. Thucydides was much too faithful to Pericles to be able to admit so strict a limit.

If, like Xenophon, Isocrates is more categorical than Thucydides in his attitude towards the evolution and the necessary end of imperialism, it is because his analysis does not go so deep. He notes that the

---

[1] Isocrates repeats the same idea in very similar terms, in paragraphs 59-60 of his *Philippus*. He shows in fact that Alcibiades is responsible for everyone's misfortunes, and especially for those of Sparta since it was on his advice that the Spartans acquired sea-power and were thus led to lose even their supremacy on land.

[2] Isocrates likes to show this progression of forces in one direction and in the other by a balance within his sentence, and by the contrast between the μέν and the δέ; thus we have

102: διὰ μὲν γὰρ τὴν κατὰ γῆν ἡγεμονίαν καὶ τὴν εὐταξίαν καὶ τὴν καρτερίαν τὴν ἐν αὑτῇ μελετωμένην ῥᾳδίως τῆς κατὰ θάλατταν δυνάμεως ἐπεκράτησαν, διὰ δὲ τὴν ἀκολασίαν τὴν ὑπὸ ταύτης τῆς ἀρχῆς αὑτοῖς ἐγγενομένην ταχέως κἀκείνης τῆς ἡγεμονίας ἀπεστερήθησαν.

108: οὐχ ἡ μὲν τῶν ἀττικιζόντων πολυπραγμοσύνη λακωνίζειν τὰς πόλεις ἐποίησεν, ἡ δὲ τῶν λακωνιζόντων ὕβρις ἀττικίζειν τὰς αὐτὰς ταύτας ἠνάγκασεν.

[3] This argument will often be repeated in political discussions. Thus Benjamin Constant (*De l'Esprit de Conquête . . .*, VIII), quotes the words of Clermont-Tonnerre in 1790: 'Everything which tends to limit the king's power is welcomed with enthusiasm, because men recall the excesses of the monarchy. A time will perhaps come when everything which tends to limit the people's power will be welcomed with the same enthusiasm, because men will have had no less intense an experience of the evils of anarchy.' This sentence recalls that of Isocrates (*On the Peace*, 108), quoted above.

same thing happened in two cases, and it is on this that he bases his argument; he does not try to take the sequence of events to pieces and to find out why things happen as they do. He is taken up by the final result, and his statements are all the more sweeping and over-generalized in that they are not based upon deductive evidence.

Nevertheless, there is a difference between Isocrates and Xeno-phon. Even though Isocrates is more superficial than Thucydides and remains unaware of the process analysed by him, he nevertheless does explain — which Xenophon does not do — how Athenian imperialis-tic policy evolved. In his view, however, this evolution corresponds to a moral transformation and to a growth in corruption: corruption produces crimes, crimes provoke hostility, and hostility brings about the fall of the empire. Now Thucydides is just as aware as Isocrates of the existence of a psychological and moral process to which the tyrant city falls victim. It is this process which defines the second law which we have mentioned, the law which explains the mistakes made by Athens and which creates the danger that she may apply the law of force incorrectly. The difference is that in Thucydides this moral law is neither the only nor the most important one to affect the development of events. The political law establishes the condi-tions under which the ruler acts, and its tenor is general; the psycho-logical law merely explains the course of the actions which he successively undertakes under the pressure of these conditions. The first law indicates the trap set for the tyrant city by the nature of empire; the second law explains why the city fails to prevent herself from falling into this trap.

The rigour of Thucydides, which puts every idea in its place, can also be found in the analysis of this second element. Isocrates[1] does not explain why this corruption occurs; doubtless it is caused by the fact that the tyrant people grows drunk with its own power, but he does not say so with any precision, any more than he states to what extent this is an inevitable evolution. Thucydides, on the other hand, gives the formula for this evolution, shows how it works and what influence it has, with a clarity that explains how all his successive judgments fit perfectly together.

[1] Elsewhere (*Panath.*, 116), Isocrates explains the loss of internal κόσμος in the city by the fact that sea-power depends on those who work the ships and who, having lost all their own possessions, live off those of others. This corruption is thus explained by economic reasons, which does not generally seem to be the case. The theory was a little vague in Isocrates' mind, and all the more so as he was interested in the event rather than in the idea.

II. The Psychological Urge

The temptation which leads man to wish for more, in defiance of all reason, is that of excess, or hubris.[1] It is something with which the Greeks are very familiar. Now in Thucydides it shows itself in the following manner: human nature being what it is, man allows himself to be so carried away by success that he conceives immoderate desires. This law is used by Thucydides to explain all the political mistakes described in his work, and those of Athens in particular.

The Spartans apply it to Athenian ambition in the warning which they give in vain in IV. 17. 4: μὴ παθεῖν ὅπερ οἱ ἀήθως τι ἀγαθὸν λαμβάνοντες τῶν ἀνθρώπων· αἰεὶ γὰρ τοῦ πλείονος ἐλπίδι ὀρέγονται διὰ τὸ καὶ τὰ παρόντα ἀδοκήτως εὐτυχῆσαι.

Thucydides himself also applies it to Athenian ambition in his analysis in IV. 65. 4: οὕτω τῇ γε παρούσῃ εὐτυχίᾳ χρώμενοι ἠξίουν σφίσι μηδὲν ἐναντιοῦσθαι, ἀλλὰ καὶ τὰ δυνατὰ ἐν ἴσῳ καὶ τὰ ἀπορώτερα μεγάλῃ τε ὁμοίως καὶ ἐνδεεστέρᾳ παρασκευῇ κατεργάζεσθαι· αἰτία δ' ἦν ἡ παρὰ λόγον τῶν πλειόνων εὐπραγία αὐτοῖς ὑποτιθεῖσα ἰσχὺν τῆς ἐλπίδος.[2]

Nicias also applies it to Athenian ambition in the remark which he makes in VI. 11. 5: ὅπερ νῦν ὑμεῖς, ὦ Ἀθηναῖοι, ἐς Λακεδαιμονίους καὶ τοὺς ξυμμάχους πεπόνθατε· διὰ τὸ παρὰ γνώμην αὐτῶν πρὸς ἃ ἐφοβεῖσθε τὸ πρῶτον περιγεγενῆσθαι, καταφρονήσαντες ἤδη καὶ Σικελίας ἐφίεσθε.

These three texts are sufficient to prove that the law in question plays a large part in 'this desire for more' to which the Athenians yield (πλειόνων ὠρέγοντο), and which controls the whole evolution of their imperialism. What we must therefore do is define its meaning and application.

First of all, it will be noted that there is a difference of nature between the law of hubris and the political law described by Thucydides: here, we are dealing with a truth based on observation. It is most frequently put forward as a general moral maxim. For a Greek of Thucydides' time, the permanence of human nature allowed men to make predictions about future behaviour, and there were general

---

[1] The word is not very often used by Thucydides, but is nevertheless sufficiently frequent for us to know to what it corresponds (cf. III. 39. 4; I. 84. 2); moreover, the Lacedaemonians actually use it to describe an ambitious policy (IV. 18. 2).

[2] And he recalls the same idea in V. 14. 1: οὐκ ἔχοντες τὴν ἐλπίδα τῆς ῥώμης πιστὴν ἔτι, ᾗπερ οὐ προσεδέχοντο πρότερον τὰς σπονδάς, δοκοῦντες τῇ παρούσῃ εὐτυχίᾳ καθυπέρτεροι γενήσεσθαι.

rules which were always valid.[1] There are some of them whose application is more or less general, but whatever may be the field of human experience under observation, it is always a question of man allowing himself to be carried away by an emotional side of his nature and no longer guiding himself by the precepts of reason. One can have, for instance, a remark on the fickleness of the crowd, which soon changes its mind about Pericles (II. 65. 4), or which suddenly becomes enthusiastic over an idea and is carried away by its present excitement in the discussion, as with Cleon (IV. 28. 3), or which soon recovers courage on losing sight of the enemy (VI. 63. 2), or which immediate fear inspires with a new taste for discipline when a disaster has taken place (VIII. 1. 4); or there is at times a comment on the ease with which, in general, men allow themselves to be led by circumstances or by words (I. 140. 1: εἰδὼς τοὺς ἀνθρώπους οὐ τῇ αὐτῇ ὀργῇ ἀναπειθομένους τε πολεμεῖν καὶ ἐν τῷ ἔργῳ πράσσοντας, πρὸς δὲ τὰς ξυμφορὰς καὶ τὰς γνώμας τρεπομένους, or VI. 34. 7: τῶν δ' ἀνθρώπων πρὸς τὰ λεγόμενα καὶ αἱ γνῶμαι ἵστανται . . . ὅπερ ἂν νῦν Ἀθηναῖοι πάθοιεν). On the whole, these are relatively facile observations, recalling the common wisdom distilled in proverbs. 'Man is by nature . . . ', 'Men usually . . . ', phrases of this type, which provide the basis for Greek εὐβουλία, are comparable to the very simple moral statements which have survived from certain of the pre-Socratics and which sum up the purely practical experience which should guide the wise man in his actions. They are valid both for individuals and for the city[2] and indicate merely habits, all too frequent ones certainly, but habits which can be remedied.

The law of hubris is no different from these remarks: it is simply at one and the same time both the most general and the most precise of all these expressions of traditional wisdom.

The mechanism corresponding to this law is very precise: what encourages men to want more is whatever induces them to believe that they can get more; that is to say, success, and especially certain

---

[1] The men of the Renaissance, struck with amazement at such knowledge of mankind, took careful note of all the maxims set down by Thucydides; in H. Estienne's edition, they are brought to the reader's attention by the design of a finger pointing at them in the margin.

[2] In general reflections of this kind, one finds the two expressions brought together:

$$\begin{cases} καὶ \ πόλει \ καὶ \ ἰδιώτῃ \ (I. \ 144. \ 3), \\ καὶ \ πόλεων \ καὶ \ ἰδιωτῶν \ (II. \ 64. \ 6), \\ αἵ \ τε \ πόλεις \ καὶ \ οἱ \ ἰδιῶται \ (III. \ 82. \ 2). \end{cases}$$

forms of success which either seem to be due to chance (men say: if it happened once, why should it not happen again?), or which come unexpectedly, and which, by the surprise that they cause, send reason to sleep (according to the analysis which Thucydides himself gives in II. 61. 3: δουλοῖ γὰρ φρόνημα τὸ αἰφνίδιον καὶ ἀπροσδόκητον καὶ τὸ πλείστῳ παραλόγῳ ξυμβαῖνον).[1] In the expressions dealing with hubris, this idea is marked by the presence of the words: εὐτυχία, παροῦσα εὐτυχία, and: ἀπροσδόκητος, παράλογος εὐπραγία; Cleon says (III. 39. 4): εἴωθε δὲ τῶν πόλεων αἷς ἂν μάλιστα ἀπροσδόκητος καὶ δι' ἐλαχίστου εὐπραξία ἔλθῃ ἐς ὕβριν τρέπειν; Athens, say the Spartans, is falling into the usual fault of men, ἀήθως τι ἀγαθὸν λαμβάνοντες; and Thucydides also speaks in IV. 65. 4 and V. 14. 1 of τῇ γε παρούσῃ εὐτυχίᾳ[2] and, still in IV. 65. 4, of: ἡ παρὰ λόγον τῶν πλειόνων εὐπραγία.

Thus, the way in which men allow themselves to be carried away by a success of this kind is especially characteristic, and the psychological mechanism is then clearer than in any other case. But all forms of prosperity can lead men into error. The very fact of being powerful is enough: ἡ δ' ἐξουσία, says Diodotus, ὕβρει τὴν πλεονεξίαν (παρέχουσα) (III. 45. 4); or the fact that one has increased one's power: οὔτε μείζονος προσγενομένης ὑβρίσαντες (IV. 18. 2): it is simply εὐπραγία by itself which then creates hubris. One thus arrives at maxims like that of Euripides in the first version of the *Hippolytus* (fr. 440 N):

> Ὁρῶ δὲ τοῖς πολλοῖσιν ἀνθρώποις ἐγώ
> τίκτουσαν ὕβριν τὴν πάροιθ' εὐπραξίαν.

The word εὐπραξία can even be replaced by any which indicates prosperity, as in the following fragment of the same play (fr. 441 N):

> ὕβριν τε τίκτει πλοῦτος, οὐ φειδὼ βίου.

---

[1] The passage describes the gloom caused by the plague; now sudden and unreasonable despondency is like an inverted form of hubris. Thucydides describes it in exactly parallel phrases, as in VII. 66. 3: καὶ τῷ παρ' ἐλπίδα τοῦ αὐχήματος σφαλλόμενοι καὶ παρὰ ἰσχὺν τῆς δυνάμεως ἐνδιδόασιν· ὃ νῦν Ἀθηναίους εἰκὸς πεπονθέναι (cf. later pp. 325-326); this error, which is the reverse of that caused by hubris at the same time as it is parallel to it, merely plays a less important role in practice. On its relationship to hubris, cf. below, p. 326, note 1.

[2] In εὐτυχία we must not neglect the idea of *luck*; it is this which explains the choice of the word in a great number of sentences, cf. I. 120. 4: ὅ τε ἐν πολέμῳ εὐτυχίᾳ πλεονάζων οὐκ ἐντεθύμηται θράσει ἀπίστῳ ἐπαιρόμενος.

This is the hubris, the πλεονεξία of prosperous men, which is referred to in the tirade of the *Suppliants* (238-245):

Τρεῖς γὰρ πολιτῶν μερίδες· οἱ μὲν ὄλβιοι
ἀνωφελεῖς τε, πλειόνων τ᾽ ἐρῶσ᾽ ἀεί.

More than for anyone else it lies in wait for the prosperous city, the one which has power and an empire. In the same way as hubris, in *Oedipus Rex*, breeds the tyrant,[1] who will also be led to ruin by it, so under the influence of her own power the tyrant city will give way to the temptations of hubris;[2] she will do so even more readily if unexpected success like that of Pylos fall to her lot.

So to allow oneself to be carried away is therefore quite clearly a mistake: men forget that they may fail,[3] and lose all ability to reason. Like all the facts noted in the maxims of Thucydides, and more so than any other of them, hubris is something that happens in man without his intervention, and without his listening to reason. It is a kind of mishap into which we are propelled by human nature, a feeling of exaltation which takes hold of us at the wrong moment in order to trick us. It is this which is marked by the presence of the word παθεῖν in almost all the phrases concerned with hubris: πάσχειν indicates an accident which happens to a man before being used to describe a feeling which he has; and this nuance is still noticeable.[4]

[1] 873: ὕβρις φυτεύει τύραννον.

[2] This is the idea which Isocrates brings out in *Antidosis*, 316: ἐπειδὴ δ᾽ αὐξηθείσης τῆς πόλεως καὶ λαβούσης τὴν ἀρχὴν οἱ πατέρες ἡμῶν μᾶλλον θαρρήσαντες τοῦ συμφέροντος ...

[3] It is always the uncertainty of chance which is invoked as a warning against hubris: the speech of the Lacedaemonians in Book IV is the best proof of this, and the theatre provides innumerable examples of maxims of this type: no one is happy for ever. See Euripides, for example, *Hecuba*, 283 and 956, quoted above, p. 183, *Auge.*, fr. 275 N; *Ino*, 424 N.

In certain cases, one even arrives at the idea of a sort of immanent justice: those who are raised up are later cast down. Between one destiny and the next there may not even be a sin of pride; this is proved by the passage in which Polydorus applies a similar reflection to his mother (*Hecuba*, 57-8):

ἀντισηκώσας δέ σε
φθείρει θεῶν τις τῆς πάροιθ᾽ εὐπραξίας.

This is an older form of hubris, in which prosperity alone *constitutes* hubris; one finds it in this form in Herodotus (see below, p. 327), but never in Thucydides, whose attitude is too scientific to accept it.

[4] One can see this by the parallelism with sentences where the word cannot designate a feeling, like I. 40. 2: ὅστις μὴ τοῖς δεξαμένοις, εἰ σωφρονοῦσι, πόλεμον ἀντ᾽ εἰρήνης ποιήσει· νῦν ὑμεῖς μὴ πειθόμενοι ἡμῖν πάθοιτε ἄν. The word retains the idea that one falls into error, an idea which appears in VII. 42. 3: οὐδὲ παθεῖν ὅπερ Νικίας ἔπαθεν — besides, for a Greek, any 'passion' is an unfortunate adventure.

Y

This word has already been noted in VI. 34. 7, and it recurs everywhere when excessive desires are mentioned:[1] thus in two of the phrases dealing with the hubris of Athens: IV. 17. 4 (μὴ παθεῖν ὅπερ . . .); VI. 11. 5 (ὅπερ νῦν ὑμεῖς . . . πεπόνθατε); and in other texts where the idea is the same, as, for example:

I. 80. 1: μήτε ἀπειρίᾳ ἐπιθυμῆσαί τινα τοῦ ἔργου, ὅπερ ἂν οἱ πολλοὶ πάθοιεν.

V. 103. 2 (it is a question of the dangers caused by false hopes): ὅ ὑμεῖς ἀσθενεῖς τε καὶ ἐπὶ ῥοπῆς μιᾶς ὄντες, μὴ βούλεσθε παθεῖν, μηδὲ ὁμοιωθῆναι τοῖς πολλοῖς, οἷς παρὸν ἀνθρωπείως ἔτι σῴζεσθαι . . .

VI. 13. 1: μηδ’ ὅπερ ἂν αὐτοὶ πάθοιεν, δυσέρωτας εἶναι τῶν ἀπόντων.

The use of the word in this case is not peculiar to Thucydides, and can be found in a large number of contemporary authors.[2]

Since hubris is characterized by the triumph of the passions over the reason, the phrases which express it are distinguished by a highly specialized affective vocabulary. Thus, one notes the words ὀρέγεσθαι and ἐφίεσθαι,[3] ἐπαίρεσθαι, ἐπιθυμία[4] (which indicates motive), ἐλπίς (which appears every time that Athens or another city allows herself to be carried away in an unreasonable manner), ἔρως (which is used in a theory as to the nature of hubris by Diodotus, and, later, in relation to Sicily), θράσος and θρασύτης (which replace τόλμα: cf. I. 120. 4; II. 61. 4 and IV. 92. 5); finally ὀργή which is contrasted with γνώμη and indicates any act performed on impulse.[5] These

---

[1] Or, on the other hand, excessive depression, which, as has been noted above, is only another aspect of the same idea. Thus VII. 69. 2: Nicias, νομίσας, ὅπερ πάσχουσιν ἐν τοῖς μεγάλοις ἀγῶσι, πάντα τε ἔργῳ ἔτι σφίσιν ἐνδεᾶ εἶναι καὶ λόγῳ αὐτοῖς οὔπω ἱκανῶ εἰρῆσθαι.

[2] To quote only thinkers very close to Thucydides, this use can be found in Thrasymachus (Diels B 1): ἀποδείξω γ᾽ ἐν τῷ λέγειν πεπονθότας πρὸς ἀλλήλους ὅπερ ἀνάγκη τοὺς ἄνευ γνώμης φιλονικοῦντας πάσχειν· οἰόμενοι γὰρ ἐναντία λέγειν ἀλλήλοις, οὐκ αἰσθάνονται τὰ αὐτὰ πράττοντες; or in the anonymous text from Iamblichus (4, p. 98, 17, 2); and, above all, naturally, in Euripides, as in the Heracleidae, 176, the Cresphontes, 460, or, with an application even closer to that now under consideration, Incert. Fab., fr. 1062 N:
πέπονθας οἷα χἄτεροι πολλοὶ βροτῶν·
τὰς γὰρ παρούσας οὐχὶ σῴζοντες τύχας
ὤλοντ᾽ ἐρῶντες μειζόνων ἀβουλίᾳ.

[3] Cf. p. 77, n. 2.

[4] See I. 84. 2; I. 120. 4; III. 45. 1; III. 45. 6; IV. 18. 4; VI. 11. 6.

[5] Zahn has a very interesting note (18) on the idea of ὀργή indicating (by contrast to γνώμη) any irrational motivation for an act; she mentions certain similar contrasts between the use by man of his rational forces, or his obedience to πάθη; such are: ἐπιθυμία – πρόνοια; φρόνημα – καταφρόνημα; αὔχημα – γνώμη; ἀμαθία – ξύνεσις.

different expressions appear in all the analyses in which Thucydides explains decisions which he finds unreasonable; many are grouped together in the long passage dealing with the Sicilian expedition in VI. 24. 3. Each one, taken alone, would be sufficient to evoke a moral climate in which men allow themselves to be carried away by hubris.

Wisdom, on the other hand, consists of resisting these different tendencies, and in 'maintaining one's happiness'. Thucydides defines it in this way on a number of occasions.[1]

If, neglecting wisdom, man gives way to his passions, he no longer takes into account what he can reasonably hope to achieve; he undertakes things without any longer being really strong enough: μεγάλη τε ὁμοίως καὶ ἐνδεεστέρᾳ παρασκευῇ (IV. 65. 4). The speeches of the Lacedaemonians or of Nicias tend to show Athens how imprudently she is acting; for irrational decisions carry their own punishment with them: failure.

Hubris, such as it is presented by Thucydides, is thus a perfectly logical mechanism which might be called an imprudence born of success. His realistic frame of mind transforms 'an attempt to rise above one's condition' into 'an undertaking beyond one's powers', and nemesis is no longer the punishment sent by the Gods but the logical result of human mistakes. The process which carries man first from success to exaltation, then from exaltation to imprudence, and finally from imprudence to failure is perfectly clear. Hubris thus becomes something strictly human.

Originally, hubris and nemesis were essentially religious ideas; the jealousy of a god was needed to give its meaning to the first and its reality to the second. Thus, in Herodotus, Artabanus explains to Xerxes (VII, 10): 'You know, my lord, that amongst living creatures it is the great ones that God smites with his thunder, out of envy for their pride. The little ones do not vex him. It is always the great buildings and the tall trees that are struck by lightning. It is God's way to bring the lofty low. Often a great army is destroyed by a little one, when God in his envy puts fear into men's hearts, or

---

[1] I. 120. 3: ἀνδρῶν γὰρ σωφρόνων μέν ἐστιν . . . μήτε τῇ κατὰ πόλεμον εὐτυχίᾳ ἐπαίρεσθαι μήτε τῷ ἡσύχῳ τῆς εἰρήνης ἡδόμενον ἀδικεῖσθαι; I. 84. 2, where it shows the σωφροσύνη ἔμφρων of Sparta; IV. 18. 4; V. 46. 1; VIII. 24. 4. This definition is repeated in almost identical terms in Thrasymachus (Diels B 1; 3rd edition, p. 279, 27) and inspires numerous comments in both prose writers and poets (cf. in particular Lysias, *Epit.*, 10; Isocr., *Panath.*, 32; Euripides, *Incert. Fab.*, fr. 955 N).

sends a thunderstorm, and they are cut to pieces in a way that they do not deserve. For God tolerates pride in none but Himself' (transl. Aubrey de Sélincourt, Penguin Classics). Then a moral idea begins to make itself felt, as high position presupposes pride and involves responsibility. In Thucydides' work, only the logical and human aspect of the notion is to be found; and we can see what becomes of the old maxims of Greek wisdom when they are passing through the hands of the sophists and the 'modern' thinkers.[1]

Of course, this does not mean that all moral disapproval of hubris has disappeared in Thucydides. Hubris stands in opposition to the old idea of moderation;[2] in so far as it leads to the desire for more than is a man's due, it contradicts the idea of justice, and in this it shocks Thucydides' feelings as it does those of any man. The only point which should be noted is that his work brings out not the moral failings which the notion involves but the political mistakes wherein it shows, the sin against reality which reality itself punishes. This explains why the phrases dealing with hubris can also apply to Athens' enemies, like the over-courageous Melians or the feather-headed subjects who allow themselves to be carried away by the taking of Amphipolis.

As a crime against reality, hubris also exists in cases where reality nevertheless seems to justify the particular undertaking: at Mytilene, at Pylos, at Melos, Athens does not seem to be presuming on her strength. The explanation is that certain mistakes, in this or in any other order, are not immediately punished. The political problem of ruling involved, as we saw, both its demands and its dangers. Therefore it is not enough for the tyrant city that its act should be temporarily successful; in its case, the problem is a more difficult one to deal with: force does not simply regulate the practical conditions of

---

[1] In Thucydides' own day, and in his work, the pious Nicias puts forward an older, both moral and religious, version of the idea: Nicias supposes, in fact (VII. 77. 3-4) that the Sicilian expedition has awoken divine jealousy (εἴ τῳ θεῶν ἐπίφθονοι ἐστρατεύσαμεν). but he comforts himself by thinking that Athens has now been sufficiently cast down: οἴκτου γὰρ ἀπ' αὐτῶν ἀξιώτεροι ἤδη ἐσμὲν ἢ φθόνου. This shows us the evolution of the idea, and at the same time reveals with what care Thucydides fitted his arguments to the people expressing them.

On the other hand, hubris is understood in Sophocles (*Oedipus Rex*, 873 ff.) almost as it is in Thucydides: 'Insolence breeds the tyrant; Insolence once vainly surfeited on wealth that is not meet nor good for it, when it has scaled the topmost ramparts, is hurled to a dire doom, wherein no service of the feet can serve' (transl. Jebb).

[2] Greek teaching was that men should 'moderate their desires'; thus Artabanus in Herodotus maintained (VII, 16, 2): ὡς κακὸν εἴη διδάσκειν τὴν ψυχὴν πλέον τι δίζησθαι αἰεὶ ἔχειν τοῦ παρεόντος; and next we have: ἐπιστάμενος ὡς κακὸν εἴη τὸ πολλῶν ἐπιθυμέειν.

effective action, but becomes a bait leading the city on to further acts of madness.

Thus power, by making its possessor drunk, incites him to acts of hubris, and, at the same time, by the problems which it imposes on him and by the appearance of impunity that it rather treacherously conveys, it makes him less conscious of the dangers threatening his position. Wisdom is thus very difficult for him to achieve, especially if he is no longer held back by any purely moral considerations.[1]

This wisdom can nevertheless be achieved, and the two laws whose mechanism we have just studied now enable us to say under what conditions; we can thus reach the very principle on which, whatever the time and circumstances, the different judgments by Thucydides on Athenian imperialism are based.

APPLICATION OF THE TWO FIRST LAWS: THE CONDITIONS OF WISDOM

In Book III, in his speech on Mytilene, Diodotus puts forward a whole theory of unreasonable ambition. What he says includes all the different aspects of hubris that we have enumerated: power giving birth to ambition, through the medium of hubris and of pride; man being led by the passion of the moment (ὀργή); hope and desire (ἥ τε ἐλπὶς καὶ ὁ ἔρως) the one leading, the other following, and both playing an equally nefarious part (πλεῖστα βλάπτουσι); chance (ἡ τύχη) providing arguments to justify exaltation (ἐς τὸ ἐπαίρειν); and, finally, an enterprise undertaken with insufficient means (ἐκ τῶν ὑποδεεστέρων): it seems indeed as if this text is deliberately written to apply to the Athenian attitude. Now Diodotus adds that this process works even more surely with cities than with individuals, and he adds that this is explicable 'because they are throwing for a higher stake, freedom or empire, and because when a man has a whole people acting with him, he magnifies himself out of all reason'.[2] This is a most important remark.

An individual can, by the use of reason, attain σωφροσύνη, and keep this 'human nature' under control, even when it 'leaps eagerly forward towards a particular act', as Diodotus has it. But can a crowd of men do this? Thucydides does not think so; he does not believe that men can act rationally when they are in a group, and he despises

[1] As we pass from Pericles to Cleon, both morality and wisdom are lost together.
[2] Similarly, he says earlier that the people cannot think in a sufficiently mature fashion (III. 43. 4): ὑμῶν τῶν δι' ὀλίγου σκοπούντων.

the mob. He likes to remind his reader of how easily it is swayed by this 'human nature', and a number of examples have already been quoted of the way he judges it, as in II. 65. 4: ὅπερ φιλεῖ ὅμιλος ποιεῖν — IV. 28. 3: οἶον ὄχλος φιλεῖ ποιεῖν — VI. 63. 2: οἶον δὴ ὄχλος φιλεῖ θαρσήσας ποιεῖν — VIII. 1. 4: ὅπερ φιλεῖ δῆμος ποιεῖν: in all these phrases, he insists on the absence of any control, on the changeability of the crowd and its swift and fleeting onsets of enthusiasm. Now, taken by itself, a city is nothing more than a vast crowd, in which each man's passions grow on contact with his neighbour's, while reason falls silent. Moreover, in another part of his speech (42), Diodotus shows how, in a city susceptible to flattery, the wise man dares not speak and seals his lips for fear of calumny: the crowd is thus incapable of guiding itself by reason, and extremely difficult to guide for those who can attain reason on their own account.

This inability of the people to follow reason is confirmed by what we have already noted in the second part of this book: that the desire for more, which is inspiring Athens' actions, is essentially the characteristic of the people.

Thus, in the same way as a wise conduct in individual matters is possible only if reason keeps the passions in check, if γνώμη governs ὀργή, so in politics wise actions are possible only if a rationally minded and personally disinterested leader can hold his own against the crowd and make his own γνώμη prevail over their ὀργαί. The Athenian crowd, as much a slave of its own passions as the young and barbarous Cyrus, needs to have, as he did, an Artabanus by their side; and the fate of the crowd will depend upon the authority which this Artabanus possesses.

It is thus in the way the Athenian constitution works that we must try to discover the origin of her foreign policy and judge the value that this has.

This truth explains not only the different opinions expressed by Thucydides in his work, but every single detail in the way in which he formulates them. When, talking of the outcome of the war in II. 65, he contrasts Pericles with his successors, he insists not on his foreign policy but solely on his relationship with the people.[1] This

---

[1] In general, in the same way as Greek wisdom depends essentially on the contrast between reason and the passions, so the action of the good leader in a democracy is considered first and foremost to be a negative and moderating force. Plutarch (Per., 39, 4) concludes his remarks about Pericles' authority (following Thucydides in this) by saying: τοσαύτη φθορὰ καὶ πλῆθος ἐπέκειτο κακίας τοῖς πράγμασιν, ἣν ἐκεῖνος ἀσθενῆ καὶ ταπεινὴν ποιῶν <u>ἀπέκρυπτε</u> καὶ <u>κατεκώλυεν</u> ἀνήκεστον ἐν ἐξουσίᾳ γενέσθαι.

passage is so important that it must be quoted in its entirety: 'The reason for the difference was that he, deriving authority from his capacity and acknowledged worth, being also a man of transparent integrity, was able to control the multitude in a free spirit; he led them rather than was led by them; for, not seeking power by dishonest means, he had no need to say pleasant things, but, on the strength of his own high character, could venture to oppose and even to anger them.[1] When he saw them unseasonably elated and arrogant (ὕβρει), his words humbled and awed them; and, when they were depressed by groundless fears, he sought to reanimate their confidence. Thus Athens, though still in name a democracy, was in fact ruled by her greatest citizen. But his successors were more on an equality with one another, and, each struggling to be first himself, they were ready to sacrifice (ἐνδιδόναι) the whole conduct of affairs to the whims of the people. Such weakness in a great and imperial city[2] led to many errors, of which the greatest was the Sicilian expedition.' The analysis I have just given of the almost abstract mechanism of the law of imperialism now makes it possible to appreciate the full meaning of this passage in all its significance.

The same thing can apply to the rest of the work. Indeed, as Rose Zahn has shown,[3] everything, from the first speech of Pericles onwards, depends upon the contrast between γνώμη and ὀργή (this ὀργή on which Archidamus is already counting to ruin Athens and which, in fact, without the authority of Pericles would have then led her to her doom): and the way in which Thucydides presents Pericles' successors, like the words which he puts into their mouths, reveals the same idea as a guiding theme running through all his work.

It is first of all noticeable in Cleon. Thucydides notes two things about him: he has no moderation himself, and he is in agreement with the people (καὶ ἐς τὰ ἄλλα βιαιότατος τῶν πολιτῶν, τῷ τε δήμῳ παρὰ πολὺ ἐν τῷ τότε πιθανώτατος). His speech on Mytilene defends a decision taken ὑπὸ ὀργῆς and defends it by denying any

---

[1] Jowett's translation is the one quoted here; the meaning adopted is the same as in Arnold and some others. Generally, one translates: 'to oppose them both with authority and *with anger*. In fact, everything that has been shown here about Thucydides' ideas would suggest that πρός has, in this sentence, a more precise meaning: '*in reply to their anger, against their anger*'. This construction is possible with ἀντιλέγειν, as we can see in Demosthenes, *Against Aphobos*, 14.

[2] That is to say, where the temptation of hubris is greater (law of hubris), and its risks more dangerous.

[3] Pp. 59-61.

right to critical examination and free discussion. It is certainly not Cleon, who blindly tells the Athenians to assume a tyrant's soul, who will be able to avoid falling into the trap of the political law. And this absolute submission of Cleon to popular opinion is made even clearer by the remarks assigned to Diodotus: this surely is the purpose of the long and at first sight rather surprising passage which opens his speech and shows the dangers of haste and anger (τάχος τε καὶ ὀργήν); the conclusion of this section sets down what circumstances are most favourable to deliberation, and Diodotus denounces the danger of trying to please the people (πρὸς χάριν – χαριζόμενός τι, III. 42. 6) exactly as Demosthenes will do later. When judged by the light of the idea with which we are now concerned, all these commentaries are seen to be never more relevant to the very essence of the question than when they appear to depart from it.

The refusal of peace in Book IV also provides the opportunity for an analysis of hubris; and this hubris is shown as being that of the people, whom Cleon merely leads in the direction which they have already chosen (ἐνῆγε).

Thus the same idea governs the composition of both episodes. As Thibaudet points out, 'Cléon s'oppose à Périclès comme le θυμός au νοῦς' (p. 203), or again: 'le gouvernement de Périclès, c'est la démocratie en confiance avec l'intelligence, le gouvernement de Cléon la démocratie en défiance avec l'intelligence'. This is because Cleon is himself unreasonable, and is neither sufficiently disinterested nor sufficiently powerful to stand out against the people's folly.

The same thing is true of Alcibiades. He cannot be a real leader, because he is no readier than Cleon to sacrifice his own interests to those of the city (V. 43. 2; VI. 15. 2), and is himself no more reasonable a man than Cleon. In Book VI, he is presented by phrases which suggest his desires (to oppose Nicias) and hope (profit from a success in Sicily and Carthage); these words already evoke the climate of hubris – and the phrase soon follows when Thucydides says of him (VI. 15. 3): ταῖς ἐπιθυμίαις μείζοσιν ἢ κατὰ τὴν ὑπάρχουσαν δύναμιν ἐχρῆτο ἔς τε τὰς ἱπποτροφίας καὶ τὰς ἄλλας δαπάνας. Neither should we forget that Alcibiades was to provide Socrates and Plato with the clearest example of an extraordinarily gifted nature lacking in wisdom and self-control.

Himself subject to the temptations of πλεονεξία, and concerned more with his own interest than with that of the people, Alcibiades is no more fitted than Cleon to hold the Athenians back on the road along which they are being driven by their passion. And here again, everything which we might find surprising in the structure of the two speeches can be explained by this fundamental idea. Nicias' criticism of Alcibiades, just like Diodotus' criticism of Cleon, puts him in a definite category of men and thus enables the reader to understand where the fault originates. The only difference is that this time the category of men subject to hubris are no longer the enemies of intelligence but simply the young. It is in opposition to the immoderate desires of these young men that Nicias repeats the phrases describing σωφροσύνη: μηδ' ὅπερ ἂν αὐτοὶ πάθοιεν, δυσέρωτας εἶναι τῶν ἀπόντων, γνόντας ὅτι ἐπιθυμίᾳ μὲν ἐλάχιστα κατορθοῦνται, προνοίᾳ δὲ πλεῖστα (VI. 13. 1).

This great duel between πρόνοια and ἐπιθυμία, between wisdom and hubris, thus dominates the history of Athenian imperialism. By acting in such a way that it was the latter which triumphed, Athens, as Thucydides tells us in II. 65, brought about her own downfall. By giving way to the tendencies driving her forward, she gave full rein to those forces which make up 'human nature' and which she should have kept under control. She thus changed and suffered corruption, like Livy's Rome; and it may be that the Funeral Oration, when placed side by side with the judgment in II. 65, finds in this very idea a new and intimate *raison d'être*.[1]

Athens could scarcely fail to bring about her own doom. As Thibaudet has very well shown (p. 112), we are in the presence of 'a will to power which had to accept the fatality imposed upon it of never being able to fix its own limits freely or to allow itself a gradual, disciplined development.[2] This ability to discipline oneself,' he continues 'does not belong naturally to man, whether an individual or a city, as some innate gift. It is something which the individual acquires through making an effort, through the help of philosophy, through

---

[1] In the conclusion of the *Antidosis*, Isocrates shows how Athens was ruined by the over-confidence which her empire gave her, and which submitted her to the influence of the sycophants; they introduce civil war into the city, treat the allies badly, cause both war and disaster. Thucydides himself does not talk about the 'sycophants', but it is roughly their reign that he is denouncing. In their view of the mechanism leading Athens to her doom, the attitude of the two authors is the same.

[2] Thibaudet does not make a clear distinction between the two ideas of political necessity (such as it has been described above) and allowing oneself to be carried away by hubris. Since her rule depends upon force, Athens cannot 'fix her own limits freely' as regards her will to power: the political necessity precludes that. But if she cannot 'allow herself a gradual, disciplined development', this is solely because she is carried away by hubris.

that of religion. And although it is less frequent, there are examples of
states which have managed to do this: under the emperors, Rome
both measured out and deliberately limited her expansion; at the
time of Vergennes, the French monarchy had attained the same
measure of wisdom; and Sparta, left to herself, would certainly not
have abandoned it'. But the first of these examples did not last, and
the third is merely hypothetical: it ceased to be true as soon as
Sparta tasted success and empire. Perhaps, indeed, wisdom can be
achieved, but only with great difficulty – and with even greater
difficulty in a democracy. The ideal constitution of Athens cannot
work without a leader of genius; [1] Periclean democracy is the finest of
regimes, but democracy without Pericles is the worst – at least from
the point of view of foreign policy, the only one, as we have seen,
with which Thucydides is concerned. Now a Pericles may appear
once or even twice but not as a general rule: [2] the day will come
when the people will no longer have wise men to guide and counsel
them, and then there will begin the reign of 'human nature', consisting in passions and doomed to disaster. Thucydides does not
establish an *a priori* link between the mistakes of a sea-power and the
existence of democracy, nor does he confuse *a priori* the two questions,
as was usually done: instead, like Isocrates, [3] he makes a clear separa-
tion between them in order to devote himself entirely to the study of
foreign policy. But, in the last resort, the study of foreign policy
brings him to the internal problem of democracy; and the two questions do come together in the final, systematic analysis which is the
result of his reflection.

Because of this, Thibaudet makes him into the predecessor of the
thinkers of the fourth century, in that we can see in his work the
origin of the idea that will then be developed of a King ruling over an
empire. 'Xenophon' writes Thibaudet (p. 201) 'will be haunted by
this idea, and will make it crystallize round Cyrus the younger,
Agesilaus, and Cyrus the elder. In the speech *Nicocles*, Isocrates will
sum up the arguments in favour of a monarchy, and even Plato, the
philosopher of the city kept within precise boundaries, the enemy
of these unwholesome and swollen empires, will place on the horizon
of his *Politicus* and his *Republic* the fine, idealized figure of a king.'

---

[1] See Werner Jaeger, *Paideia*, I. p. 409 of the English translation.

[2] There is no way of obtaining such a result, if it is true that political wisdom (such as it
is envisaged here) cannot be transmitted (*Meno*, 93-94).

[3] Cf. Mathieu, *Les idées* . . . , p. 120.

In fact, one occasionally does find in philosophers, and especially in Plato, this mistrust which the intellectual feels towards the mob, and which characterizes the ideas of Thucydides; in the *Politicus* (300 e), Plato declares that the crowd could obviously never learn the art of the King or the art of politics. But we must beware of making any over-hasty comparisons. Only Plato can be compared to Thucydides, because like him he places the quality of a regime not in its form but in how it works.[1] And Thucydides had even less intention than Plato of providing a formula that would say what is actually to be done. He did not even try to make men understand where imperialism should have stopped: the great effort of Isocrates to define a system of rule which did not repeat the mistakes of the first Athenian empire would have been quite foreign to him;[2] in his eyes, this is not a problem that men can hope to solve or settle in advance. Wishing to make his work a κτῆμα εἰς αἰεί, he wanted to rise, by a process of abstraction and generalization, to an intellectual notion that would enable men to understand, not only the pattern of the Peloponnesian War, but any facts that might follow this pattern in the future. And the final notion which he attains is less a solution for future problems than an explanation of what happened. By the definition which it gives of the fundamental principle which lies behind all the mistakes made by imperialism, his work does, it is true, tend to forestall them in the future; but this is a task which demands the presence of a man of the highest talents. The History thus provides only rather a vague plan for successful action, since it makes the realization of this plan depend upon the exceptional merit of a single individual.[3]

As the two laws which provide arguments both for the supporters

[1] Cf. The definition given in the *Politicus* (293 c): ἀναγκαῖον δὴ καὶ πολιτειῶν, ὡς ἔοικε, ταύτην διαφερόντως ὀρθὴν εἶναι καὶ μόνην πολιτείαν, ἐν ᾗ τις ἂν εὑρίσκοι τοὺς ἄρχοντας ἀληθῶς ἐπιστήμονας καὶ οὐ δοκοῦντας μόνον, ἐάντε κατὰ νόμους ἐάντε ἄνευ νόμων ἄρχωσι, καὶ ἑκόντων ἢ ἀκόντων, ἢ πενόμενοι ἢ πλουτοῦντες, τούτων ὑπολογιστέον οὐδὲν οὐδαμῶς εἶναι κατ' οὐδεμίαν ὀρθότητα.

[2] Eight years after her defeat, Athens will leap at the chance of going to war again in order to recover her empire (Xen., *Hell.*, III, 5, 10: ὅτι μέν, ὦ ἄνδρες Ἀθηναῖοι, βούλοισθ' ἂν τὴν ἀρχὴν ἣν πρότερον ἐκέκτησθε ἀναλαμβάνειν, πάντες ἐπιστάμεθα): no better confirmation could be found for the validity of Thucydides' analysis. When Deonna writes (*L'éternel Présent*, R.E.G., 1922, p. 6): 'The lesson was not heeded ... and the second Athenian empire repeated the mistakes of the first', one must point out that this fact was foreseen in the very 'lesson' that was not heeded.

[3] In this respect, the only theoretician who can be compared to him is Aristotle. When it is a question of choosing between the different forms of government, Aristotle makes their respective merits clearly depend upon the existence in a citizen, a family or a people, of a superior virtue which can impose itself for the sake of the general good (*Pol.*, 1288 a, 34).

and the opponents of imperialism come together, the truth stands out in its frightening impartiality. Less sweeping than Isocrates in his condemnation of Athenian imperialism — in that he still considers that it could have been governed wisely — Thucydides is also less optimistic: he does not believe in the wise system of rule that Isocrates would like to see established, and which would always be so well organized that it would be a real rule and yet never turn into an empire. He does not believe that a political reform can provide a fundamental remedy for evils which spring from the nature of man himself.

In so far as it here comes into contact with a fundamental human element, the analysis of hubris links up with the third law of imperialism, the one that we have called the philosophical law.

III. THE PHILOSOPHICAL LAW

The philosophical law, which speaks of ruling because one is stronger, is strangely close in content to the law of hubris, which speaks of allowing oneself to be carried away by one's own power. And this similarity is all the more surprising since the first is invoked by the supporters and the second by the enemies of imperialism: it is thus on the difference between the two laws that the final value of the process analysed must rest.

The law of strength, or philosophical law, depends like the law of hubris on an observation of 'human nature'. The Athenians in Book I speak of τοῦ ἀνθρωπείου τρόπου (I. 76. 2) and of τῇ ἀνθρωπείᾳ φύσει (I. 76. 3); the Athenians in Book V speak of τὸ ἀνθρώπειον, and show this ἀνθρώπειον as determined by a necessity of its own nature: ἀπὸ φύσεως ἀναγκαίας (V. 105). Similarly, Hermocrates explains the principle in question by announcing: πέφυκε γὰρ τὸ ἀνθρώπειον (IV. 61. 5).

On the other hand, like that of hubris, this law impels man to undertake action (I. 76. 2: ἰσχύϊ τι κτήσασθαι; V. 89: οἱ προύχοντες πράσσουσι; V. 105: δρῶντας ἂν ταὐτό). It thus shows itself in facts, as hubris does, by the action of πλεονεξία. Πλεονεξία is a fault, into which Athens falls, and which is indicated by the expression πλείονος ὀρέγεσθαι, the one which Diodotus explains by hubris: ἡ δ' ἐξουσία ὕβρει τὴν πλεονεξίαν καὶ φρονήματι (παρέχουσα), and the one which Thucydides attacks in individuals (III. 82. 8: moral disorder comes from πλεονεξίαν καὶ φιλοτιμίαν); but, in the eyes of the law with which we are at the moment concerned, it is a legitimate attitude, before which considerations of justice give way (justice, ὃν οὐδείς πω προθεὶς τοῦ μὴ <u>πλέον ἔχειν</u> ἀπετράπετο says I. 76. 2); and which should be <u>excused</u> rather than blamed (καὶ τοὺς μὲν Ἀθηναίους ταῦτα πλεονεκτεῖν τε καὶ προνοεῖσθαι πολλὴ ξυγγνώμη καὶ οὐ τοῖς ἄρχειν <u>βουλομένοις</u> μέμφομαι, ἀλλὰ . . . IV. 61. 5).

Nevertheless, this πλεονεξία presents a different aspect in each of the two cases.

The πλεονεξία due to hubris was an accident, an unfortunate occurrence which the wise man avoided. Men only gave themselves over to it when they were lured on by a lucky chance, carried away by surprise, drunk with power; it was part of human nature as one might say that boastfulness is part of human nature (V. 68. 2: τὸ ἀνθρώπειον κομπῶδες). This does not mean that it is an integral part of man's essence. The law of force, on the other hand, is given as the rule of the world: αἰεὶ καθεστῶτος – οὐδείς πω . . . ἀπετράπετο, these indications in Book I correspond to the expression in Book V: οὔτε θέντες τὸν νόμον οὔτε κειμένῳ πρῶτοι χρησάμενοι, ὄντα δὲ παραλαβόντες καὶ ἐσόμενον ἐς αἰεὶ καταλείψοντες χρώμεθα αὐτῷ, εἰδότες καὶ ὑμᾶς ἂν καὶ ἄλλους ἐν τῇ αὐτῇ δυνάμει ἡμῖν γενομένους δρῶντας ἂν ταὐτό. It is by this universal character that the law of force can be invoked as an excuse, and πλεονεξία considered as legitimate.

But this universal quality is conferred on the law of force only by those who observe it, and every man is free to become an exception. The law is valid only if one accepts the ἀνθρωπεία φύσις, if one has no ideal which transcends it, and if one does not introduce a new and freely chosen norm into this process which otherwise tends to govern human actions as the law of gravity governs the behaviour of objects. The Boeotians and the Melians may perhaps only speak of justice because they are weak, but Pericles speaks of a glory which presumes some form of disinterested feelings, and the Athenians in Book I speak of moderation. When Thucydides puts forward the law of force he is expressing a principle on which any imperialism conceived as tyranny necessarily depends to a greater or lesser extent, but which tells us less what we ought to think than how imperialists think themselves. While the law of hubris was recognized by everybody but did not apply to everybody, the law of force is not recognized by everybody, but nevertheless whoever recognizes it has to give it universal application: according to Thucydides, this is the attitude adopted by imperialism, when it acts according to its essence.

But for πλεονεξία to receive this character of universality, it must cease to be simply a sort of mishap and must be in some way rectified, so that it can be practically carried out and, in some way at least, justified: the πλεονεξία which is based on force does have something of this quality. Hubris, such as it is presented in Thucydides, only incidentally assumes the aspect of a moral failing: it ignores wisdom and prudence, leads men to neglect reality, to undertake plans which are beyond their means, so that eventually it is reality itself which punishes them. The law of force, on the other hand, which contradicts law and justice exactly as hubris does, nevertheless conforms very closely to reality. Hubris acts παρὰ ἰσχὺν τῆς δυνάμεως (cf. VII. 66. 3); the law of force, on the other hand, presumes that one undertakes only what is exactly within one's means: παρατυχὸν ἰσχύϊ τι κτήσα-σθαι — δυνατὰ δὲ οἱ προύχοντες πράσσουσι — οὗ ἂν κρατῇ ἄρχειν; on this point, the texts are extremely precise, and it is here that the great difference between the two domains is to be found. In the Melian dialogue, all the affective vocabulary which indicates political error is used to describe the Melians' attitude; the Athenians may be making a mistake, but not if one considers only the particular occasion and their immediate success. Consequently, we can say that if both hubris and the law of force bring about actions of similar nature, the difference between them lies in the fact that those undertaken according to the law of force are well calculated to succeed, while those undertaken through hubris are badly calculated and therefore predestined to failure.

In practice, of course, one set may mingle with the other, and we have already seen that when the law of force is applied clumsily, it can become the instrument of hubris (Thucydides hints that this is the case in the affair of Melos). The use of force on one occasion may indirectly bring about failure in the future, and the respect which men pay to force is often merely a symptom of excess, a predisposition to hubris on their part.

Taken by itself, however, the law of force does not simply come down to being an unconscious form of hubris. Like the political law, it creates the opportunity for error but is not directly the cause of it and does not make it inevitable. The phrases used by Thucydides to describe it are intended less to show the folly of Athens' conduct than to bring out the principle on which she acts, such as both the Athenians and others may recognize it and admit its existence. In principle at least, no two things are wider apart than an act committed under the influence of hubris (in the sense which we have given to this concept up to now), and an act performed according to force. Certainly the real difference between the two lies only in two different attitudes to reality, but it is a difference whose importance is essential.[1]

Thucydides certainly looks upon action based on the principles of force with the same emotional and moral disapproval which, in spite of everything, he still has towards hubris; in him as in other writers, the word πλεονεξία has a disparaging sense, and his feelings are revealed quite clearly in the words which he puts into the mouth of the Theban Pagondas (IV. 92. 7), or even in the distinction which he makes between an imperialism which is still controlled by the presence of an ideal, like that of Pericles and the Athenians in Book I, and an imperialism which gives itself entirely over to principles of realism in politics, like that of Cleon or of the Athenians in Book V. But this moral disapproval is somehow independent of his political judgment; in the same way as his actual denunciation of hubris is based solely on reality, so whatever is performed in accordance with reality receives his intellectual approval, however reluctantly he may give it; and he cannot denounce acts based on real force as he does those committed under the effect of hubris. As long as it remains prudent, imperialism merely follows the way of the world.

If the law of force has so much wider a field of application than that of hubris, it does not seem to allow either the law of hubris or that of political necessity a very large place in the system of imperialism. And, in fact, since the imperialists themselves recognize it as a universal and inevitable principle, it is alone sufficient to explain the evolution of imperialism, and makes all other considerations unnecessary. There is no need to speak of a necessity which is peculiar to an empire or of a tendency to hubris which is peculiar to those who experience success: Athens behaves exactly as everyone else does, by acting in accordance with her strength; her ambition is to be explained neither by circumstances which blind her to reality nor by

[1] Some writers have completely identified action according to one's force with hubris. Thus Thibaudet states (pp. 74-75): 'The hubris which Herodotus puts up on a royal stage in order to have it struck down with lightning by the Gods is seen by the cool realism of Thucydides to be merely an ordinary part of the activity and behaviour of states. It has a definite name, which is the nature peculiar to man, the ἀνθρώπειον.' The analysis made of the notion in this chapter shows that such an identification is impossible. The two spheres of influence are often difficult to distinguish from each other, but they can in no way be confused as far as political theory is concerned.

cumstances which impose themselves upon her: this ambition is in her, it is part of the human nature which she allows to reign over her as sovereign mistress. We then wonder how Thucydides can reconcile two explanations which appear to be so different in nature.

In fact, however, these explanations seem to be so difficult to reconcile only if we consider them as having an equal importance, which was certainly not Thucydides' intention: the very difference between the functions that each fulfils makes it impossible for us to bring them in direct contrast with one another.[1]

The first two laws have this in common: that they both define to what extent an act is wise, prudent or useful. The first analyses a situation whose demands provide Athens with an excuse: an imperial city cannot remain in existence without continuing to act by force. The second defines the danger and provides an argument for criticizing Athens: a prosperous city, drunk with sight of power, allows herself to be carried away and use her force incorrectly. In both cases, Athens is presumed to be seeking her own interest and the best use of her power; if this is not stated in so many words, it is because it is a natural assumption. And, in fact, we generally find these assertions in debates which are held inside Athens and which are concerned with Athenian interests: if the act under discussion serves these interests, everyone will approve of it.

It is probably for this reason that, in the arguments by which Thucydides presents the contrasting views put forward in the Athenian debates, he refrains from considering hubris as anything but the enemy of enlightened political self-interest and prudence: he does not take into consideration factors which in fact played no part in the debate.

It is this unspoken assumption governing all these debates which it is the function of the third law to state openly. Everything that men can do, they do, it says. The statement of this law in the Melian dialogue merely tends to establish that the basis for the discussion will be the ξυμφέρον.[2]

Although it occupies third place in this analysis of the theory

---

[1] Thus, in so far as the law of force is only the instrument whereby hubris works, both do mingle together; but as soon as one looks at the difference which separates them in theory, it is immediately confirmed by such a difference of function in Thucydides' system that it becomes equally impossible to bring them in conflict with each other.

[2] In fact the Melians reply: Ἦι μὲν δὴ νομίζομέν γε, χρήσιμον (ἀνάγκη γὰρ ἐπειδὴ ὑμεῖς οὕτω παρὰ τὸ δίκαιον τὸ ξυμφέρον λέγειν ὑπέθεσθε) μὴ καταλύειν ὑμᾶς τὸ κοινὸν ἀγαθόν.

implicit in Thucydides' work, precisely because it is the most abstract, this law ought nevertheless, in a general and theoretical reconstruction of political action, to be put in the first place, since it provides the very basis of it all. It indicates the fundamental principle which lies at the root of Athenian policy, while the other two laws determine the practical conditions under which this policy has to be carried out.

The difference of function explains the position of the law of force in Thucydides' work: it occurs, in fact, only in the two general analyses dealing with the development of Athenian imperialism, looked at outside Athens. While the two other laws could provide arguments for a discussion conducted among Athenians, the law of force assumes that the whole problem is now called into question and that even the end pursued must be discussed and justified. While the first two laws analysed the almost mechanical process giving rise to either right or wrong actions, the third law provides the general principle inspiring them all.

At the same time, this law presupposes an attempt at extremely profound analysis on the part of Thucydides, and an effort to formulate a philosophy of action, which is clearly quite an exceptional undertaking in a historical work. It stands out in full contrast to the purely political level of analysis to which the two other laws belong.

It thus reveals intellectual affinities which are different from those of the first two laws: the conditions of wisdom, such as they have been analysed here, constantly took us back to the wise men of older times and to their γνῶμαι, to the advice of an Artabanus, the aphorisms of poets and the teaching of the pre-Socratics. If one found an echo of Thucydides' ideas in sophists like Thrasymachus, or in 'modern' writers like Euripides, it was only to the extent that they also, like Thucydides, were repeating these older, and perhaps permanent, ideas of the Greeks. The law of force, on the other hand, in the form in which the Athenians express it at Melos, does not seem to have been developed except by the most revolutionary of the thinkers who came towards the end of the fifth century. As long as Thucydides talks only of hubris, there is little originality in what he says; but as his ideas go deeper, he achieves a progress which puts him into a definite intellectual group. Here again, the law of force appears as a final achievement.

This difference in nature and function between the law of force

z

and the other two laws also corresponds to the suggestions that I have put forward concerning the composition of the work.

The idea of political necessity makes itself felt essentially in texts which we have seen to be late (as Pericles' speech, for example); but it also occurs in others (like Cleon's speech on Mytilene); and it can be admitted that while this idea was present in Thucydides' mind from the very beginning, it acquired, with the passage of time, more clarity and precision than it had ever had originally. At the same time it also constituted a defence of imperialism, and in particular of the form which this assumed under Pericles, and therefore could easily take up greater importance after 404. However, as he developed the terms of this law, Thucydides did little more than make his earlier ideas deeper and more far-reaching.

The idea of the influence of hubris is not peculiar to Thucydides. The phrases denouncing it define a type of wisdom which belonged to Pericles, and which Thucydides himself used from the very beginning as a criterion in judging political actions. Thus, the notion of such a process can be found throughout his work: it makes itself felt in sections which we have seen to be 'early', like the debate on Mytilene, as well as in II. 65, the passage which can be most certainly ascribed to a 'late' period. As has been seen in this chapter, it links together in a coherent whole the successive judgments which Thucydides makes. And there is nothing which better underlines the firm and constant unity of his thought than to see the criterion remaining exactly the same, even down to the very detail of the phrases which express it, from one end to the other of his long work.

At the same time, however, the late passages do seem to mark an advance on the others, and as the idea of political necessity grows more precise, the philosophical law also makes its appearance. With it, we reach the final stage in Thucydides' moral and philosophical ideas. This law is, in fact, to be found only in two passages, which have both seemed to be of late inspiration. It still remains consistent with the other ideas, and if it differs from them in any way it is rather by the higher level of analysis which it attains than by its actual content. It carries us to the most abstract point and to what is essential in man — to the ἀνθρώπειον.[1]

---

[1] The difference between these two analyses and the rest can partly be explained by circumstances; but if circumstances make such an analysis possible in these two cases, and not in others, which are nevertheless also 'late', they cannot account for them completely.

The dates which have been put forward for the composition of the work thus provide a fairly reasonable explanation for the intellectual development which accompanied its growth. Thucydides' thought shows as complete a unity and coherence in the realm of theoretical analysis as it had done in that of political opinion, and in both cases it merely developed characteristics that were already inherent. Thucydides had always tended, from the very beginning, to analyse events in a general and abstract manner so as to bring out the principles which lay behind them; as the years went by and his work progressed, he carried this tendency to its fullest extent: the continuity and consistency of his own intellectual attitude enabled his work to evolve in accordance with the principles first inspiring it, so that chronological evolution and logical progress are, with him, identical.

CONCLUSION

404: THE DIVIDING LINE

IT has been taken for granted, in all the previous chapters of this book, that different levels could be distinguished in Thucydides' work, levels which corresponded to different periods of composition. This assumption has, in my view, been able to provide a good account both of the textual details of the History and of its deeper meaning. More particularly, a distinction can apparently be made, from the beginning to the end of the work, between an early level, written in some form or other before 404, and a series of later elements, added after 404.

No claim has been made that the exact nature and extent of these elements could be determined: to begin with, such an ambition was irrelevant to the main aim of this work, and even if it had been relevant the margin of uncertainty would still have remained very wide. Nevertheless, once these reservations have been made, some of these elements did in fact seem to emerge, in particular in Book I, where they can be seen in the Pentecontaëtia and in the second part of the speech of the Athenians; in Book II, in Pericles' Funeral Oration, in all or part of his last speech, together with the praise for him which follows it; in Book IV, in certain details about Brasidas; in Book V, in the Melian dialogue; and finally, in Books VI and VII, in a few isolated passages where Thucydides insists either on the personality of Alcibiades, or on the extent of Athenian power. In each of these cases, mention has been made of 'later' passages, which have been contrasted with an 'earlier' version.

But if, in fact, after this long analysis has been made, Thucydides' work finally seems to be constructed round one idea and one system; if, in fact, the progress of the work in time does coincide so exactly with the development of the logic of Thucydides' ideas, we might well have occasion to wonder just what is the relevance of this distinction established between the two levels of the work, both as far as material and intellectual questions are concerned. In other words, we may well wonder what right we have to maintain that at a certain moment in time a particular event occurred which interrupted

344

Thucydides in the midst of his composition of the History and gave a new turn to his ideas, thus determining, in a piece of work that extended in fact over decades, a complete change of level, a break, a dividing line.

It is only the way they see the practical nature of this break, which distinguishes those who think that the work was written in separate sections from those who consider that it was written as a whole. However, once we reduce it to its correct proportions, it is not certain that this problem remains a valid one.

The general trend of all recent research has been to acknowledge more and more the profound unity of Thucydides' work. According to Ullrich's theory, Thucydides introduced into his first version only a few remarks caused by the greater dimensions assumed by the war: the discovery of ever more numerous 'later' elements finally gave rise, in Schwartz, to the idea that Thucydides had rewritten his work almost completely, though without finishing this rewriting, and that what remained was just a collection of bits and pieces in contradiction with one another. This involved denying the unity of the work, and philologists soon showed that this was impossible. Since Schwartz's book was published, there has been a strong reaction which has tended to suppress the contradictions which he listed.[1] Scholars questioned the idea that these contradictions were the work of an unintelligent editor: some (like Kolbe) proved the coherence of the narrative; Pohlenz demonstrated the unity of a large single passage like that of the debate at Sparta in Book I, as did Schadewaldt for an even larger one like the Sicilian books; Rose Zahn and Jacoby even came to the conclusion that passages which had been rewritten might well have been very numerous, but that because of their very multiplicity they tended to merge into a new unity. Finally, the change which Schwartz had attributed to Thucydides' actual ideas was restricted by Pohlenz to the realm of his personal attitude to events, and by Schadewaldt to his methods of presenting a historical narrative and to his notion of truth; soon, Grosskinski denied the validity even of this particular difference. Thus, all the contradictions became less glaring or even disappeared. The very history of the solutions put forward conveyed a very obvious

[1] With exceptions like that of Laqueur, who in 1937 still finds contradictions even inside a single group of words.

objection to the non-unitarian theory: for the more one tried to put it into practice, the more one was brought back to the opposite view, and obliged to admit the unity of Thucydides' work. This is proved by Patzer's book.

But this idea is no more acceptable in Patzer's case than it was in that of Eduard Meyer, since it does not take sufficient account of the existence of 'earlier' passages. Probability alone seems to demand that such passages do exist, and a scrutiny of the text provides traces of their existence, as, for example, in I. 23. Scholars who maintain that the work was written as a whole have felt the existence of this difficulty, and have recognized it by talking about 'notes reproduced without modifications'. Thus, Eduard Meyer assumes it to be obvious that Thucydides did not wait for years before writing a single word about the events that he intended to relate; he argues that Thucydides could not have considered any version as final or completed before the war (either the Archidamian or the Decelean War) was over, but that he may have repeated these earlier versions without altering them, and may even have kept certain expressions which were no longer very suitable to the new situation (although, according to Eduard Meyer, there are not very many of these, and any modern work, subjected to the same amount of criticism applied to that of Thucydides would reveal many more).[1] Similarly, Patzer, in his effort to eliminate the 'earlier' passages, repeats the hypothesis of the 'note reproduced unchanged'.[2] In fact, this involves opening the door to the theory that the work was not written as a whole, since if it is true that one particular passage comes from a note reproduced unchanged, where are we going to stop? In spite of Thucydides' own intentions, this note could indicate an earlier aspect of his ideas, and differ from such and such another passage. The field is therefore open to the kind of research that scholars had tried to banish.

We are thus brought by a continuous and logical movement from the view that the work was written at different times and with different intentions to the view that it was written as a single unit, and vice versa. And this is only normal; for if we are going to take into account the various features of the text, we must reckon both with the unity of the work as a whole and with the slight differences which it reveals in certain places. This means that, as each scholar

---

[1] Eduard Meyer, *Forsch.*, p. 272 and p. 318, note 2.
[2] H. Patzer, pp. 14-15.

tries to improve on the other's interpretation, we gradually pass through all the different stages which separate one theory from the other. Thus, there only remain differences of detail and emphasis between the two: scholars who are more conscious of the unity of the work will call the earlier passages 'notes'; they will tend to minimize their number, and to emphasize the extent to which they agree with the 'late' passages; on the other hand, scholars who are more conscious of the different shades of meaning which indicate an earlier date of composition will talk about an 'earlier version' or an 'earlier plan'; they will tend to emphasize both the number of these passages and the significance of the differences between 'earlier' and 'later' versions.

Thus, the problem comes down to deciding to what extent these earlier 'notes', or this earlier 'plan' or 'version' were already completed when Thucydides began the 'later' part of his work.

Such a problem certainly cannot be solved. If it does seem obvious that in certain cases there are differences of intention between one text and another, then we can say that there probably was an original version. But what are these cases? how important are they? what must we understand by 'version'? It is extremely difficult to decide, and depends upon the personal opinion of each scholar; in fact, as we saw in the case of the Sicilian expedition, the question is of secondary importance. It can only be a question of probability, and that is why I have not allowed my own personal hypothesis to play a part in the discussion up to now. This hypothesis is based both upon the nature of the differences noted in the first books and on general probability. It consists of the idea that Thucydides first considered the ten-years war as his subject and started to write its history in what he thought would be a definitive version: this included, by the side of the account of what happened, an analysis of the causes of the war. When he then saw events starting up again, he naturally went on with his work, but limited himself to writing up certain episodes in a more provisional fashion, with making notes and essays, and only put these in order after 404. Thus, as far as the first books are concerned, he had to correct and revise an earlier version;[1] as far as the later books are

---

[1] Thus there would be, to put it roughly, three stages through which these notes passed: notes made almost on the spot and reflecting Thucydides' immediate opinion; an 'early' version; and a revision after 404. This is more or less the feeling of Wilamowitz as far as the opening of Book II is concerned (*Lesefrüchte*, LXVII, *Hermes*, 35, 1900, p. 560), since he detects in these pages the traces of Thucydides' immediate impressions during the first summer, and distinguishes two stages, both earlier than 404.

concerned, he simply had to provide a framework for the passages he had already composed.[1]

In fact, I have kept this hypothesis strictly to one side because such a reconstruction of Thucydides' work can offer only a curiosity interest. Among a number of equally possible solutions, it implies an almost gratuitous choice and makes no difference in the interpretation of the actual History. The important question is whether or not a particular passage does or does not correspond to an earlier version, not under what form this earlier version which has now disappeared or been transcended originally existed. It is not even very important to say exactly when this original version was written down, since, as we saw in the case of Pylos, any 'earlier' version generally re-produces what was Thucydides' view at the time of the event. What is important is to find out whether we are dealing with this con-temporary view or with a later one, whether the passage did exist in an earlier version or not, whether it forms part of the general sequence of the work or whether it stands out as a passage obviously rewritten later. And what we have to do is to ask not when such a passage was *written* but when it was *conceived*, and when Thucydides realized that its presence in his work was necessary: whether this was immedi-ately after the event occurred or only some time afterwards.

Thus, it is possible that the speech of Euphemus and that of the Athenians in Book I were both written at about the same time. But the first fits into the narrative, and does not go beyond the precise function assigned to it, a function which is, moreover, essential in the analysis of the political circumstances of that period; Thucydides therefore probably foresaw it, prepared it, and also wrote it from the very beginning. The speech of the Athenians, on the other hand, at least so far as the second part is concerned, has a significance which goes beyond the immediate debate, to which it is not really relevant. Its presence seems to be explicable by a series of new preoccupations on the part of the historian rather than by the normal course of the narrative: it is this difference which is important, and which gives a meaning to the distinction between 'early' and 'late' passages. It is this which really implies a break in the composition of the work, and the existence of a dividing line.

[1] Thus he may have written late (although before 404), and his first version may have needed little more than a few minor revisions, or he may not have written until after 404, although using plans that were practically complete: there is here a margin of uncertainty which could only be reduced, in the present state of our knowledge, by a gratuitous assumption.

This is why the distinction can be so precise and clear cut. Thucydides may have worked on his History for thirty years, he may have written such and such an episode at one particular time and others very much later, he may have prepared notes, then collected them together, then revised them. But it is certain that he brought all those together after 404 in order to achieve the final unit. And it is the different nature of the work which is then carried out that enables us to distinguish two levels in the whole of his History: the first one includes all the different basic elements collected together either in one form or in another; and the second includes everything that was introduced or altered after the end of the war.

The end of the war must, in fact, have brought about a number of modifications in the principles according to which Thucydides was writing his work.

First of all, the very nature of the work which he did after 404 implies that he himself could intervene more freely and more directly in what he was writing. As soon as he was no longer mainly concerned with accurate documentation, then all the additions and alterations must correspond to an artistic, political or philosophical aim on the part of Thucydides himself. The circumstantial accuracy of the annalist gives way to the deliberate presentation of events by the historian.[1]

Moreover, Thucydides not only intervenes more freely after 404; the end of the war also determines the nature of his interventions, and does so in three different ways.

First of all, the very fact that the war is over gives finality to the subject which he is treating. By assigning a definite limit to the war, it enabled him to modify certain of his opinions as to its causes or the factors influencing the course of events; in particular, the complete collapse of the Athenian empire now made it clear that the war had really been the crisis of imperialism. Thucydides, who had always made imperialism play an important part in his work, could then show even more exactly what had been its nature and influence. It thus became natural and legitimate for him to include in the first part of his work a historical passage dealing with the growth and

---

[1] This explains why even stylistic differences may correspond to this purely intellectual dividing line. This type of research is necessarily difficult; see, however, Zahn, pp. 33-35, for a comparison between the style of the Funeral Oration and that of the Melian dialogue, both being contrasted with that of the debate between the Corcyraeans and the Corinthians in Book I.

development of this empire: this is the explanation I have put forward to account for the presence of the Pentecontaëtia.[1] This attitude is one that Thucydides always had, but the events of 404 confirmed its validity and reinforced it in a startling manner. We are therefore in the presence, not of a slow progress and maturation, but of a clear-cut change, brought out by an actual event.

It is this first type of modification, caused by the transformation of the actual object of Thucydides' study, that has been brought out by Ullrich and by those scholars who have adopted very much the same line of research (Ćwikliński, Breitenbach, Leske, Wilamowitz).[2] Since these modifications affected the History by a change in its subject matter, they emerged in the first part of this book, which was devoted to the attitude adopted by Thucydides, the historian, towards Athenian imperialism.

However, the disaster which overtook Athens in 404 did not influence Thucydides merely as a historical event. By the repercussions which it had upon Athenian opinion, it also changed the conditions under which he was writing. He had always remained faithful to the imperialist ideal such as it had been incarnated in Pericles; he had only criticized Pericles' successors and the mistakes they made. When he was allowed to come back to Athens, nothing of this ideal remained: the opponents of imperialism were triumphant, and they were denigrating not only democratic leaders and democracy itself, but the dreams of greatness that had brought Athens to her ruin. They were full of praise for the moderate and oligarchical city of Sparta, which had been Athens' rival but which had always been their model, and full of regret for the friendship which Athens ought to have cultivated for her. Thucydides, who had always defended Pericles and Athens against criticism of this type when it had been put forward by an Aristophanes, was now inspired to reject it even more forcibly than before. The very resistance which he everywhere encountered must have made him even more aware of the need to exalt everything which seemed so unjustly cast down. He wished first of all to defend both Pericles, his ideal statesman, and everything to which Pericles had imparted such incomparable splendour: imperialism, to the extent that it remained lucid and

[1] This is what Cwiklinski noted in his first study, in 1873, and which enabled him to go much further than the purely mechanistic thesis of Ullrich.

[2] These scholars, however, and especially Ullrich, supposed that the evidence for these changes would show itself in too brutal and simplified a way; this accounts for the amount of justified criticism that they received.

rested on a living ideal; democracy, so long as it can be brought back
to some general principles, and is distinct from demagogy; the very
figure of Athens, so long as her taste for action can appear generous.
This is the explanation I have suggested for the alterations made in the
sections dealing with Pericles, and which include the new version of
his last speech, together with the praise for him which concludes it;
the Funeral Oration; and, finally, all the signs of a greater severity
towards Sparta,[1] either in this speech, or in that of the Athenians in
Book I, or in the Melian dialogue. Finally, it is this desire to justify
and defend Pericles which seems to have inspired all the comments
introduced into the account of the Sicilian expedition, comments
which tended to underline either the idea of the power of Athens or
the fact that she owed her final defeat only to an accumulation of
errors. There is nothing in these texts which differs from the ideas
that Thucydides had always expressed, but in the circumstances
born of Athenian defeat these ideas met an obstacle which had the
effect of giving them a new vitality. Here again, we are in the
presence not of a slow progress, but of a definite change.

This second type of modifications, brought about by the circumstances under which Thucydides is writing, is the one that has been
most emphasized by Schwartz.[2] Since these changes affected the
History by altering Thucydides' attitude towards Athenian politics,
they emerged in the second part of this thesis, which was devoted to
the political judgments expressed by Thucydides on the successive
problems encountered by Athenian imperialism and the different
solutions put forward to solve them.

The end of the war, however, had yet another effect upon the
writing of the History. By making imperialism entirely a thing of the
past, something which no longer existed, it gave much more freedom
to Thucydides' ideas, liberated them from any immediate preoccupations, and allowed him to see events from a distance; it
turned him away from the ephemeral debates about the present and
future of imperialism, in which he would appear simply as another

---

[1] This severity can be explained not only by a very sharp awareness of the cultural
differences between Sparta and Athens, to which the Funeral Oration bears witness
(Schwartz) and by the desire to denigrate Sparta: it is also an indirect reply to the enemies
of imperialism who were criticizing it from a moralizing point of view; the insistence on
the self-centred character of Sparta is in fact an argument against such a point of view
(Pohlenz, I, p. 136).

[2] Schwartz, however, saw too clean a break between these two attitudes of Thucydides,
and it is this which explains the amount of justified criticism which he received.

Athenian citizen, and, making him into a disinterested thinker by the very force of circumstances, linked him to the philosophers and theoreticians of the years to come. Then, as Thibaudet writes with such powerful words, 'tout se compense; il faut envisager la guerre comme un événement inévitable, et qui, quels qu'aient été les efforts des uns et des autres pour en modifier le cours, fut; il n'est plus temps, il n'y a plus de temps, et tout s'incline, comme les lignes du Parthénon, vers le point aérien du κτῆμα ἐς αἰεί'.[1] Thucydides' analysis is henceforth concerned not with the particular but with the general; it neglects specific details in order to reach a deeper truth which it understands more completely, in a wider and more impartial manner. This is the explanation that has been suggested here for the introduction into his work of a passage like the Melian dialogue, as well as for Thucydides' well-marked tendency, in the later parts of his work, to insist on the 'laws' valid for all forms of imperialism, and to link philosophy with psychology and politics in the study of these laws. Certainly, there is nothing in these later texts which differs from what had always been Thucydides' attitude of mind; his aim had always been to reach a truth that went beyond mere historical accuracy; his intention had always been to bring out the deeper meaning of the events he was describing, to insist upon their eternal nature and upon the lessons that could be drawn from them. But as Athenian imperialism came to an end, it gave much wider scope for Thucydides to develop the implications of this attitude. And, once again, it is the events of 404 which mark a definite dividing line.

This last kind of change, which has to do with the intellectual attitude of Thucydides himself, is that on which Pohlenz, and after him Schadewaldt, have most insisted.[2] Since it affected the work through the intellectual conditions in which Thucydides was placed in relation to his subject, it emerged in the third part of this book, devoted to Thucydides' general ideas on Athenian imperialism.

Thus the various explanations put forward to account for the difference between 'earlier' and 'later' passages are all valid to a certain extent, but none of them is wholly acceptable unless one goes back to the point at which they cease to contradict one another and come

[1] Thibaudet wrote these lines (p. 117) under the impression that the whole of the work was written late. They are perfectly applicable to those passages which are late.

[2] However, they saw too general and too clear a difference when they maintained that the 'programme' of I. 22 fitted only some of the speeches. This explains the justified criticism that they received.

together to confirm their respective findings. We then see how the end of the war, by influencing both Thucydides' own political and intellectual attitude and the exact range of his subject, necessarily changed everything which was written after it, and established a genuine dividing line between the twenty-seven years of work that had gone before it and the alterations which were then made.

However, in the three domains in which we have seen this dividing line to be valid, it has never been a question of a complete reversal of Thucydides' attitude. He was in no way surprised or proved wrong by what had happened; neither his attitude as a historian, nor his opinions as an Athenian citizen, nor his theoretical views and historical method were changed by the defeat of Athens, but were simply given greater intensity and precision. Instead of revising his work because he had ceased to agree with either the method or the ideas of what he had already written, he rewrote it only in order to express these earlier ideas more clearly and carry even further the intellectual method he had adopted.

Such a conclusion enables us to see the nature of Thucydides' mind in its true light: in his firm, rational, coherent, systematic and self-confident attitude, he is not the man to have yielded to the inconstant vacillations attributed to him by the failure of certain scholars to understand his work. The collapse of everything which had been most dear to him found a place already waiting for it in his intellectual system, and fitted into it with no disturbance to the other factors. In his work, intellect is independent and all-powerful, dominating the diversity of the individual events, so that they are necessarily submitted to the unity which it creates and which it emphasizes with ever-increasing force.

This firm and commanding role played by intellect and understanding in Thucydides' work nevertheless implies some limitations: Thucydides' ideas could not be shaken by what happened, but not renewed either; they could not reach conclusions that would have been very far removed from his original attitude.[1] Thucydides remains faithful to his early ideas, but he does not go beyond them. He does not rise above the actual conditions of the experience he has witnessed and analysed; and we see in him the perfection of a type

---

[1] Thucydides has often been criticized for the mistakes that an excessively intellectual approach made him commit, in particular as far as civilizations preceding that of Athens are concerned. He has too great a tendency to consider that reality is perfectly intelligible, and here again it is his very strength which leads to his weak point.

of meditation which is itself limited and which only the philosophers of the fourth century were eventually to widen.

Yet he and he alone displayed in his work this triumph of a mind which is constantly at grips with the facts and which, going on — as the people he describes — from conquest to conquest, always subjugates them to its sovereign power.

General Conclusion

FROM POLITICS TO ETHICS

THUCYDIDES is, in a way, outside the main stream of intellectual relationships which allow us to follow the influence of different minds on one another. However, his ideas are not completely separated from those which were expressed in the following century, and as we reach the end of this study the task remains of trying to sum up the general account of his ideas by defining his relationship with these later thinkers.

The passages in Thucydides' work which analyse Athenian imperialism are not lacking either in fervour or confidence. Nevertheless, the deeper and more universal element which they tend to bring out implies a pessimistic conclusion, and this is the nature of the final lesson which the History conveys. He himself presents the object of his admiration and belief as an exception, at the same time as he shows the existence of an almost inevitable rule which brings about the triumph of certain human tendencies which are opposed to justice and which soon bring about the disappearance of wisdom. Thus, in spite of the great achievement which he celebrates in the character of Pericles and of the imperialism of his day, his work is above all the record of a failure, a failure which he makes into a failure on the part of man.

Moreover, nothing seems to lie beyond this failure, except the hope to begin all over again, as Athens later tried to do, and, if possible, to do better in the future. Nowhere does he suggest that other solutions are possible, and he sees no further than the boundaries of this city whose attempt to assert its own being is so dramatic. In this, he remains fully a man of the fifth century. At a time when the Athenians were setting up the state, or rather, the city, as the essential object and framework of their ideas, Thucydides was rising to an intellectual theory of the nature of action. However, this theory tends only to explain the events in which he himself was involved, and hardly at all to correct them with the future in mind. Thus, he approaches problems only from within the city, and never reaches any conclusions which might call her existence into question. It is this fact which provides the key to his pessimism, for it is the problem of the city, a problem brought forward by Athenian imperialism, which gives this pessimistic conclusion to Thucydides' ideas. It is the city, such as it was, which explains the general failure noted in the History; and we can say that, whether consciously or not, it is the defeat of the city as such which Thucydides is recording.

The only escape from this pessimism lay, therefore, in the direction of a movement away from the narrow and limited framework of the city. In fact, thinkers of the fourth century followed that direction; and this explains the nature of the two solutions actually put forward.

The first of these was purely political, and owed nothing to Thucydides. It already existed in his time, and he had preferred to know nothing about it: it is the Panhellenic solution. In the fourth century, circumstances gave it a new importance, first of all by developing an international civilization, and secondly by setting the Greeks, with the appearance of Philip of Macedon, problems which concerned them all. The Panhellenic ideas of the sophists are linked with the first set of circumstances, the development of an international civilization, which inspires the whole series of panegyric speeches ranging from Gorgias to Lysias and Isocrates. The political ideas of the latter are probably all to be explained in that way, for if he constantly changes his mind about the form which the union of all the Greeks ought to take, or on the leader who ought to direct it, the idea of this union itself never left him. Philip himself was only one of the possible incarnations, and when he appeared Isocrates wanted to achieve under his direction the union which Demosthenes wanted to create in order to oppose him. However that may be, it is no longer possible in the fourth century to treat Athenian politics without treating Greek politics at the same time, and in this respect Isocrates and Xenophon, Demosthenes and Aeschines differ from Thucydides. They may have borrowed something from him, Isocrates some of his criticisms of Athenian imperialism,[1] Demosthenes some of his themes concerning Athenian tradition,[2] but both thinkers use these elements to put forward ideas which Thucydides' work did not

[1] Mathieu, *Isocrate et Thucydide*. We have already seen (p. 261) that Isocrates also borrows themes concerning the glory of Athens from Thucydides.

[2] He borrows everything which represents the Athenian ideal of an active but personally disinterested and generous policy inspired by the idea of glory — Athenian policy such as it is expressed in the Funeral Oration. He also puts forward very similar ideas on the right conditions for political debates and the duties of the orator. As far as Athenian imperialism is concerned, he scarcely has occasion to return to it. The only thing which he does is occasionally to repeat, applying them to Philip, expressions which applied to Athenian imperialism in Thucydides (cf. for example in *Crown*, 66). But if the whole seems to bear in certain sections traces of a precise memory of Thucydides, it is impossible to tell when we must talk of influence and when of coincidence.

mention, and which owed their diffusion only to circumstances that were foreign to it.

The moral solution proposed, on the other hand, seems almost a direct reply to Thucydides. He had emphasized the fact that both the greatness and the happiness of the city came up against difficulties born of human nature itself, and which, in the final analysis, were essentially moral. In order to remedy these defects, men had to turn away from the city as it actually existed and begin by imposing a moral reform upon it. This is what the theorists of the fourth century proceeded to do. They contrasted the real city, with its continual agitation and perturbations, with the need for profound reforms. The balance between the intellect and the state, which had characterized the thought of Thucydides, was broken in favour of the mind.[1] The thinkers retired from public life in order to become philosophers. They were no longer fifth-century Athenians incessantly discussing on the city streets the day-to-day problems affecting their welfare — if we are to believe the unanimous testimony of Thucydides and other writers of the time. Instead, these thinkers turned away from the immediate problems of political action, and argued that they must first of all change the very principles which guided men's actions. They were as much or more moralists than politicians. Now this may not have been the result of reading Thucydides, but his work nevertheless led logically to such an attitude. And one can find a perfect confirmation for the validity of Thucydides' analysis in the fact that, taken by themselves, events had the same influence on men's minds that they would have had when presented through his work.

However, we must distinguish two different steps in this movement of moral reform. Some thinkers sought only a partial reform, and tried simply to avoid the influence of hubris. Others attempted a more radical reform, and made a direct effort to solve the problem of justice and force. Thus both sets of thinkers replied to Thucydides, but on different levels.

In the first category, we can include almost all the orators and theorists,[2] for in the fourth century political and moral ideas mingled closely together in everybody. No-one, however, provides a more obvious example of this than Isocrates.

Isocrates had the most vivid awareness of the need for an education

[1] W. Jaeger, *Staat und Kultur, Die Antike*, VIII, 1932, p. 81.
[2] Xenophon in particular.

based on morality, and his political theories show detailed evidence
of this. Mathieu has written (*Les Idées politiques d'Isocrate*, p. 129):
'There is one thing which strikes the reader first of all in Isocrates'
ideas on the organization of the city, and that is the importance
which he attributes to moral questions: such an attitude was only
normal for a man so profoundly concerned with education. In his
eyes, the moral duties of the state are the same as those of the individual, and in both cases there is no virtue higher than a respect for
general rules (σωφροσύνη), and no crime worse than the lack of
moderation (ὕβρις).'

Such a summary shows clearly the debt that Isocrates' ideas owe to
Thucydides', or at least the exact connection which exists between
both, the former being the natural complement of the latter. The
only difference lies in the fact that Isocrates thinks in a more optimistic way than Thucydides, and tries to formulate prescriptions that
will cure the evils described by the historian. However, he is concerned with the same symptoms, and the remedies which he proposes
seem to come directly from Thucydides' analyses. In the treatise *On
the Peace* (133-135) he lays down with great precision what these
remedies should be: the first essential is that the city must be able to
choose correctly those who will advise her — a remark which merely
resumes the message of II. 65 and corresponds to Thucydides'
conception of the conditions of political wisdom; the second and
third are more directly concerned with foreign policy, but they bring
out only the general principles governing it; in fact, the second
recommends the ruling city to act as a friend and not as a master
towards her allies, and the third that she should always try to honour
the Gods and deserve the high opinion of all the Greeks: that is to
say, everything that Athens failed to do, and everything which
Thucydides — without nevertheless thinking that such faults were
easy to avoid — criticized her for not doing, everything which he
emphasizes in texts like the debate on Mytilene and, above all, the
Melian dialogue. The conclusion which Isocrates reaches in this text[1]
could thus be taken directly from Thucydides, and it would seem
that Isocrates owes at least certain guiding ideas to the History.[2]

[1] Similarly in the *Areopagiticus* where he shows the moral superiority of the men of
the past.

[2] Did Isocrates know Thucydides' work? Blass does not commit himself, and Wilamowitz thinks not (*A. und A.*, I, 99). My own view, like that of Mathieu and Bodin (*Isocrate
et Thucydide; Isocrate et Thucydide*) is that he several times bases his arguments on
passages from Thucydides' work.

However, Isocrates did not make full use of the whole of Thucydides' analysis. He is acquainted only with the psychological law which leads imperialism to its ruin, and tries merely to avoid making mistakes or falling into error; to achieve this, he tries to restore wisdom and to remedy immorality. His aim, however, is not very revolutionary, and he thinks it can be attained simply by going back to the past. Thus, like Thucydides, he finally remains within the framework of the city whose evils he sets out to cure. His optimism is valid for what is going to happen in the immediate future, in a year or in a month: if men would only listen to him, then everything would be all right; a speech can persuade the responsible people, and virtue can become a reality; a partial reform is possible, and the basic situation is sound.

He thus does not take into account the ideas which Thucydides brings out in what we have called the philosophical law, and he thus does not treat the great moral problem which it raises; in this respect he is inferior to Thucydides, for he does not understand the nature of this problem, and one might almost go so far as to say that he does not realize that it even exists. Sometimes he states that it is better to be defeated when fighting for what is right rather than to win an unjust victory (*Panath.*, 185); elsewhere, and even in the same speech, he states that it is better to do evil than to endure it (*Panath.*, 117). Certainly, he is here talking about foreign policy, and that does make a difference; but by the very way in which he discusses it, he shows that he has failed to grasp this purely moral aspect of the problem, and failed to perceive the real importance of the Socratic themes; he calls those who could choose to endure evil 'the so-called philosophers'.[1] On the whole, he shows a complete lack of consistency on this question throughout all his works, and his moral and philosophical opinions are dominated by his political ones: when he defends the empire, he does so in the name of reality; but when circumstances lead him round to wishing to condemn it and trying to dissuade the Athenians from following an imperialistic policy, he then starts to talk about justice again, as, for example, in *On the Peace* (69): οὐ δίκαιόν ἐστι τοὺς κρείττους τῶν ἡττόνων ἄρχειν.[2]

If he had been more clearly aware of the fundamental choice with

---

[1] 118: τῶν προσποιουμένων εἶναι σοφῶν.

[2] Whatever may be his final view, Isocrates nevertheless confirms the validity of Thucydides' analysis by the very fact that he is obliged, against his will, to take up a position on this question of justice and force.

which he was confronted, he would have given up trying to base his arguments on justice, and would have acted like the Athenians in Thucydides; or else, he would have given up the idea of exercising an immediate effect upon the city of his day, and would have done what Plato did.

Plato did understand the problem created by the third law, and he solved it in the only domain in which an answer could be found: that of pure thought. He did not believe in the possibility of isolated, piecemeal reforms.[1] Like Thucydides himself,[2] he turned away from immediate action in order to move towards a κτῆμα ἐς αἰεί.[3] In this respect, he resolutely turns his back on men like Isocrates, and has no time for any half-way house between philosophy and politics.[4] He sets out resolutely from Thucydides' third law, and by a kind of living and logical sequence of ideas, he deals with the moral problem which concludes Thucydides' work. Thus, by following the paths of pure thought, he comes closer than anyone else to Thucydides, who, as a historian, is necessarily concerned with concrete facts.

Even though his ideas may stand in contrast with those of Thucydides, this very circumstance confirms the validity of the historians' analysis, for the contrast itself is clear proof that the direction of the whole intellectual system actually depended on the solution of the fundamental moral problem put forward by each thinker. Clearly this solution cannot be the same for Thucydides, who studies reality, as for Plato, who creates it anew according to his ideals.

[1] See *Republic*, 425 and Mathieu, *Les idées . . .*, p. 178.

[2] It may be that in Thucydides' case this detachment is due to the circumstances and results of his exile, but his highly abstract and analytical intelligence seems to have predisposed him to it in advance; his History could well have been inspired by party considerations if such had been his nature, and if he had seen it only as an accidental substitute for action.

[3] This naturally does not exclude the famous (but vain) attempts to undertake a vast reform which would actually achieve something resembling as much as possible the ideal city.

[4] The relationship between the two men confirms this relationship between their ideas. They began by being unaware of each other's existence, since Isocrates remained preoccupied with action. Mathieu writes of this period (*Les premiers conflits entre Platon et Isocrate et la date de l'Euthydème*, Mél. *Glotz*, II, p. 558): 'Moreover, since Isocrates was aiming at being a man of action, it was natural for him to keep both his attention and his criticisms for practical moralists and professional legal theorists rather than for a pure theoretician like Plato. The difference in both character and activity between the two men was so great that they should really have never come into conflict.' Soon, however, the semi-philosopher revealed by the *Panegyricus* attracted Plato's severity, which showed itself in an allusion in the *Euthydemus* (304 d-306 d) to the person who is 'between the philosopher and the statesman' (see Mathieu, loc. cit.).

While in Thucydides this moral problem is the crowning point of his analysis, in Plato it provides the basis for all his political views. Plato dismisses any other consideration from the very beginning, and refuses to take account of the actual state, whose mechanism Thucydides had analysed. He not only reconstructs the ideal state, but he does so from the very foundations.[1] In the *Republic*, he asks first: what is a good man? then: what is a good state? The problem of the relationship between justice and force thus determines everything else.[2] This order is indeed one of the fundamental principles of the Socratic method, for how often do we not see Socrates holding back young men who, like Alcibiades, are eager to plunge into public life, by asking them: 'But do you even know what the best is?'

And if the best is justice and not force, then everything which the Athenians, and even Pericles, spent their lives searching for immediately loses its meaning. The city should look inside, not outside.[3] In this respect, the *Gorgias* shows how far Plato's aim differs from that of Thucydides: the aim of the man who takes part in politics should be to improve the moral quality of the citizens (*Gorgias* 515 a, cf. *Politicus* 293 d). Certainly, if he wishes to do this, he must follow Thucydides' advice and stand up against the city by resisting its desires (*Gorgias* 517 b: μεταβιβάζειν τὰς ἐπιθυμίας καὶ μὴ ἐπιτρέπειν),[4] but he must do this solely in order to improve the city. Pericles, Cimon, Miltiades, Themistocles, the undoubted leaders whom Thucydides admires with all the force of his intelligence, were no

[1] This is what distinguishes his views not only from those of empirical works like the *Constitution of the Athenians* by the Pseudo-Xenophon, but also from the ideal states whose various models were put forward by the philosophers of that time. We know of the attempt of Hippodamus of Miletus, and, through Aristotle, those of Phaleas of Chalcedon and of Telecles of Miletus: these works seems to have aimed at a purely political re-organization. In a historical form, the *Cyropaedia* of Xenophon represents a similar attempt, but in which moral ideas also play their part. However, there is no question of a system either so complete or so wholly based on first principles as that of Plato, and Xenophon's ideas are much closer to those of Isocrates than to those of Plato.

[2] This is confirmed by the position of the debate in his work — in the very heart and centre of the *Gorgias*, which discusses whether or not political virtue can be taught, and at the beginning of the *Republic*, which aims at constructing the ideal city: that is to say in the two places where he lays the foundations of any kind of political theory by defining the very aim which men should pursue in political matters.

[3] *Laws*, 630 d, ff.

[4] This is an idea on which Plato insists on a number of occasions, as, for example, in the *Gorgias* itself, in pages 502 e-505 c, where he introduces the discussion of the duties of the statesman, setting out from the distinction between two kinds of eloquence: the first is 'flattery and something ugly; only the other is something beautiful, since it tries to improve the souls of the citizens and to say what is best, whether this pleases the listener or not'.

more successful than any others in achieving this aim. A man like Pericles did not improve the citizens of Athens, since under his guidance they grew so ferocious as to prosecute and condemn him (515 e-516 b). The reason for this is that, like other leaders, Pericles failed to recognize the true end of political action: 'You praise the men who feasted the citizens and satisfied their desires, and people say that they have made the city great, not seeing that the swollen and ulcerated condition of the State[1] is to be attributed to these elder statesmen; for they have filled the city full of harbours and docks and walls and revenues and all that, and have left no room for justice and temperance' (518 e). Harbours and docks and walls and revenues – these indeed are what Thucydides admires; the great men of former days are those who seem to him, as to Isocrates, models who should be imitated; increasing the power of the city (φασὶ μεγάλην τὴν πόλιν πεποιηκέναι αὐτούς) is exactly what he glorifies Pericles for having done. Perhaps not without dismay, but with remarkable steadfastness of purpose, Thucydides brings to the light of day the motives and aims which make the city act; yet, unlike Plato, he cannot turn his back on these, for he cannot turn his back on action.

Since he remains constantly taken up with reality, he finds wisdom infinitely difficult to achieve; for Plato, on the other hand, whose aim is essentially simple and concerned solely with the realm of ideas, wisdom can be the object of human knowledge. For there is a science of the good, and the whole of Plato's work is dedicated to discovering it. This science must rest on certain principles, and can consequently be handed down from one person to another; the fate of cities no longer depends upon chance, and on whether or not they find the right man to deal with the particular crisis facing them. Instead of the art of the cook, one has that of the doctor: 'Whereas medicine is an art, and attends to the nature and constitution of the patient, and has principles of action and reason in each case, cookery in attending upon pleasure never regards either the nature or reason of that pleasure to which she devotes herself, but goes straight to her end, nor ever considers or calculates anything, but works by experience

---

[1] Plato had nothing of what has been referred to in this book as 'imperialist feeling'. He considers that when men give way to it they are pursuing a vain and despicable end which cannot make them happy. The pleasure of extending one's power is one which cannot be made into an end in itself, and is in this respect like the pleasure one takes in scratching oneself when one has the itch: 'Tell me first of all' asks Socrates in the *Gorgias* (494 c) 'whether a happy life consists of having the itch, feeling the need to scratch oneself, being able to do so to one's heart's content, and to spend one's life scratching oneself?'

and routine, and just preserves the recollection of what she has usually done when producing pleasure.'[1] The *Republic* and the *Laws* belong to the art of medicine; but the wisdom of Thucydides, limited to the framework of the city, is but a cookery recipe by comparison.[2]

Following two opposite directions, pursuing contrary aims and setting out different lessons, Thucydides and Plato are linked together by one essential problem. The courses taken by their ideas seem to represent opposite slopes which are joined together only at their summit, so that as the first ends his climb the second begins his descent. But the descent follows straight on from the rise, and they meet at a point which is exactly common to both of them. In different terms and on different levels, the opposition between justice and force which stands out as the crowning point of Thucydides' work affords an intellectual point of departure for Plato.

Working as a historian, Thucydides necessarily studies human behaviour, and bases his conclusions on data provided by international relations; as a philosopher, Plato studies the very nature of justice and force, and uses the simplest examples which he can find, selected to suit his own purpose from the domain of private and individual activity. Nevertheless, the arguments which the two men put forward are practically the same: Thrasymachus and Callicles speak like the Athenians, and Socrates not unlike the Melians; it is one and the same debate, which here takes place in a political and there in a philosophical framework.

This junction is all the more surprising since Plato certainly does not set out from Thucydides, as would seem logically to be the case. Attempts have sometimes been made to show that Plato knew Thucydides' work;[3] but they were based on passages like the one where Plato, as did Thucydides, analyses the moral disorder which accompanies periods of political crisis. If this is the only proof offered, such a parallel is no more striking than this sort of continuity linking together the ideas of both authors, and should simply be brought in relation with it. Such a deep similarity in intellectual

---

[1] *Gorgias*, 501 a. The translation, for this passage and the one before, is Jowett's.

[2] The *Politicus* distinguishes between two degrees of evil: in the first, the statesman does not act κατὰ τέχνην; in the second, which is obviously much more serious, he pays no attention to rules and gives himself over to corruption and personal favours. Isocrates and Thucydides aimed only at curing the second evil: their ideal city is to that of Plato what Purgatory is to Paradise.

[3] Cf. Pohlenz, *Aus Platos Werdezeit*, pp. 240 ff. and Barker, p. 250, note 2. For an opposite view, see Schwartz, pp. 152-153; Wilamowitz, *Hermes*, XII, p. 328.

approach — visible even when the two texts are arguing opposite points of view — is sufficient explanation for any number of such parallels, and deprives them of any conclusive force. In fact, there is not a single word in Plato which shows that he is acquainted with Thucydides' work, and this is even more significant when one considers that the analysis of political events made by Thucydides is very close to Plato's ideas, and that it tends to confirm the general theses put forward in the dialogues while at the same time departing from the views inspiring them. In the absence of a definite quotation,[1] there is not a hint, not an allusion, not an echo. Thucydides seems to be unknown to Plato, as indeed to all his contemporaries, except Isocrates and Demosthenes.

The fact is that Plato's point of departure is to be found neither in the analyses of the History nor in the ideas put forward by political thinkers writing against imperialism,[2] but in the debates of the fifth century where, as we have seen, this theory of the right of the strongest was first brought out, largely under the inspiration of political events; it was popularized in 'modern' circles by certain sophists, who are as well represented by the Athenians in the Melian dialogue as by Callicles in the *Gorgias* and Thrasymachus in the *Republic*. And Plato's own reply is in all probability simply the one that the fifth century refused to hear: the reply of Socrates.

In the same way that Plato does not know the work of Thucydides, so Thucydides is unaware of the existence of Socrates.[3] And, when one considers the general direction of his ideas, this seems fully comprehensible.

As a man of the fifth century, Thucydides was not yet ready to understand Socrates' message. In this, he was no different from the Aristophanes who wrote the *Clouds*, or from the judges who condemned Socrates, or from the citizens who went and applauded at the *Clouds* and allowed the philosopher to be condemned to death. Socrates was a good citizen, who respected the laws; but, in a way

[1] The Greeks do not often mention their sources.

[2] Eduard Meyer (*Forsch.*, II, 393) says that it is the idea put forward by the anti-imperialist theoreticians which triumphs in Plato and which provides the centre of Aristotle's ideas, whereby he differs from Thucydides. In fact, if Plato condemns the very principle of Athenian imperialism far more than Thucydides does, it is from a point of view to which he could have been led by reading Thucydides, but not by reading any of the theoreticians opposed to imperialism.

[3] It is quite useless to try, as Ullrich does (in his *Beiträge*, p. 137), to see in the words of VIII. 68. 2 on the defence of Antiphon an allusion to the trial of Socrates.

that those who were concerned with other problems were unable to understand, he was no longer a man of the city. This was the reason for their failure to understand his greatness. People saw him discussing new ideas with young men, but were unaware of the things this clever talker was teaching and how he differed from his fellows: for ordinary people, he was a just sophist like the others.

When the crisis of 404 had marked the collapse of imperialism and the defeat of Athens, it cast men's minds in the direction of pure thought and freed them from the ardent pragmatism of earlier times; in the fourth century, the century of the philosophers, the figure of Socrates then took on, by reaction, a wide and striking appeal. There appeared the Socrates of Plato, the Socrates of Xenophon, and the school of Socratic thinkers. Military defeat had, as it were, laid the foundations for the development of ethics, while Socrates, the sophist who did not consider practical profit, was finally being granted his place of honour in the prytaneum of intelligence. His influence had been made possible, even natural, by the political disaster. And the city, by condemning him to death, ultimately destroyed what was left of its reputation in the eyes of the philosophers. Thus, among the various disciples of Socrates who wanted to devote themselves to politics, Alcibiades was not dissuaded by him, while Plato, who came later, was.

Thucydides was older than these young men. He may one day have spoken with Socrates. But there was in him no place for what Socrates had to offer. In Thibaudet's view, Thucydides' ideas on morality are those of a 'modernist'. 'The ideas of Aristeides and of the older Diacrians', he writes, 'those for which Socrates lived and died are out of date. By his realism and his dry chrematism, Thucydides stands out clearly in our eyes as the son of the Athenian sea-power.' This shows too easy a confusion between the ideas 'of Aristeides and the old Diacrians' and those of Socrates. Between the two, there was a complete renewal of the ethical problem, the discovery of this extreme realism which demands an equally extreme refusal. Thucydides comes up against this realism, and has nothing to help him to dismiss it; for he remains taken up with reality, and is still unaware of the possibilities hidden in the Socratic mode of inquiry. As they talked, at about the same time, in the streets of Athens, the two men came into contact with the same ideas; but for Thucydides, these ideas were still part of the domain of action and of politics, while for Socrates they lay in the still little frequented field of philosophical principles.

We might thus place by the side of the couple formed by Socrates and Alcibiades, and which will represent for all time the conflict between thought and action, a second couple consisting of Socrates and Thucydides; the two men will there remain closely linked as Athenians and as contemporaries, united in their brotherhood, but each looking in the opposite direction like the two faces of Janus.

ADDITIONAL REMARKS

AFTER twenty years there is much that one would like to alter in a book. In fact, there is so much that it would almost be easier to write a new one. And more honest, too. I have therefore decided to leave this one unchanged, and only explain briefly in what ways the views put forward in recent publications can be considered as complementary or contrary to those expressed here.

Twenty years is a long time. And it ought to be mentioned that, although this book was first published in 1947, it had been written during the first years of the war, and without the knowledge of works (especially foreign) later than 1939.[1] Among them were a number of short essays, some of which were closely connected with my subject, such as Deininger's most interesting study of the Melian dialogue,[2] or Méautis' inaugural lecture, precisely entitled *Thucydide et l'Impérialisme athénien*. Deininger, indeed, by comparing the discussions on imperialism in the Melian dialogue and elsewhere in Thucydides, as well as by comparing the ethical discussions in it and the texts of Plato, showed a purpose similar to mine, and our conclusions were often the same.[3] Further, before my book was issued, not only articles or particular studies were to be published about Thucydides: two books of considerable importance and value, both of them in English, appeared towards the end of the war. One was the first volume of Gomme's Commentary,[4] and the other was Finley's *Thucydides*.[5] The latter had been preceded by various articles in the *Harvard Classical Studies*.[6] The former had been prepared for by a number of articles, while some others were published later, and were

[1] This was explained in p. 307 of the French edition. The same thing happened to many books of that time: cf. Schmid (List, Nr 40), published in 1948. It should be added that the chapter on Thucydides in de Sanctis' *Storia dei Greci*, first published precisely in 1939, was not quoted either, for similar reasons; yet it gives in III, 14 a rather precise — if hasty — reconstruction of the way Thucydides wrote his work.

[2] List, Nr 8.

[3] He did not deal with the time of composition, but admitted that a late date was 'mit Recht allgemein angenommen' (p. 17, n. 26).

[4] List, Nr 16.

[5] List, Nr 15.

[6] List, Nrs 12, 13, 14.

soon followed by the next two volumes.[1] Meanwhile Gomme's
elegant and suggestive study on *The Greek Attitude to Poetry and
History* had appeared in 1954.[2] No passage in the History of Thucydides can now be properly considered without consulting the
Commentary. And the fact that these two important items are to be
included in the literature posterior to my book makes it all the more
necessary for me to add one or two words here about this literature,
and about its tendencies or results, at least in so far as they have some
precise bearing on the subject I had endeavoured to treat.[3]

I had tried, in my book, to subordinate one problem to another,
i.e. the problem of composition (which, at the time, dominated all
studies, and particularly German studies) to the problem of political
interpretation. And I had tried to show that, although written at
different times, Thucydides' work showed a great unity of thought. I
could not, therefore, be either shocked or sorry to see this much vexed
problem of composition now cast aside — or even to see that various
scholars, impressed by that same unity of thought, inferred from it
the conclusion that there had also been unity of composition. That all
the work had been written at one and the same time was the view
brilliantly advocated by Finley, and adopted by a number of other
scholars (as, for instance, Maddalena or Lord).[4] In fact I had been
careful to keep the unitarian hypothesis in view all along, until the
concluding section, as a possible explanation and one that would
not greatly change the main interpretation.

Yet it is a fact that many, among those who have to deal with the
very detail of the text, still feel that things cannot be quite so simple
as they seem to be. Gomme, though not putting the question in the
foreground, indicates often enough[5] the possibility, or probability,

[1] They were published in 1956 and go on to ch. V. 24. All scholars will be greatly
indebted to those who are now preparing, in Gomme's place and with his notes, the end
of this precious Commentary.

[2] List, Nr 18.

[3] This is no review of all the literature on Thucydides, such as one can find, for instance,
in Wassermann, List, Nr 51. That is why even some important books are not mentioned
here, although immediately after the two books just quoted there followed — to mention
but these — Schmid's analysis (List, Nr 40) and Grundy's second volume (List, Nr 20),
both, of course, worthy of attention.

[4] List, Nrs 30 and 29.

[5] There was to be an Appendix dealing with that question at the end of the third
volume, but even without it many indications have been published here and there in the
Commentary (and cf. List, Nr 17); I also had very illuminating letters from him discussing
the question.

that such and such passages were not written at the same time. And
scholars like Hammond, Adcock and Westlake still try to distinguish
between ancient and late passages in Book I,[1] while Treu discovers
them in proximity to one another in certain chapters of Book VI.[2]
This kind of interpretation, then, still seems, on the whole, to be not
only the best general hypothesis but the most satisfactory in some
matters of detail. Only, no scholar of recent times would incline to
see – as the previous analysts did – Thucydides' work as made up of
independent and incoherent pieces; and no one among them would
believe – as the previous analysts did – that it is easy to find a date or
a system of dates. The general tendency would, I think, easily fit in with
the method I have tried to use, which tends to consider, not so much
when a passage was finally written, but whether or not its conception
and design implied any knowledge of the final issue of the war.[3]

But this does not mean that there has been no disagreement as to
the results of such research: it only means that these disagreements are
not necessarily of great consequence. Still, it would be only fair to
indicate here which were the main ones between what had been
written in this book and what was later suggested by the above
mentioned scholars. It had been said, here (p. 19) that the Pentecontaëtia was generally admitted to be 'late': this would seem to be
wrong, according to Hammond, Gomme, Adcock and Westlake,
who all draw their conclusions from the sources of information used
by Thucydides (although their arguments are rather divergent, and
even their precise conclusions);[4] in their view, if there are references
to later events (93. 5 or 97. 1), these might be only additions. – This
interpretation, if valid, would of course give less authority to the idea
that the stress laid by Thucydides on Athenian imperialism grew
greater as time passed, and particularly after 404.[5]

[1] List, Nrs 21, 1, and 53.

[2] List, Nr 46.

[3] Not that even this is easy: cf. G. E. M. de Ste Croix (List, Nr 38), p. 31 (about
attempts made to sketch Thucydides' development): 'But they are all subjective, and
agreement has not been reached on any of the major problems involved.' Perhaps this is
altogether a pessimistic view of the situation.

[4] Was this information collected in exile or before the exile? Was the Pentecontaëtia
written at one time as a whole or not? These questions are dealt with in different manners
by those four authors.

[5] F. E. Adcock does not believe the Pentecontaëtia to be part of the ἀληθεστάτη
πρόφασις. But it undoubtedly serves to demonstrate the existence of a deep and ancient
conflict centred on imperialism. – In my opinion, Thucydides (who did not lack historical
curiosity) could well have got his information when in exile, without deciding before
404 exactly how and where he would use it.

About other passages or sections of the work, other views have
been put forward, more or less firmly, by Gomme, most of which
would result in having more 'ancient' passages than I suggested.
Thus,[1] he did not feel convinced, for instance, that I. 77.6 was late[2]
(see here, p. 263), or, for that matter, II. 64. 3 (see here, p. 149); and
he believed the Funeral Oration to be ancient (here, p. 146).[3] The
result, as one can notice, would in each case, involve the same kind of
consequences as the disagreement about the Pentecontaëtia. Now
none of these different points can be properly established, either way;
and nobody can pretend, in that field, to any certainty. I can only say
that, in my opinion, the fact that the Funeral Oration is in the manner
and style of Periclean times can in no way prove it to have been
written 'early'; nor does the idea of glory outliving power seem to
me to be in the least out of place after 404; on the contrary.[4] Also, it
still appears to me that very general or far-reaching texts like the
Pentecontaëtia and the Funeral Oration would not have been a quite
adequate introduction or complement to the history of the ten years'
war.

But, as I have tried to remind the reader in each instance, nothing
can ever be absolutely certain in this matter of dating, and no discrepancy can therefore prove disastrous. Also, these were not the
points to which recent studies directed their main attention.

Many other subjects have been considered or reconsidered, some
of which can add complementary information to the conclusions I
have tried to draw, while others would raise problems and doubts
about their validity.

The first kind of studies I can only mention briefly, hoping that
scholars interested in the matter will thus be able to see how and why
the discussions developed here should now be enriched by further
references and arguments. I shall not repeat what I have just said
about the need of always consulting Gomme's Commentary if one
wants to look into a passage with some detail (although it would be
particularly useful about economic matters, for instance those dis-

---

[1] Leaving out smaller discrepancies, or differences in stress.

[2] Nor does Adcock, op. cit.

[3] He also believes there is more difference than I suggest (here, p. 213) between the late
remarks of II. 65 and the Sicilian narrative. Three passages seem to him manifestly late,
and also lacking in real coherence with the context: II. 65. 5-10; IV. 81. 2-3; VI. 15. 3-5.

[4] It seems to me no more out of place than is the same ideal of glory after Chaironeia,
in Demosthenes' speech *On the Crown*, which owes so much to Thucydidean Pericles.

cussed here, pp. 89 ff.). Nor shall I quote a number of books or articles, which could, directly or indirectly, have some bearing on the matters examined here: I shall just add a few titles, which have particular relationship to the topics treated here, and mention them in the order in which these topics appear in the book.

About the general features of Athenian imperialism, I should like to cite two articles, one dealing with economic factors in Thucydides, and published by S. B. Smith in the *Harvard Studies*[1] and the other one commenting on the love of action which inspired Athenian imperialism (here, p. 78): that was Ehrenberg's important article on πολυπραγμοσύνη.[2]

More has been published, as would be expected, on particular sections or persons. Leaving Pericles aside for the moment,[3] I should like to mention the three main sections which have been more thoroughly examined in recent years.

First, the discussion between Cleon and Diodotus (see here, pp. 156-171). It has been often studied and analysed;[4] and it should be said that most of the authors (including Gomme) believed the resemblance between some sentences of Cleon and Pericles to have been put there on purpose, so as to make clear a contrast between the two men (here, pp. 164 ff.). Perhaps I should have explained my opinion more clearly, and shown in a more satisfactory way what I meant — which was that this resemblance might be there on purpose, without the comparison being systematic, that is to say without aiming, on the whole, and all through the speeches, at a clear contrast of policies. Thucydides could have welcomed the opportunity of playing on a difference: it does not mean that this is a clue to his main intention in this section.

Still more important is the literature about the Melian dialogue; and it is even difficult to give a complete list in such a short summary. We can but draw up a list of titles,[5] some of them only dealing with philological explanation, others taking sides either against Athens or for her;[6] one of them, Max Treu, indeed takes sides against Thucydides

---

[1] List, Nr 41.

[2] List, Nr 11.

[3] See below, pp. 375-376.

[4] List, Nrs 37, 34, 9, 50.

[5] Together with Deininger (already mentioned) one could mention here several articles, such as List, Nrs 3, 49, 25, 30, 28, 5, 24, 45 (the list being far from complete). To these should be added, on a different level, Heinimann's important study (List, Nr. 22).

[6] Yet, most of them show (as we tried to do) the existence of the antinomy.

himself, as he endeavours to show that Athens' policy rested mainly on the fact that Melos had already been paying tribute since 425. But even her presence on a list would not, in my opinion be sufficiently clear, without any other explanation or commentary, to prevail against the general tradition.[1]

About the Sicilian expedition and its political interpretation, apart from general historical research in that field, there have been some useful or personal studies – either about Nicias[2] or about Alcibiades. Among the last ones, two have presented audacious conclusions. Brunt[3] believes that there is in Thucydides some bias in favour of Alcibiades, owing to the nature of his information (but, in any case, I am not sure that information, with a man like Thucydides, would be quite so simple and one-sided as all that), whereas Max Treu[4] thinks Thucydides first put on an 'interpretatio maligna' and only came later to a more favourable one, when he showed the importance of the plan of general coalition (not of conquest) made by Alcibiades.[5] This, of course, would be important – provided it were possible to admit such sharp contrasts in the History – or, for that matter, in the very facts.[6]

Strange to say, the last chapter is that on which there is comparatively important literature to add (here, pp. 311 ff.). It seems that the philosophical problems of politics and morals in Thucydides were indeed coming to the fore when I was writing this last chapter. For, apart from the comparison between Thucydides and Plato, which I tried to draw in the conclusion and which was the subject-matter of Grene's book, *Man in his Pride*,[7] there have been quite a number of studies about the laws of history in Thucydides, and human nature, and similar subjects, which pointed to a sort of converging and common preoccupation.[8]

---

[1] Isocrates, even when he tries to justify what was done at Melos, either in the *Panegyricus*, 10 ff., or in the *Panathenaicus*, 70 ff., 88 ff., never suggests anything of the sort. Other authors try to excuse Athens on the view that Melos had paid money to Sparta.

[2] See Westlake, List, Nr 52.

[3] List, Nr 6.

[4] List, Nr 46.

[5] The article admits rather easily that all the speeches might be late. For reasons of literary composition (which I have dealt with partly in this book, but mainly in another one: List, Nr 35) this seems to me quite impossible.

[6] Between coalition and conquest, it is easy enough to have combinations, evolutions and uncertainty.

[7] List, Nr 19.

[8] See List, Nrs 10, 44, 23, 47, 31, and mainly 42, which gives an important characterization of Thucydides as opposed to Herodotus (see also my own contribution, List, Nr 36).

But apart from these more or less important contributions, which could add useful details to some of the discussions, it has to be acknowledged that two central questions have been raised, and that no person interested in Thucydides and Athenian imperialism should ignore them. One bears on the signification and validity of Thucydides' Pericles, the other on the validity of his whole interpretation of the Athenian empire. Both deserve a fuller treatment than can be given here.

As it is, I can only hope to show, in a few words, where the discrepancy lies and what are the main arguments for both sides: then I can leave the matter to the readers, as one did in a Greek ἀντιλογία.

First, about Pericles. Two questions have been raised in connection with him — both in Germany, and both inspired, one would think, by a sort of suspicion against the man who represented Athens' power and imperialistic views at their brightest.

The first is of historical nature. It has been doubted whether Thucydides' approval of Pericles was not somewhat exaggerated and undeserved. Vogt presented a whole case against Pericles,[1] insisting on his responsibility as regards the war, on his imperialism, on his private difficulties, and attacking even the quality of his military plans. The case — which is not quite new, as one can see from fifth-century evidence[2] — cannot be discussed here. But it can be noted that the very possibility of presenting such a case shows how important is the part played, in Thucydidean history, by personal choice and personal interpretation. And it suggests that this choice and interpretation is here very strongly directed towards a defence and approval of Pericles. In fact, it suggests bias where I should only speak of judgment; but there is agreement about the text itself.

This is not the case with the second question raised. For Strasburger has precisely doubted whether Thucydides' approval of Pericles was really complete and sincere. He has noticed[3] that all Athenian speakers in Thucydides — including Pericles — spoke a hard and realistic language, quite different from what we can know about their real themes;[4] and he has come to think that none of them can

[1] List, Nr 48.
[2] But the importance of Panhellenism would not have appeared there.
[3] List, Nr 43 (for the contrary view, see, in particular, Nrs 4 and 7).
[4] But of course we do not possess any single line from a political *discussion* in Athens at that time.

be approved by Thucydides: the historian says that Pericles would have won the war and he does not mean to praise him for anything more. — Now, this is exactly the contrary of what has been maintained in this book (here, pp. 136 ff.); and I must confess that even now I do not think that Thucydides would have been such an imprudent writer as to write so much about Pericles' qualities and personal superiority, had he not felt any sympathy, or real admiration, for the man and his ideas. And I still do not think he would have written the Funeral Oration — which arouses, even now, so much emotion and enthusiasm that I have of set purpose given up mentioning the recent literature about it[1] — had it not meant something important to him and had it only been a piece of rhetoric, rather incoherent and out of tune. And the whole composition of the two first books, in their very detail, points to the same spirit of deep and systematic laudation. But, after all, why not? Is it not possible to approve of power, and yet admit of its inherent difficulties and necessities? In French, at least, words like 'grandeur', 'prestige', and the like do not imply any moral aim or justification, yet they often stir a generous and idealistic enthusiasm. These questions of degrees and spiritual atmosphere do make a difference. And I, for one, feel quite unable not to see a real opposition, in this matter, between the different moments of Athenian imperialism. So this remains a question for others to judge.

So is the last question, which involves an even more serious difficulty. It throws doubt on the whole of Thucydides' views about Athenian imperialism. This doubt has been raised by an article of Mr de Ste Croix,[2] which has excited some notice (as well as by a similar article of A. H. M. Jones).[3] The author endeavours to show that all the interpretation put forward by Thucydides, with Athens acting as a tyrant, and enslaving the subject cities, and their hating her, and wanting to revolt, was in fact the interpretation of a rich and important man, living in oligarchic circles, hostile to Athenian democracy, and getting his information about the subject cities from

[1] There are some bibliographical indications in the recent and important study published by Kakridis and developing in fuller fashion the conclusions of his former work: List, Nr 27. — According to Strasburger, parts of the Funeral Oration are not to be read too ingenuously, while others clearly show the usual spirit of competition and selfishness (pp. 34-35). The interpretation which I give in the Budé edition is of course very different (although the spirit of competition I acknowledge, without thinking it implies any blame).

[2] List, Nr 38.

[3] List, Nr 26. Mr de Ste Croix's article was written before, and known to the other author, although it appeared just after.

people equally hostile to this democracy; whereas, in fact, all democratic people in the cities highly valued Athens' authority, and benefited by it, and were therefore loyal to Athens — as appears from the
very history of Thucydides, whose facts are correct, if not his
interpretation.

Now, this would not mean altering much in the description which
I gave of Thucydides' interpretation;[1] but it would mean adding a
most important criticism, while showing that this representation
rested on bias and was, ultimately, a misrepresentation.

Although I should not be at all ready to go that far, I think — and I
confess — that this question should have been raised in the book, and
that a comment should have been added concerning the validity of
the views here described. For the problem exists.

But the conclusion would not have to be necessarily as severe as
has just been stated. For both things are true: many of Athens' allies
had revolted in the past and more did revolt after the disaster in
Sicily — but yet, democratic parties in the cities were everywhere in
favour of Athens (Thucydides not only gives facts, but he acknowledges it, several times[2]) and the greatest part of these cities showed, on
the whole, a rather long and obstinate fidelity. Between these two
ideas, which is the most characteristic, and the most important?
Thucydides thought it was the first, the new interpretation suggests
it is the second one. Or, to put it in other words, there existed a
political opposition between democrats and oligarchs, which created
strong ties, regardless of national problems; but there also existed
national oppositions, when the interests of the whole city were at
stake. How is one to judge which was the prevailing feature or how
exactly they combined? The new interpretation suggests doing it by
considering the facts. But do we know them well enough, when it is
a matter of degree? Can they tell us whether the important thing
was that Brasidas did obtain so many secessions, or that he had such
difficulty in obtaining them? Can they tell us whether the capital
feature was that only one part of the city imposed a secession, or that
it finally took place? All these are facts. And such facts are difficult
enough to appreciate in our own time, with all kinds of information.[3]

[1] Only it would make the alliance of democracies (here p. 84) a much more important
feature.
[2] See here, p. 84.
[3] Lawrence Durrell's recent book on Cyprus (considered apart from any historical
or political views about the question) affords a good example of some of the ambiguities
that can be found in a subject's μῖσος.

One can therefore wonder whether, since the matter is in any case subjective, it is not safest to rely, precisely, on the subjective appreciation of the people of the time.

Of course, it is true that most of our ancient sources come from the same social and political class as Thucydides and may show the same kind of bias. Nevertheless, they often have different aims or opinions, or minds; that makes their agreement seem striking. Why, for instance, does the Pseudo-Xenophon who knows well enough about this general association between democrats, instead of denouncing their shrewd cohesion, insist on Athens' despotism?[1] Why does Isocrates, when he wants to write a defence for Athenian imperialism, miss the opportunity of insisting on the existence of this 'εὔνοια', for 'εὔνοια' in his opinion, is one of the main achievements in politics?[2] And why does he devote his whole life effort to the advocacy of this idea, if no remedy was required? Why should so many speeches mention autonomy as an ideal, at all periods, if it had been really outdone by political opposition, so as to have but a second place in the people's thought?[3] And why should we deny the right of calling 'δουλεία' or 'δούλωσις' the paying of a tribute, when Pericles called by the same names the acceptance of Sparta's complaints, or the sheer loss of the empire (I. 141. 1; II. 63. 3)? When it is a matter of appreciating ideas and interpretations, we must indeed be careful not to forget that subjectivity is only a symptom — and an alarming symptom — when it is but one person's subjectivity. And finally, if we are to question the validity of Thucydides' interpretation (as indeed we should), not history alone affords clues, but also, and perhaps mainly, history of ideas. For it could be shown — and presented as a final plea for Thucydides (and for myself) — that his theory fits in remarkably well with a general history of the theories about power as a whole and sea-power in particular.[4]

Thucydides' firmly expounded doctrine about sea-power, its means, and its dangers, is indeed the latest and most complete

---

[1] Whatever be the meaning of μισεῖσθαι μὲν ἀνάγη τὸν ἄρχοντα ὑπὸ τοῦ ἀρχομένου, in I, 14, which I understand as a statement (obvious to the author) about the relation between Athens and the cities.

[2] See my article in *J.H.S.*, 78 (1958), 92-101. Of course, he strongly denounces the μῖσος when he criticizes Athenian imperialism in *On the Peace*.

[3] See Ehrenberg, op. cit., p. 48. See also, recently, Adkins, List, Nr 2.

[4] I have been holding a seminar on this subject for the last three years. For a general view of the subject, see Momigliano, List, Nr 33.

expression of a system of ideas, which one can see growing and developing in Greece, in a regular way, as each circumstance affords an opportunity for its progress. Indications are given, ideas appear, the vocabulary grows more insistent and more precise,[1] some notions are presented by Herodotus, others by the Pseudo-Xenophon; but only in Thucydides are they all linked together in the close and tight system, which we tried to describe in this book, and which corresponds to the intellectual pride of this utmost and final experience: Athens' sea-power confronting her enemies. — Then comes the ruin of the system. Something went wrong. Sea-power finally collapsed. Thucydides, who saw it happening, suggests it was because of the hatreds (μῖσος). And in fact the various theories (as well as the disorder) of the fourth century can all be interpreted as an answer to that experience and a remodelling of previous ideals. How could hatred be avoided, or power shared, or glory preserved? such seem to be the problems dealt with by Isocrates, or Xenophon (when he is interested), or Demosthenes — not to mention Plato's more drastic remedies.

In that light, one can see that 'Thucydides and Athenian imperialism' is only part of a wider history, in which the historian's interpretation marks both a time of perfection and a crisis.

This notion might perhaps enhance the interest of the problem treated in the book. One could also hope that it might direct readers to problems of a higher order, thereby diverting their attention — at last — from the book itself and its many imperfections.

---

[1] Without entering here into details, it could be mentioned that the vocabulary shows the growing insistence on power from Herodotus to Thucydides: Ισχύς, from 4 to 39; δύναμις, from 51 to 145; κρατεῖν, from 29 to 173.

SELECT BIBLIOGRAPHY GIVEN IN THE FRENCH EDITION

I — STUDIES DEALING WITH THE PROBLEM OF HOW THE WORK WAS WRITTEN

W. ALY. 'Form und Stoff bei Thukydides', *Rh. M.*, 77, 1928, pp. 361-383.

V. BARTOLETTI. 'Potenza della Sicilia e Ardore degli Ateniesi in Tucidide', *St. It. di Fil. Class*, XIV, 3, 1937, pp. 227-235.

L. BODIN. 'Thucydide et la Genèse de son Œuvre', *R. E. A.*, 1912, pp. 1-40.

L. BREITENBACH. 'Ueber die Abfassungszeit des Thuk. Geschichtswerkes', *N. Jhb. für Phil.*, 1873, pp. 185-191.

L. ĆWIKLINSKI. *Quaestiones de tempore quo Thuc. priorem historiae suae partem composuerit*, Berlin, 1873, 58 pp. in-8. — cited as: Ćwikliński I.

— 'Ueber die Entstehungswiese des zweiten Theiles der Thuk. Geschichte', *Hermes*, 12, 1877, pp. 23-87.

J. DAVID. 'Rapport sur l'État présent des Études relatives à Thucydide', *Congrès de Strasbourg de l'Association Guillaume Budé, Actes du Congrès*, Paris, 1939, pp. 64-80.

A. GROSSKINSKY. *Das Programm des Thukydides*, Neue Deutsche Forschungen, Abteilung klassische phil., Berlin, 1936, 108 pp. in-8.

G. B. GRUNDY. *Thucydides and the History of his Age*, London, 1911, 535 pp. in-8.

L. HOLZAPFEL. 'Doppelte Redaktionen im VIII Buch des Thukydides', *Hermes*, 28, 1893, pp. 435-464.

A. KIRCHHOFF. *Thukydides und sein Urkundenmaterial. Ein Beitrag zur Entstehungsgeschichte seines Werkes*, Berlin, 1895, 179 pp. in-8.

W. KOLBE. *Thukydides im Lichte der Urkunden*, Stuttgart, 1930, IV-103, pp. in-8.

R. LAQUEUR. 'Forschungen zu Thukydides', *Rh. M.*, 86. 1937, pp. 316-358.

P. LESKE. *Ueber die Verschiedene Abfassungszeit der Theile des thuk. Geschichtswerkes*, König-Ritter Ak. zu Liegnitz-Oster Progr., 1875, 42 pp. in-4.

Ed. MEYER. *Forschungen*, II, 1899, pp. 269-436.

A. MOMIGLIANO. 'La composizione della Storia di Tucidide', *Mem. della Reale Acc. delle Scienze di Torino*, II, LXVII, 1930, pp. 1-48.

H. PATZER. *Das Problem der Geschichtsschreibung des Thuk. und die Thuk. Frage*, Neue Deutsche Forschungen, Abteilung klassische phil., Berlin, 1937, 118 pp. in-8.

M. POHLENZ. 'Thukydidesstudien I', *G. G. N.*, 1919, pp. 95-138 — cited as: Pohlenz I.

— 'Thukydidesstudien II-III', *G. G. N.*, 1920, pp. 56-83 — cited as: Pohlenz II.

— 'Die Thuk. Frage im Lichte der neueren Forschung', *G. G. A.*, 1936, pp. 281-300 — cited as: Pohlenz III.

G. DE SANCTIS. 'Postille Tucididee', *Rendi Conti della Reale Acc. dei Lincei. Cl. di Scienze Mor. stor. e fil.*, ser. VI, vol. VI, 1930, pp. 299-341.

— 'I Precedenti della grande Spedizione Ateniese in Sicilia', *Riv. di Fil. Class.*, 1929; reprinted in: *Problemi di Storia Antica*, Bari, 1932, pp. 113-136.

W. SCHADEWALDT. *Die Geschichtsschreibung des Thuk.*, Berlin, 1929, 106 pp. in-8.

A. REHM. 'Ueber die Sizilischen Bücher des Thukydides', *Philol.*, 89, 1934, pp. 133-160.

Ed. SCHWARTZ. *Das Geschichtswerk des Thukydides*, Bonn 1919 and 1929, 365 pp. in-8.

—'Ueber das erste Buch des Thuk.', *Rh. M.*, 41, 1886, pp. 203-222.

F. W. ULLRICH. *Beiträge zur Erklärung des Thukydides*, Hamburg, 1846, VIII-183 pp. in-8.

U. von WILAMOWITZ-MÖLLENDORF. 'Lesefrüchte LXVII', *Hermes*, 35, 1900, pp. 553-561 (about Book II).

— 'Thukydides VIII', *Hermes*, 43, 1908, pp. 578-618.

— 'Lesefrüchte CXCV', *Hermes*, 60, 1925, pp. 297-390 (on Book VI).

R. ZAHN. *Die erste Periklesrede (Thuk. I. 140-144). Interpretation und Versuch einer Einordnung in den Zusammenhang des Werkes*, Inaug. Diss. Kiel, 1934, 116 pp. in-8.

II — VARIOUS OTHER STUDIES

G. F. ABBOTT. *Thucydides. A Study in Historical Reality*, London, 1925, 236 pp. in-8.

E. BARKER. *Greek Political Theory, Plato and his Predecessors*, London, 1925, 403 pp. in-8.

J. BELOCH. *Die Attische Politik seit Perikles*, Leipzig, 1884, 369 pp. in-8.

G. F. BENDER. *Der Begriff des Staatsmannes bei Thuk.*, Würzburg, 1938, 114 pp. in-8.

L. BODIN. 'Autour du Décret Mégarien', *Mélanges littéraires Fac. L. Clermont-Ferrand*, 1910, pp. 169-182.

— 'Histoire et Biographie. Phanias d'Erèse', *R. E. G.*, 1937, pp. 1-73.

— 'Isocrate et Thucydide', *Mélanges Glotz*, Paris, 1932, pp. 93-102.

— 'Thucydide et la Campagne de Brasidas en Thrace, Remarques sur la Composition de l'Exposé', *Mélanges Navarre*, Toulouse, 1935, pp. 47-55.

— 'Thucydide I. 84', *Mélanges Desrousseaux*, Paris, 1937, pp. 19-25.

— 'Diodote contre Cléon. Quelques aperçus sur la dialectique de Thucydide', *Mélanges Radet, R. E. A.*, XLII, Paris, 1940, pp. 36-52.

— 'Alcibiade interprète à Sparte de l'appel des Syracusains au Péloponnèse', *Congrès de Strasbourg de l'Ass. G. Budé, Actes du Congrès*. Paris 1939, pp. 89-90. — cited as: *Alcibiade interprète*.

E. CAVAIGNAC. *Études sur l'Histoire financière d'Athènes au Ve siècle*, B. Ec. fr. de Rome et d'Athènes, fasc. 100, Paris, 1908, 192 pp. in-8.

— Miltiade et Thucydide, *R. Phil.*, 1929, pp. 281-285.

H. DROYSEN. *Athen und der Westen vor der Sicilischen Expedition*, Berlin, 1882, 59 pp. in-8.

W. FERGUSON. *Greek Imperialism*, Boston and New York, 1913, 258 pp. in-8.

A. FERRABINO. *L'Impero Ateniese*, Turin, 1927, 470 pp. in-8.

L. GERNET. *L'approvisionnement d'Athènes en blé au Ve et au IVe siècles*, Mél. hist. anc. Bibl. Fac. L. Paris, 1909, 391 pp. in-8.

G. GILBERT. *Beiträge zur inneren Geschichte Athens im Zeitalter d. Pel. Krieges*, Leipzig, 1877, 399 pp. in-8.

A. W. GOMME. *Essays in Greek History and Litterature*, Oxford, 1936, 298 pp. in-8.

H. GOMPERZ. *Sophistik und Rhetorik. Das Bildungsideal des εὖ λέγειν in seinem Verhältnis zur Philos. des V Iahrh.*, Leipzig, 1912, 292 pp. in-8.

Th. GOMPERZ. *Griechische Denker* (3d ed. Leipzig, 1909-1912).

J. HATZFELD. *Alcibiade*, Paris, 1940, 376 p. in-8.

B. W. HENDERSON. *The great War between Athens and Sparta. A companion to the military Hist. of Thucydides*, London, 1927, 491 pp. in-8.

W. JAEGER. *Paideia*, Berlin, 1934, II, pp. 479-513 (Tr: Oxford, 1954, I, 382-411).

W. JUDEICH. 'Griechische Politik und Persische Politik im V Jahrh.', *Hermes*, 58, 1923, pp. 1-19.

A. KIRCHHOFF. 'Untersuchung über den Delischen Bund im ersten Decennium seines Bestehens', *Hermes*, 11, 1876, pp. 1-48.

G. P. Landmann. *Eine Rede des Thukydides. Die Friedensmahnung des Hermokrates*, Kiel, 1932, 82 pp. in-8.

E. Lange. 'Thukydides und die Parteien', *Philol.* 52, 1894, pp. 616-651.

H. Lipsius. *Attisches Recht und Rechtverfahren*, III, 1915, pp. 969 ff.

G. Mathieu. *Les Idées politiques d'Isocrate*, Paris, 1925, 228 pp. in-8 — cited as: *Les Idées*.

— 'Survivances des luttes politiques du Ve s. chez les orateurs du IVe s.', *Rev. Phil.* 1914, XXXVIII, pp. 182-205. — cited as: *Survivances*.

— 'Isocrate et Thucydide', *Rev. Phil.*, 1918, XLII, pp. 122-129.

Ad. Menzel. *Kallikles. Ein Studie zur Geschichte der Lehre vom Recht des Stärkeren*, Vienna-Leipzig, 1922, 101 pp. in-8.

H. Müller-Strübing. 'Die Kerk. Händel bei Thuk., *Jhb für Phil.*, 1886, pp. 586 ff.

— *Thuk. Forschungen*, Vienna, 1881, 276 pp. in-8. — cited as: *Th.*

— *Aristophanes und die historische Kritik*, Leipzig, 1873, 735 pp. in-8. — cited as: Müller-Strübing.

W. Nestle. 'Thuk, und die Sophistik', *N. Jhb.*, 1914, pp. 648-685.

— 'Politik und Aufklärung in Gr. im Ausg. der V Jahrh., *N. Jhb.*, 1909, pp. 1-22.

H. Nissen. 'Der Ausbruch des Pel. Krieges', *Histor. Zeitschrift*, 1890, pp. 385-427.

G. Pasquali. 'L'ultimatum spartano ad Atene nell' inverno 431-430', *Stud. It di Fil. Cl.* N. S., V, 1927, pp. 299-315.

M. Pohlenz. 'Thukydides und wir', *N. Jhb. für Paed.*, 1920, pp. 57-82.

— *Aus Platos Werdezeit*, Berlin, 1913, 427 pp. in-8.

J. Ros S. J. *Die μεταβολή (Variatio) als Stilprinzip des Thuk.*, Rhet. Studien, Ergänzungsband I, 1938, 512 pp. in-8.

J. M. Stahl. *De Sociorum Atheniensum Judiciis*, Index lectt. v. Munster, 1881.

J. H. Sussmann. *Die Grundzüge der Panhellenischen Idee im V und IV Jahr. v. Chr.*, Zurich, 1921, 74 pp. in-8.

A. Thibaudet. *La Campagne avec Thucydide*, Paris, 1922, 285 pp. in-12.

H. Weil. *De Tragoedarium Graecarum cum rebus publicis conjunctione*, Paris, 1884. — cited as: Thèse.

— *Etudes sur le Drame antique*, Paris, 1897.

A. B. West. 'Pericles' political Heirs', *Class. Phil.*, XIX, 1924, pp. 120 ff.

U. von Wilamowitz-Möllendorff. *Aristoteles und Athen*, Berlin, 1893, 2 vol. cited as: *A. u A.*

Studies Mentioned in the Additional Remarks

1. F. E. Adcock, 'Thucydides in Book I', *J.H.S.*, 71 (1951), 2-12.
2. A. W. Adkins, *Merit and Responsibility. A study in Greek Values*, Oxford, 1960, 380 pp.
3. V. Bartoletti, 'Il dialogo degli Ateniesi e dei Meli nella Storia di Tucidide', *R.F.I.C.*, 1939, 301-318.
4. E. Bayer, 'Thukydides und Perikles', *Würzburger Jahrbücher*, 3 (1948), 1-57.
5. E. Braun, 'Nachlese zum Melierdialog', *Jahreshefte*, XL (1953), 233-242.
6. P. A. Brunt, 'Thucydides and Alcibiades', *R.E.G.*, 65 (1952), 59-96.
7. M. H. Chambers, 'Thucydides and Pericles', *Harv. St. in Cl. Phil.*, 62 (1957), 79-92.
8. G. Deininger, 'Der Melier-Dialog (Thuk., V, 85-113)', *In. Diss. Erlangen*, 1939, 3, 144 pp.
9. D. Ebener, 'Kleon und Diodotos. Zum Aufbau und zur Gedankenführung eines Redepaares bei Thukydides (Thuk., III, 37-48)', *Wissenschaftliche Zeitschrift der Martin Luther Universität*, Halle-Wittenberg, V, 1955-1956, pp. 1085-1160.
10. F. Egermann, 'Die Geschichtsschreibung des Thukydides', *Das Neue Bild der Antike*, Leipzig, 1942, I, 272-302.
11. V. Ehrenberg, 'Polypragmosyne, A Study in Greek Politics', *J.H.S.*, 67 (1957), 46-67.
12. J. H. Finley, Jr., 'Euripides and Thucydides', *Harv. St. in Cl. Phil.*, 49 (1938), pp. 23-68.
13. J. H. Finley, Jr., 'The Origins of Thucydides' Style', *Harv. St. in Cl. Phil.*, 50 (1939), pp. 35-84.
14. J. H. Finley, Jr., 'The Unity of Thucydides' History', *Harv. St. in Cl. Phil.*, Suppl. vol. I (1940), pp. 255-298.
15. J. H. Finley, Jr., *Thucydides*, Harv. Univ. Press, 1947, 344 pp.
16. A. W. Gomme, *A Historical Commentary on Thucydides*, Oxford, Clarendon Press, volume I, 1945, 480 pp. — volumes II and III, 1956, 748 pp.
17. A. W. Gomme, 'Four Passages in Thucydides', *J.H.S.*, 71 (1951), 70-80.

18. A. W. GOMME, 'The Greek Attitude to Poetry and History', Sather Classical Lectures, 27 (1954), 190 pp.

19. D. GRENE, Man in his Pride. A Study in the political philosophy of Thucydides and Plato, Chicago, 1950, 231 pp.

20. G. B. GRUNDY, Thucydides and the History of his Age, II, Oxford, 1948, 256 pp.

21. N. G. L. HAMMOND, 'The Composition of Thucydides' History', Cl. Q., 34 (1940), 146-152.

22. F. HEINIMANN, Nomos und Physis, Basel, 1945, 221 pp.

23. H. HERTER, 'Freiheit und Gebundenheit des Staatsmannes bei Thukydides', Rh. M., 93 (1949), 133-153.

24. H. HERTER, 'Pylos und Melos. Ein Betrag zur Thuk. Interpretationen, Rh. M., 1954, 316-343.

25. H. C. HUDSON-WILLIAMS, 'Conventional Forms of Debate and the Melian Dialogue', Am. J. Ph., 71 (1950), pp. 156 ff.

26. A. H. M. JONES, 'The Athenian Democracy and its Critics', C.H.J., XI (1953), 1-26.

27. J. T. KAKRIDIS, 'Der Thukydideische Epitaphios, ein stilistischer Kommentar', Zetemata, 26, 1961, 119 pp.

28. M. A. LEVI, 'Il Dialogo dei Meli', La Parola del Passato, 8 (1953), 5-16.

29. L. E. LORD, 'Thucydides and the World War', Martin Classical Lectures, 1945, 300 pp.

30. A. MADDALENA, 'Introduction to his edition, Biblioteca di Studi superiori, XV', La Nuova Italia, Florence, 1951.

31. A. MADDALENA, 'Tempo ed Eternità in Tucidide', R.H.I., 55 (1953), 7-18.

32. G. MÉAUTIS, Thucydide et l'Impérialisme athénien, Discours inaugural, Neuchâtel, 1939, 31 pp.

33. A. MOMIGLIANO, 'Sea-Power in Greek Thought', Class. Rev., 58 (1944), 1-7; reprinted in Secondo Contributo alla Storia degli Studi Classici, Rome, 1960, pp. 57-68.

34. P. MORAUX, 'Thucydide et la rhétorique. Essai sur la structure des deux discours III, 37-48', Les Et. class., 22 (1954), 3-22.

35. J. DE ROMILLY, Histoire et Raison chez Thucydide, Paris, les Belles Lettres, 1956, 314 pp.

36. J. DE ROMILLY, 'L'Utilité de l'histoire selon Thucydide, dans Histoire et historiens dans l'antiquité, Entretiens sur l'antiquité classique', IV, Vandœuvres-Genève, 1958, 41-66.

37. H. G. SAAR, 'Die Reden des Kleon und Diodotos und ihre Stellung im Gesamtwerk des Thukydides', diss. Hamburg, 1953 (not printed).

38. G. E. M. DE STE CROIX, 'The Character of the Athenian Empire', *Historia*, III (1954), 1-41.

39. G. DE SANCTIS, *Storia dei Greci*, 1939 (6th ed. 1961), Florence, 2 vol.

40. W. SCHMID, *Thukydides, Handbuch der Altertumswissenschaft*, VII, 1, 5, 1948.

41. S. B. SMITH, 'The Economic Motive in Thucydides, *Harv. St. in Cl. Phil.*, 51 (1940), 267-301.

42. H. STRASBURGER, 'Die Entdeckung der politischen Geschichte durch Thukydides', *Saeculum*, V, 1954, 395-428.

43. H. STRASBURGER, 'Thukydides und die Selbstdarstellung der Athener', *Hermes*, 86 (1958), 17-40.

44. E. TOPITSCH, 'Ἀνθρωπεία φύσις und Ethik bei Thukydides', *W. St.*, 1943-1947, 50-68.

45. M. TREU, 'Athen und Melos und der Melierdialog des Thukydides', *Historia*, 2 (1953), 253-273 and 3 (1954), 58-59.

46. M. TREU, 'Athen und Karthago in der Thuk. Darstellung', *Historia*, 3 (1954), 41-57.

47. J. VOGT, 'Dämonie der Macht und Weisheit der Antike', *W.G.*, 1950, 1-17.

48. J. VOGT, 'Das Bild des Perikles bei Thukydides', *Hist. Zeitschrift*, 1956, 249-256.

49. F. WASSERMANN, 'The Melian Dialogue', *Trans. of the Am. Phil. Ass.*, 78 (1947), 18-36.

50. F. WASSERMANN, 'Post-Periclean Democracy in Action: the Mytilenean Debate' (Thuc., III, 37-48), *Trans. of the Am. Phil. Ass.*, 87 (1956), 27-41.

51. F. M. WASSERMANN, 'Thucydidean Scholarship 1942-1956', *Classical Weekly*, 1956, 65-70 and 1957, 89-101.

52. H. D. WESTLAKE, 'Nicias in Thucydides', *Class. Q.*, 1941, 58-65.

53. H. D. WESTLAKE, 'Thucydides and the Pentecontaëtia', *Class. Q.*, N. S. 5 (1955), 53-67.

INDEX I

Passages in Thucydides

The figures in italics refer to Thucydides' work, the others to the pages of this book. Figures in heavy type are used when the pages concerned are dealing particularly and directly with the corresponding passage in Thucydides, so that they include a number of detailed quotations and discussions, which are not listed here separately.

BOOK I

Book III

INDEX II

Other Greek Authors